ARTHURIAN WOMEN

ARTHURIAN CHARACTERS AND THEMES
VOLUME 3
GARLAND REFERENCE LIBRARY OF THE HUMANITIES
VOLUME 1499

ARTHURIAN CHARACTERS AND THEMES
NORRIS J. LACY, *Series Editor*

ARTHURIAN WOMEN
A CASEBOOK

EDITED WITH AN INTRODUCTION BY
THELMA S. FENSTER

GARLAND PUBLISHING, INC.
NEW YORK AND LONDON
1996

Library of Congress Cataloging-in-Publication Data

Arthurian women : a casebook / edited with an introduction by Thelma S.
Fenster.
        p.   cm. — (Arthurian characters and themes ; vol. 3)
(Garland reference library of the humanities ; vol. 1499)
    Includes bibliographical references.
    ISBN 0-8153-0623-7 (alk. paper)
    1. Literature, Medieval—History and criticism.   2. Women in literature.
3. Sex roles in literature.   I. Fenster, Thelma S.   II. Series.   III. Series:
Garland reference library of the humanities ; vol. 1499.
PN682.W6A78   1996
809'.93352042'0902—dc20   95-52563
                                           CIP

Cover photograph: Collection of the J. Paul Getty Museum, Malibu,
California, Julia Margaret Cameron, "And Enid Sang," 1874,
Albumen, 13⁷/₈ × 11¹/₄ in.

Printed on acid-free, 250-year-life paper
Manufactured in the United States of America

Contents

STORY, GENDER, AND CULTURE

FAIRIES' TALES

ISEULT AND GUENEVERE IN THE
NINETEENTH CENTURY

ANOTHER LOOK

REVISIONARY TALES: GUENEVERE AND MORGAN
IN THE TWENTIETH CENTURY

Series Editor's Preface

This is Volume III of Arthurian Characters and Themes, a series of casebooks from Garland Publishing. The series includes volumes devoted to the best-known characters from Arthurian legend: Tristan and Isolde, Arthur, Lancelot and Guenevere, Merlin, Gawain, and Perceval; one volume will deal with the Grail.

Each volume offers an extended introductory survey and a bibliography and presents some twenty major essays on its subject. Several of the essays in each are newly commissioned for the series; the others are reprinted from their original sources. All contributions are presented in English, and each volume includes essays that are translated here for the first time.

The proliferation of research devoted to Arthurian material is daunting. At present, each number of the annual *Bibliographical Bulletin of the International Arthurian Society* lists some seven hundred scholarly items (books, articles, and reviews). This increase, which shows no sign of abating, makes it extraordinarily difficult for even the professional medievalist to keep abreast of Arthurian scholarship, and it would be very nearly impossible for the nonscholar with serious Arthurian interests to select and locate fifteen or twenty of the major scholarly contributions devoted to a particular character or theme.

These difficulties clearly dramatize the value of this series, but they also remain an insistent reminder that even the most informed selection of about twenty major essays requires us to omit many dozens of studies that may be equally instructive and engaging. Editors have attempted to remedy this situation insofar as possible by providing introductions that present other writers and texts, as well as bibliographies that document a good many important studies that could find no room in these volumes. In addition, many of the contributions that are included here will provide discussions of, or references to, other treatments that will be of interest to readers.

This volume, edited by Thelma S. Fenster, provides a very full and detailed introduction surveying the question of the women of Arthurian legend. (In that introduction and in the bibliography that follows it, an asterisk preceding a title or an author's name identifies studies that are reprinted in this book.) Interest in female characters has increased markedly in recent years; accordingly, all the studies included in this volume date from 1978 or later, and most of them are from the past dozen years. Characters who are treated here include Guenevere, Iseult, Nymue, Morgan, and Elaine; the authors and artists who are discussed range from Chrétien de Troyes to Gottfried von Strassburg to Malory, and from Matthew Arnold to William Morris to Julia Margaret Cameron to Marion Zimmer Bradley. There is a foreword by Sharan Newman, the author of a widely read Guinevere trilogy.

Unless otherwise indicated, the essays reprinted here from other sources are presented in their original form, with changes generally limited to the correction of typographical errors. However, in some cases authors have, with permission, chosen to update, expand, or rework their contributions. All such treatments, as well as the translation of some articles into English, are clearly documented.

The necessity, sometimes imposed by the original publishers, to reproduce many essays in the exact form of their first appearance yields results that, although inevitable, may perturb some editorial sensibilities. First, in most of the volumes there are a few instances in which a reprinted book chapter refers to a passage that is not to be found in this volume. Second, note form will vary widely from one to another. Finally, style, usage, and even spelling (British vs. American) vary as well. Offsetting these inconsistencies is the advantage of having in one's hand a substantial selection of the finest available studies, new as well as previously published, of Arthurian characters and themes.

Herewith, then, a score of contributions to our understanding of women in Arthurian literature, art, and criticism.

Such a volume could not be produced without the generosity of museum officials and editors of presses and journals, who kindly gave us permission to reproduce illustrations and articles. We are pleased to express our gratitude to all of them.

Norris J. Lacy

FOREWORD

I can't remember when I first heard of King Arthur, or the knights of the Round Table. They were always part of the culture, like Santa Claus or George Washington. Arthur and Lancelot, Camelot and Guinevere are part of our Western tradition; Arthur the perfect king, Lancelot the perfect knight, Camelot the perfect kingdom, and Guinevere . . . well, what was Guinevere? She could hardly be the perfect queen. She didn't rule, had no children, and was unfaithful to her husband. In most of the stories I read or saw dramatized, she was childish or selfishly imperious. Her romance with Lancelot was the catalyst for the downfall of the perfect society. So how did Guinevere fit into the legend?

In graduate school, I was fortunate enough to take several excellent courses on various forms of the Arthurian legend, and I became aware of how it had changed over the centuries to suit each generation. But, unlike the interpretations of Arthur, Merlin, Galahad, and the other men, the figure of Guinevere never varied. She was beautiful and regal, but petty, selfish, and demanding. I wanted to know why, but the stories provided no answer.

Since the time I began my first book on Guinevere, there has been some work, both in fiction and nonfiction, that deals with the major feminine characters of the Arthurian legend. But at the time, I could find nothing. I therefore set out to create my own Guinevere, to start from her childhood and to try to discover for myself why she became this rather unlikable woman. I also wanted to carry the story beyond the end of Camelot and show the kind of person Guinevere became after Arthur's death. I wanted her to grow beyond the legend, to become real.

But, in creating Guinevere, I realized that I also had to create a number of other people. With the men of the story, I thought I had a fair amount to work with. But, with the exceptions of Elaine, the sacrifice, and Morgan, the witch, few of the women of the central story even had names. To create Guinevere, I also had to create her mother. I had to give names and personalities to her maids and friends. To understand her, I also had to understand Morgan and Elaine, and then I realized that it would be necessary to reinterpret the men in the story in the light of what I had found out about the women.

So, instead of exploring one puzzling character, I ended up mounting a full expedition to Camelot. When I understood my Guinevere's point of view, I couldn't ignore Arthur's or Merlin's or even Mordred's. If she became a real person, then Morgan had to be one, too.

Like too many other bodies of accepted wisdom, up until this century the canon of Arthurian legend has marginalized or ejected women. I wanted to put them back where they belonged. By abandoning the female, the story was diminished. The lack of serious studies of the feminine side of Camelot has meant that Arthur, Merlin, Lancelot, and the other knights have received a disproportionate amount of attention. The essays in this book go a long way toward restoring the balance.

Sharan Newman

Other studies took a documentary and folklorist approach to medieval literature. Lucy Paton's analysis of the character of Morgan le Fay, for example, in her *Studies in the Fairy Mythology of Arthurian Romance* (1903), examined the (gradually more and more defamed) French Morgan character in twelfth- and thirteenth-century material and found her origins in earlier Celtic sources. In 1969, Fanni Bogdanow objected, arguing that the variations in Morgan's character (see below, Morgan le Fay) were due to the use made of her by each work in which she appeared, primarily by its plot, and not to an enigma in the character's source (123–33). Although Bogdanow did not look outside the text for explanations, her protestation implicitly shifted emphasis from ancient sources to a valuing of the medieval French texts themselves.

A more recent example than Paton's, Pierre Jonin's substantial study, *Les Personnages féminins dans les romans français de Tristan au XIIᵉ siècle: étude des influences contemporaines,* contains many interesting observations about the women characters of the French Tristan poems. Jonin concentrates first, however, upon arguing the originality of twelfth-century French Tristan poems as compared with the German version by Eilhart, and second, upon demonstrating "the influence of historical reality, literary currents, and religious climate upon each episode or event in which female characters appear" (14).

But all too often critical scholarship neglected the female characters of Arthurian literature, or undervalued them. At least two contributors to this volume bear witness: in her 1988 essay reprinted here, Sheila Fisher points out that book-length studies of *Sir Gawain and the Green Knight* had seldom treated Morgan with the depth necessary to an important character in the poem. Sue Ellen Holbrook found, when she wrote her 1978 essay on Malory's Nymue, also reprinted here, that attention to the fairy character had been only "incidental," since such minor characters were more usually explored for clues to sources, chronology, biography, or unity.

As a whole, and always with the possibility of exceptions, the study of female literary characters had been regarded until recently as a minor critical genre. It does not seem exaggerated to say that the advent of feminist literary criticism has helped to establish both the intellectual and the institutional validity of such studies. Analyses of female characters written during more than two decades now have often come under the umbrella of feminist literary history and theory, and/or have heeded its call to attend to women in literature, or have simply enjoyed the freedom that feminist critical praxis has made possible. The present volume offers an outline of what has been written and, in the best of consequences, will encourage others.

INTRODUCTION

Thelma S. Fenster

Arthurian Women brings together essays that focus on female characters in Arthurian literature from the twelfth through the twentieth centuries, and it includes two essays that deal with the visual arts. Each demonstrates, explicitly or implicitly, the importance of Arthurian legend's women characters. Taken as a collection, they chart the direction of ideas about Arthurian women characters over time, ending with some of the changes added most recently, as real women became writers and illustrators of Arthurian stories.

Studies of female characters in medieval Arthurian literature have existed since the turn of the century, when modern editions, for the first time in history, made medieval texts available to a large number of readers. Those early, groundbreaking interpretations reflected contemporary interests and approaches, and sometimes restraints. A few examples may suggest how they proceeded. Shortly after publication of the first modern edition of the works of Chrétien de Troyes, considered the creator of the Arthurian romance, Myrrha Lot-Borodine devoted her book published in 1909, *La Femme dans l'œuvre de Chrétien de Troyes*, to analyzing his women characters. Conceived as a study of the psychology of feeling as applied to the twelfth-century courtly romance, the book attempts to provide a psychologically credible and rounded interpretation of Chrétien's female (and male) characters. The author says that her book does not aim to offer a thorough study, but that it analyzes "only" Chrétien's conception of woman (vi).[1] Enid's character, in Chrétien's *Erec et Enide*, turns out to be notable for her "self-effacement" and "abnegation," and for her desire "to live in the shadow of her lord's glory" (75). But if, in Lot-Borodine's opinion, the message of the work is that "man must never sacrifice his prowess to his love for a woman," there remains room for "the proud knight [to return] to his vocation softened by the beneficent influence of love and suffering" (76).

Acknowledgments

A number of people assisted me with this volume and I would like to thank them here. Joan Grimbert, Constance Hassett, and Kathryn Heleniak gave useful advice and information. Joanne Lukitsh took over from me the task of obtaining a new set of photographs to accompany her reprinted article. Roberta Krueger and Clare Lees offered helpful reactions to the introduction. My assistant Louis DiGiorno wrestled uncomplainingly with the optical scanner for most articles, and then with mop-up and reformatting. My assistant Holly Gilbert researched articles. Norris J. Lacy, general editor for the Arthurian Characters and Themes series, was always encouraging and helpful, both in his reading of the introduction and in other matters. Working with Gary Kuris of Garland Publishing has been an especially positive experience. The Falmouth Public Library, and Jill Ericson in particular, earned my admiration and thanks. The Woods Hole Oceanographic Institution kindly provided technical support.

I am grateful to the editors of the following journals, presses, and books for permission to reproduce, and in some instances translate, the previously published articles and sections of books included here: *Médiévales: Langue, Textes, Histoire*; *Romance Notes*; *Speculum*; *Victorian Poetry*; Bowling Green State University Popular Press; Boydell & Brewer; Champion; Garland Publishing; John Benjamins; Leuven University Press; New York University Press; The Ohio University Press/Swallow Press; University of Pennsylvania Press; and Christopher Baswell and Debra Mancoff. Fordham University generously paid a number of reprint fees.

I am further grateful to the following for permission to reprint illustrations: Associated University Presses; the J. Paul Getty Museum; the University of Alberta Library in Edmonton; Carolynne Poon; and the Lincolnshire County Council.

genres have underscored the complex relationship between the legend and its female actors. Consideration of the so-called "chivalry topos" alone may suggest the contours of the problem. In the twelfth century, in Geoffrey of Monmouth's *Historia Regum Britanniae* (*History of the Kings of Britain*), ca. 1138, ladies are said to require that a knight prove himself three times in battle before being worthy of love. This chivalry topos, according to which a lady might inspire a knight to perform more impressive martial deeds, became a staple of the romance form, Arthurian or not. But it also quickly became intertwined with the quest for the lady's love, so that in the second half of the twelfth century, in Chrétien de Troyes's *Lancelot ou le Chevalier de la charrete* (*Lancelot, or the Knight of the Cart*), Lancelot's efforts to win the love of a seemingly unreasonable Guenevere show how the knight must accomplish more and more impossible feats to win his lady's love. The topos contained the seeds for several developments, one of which led to the lady's being depicted as imperious and unsatisfiable: the cruel and exacting *dame*. In this, in fact, female "human" characters began to share with certain fairy ones an exigent and unpredictable cast. But, oddly, Guenevere's adulterous relationship with Lancelot also seems to free her: as Arthur's wife she submits to his will (it is she whom Arthur sends to plead with Kay, demeaningly enough, when the vain seneschal threatens to leave the court) and often appears as a pawn between men; but as Lancelot's lover Guenevere enjoys a degree of power and authority that she loses as a married woman at court. Thus, although Chrétien's work no doubt reflects a masculine perspective, it does not do so monolithically.

In fact, the very term "Arthurian Women," virtually unavoidable, itself captures a textual reality. Its nearly oxymoronic flavor (cf., at the opposite extreme, the wholly different-sounding "Arthurian Men," a collocation apparently so redundant that it is almost never used) suggests a bracketing-off, a containing, of female figures. The term mirrors the texts: in spite of their extraordinary malleability from culture to culture and through the centuries, female Arthurian figures seem to arrive in each new work with a full set of already-givens that carry the freight of the problem that is woman. That was so from the beginning—at least insofar as the extant written record of the Middle Ages is concerned. Among contributors to this collection inspired by medieval texts, *E. Jane Burns observes that Chrétien's female characters act as the site where masculinity is constructed, a site valuable mostly for its silence and its beauty—a place rather for *imaging*. Female characters are diminished in importance when, unlike most male Arthurian characters, they lack

---

*An asterisk preceding a title or an author's name indicates articles printed in this volume.

Francesca, as Dante tells us in Canto V of the *Inferno*, was a reader of Arthurian romance, for she knew the story of Lancelot and Guenevere: she imi-
tated their illicit kiss with her brother-in-law, Paolo. This famous canto, el-
evating Francesca and Paolo to the level of a canonical adulterous pair, has
provoked a good deal of modern critical commentary. Among these, Susan
Noakes points out that for Dante and his contemporaries the kiss made of
Francesca not a reader but a misreader, someone who understood only the
surface of the text, not its inner meaning. So often has that characterization
been applied to women in Western tradition that Noakes has dubbed it the
"topos of the woman as misreader."[2] The intimidating construction of the
female as a shallow reader would have distanced her from the book and from
commenting, sometimes upon the very works that construed her as misreader. In the nineteenth century, in *Madame Bovary*, Gustave Flaubert created the adulteress Emma Bovary, who as a girl had read and idolized
historical novels while in the convent school; she is perhaps among the bet-
ter-known examples of a "misreader" in the style of Francesca. The assertions among scholars even today that the fifteenth-century French author
Christine de Pizan—as an example of a woman reading more "serious"
material—did not comprehend the subtleties of Jean de Meun's *Romance
of the Rose*, a work written late in the thirteenth century in a learned and
ironic university style, remind us that the topos lives. Nor was the point
wasted on the witty T.H. White, who, in the fourth book of *The Once and
Future King*,[3] writes that in the Queen's chamber at Carlisle was a book,
"perhaps the Galeotto one[4] which Dante mentions," but, adds the narrator,
"as Guenever had already read it seven times, it was no longer exciting" (604).

There is much more to be said about Francesca of course, for she may
well have represented to some the disruptive desire of a female reader,[5] the
movement of difference from and resistance to a learned male reading.
Francesca, Paolo with her, responds not to the text of scholarly masculine
readings but to her own pleasure in the text. Her reading releases what is
fleshly and erotic, and it makes Francesca herself the subject—that is, agent—
of that desire.

Arthurian literature itself often reveals some of these same tensions:
its earliest avatar, medieval romance narrative, suggested woman's desirability but could nonetheless cast woman's desire as a problem. Abetted
by the contemporary interest in love and encouraged perhaps by some real
historical women, Arthurian romance praised feminine beauty and made
women centrally important in Arthur's court (Lacy et al., eds. 524–26).
But numerous modern critical treatments of romance and other Arthurian

a heroic dimension, as *Maureen Fries notes, or when their lineage is but sketchy at best, as *Ann Marie Rasmussen writes and as Sharan Newman corroborates in her preface to this volume. When situated against the history of actual women, female characters remain the locus of manifold tensions, the record of an ambivalence about women's real position in medieval court life, in *Roberta Krueger's view. *Fisher's reading of *Sir Gawain and the Green Knight* argues that to save the Arthurian kingdom feminine power must be written out of the tale. *Regina Psaki relates that in Italian medieval Arthurian literature the reader almost never sees the action of a tale through the eyes of its female characters, for they are not "narrative focalizers"; Psaki notes, too, the curious intractability from text to text of Guenevere's sin. To grapple with such contradictories—that is, with the apparently valorized but paradoxically always-already-condemned female characters—is to rewrite the Arthurian paradigm, to see it differently, a project that twentieth-century fiction and scholarly criticism have in fact already begun.

II

Who are the "Arthurian Women"? Certainly the best known will be Guenevere, Arthur's queen; Iseult, of the legend of Tristan and Iseult, which came to be associated with the Arthurian legend, and the second Iseult, called Iseult of Brittany or Iseult of the White Hands, along with Brangain, Iseult's faithful confidante; and Morgan le Fay, Arthur's sometime sister and frequent nemesis, as well as Morgause, Arthur's half-sister, who often seconds Morgan in a variety of ways. Beside those, other named female characters can be encountered frequently in Arthurian legend; many are discussed centrally or incidentally in this volume. Elaine, the Maid of Astolat, and Elaine of Corbenic enjoyed prominence both in the medieval period and in the nineteenth century. Enid, Erec's patient wife, Igerne, Arthur's mother, and Laudine, the lady who owned a magic fountain and was loved by Ywain, furnish important medieval examples in particular, as does Lunette, Laudine's confidante. Named Fairy Women other than Morgan include Nymue, variously Lady of the Lake, Nyneve, Niniane, Niviane, or Viviane, and the somewhat recondite Argante.†

Guenevere

Guenevere is identified in Geoffrey of Monmouth's *Historia Regum Britanniae* as Arthur's wife, whom Arthur's nephew Mordred also married after seizing the throne; though that should have made her primarily a victim, she

---

†The figure known as the Loathly Lady is not treated in this volume.

nonetheless early stood for a zone of vulnerability in Arthur's realm, and some of the literature that followed was quick to cast her as Mordred's accomplice. It is possible that an even earlier work, a visual depiction (ca. 1120–40), the carvings on the north portal of the Cathedral of Modena in Italy, and referred to as the Modena Archivolt (an ornamental band or molding surrounding an arch), depicts Mordred's abduction of the queen. Though scholars do not agree upon the meaning of the relief, the inscribed names Winlogee and Mardoc have often been interpreted to refer to Guenevere and Mordred (Lacy et al., eds. 324–26).

In fact, a theme associated with Guenevere in the early medieval versions of the legend was that of her abduction.[6] In addition to her kidnapping by Mordred, Guenevere is carried off by Meleagant in Chrétien's *Lancelot*, by Valerîn in Ulrich von Zatzikoven's German *Lanzelet* (1194–1205), and by Gasozein in Heinrich von dem Türlin's German *Diu Crône* (*The Crown*, ca. 1220).

Among Guenevere's attributes is of course her great beauty, such that the mere visualizing of her puts her lover Lancelot into a trance in both Chrétien de Troyes's *Lancelot*, the first work to mention an affair between the queen and the great knight, and in the thirteenth-century Prose *Lancelot*, which, with the *Queste del saint Graal* ("The Quest for the Holy Grail") and the *Mort Artu* ("Death of King Arthur"), comprises the French Vulgate Cycle (ca. 1215–35; also called the Lancelot-Grail Cycle, the Prose *Lancelot*, or the Pseudo-Map Cycle). Ulrich von Zatzikhoven's *Lanzelet*, based on a lost version of the story, recounts no such affair. Because of Lancelot's love for the queen in Chrétien's *Lancelot*, the nineteenth-century French scholar Gaston Paris took that work to be a template of "courtly love"; later generations of scholars have nonetheless wondered about Chrétien's intentions. And if in the Vulgate Cycle the famous affair was at first glorified, it subsequently became the cause of Lancelot's failure to find the Grail. In the *Mort Artu*, the final romance of the Cycle, it contributes to the fall of the Round Table. By "positing the love of women as a hindrance to male chivalric success," the Vulgate Cycle as a whole shows how "courtly love, even in the earliest Arthurian texts, introduced more problems than solutions to the charged interaction between male and female protagonists."[7] It has further been suggested that in the *Lancelot* the hero's feelings for Galahad hold him more surely than does his tie to the queen.[8] The Post-Vulgate Cycle, which followed upon the Vulgate, omitted the affair between Lancelot and Guenevere and abridged the *Mort Artu*.

A number of important Arthurian female characters have doubles, and Guenevere is one of them. Doubling is a term widely used to denote the

"splitting" of a character into two characters, or the copying of traits from one character to another, sometimes in order to present the character's opposite face, or for other purposes. Guenevere is doubled by a character known as the False Guenevere, whose appearance, not generalized in the legend, is limited to the Vulgate Cycle. The False Guenevere is a half-sister of Guenevere, born of the same father but of a lower-ranking mother. She accuses her half-sister of not being Arthur's true wife, and for a time the king believes that she, the False Guenevere, is his wife. Later, the impostor confesses her lie.

Not motivated by interests of plot, however, are the three Gueneveres of Triad 56 of the collected Welsh *Triads*, a body of teaching in the bardic schools in which each item occurs in a triple grouping, for mnemonic purposes:

> Gwennhwyfar daughter of (Cywryd) Gwent,
> and Gwenhwyfar daughter of (Gwythyr) son of Greidiawl,
> and Gwenhwyfar daughter of (G)ogfran the Giant.

This literary convention, among the Welsh and Irish, has led some to posit a mythological origin for characters that show such "multiple personalities," since deities could be portrayed in single or in triple form.[9] In a distant way, too, the doubling of named female characters recalls the many nameless fairy women who flit through medieval Arthurian romance, from Chrétien to Malory, and whom the reader is often hard-pressed to distinguish from one another (see *Berthelot). Constance B. Hieatt and Raymond H. Thompson note that a modern writer, David Lodge, refers to Spenser's *The Faerie Queene* (2.66.6 [Lacy et al., eds. 281]) when in *Small World* (1984) Persse McGarrigle (Percival) seeks Angelica Pabst, identical twin of Lily, with the result that he sleeps with the wrong twin during a New York convention of the Modern Language Association; in a larger sense the episode captures the medieval text's doubling of its female characters and its studied replication of "damsels."

The *Mort Artu* contains another motif that crystallized around Guenevere. Here, she offers an apple to one of Arthur's knights, but unbeknownst to her, the apple is poisoned and the young man dies. The ensuing strife among men emblematizes the difficult encounter between Arthurian knights and women. For her crime, Guenevere is threatened with death at the stake, a punishment often associated with those thought to have practiced magic.[10]

In English literature, Guenevere appears in both Laȝamon's *Brut* of the thirteenth century and in *Sir Gawain and the Green Knight* of the four-

teenth. Sir Thomas Malory, writing his *Morte Darthur* toward the end of the fifteenth century, paints perhaps a more flattering portrait of Guenevere than do earlier writers, emphasizing the true love between Lancelot and the queen. The following observation about the queen by Malory's narrator has often prompted scholars to find that the author is sympathetic toward the queen:

> And therefore all ye that be lovers, calle unto youre remembraunce the monethe of May, lyke as ded quene Gwenyver, for whom I make here a lytyll mencion, that whyle she lyved she was a trew lover, and therefor she had a good ende.[11]

Yet this brief comment about Guenevere's personal life is not the rule in Malory, for he prefers a public portrait of the queen that shows little of the character as wife and mistress.[12]

Malory's version of the legend was to influence modern English ones, as the French material fell into neglect. Early in the nineteenth century, the *Morte Darthur* was republished for the first time in almost two centuries. A pair of editions in 1816 and Southey's in 1817 signaled an Arthurian revival, encouraging a rewriting of medieval sources. But polar views of women centered on sexuality were to persist and perhaps even sharpen in the work of some authors. As *Barbara Fass Leavy comments, Victorian times added to the traditional splitting of woman into Eve or Mary a "social system" that created "polar opposites in woman": "one side denied the desires that were in reaction projected so emphatically onto her opposite that she could be conceived of as a diabolical temptress." A common thread is the attribution to these "Victorian Spellbinders," in Carole Silver's term, of preternatural faylike powers, which helped to exonerate them. Silver suggests that their powerful resonance in the work of Morris and Swinburne and in the paintings of Burne-Jones (they were "great in stature and rising in their fall" ["Victorian Spellbinders" 259]) may have offered the freedom to imagine to a Victorian female audience, as it apparently did to some of their male creators.

Malory's depiction of Guenevere is the point of departure for William Morris's heroine in *The Defence of Guenevere* (1858), a figure of intriguing complexity (see *Silver). Alfred Lord Tennyson in his *Idylls of the King* makes of Guenevere an abased fallen woman. Nina Auerbach finds the abased woman so pervasive a theme in the *Idylls* that "it transmutes a woman's fall from a personal to a national event, one that inspires and symbolizes Victorian England's epic portrait of its own doom" (157). So harshly

seen in its own time was Tennyson's portrait of Guenevere, however, that a contemporary editor, F. J. Furnivall, criticized it, saying that Arthur's own sin was the cause of the fall, and "Guenevere's the means only through which that cause worked itself out" (Gordon-Wise 52). It is worth noting that Tennyson's first Arthurian poem, "The Lady of Shalott," and his first four idylls, "Enid," "Vivien," "Guinevere," and "Elaine," which formed the foundation for his Arthurian epic, all show the poet drawn to female subjects: these he depicted contrastively, female destructiveness (Vivien, Guenevere) as against female virtue (Enid, Elaine), although Guenevere "partakes of both Enid's ennobling goodness and Vivien's destructive sensuality" (Lacy et al., eds. 447).

With the Arthurian literary revival of the nineteenth century came the development of a companion iconography, in the 1860s and 1870s, in both painting and book illustration. Pre-Raphaelites like Edward Burne-Jones, William Morris, and Dante Gabriel Rossetti developed, in paintings and in the decorative arts, their absorbing interest in the reborn stories. Book illustration enjoyed special popularity and included the Moxon Tennyson—the collected early writings of the poet, illustrated by artists of his choosing; Moxon was the publisher—and the Gustave Doré engravings and Julia Margaret Cameron photographs accompanying editions of Tennyson's *Idylls of the King.*

In Victorian art, Guenevere did not enjoy the popularity of a figure like Elaine or the Lady of Shalott, whose purity and suffering probably seemed a more suitable theme. But Guenevere figures later in paintings by Rossetti and Morris, where her seductive qualities often dominate (Gordon-Wise 108–15). Other works favored her portrait as a nun, a theme developed in literature as early as the thirteenth century when the queen withdrew to a convent after the fall of the realm.

Twentieth-century Gueneveres include T. H. White's Jenny in his *Once and Future King* (1939–40). In his notes, White wrote that when Morgause and Arthur, who did not know one another, went to bed together and produced Mordred, "The sin was incest, the punishment Guinever, and the instrument of punishment Mordred, the fruit of the sin."[13] If "White endeavoured to depict Guenevere with the psychological realism of the modern novel," as *Elisabeth Brewer argues, his "realism" nonetheless produces a female character whose negative qualities are much in tune with a type of twentieth-century antifeminism: his queen can be frivolous and shallow (she cannot understand Lancelot's spiritual side—again, the "woman as misreader"); vain and ugly as an older woman wearing excessive makeup, she is shown to be bored perhaps because she has had no children. White's

depiction of Guenevere does little to improve her, however sympathetic he may have been to the character he created.

Rosemary Sutcliff's *Sword at Sunset* (1963)[14] depicts a marriage between Arthur and Guenhumara (Guenevere) that is uniquely stripped of all courtly elements. Set in early Britain, the story of the "Count of Britain" features a fighting man who is sometimes less comfortable with his wife than with his dog, upon whose belly he likes to place his head to sleep. Obliged to marry Guenhumara after her father offers her to him publicly, then a reluctant lover in part because of his guilt at having slept with his half-sister, named Ygerna, he produces a daughter, who later dies. Thus when plain Guenhumara later takes not "Lancelot" (there is no such character in this version) but a far from handsome "Bedwyr" for her lover, a subtle shift of blame has occurred in more than one sphere. Guenevere's legendary barrenness, implicit in the French sources and in Malory (because in so much medieval literature conception is often quick work [McCarthy 115]—compare Guenevere with Elaine of Corbenic, who conceives Galahad after sleeping with Lancelot just once), has been utterly displaced by Arthur's admission that he has failed his wife. The disappointment that eventually turns Guenhumara toward Bedwyr is bred of Arthur's absence at both the birth and death of his child—a death, moreover, for which Guenhumara blames Arthur.[15]

Sutcliff's heroine has not been romanticized: relatively late to marry and not pretty, she tells Arthur on their wedding night that he is beautiful, a compliment he does not—indeed, cannot—return. Steering a course between her father and Arthur, Guenhumara endeavors to author her own fate to the extent possible. In the hard war camps of Arthur's existence, she is as tough and resilient as her husband, and her outlook on life is no less painfully grim. The enmeshing of errors and decisions that catches Guenhumara and Arthur from the beginning is symbolized in her tawny braids, fastened at their ends with small golden apples (208), and made explicit by her reference to their situation as "the tangle" (232). Most important, in confronting the events that life has planned for her, Sutcliff's heroine is no less heroic than Arthur; but unlike Arthur Guenhumara can expect no kingdom.

Among more recent depictions of Guenevere, Sharan Newman's Guinevere Trilogy (*Guinevere*, 1981; *The Chessboard Queen*, 1983; *Guinevere Evermore*, 1985),[16] tells Arthurian history from the queen's point of view, and Wendy Mnookin's *Guenever Speaks* (1991)[17] tells the queen's story poetically. Marion Zimmer Bradley's *The Mists of Avalon* (1982)[18] does not try to exonerate Guenevere for her role in the fall of Arthur's kingdom; rather, the queen's motive springs from the barrenness

she so deeply regrets. In other twentieth-century historical fiction, Guenevere can be portrayed as a prostitute.[19]

Iseult, Iseult of Brittany, Brangain

A second important example is Iseult, daughter of the king of Ireland and initially a healer.[20] She first crosses paths with Tristan when she salves the wounds he sustained in battle with the Irish champion Morholt, Iseult's uncle. She does not know the origin of the wounds, nor does she know the identity of her patient. Again later, when Tristan is overcome by poisonous fumes from the body of a dragon he has slain, Iseult restores him to health, eventually learning his identity. It is Iseult's mother who prepares the love potion intended for Iseult and her husband-to-be, King Mark. Tristan and Iseult accidentally imbibe the liquid and become adulterous lovers. The pair practice many deceptions to keep Mark from knowing the truth. Probably the most troubling initiative belongs to Iseult alone who, having persuaded her governess, the faithful and virginal Brangain, to take her place with Mark on the wedding night, subsequently fears exposure and arranges Brangain's murder. The governess is later spared. If Iseult here has revealed a cruel, though frightened, nature, it is also true that in the hands of the tradition's male writers, Arthurian women characters including Guenevere (and, it goes without saying, Morgan le Fay), do not always enjoy smooth relationships with one another.

Iseult is the only one of the three major female characters to have a mother portrayed in the medieval material. In some texts, her mother merely prepares the famous love potion, but in others she also helps to cure Tristan and/or is among the first to recognize Tristan's identity as killer of Morholt.

The legend is preserved in important French and German variants of the twelfth and thirteenth centuries,[21] although antecedents for the character of Iseult may be found in the tenth-century Irish *The Wooing of Emer* and in the ninth-century *The Pursuit after Diarmaid and Gráinne*. An archetype of the Tristan story may have been composed around 1150 in France, followed by the verse romances of what is now referred to as the "common" version, especially Eilhart von Oberg's German *Tristrant* (ca. 1170) and Béroul's Anglo-Norman *Roman de Tristan* (late twelfth century). Béroul's poem, highly episodic and containing some apparent inconsistencies in characterization, portrays Iseult as linguistically resourceful and quick-witted, if duplicitous—the crafter of the "truthful lie" that Tristan then embroiders (Burns, "How Lovers Lie Together," 26).

The extant fragment of Béroul's poem does not contain the end of the story. Among French versions, it is left to the "courtly" rationalized

Anglo-Norman version by Thomas d'Angleterre (ca. 1170) to introduce Iseult's important double, Iseult of the White Hands (Iseult of the Fair Hands, Iseult of Brittany; see below, Iseult of Brittany), and thus to bring the tale to its tragic conclusion off the Breton coast. But Thomas's version also augments the conflict between Iseult and Brangain: as Emmanuèle Baumgartner notes, the disagreement affords Thomas the chance to present a different point of view about the lovers, for Brangain condemns their love, calling it a bad and foolish thing. Before the dispute ends, Brangain will have created an obstacle to their love, thereby, in Baumgartner's view, prefiguring the second Iseult (*Tristan et Iseut: De la légende aux récits en vers*, 96–97).

Thomas's version provided inspiration for Gottfried von Strassburg's German *Tristan und Isold* (ca. 1210), considered possibly the best of the medieval Tristan texts. In Gottfried's work, Tristan's courtly and learned accomplishments set him apart: his abilities with languages, both those of different groups of people and Latin, as well as his musical skill, make him the perfect tutor for Isold, who learns from him "the whole art of writing . . . and Latin and stringed instruments."[22] Gottfried's Isold, a charmingly beautiful and generally sympathetic character, is seconded by a strong mother figure, also named Isold, thereby increasing the doubling around Isold's figure. Queen Isold, who clearly possesses magical powers, saves her daughter from marriage with a wicked steward; such a mother-daughter effort constitutes a rare scenario in Arthurian literature (see *Rasmussen). On the whole, Queen Isold's resourcefulness, and that of the princess's lady-in-waiting, Brangain, outstrips Isold's own.

In the thirteenth-century French Prose *Tristan*, the heroine generally resembles her predecessors. As for her feelings for her husband Mark, however, Iseult of the prose story has changed: in the poems she simply did not seem to mind betraying Mark, but now she is filled with hatred for him (Baumgartner, *Le "Tristan en prose,"* 223).

The legend was retold in Norway in the early thirteenth century as *Tristrams saga ok Ísöndar* ("The Saga of Tristram and Isold"), a translation of Thomas's *Tristan* by a certain Brother Robert. Echoes of it could again be heard in Danish, Icelandic, and Faroese ballads of the end of the Middle Ages (Lacy et al., eds. 398, 400). Italian medieval literature preserves aspects of the legend in the *cantari* ("songs"), which present episodes of the Prose *Tristan*; in the *Tristano Riccardiano* ("Tristan" [of the Riccardiano Codex 2543]) of the late thirteenth century; and in the *Tavola Ritonda* ("Round Table") of the second quarter of the fourteenth century. The Italian texts favored Tristan over Lancelot, and thus Isotta over Ginevra; when, in the *Tavola Ritonda* (CVI), the two queens hear that

Lancillotto and Tristano are dead, Ginevra's lament is four lines long and Isotta's twenty-four (see *Psaki).

Malory's main source for his lengthy story of Tristan was the Prose *Tristan*, and his emphasis thus falls upon chivalric service, not adultery (Grimbert xliii–xliv). He augments both Tristan's role as warrior and the hostility between the hero and King Mark, who is often portrayed as evil. He effaces the actuality of his heroine: although La Beale Isoud as a character appears from time to time, it is her reputation as a superlatively beautiful and good woman, the *idea* of her, that wafts through the romance. She is often compared with Guenevere and is loved, though from afar, by several men, among them Sir Palomides and Sir Kehydius, a precedent that had already been set by earlier French variants.

Among re-creations of the Tristan and Iseult story in the modern era probably none has influenced the contemporary grasp of it more than Richard Wagner's opera *Tristan und Isolde* (1865), which heightened the impossibility of the amorous liaison. Unlike medieval renditions, Wagner's allowed the lovers no consummation of their love in life, and it left them craving a physical and spiritual joining that death alone could provide (Grimbert lviii). The opera ends on Isolde's famous *Liebestod* ("love-death"), the highly sensual final piece that brings fulfillment to the lovers' death-wish.

English-language retellings of the story in the nineteenth century include those by Matthew Arnold and the version that Alfred Lord Tennyson included in his idyll "The Last Tournament." In the earlier twentieth century, the American poet Edwin Arlington Robinson wrote three Arthurian poems, of which *Tristram* (1927) is thought to be the most original. In it, the heroines—Isolt and Isolt of the White Hands—are better able than the hero to see that the love affair must end in death (Lacy et al., eds. 388).

In France, Joseph Bédier's reconstruction of the legend in his *Roman de Tristan et Iseut* (1900),[23] based primarily but not exclusively on Béroul and Eilhart, depicts the heroine sympathetically. Modern French versions of the tale include Jean Cocteau's screenplay *L'Eternel Retour* ("The Eternal Return")(1943)[24] in which Patrice (Tristan) and Nathalie (Iseut), the latter married to Patrice's uncle Marc, must endure the jealousy of the Frossin family, whose dislike of the lovers is carried forward most aggressively by the mother and her dwarf son, Achille. Nathalie herself has a foster mother, who helps to prepare the love potion. When Patrice meets Nathalie, she is in a bar in the company of Morolt, a battering bully. Patrice rescues her and takes her back to marry his uncle Marc. Interestingly, though, Nathalie remains sexually pure, having contracted an illness that prevents her from ever having relations with Marc *or* Patrice.

Among the most recent versions is John Updike's *Brazil* (1994),[25] in which a poor but handsome black youth named Tristão, raised in a *favela* shanty of Rio de Janeiro, meets the pale and beautiful, upper-class Isabel on the beach. Having decided to be rid of her virginity, Isabel invites Tristão home. She quickly takes to sex and to Tristão, eventually wishing to be his love slave. They run away but are found by her father's hired guns and separated. After a time, Tristão finds Isabel again and the couple flee into the Brazilian hinterland, living among prospectors and indigenous groups, on a journey in which geography intersects with time.[26] To supplement their meager income Isabel turns to prostitution, through which she gives birth to several children. None of her numerous children belongs to Tristão, who produces no offspring in spite of his remarkable (and often mentioned) "yam." *Brazil* has been criticized for its perceived racial stereotyping.

"Revisionist" Iseults would include the heroine of Martha Kinross's play *Tristram and Isoult* (1913),[27] in which the heroine, notably independent, forthrightly reveals to Mark her love for Tristan. In this retelling, Iseult regrets the harm she has done to Iseult of Brittany (Grimbert lxxxiii). A modern version of the legend with a title that seems to announce an unaccustomed emphasis is Dee Morrison Meaney's *Iseut: Dreams That Are Done* (1985)[28] in which the story is told from the heroine's perspective (Lacy et al., eds. 316). In film,[29] Agnès Verlet's poetic *Yseult et Tristan* reverses the traditional hierarchy to produce a work that, as Jean Markale comments in his preface to the screenplay, concentrates upon woman.[30] In this version of the story, Yseult grows angry when she realizes that Tristan wants her not for himself, but for Mark. She says that Tristan has chosen the love of a father over that of a woman: he has killed the dragon and therefore has the right to take Yseult, but instead prefers to bring her to his lord, as if she were a slave.

Iseult of Brittany

Iseult's famous perceived double is Iseult of Brittany (Iseult of the White Hands, Iseult of the Fair Hands), the woman Tristan marries after he is forced to leave Cornwall, where the first Iseult resides with Mark. The marriage is never consummated. When Tristan falls gravely ill, he sends his wife's brother to bring back his first love, knowing well her healing powers. But Iseult of Brittany, jealous and feeling spurned, betrays Tristan when she tells him that the approaching ship bearing Iseult flies a black sail, for in fact its sail is white, the signal that was to tell Tristan of the first Iseult's imminent arrival.

The doubling of Iseult's character has sometimes lent itself to a play of contrasts, with one or the other Iseult cast as the good or evil "twin." Although the second Iseult is often seen as responsible for the deaths of the lovers, she can also be portrayed as patient and long-suffering (see *Fass Leavy). A modern retelling in which the first Iseult's initiative in the love affair is played off against the second Iseult's forbearing nature is Rosemary Sutcliff's *Tristan and Iseult* (1971).[31]

Brangain

Brangain (Brangien, Brangaene), Iseult's confidante, who in a number of versions accidentally gives the love potion to the young couple, takes on a significant role in Thomas's and in Gottfried von Strassburg's redactions. In Thomas's version, where Brangain is far from a mere compliant servant, there is a certain amount of strife between her and Iseult. In Gottfried's story, she assumes a courtly and wise demeanor, sometimes alert when the heroine is not. Of special note is the episode in which Isold has ordered the murder of Brangain, whose ability to talk her way out of being killed is handled in a particularly interesting way.[32] A modern work in which Brangain plays an expanded role is John Erskine's *Tristan and Isolde: Restoring Palamede* (1932)[33] (Thompson, *Return from Avalon* 58–59).

Morgan le Fay

The third major, complex example is Morgan le Fay. In her first appearance, in Geoffrey of Monmouth's *Vita Merlini* ("The Life of Merlin"), Morgan is the most beautiful of nine sisters, a kind and magically talented being who can change her shape.[34] After the battle of Camlann, Arthur voyages to Morgan's residence on the Isle of Avalon to be healed of his wounds by her special arts. In Chrétien de Troyes and elsewhere, it is suggested that Morgan is Arthur's sister.

In the French prose romances of the thirteenth century, Morgan's image suffers a decline. She becomes treacherous, wishing to harm Lancelot and Guenevere, Arthur, and Tristan by turns. In the Prose *Lancelot*, Morgan's enmity toward Lancelot and Guenevere is explained by the queen's interference in Morgan's love affair with the queen's cousin Guiomar. Guenevere threatens Guiomar with death unless he leaves court, which he does. From that time forward, Morgan nurtures a *grant hayne* ("great hatred") toward the queen. In one of three imprisonments that Morgan inflicts upon Lancelot, sometimes in the hope of seducing him, the knight consoles himself by illustrating the walls of his chamber with the deeds he has accomplished for Guenevere's love. Later, in the *Mort Artu*, Morgan is able to show these drawings to Arthur and to reveal thereby the secret love affair.

In the Prose *Tristan* of the thirteenth century, Morgan has a role to play in Tristan's death at Mark's hand. She also instigates a chastity test to try to unmask Guenevere: to Arthur's court she sends a magic drinking horn from which no disloyal lady can drink without spilling its contents. In the Post-Vulgate Cycle, in which Morgan is pictured as Urien's wife and Ywain's mother, Morgan becomes Arthur's enemy, inciting Accolon, another of her lovers, to kill him. In the section known as the *Suite du Merlin* ("Merlin Continuation"), Arthur entrusts to Morgan a precious scabbard, which protects its bearer from shedding even a drop of blood. A complex series of events built around the scabbard underlines the conflict between Arthur and Morgan. In the end, Morgan, having lost control of the scabbard, steals it back, then tosses it into a deep lake, thus disposing of the object that might have saved Arthur's life. (Malory's work, too, contains the scabbard; see *Heng.) In certain of these works, Morgan is on good terms with Merlin, who is fond of her, but she is occasionally thwarted by Niviene.

Morgan's decline is informed by her passage from immortal fay to human woman. In her human aspect, she hides the traits of age with magic, and she schemes to harm others. In the *Prophecies de Merlin* ("Prophecies of Merlin") of the late thirteenth century, Morgan is finally humiliated by the Lady of Avalon, who forces her to appear naked, when all may see the signs of her age, that is, her pendulous breasts and sagging belly. It is thus an ancient and withered Morgan who controls events in the fourteenth-century English poem *Sir Gawain and the Green Knight* (see *Fisher).

Among modern writers of fantasy, T.H. White depicted an unredeemed Morgan. Thomas Berger's ironic fantasy *Arthur Rex* (1978)[35] shows a Morgan La Fey who reforms, having decided that "corruption were sooner brought amongst mankind by the forces of virtue" (Lacy et al., eds. 35). Raymond Thompson observes that Phyllis Ann Karr in *The Idylls of the Queen* (1982) and Parke Godwin in *Firelord* (1980)[36] view Morgan favorably, even sympathetically (*Return from Avalon* 136). Modern fantasy writers have been attracted to the figure of Morgan. Among these, Fay Sampson casts her as the protagonist of a series of novels: *Wise Woman's Telling* (1989) depicts her attachment to her father, and *White Nun's Telling* (also 1989)[37] shows Morgan as a child with a powerful personality (Lacy et al., eds. 396).

Perhaps the most extensive and imaginative modern Arthurian reshaping in which Morgan plays a central role is Marion Zimmer Bradley's *The Mists of Avalon*. This novel tells the Arthurian story through the eyes of Morgaine, daughter of Igraine and half-sister to Arthur, and sets it against the struggle between the matriarchal religion of Goddess-worship and a male Christianity that seeks exclusivity. In this work, Viviane is the Lady of the Lake and High Priestess of Avalon who chooses Morgaine to succeed her.

Impelled by a dream vision in which she has seen Britain ruled by a high king true to Avalon and its Goddess-religion, but tolerant of the Christian religion, with its male god Jesus Christ, Viviane arranges for Arthur's heir: for the pagan ritual that will seal Arthur's kingship, Viviane chooses Morgaine as the priestess to be deflowered, thereby engineering the incest—immaterial to the old religion—that produces Mordred. But when Morgaine realizes what has happened, she abandons Avalon, Viviane, and her role as priestess. Later, however, after Arthur has broken his oath to protect Goddess-worship and adopts Christianity exclusively—largely through the urgings of a Gwenhwyfar so nervous about her own barrenness that she feels compelled to expel the ancient religion—Morgaine determines to bring down his kingship. It is thus through the female characters that new motivations are introduced for the hallowed events of Arthurian legend.

Because of these new motivations, which, for those familiar with medieval Arthurian literature, seem to explain in a plausible way some of the conundrums of the medieval inheritance, *The Mists of Avalon* seems almost to be the rediscovered manuscript of a lost or suppressed story; as "the plot behind the plot of the Arthurian story as we have known it," it is written so that "we realize [Arthur's story] has always also been the story of [Arthur's] sister, the Fairy Queen."[38] The extent to which female characters therefore determine the outcome of events is unprecedented. Although the male characters (a large cast of them) populate the novel as ever, they are characterized only externally and are seen by the reader through their outward appearance and acts. On the other hand, the reader comes to know the female characters through their thoughts, fears, and desires (Spivack 158–59), and in this way Morgaine emerges as a rounded female protagonist.[39]

A most unusual modern treatment of Morgan can be found in George Romero's film *Knightriders* (1981). Here, Morgan is cast as a man, "the infamous black knight," who has shades of the Mordred figure and who disputes the kingship with "Billy the King" in a story about a traveling carnivalesque motorcycle-jousting, stunt-riding group.[40] Morgan eschews Billy's high ideals concerning the purity of the jousts, claiming that Billy wears the "crown of thorns." (Guenevere, who has no speaking part to speak of, is recognizable by the air of frightened concern she wears throughout the film.)

Morgause

Sometimes Morgause (Morgawse, Margause) appears as Morgan's double. Supposedly one of three daughters of Gorlois and Igraine, the other two being Morgan herself and Elayne (all three are named by Malory), Morgause is Arthur's half-sister. The Vulgate *Merlin* makes of (an unnamed) Morgause, the wife of King Lot and the mother of Gawain, Agravain, Gareth, Gaheris, and Mordred. In some versions she is simply conflated with Morgan (Lacy et al., eds. 329). In *The Mists of Avalon* Morgause takes Morgaine's son, Gwydion (later Mordred), away from Morgaine at birth and raises him herself, thereby linking herself to an evil force early in the novel.

Elaine of Astolat and Elaine of Corbenic

Arthurian tradition knows two significant characters called Elaine. Elaine of Astolat (demoiselle d'Ascolat, Fair Maid of Astolat) is the woman who dies of unrequited love for Lancelot. A barge bearing her dead body arrives at Camelot, and in it is a letter explaining that Lancelot's rejection of her caused Elaine's death. In Malory's retelling, where Elaine is first named (Elaine le Blank, Fair Maid of Astolat), her story is simply and eloquently told, and in a long deathbed speech Elaine herself explains her passion, declaring that she loved Lancelot "oute of mesure." Authors sometimes found in Elaine's selflessness a foil for Guenevere's apparent selfishness, and the two were easily targeted as a contrasting pair.

Elaine became particularly interesting to Tennyson and his contemporary writers and artists (see *Lukitsh). In creating his "Lady of Shalott" (see *Hassett and Richardson), Tennyson added to the portrait he found in his source, the medieval Italian *Donna di Scalotta* (Gribble 2) (at the beginning of his career Tennyson did not yet know Malory's Fair Maid of Astolat), the famous "magic web" (l. 38) that she weaves "by night and day" (l. 37), the curse whose nature "she knows not" (l. 42), and the mirror "That hangs before her all the year" (l. 47) in which "Shadows of the world appear" (l. 48), so that when Lancelot first arrives:

> Out flew the web and floated wide;
> The mirror crack'd from side to side;
> "The curse is come upon me," cried
> The Lady of Shalott. (ll. 114–17[41])

The second Elaine is Elaine of Corbenic, mother of Galahad, who goes unnamed in French texts but is named by Malory. Her pedigree is excellent: descended from Joseph of Arimathea, to whom legend attributes the bringing of the Grail to Britain, and daughter of King Pelles (in some texts, one of the Fisher Kings), she is born of a holy line. To her falls the task of uniting Lancelot's line to her own. This is accomplished through an enchantment persuading Lancelot that Elaine is Guenevere. In modern literature, this

Elaine can be portrayed as naive (Bradley) or sanctimonious (Godwin); sometimes she is one with Elaine of Astolat (Godwin; Lacy et al., eds. 130). John Erskine's novel *Galahad* (1926) portrays this Elaine as clever and determined, bent on having a child with Lancelot (Lacy et al., eds. 146).

Lancelot's mother may also be named Elaine. That is the case in the Prose *Lancelot*, where Elaine of Benoic, wife of King Ban, suffers a double blow when her husband's death is followed immediately by the loss of her son, whom she sees carried down into the lake by the Lady of the Lake.

Enid

Enid's role is that of wife and companion to a knight of Arthur's court, who tests her devotion to him and her ability to manifest it properly. She appears as Geraint's wife in the Welsh *Geraint* and as Erec's wife in Chrétien de Troyes's *Erec et Enide*, in Hartmann von Aue's *Erec*, in the Old Icelandic *Erex Saga*, in Tennyson's *Idylls of the King*, and elsewhere. In Chrétien's poem, Enid is the beautiful daughter of a poor vavassor whom Erec brings back to Arthur's court and marries. After their marriage, the men of the court whisper that Erec spends too much time with Enid, gossip that Enid alone has noticed. When she reports this reluctantly to Erec, he sets off to seek adventure; by Erec's own order, Enid accompanies him, for he wishes to prove, with her as witness, that he has not relinquished his manhood. (By contrast, Enid's womanhood was established the first time Erec made love to her.) In the end, with Erec tested and proven by the adventures he has sought, and with Enid's loyalty demonstrated, the couple assume positions as king and queen of Erec's land.

In the *Erex Saga*, a prose rendering of Chrétien's poem, the story follows the general shape of its model, but in the episode where, in the French version, the Count of Limors forces Enid to marry him (in one of the events that test both her skill and faithfulness), the Scandinavian text makes an important change: Earl Placidus instead agrees with the court that it is against God's law to marry Evida (Enid) without her consent (Lacy et al., eds. 399).

Igerne

Igerne (Ygerne, Yguerne, Igraine) is Arthur's mother. In Geoffrey of Monmouth, Wace, the *Estoire de Merlin*, and the *Suite du Merlin*, Igerne is at first married to Gorlois, Duke of Tintagel; through Merlin's magic arts, she is tricked into believing that Uther Pendragon is Gorlois and sleeps with him, conceiving Arthur. That same night Gorlois is killed in battle and Uther soon marries Igerne.[42] Igerne's "adultery" is handled differently by different medieval texts.

In modern literature, Igraine in Marion Zimmer Bradley's *The Mists of Avalon* is something of a *mal-mariée*, a much younger woman married to an older man, who is Gorlois, here a Romanized Christian leader. Igraine falls in love with Uther and remains devoted to him for the rest of her life. Some have seen in this portrayal of Igraine an aspect of the triple goddess worshiped by her people: with Viviane, her older sister, as wise woman and Morgaine, her child, as maiden, Igraine is mother. Igraine's role, therefore, the destiny from which she may not swerve, requires her to give birth to the High King of Britain (Spivack 151).

Laudine and Lunette

The beautiful Laudine, in Chrétien de Troyes's *Yvain, ou le chevalier au lion* (*Ywain, or the Knight with the Lion*) and in the German story it inspired, Hartmann von Aue's *Iwein* of the late twelfth century, marries Ywain after he has killed her husband, defender of the magic fountain. Her confidante, Lunette, has persuaded Laudine that no man could better protect the fountain than the man who defeated her husband. Thus begins a marriage based on Ywain's sexual desire for Laudine and on Laudine's need for a new defender of the fountain. Related to the French *Yvain* is a Middle Welsh tale about Owain and Lunet, or the Lady of the Fountain, probably composed in the thirteenth century.

Fairy Women

The Lady of the Lake, or the Dame du Lac, is a title that designates several female characters whose frequent namelessness, which makes it difficult to tell them apart, may betray their fairy or quasi-fairy nature. When the Lady is named, she can be Eviène, Niviane (or Niniane), Nyneve, Viviane (see below), or Nymue (see below). She appears in William Wordsworth's poem "The Egyptian Maid" (1835) as Nina, where she instructs Merlin to take the heroine to Arthur's court (Lacy et al., eds. 526). Arthurian legend knows the Lady of the Lake as the fairy woman who gave Excalibur to Arthur and, sometimes, as the person who raised Lancelot. Some see her as a "split-off double" of Morgan, a benevolent anti-Morgan prominent especially in Malory (Fries, "From The Lady to The Tramp," 13).

In the Prose *Lancelot* Ninianne (elsewhere, variously Niniane, Niviane, Nyneve, or Viviane) is one of the fairies, who "knew the powers of words and stones and herbs, which allowed them to retain youth and beauty and enjoy whatever wealth they wished."[43] In that work, too, she is the same as the Lady of the Lake, who takes Lancelot from his mother and raises him. As a mentor, she is highly christianized, emphasizing to Lancelot that "knighthood was established to defend the Holy Church" (*Lancelot-Grail* 59). Among modern French works, Viviane re-appears in Guillaume Apollinaire's *L'Enchanteur pourrissant* ("The Rotting Magician," 1904; Lacy et al., eds. 9[44]) and in René Barjavel's *L'Enchanteur* ("The Magician," 1984; Lacy et al., eds. 32[45]), which centers in part on Merlin's relationship with Viviane. Canadian author Margaret Atwood devoted a short poem to "Recollections of Vivien."[46] In Bradley's *The Mists of Avalon*, where Viviane is High Priestess of Avalon, Nimue, Niviane, and Viviane are separate characters.

Nymue is the name that Malory gave to his "Chief Lady of the Lake" (see *Holbrook). It is she who entombs Merlin, in an effort to preserve her virginity.

Finally, an infrequent fairy figure, who appears in Laȝamon's *Brut* and in Spenser's *Faerie Queene*, is Argante. Most fairies, however, although an indispensable element of the Arthurian world, go unnamed.

III

Bradley's *The Mists of Avalon* and other modern works redeem the feminine face of Arthurian legend, a face that was always there, paradoxically both oppositional yet complementary, and certainly integral. Discussing the characters of Morgaine and the Lady of the Lake, Bradley has observed that "Malory could not imagine telling tales of Arthur without them. In other words, they were so much a part of the Arthurian legends that their absence could not be imagined" (107). A certain play of values was held in tension by the medieval Arthurian gendered paradigm, in a network of irreconcilables that, in some ways, characterizes the Arthurian phenomenon. One place where the female characters sometimes assume their full measure is in depictions of the fairy world, which may then cast light on the romance.

In all five of Chrétien de Troyes's Arthurian romances—*Erec et Enide*, *Cligés*, *Yvain*, *Lancelot*, *Le Conte du Graal* (*Perceval*)—emphasis falls upon the education of a young man and his responsibilities toward society. But Chrétien's irony, and his generally unimpressive portraits of Arthur, suggest that already in the twelfth century there existed an amused skepticism about aspects of the legend, one that, as inheritors of a more reverent tradition based on Malory's *Morte Darthur*, we may be slower than the medieval public to perceive. Beside the human world depicted in Chrétien's work, there existed a fairy one, and it provided a host of otherworld women who often interacted with Chrétien's human heroes. The romance world may have depended upon its audience's knowledge of the fairy one, for the romance offered itself as an improvement over that world, even as it often sought amelioration and enhancement from the magic ladies. Yet the separation was neither neat nor uncomplicated, for in the twelfth and thirteenth centuries the romance drew upon faery in numerous ways.

Certain short, anonymous tales, called lais, showcase a female character with magic powers, though not all such tales are Arthurian. In most of these stories, the human world prevails in the end, but there is one, Marie de France's *Lanval*, in which it does not. Unlike her contemporary Chrétien, Marie did not generally use Arthurian material in her lais, so it is significant that *Lanval* is one of only two among her tales that she situated in the Arthurian realm (the other, *Chievrefoil*, recounts an episode in the Tristan and Iseult legend).[47]

In *Lanval*, the hero, alone of Arthur's knights to be unrewarded by the king, wanders dejectedly into a meadow. Asleep next to a stream, he is summoned by a beautiful fairy, who in the comfort of her magnificent pavilion offers her love to him. She sets the terms: he may have her any time he thinks of her, and she will provide him with great wealth so long as he keeps their love secret. Lanval agrees. But Arthur's queen, like Potiphar's wife[48] (and who, like Potiphar's wife, is unnamed), importunes Lanval for his love; faced with his refusal, she implies that he must be homosexual. Finally irritated, Lanval blurts out the truth of his love, claiming at the same time that his lover is more beautiful than the queen. Lanval is now doubly condemned: the queen accuses him before Arthur of having made advances to her, which means that Lanval will have to stand trial; and, he has lost his fairy lover. In this trial, only the appearance—in both senses of the term—of Lanval's lover can save him, and he cannot summon her. In the end, of course, just when Lanval has resigned himself to his perdition, his lover exonerates him, then transports him away from Arthur's court on a palfrey that seems to fly.

Lanval has inspired a great number of interpretations. Nearly all of them take the lai to be an entirely serious work, and some of them find complex symbolism in it.[49] A few voices have dissented from these analyses. Elizabeth Poe, for example, lamenting that some of the more metaphysical glosses especially "serve more to obscure than to elucidate the text," has wondered why readers rarely consider the humor in *Lanval*; she finds, significantly, that the humor depends upon inversions. Poe shows that *Lanval* inverts what Matilda Bruckner has called the Hospitality Sequence: the Welcome, Suppertime, Bedtime, and Departure become instead the Welcome, Bedtime first, then Suppertime and Departure. Alterations in other details of the sequence suggest to Poe that Marie has infused "playful irony" into the flow of events.[50] And without going into detail, it can also be noted that the physical description of the fairy reverses the usual descending order of items established by Alice Colby in her study of the portrait in twelfth-century French literature.[51] In short, *Lanval* may contain a certain play element that depends upon inversion, or reversal of expectation.

And in fact, further inversions can be noted of a less rhetorical nature. The two spheres into which Marie places the action of her tale—the Arthurian court and the fairy otherworld—oppose one another. In this type of tale, in which a fay ventures out of her realm and into the courtly, human one, the female is seen outside the contained space that is often her place by medieval literary convention (e.g., the lady in the tower). In *Lanval*, it is rather Arthur's court that appears interiorized, small, and static; its members leave only to go into a garden below the castle, where the queen spies Lanval with the other knights. The fay's world, on the other hand, occupies open space—in the romance, the space where the hero's adventure unfolds. Lanval first meets the fay in a meadow, by a stream, and she and her damsels are the only characters in the tale who ride boldly upon horseback. The court's horizons open only to look upon the fairy and her ladies as they enter, and once more to watch as the fay sweeps Lanval away, leaving Arthur and his knights behind.[52]

Such contrasts point to a deeper one between the human and fairy worlds. With *Lanval*, a narrative schema drawn from tales of the marvelous enters into French *literary* expression, according to Laurence Harf-Lancner's study of the Morganian fairy tale, that is, one in which a fairy loves a mortal, whom she carries off with her into the otherworld (*Les Fées au moyen âge* 266). The beyond itself is portrayed as an ideal world whose inhabitants live in eternal happiness. In that regard, *Lanval* contrasts with the romance, which interprets such notions in the light of a new ethics: the hero must fulfill his role in *human* society, where the appeal of the otherworld is but a dangerous temptation from which he must withdraw (330). Indeed, in Chrétien's romances generally, the Arthurian court "has become a guarantee of the superiority of chivalric society," and it serves as a bulwark against such "irruptions from the other world" (267). One axis of *Lanval*, therefore, lies along a line opposing the supernatural to the human: *Lanval*, like certain other medieval lais and short tales, shows that the goodness of supernatural women can remedy human perversity. It is in fact such series of inversions that may point to a contrast between the romance model and the lai in *Lanval*.[53] An early reader of *Lanval* in that way was W.T.H. Jackson.[54]

In Jackson's view, *Lanval* contrasts with Arthurian chivalric mores in several ways. One of these is "the beauty contest" that presents a combat between women resembling those fought by knights to save a lady. The contest between the champions, queen and fairy, begins when the fairy removes her cloak, so that all may behold her beauty; the queen is judged less beautiful; Lanval is saved by his "champion"! The "lady performs service for the man," and a "man's honor is vindicated in a lady's beauty contest." During all this, the hero, like the ladies in an Arthurian romance (like Guenevere herself in so many other circumstances), stands by as his champion rescues him and carries him off to Avalon—indeed, perhaps in fact "abducts" him from Arthur's court, as Guenevere has so often been abducted. Here, according to Jackson, Marie does no more than push the Arthurian ethic to its logical conclusion: "If women dominate the Arthurian court and determine its values, then it is they who should contest for the possession of man, not vice versa" (16–17).

A competing pair is formed, therefore, by Arthur and the fairy mistress, in a nearly overdetermined distinction that must be thought of as at least partly gendered. Although Marie's portrait of the Arthurian court and of its ineffectual, even pusillanimous, king may be comparable to Chrétien's, as some critics believe,[55] it in fact goes farther: in Chrétien's depiction, an aging Arthur is degraded in favor of the group of younger knights and, in each work, of one or two younger knights especially—in short, in favor of another male character; but in Marie's *Lanval*, Arthur is bested not by one of his knights but by a fairy *woman*. Further, when the humanness of Arthur's finite and bounded world, accounting for his relatively more limited resources, causes him to fall short of the medieval ideal of generosity toward one's retainers, there is also a gendered note, for such magnanimity marks a lord in particular; yet the fay, a woman, can easily outmatch him. In the end, even Arthur's status as Lanval's lord is challenged when, in the trial scene, the fay performs as Lanval's legal "warrantor." That is, to exonerate himself Lanval must produce a warrantor—someone who will state formally that he spoke the truth. The fay does so. Since the function of warrantor was generally filled by an overlord,[56] a medieval audience would no doubt have recognized the important exchange that occurs at Lanval's trial, with the fairy replacing Arthur as the hero's "lord."

Although in the end the fay's superiority to Arthur belongs to a tale-type in which fairy women predominate, *Lanval* remains unique in making fewest concessions to the romance. A special interest of the lai lies in the way it presents female desire, for the fairy is a desiring subject, a custodian of her own pleasure who, unlike "human" women characters in the romance, participates neither in marriage nor in life at court. The fay helps the hero in part because he is fundamentally worthy of her ministrations; but she also acts in his behalf because she loves him and wishes to gratify her own sexual desires. As Lucy Paton had already observed, a "fairy is never a disinterested actor. Her influence on the hero's life is for the gratification of her own love for him" (193). If, structurally, the tale seems to reverse the terms of the romance, and if it mocks a decadent Arthurian court, at another level it demonstrates the complementary indispensability of the woman's realm. That is, the satisfying of the female subject's own desires, not masked or written out of the text, appears confrontational but in fact resonates to the betterment of Arthur's court, or at least to that of one of its premier knights. *Lanval* turns the romance fabric inside out, revealing, with a certain deliberateness, the feminine desire that the romance strives to contain.

IV

In a line stretching from *Lanval* and other medieval works to much recent fiction, female characters, previously hidden behind the critical assumption that what happens to men is more important, somehow more *universally* relevant, than what happens to women (Felman 29–30), emerge as essential to the Arthurian idea. Thus a good portion of recent Arthurian criticism has set itself the task of questioning the received opinion that undervalued or overlooked the Arthurian feminine. In this collection, many essays present readings of Arthurian texts that depart from traditional or canonical ones. Not all the literature essays here are avowedly feminist or theoretical; but all concentrate interpretation upon a female character or characters. All but four of the essays have already appeared elsewhere. The four explore areas overlooked by the existing literature or they challenge, from a newer perspective, the assumptions underlying essays published earlier.

Contents of This Volume

A number of essays here will be of interest both to the medieval or period scholar and to the modern theoretically oriented critic and/or feminist. As a group they may supplement each other, or they can be seen to engage in dialectical readings. The matter of women as readers and/or writers, for example, has recently held the attention of theorists and historians. Three articles in the volume deal with or include the theory of the woman reader: representing the American historical and empirical school, Roberta Krueger is concerned to recover the woman writer or reader, and the conditions of text reception. Raymond Thompson views twentieth-century women writers and readers as having brought a new shape to Arthuriana. Yet the Constance Hassett and James Richardson interpretation of Tennyson's "The Lady of Shalott" asks whether there can be a properly gendered response to a given text. As for women as "authors," E. Jane Burns's reading here of

Chrétien de Troyes's Enid as a teller of the chivalric story who undercuts the ground of the masculine tale is coincidentally paralleled in some ways by Carole Silver's interpretation of William Morris's Guenevere, whose self-defense reverses her accusers' terms.

The theoretical thrust of modern French approaches is represented in this collection by four essays. Ann Marie Rasmussen's analysis of Gottfried von Strassburg's *Tristan* is grounded in the work of French thinker Julia Kristeva, particularly in Kristeva's ideas about "Women's Time."[57] The writings of French philosopher Luce Irigaray[58] have influenced Burns's reading of Chrétien de Troyes's *Erec et Enide* and Marilyn Farwell's essay on Bradley's *The Mists of Avalon*. The ideas of French psychoanalyst Jacques Lacan[59] have encouraged readings that find a theoretical feminine existing in textual discourse,[60] as in Geraldine Heng's treatment of Malory.

The volume offers the varied analyses of Sheila Fisher and Geraldine Heng, centered upon questions of the gender of the Arthurian text itself. Fisher gives a historicized reading of *Sir Gawain and the Green Knight* in which she attends to the politics of Morgan's representation in the poem and thus to the character's medieval reception. Heng here interprets Malory but has written elsewhere on *Gawain*. Fisher's text further provides an example of recent feminist studies of (masculine) public and (feminine) private space. Regina Psaki's contribution contains a two-part program: to describe Italian medieval Arthurian literature's independence from the French tradition, and to open discussion of its female characters.

Some essays in the volume, less overtly theoretical in orientation, cluster around enduring concerns and have both historical and contemporary relevance. Elisabeth Brewer rightly observes, in her study of the modern Guenevere, that Western culture's changing view of women and sexuality is often imprinted upon the female characters of powerful myths. Sue Ellen Holbrook's analysis of Malory's Nimue, the article of earliest date in the collection, Anne Berthelot's examination of the Damsel of the Fountain in the Prose *Lancelot*, and Judith Anderson's analysis of Spenser's Argante in *The Faerie Queene* all emphasize the importance of paying serious attention even to perceivedly "minor" female characters, against their traditional elision in the scholarly literature. They show how characters who are not principal—as may frequently be the case for female portraits—can nonetheless play a significant role in a reading of the text. In a similar vein, Maureen Fries's point of departure here is Georges Dumézil's categorization of heroic roles in Indo-European literature, a classification that, as Fries states, omits the female. Laurence Harf-Lancner's prominent book-length analysis of the fairy figures Morgan and Melusine, represented here by a translated excerpt,

is one of several substantial studies that testify to modern interest in the fairy phenomenon,[61] a subject that is frequently related to issues of women and literature.

In the nineteenth-century section of the collection, Barbara Fass Leavy's reading of Matthew Arnold's Iseult of Brittany as a character who relates in part to Arnold's own personal concerns represents a type of cross-gendered analysis. That sort of interpretation is taken up again for Tennyson's Elaine by Hassett and Richardson.

The articles in this gathering by art historians Joanne Lukitsh and Muriel Whitaker, with their attention to the female creators of art, and perhaps even more specifically to the ways in which such artists deal with female and male subjects, exemplify a trend in art-historical studies. While Whitaker in particular, in her article written for *Arthurian Women*, takes off from the notion of a "woman's eye," Hassett and Richardson examine critically the part of gaze theory that takes the gazer to be masculine and appropriative, the gazed-upon feminine, passive, and appropriated.

The individual summaries that follow may help to bring out further the relevant themes.

Resisting Tales

Essays in this first section challenge the way modern criticism has read certain medieval Arthurian texts. Traditional interpretation, wherever it stands along the critical continuum, has generally sought and argued over, and then sought to fine-tune, what strikes some feminist critics as a rather uniform reading of the medieval text. In assuming a univocal reception of texts by a Medieval Reader, a corpus of like-minded views becomes constituted through elaborations upon previous criticism. Such criticism, seeming to speak for a homogeneous medieval audience, misses a chance to explore the multiplicity of possible reader responses, no less available to the medieval public than to the modern. What is required, as Roberta Krueger puts it in her contribution, is an approach that allows for the play of the text's dialectics, a multilateral response that captures the complexities and sophistication of the text itself.

One of the strengths of American feminist criticism has been its eagerness to historicize, to try to recover both female writing and to reconstruct what may have been female reading, unlike the more theoretical French and perhaps British feminisms. Of course, the need for historical reconstruction and the concomitant difficulty of performing it become more acute in medieval studies. Thus Krueger tries to learn something about the position of noblewomen in courtly society by careful study of Chrétien de Troyes's

romances.[62] She argues that by simultaneously privileging and marginalizing their female characters, Chrétien's romances record the ambiguous position of noblewomen. Did women listeners/readers of Chrétien's tales act as accomplices to their fictional representation as subordinate? Or did Chrétien, who often seems to have held an ironic view of courtly convention, invite his female public to share that view as it related, for one, to his notable female creations—Enid, Fenice (in *Cligès*), Laudine, Guenevere—and their responses to courtliness? To be sure, Chrétien shares his culture's acceptance of men's hegemony; but by casting female characters and women readers as *problems*, he may have provoked some women readers to question what they were hearing. An approach to the text that accounts for several possible, even conflicting, readings would be desirable: the knight-listener (who, it is assumed, identifies with the hero) could have enjoyed the text, while an alert female listener (who may identify with Laudine) might have felt excluded from its proffered privileges.

Implicit in Krueger's analysis is the idea of a woman's *resistance*, a notion that also grounds E. Jane Burns's reading of Chrétien de Troyes's *Erec et Enide*, adapted for this volume from chapter four of Burns's *Bodytalk: When Women Speak in Old French Literature*. Taking off primarily but not exclusively from the work of Luce Irigaray, and accepting the predominance of the masculine in the romance, Burns listens for a dissenting and "resistant doubled discourse," a "bodytalk." The female body, in romance the site of the construction of a bolstered male identity as the male gazes upon the female (a "headless, mindless" body[63]), necessarily becomes the locus of an alternative reading through which female voices (in an Irigarayan move that is neither one nor the other, yet is both) "neither fully underwrite the specular basis of male subjectivity nor thoroughly repudiate the culturally constructed female." Burns calls upon Irigaray's strategy of mimicry—that is, what happens when a man's words or a male writer's text are framed within a woman's discourse or a female writer's text[64]—and she wonders what would happen if *Erec et Enide* were "Enide's Romance?" What she sees in Chrétien's first romance is a rivalry between men's and women's stories, one that is obscured by the tale of love, which in turn may be a screen for the hero's reputation. But what if we were to read *Erec et Enide* as a tale of female voices raised against the masculine tradition of storytelling? (Can we be sure that none of the female audience heard it that way?) Enid's repeated warnings to Erec in the forest cast him as a loser, and they tell a chivalric tale quite different from that of Chrétien's narrator. For Enid, Chrétien's famous formulation, *bele conjointure* ("fine conjoining"), through which he describes in part the process of writing, is "a simultaneous coming together and holding apart

of the female flesh and its supposedly antithetical speech," a description that captures Irigaray's positing of a feminine discourse having the structure of the female genitalia.

The idea that an apparent compliance may mask a deep resistance reappears in Ann Marie Rasmussen's article, prepared especially for this group of essays. She examines Gottfried von Strassburg's *Tristan*, attending to the strains of cooperation and resistance that constitute Isolde's inheritance from her mother, also named Isolde. Basing her analysis upon Julia Kristeva's notion of "Women's Time," Rasmussen proposes that the male Arthurian world occupies the horizontal axis—that is, what Kristeva calls "linear time": genealogy, chronology, synchronic movement through time. The female Arthurian world fills a vertical axis: that is, "cyclical time": space, eternity, biological rhythm, seasonal return. But what if we suppose that the love potion, prepared by Queen Isolde, sister of Morold and wife of King Gurmun, for her daughter, is rather an outcome of a mother-daughter *genealogical* relationship—that is, of a *horizontal* female relation?

In German medieval literature, the "sexual apprenticeship model" of mother-daughter relations dominates: mothers educate their daughters and guide them into marriage. In that way the mother herself is replicated, and the process recapitulates woman's function as bearer of Kristeva's monumental time. But that ideal may also be ripe for subversion. Queen Isolde's practical and political cleverness appears when she outsmarts the disreputable seneschal who, hoping to marry Princess Isolde, stole the tongue of the dragon Tristan slew in order to fulfill the terms of the marriage bargain. The queen's manipulation of events suggests that women may both collude with and resist male authority. And the potion, called a love philter, has, for the queen, both sentimental *and* political efficacy. It bears the queen's hope that her daughter will enjoy not only love but that she will also learn to manipulate her necessarily limited access to political power. The plan miscarries, however, and Princess Isolde earns not honor and love but suspicion and condescension; hardly following in her mother's footsteps, the young Isolde is instead removed from oneness with her mother. As a result, in a "paradox of contrasts and sameness," the Isolde-Isolde continuity is both deeply affirmed and startlingly disrupted.

Maureen Fries, like Burns and Krueger, and again drawn by the idea of female resistance, here discusses Enid in Chrétien de Troyes's *Erec et Enide* and the characters of Laudine and Lunette in his *Yvain*, and she takes up the character of Morgan in *Sir Gawain and the Green Knight*, as does Sheila Fisher in the next section. But Fries's interest lies in pursuing the results to be obtained from classification and synthesis. She asks whether the image

of the Arthurian woman as passive, conforming supporter of the masculine experience—in short, the heroine's adherence to an identifiably female role—is the only one we may expect. Georges Dumézil's well-known categorization of heroic roles, based upon masculine functions in Indo-European society, left to women a "vague and contrapuntal" position at best; were there not others, to which Dumézil was not particularly attuned?

Fries divides her samples into heroines, female heroes, and female counter-heroes. Briefly put, the heroine respects the virtues of chastity, obedience, and silence; her principal attraction is her beauty; she is an instrument rather than an agent. The female hero, whether wife or virgin, may be a surpassing example of a female, but she still serves patriarchal culture. Only the female counter-hero, who may hold values at variance with the male culture "in which she must exist," paradoxically may also fill roles usually open only to men. The preeminent example of the female counter-hero is Morgan, and the price of her insurgency is a quick downward turn in her character, from beauty to crone.[65]

Story, Gender, and Culture

Most critical treatments of female characters in Arthurian legend begin by assuming the stories' masculine orientation. Essays in the preceding section posited a female resistance to submergence in a masculine field. In this section Sheila Fisher's article on *Sir Gawain and the Green Knight*, one of two important articles that Fisher has published on that Middle English text, agrees with estimates in the first section that figure medieval Arthurian literature as masculine. Fisher's approach is again an example of American historical feminist analysis. Geraldine Heng's essay on Malory's *Morte Darthur* argues instead for a "feminine subtext," and two other Heng essays, not reprinted here but summarized below, posit such a subtext in *Sir Gawain*. The third article, Regina Psaki's, offers a different kind of resistance, and is the only one of the collection to do so. Psaki's "multicultural" stance rejects the marginalizing of Italian medieval Arthurian literature, measured against the French "ideal," the romances of Chrétien de Troyes.

Fisher's "Leaving Morgan Aside: Women, History, and Revisionism in *Sir Gawain and the Green Knight*" appeared in 1988, preceding her "Taken Men and Token Women in *Sir Gawain and the Green Knight*" and Heng's two articles on *Sir Gawain*. Fisher broke ground by drawing attention to Morgan's importance to the poem, for "Leaving Morgan Aside" undertook a study ignored by book-length treatments and discussed by only a handful of earlier articles. As Fisher observes, Morgan le Fay, not named until close to the end of the poem, and who turns out to be its "generator," had

been as marginalized by modern criticism as by the text itself. What does it mean that Morgan, jettisoned from a central *narrative* position, becomes central to the text's revision of Arthurian history? *Gawain* seeks to demonstrate how the Arthurian paradigm might have assured its own continuation by conforming to the tenets of Christian chivalry: since women were implicated in the fall of the Round Table, the Arthurian kingdom might be saved if women can be placed at the periphery: "To deny the female would be to save the kingdom."

In Fisher's reading, a silent Guenevere, displaced to the beginning of the poem, is thus marginalized even as it opens. When the Lady who will soon test Gawain and who occupies the center section of the poem first appears, she is accompanied on either side—framed, as it were—by Guenevere and Morgan, this latter displaced to the end of the poem. Eventually, if the Christian chivalric revision is to succeed, the Lady too, who is "femaleness itself," must be relegated to the periphery.

"Contained" between Guenevere and Morgan, the Lady operates from within interior space, from which, or so it seems, she can exercise power. In this way her femaleness becomes linked with privateness, itself joined to female sexuality. By redefining this privateness—and with it the emblematic and enigmatic girdle that issues from it—the poem revises Arthurian legend as it must, for the kingdom is doomed when private desire overwhelms public responsibility. The girdle, which reveals Gawain's private desire, is linked to the privateness of the Lady. When in the end Gawain returns to the court, the Lady vanished, the girdle has become a "sign now not of the woman, but of the tested man, who has not been found so wanting after all."

In "Taken Men and Token Women," published a year later, Fisher developed further certain of the points made in "Leaving Morgan Aside." Here, she situates the Lady against the extratextual background of women's relative powerlessness, for in "real life" aristocratic women did not have the sort of power the Lady deploys. Contrasting the feudal and money economies, Fisher finds that the gift economy, basis of "idealized feudal bonding," is replaced during the Lady's negotiations with Gawain by a money economy, one that medieval theorists thought gave "too much power and self-determination to the individual subject." Had the Lady succeeded, the feudal system of exchange would have succumbed—another reason to bracket her off.[66]

These readings receive a challenge from Heng's psychoanalytic work, as do other essays that suppose the medieval Arthurian text to be always about its male characters. In "Feminine Knots and the Other *Sir Gawain and the Green Knight,*" Heng hopes to explode what she calls "phallocentric" interpretations. She supplants the notion of feminine marginalized figures with that of the feminine "countertext," and she argues for "another desire," expressed in a "feminine narrative folding into and between the masculine." In a "feminine relay," the work is the "theater of its feminine figures," whose example is one of "identity as plural, heterogeneous, and provisional," an idea that, in its philosophical origins, seeks to unsettle the Cartesian Subject, and one that seems to obliterate the possibility of a historical approach. Whereas in Fisher's analysis here the Lady's "luf lace" (girdle) was a private index that had to become public, and the pentangle the place where private masculine virtues were conjoined with the public good, for Heng the girdle signifies in a protean way and unsettles identities, while the pentangle, on the other hand, is a closed masculine sign that aims at guaranteeing a stable identity.[67] In "A Woman Wants: The Lady, *Gawain,* and the Forms of Seduction," Heng takes the argument farther: *Gawain,* through the Lady's desire, erases the borders of gendered identity. In a seduction that does indeed occur, but through language, *Gawain* answers the Freudian-Lacanian question "What does woman want?" not with the usual "single, unendurably banal, requisite response"—the phallus—but by discovering new avenues. The Lady is both a woman playing a man in the act of courtship and a woman playing a woman; the fixed, gendered courtly subject is not sustainable. "By putting in jeopardy, and under the stress of constant revision, received definitions of gender, identity, and the subject, the Lady turns away the demand that would make feminine desire finite and reducible, a transparent object of knowledge, and vulnerable therefore to mastery and assimilation" (123).

When Heng turns to Malory's *Morte Darthur,* the subject of her article reprinted in this volume, she once more examines "the feminine," discussing first the numerous gifts and objects provided by female characters. But it is the notion of enchantment that works doubly to describe two "kinds of feminine play": the term refers both to magic and to the "enchantment of love." In Malorian Arthurian society, love is so fundamental that those who eschew it, like Balyn, are cast out. Once a knight dedicates himself to a lady, she becomes "immanent in his deeds." The example of Lancelot is telling, as he surrenders his identity to Guenevere. Lancelot's behavior "translates polysemously for him into dedication to a feminine principle." If Lancelot did not exist "within a world of feminine purpose," the character as he is known to us would be unimaginable.

Magic, an independent force privileged in Malory's text, is a more "direct mode of feminine play," and it is far more powerful than the practice of arms. And it is significant that its male practitioner, Merlin, is replaced by female users of magic early in the narrative. Both Nyneve and Morgan supplant Merlin (Morgan in particular takes pleasure in staging the effects of her powers on Arthur's realm), and their mere presence recognizes "alterity in the Arthurian worldview" and "the active pressure of submerged discourses." It is when she discusses the final scene, in the barge to Avilion, that Heng touches on themes raised in her two Gawain articles, for in this final scene may be "discerned a suggestion of the final instability and impermanence of all constructed identity." Concluding on an Irigarayan note, Heng sees in the "subtext of feminine presences" a "range of play" that may yield "the recovery of a possible operation of the feminine in language."

In her contribution written for *Arthurian Women*, Psaki laments the bias among Italian critics who find that "true" Arthurian expression is French. Because the critics' francophilic commentary implies that the twelfth-century French texts offer an enhancement of the female beloved nearly to the status of the knight, Psaki points to recent critical readers of French Arthuriana (such as Krueger) who demonstrate the opposite.

Examining the Italian works narratologically and discussing the narrative partly from the perspective of gaze theory, Psaki finds that "narrators, focalization, plot, characterization" all prevent a focus on female characters independent of the male characters in the *Tristano Riccardiano, Tavola Ritonda*, and *cantari*, as well as in *cantari* set in or mentioning Arthur's realm. Those secondary female characters the hero is likely to meet in the forest are the protagonist's "burdens or rewards." Among men, the heroine herself provokes quarrels more often than anything else; if a modern reader might indict Mordred sooner than Guenevere for the fall of Arthur's kingdom, the Italian medieval reader *knew* it was Guenevere's transgressions that constituted the "flaw at the heart of the Arthurian dream of chivalry." Women could not be "narrative focalizers"—we hardly ever see the story from their perspective—and this is a "vital index of the author's presentation of women." In general, the medieval text does not explore a character's thoughts; but the female character whose private ruminations the text may happen to reveal is likely to be an antagonist. And when "women in the Italian romances articulate an active desire that is not mutual, they disturb the universe far more than the knight who rapes or abducts."

Finally, in an observation that works as well for French versions, Psaki notes that women are related not only causally to adventure and to mystery, but metaphorically as well. Like the lady's demands, which have no logic of their own, the terms of adventures are inflexible, arbitrary, and unreasonable; such an unfathomable posture locates women in the world of the Other.

Many of medieval Arthurian literature's female characters have fairylike qualities and supernatural powers, as summaries of the articles by Fries, Rasmussen, Fisher, and Heng have already shown. The special healing and occult powers of Iseult and/or her mother, for example, make them kin to those enchantresses who reign without men in a place beyond but contiguous to Arthur's world. In many Arthurian romances, such fairy women live apart from men; they are more powerful than humans and often test the mettle of mortal men.[68] In this section, Laurence Harf-Lancner's philological inquiry into two types of fairies in Old French literature constitutes the only essay in the volume to deal with origins. Anne Berthelot, analyzing the Damsel of the Fountain in the thirteenth-century Prose *Lancelot*, suggests some of the problems surrounding the fairy figures, whose narrative replicability and anonymity are a feature of their representation in romance. Sue Ellen Holbrook then sorts Nymue out from Malory's myriad ladies of the lake and shows how the fifteenth-century author rewrote her character and gave it both continuity and shape. The character Argante, who figures as a lustful giantess in Book III of Spenser's *The Faerie Queene*, is the subject of Judith Anderson's essay.

The selection from Harf-Lancner incidentally reminds us, through its range over several literary worlds, that Arthurian material is not always discrete. Rather, the subject of fairies embraces and incorporates the Arthurian phenomenon, even as it seems to characterize it. Harf-Lancner's book has been called "a complete file on fairies in French literature from the twelfth to the fourteenth centuries."[69] The portions translated here are drawn from the early part of the book, where Harf-Lancner discusses the figures of fairy godmother and fairy lover. She points out that learned culture preserved the image of the classical Parcae, while another concept was taking form in the collective imagination: that of the *fata* who was mistress of destiny but who was also tied to fertility cults and to abundance, and who might make nocturnal visits to welcoming households, where she gathered propitiatory offerings. At the same time, popular culture knew other figures, forest divinities who bestowed their love upon fortunate mortals. By the twelfth century, these last two had been united into one. But in the twelfth century, too, with the taste for the Matter of Britain and its Arthurian substance, folklore themes and characters were incorporated into written literature. At that point, two types of fairies emerge: fairy godmothers—the Parcae revised and corrected by ten centuries of popular culture—and the supernatural lover, whose relations with the world of humans are retold in two types of narratives, the Melusinian (denoting the passage of the fairy woman into the world

of mortals), and the Morganian (denoting the passage of the hero into the otherworld of fairies) (76–77).

In Berthelot's view, the Prose *Lancelot*, the lengthy third part of the Vulgate Cycle, has too often been studied for the episode of Galahad's conception at Corbenic, when a drugged Lancelot makes love to the Fisher King's daughter, thinking that she is Guenevere. In a complex analysis that brings out the multilayered richness of the text itself, Berthelot studies instead the episode of the Damsel of the Fountain, longer and more meaningful to a reading of the hero's relationship with Guenevere and to an interpretation of her character.

In some ways, the Damsel of the Fountain portion seems to rehearse the later event at Corbenic, which "inverts the sign of an already-encountered section." The anonymity of the Damsel, and the resemblance of Lancelot's adventure with her to so many others, could leave her overlooked; but in fact, the adventure is nothing less than a "matrice" (in French, both "matrix" and "womb") for events that follow: these include not only what happens at Corbenic but also an episode with a third damsel, called the Damsel of the Well. Significantly, if a mystical element surrounds events with the two damsels, that is not true for events at Corbenic.

In addition to other parallels among the three, Lancelot is each time made to drink a substance: the episodes at the fountain and the well participate in a magic causality that brings with it a supernatural logic, one that intersects with the text's chivalric logic. While the Damsel of the Fountain, also called the Healer Damsel, lies close to death because of her unrequited love for Lancelot, she is unable to tend to the ailing hero; her recovery puts her into a position of enormous strength, for she holds in her hand not only the life of the hero but that of the romance written about him. The proliferation of damsels—the multiform figure of the fountain damsel—in fact erects "a series of obstacles that parallel the obvious meaning of the story," whose reason for being is to turn Lancelot "away from a univocal courtly love." The hero himself passes through these tests without realizing what they are, true to his "type." A certain suppleness characterizes those around him, however, who participate in a text—a "matrix" of a different sort— that acts upon and "for" the "queen's knight."

Holbrook's "Nymue, Chief Lady of the Lake, in Malory's *Le Morte Darthur*," published earlier (1978) than other medieval essays in this collection, endures as a first serious, recuperative look at one Arthurian female character. Holbrook was concerned to rescue Nymue from certain pejorative assumptions of modern criticism, made either through inattention or unexamined expectation.

Malory offers two Ladies of the Lake, according to Holbrook, and one of these is Nymue. In responding to his sources, Malory improves Nymue's part in Merlin's disappearance and expands her role as benevolent helper. Nymue evolves from a helpless figure to one who, when she has attained her full powers, cleaves to good knights and Arthur's in particular, as a helpful influence. In Holbrook's view, Nymue's role as Pelleas's wife thus becomes more memorable than her relationship with Merlin. It is in Nymue's appearance in the story of Gawain, Ettard, and Pelleas, that Malory delineates a unique role for her as "the savior and beloved wife of Sir Pelleas." She thus becomes Pelleas's lover and his good guardian—in a collapsing of roles that recalls Harf-Lancner's observations about the conflation of the originally separate fairy-godmother and fairy-lover figures. Whether "by craft or by accident," Malory surpassed his predecessors by creating a minor character whose various appearances achieve a pattern that itself emanates from a "single, unambiguously benign character."

Argante, whose appearance in Spenser's *The Faerie Queene* is the subject of Anderson's discussion, is but a minor character in recorded Arthurian tradition, having been mentioned only in Laȝamon's *Brut*, though her name may reach back into oral literature.[70] Laȝamon made of her the queen of Avalon, whose role was to heal Arthur after he had been wounded in battle. She thus took the role traditionally held by Morgan, and written tradition generally knows of her therefore as a Morgan analogue. Anderson rejects as conjecture the suggestion that Spenser's readers would have seen in the name *Argante* a variation on the sea-dwelling *morgans*; she believes that the elf-queen of Laȝamon's *Brut* is the source for the name.

Arthurian literature has always been able to lend itself to political purpose, and *The Faerie Queene* is no exception. In Edmund Spenser's unfinished allegorical epic, begun during the 1570s, Arthur, who represents the virtue of magnanimity, searches for Gloriana, the Faerie Queene, whom he has seen in a dream. Argante, seen as an antitype of the chaste Belphoebe, and through a distant tie to the elf-queen Gloriana, "parodically aproaches the idea of" Queen Elizabeth I of England. In "radically . . . deflected ways," Argante can be read as a reflection on the queen's courtly flirtations, involving the younger men of the court. This parody is reinforced by knowledge of the origin of Argante's name as Laȝamon's elf-queen of the fairies.

Once Argante is recognized as a distortion of Gloriana, Arthur's dream of her as Faerie Queene may be explored for its allusions to comic passages in Chaucer's work, passages that qualify the dream by threatening or enriching it. Certain ambivalences and parodic touches cluster

around the figure of Arthur and around his ideal, the elf-queen. Argante, whose figure parodies this dream, is a "more destructive instance of [a] broader parody."

Guenevere and Iseult in the Nineteenth Century

Two poems in particular reveal some of the complexities of the nineteenth-century view of Arthurian womanhood. These are Matthew Arnold's *Tristram and Iseult* (1852), the first modern version in English of the legend, studied here by Barbara Fass Leavy, and William Morris's "The Defence of Guenevere" (1858), the subject of Carole Silver's essay in this volume.

At the end of *Tristram and Iseult*, Iseult of Brittany (also known in the tradition as Iseult of the White Hands), now widowed, tells her children the story of Vivian and Merlin—how Vivian imprisoned the old magician, then went her own way. The enigma of the tale's presence in the third and final part of Arnold's hauntingly difficult poem has called up varying explanations. Though the three parts of the poem are devoted, as their subtitles show, to "Tristram," "Iseult of Ireland," and "Iseult of Brittany," Fass Leavy argues that it is Iseult of Brittany who is Arnold's focus.

Iseult of Brittany's character is that of stoical wife and mother, obliged to spend her days at "female" tasks. But she enjoys a rich fantasy life, conjuring the Merlin-Vivian tale to imagine a relationship in which she may leave her submissive state and become adventurous. Arnold conceived of Iseult as a mother who is a frustrated Vivian—who is cast as a shape-changing fairy in one of Arnold's sources—something to which a proper Victorian wife could never confess.

Arnold develops an identification between Iseult of Brittany and Keats's Belle Dame, thus preparing the conclusion in which Iseult may imagine herself a Vivian whose freedom is like the "light-footedness" of Keats's figure. But Keats's ballad and the story of Tristan and Iseult both fit a larger pattern, that of the story of the man who leaves the world "to seek a more blissful existence" with an otherworldly mistress, a common narrative in nineteenth-century Europe. Fass Leavy suggests the theme's "unique applicability [in Arnold] to the life of women." She further argues that Homer's *Odyssey* was a more important influence on *Tristram and Iseult* than was previously acknowledged: in her fantasy, Iseult abandons her role as the faithful, patient Penelope in order to take on the role of a female Odysseus. Penelope may well constitute the Victorian model of sexual innocence and motherhood: innocence in Arnold's poem is still death. Sexuality alone bestows life, for "what Arnold has depicted in this poem is the double tragedy, for man and for woman, of Victorian attitudes toward sexuality."

William Morris's "The Defence of Guenevere," the only dramatic monologue studied in this collection, is also the only work in which the heroine tells her own story. Although Guenevere is traditionally a guilty party, Morris's character sees her own transgression in a *different* light, and she proceeds by "shifting the very ground on which judgment is to be passed" (Freedman 242). Her evasions, distantly like those of the medieval Iseult, are linguistic and in the domain of rhetoric, not in that of "empirical verification or logic" (Freedman 243).

Silver's essay on "The Defence of Guenevere" and "King Arthur's Tomb," drawn from her book *The Romance of William Morris*, emphasizes the poet's preoccupation with character motivation, as he analyzes emotions left sketchy in his Malorian source. Silver's analysis "lifts the discussion of the poems beyond the point where too many critics of the dramatic monologue have stopped: that is, with the question of Guenevere's literal guilt."[71] For Silver, Guenevere steps off Morris's page as a speaking subject and nearly as her own person, one whose motivations, almost *sui generis*, escape the control of Morris's pen: "The moral ambiguities within the poem are quite deliberate; they stem from Guenevere's character, not Morris's uncertainty about it."

Integral to the psychological complexity of Morris's poem is its construction as a dramatic monologue: as Guenevere stands trial, she speaks her own story; it is from her defense of herself that the "moral ambiguities" spring, for Guenevere is not sure of her moral guilt, only of the strength of her love. She slides between temporarily admitting her guilt and assuming an innocent stance. The queen represents the poet's "mixed anima," "creative and destructive, deadly and life-giving both."

Guenevere bases her defense upon the "moral confusion in the universe," for "things are not what they seem." She describes her love for Lancelot as a madness and a fall: she "slips" into love with him. Ironically, however, in dwelling upon the mitigating circumstances, Guenevere persuades the reader that she is guilty. But there is a final turn: the reader is obliged to understand that the "adultery is less meaningful than the love itself." In "King Arthur's Tomb," a sequel to the "Defence" and a further analysis of mortal love, Guenevere comes to know herself better, passing first through "an intricate process of self-vindication."

Another Look

Preceding the women authors of Arthuriana who have flourished in the late twentieth century, the photographer Julia Margaret Cameron and a number of women book illustrators have, it is argued in essays by Joanne Lukitsh and Muriel Whitaker, brought a particular vision to Arthurian visual art. On the other hand, co-authors Constance Hassett and James Richardson, in a literary discussion, wonder whether there can be such a thing as gendered looking.

The Arthurian photographs of Julia Margaret Cameron, like her work in general, mark her as one of the "passionate Victorians" who "sought to sublimate desire and to make desire sublime, both at the same time" (Weaver 23). According to Lukitsh, in Cameron's oeuvre "womanly" subjects provided a major theme, as she illustrated inspirational and heroic female characters. In Lukitsh's discussion of Cameron's illustrations for the *Idylls of the King*, the photographer emerges as especially interested in the women characters who inhabited Camelot. Though no revolutionaries (and Cameron no revolutionary herself), the women characters that Cameron interpreted "exert power over the men." Of the fifteen photographic illustrations to the *Idylls*, eleven, or more than two-thirds, are from the idylls of Enid, Vivien, Elaine, and Guenevere. In particular, Elaine's idyll bears four photographic illustrations, the greatest number for any character. In Lukitsh's view, Cameron draws out, in an explicitly visual way, the parallels between Arthur's dream of the ideal kingdom and Elaine's dream of the ideal love.

Implicit in Lukitsh's essay is the matter of an original woman working in traditions that were masculine. These include Arthurian history (and Tennyson's interpretation of it) and painting and graphic arts in general. Having taken some of her inspiration from the contemporary engravings of Gustave Doré, by then an internationally recognized figure, Cameron worked to assert the superiority of her renditions over his; a posterity that has found Doré's "depiction of women often weak"—in one illustration Elaine looks "more besotted than dead" (Lacy et al., eds. 118)—might well judge that she surpassed Doré in at least one way.

Indeed, in the nineteenth and early twentieth centuries women seem often to have found their niche in book illustration. The women illustrators and designers of bindings for Arthurian texts who came after Cameron flourished under the umbrella of the Arts and Crafts movement. Many shed their amateur status to become partners or competitors of professional men. Four who did so illustrated Arthurian works—Eleanor Fortescue Brickdale, Jessie M. King, Dorothea Braby, and Annegret Hunter-Elsenbach.

Whitaker proposes that a "woman's eye" often informs both the woman artist's choice of subject and the way it is treated. Brickdale, for example, who represented "the third generation of the Pre-Raphaelite Arthurian vision" (Lacy et al., eds. 53), chose to illustrate lines of text that presented women characters in emotionally charged situations, and she made women the central figures in her interpretation (Gordon-Wise 111). Jessie M. King, today regarded as the finest book illustrator that Scotland has produced, illustrated *The High History of the Holy Graal* and contributed her designs for William Morris's *The Defence of Guenevere and Other Poems*. Her illustration for the line "He did not hear her coming as he lay," in particular, effects a role reversal: Guenevere as nun encroaches formally and symbolically on the white space that contains Lancelot in a posture of abasement at the queen's feet. Dorothea Braby (b. 1909) is a wood engraver, portrait painter, and book illustrator who provided six color engravings for Gwyn Jones's prose translation of the Middle English romance *Sir Gawain and the Green Knight* (1952) published by the Golden Cockerel Press. Annegret Hunter-Elsenbach (b. 1948) is a Canadian painter and bookbinder who created an illustrated edition of Tennyson's early poem, *Morte Darthur* (1842).

But the conundrum of gendered looking may not offer easy resolution. In an article written for this collection from the perspective of literary gender studies, Constance Hassett and James Richardson engage with recent feminist thinking about the gaze in a way that also implicates theories of the woman reader. Through their reading of Alfred Lord Tennyson's poem "The Lady of Shalott," they reject the idea that there exists a special sympathy between reader and literary character that depends upon gender. Their work therefore departs from and revises certain feminist assumptions about the gaze, made current first and most notably, but not exclusively, by Laura Mulvey,[72] namely, that the gazer is always male and always dominant, the female always the passive gazed-upon. Noting that those and other, similar suppositions paradoxically reinforce "representations of gender imbalance" as much as they resist "the sadistic-aggressive impulses underlying" some representations of women, the coauthors implicitly question a feminist criticism that would flatten the complexity of gendered responses to works of art. Centrally important to any such discussion is the idea, as Linda Williams has concluded from research that marks a new departure in American feminist criticism,[73] that both male and female viewers identify with the principals of any scenario, regardless of gender. In short, for Hassett and Richardson, there is no "rigidly coherent and gendered self whose response to art is determined entirely by its biological sex."[74]

In the wake of feminists who applaud the collapse in theory of the male/female binarism, Hassett and Richardson here propose a cross-gendered reading of Tennyson's "Lady," finding that the gaze, rather than being simply masculine and appropriative, includes "the anxiety of being looked at." They approach Tennyson's poem through Keats's "The Eve of St Agnes": there, Porphyro's gaze upon Madeline will not be riskless. The yearning of

Porphyro and Madeline, who do not see each other but rather a dream of love, is without an object, for "particularization" brings limitation. Paralleling the "dissolved" object and the "dissolved self" of the author is a vagueness of poetic visualizing: the single perspective required by the gaze is in fact an unstable construct in both Keats and Tennyson. Especially in Tennyson, one sees the "dissolution of poetic (and readerly) identity," for his poetry "revises the rigid binary of 'active' and 'passive.'" In female surrogates, Keats and Tennyson find their own dissolution. Though the Lady's death *looks* passive, therefore, she becomes "a terrible prophet" and her dying becomes "the source of poetic authority."

Revisionary Tales: Guenevere and Morgan in the Twentieth Century

The twentieth century may have brought to Arthurian legend some of its most profound alterations. The medium of film, the wide market in books for children, and the advent of the paperback book have all helped the proliferation in kind and number of the Arthurian legend's vehicles. In the thirty or so years after the mid-century, more than one hundred novels retold the Arthurian legend (Thompson, *Return from Avalon* 3). No less noteworthy is the documentable entrance of women as an influential reading public, and then as authors and revisers of Arthurian material. The three articles in this section, by Elisabeth Brewer, Marilyn Farwell, and Raymond Thompson, explore the fortunes of the Arthurian legend in the late nineteenth and twentieth centuries.

In her article, Brewer observes that in both medieval and modern fiction, "the figure of Guenevere personifies the feminine ideal, and in so doing indicates our changing attitudes to women and to sexual morality." She surveys briefly the changes in the portrait of Guenevere from the mid-nineteenth century, when Tennyson wrote, to the end of the nineteenth, and from then until the 1980s.

In the late nineteenth century, although Guenevere was the "weak little woman," her infidelity prompted greater tolerance than it had in Tennyson's era, in part because of the research into sexual relationships undertaken by Havelock Ellis. In many plays the sweep and grandeur of the medieval story is reduced and "domesticated." In others, a new pastoralism places Guenevere under the leaves and stars, making of her an innocent whose passion is "pure" and "elemental." Richard Wagner's promotion of the love-death motif in his opera *Tristan und Isolde* seeps into representations of the Lancelot-Guenevere liaison.

More recent retellings update Guenevere to reflect images found in modern media. Brewer discovers a "Laura Ashley Guenevere" in Mary

Stewart's *The Wicked Day* (1983). Sexual matters are treated at greater length and pitch in modern novels, which feature a "new race of liberated young Gueneveres." The Guenevere of the 1980s has become an Arthurian superwoman: executive and administrator, efficient organizer and even fundraiser, she must also have known pregnancy and childbirth, for "even the experience of motherhood is seen in terms of a career." Though freed from the harsh demands of Victorianism, Guenevere has sometimes been "vulgarized" and made "less interesting." In Brewer's estimation, there has been some loss: "We no longer censure Guenevere—all is understood, all forgiven."

One result of the presence of women as readers, authors, and revisers of Arthuriana is perhaps an affection for the figure of Morgan, long the marginalized but powerful archvillain of Arthurian legend. At the same time, previously silenced criticism has become admissible. Farwell analyzes a passage of only two pages from Marion Zimmer Bradley's *The Mists of Avalon* that in her view is "an unmistakably charged lesbian scene." From this exchange between the characters of Raven, a woman sworn to serve the goddess, and Morgaine, Farwell carves out a theory of lesbian narrative space (that is, a privileged place in the narrative from which a lesbian voice, or point of view, speaks). Farwell asks: how is the reader to understand what (as she argues) is probably the crucial scene of an otherwise heterosexual book?

In current poststructural French theory, the space of "alterity"—"otherness"—is female. Some feminists have seen this differently, however. French theorists Monique Wittig and Luce Irigaray urge the privileging of "lesbian as the place of the new alterity" and the revision of the binary structures male/female, subject/other, presence/absence. Farwell therefore proposes the idea of "lesbian narrative space as a . . . space of sameness," where such binary structures are collapsed.

Traditional analyses define narrative as traditionally gendered: active (male) and passive (female, that which is overcome, such as the monster or the princess). This same narrative structure that "identifies narrative space in gendered terms" "reinforces heterosexuality, for in defining the movement of male desire, the active space, into and through the passive space, morphologically female, we have a narrative reenactment of the heterosexual act." But lesbian space is not created simply when a female character steps into traditionally masculine space. Here, Irigaray's "neither one nor two" denotes a fluctuation in the boundaries between subject/object, lover/beloved, undercutting the heterosexuality that is based on this dualism. The point at which this deconstruction begins is what Farwell denotes lesbian narrative space.

Bradley's text has the male Christian world of Britain, on the one hand, "assuring the sexual dichotomization of a world that had once been ruled by women." On the other, though Avalon is fading because its values are no longer accepted, it remains "the sanctuary for strong feminist values." A "sameness," of which the relationship between Raven and Morgaine becomes the essence, forms "the core of Avalon." Depictions of women loving women in Avalon are made without negative comment, whereas in the Christian world homoerotic desire is accompanied by tension. So in the end it is through the act of love with Raven that Morgaine is given the strength to complete her task.

As if to underscore Morgan's importance in the late twentieth century, this volume comes to a close with a second essay devoted to her, Thompson's survey of modern treatments of Morgan and her relationship with Arthur. Thompson covers five works, all published in the 1980s. All, again, take up a theme not generally acceptable before the late twentieth century; that is, they "take the final step of focusing upon the love between Morgan le Fay and Arthur." These are Parke Godwin's *Firelord*, Marion Zimmer Bradley's *The Mists of Avalon*, Joy Chant's *The High Kings*, Joan Wolf's *The Road to Avalon*, and Welwyn Wilton Katz's *The Third Magic*.

The love between Morgan and Arthur is developed in these modern tales primarily by modifying traditional accounts of their youth. Medieval literature, laconic about the earlier years of both Morgan and Arthur, leaves modern authors free to introduce new material without violating firmly established tradition. The idea of a first, forbidden love between the two also offers a credible, modern psychological explanation for the failure of Arthur's marriage to Guenevere and for the curious love-hate relationship between sister and brother.

Thompson finds a number of explanations for this modern change, including widespread sympathy for the figure of Arthur and the recent popularity of fantasy as a literary genre, combined with the growth of interest in the occult and in pagan religions, such as Wicca. But he devotes the greatest attention to the matter of the woman author and the woman reader, noting that the overwhelming majority of the authors he studies are women. He concludes that the rejection of "essentially passive" heroines like Guenevere, Iseult, and Ygraine, in favor of the more independent-minded Morgan le Fay "would seem to reflect changing attitudes on the part of a growing number of women in contemporary society."

It is to the trajectory from the medieval to the modern Arthurian text that we now turn, to survey the varying presentations of Arthurian women over the centuries, as viewed by modern criticism's diverse approaches.

1. "L'auteur de ce petit livre n'a point prétendu si haut, mais seulement analyser la conception que Chrétien de Troyes s'est faite de la femme, conception qui dépend des théories sentimentales inspiratrices de son œuvre" (pp. v–vi). In this introduction all translations from French are mine.

2. "On the Superficiality of Women," in *The Comparative Perspective on Literature: Approaches to Theory and Practice,* ed. Clayton Koelb and Susan Noakes (Ithaca, N.Y.: Cornell University Press, 1988), pp. 339–55. See also Noakes's "The Double Meaning of Paolo and Francesca," *Philological Quarterly,* 62 (1983), 221–39.

3. New York: Ace Books, 1987.

4. "Galeotto," or Galehaut, is the name of the book that Francesca and Paolo are reading; it refers to the character Galehaut, who arranged the first passionate meeting between Lancelot and Guenevere. In the canto, Francesca, speaking for both lovers, says that the book in which they read the story of Lancelot was a "Galehaut,"— that is, an intermediary or messenger between the desiring lovers—as was whoever wrote it (*Galeotto fu 'l libro e chi lo scrisse*). In French Galehaut has come to be synonymous with "pander."

5. For a compelling discussion of this problem from a psychoanalytic perspective, see Shoshana Felman's *What Does a Woman Want? Reading and Sexual Difference* (Baltimore: Johns Hopkins University Press, 1993).

6. See the early studies by Tom Peete Cross and William Albert Nitze, *Lancelot and Guenevere: A Study on the Origins of Courtly Love,* pp. 20–62; and Kenneth G.T. Webster, *Guenevere: A Study of Her Abductions.*

7. E. Jane Burns, introduction to *Lancelot-Grail: The Old French Arthurian Vulgate and Post-Vulgate in Translation,* ed. Norris J. Lacy. Vol. 1 (New York: Garland, 1993), p. xxvi.

8. Burns cites Jean Frappier, "La Mort Galehot," *Histoire, mythes et symboles: Etudes de littérature françaises* (Geneva: Droz, 1976), pp. 137–47; and Christiane Marcello-Nizia, "Amour courtois, société masculine et figures du pouvoir," *Annales, économies, sociétés, civilisations,* 36 (1981), 969–82.

9. See Rachel Bromwich's introduction to *Trioedd Ynys Pridein: The Welsh Triads,* ed. Rachel Bromwich (Cardiff: University of Wales Press, 1961; rev. 1978), p. lxx, p. 155.

10. The possible connection between the character of Guenevere and witchcraft is made by Barbara Ann Gordon-Wise in *Reclamation of a Queen: Guinevere in Modern Fantasy,* pp. 74–81; she adds that in Arthurian literature burning seems restricted to female characters. Lunette in Chrétien's *Erec et Enide* and Iseut both are saved from burning; see in particular p. 81, n. 28.

11. Cited by John Lawlor in his introduction to *Le Morte D'Arthur* (Harmondsworth: Penguin, 1969), p. xxii. Lawlor argues that Malory here demonstrates his independence from the French sources, which do not present Guenevere's love for Lancelot in this way (xvi).

12. See Terence McCarthy's brief comments concerning Guenevere in *An Introduction to Malory,* pp. 114–17.

13. "The Story of the Book," Sylvia Townsend Warner's introduction to T.H. White, *The Book of Merlyn* (London: Fontana [HarperCollins], 1978), p. 12.

14. New York: Coward-McCann.

15. The blame is based in part upon an episode in the Hollow Hills, about which Sutcliff herself was vague. In an interview, she said about Guenhumara that "she was, she is, an overwrought woman undergoing childbirth . . . I never made up my own mind whether anything happened or not." (John Withrington, "An Interview with Rosemary Sutcliff," *Quondam et Futurus: A Journal of Arthurian Interpretations,* 1.4 [Winter 1991], 53–60.)

16. New York: St. Martin's.

17. Rochester, N.Y.: Round Table.

18. New York: Knopf; rpt. New York: Ballantine.

19. In the work of Henry Treece and Peter Vansittart; cited by Raymond Thompson, *The Return from Avalon*, p. 43.

20. A thorough history of the legend of Tristan and Isolde may be found in Joan Tasker Grimbert's introduction to *Tristan and Iseut: A Casebook*.

21. Joan Ferrante's *The Conflict of Love and Honor: The Medieval Tristan Legend in France, Germany and Italy* contains useful observations throughout about the heroines of these medieval variants.

22. Gottfried von Strassburg, *Tristan*, tr. A.T. Hatto (Harmondsworth: Penguin, 1967).

23. Paris: Piazza.

24. In *Three Screenplays*, tr. Carol Martin-Sperry. New York: Grossman, 1972.

25. New York: Knopf.

26. Reviewer Michael Dirda comments that the more deeply they penetrate inland, the farther they voyage into Brazil's past (*The Washington Post*, February 13, 1994, p. 14).

27. London: Macmillan.

28. New York: Ace.

29. Danish director Jytte Rex's *Isolde* (1989) is discussed briefly by Kevin J. Harty, "The Arthurian Legends on Film," in *Cinema Arthuriana*, ed. Kevin J. Harty (New York: Garland, 1991), p. 22.

30. Jean Markale, preface to Agnès Verlet's *Iseult et Tristan* (Paris: Harmattan, n.d.), pp. 6–7.

31. London: Bodley Head.

32. C. Stephen Jaeger likens Brangaene to Griselda, who satisfies the medieval audience's love for "scenes of fanatical devotion," while Brangaene "cunningly plays upon it." To a scene of "undeserved suffering nobly borne," therefore, Gottfried added "the cunning of the innocent" ("The Testing of Brangaene: Cunning and Innocence in Gottfried's *Tristan*," p. 202, p. 206).

33. Indianapolis: Bobbs-Merrill.

34. The vicissitudes of Morgan's character in the twelfth- and thirteenth-century French works are concisely outlined by Fanni Bogdanow in "Morgain's Role in the Thirteenth-Century French Prose Romances of the Arthurian Cycle," from which selected details are presented here. See also Maureen Fries's discussion in "From The Lady to The Tramp."

35. New York: Delacorte.

36. New York: Ace; Garden City, N.Y.: Doubleday, rpt. New York: Avon, 1994.

37. These are followed in the sequence by *Black Smith's Telling* (1990) and *Taliesin's Telling* (1991); London: Headline.

38. Maureen Quilligan, *New York Times Book Review*, January 30, 1983, p. 11, p. 30.

39. Charlotte Spivack comments that "through the character of Morgaine the reader encounters the complete circle of feminine experience; birth and death, love and hate, attack and surrender, nurture and killing. Morgaine's social passivity and private activism is an image that modern women may easily identify with. And, as both Morgaine and Viviane in turn see themselves as the 'death crone,' that image evokes the experience of the aging woman, so rarely presented in fiction, either realism or fantasy." Spivack observes that such "realistic" concerns as the psychological needs of women may seem "the prerogative of realistic fiction rather than fantasy," but Bradley's novel, which is indeed fantasy, manages to achieve an integration of the magical and the mundane (p. 160).

40. Harty, "The Arthurian Legends on Film," *Cinema Arthuriana*, pp. 20–21.

41. "The Lady of Shalott," *Tennyson's Poetry*, ed. Robert W. Hill, Jr. (New York: Norton, 1971), pp. 13–17.

42. For further discussion of this character, see Rosemary Morris, "Uther and Igerne: A Study in Uncourtly Love."

43. *Lancelot-Grail: The Old French Arthurian Vulgate and Post-Vulgate in Translation. Lancelot,* Part I, tr. Samuel N. Rosenberg (New York: Garland, 1993), p. 11.

44. Paris: Minard, 1972.

45. Paris: Denoël.

46. "Avalon Revisited," *The Fiddlehead* 55 (1963): 10–13.

47. As Michelle Freeman has pointed out in her analysis of *Chievrefoil* and another of Marie's lais, *Laüstic,* Marie seems to have consciously chosen "at least nominally Celtic but non-Arthurian material over Roman or French." ("Marie de France's Poetics of Silence" p. 879, n. 8.)

48. In the Bible, Potiphar was an Egyptian officer for whom Joseph was overseer (*Genesis* 39:4). Joseph had to reject the amorous advances of Potiphar's wife, who then complained to Potiphar that Joseph had behaved inappropriately toward her.

49. See, among others, Michèle Koubichkine, "A propos du Lai de *Lanval,*" *Le Moyen Age,* 78 (1972), 467–88; D.A. Monson, "L'Idéologie du lai de *Lanval,*" *Le Moyen Age,* 93 (1987), 349–72; Jacques Ribard, "Le Lai de *Lanval*: essai d'interprétation polysémique," in *Marche Romane: Mélanges de philologie et de littératures romanes offerts à Jeanne Wathelet-Willem* (Liège: Cahiers de l'A.R.U.L.G., 1978), pp. 529–44; Edgar Sienaert, *Les lais de Marie de France: du conte merveilleux à la nouvelle psychologique* (Paris: Champion, 1978).

50. "Love in the Afternoon: Courtly Play in the 'Lai de *Lanval,*'" *Neuphilologische Mitteilungen,* 84 (1983), 301–10; here, p. 307. Poe's emphasis upon the humor of *Lanval* receives independent support from Emanuel J. Mickel's earlier treatment of the sexual double meaning of two lines, uttered by the narrator after Lanval has secured the favors of his fairy mistress: *Ore est Lanval en dreite voie!* ("Now Lanval is on the right/straight road!" line 134), and *Ore est Lanval bien herbergez* ("Now Lanval is well-domiciled/well-lodged," line 154). See "Marie de France's Use of Irony as a Stylistic and Narrative Device," *Studies in Philology,* 71 (1974), 265–90, here 288–89.

51. *The Portrait in Twelfth-Century French Literature* (Geneva: Droz, 1965), p. 20.

52. Jean Rychner calls *Lanval* a *conte de plein air* ("open-air tale"), in "La présence et le point de vue du narrateur dans deux récits courts: le *Lai de Lanval* et la *Châtelaine de Vergi,*" *Vox Romanica: Annales Helvetici Explorandis Linguis Romanicis Destinati,* 39 (1980), 88.

53. At least two articles deal in whole or in part with this contrast: Eva Rosenn, "The Sexual and Textual Politics of Marie's Poetics," *In Quest of Marie de France, a Twelfth-Century Poet,* ed. Chantal Maréchal (Lewiston, Maine: Mellen, 1992), pp. 225–42; Tilde Sankovitch argues that Marie's use of Celtic material marks out her "wild zone," and her "determination to belong to the male world of conventional literature while implanting in that world her female sphere of unconventional wildness" ("Marie de France: The Myth of the Wild," *French Women Writers and the Book: Myths of Access and Desire,* ed. Tilde A. Sankovitch [Syracuse: Syracuse University Press, 1988], pp. 15–41).

54. "The Arthuricity of Marie de France."

55. As Joan Ferrante observes in *A New History of French Literature,* ed. Denis Hollier (Cambridge: Harvard University Press, 1989), p. 52.

56. See E.A. Francis, "The Trial in *Lanval,*" *Studies in French Language and Mediaeval Literature Presented to Professor Mildred K. Pope* (Manchester: Manchester University Press, 1939), pp. 115–24.

57. See note 3 of *Rasmussen's essay for a brief explanation of "Women's Time." Julia Kristeva has written a number of books that put forward her thinking from the 1960s through the 1980s, and many of these have been translated into English. A sampling includes *La Révolution du langage poétique,* translated as *Revolution in Poetic Language,* tr. Margaret Waller (New York: Columbia University Press, 1984); eight essays from *Polylogue* have been translated as *Desire in Language: A*

Semiotic Approach to Literature and Art, tr. Thomas S. Gora, Alice Jardine, Leon S. Roudiez (Oxford: Blackwell, 1984); *Pouvoirs de l'horreur: Essai sur l'abjection*, translated as *Powers of Horror: An Essay on Abjection*, tr. Leon S. Roudiez (New York: Columbia University Press, 1982); *Histoires d'amour*, translated as *Tales of Love*, tr. Leon S. Roudiez (New York: Columbia University Press, 1987). A useful anthology of Kristeva's essays, including "Women's Time" (pp. 187–213), is *The Kristeva Reader*, ed. Toril Moi (Oxford: Blackwell, 1986). ("Women's Time" is also reprinted in the more general *Feminisms: An Anthology of Literary Theory and Criticism*, ed. Robyn R. Warhol and Diane Price Herndl [New Brusnwick, N.J.: Rutgers University Press, 1991], pp. 443–62.) John Lechte provides an introduction to Kristeva's thought in *Julia Kristeva* (London: Routledge, 1990).

58. Philosopher and psychoanalyst Luce Irigaray's ideas have been elaborated primarily in two books, *Ce Sexe qui n'en est pas un*, translated as *This Sex Which Is Not One*, tr. Catherine Porter (Ithaca, N.Y.: Cornell University Press, 1985), and *Speculum de l'autre femme*, translated as *Speculum of the Other Woman*, tr. Gillian G. Gill (Ithaca, N.Y.: Cornell University Press, 1985).

59. An accessible introduction to aspects of Lacan's thought is Juliet Flower MacCannell, *Figuring Lacan: Criticism and the Critical Unconscious* (Lincoln: University of Nebraska Press, 1986). The introduction and first chapter indicate further readings.

60. For an introduction to the notion of "discourse" and a helpful list of further readings, see Paul A. Bové's entry in *Critical Terms for Literary Study*, ed. Frank Lentricchia and Thomas McLaughlin (Chicago: University of Chicago Press, 1990), pp. 50–65.

61. For books alone, see Aubailly, Chandès, Gallais, and Lecouteux in the bibiliography to this volume.

62. *Krueger's article should be read with her "Desire, Meaning, and the Female Reader: The Problem in Chrétien's *Charrete*," in Baswell and Sharp, eds.; rpt. in *Lancelot and Guenevere: A Casebook*, ed. Lori Walters (New York: Garland, 1996).

63. Nancy A. Jones's review of *Bodytalk*, in *Medieval Feminist Newsletter*, 17 (Spring 1994), 11.

64. Nancy A. Jones's review of *Bodytalk*.

65. See also Fries's essay, "From The Lady to The Tramp."

66. In this article too, Fisher briefly mentions "the veiled possibility of a homosexual act," in case Gawain had made love to the Lady and then had to pay Bertilak in kind; this observation is echoed in some recent analyses of the poem (see, for example, David Lorenzo Boyd, "On Lesbian and Gay/Queer Medieval Studies," *Medieval Feminist Newsletter*, 15 (Spring 1993), 13.

67. In her own synopsis of the article, written for the annual *Bibliographical Bulletin of the International Arthurian Society*, Heng states that her reading of the poem restores to it a strangeness that had been eradicated by "settled conventions of reading" and "the consolidation of criticism over time" (121).

68. Lucy Paton's general description of the Celtic fairy queen and the fairy of medieval romance remains useful; see *Studies*, pp. 4–6.

69. Pierre Gallais, "Les fées seraient-elles nées au XIIe siècle? (A propos d'un ouvrage récent)," *Cahiers de Civilisation Médiévale X^e–XIIe Siècles*, 29 (1986), 355–71.

70. See Caitlin Matthews and John Matthews, *Ladies of the Lake*.

71. Constance Hassett (personal communication).

72. "Visual Pleasure and Narrative Cinema," *Screen*, 16 (1975), 6–18. Mulvey's influential article has been reprinted in *Visual and Other Pleasures* (Bloomington: Indiana University Press, 1989), pp. 14–26, and elsewhere, including *Feminisms: An Anthology of Literary Theory and Criticism*, pp. 432–42 (see note 43).

73. *Hard Core: Power, Pleasure, and the "Frenzy of the Visible"* (Berkeley: University of California Press, 1989), p. 215.

74. Mary Jacobus has summarized the problem succinctly: "The assumption [in American empiricist feminist criticism] is of an unbroken continuity between 'life' and 'text'—a mimetic relation whereby women's writing, reading, or culture, instead of being produced, reflect a knowable reality. Just as one can identify a woman biologically (the unstated argument would run), so one can with a little extra labor identify a woman's text, a woman reader, the essence of female culture" (*Reading Woman: Essays in Feminist Criticism* [New York: Columbia University Press, 1986], p. 108).

SELECT BIBLIOGRAPHY

With certain exceptions, the present bibliography concentrates on publications that appeared after 1975. Items preceded by an asterisk are printed in this volume.

GENERAL REFERENCE

Grimbert, Joan, ed. *Tristan and Isolde: A Casebook.* Arthurian Characters and Themes, 2. Garland Reference Library of the Humanities, 1514. New York: Garland, 1995.

Lacy, Norris J., Geoffrey Ashe, Sandra Ness Ihle, Marianne E. Kalinke, and Raymond H. Thompson, eds. *The New Arthurian Encyclopedia.* Garland Reference Library of the Humanities, 931. New York: Garland, 1991.

MEDIEVAL PERIOD

Alamichel, Marie-Françoise. "The Function and Activities of Women in Laʒamon's *Brut.*" In *A Wyf Ther Was: Essays in Honour of Paule Mertens-Fonck,* ed. Juliette Dor. Liège: Liège Language and Literature, 1992, pp. 11–22.

Allen, Peter L. "The Ambiguity of Silence: Gender, Writing, and *Le roman de Silence.*" In *Sign, Sentence, Discourse: Language in Medieval Thought and Literature,* ed. Julian N. Wasserman and Lois Roney. Syracuse, N.Y.: Syracuse University Press, 1989, pp. 98–112.

Allen, Rosamund. "Female Perspectives in Romance and History." In *Romance in Medieval England,* ed. Maldwyn Mills, Jennifer Fellows, and Carol Meale. Cambridge: Brewer, 1991, pp. 133–47.

Archibald, Elizabeth. "Women and Romance." In *Companion to Middle English Romance,* ed. Henk Aertsen and Alasdair A. MacDonald. Amsterdam: VU University Press, 1990, pp. 153–69.

Armstrong, Grace M. "Enide and Solomon's Wife: Figures of Romance *Sapientia.*" *The Philology of the Couple,* vol. 14 of *French Forum* (1989), 401–18.

———. "Women of Power: Chrétien de Troyes's Female Clerks." *Women in French Literature,* ed. Michel Guggenheim, vol. 58 of Stanford French and Italian Studies, vol. 58. Stanford: Anma Libri, 1988, pp. 29–46.

Aronstein, Susan. "Prize or Pawn?: Homosocial Order, Marriage and the Redefinition of Women in the *Gawain Continuation.*" *Romanic Review,* 82 (1991), 115–26.

Aubailly, Jean-Claude. *La fée et le chevalier: essai de mythanalyse de quelques lais féeriques des XIIᵉ et XIIIᵉ siècles.* Paris: Champion, 1986.

Baughan, Denver Ewing. "The Role of Morgan la Faye in *Sir Gawain and the Green Knight.*" *English Literary History,* 17 (1950), 241–51.

Baumgartner, Emmanuèle. "Des femmes et des chiens." In *Le Rire au Moyen Age dans la littérature et dans les arts.*: *Actes du colloque international des 17–19 novembre 1988*, ed. Thérèse Bouché and Hélène Charpentier. Talence: Presses Universitaires de Bordeaux, 1990, pp. 43–51.

————. *Le "Tristan en prose": Essai d'interprétation d'un roman médiéval.* Publications romanes et françaises, 133. Geneva: Droz, 1975.

————. *Tristan et Yseut: De la légende aux récits en vers.* Paris: Presses Universitaires de France, 1987.

Bayard, Marie-José. "La place de la femme dans le *Livre d'Artus*: un exemple de la transposition littéraire des structures sociales dans les romans en prose du XIIIe siècle." In *Actes du XIVe Congrès International Arthurien, Rennes, 1985*, ed. Charles Foulon, Jean-Claude Lozac'hmeur, Maud Ovazza, Annick Richard, Michel Rousse. Rennes: Presses Universitaires de Rennes, 1985, vol. I, 44–58.

*Berthelot, Anne. "Du lac à la fontaine: Lancelot et la fée-amante." *Au pays d'Arthur*, vol. 6 of *Médiévales: Langue, Textes, Histoire* (1984), 5–17.

Blakeslee, Merritt R. "Misogynie, fin'amur, et ambiguïté dans le *Tristan* de Thomas." PRIS-MA, 7 (1991), 1–16.

Bloch, R. Howard. "The Arthurian Fabliau and the Poetics of Virginity." In *Continuations: Essays on Medieval French Literature and Language in Honor of John L. Grigsby*, ed. Norris J. Lacy and Gloria Torrini-Roblin. Birmingham, Al.: Summa, 1989, pp. 231–49.

Bogdanow, Fanni. "Morgan's Role in the 13th Century French Prose Romances of the Arthurian Cycle." *Medium Aevum*, 38 (1969), 123–33.

————. "The Tradition of the Troubadour Lyrics and the Treatment of the Love Theme in Chrétien de Troyes' *Erec et Enide*." In *Court and Poet. Proceedings of the Third Congress of the International Courtly Literature Society* (Liverpool 1980), ed. Glyn Burgess. ARCA Classical and Medieval Texts, Papers, and Monographs, 5. Liverpool: Cairns, 1981, pp. 79–92.

Boivin, Jeanne-Marie. "La Dame du Lac, Morgane et Galehaut; symbolique de trois figures emblématiques de l'Autre Monde dans le *Lancelot*." *Au pays d'Arthur*, vol. 6 of *Médiévales: Langue, Textes, Histoire* (1984), 18–25.

Bossy, Michel-André. "The Elaboration of Female Narrative Functions in *Erec et Enide*." In *Courtly Literature: Culture and Context. Selected papers from the 5th Triennial Congress of the International Courtly Literature Society, Dalfsen, The Netherlands*, 1986, ed. Keith Busby and Erik Kooper. Amsterdam: Benjamins, 1990, pp. 23–38.

Burg, Irene von. "Tristan und seine Mütter." *Etudes de Lettres*, 3 (1990), 79–90.

Burns, E. Jane. "How Lovers Lie Together: Infidelity and Fictive Discourse in the *Roman de Tristan*." *Tristania*, 8.2 (Spring 1983), 15–30.

*————. "Rewriting Men's Stories: Enide's Disruptive Mouths," and "Why Beauty Laughs: Iseut's Enormous Thighs." In *Bodytalk: When Women Speak in Old French Literature*. New Cultural Studies. Philadelphia: University of Pennsylvania Press, 1993, ch. 4 and 5.

————. "*La Voie de la Voix*: The Aesthetics of Indirection in the Vulgate Cycle." In *The Legacy of Chrétien de Troyes*, ed. Norris Lacy, Douglas Kelly, and Keith Busby. Amsterdam: Rodopi, 1988, vol. II, 151–67.

————, and Roberta L. Krueger. Introduction, *Courtly Ideology and Woman's Place in Old French Literature*, vol. 25 of *Romance Notes* (1985), 205–11.

Burrell, Margaret. "The Participation of Chrétien's Heroines in Love's 'covant.'" *Nottingham French Studies*, 30 (1991), 24–33.

Buschinger, Danielle, and Wolfgang Spiewok, eds. *Le monde des fées dans la culture médiévale*. Greifswald: Reineke, forthcoming.

Cadot-Colin, Anne-Marie. "Images de la femme dans la *Vengeance Raguidel*." In *Farai chansoneta novele: Hommage à Jean-Charles Payen*. Caen: Centre de Publications de l'Université de Caen, 1989, pp. 113–21.

Caples, C.B. "Brangaene and Isold in Gottfried von Strassburg's *Tristan*." *Colloquia Germanica*, 9 (1975), 167–76.

Carne, Eva-Marie. *Die Frauengestalten bei Hartmann von Aue: Ihre Bedeutung im Aufbau und Gehalt der Epen*. Marburger Beiträge zur Germanistik, 31. Marburg: Elwert, 1970.

Carson, Mother Angela, O.S.U. "Morgain la Fee as the Principle of Unity in *Gawain and the Green Knight*." *Modern Language Quarterly*, 23 (1962), 3–16.

Cazenave, Annie. "Iseut et Héloïse, ou la passion et l'amour." In *Tristan et Iseut, mythe européen et mondial. Actes du Colloque des 10, 11 et 12 janvier 1986*, ed. Danielle Buschinger, pp. 87–96. Göppingen: Kümmerle, 1987.

Chandès, Gérard. *Le serpent, la femme et l'épée: Recherches sur l'imagination symbolique d'un romancier médiéval, Chrétien de Troyes*. Amsterdam: Rodopi, 1986.

Chocheyras, Jacques. "Sur le nom d'Iseut dans Béroul." *Bibliographical Bulletin of the International Arthurian Society*, 40 (1988), 265–67.

Classen, Albrecht. "Matriarchy vs. Patriarchy: The Role of the Irish Queen Isolde in Gottfried von Strassburg's 'Tristan.'" *Neophilologus*, 73 (1989), 77–89.

Cross, Tom Peete, and William Albert Nitze. *Lancelot and Guenevere: A Study on the Origins of Courtly Love*. Chicago: University of Chicago Press, 1930; rpt. New York: Phaeton, 1970.

Dayan, Joan. "The Figure of Isolde in Gottfried's Tristan: Toward a Paradigm of Minne." *Tristania*, 6.2 (Spring 1981), 23–36.

Dembowski, Peter F. "Women," "Code of Feminine Behavior." In *Jean Froissart and His Méliador: Context, Craft, and Sense*. Lexington, Ky.: French Forum Publishers, 1983, pp. 113–18.

Dick, Ernst S. "Gottfried's Isolde: Coincidentia Oppositorum?" *Tristania*, 12 (1986–87), 15–24.

DiPasquale, Pasquale, Jr. "Malory's Guinevere: Epic Queen, Romance Heroine and Tragic Mistress." *Bucknell Review*, 16 (1968), 86–102.

Dobyns, Ann. "The Rhetoric of Character in Malory's *Morte Darthur*." *Texas Studies in Language and Literature*, 28 (1986), 339–52.

Dulac, Liliane. "Peut-on comprendre les relations entre Erec et Enide?" *Le Moyen-Age*, 100 (1994), 37–50.

Ehlert, Trude. "Die Frau als Arznei. Zum Bild der Frau in hochmittelalterlicher deutscher Lehrdichtung." *Zeitschrift für deutsche Philologie*, 105 (1986), 42–62.

Ehrismann, Otfrid. "'Tandarei,' 'hêre vrouwe' und die 'Schwelle des Allerheiligsten': Frau und Tabu." *Sprache und Literatur*, 18 (1987), 36–54.

Farrier, Susan E. "*Erex Saga* and the Reshaping of Chrétien's *Erec et Enide*." *Arthurian Interpretations*, 4.2 (Spring 1990), 1–11.

Ferrante, Joan. *The Conflict of Love and Honor: The Medieval Tristan Legend in France, Germany and Italy*. The Hague: Mouton: 1973.

———. "Courtly Literature" and "In the Thirteenth Century." In *Woman as Image in Medieval Literature: From the Twelfth Century to Dante*. New York: Columbia University Press, 1975, ch. 3 and 4.

Field, P.J.C. "Time and Elaine of Astolat." In *Studies in Malory*, ed. James W. Spisak. Kalamazoo: Medieval Institute Publications, 1985, pp. 231–36.

Finke, Laurie. "Towards a Cultural Poetics of Romance." *Genre*, 22 (1989), 109–27.

Firestone, Ruth. "Chrétien's Enide, Hartmann's Enite and Boethii *Philosophiae Consolatio*." *Amsterdamer Beiträge zur älteren Germanistik*, 26 (1987), 69–106.

Fisher, Rodney. "Erecs Schuld und Enitens Unschuld bei Hartmann." *Euphorion*, 69 (1975), 160–74.

*Fisher, Sheila. "Leaving Morgan Aside: Women, History, and Revisionism in *Sir Gawain and the Green Knight*." In *The Passing of Arthur: New Essays in*

Arthurian Tradition, ed. Christopher Baswell and William Sharpe. New York: Garland, 1988, pp. 129–51.

———. "Taken Men and Token Women in *Sir Gawain and the Green Knight*." In *Seeking the Woman in Late Medieval and Renaissance Writings: Essays in Feminist Contextual Criticism*, ed. Sheila Fisher and Janet E. Halley. Knoxville: University of Tennessee Press, 1989, pp. 71–105.

Francke, Walter K. "Orgeluse's Predicament." *Michigan Germanic Studies*, 9 (1983), 18–32.

Freeman, Michelle. "Marie de France's Poetics of Silence: The Implications for a Feminine *Translatio*." *PMLA*, 99 (1984), 860–83.

Friedman, Albert B. "Morgan la Faye in *Sir Gawain and the Green Knight*." *Speculum*, 35 (1960), 260–74.

*Fries, Maureen. "Female Heroes, Heroines, and Counter-Heroes: Images of Women in Arthurian Tradition." In *Popular Arthurian Traditions*, ed. Sally K. Slocum. Bowling Green, Ohio: Bowling Green State University Popular Press, 1992, pp. 5–17.

———. "From the Lady to The Tramp: The Decline of Morgan le Fay in Medieval Romance." *Arthuriana*, 1 (1994), 1–18.

Gallais, Pierre. *La Fée à la fontaine et à l'arbre: un archétype du conte merveilleux et du récit courtois*. Cermeil. Amsterdam: Rodopi, 1992.

Germain, Ellen. "Lunete, Women, and Power in Chrétien's *Yvain*." *Romance Quarterly*, 38 (1991), 15–25.

Gibbs, Marion E. *"Wiplîchez wîbes reht": A Study of the Women Characters in the Works of Wolfram von Eschenbach*. Duquesne Studies, Philological Series, 15. Pittsburgh: Duquesne University Press, 1972.

Gravdal, Kathryn. "The Poetics of Rape Law: Chrétien de Troyes's Arthurian Romance." In *Ravishing Maidens: Writing Rape in Medieval French Literature and Law*. Philadelphia: University of Pennsylvania Press, 1991, ch. 2.

Greenwood, Maria K. "Women in Love, or Three Courtly Heroines in Chaucer and Malory: Elaine, Criseyde and Guinevere." In *A Wyf Ther Was: Essays in Honour of Paule Mertens-Fonck*, ed. Juliette Dor. Liège: Liège Language and Literature, 1992, pp. 167–77.

Guidot, Bertrand. "Pouvoirs et séductions, pouvoir de séduction dans les *Lais* de Marie de France." *Romanische Forschungen*, 102 (1990), 425–33.

Guyonvarc'h, Christian J. "Mythologie celtique et littérature arthurienne." In *Actes du XIVe Congrès International Arthurien*. Rennes: Presses Universitaires de Rennes, 1985, vol. II, 753–57.

Hahn, Ingrid. "Die Frauenrolle in Hartmanns 'Erec.'" In *Sprache und Recht. Beiträge zur Kulturgeschichte des Mittelalters: Festschrift für Ruth Schmidt-Wiegand zum 60. Geburtstag*, ed. Karl Hauck, et al. Berlin: de Gruyter, 1986, vol. 1, pp. 172–90.

Hahn, Stacey L. "The Motif of the Errant Knight and the Royal Maiden in the Prose *Lancelot*." *Arthurian Interpretations*, 3.1 (Fall 1988), 1–15.

Hale, William C. "Origins: Morgaine, Morgana, Morgause." *Avalon to Camelot*, 1 (1984), 35–36.

Harf-Lancner, Laurence. "*Le Chevalier au lion*, un conte morganien." *Bien dire et bien aprandre*, 7 (1989), 107–16.

———. "L'Eau magique et la Femme-Fée, le mythe fondateur du Tristan en prose." *L'Eau au Moyen Age*, vol. 15 of *Sénéfiance*. Aix-en-Provence: CUER MA, 1985, pp. 201–12.

*———. *Les Fées au Moyen Age: Morgane et Mélusine: La Naissance des Fées*. Nouvelle Bibliothèque du Moyen Age, 8. Paris: Champion, 1984.

———. "Lancelot et la Dame du Lac." *Romania*, 105 (1984), 16–33.

———. "Le Val sans Retour et la prise du pouvoir par les femmes." In *Amour, mariage et transgressions au Moyen Age. Université de Picardie. Actes du colloque des 24,*

25, 26 et 27 mars 1983, ed. Danielle Buschinger and André Crepin. Göppinger Arbeiten zur Germanistik, 420. Göppingen: Kümmerle, 1984, pp. 185–93.

Harrison, Ann Tukey. "Arthurian Women in *Jaufre*." In *Studia Occitanica in memoriam Paul Remy. Vol. 2. The Narrative-Philology*, ed. Hans-Erich Keller with Jean-Marie D'Heur, Guy R. Mermier, Marc Vuijlsteke. Kalamazoo: Medieval Institute Publications, 1986, pp. 65–73.

Helm, Joan. "The Celestial Circle: Fées, Philosophy, and Numerical Circularity." *Arthurian Interpretations*, 3.1 (Fall 1988), 25–36.

———. "Nature's Marvel: Enide as Earth Measure in an Early Arthurian Manuscript." *Quondam et Futurus: A Journal of Arthurian Interpretations*, 1.3 (Fall 1991), 1–24.

Hemmi, Yoko. "Morgain la Fée's Water Connection." *Studies in Medieval English Language and Literature*, 6 (1991), 19–36.

*Heng, Geraldine. "Enchanted Ground: The Feminine Subtext in Malory." In *Courtly Literature: Culture and Context. Selected papers from the ICLS conference, Dalfsen, The Netherlands, 9–16 August, 1986*, ed. Keith Busby and Erik Kooper. Amsterdam: Benjamins, 1990, pp. 283–300.

———. "Feminine Knots and the Other *Sir Gawain and the Green Knight*." *PMLA*, 106 (1991), 500–14.

———. "A Woman Wants: The Lady, Gawain, and the Forms of Seduction." *Yale Journal of Criticism*, 5 (1992), 101–34.

Hill, Sarah J. "Recovering Malory's Guenevere." In *Proceedings of the Medieval Association of the Midwest*, ed. John McCully, with Earl Anderson, Ruth Hamilton, Robert Kindrick. Ames: Iowa State University Press, 1991, vol. I, 131–48.

Hoffman, Donald L. "The Ogre and the Virgin: Varieties of Sexual Experience in Malory's *Morte Darthur*." *Arthurian Interpretations*, 1.1 (Fall 1986), 19–25.

*Holbrook, Sue Ellen. "Nymue, Chief Lady of the Lake in Malory's *Morte Darthur*" *Speculum*, 53 (1978), 761–77.

Holichek, Lindsay E. "Malory's Gwenevere: After Long Silence." *Annuale Mediaevale*, 22 (1982), 112–26.

Hollandt, Gisela. *Die Hauptgestalten in Gottfrieds 'Tristan': Wesenzüge, Handlungsfunktion, Motiv der List*. Philologische Studien und Quellen, 30. Berlin: Schmidt, 1966.

Houstin, Françoise. "Le drame de la mère de Perceval: Chrétien de Troyes, *Le Conte du Graal*." PRIS-MA, *Bulletin de liaison de l'équipe de recherche sur la littérature d'imagination du Moyen Age* (Poitiers, CESCM), 1.2 (1985), 72–78.

Imbs, Paul. "La reine Guenièvre dans le *Conte du Graal* de Chrétien de Troyes." In *Mélanges de langue et de littérature du moyen âge offerts à Teruo Sato*. Nagoya: Centre d'Etudes Médiévales et Romanes, 1973, pp. 41–60.

———. "La reine Iseut dans le Tristan de Béroul." *Romance Philology*, 26.2 (1972), 215–28.

Jackson, W.T.H. "The Arthuricity of Marie de France." *Romanic Review*, 70 (1979), 1–18. Rpt. in W.T.H. Jackson, *The Challenge of the Medieval Text: Studies in Genre and Interpretation*, ed. Joan M. Ferrante and Robert W. Hanning. New York: Columbia University Press, 1985, pp. 197–217.

Jaeger, C. Stephen. "The Testing of Brangaene: Cunning and Innocence in Gottfried's *Tristan*." *Journal of English and Germanic Philology*, 70 (1971), 189–206.

Jennings, Margaret. "'Heavens defend me from that Welsh Fairy' (*Merry Wives of Windsor*, V, v, 85): The Metamorphosis of Morgain La Fee in the Romances." In *Court and Poet: Proceedings of the Third Congress of the International Courtly Literature Society (Liverpool 1980)*, ed. Glyn Burgess. ARCA Classical and Medieval Texts, Papers, and Monographs, 5. Liverpool: Cairns, 1981, pp. 197–205.

Jezewski, Mary Ann. "Traits of the Female Hero: The Application of Raglan's Concept of Hero Trait Patterning." *New York Folklore Quarterly*, 10 (1984), 55–73.

Jillings, Lewis. "The Ideal of Queenship in Hartmann's *Erec*." In *The Legend of Arthur in the Middle Ages. Studies presented to A.H. Diverres by colleagues, pupils, friends*, ed. P.B. Grout, R.A. Lodge, C.E. Pickford, and E.K.C. Varty. Woodbridge, Suffolk: Boydell and Brewer, 1983, pp. 113–28.

Jonin, Pierre. *Les personnages féminins dans les romans français de Tristan au XIIe siècle: Etude des influences contemporaines*. Publications des annales de la Faculté des Lettres, n.s. 22. Aix-en-Provence: Editions Ophrys, 1958.

Kamps, Ivo. "Magic, Women, and Incest: The Real Challenges in *Sir Gawain and the Green Knight*." *Exemplaria*, 1 (1989), 313–36.

Kasten, Ingrid. "Hässliche Frauenfiguren in der Literatur des Mittelalters." In *Auf der Suche nach der Frau im Mittelalter: Fragen, Quellen, Antworten*, ed. Bea Lundt. Munich: Fink, 1991, pp. 255–76.

Korrel, Peter. *An Arthurian Triangle. A Study of the Origin, Development and Characterization of Arthur, Guinevere and Modred*. Leiden: Brill, 1984.

Krawutschke, Peter W. *Liebe, Ehe und Familie im deutschen "Prosa-Lancelot" I*. European University Papers, Series 1, German Language and Literature, 229. Bern: Peter Lang, 1978.

Krueger, Roberta L. "Desire, Meaning, and the Female Reader: The Problem in Chrétien's *Charrete*." In *The Passing of Arthur: New Essays in Arthurian Tradition*, ed. Christopher Baswell and William Sharpe. New York: Garland, 1988, pp. 31–51.

*———. "Love, Honor, and the Exchange of Women in *Yvain*: Some Remarks on the Female Reader." In *Courtly Ideology and Woman's Place in Old French Literature*, special issue of *Romance Notes*, 25 (1985), 302–17.

———. *Women Readers and the Ideology of Gender in Old French Verse Romance*. Cambridge: Cambridge University Press, 1993.

LaFarge, Catherine. "The Hand of the Huntress: Repetition and Malory's *Morte Darthur*. In *New Feminist Discourses: Critical Essays on Theories and Texts*, ed. Isobel Armstrong. London: Routledge, 1992, pp. 263–79.

Lazar, Moshé. "Lancelot et la 'mulier mediatrix': La quête de soi à travers la femme." *L'Esprit Createur*, 9 (1969), 243–56.

Le Merrer, Madeleine. "Iseut et le pouvoir: du mythe reçu aux poèmes de Béroul et de Thomas." In *Actes du cent cinquième congrès national des sociétés savantes, Caen 1980*. Paris: Bibliothèque Nationale, 1984, pp. 29–44.

Lecouteux, Claude. *Fées, sorcières et loups-garous au Moyen Age*. Paris: Imago, 1992.

Lefay-Toury, Marie-Noëlle. "Roman breton et mythes courtois: L'évolution du personnage féminin dans les romans de Chrétien de Troyes." *Cahiers de Civilisation Médiévale*, 15 (1972), 193–204 and 283–93.

Lie, O.S.H. "Guinevere." In *Middeleeuwers over vrouwen*, ed. R.E.V. Stuip and C. Vellekoop. Utrecht: HES, 1985, vol. I, 27–40.

Lot-Borodine, Myrrha. *La Femme dans l'oeuvre de Chrétien de Troyes*. Paris: A. Picard, 1909.

Mälzer, Marion. *Die Isolde-Gestalten in den mittelalterlichen deutschen Tristan-Dictungen: Ein Beitrag zum diachronischen Wandel*. Heidelberg: Winter, 1991.

Markale, Jean. "L'étrange rôle de la reine Guenievre." *Europe: Revue Littéraire Mensuelle*, 642 (October 1982), 96–105.

Mathewson, Jeanne T. "Displacement of the Feminine in *Golagros and Gawane* and the *Awntyrs off Arthur*." *Arthurian Interpretations*, 1.2 (Spring 1987), 23–28.

Matthews, Caitlin, and John Matthews. *Ladies of the Lake*. London: Aquarian, 1992.

McCarthy, Terence. *An Introduction to Malory*. Cambridge: Brewer, 1988.

McCash, June Hall. "The Flowering of Romance: Women and the Development of Medieval Arthurian Literature." *Avalon to Camelot*, 1.4 (Summer 1984), 4–8.

McConecky, Patrick. "Women's Speech and Silence in Hartmann von Aue's *Erec*." *PMLA*, 102 (1987), 772–83.

McMahon, James V. "Enite's Relatives: The Girl in the Garden." *Modern Language Notes*, 85 (1970), 367–72.

Meister, Peter. *The Healing Female in the German Courtly Romance.* Göppinger Arbeiten zur Germanistik, 523. Göppingen: Kümmerle, 1990.

———, and Mary Lynne Ditmar. "A Little-Acknowledged Theme in the Courtly Romance: Rape." *Quondam et Futurus: A Journal of Arthurian Interpretations*, 1.4 (Winter 1991), 23–35.

Méla, Charles. *La Reine et le Graal: La "conjointure" dans les romans du Graal de Chrétien de Troyes au Livre de Lancelot.* Paris: Seuil, 1984.

Mertens, Volker. *Laudine: Soziale Problematik im* Iwein *Hartmanns von Aue.* Zeitschrift für deutsche Philologie, Beihefte, vol. 3. Berlin: Schmidt, 1978.

Milin, Gaël. "Le bon chevalier loup-garou et la mauvaise femme dans l'histoire de Sir Marrok dans *La Mort d'Arthur* de Thomas Malory." *Le Moyen-Age*, 8 (1994), 65–80.

Moi, Toril. "'She Died because She Came too Late . . .': Knowledge, Doubles and Death in Thomas's *Tristan.*" *Exemplaria*, 4 (1992), 105–33.

Moon, Douglas. "The Role of Morgan la Faye in *Gawain and the Green Knight.*" *Neuphilologische Metteilungen*, 67 (1966), 31–57.

Moore, Dennis. "Making Sense of an Ending: Morgan Le Fay in *Sir Gawain and the Green Knight.*" *Mediaevalia: A Journal of Mediaeval Studies*, 10 (1988), 213–33.

Morris, Rosemary. "The Knight and the Superfluous Lady: A Problem of Disposal." *Reading Medieval Studies*, 14 (1988), 111–24.

———. "Uther and Igerne: A Study in Uncourtly Love." In *Arthurian Literature*, 4 (1985), 70–92.

Mowatt, D.G. "Tristan's Mothers and Iwein's Daughters," *German Life and Letters*, 23 (1969), 18–31.

Müller, Irmgard. "Liebestränke, Liebeszauber und Schlafmittel in der mittelalterlichen Literatur." In *Liebe—Ehe—Ehebruch*, ed. Xenja von Ertzdorff and Marianne Wynn. Beiträge zur Deutsche Philologie, 58. Giessen: Schmitz, 1984, pp. 71–87.

Musseter, Sally. "The Education of Chrétien's Enide." *Romanic Review*, 73 (1982), 147–66.

Newstead, Helaine. "The Besieged Ladies in Arthurian Romance." *PMLA*, 63 (1948), 803–30.

Nickel, Helmut. "Arthurian Heraldry: Ladies' Service and Ladies' Favors." *Avalon to Camelot*, 1.4 (Summer 1984), 31–34.

Paradis, Françoise. "La triple mise au monde d'un héros ou trois images d'une féminité maîtrisée dans le début du *Lancelot en prose.*" In *Approches du "Lancelot en prose": Etudes recueillies par J. Dufournet*, pp. 157–76. Geneva: Slatkine, 1984.

Pastre, Jean-Marc. "La beauté d'Iseut." In *Tristan et Iseut, mythe européen et mondial. Actes du Colloque des 10, 11 et 12 janvier 1986*, ed. Danielle Buschinger. Göppingen: Kümmerle, 1987, pp. 326–40.

Paton, Lucy Allen. *Studies in the Fairy Mythology of Arthurian Romance.* Radcliffe College Monographs, 13. Boston: Ginn, 1903. 2nd ed., ed. Roger Sherman Loomis. New York: Franklin, 1960.

Payen, Jean-Charles. "La Destruction des mythes courtois dans le roman arthurien: la femme dans le roman en vers après Chrétien de Troyes." *Revue des Langues Romanes*, 78 (1969), 213–228.

Peschel-Rentsch, Dietmar. *Gott, Autor, Ich. Skizzen zur Genese von Autorbewusstsein und Erzählerfigur im Mittelalter.* Erlanger Studien, 89. Erlangen: Palm and Enke, 1991.

Press, A.R. "Chrétien de Troyes' Laudine: A 'belle dame sans merci.'" *Forum for Modern Language Studies*, 19 (1983), 158–71.

Quinn, Esther C. "Chaucer's Arthurian Romance." *The Chaucer Review*, 18 (1984), 211–20.

Rabine, Leslie W. "Love and the New Patriarchy: *Tristan and Isolde.*" In Leslie W. Rabine, *Reading the Romantic Heroine: Text, History, Ideology* (Ann Arbor: University of Michigan Press, 1985), pp. 20–49; rpt. in *Tristan and Isolde: A Casebook,* ed. Joan Tasker Grimbert. New York, Garland, 1995, pp. 37–74.

Ribard, Jacques. "Figures de la femme dans la *Quête du Saint Graal.*" In *Figures féminines et roman,* ed. Jean Bessière. University of Picardy Centre d'Etudes du Roman et du Romanesque. Paris: Presses Universitaires de France, 1982, pp. 33–48.

Riddy, Felicity. "Structure and Meaning in Malory's 'The Fair Maid of Astolat.'" *Forum for Modern Language Studies,* 12 (1976), 354–66.

Rocher, Daniel. "La Femme Mariée entre deux familles dans la littérature narrative allemande au Moyen Age." In *Sénéfiance,* 26, *Les Relations de parenté dans le monde médiéval.* Aix-en-Provence: CUER MA, 1989, pp. 247–55.

Rothschild, Judith Rice. "The 'Controlling Woman' in Marie de France's *Lais*: A New Perspective on Narrative Technique." *Fifteenth-Century Studies,* 17 (1990), 337–49.

———. "Manipulative Gestures and Behaviors in the *Lais* of Marie de France." In *The Spirit of the Court: Selected Proceedings of the Fourth Congress of the International Courtly Literature Society (Toronto 1983),* ed. Glyn S. Burgess, Alan Deyermond, Dennis Green, Beryl Rowland, and Robert A. Taylor. Woodbridge, Suffolk: Boydell and Brewer, 1985, pp. 283–88.

Rousse, Michel. "Chrétien de Troyes, les femmes et le politique." In *Actes du 14ᵉ congrès international Arthurien.* Rennes, 16–21 August 1984, ed. Charles Foulon, Jean-Claude Lozac'hmeur, Maud Ovazza, Annick Richard, and Michel Rousse. Rennes: Presses Universitaires de Rennes, 1984, pp. 739–52.

Saint Paul, Thérèse. "A Forgotten Heroine in Medieval English Literature." In *A Wyf Ther Was: Essays in Honour of Paule Mertens-Fonck,* ed. Juliette Dor. Liège: Liège Language and Literature, 1992, pp. 247–55.

Sargent-Baur, Barbara Nelson. "Erec's Enide: 'sa fame ou s'amie'?" *Romance Philology,* 33 (1979–80), 373–87.

Schichtman, Martin R. "Elaine and Guenevere: Gender and Historical Consciousness in the Middle Ages." In *New Images of Medieval Women: Essays Towards a Cultural Anthropology,* ed. Edelgard E. DuBruck. Lewiston, N.Y.: Mellen, 1989, pp. 255–71.

Schnell, Rüdiger. "Der Frauenexkurs in Gottfrieds *Tristan* (v. 17858–18114): Ein kritischer Kommentar." *Zeitschrift für Deutsche Philologie,* 103 (1984), 1–26.

Scott, Brigitte. "'Reclaim the (K)night!' König Artus und seine Tafelrunde aus wieblicher Sicht." In *Der frauwen buoch: Versuch zu einer feministischen Mediävistik,* ed. Ingrid Bennewitz. Göppinger Arbeiten zur Germanistik, 517. Göppingen: Kümmerle, 1989, pp. 457–71.

Scott, Mary Etta. "The Good, the Bad, and the Ugly: A Study of Malory's Women." *Mid-Hudson Language Studies,* 5 (1982), 21–29.

Seiffert, Leslie. "Finding, Guarding and Betraying the Truth: Isolde's Art and Skill, and the Sweet Discretion of Her Lying in Gottfried's *Tristan.*" In *Gottfried von Strassburg and the Medieval Tristan Legend: Papers from an Anglo-North American Symposium,* ed. Adrian Stevens and Roy Wisbey. Cambridge; London: The Institute of Germanic Studies, 1990, pp. 181–207.

Shenk, Robert. "The Liberation of the Loathly Lady of Medieval Romance." *Journal of the Rocky Mountain Medieval and Renaissance Association,* 2 (1981), 69–77.

Smits, Kathryn. "Enite als christliche Ehefrau." In *Interpretation und Edition deutscher Texte des Mittelalters: Festschrift für John Asher,* ed. Kathryn Smits, Werner Besch, and Victor Lange. Berlin: Schmidt, 1981, pp. 13–25.

———. "Die Schönheit der Frau in Hartmanns *Erec.*" *Zeitschrift für Deutsche Philologie,* 101 (1982), 1–28.

Sterba, Wendy. "The Question of Enite's Transgression: Female Voice and Male Gaze as Determining Factors in Hartmann's *Erec.*" In *Women as Protagonists and*

Poets in the German Middle Ages: An Anthology of Feminist Approaches to Middle High German Literature, ed. Albrecht Classen, pp. 57–68. Göppinger Arbeiten zur Germanistik, 528. Göppingen: Kümmerle, 1991.

Subrenat, Jean. "Chrétien de Troyes et Guenièvre: un romancier et son personnage." In Chrétien de Troyes et le Graal: Colloque arthurien de Bruges. Paris: Nizet, 1984, pp. 45–59.

Sullivan, Penny. "The Presentation of Enide in the Premier Vers of Chrétien's Erec et Enide." Medium Aevum, 52 (1983), 77–89.

Swilling, Paula. "Arthur and Ancient Britain: Images of the Great Goddess." Avalon to Camelot, 1.4 (Summer 1984), 26–27.

Thoran, Barbara. "Diu ir man verrâten hat—Zum Problem von Enîtes Schuld im 'Erec' Hartmanns von Aue." Wirkendes Wort, 25 (1975), 255–68.

Tigges, Wim. "'Lat the Womman Telle Hir Tale': A Reading of The Wife of Bath's Tale." English Studies, 73 (1992), 97–103.

Unzeitig-Herzog, Monika. "Parzivals Schwester in der Queste: Die Konzeption der Figur aus intertextueller Perspektive." In Artusroman und Intertextualität. Beiträge der Deutschen Sektionstagung der Internationalen Artusgesellschaft, ed. Friedrich Wolfzettel. Giessen: Schmitz, 1990, pp. 181–93.

Wade, Marjorie. "Gottfried von Strassburg's Elder Isolde: Daz Wîse Wîp." Tristania, 3.1 (November 1977), 17–27.

Walsh, John Michael. "Malory's Characterization of Elaine of Astolat." Philological Quarterly, 59 (1980), 140–49.

Wathelet-Willem, Jeanne. "Le personnage de Guenièvre chez Marie de France." Marche Romane, 13 (1963), 119–31.

Watson, Jeanie. "Enid the Disobedient: The Mabinogion's Gereint and Enid." In Ambiguous Realities, ed. Jeanie Watson and Carole Levin. Detroit, Mich: Wayne State University Press, 1987, pp. 114–32.

Webster, Kenneth G.T. Guenevere: A Study of Her Abductions. Milton, Mass.: Turtle, 1951.

Westoby, Kathryn S. "A New Look at the Role of the Fée in Medieval French Arthurian Romance." In The Spirit of the Court: Selected Proceedings of the Fourth Congress of the International Courtly Literature Society (Toronto 1983), ed. Glyn S. Burgess, Alan Deyermond, Dennis Green, Beryl Rowland, Robert A. Taylor. Woodbridge, Suffolk: Boydell and Brewer, 1985, pp. 373–85.

Westphal-Wihl, Sarah. "Smut and Armor." In Discours social/Social Discourse: The International Research Papers in Comparative Literature, 1 (1988), 149–71.

Whitaker, Muriel. The Legends of King Arthur in Art. Arthurian Studies, 23. Cambridge: Brewer, 1990.

Williams, Edith Whitehurst. "Morgan La Fee as Trickster in Sir Gawain and the Green Knight." Folklore, 96 (1985), 38–56.

Willson, H.B. "Adventure and Enite's Guilt in Hartmann's Erec." In Arturus Rex: Acta Conventus Lovaniensis 1987, ed. Willy Van Hoecke, Gilbert Tournoy, Werner Verbeke. Mediaevalia Lovaniensia Series I/Studia XVII. Leuven: Leuven University Press, 1991, pp. 164–71.

Wolfzettel, Friedrich, ed. Arthurian Romance and Gender. Selected Proceedings of the XVIIth International Arthurian Congress. Amsterdam: Rodopi, 1995.

Wurtele, Douglas J. "Chaucer's Wife of Bath and her Distorted Arthurian Motifs." Arthurian Interpretations, 2.1 (Fall 1987), 47–61.

Wynn, Marianne. "Gottfried's Heroine." In Gottfried von Strassburg and the Medieval Tristan Legend: Papers from an Anglo-North American Syposium, ed. Adrian Stevens and Roy Wisbey. Cambridge: Brewer; London: The Institute of Germanic Studies, 1990, pp. 127–41.

———. "Nicht-Tristanische Liebe in Gottfrieds Tristan: Liebesleidenschaft in Gotffrieds Elterngeschichte." In Liebe—Ehe—Ehebruch in der Literatur des

Mittelalters, ed. Xenja von Ertzdorff and Marianne Wynn. Giessen: Schmitz, 1984, pp. 56–70.

Zaddy, Z.P. "Enide's Role in the Romance." In Problems of Form and Meaning in "Erec," "Yvain," "Cligés," and the "Charrete." Chrétien Studies. Glasgow: University of Glasgow Press, 1973, pp. 23–39.

———. "Pourquoi Erec se décide-t-il à partir en voyage avec Enide?" Cahiers de Civilisation Médiévale, 7 (1964), 179–85.

Zak, Nancy C. The Portrayal of the Heroine in Chrétien de Troyes's "Erec et Enide," Gottfried von Strassburg's "Tristan," and "Flamenca." Göppinger Arbeiten zur Germanistik, 347. Göppingen: Kümmerle, 1983.

SEVENTEENTH CENTURY

*Anderson, Judith H. "Arthur, Argante, and the Ideal Vision: An Exercise in Speculation and Parody." In The Passing of Arthur: New Essays in Arthurian Tradition, ed. Christopher Baswell and William Sharpe. New York: Garland, 1988, pp. 193–206.

Cavanagh, Sheila T. "'Beauties Chace': Arthur and Women in The Faerie Queene." In The Passing of Arthur: New Essays in Arthurian Tradition, ed. Christopher Baswell and William Sharpe. New York: Garland, 1988, pp. 207–18.

———. Wanton Eyes and Chaste Desires: Female Sexuality in The Faerie Queene. Bloomington: Indiana University Press, 1994.

NINETEENTH CENTURY

Auerbach, Nina. Woman and the Demon: The Life of a Victorian Myth. Cambridge, Mass.: Harvard University Press, 1982.

Balch, Denis R. "Guenevere's Fidelity to Arthur in 'The Defence of Guenevere' and 'King Arthur's Tomb.'" Victorian Poetry, 13 (1975), 61–70.

Boos, Florence S. "Justice and Vindication in William Morris's 'The Defense of Guenevere.'" In King Arthur through the Ages, ed. Valerie M. Lagorio and Mildred Leake Day. Garland Reference Library of the Humanities, 1269, 1301. New York: Garland, 1990, II, 83–104.

———. "Sexual Polarities in The Defence of Guenevere." Browning Institute Studies, 13 (1985), 181–200.

Carson, Mother Angela. "Morris's Guenevere: A Further Note." Philological Quarterly, 42 (1963), 131–34.

Dillon, Steven C. "Milton and Tennyson's 'Guinevere.'" English Literary History, 54 (1987), 129–55.

Fontana, Ernest. "William Morris's Guenevere and Dante's Francesca: Allusion as Revision." English Miscellany: A Symposium of History, Literature and the Arts (1979–80), 28–29, 283–92.

Freedman, Jonathan. "Ideological Battleground: Tennyson, Morris, and the Pastness of the Past." In The Passing of Arthur: New Essays in Arthurian Tradition, ed. Christopher Baswell and William Sharpe. New York: Garland, 1988, pp. 235–48.

Fries, Maureen. "What Tennyson Really Did to Malory's Women." Quondam et Futurus: A Journal of Arthurian Interpretations, 1.1 (Spring 1991), 44–55.

Gilbert, Elliott L. "The Female King: Tennyson's Arthurian Apocalypse." In Speaking of Gender, ed. Elaine Showalter. New York: Routledge, 1989, pp. 163–86.

Gribble, Jennifer. The Lady of Shalott in the Victorian Novel. London: Macmillan, 1983.

Harris, Jack T. "'I Have Never Seen a Naked Lady of Shalott.'" The Pre-Raphaelite Review, 5 (1984), 76–87.

Hoberg, Thomas. "Duessa or Lilith: The Two Faces of Tennyson's Vivien." Victorian Poetry, 25, 17–25.

*Leavy, Barbara Fass. "Iseult of Brittany: A New Interpretation of Matthew Arnold's *Tristram and Iseult*." *Victorian Poetry*, 18 (1980), 1–22.

Linley, Margaret. "Sexuality and Nationality in Tennyson's *Idylls of the King*." *Victorian Poetry*, 30 (1992), 365–81.

*Lukitsh, Joanne. "Julia Margaret Cameron's Photographic Illustrations to Alfred Tennyson's 'The Idylls of the King.'" In *Arthurian Literature*, 7 (1987), 145–57.

Marsh, Jan. *Pre-Raphaelite Women: Images of Femininity*. New York: Harmony, 1987.

Millard, Charles W. "Julia Margaret Cameron and Tennyson's *Idylls of the King*." *Harvard Library Bulletin*, 21 (1973), 187–201.

Perrine, Laurence. "Morris's Guenevere: An Interpretation." *Philological Quarterly*, 39 (1960), 234–41.

Plasa, Carl. "'Cracked from Side to Side': Sexual Politics in 'The Lady of Shalott.'" *Victorian Poetry*, 30 (1992), 247–63.

Raymond, Meredith. "The Arthurian Group in *The Defence of Guenevere and Other Poems*." *Victorian Poetry*, 4 (1966), 213–18.

Relihan, Constance C. "Vivien, Elaine, and the Model's Gaze: Cameron's Reading of *Idylls of the King*." *Popular Arthurian Traditions*, ed. Sally K. Slocum. Bowling Green, Ohio: Bowling Green State University Popular Press, 1992, pp. 111–31.

Silver, Carole G. "'The Defence of Guenevere': A Further Interpretation." *Studies in English Literature*, 9 (1969), 695–702.

*———. *The Romance of William Morris*. Athens: Ohio University Press, 1982.

———. "Victorian Spellbinders: Arthurian Women and the Pre-Raphaelite Circle." In *The Passing of Arthur: New Essays in Arthurian Tradition*, ed. Christopher Baswell and William Sharpe. New York: Garland, 1988, pp. 249–63.

Simpson, Arthur L. "Elaine the Unfair, Elaine the Unlovable: The Socially Destructive Artist/Woman in *Idylls of the King*." *Modern Philology*, 89 (1992), 341–62.

Smith, Lindsay. "The Politics of Focus: Feminism and Photography Theory" [Lewis Carroll, Julia Margaret Cameron]. In *New Feminist Discourses: Critical Essays on Theories and Texts*, ed. Isobel Armstrong. London: Routledge, 1992, pp. 238–62.

Stallman, Robert L. "The Lovers' Progress: An Investigation of William Morris' 'The Defence of Guenevere' and 'King Arthur's Tomb.'" *Studies in English Literature: 1500–1900*, 15 (1975), 657–70.

Weaver, Mike. *Julia Margaret Cameron 1815–1879*. Boston: Little, Brown, 1984.

TWENTIETH CENTURY

Alama, Pauline J. "A Woman in King Arthur's Court: Wendy Mnookin's *Guenever Speaks*." *Quondam et Futurus: A Journal of Arthurian Interpretations*, 2.2 (Summer 1992), 81–88.

Blanch, Robert J. "George Romero's *Knightriders*: A Contemporary Arthurian Romance." *Quondam et Futurus: A Journal of Arthurian Interpretations*, 1.4 (Winter 1991), 61–69.

Boyle, Sara. "From Victim to Avenger: The Women in John Boorman's *Excalibur*." *Avalon to Camelot*, 1.4 (Summer 1984), 42–43.

Bradley, Marion Zimmer. "My Search for Morgaine Le Fay." In *The Vitality of the Arthurian Legend*. Odense: Odense University Press, 1988, pp. 105–09.

*Brewer, Elisabeth. "The Figure of Guenevere in Modern Drama and Fiction." In *Arturus Rex: Acta Conventus Lovaniensis 1987*, ed. Willy Van Hoecke, Gilbert Tournoy, Werner Verbeke. Mediaevalia Lovaniensia Series I/Studia XVII. Leuven: Leuven University Press, 1991, pp. 479–90.

de Weever, Jacqueline. "Morgan and the Problem of Incest." *Cinema Arthuriana: Essays on Arthurian Film*, ed. Kevin J. Harty. New York: Garland, 1991, pp. 145–56.

*Farwell, Marilyn R. "Heterosexual Plots and Lesbian Subtexts: Toward a Theory of Lesbian Narrative Space." In *Lesbian Texts and Contexts: Radical Revisions*, ed. Karla Jay and Joanne Glasgow. New York: New York University Press, 1990, pp. 91–103.

Fuog, Karen E.C. "Imprisoned in the Phallic Oak: Marion Zimmer Bradley and Merlin's Seductress." *Quondam et Futurus: A Journal of Arthurian Interpretations*, 1.1 (Spring 1991), 73–88.

Gordon-Wise, Barbara Ann. *The Reclamation of a Queen: Guinevere in Modern Fantasy*. Contributions to the Study of Science Fiction and Fantasy, 44. New York: Greenwood, 1991.

Herman, Harold J. "Sharan Newman's Guinevere Trilogy." *Arthurian Interpretations*, 1.2 (Spring 1987), 39–55.

———. "The Women in Mary Stewart's Merlin Trilogy." *Interpretations: A Journal of Ideas, Analysis, and Criticism*, 15 (1984), 101–14.

Hoberg, Tom. "In Her Own Right: The Guenevere of Parke Godwin." *Popular Arthurian Traditions,* ed. Sally K. Slocum. Bowling Green, Ohio: Bowling Green State University Popular Press, 1992, pp. 68–79.

MacCurdy, Marian. "Bitch or Goddess: Polarized Images of Women in Arthurian Literature and Films." *Platte Valley Review*, 18 (1990), 3–24.

Morrison, Susan Signe. "Morgan Le Fay's Champion: Marion Zimmer Bradley's 'The Mists of Avalon' as Challenge to Sir Thomas Malory's 'Le Morte D'Arthur.'" In *Mittelalter-Rezeption IV*, ed. Irene von Burg, Jürgen Kühnel, Ulrich Müller, and Alexander Schwartz. Göppinger Arbeiten zur Germanistik, 550. Göppingen: Kümmerle, 1991, pp. 133–54.

O'Valle, Violet. "Bernard Malamud's 'The Lady of the Lake' and the Lake Legends of Wales." *Language and Literature*, 7 (1982), 63–80.

Podroschko, Sirikit. "Ein mittelalterlicher Mythos im Film. John Boorman und die Arthurische Tafelrunde." In *Der frauwen buoch: Versuch zu einer feministischen Mediävistik*, ed. Ingrid Bennewitz. Göppinger Arbeiten zur Germanistik, 517. Göppingen: Kümmerle, 1989, pp. 473–89.

Rétif, Françoise. "Affleurement d'un mythe: Tristan chez Simone de Beauvoir et Ingeborg Bachmann." *Revue de Littérature Comparée*, 63 (1989), 357–67.

Samples, Susann. "Guenevere: A Re-Appraisal." *Arthurian Interpretations*, 3.2 (Spring 1989), 106–18.

———. "Guinevere: A Germanic Heroine." *Quondam et Futurus: A Journal of Arthurian Interpretations*, 1.4 (Winter 1991), 9–22.

Sklar, Elizabeth S. "Thoroughly Modern Morgan: Morgan le Fey in Twentieth-Century Popular Arthuriana." *Popular Arthurian Traditions*, ed. Sally K. Slocum. Bowling Green, Ohio: Bowling Green State University Popular Press, 1992, pp. 24–35.

Spivack, Charlotte. *Merlin's Daughters: Contemporary Women Writers of Fantasy*. Contributions to the Study of Science Fiction and Fantasy, 23. New York: Greenwood, 1987.

———. "Morgan Le Fay": Goddess or Witch?" *Popular Arthurian Traditions*, ed. Sally K. Slocum. Bowling Green, Ohio: Bowling Green State University Popular Press, 1992, pp. 18–23.

Starr, Nathan Comfort. "Edwin Arlington Robinson's Arthurian Heroines: Vivian, Guenevere, and the Two Isolts." *Philological Quarterly*, 56 (1977), 231–49.

Thomas, Patrick Michael. "*Tristan* and the Avatars of the Lunar Goddess." *Quondam et Futurus: A Journal of Arthurian Interpretations*, 2.3 (Fall 1992), 15–20.

*Thompson, Raymond H. "The First and Last Love: Morgan le Fay and Arthur." *The Arthurian Revival: Essays on Form, Tradition and Transformation*, ed. Debra Mancoff. New York: Garland, 1992, pp. 230–47.

———. *The Return from Avalon: A Study of the Arthurian Legend in Modern Fiction*. Westport, Conn.: Greenwood, 1985.

Tuczay, Christa. "Die Frauengestalten in Godwins, Newmans, Bradshaws, Stewarts und Zimmer-Bradleys Artusromanen." In *Mittelalter-Rezeption III*, ed. Jürgen Kühnel, Hans-Dieter Mück, and Ursula Müller. Göppinger Arbeiten zur Germanistik, 479. Göppingen: Kümmerle, 1988, pp. 663–81.

Walker, Jeanne Murray. "The Demoness and the Grail: Deciphering MacDonald's Lilith." In *The Scope of the Fantastic: Culture, Biography, Themes, Children's Literature*, ed. Robert A. Collins and Howard D. Pearce, III. Westport, Conn.: Greenwood, 1985, pp. 179–90.

Williams, Mary C. "Lessons from Ladies in Steinbeck's 'Gawain, Ewain, and Morholt.'" *Avalon to Camelot*, 1.4 (Summer 1984), 40–41.

RESISTING TALES

Love, Honor, and the Exchange of Women in *Yvain*

Some Remarks on the Female Reader

Roberta L. Krueger

AUTHOR'S PREFACE

This article about Chrétien de Troyes' Yvain, or The Knight of the Lion, *first published in 1985, was the beginning of what ultimately became a book-length study of Old French courtly romance and its female audience.* Women Readers and the Ideology of Gender in Old French Verse Romance *(Cambridge University Press, 1993) analyzes the problem of female reception of courtly ideology in selected verse narratives from Chrétien de Troyes to Christine de Pizan. It argues that many romances present a surface that is more complex than the simple promotion or devalorization of women: they simultaneously invite women readers' complicity with and resistance to the texts' idealized constructions of gender.*

Since "Love, Honor, and the Exchange of Women" was published, a lively debate in feminist criticism has questioned the very notions of a "female subject" or "female reader." Some critics have cautioned against drawing a necessary link between a reader's gender and a particular mode of identification or subjectivity; but others have warned of the dangers of erasing the different voices of historical women. The terms of this debate inform Women Readers and the Ideology of Gender in Old French Verse Romance. *In it I reject the notion of an "essentially" feminine way of reading but I also argue that to overlook the problematic position of women readers of medieval romance (a genre written for a mixed audience of knights and ladies) contributes to women's effacement in history. If courtly women did not have essentially different ways of reading, nonetheless they occupied a different position with respect to textual production and performance, traditionally male domains. European medieval women were normally displaced from the subject position in writing; so, too, the apparently*

Reprinted by permission from *Romance Notes*, 25, 3 (1985), 302–17.

privileged fictional women within *French medieval romances were usually displaced as objects within the masculine chivalric plot.*

As the author of the first full-length Arthurian romances, Chrétien de Troyes in fact inscribes the female audience's displacement at the genre's inception. But, as I show here and in an analysis of a companion romance, Le Chevalier de la Charrete,* *which together form Chapter 2, "The Question of Women in* Yvain *and* Le Chevalier de la charrete," *of* Women Readers, *Chrétien's romances invite his readers to question the processes by which women are marginalized. He inscribes female characters and female readers as a* problem. *He creates complex female characters (Laudine in* Yvain, *Guenevere in the* Charrete) *who do not accede instantly to the knight's desire. He further explicitly presents courtly women as a problematic audience for chivalric stories of love and honor, both in the Prologues and Epilogues to each work and in each text's depiction of women as readers, listeners and spectators. Chrétien's romances may eventually have done more than inculcate gender identities in their aristocratic audience: they may have challenged their readers to question their own identification with courtly fictions.*

Yvain's *marriage quest and the* Chevalier de la Charrete's *adulterous love quest set the stage for the continuation, imitation, adaptation, and translation of the Arthurian legend throughout the Middle Ages. The story of the Knight of the Lion became a prototype for Arthurian romances that recount the adventures of an individual knight who increases his status through combat and marriage; the fictional adultery between Lancelot and Guenevere forms the core of the immense recasting of Arthurian legend in the thirteenth-century Prose* Lancelot. *In both types of quest narrative, the women's subjective autonomy is subsumed within the masculine adventure. But if Chrétien's narratives lay the groundwork for women's subsequent displacement in Arthurian fiction, so, too, do they create a discursive space where courtly ideology can be examined and questioned.* Yvain *and* Le Chevalier de la Charrete *inaugurate a tradition of debate about gender roles, a debate catalyzed by the displacement of the female reader.*

Roberta L. Krueger

---

*Originally published as "Desire, Meaning, and the Female Reader: The Problem in Chrétien's *Charrete.*" *The Passing of Arthur. New Essays in Arthurian Tradition.* Eds. Christopher Baswell, William Sharpe. New York, London: Garland, 1988. Pp. 31–51. (Ed.)

If Old French courtly romances were addressed to audiences of men and women, and if a text's ideological function depends upon the relationship it establishes with its readers, how does the *sens* of a romance differ when the implied reader is a woman? The hypothesis of the female reader[1] focuses our attention on the problem of gender in romance and reveals sexual tensions which qualify the ideology of chivalry. Such an approach draws its theoretical justification from the critical perspective of a modern female reader, from the historic conditions of romances' reception, and, preeminently, from the problematic inscription of women as readers and as characters in particular texts.

The debate about the promotion of women in courtly literature[2] finds much fuel to feed its fires in Chrétien de Troyes' *Yvain*,[3] where a profound ambivalence about woman's position in court life is established in the first lines of the Prologue. The narrator's invocation of Arthur's prowess for "our" instruction—"la cui prœsce *nos* enseigne" (2)—appeals to an implied audience of knights. But the fictional knights assembled at Arthur's court on Pentecost have gathered where the *ladies* have called them—"cil chevalier s'atropelerent / la ou dames les apelerent / ou dameiseles ou puceles" (9–11)—and they discuss not honor but Love (12–17). Arthur's negligent absence from the court at Pentecost because the Queen has detained him in bed—"que la reïne le detint" (50)—bespeaks the power of feminine wiles to influence court life for better or worse. Then, when Guenevere sneaks in, "tot a celee" (64), to listen to the story that Calogrenant recounts before an exclusively male audience (as described in 53–60), her appearance occasions a display of *courtoisie* which degenerates into uncourtly bickering among the knights (69–130). From the perspective of the knights, the intrusion of the feminine threatens to ruin the ambiance of the male gathering, as Keu warns: "Dame, se nos n' i gaeignons, / fet Kex, an vostre conpaignie, / gardez que nos n' i perdiens mie" ("Lady, says Kay, if we do not gain by your company, be careful that we do not lose because of it," 92–94).

Guenevere's presence is a troublesome influence, but her power to act is sanctioned by the knights' approval. Although she commands Calogrenant to resume his storytelling, after he has begged that she leave him "an pes" ("in peace," 120) and that she "s'an teise" ("be quiet," 121), her command is reinforced by Keu. The seneschal invokes the faith she owes the King "le vostre seignor et le mien" ("your lord and mine," 129) to entreat her to order Calogrenant, "comandez li, si feroiz bien" ("command him, you would do well," 130). By making her love conditional upon the knight's recounting of his adventures, "se de m'amor volez joïr" ("if you wish to have my love," 140), Guenevere appears to act as the sovereign patron of Calogrenant's tale. But Calogrenant's principal *destinataires* are the Arthurian knights, whose reputation for honor rests upon their successful vindication of his shame. If the Queen enjoys a privileged position where she influences court life, she is no less subordinate to the action of knights vying for honor.

Chrétien's presentation of fictional woman's problematic status in court life may be in keeping with historians' differing conceptions of noblewomen's power in medieval France.[4] But Chrétien's work does more than "reflect" an historical paradox. In the subsequent adventures of Yvain, the narrator explores the process by which the tensions between men and women become masked by an ideology of love and honor. This embellishment or "mystification" of sexual division is a textual strategy which Chrétien simultaneously adopts and debunks. As will be shown in an analysis of three episodes—Yvain's lovesickness and marriage with Laudine, Yvain's exploits at Pesme Aventure, and Yvain's return to the Fountain and "reconciliation" with Laudine—the narrator calls our attention to the romance's mystification of woman's place at the same time that he reveals the underlying reality of her status as an object of exchange. Chrétien's dialectical presentation produces a romance with a double vision which calls forth several possible responses among the women who heard or read it. If one woman reader or listener may have admired an idealized image of chivalry, another may have perceived the narrator's critical analysis of a system which constrains both sexes.

A paradigm for the dynamics of sexual exchange can be found in the *costume* ("custom") of the immodest damsel in *Yvain*'s companion romance, *Le Chevalier de la Charrete*.[5] A nameless maiden who has staged a mock rape the previous night in order to attract Lancelot's attention requests that Lancelot allow her to accompany him and that he protect her, according to a *costume* which seems perhaps as uncourtly as the damsel's former behavior (see lines 1302–16). The *costume*'s two propositions can be restated as follows: 1) A knight will be dishonored in court if he seizes a woman who is alone (1302–10). But, 2) If a knight conquers a woman from another knight in battle, he may do with her as he pleases without incurring shame or blame (1311–16).

From one perspective, the custom is another ruse by which the damsel attempts to secure Lancelot's affections; it is one of a number of constraints in which the knight finds himself enmeshed. But on a deeper level, the custom—recounted here by the third-person narrator—describes how a system which may seem to protect damsels regulates instead the ascription of honor to knights.

If a knight wishes to be of good reputation he will not dishonor a woman alone: ". . . ne feïst se tote enor non, / *s'estre volsist de bœn renon*" ("he should do only what is honorable, if he would like to be of good renown," 1307–08, emphasis added). As stated, the custom's first tenet implies the existence of *some* dishonorable knights who will harm women alone. A resultant corollary is that prudent damsels would be well-advised to seek a strong knight's protection. But, under the terms of the second proposition, a maiden appended to a knight becomes fair game for any other knight willing to do battle for her: ". . . sa volenté an poïst faire / sanz honte et sanz blasme retraire" (". . . he might do his will without earning shame or blame," 1315–16).

The custom thus assures not the protection of a maiden's autonomy, but her value as a possession or prize for those knights between whom she is the object of dispute. Within the chivalric honor system, the woman becomes an object of exchange.[6] The damsel's custom describes not only Guenevere's situation with regard to Meleagant and Lancelot in the *Charrete;* it also describes Laudine's position with respect to Esclados le Ros and Yvain in *Le Chevalier au Lion.*[7]

Yvain's *coup de foudre* and marriage to Laudine exemplify how the romance mystifies the exchange of women at the same time that it lays bare the mechanism for our analysis. Yvain's adventure in Brocéliande fulfills what Duby might call a *rêve de jeunesse:* he marries the wife of the knight he has slain in combat. His conquest of his rival's wife and possession of her domain resembles a marriage by capture in early Germanic society which, if it is antithetical to the doctrine of consent in the twelfth century,[8] is not without historic example as late as the eleventh century in Northern France.[9] Chrétien's courtly romance transforms the unchivalrous practice of *rapt* into an artfully negotiated exchange between Lunete and Yvain.

That exchange is further transformed by a narrative presentation which allows the reader to create the fiction of a widow in love with Yvain by her own desire and for her own good. The mystification of the exchange occurs in three steps through a narrative progression from Yvain's lovesickness, to Lunete's negotiations, to Laudine's quick change of heart. In each step, Chrétien's narrative embellishes the marriage by coercion at the same time that it points up the constraints of the custom imposed on Laudine.

For some critics, the courtly manner in which Yvain falls in love, while peering from his hiding place through a little window to marvel at the beauty of the bereaved Laudine as the mourning procession for her husband passes beneath, legitimates his desire for his rival's widow.[10] It does so by reversing the terms of the capture: Yvain is the prisoner, the victim of Amors, and Laudine is the unwitting agent of vengeance for her husband's death: "Bien a vangiee, et si nel set / la dame la mort son seignor" ("The lady has indeed avenged—and doesn't know it—the death of her lord," 1366–67). Chrétien's artful overlay of Ovidian conceit and lyric form effectively transforms the knight's claim to a war prize into the lady's sexual conquest of the submissive, lovestruck knight: "Cele plaie a mes sire Yvains, / dom il ne sera ja mes sains, / qu'Amors s'est tote a lui randue" ("My lord Yvain has a wound from which he will never recover, because Love has given herself to him completely," 1379–81).[11]

Chrétien's amplification of *amors* is double-edged both in metaphoric content and in its narrative function. Even as Yvain's new love "sweetens" the knight's shameful memory of Keu's taunts with its sugar and honey ("Mes de son çucre et de ses bresches / li radolcist novele amors," ["With its sugar and honey, new love sweetens him up,"] 1360–61), it simultaneously hunts him down like prey, "s'a tote sa proie acoillie" (1363). So does Chrétien's amplification both "soften" the moment when Yvain falls in love with Laudine and underscore the bitter tensions between this knight and lady. As Tony Hunt has shown for the play of dialectic throughout *Yvain,* Chrétien's rhetorical display is often an "allusive technique" which calls the reader's attention to "the realities underlying paradoxes."[12] In the context of Yvain's recent victory over Esclados, the Ovidian conceit "son cuer a o soi s'anemie, / s'aimme la rien qui plus le het" ("his heart has its enemy with it, for he loves the creature who most hates him," 1364–65) is concretized. Further variations upon the oxymoronic pairing "amie" / "anemie" (1453–64) underscore the sexual dialectics of Yvain's *coup de foudre.*

If Yvain does not here employ physical force to win Laudine, neither does he *court* her, gradually earning her consent through a sustained demonstration of love or merit. He instead comes to ask for her hand as a result of negotiations made by a go-between, Lunete. Lunete serves Yvain in repayment for the honor he alone showed her once at Arthur's court, as she explains (996–1025): "Et sachiez bien, se je pooie, / servise et enor vos feroie, / car vos la feïstes ja moi" ("And know well that if I could, I would render you service and do you honor, for you have already done so for me," 1001–03); ". . . de l' enor que vos m'i feïstes / vos randrai ja le guerredon" (". . . for the honor that you did me there I will give you the reward," 1014–15). Her role as servant and intermediary is the second way in which the narrative creates the fiction of the "good marriage" for Laudine. Because Lunete's faithful service to Yvain is equaled only by that of the Lion, and because she is reputed to be on excellent terms with Laudine (1593–97), we might believe that acts in the interest of both Yvain and her lady.

But Lunete, who has promised to give Yvain whatever he needs—"si li fist creance et despans / de tot quan que il li convint" ("thus she gave him credit and provision for whatever he needed," 1586–87)—serves first of all Yvain and the system of knightly honor when she convinces Laudine to marry the man who has killed her husband. Her argument—that Laudine must marry to defend her Fountain from King Arthur and that the strongest knight would be the one who has proved himself victorious (1690–1703; 1706–13)—restates the double bind of the immodest damsel's custom in the *Charrete*. Here the protector and the enemy are the same man. Lunete's language in this section, tinged with proverbial misogyny, resembles that of Laudine's male adviser. She begs Laudine to take counsel—"vos deüssiez or consoil prendre / de vostre fontainne desfendre" ("you ought to take counsel now to defend your fountain," 1627–28; cf. 1850–51)—just as the seneschal cites woman's inability to carry a sword or strike with a lance as the reason why Laudine must maintain the custom and marry: "Fame ne set porter escu / ne ne set de lance ferir; / molt amander, et ancherir, / se puet de panre un bœn seignor" ("A woman does not know how to carry a shield nor does she know how to strike with a lance; she can repair much damage and raise herself in dignity in taking a good lord," 2098–2101).

Laudine initially feels trapped by Lunete's arguments—"Il m' est avis que tu m'agueites, / si me viax a parole prandre" ("I think that you are watching me and trying to trip me on my own words," 1704–05)—and becomes furious when she understands the "desreison" ("insulting, unreasonable thing") which Lunete has proposed, "la plus grant c'onques mes fust dite" ("the greatest that ever was uttered," 1715), that she marry her husband's assassin. But the narrator tells us, voicing Laudine's thoughts, that Lunete loves her lady more than Yvain and is too loyal to advise action that would harm or shame her, ". . . trop est sa leax amie" "[she is] very much her loyal friend," 1750). After her lady has banished her, Lunete laments to Yvain that she believed she acted more in Laudine's interests than in Yvain's, "plus por son preu que por le vostre / le cuidai feire et cuit ancor" ("I believed and believe still that I did it more for her profit than for yours," 3650–51). But, even as the reader may sympathize with Lunete's intentions as she plays the role of the good counselor, in the terms of the romance's structure of exchanges, she acts as a relative who hands a daughter or sister over for marriage, to honor a peer or appease an opponent.

The third reason we believe in the fiction of Laudine's love for Yvain—the third way in which the *exchange* of the woman is obscured—is that

Laudine, after initially acting with outrage at Lunete's suggestion that she marry her husband's slayer, becomes extremely impatient to meet him. The narrator again describes a character's emotional state by means of rhetorical adornment. The litote which tells us that Laudine has proved to herself by reason that she should not hate Yvain and may have what she desires (1773–78) is followed by the simile of the fire which bursts into flame as soon as it is sparked, like Laudine's desire:

> et par li meïsmes s'alume
> ensi come li feus qui fume
> tant que la flame s'i est mise,
> que nus ne la soufle n'atise.

["And by herself she catches fire like the fire that smokes until the flame catches, without anyone blowing on it or stoking it," 1779–82.]

Narrative indirection thus leads the reader to believe that Laudine loves Yvain, although she never tells the knight this before their marriage. The implication that women really desire what necessity dictates to them conforms to the misogynist comments, reminiscent of the *Ars Amatoria*,[13] which punctuate this episode—that Laudine may come to desire Yvain because women often change their minds as Yvain muses (1439–40), that women say no to what they really want, as the narrator insinuates (1644–48), that women get mad when they hear what is good for them, as Lunete tells Laudine (1653–56).

From one perspective, Laudine's "choice" comes to seem natural and laudable. When the narrator announces: "Ez vos ja la dame changiee" ("There before you is the lady, changed," 1751), the text signals its own transformation of woman's status, one in which its readers, credulous or skeptical, may participate. Laudine's coerced marriage, an exchange between Lunete and Yvain, has been embellished to be perceived as a sentimental *change* in Laudine's feelings, fostered by the good counsel of another woman. The romance mystifies the knight's desire and Laudine's powerlessness by transposing the latter onto Yvain, who appears tongue-tied and contrite before his lady, as he falls to his feet and submits himself to her will (1952–80).

If critical reactions to this episode have recognized the political necessity of Laudine's marriage, many critics would agree with Lot-Borodine's early assessment that if we do not accept the fact that Laudine loves Yvain, then we cannot find a *sens* for the romance's subsequent events[14] and with Frappier's later contention that Laudine is "très sincèrement éprise d'Yvain," ("very sincerely smitten with Yvain") even if she never admits it to herself.[15]

Such critical explanations seem to compensate for the paucity of sentimental development in Laudine in the text. For, although the narrator embellishes Laudine's sentimental transformation with the image of the spontaneous fire and later says that "Amors" has motivated her (2141), Laudine herself never directly expresses her affections to Yvain before their marriage. Only as Yvain's wife does she speak once of her "love" turning to hate if the knight does not return by the end of his term, "Mes l'amors devanra haïne, / que j'ai en vous. . ." ("But the love I have for you will become hate," 2566–67).

Throughout the *coup de foudre* and marriage episode, the narrator's presentation emphasizes the disparity and inequality of Yvain's and Laudine's love. We need only compare the nearly two hundred verses which explore Yvain's *amor* (1361–1544) to the thirty-odd verses which recount Laudine's sentimental change (1751–83) to see how this difference is structurally present; Yvain's love monologue occupies seventy-nine lines (1432–1510); Laudine's internal "reasoning" comprises only thirteen lines (1762–74). As Marie-Noëlle Lefay-Toury has remarked, emotional encounters between husband and wife are truncated in *Yvain,* as compared, for example, to the poignant interactions between Yvain and his Lion, whose fidelity and gratefulness replace Laudine's more troublesome companionship.[16] Such a textual imbalance seems to justify the position of those who question the equality of Laudine and Yvain's marriage[17] and those who construe the central issue in *Yvain* not as love but as the sovereignty of the knight in love.[18]

Chrétien's sentimental overlay does nothing to change Laudine's dependent political status, as the language of the text insists. She asks Yvain not for love but that he defend her fountain, "—Et oserïez vos enprandre / por moi ma fontainne a desfandre?" ("And would you dare to undertake for me the defense of my fountain?" 2035–36), and she agrees to make him "seignor de ma terre et de moi" ("lord of my land and of myself," 1808). In the episode's final lines, Lunete recounts to Gauvain how she has "conquered" Laudine, "Et ele li conte et devise / a con grant poinne ele *conquist* / sa dame" ("And she tells him and describes to him how with great difficulty she *conquered* her lady," 2426–28, emphasis added). The narrator also describes how Arthur's knights visit the land "que mes sire Yvains ot *conquise* / en la dame que il ot *prise*" ("that my lord Yvain had *conquered*, with the lady that he had *taken*," 2473–74, emphasis added). Beneath the fiction of Laudine's and Yvain's mutual desire, the text describes coercion and possession.

The Pesme Aventure episode further exemplifies *Yvain's* double vision of woman's place and provides an image of a female reader appropriated by the ideology of love. The *pucele* ("maiden") whom Yvain discovers reading a romance to her parents in a garden appears to be the center of value in this privileged world. Her beauty occasions the narrator's digression on the "plaie" ("wound") which the God of Love would inflict upon himself if he saw her and about which the narrator would speak further if he did not fear that his audience would accuse him of talking about dreams (5369–5390). As we have seen earlier, rhetorical amplification accompanies the narrator's idealization of love, which is underscored here by a self-conscious, ironic intervention.

From the perspective of the maiden and her family, Pesme Aventure's oppressive custom will reward the girl as a prize to the knight who will conquer the two *fils de netun* ("sons of a demon"). But the same custom which elevates the *pucele* into a valued prize has condemned three hundred silkworkers (also called *puceles)* to enforced labor in the castle's workroom. If Chrétien's embellished presentation of the maiden reading in the garden on a silk rug idealizes the female as privileged subject, then his portrayal of the three hundred silkworkers superimposed upon the single *pucele* invites our demystification of that idealization. The fiction of female privilege in romance is undercut by the hyper-realism of the silkworkers' oppression. The damsels' torn clothing and pale faces (5188–99) echo Laudine's anguished mourning (1155–64). The text again lays bare the double bind of women's relationship to the knights who protect them. The silkworkers owe their oppression to the cowardice of a foolhardy young knight, king of the Isle of the Damsels, who each year trades thirty of them into labor in exchange for his refusal to fight the *fils de netun* (5250–88); the dishonor of that knight necessitates Yvain's chivalrous service.

Yvain's victory over the devils liberates the silkworkers from servitude and at the same time transforms the *pucele* in the garden into an item on the marriage market. When the lord offers Yvain the maiden as a reward—"et nostre fille iert vostre dame / car nos la vos donrons a fame" ("and our daughter will be your lady, *for we give her to you for your wife,*" 5695–96, emphasis added)—Yvain immediately returns the gift—"Et je, fet il, la vos redoing" ("And I, he says, give her back to you," 5697)—and asks instead that the other damsels be freed (5702–05).

The father sings the praises of his daughter—"mes prenez, si feroiz savoir / ma fille . . . / qui est molt bele, et riche, et sage" ("but take my daughter . . .who is very beautiful, rich and prudent," 5709–11)—saying that Yvain will miss his chance for a rich marriage if he does not take her, "ja mes si riche mariage / n'avroiz, se vos cestui, n'avez" ("never will you have such a rich marriage if you don't have this one," 5712–13). Yvain's second refusal (5714–30) provokes the lord's wrath and his threat to imprison Yvain for his disdain of the girl (5731–38). Only after Yvain promises to return "se j'onques puis" ("if ever I can," 5747) to take the damsel does her father retreat, saying that he refuses to give his daughter "par force" ("by force," 5761).

Throughout this altercation between the two men, the daughter's opinion on the matter is never solicited. The young girl who was actively reading a romance aloud to her parents here becomes the passive object of verbal exchange between two knights seeking honor. The episode ends with Yvain's liberation of the silkworkers, who leave their imprisonment with "grant joie" ("great joy," 5803), but whose future welfare remains as unclear as the daughter's.[19] If the evil *costume* of the castle has been abolished along with a virulent form of female servitude, the narrative provides no details about the women's place after liberation. The episode's final lines recount the exchange of salutations between Yvain and the silkworkers, who display more "joie" than if Yvain had descended from the heavens (5775–77), thus multiplying hundredfold the honor shown him.

At the end of his adventures, Yvain has grown in stature as a knight. However, although he has fought victoriously on behalf of other women threatened by dishonorable men in the intricately interlaced episodes of the romance's second half,[20] it does not necessarily follow that Yvain now deserves Laudine, as many critics maintain.[21] The comic interpretation of Yvain's moral progress, whether viewed as a result of the hero's "sens de la réflexion" and "self-control"[22] as the expiation of broken promise,[23] or as the Subject's "accumulation of value,"[24] derives from a perspective focused sympathetically on the knight.[25] While this view is not excluded by a romance whose complexities admit multiple interpretations, it overlooks the narrative's explicit inscription of persistent sexual tensions.

Despite the Chevalier au Lion's moving encounter with Laudine after Lunete's rescue (4582–4628), the knight's relationship to his wife has not ameliorated any more than woman's place within the exchange system has improved. Laudine, during and after all of her husband's exploits, remains where she always was—in a castle near the fountain, the locus of male desire and the playfield of knightly honor; she is still subject to its storms and tremblings. When Yvain, possessed by "Amors," decides to make the fountain storm so much that Laudine will have to make "peace" with him (6500–16), the aggressor turned defender of the Fountain reverts to the role of aggressor.

Just as Yvain's marriage with his victim's wife was enhanced by his manner of loving her, so "amors" would seem to some to justify his desperate blackmail: his heart has been "mis en Amor" ("put in Love," 6502) so that if he does not have Laudine back he will die, "et par Amor an fin morroit, / se sa dame n'avoit merci / de lui . . ." ("and in the end through Love he would die, if his lady had no mercy on him," 6504–06). Nevertheless, Yvain wars against Laudine in the same way that his defeated enemies warred against other defenseless women; the verb *guerroier* ("to make war") employed to recount Yvain's plan—"et si iroit / a sa fontainne guerroier" ("and so he would go to make war at her fountain," 6508–09)—is the same as that the damsel of Norison used to describe the malicious actions of the rapacious Count Alier, Yvain's first enemy, to her lady, "Car trop vos a mal envaïe li cuens Aliers qui vos guerroie" ("For count Aliers, who was warring against you, has very evilly invaded you," 2934–35). Chrétien portrays Yvain's amorous reconciliation as an act of physical coercion.

Lunete's clever verbal manipulations again allow her to hand Laudine over to Yvain, as one knight might to another. Her stratagem— she convinces Laudine to swear on relics that she will reconcile the Knight of the Lion with his lady in order to enlist his services—may be seen as a clever and courtly move by the narrator, who deems Lunete "molt cortoise" ("very courteous," 6620), but it serves Yvain's desires more than it honors his wife. In her angry reaction (6750–66), Laudine claims that she has been trapped, "au hoquerel prise" ("caught in a trap," 6751), comments ironically that Lunete has "esploitié molt bien" ("succeeded very cleverly," 6754), and states that, if she did not fear perjury, she would rather endure "vanz et orage" ("winds and storms") her whole life than make her peace with Yvain (6756–61). Such words make it difficult to believe that Laudine accepts Lunete's trick as a pretext to rekindle a love repressed by pride.[26] Laudine's own transformation of the fire image (used earlier by the narrator to describe her feelings) into smoldering ashes bespeaks her continued resentment, "Toz jorz mes el cors me covast, / si con li feus cove an la cendre, / ce don ge ne voel ore aprendre . . ." (6762–64). Laudine pardons Yvain not out of love for him, but for fear of perjuring herself before Lunete.

The romance's dénouement occupies some three hundred lines of verse (6500–6808) and of those, roughly two hundred and eighty describe Yvain's warring and Lunete's manipulation. Readers and critics who believe that a transformation has taken place in the married couple's relationship do not derive this view from any dramatic encounter in the narrative. Their feeling that all is well comes rather from a willingness to believe the twenty-line epilogue with which the poem concludes. In these final lines, the narrator assures us that Yvain and Laudine are at peace, loved and cherished one by the other: "Molt an est a boen chief venuz / qu' il est amez et chier tenuz /

de sa dame, et ele de lui" ("He has come to a good conclusion because he is loved by his lady, and she by him," 6793–95).

But the narrative's harmonious closure is undercut by the disposition of the last twenty lines of verse, which divide into two indicative propositions inscribing the names of Yvain and Lunete: "Or a mes sire Yvains sa pes" ("Now my lord Yvain has his peace," 6789) and "Et Lunete rest molt a eise" ("And Lunete remains very comfortable," 6799). Laudine, the lady of the Fountain, is not named in the romance's concluding lines.[27] Structurally, the romance's conclusion valorizes the exchange of service and honor between Yvain and Lunete more than it celebrates the mutual love of Yvain and Laudine. Yvain and Lunete's courtly reciprocity finds its final expression in the gift Lunete makes of Laudine to Yvain, a gift for which Yvain has said he can never repay her (6697–98). If Lunete's verbal manipulations exemplify female strength,[28] we should not forget that she derives her momentary parity with Yvain by exploiting another woman's powerlessness in repayment for the protection the knight has offered her. Laudine, ostensibly the sovereign lady of the Fountain, who has vowed she can make peace between the Knight of the Lion and his lady, finds herself displaced as an object of exchange: *she herself* is the lady whom she had pledged to bring back to Yvain.

The romance's conclusion allows the reader either to mystify this appropriation of woman as an object by believing in the enduring happiness of Laudine and Yvain's marriage, or to criticize it by analyzing its paradoxical structure. The narrator's ambiguous attitude toward his material, no easier to discern in the epilogue than in the Prologue, resists our efforts to categorize him as a proponent of chivalric ideals or to assess his degree of "misogyny" or "feminism."[29] By calling attention to his rhetorical display in the final lines with the *annominatio* of "fin" / "fine" (which insists four times in as many verses on the happy ending [6801–04]), Chrétien dramatizes his narrator's self-conscious manipulation of a felicitous conclusion. His overinscription of closure thus implicitly acknowledges the complicity or resistance of the audience in creating the ideology of courtly romance.

As with all of Chrétien's romances, the *sens* of *Yvain* rests upon the reader's relationship to its ideological structures and content. A knight identifying with Yvain's increasing honor would be likely to find his dreams of sovereignty fulfilled by the narrative's episodic repetitions and evolution, with no conflict apparent to him in the ending; the romance would confirm his desire to be the active subject. To the extent that the implied female reader identified with this romance, she may have found herself displaced from her ostensible role as the privileged audience and appropriated by the romance's textual exchange, like the young girl reading at Pesme Aventure or like Laudine. But female or male readers who resisted identification and focussed instead on Chrétien's structural paradoxes, may have discovered a *mise en question* of the gender relationships embodied in marriage and chivalry.

NOTES

1. See Elaine Showalter, "Towards a Feminist Poetics," in *Women Writing and Writing about Women,* ed. Mary Jacobus (London: Croom Helm, 1979), p. 25.

2. The debate centers around whether aristocratic women's interests were advanced or thwarted by courtly literature. The promotion of women is maintained by Reto Bezzola, "La Transformation des mœurs et la rôle de la femme dans la classe féodale du XIe au XIIe siècle," *Les Origines et la formation de la littérature courtoise en Occident (500–1200)* (Paris: Champion, 1960), II, 461–484; Myrrha Lot-Borodine, *De l'Amour profane à l'amour sacré: études de psychologie sentimentale au Moyen-Age* (Paris: Nizet, 1961), 15–28; Joan Kelly-Gadol, "Did Women Have a Renaissance?" in *Becoming Visible: Women in European History,* ed. Renate Bridenthal and Claudia Koonz (Boston: Houghton Mifflin, 1977), 141–148; and Rita Lejeune, "La Femme dans les littératures française et occitane du XIe au XIIIe siècle," *Cahiers de Civilisation Médiévale* 20 (1977), 201–208, among others. The opposing argument has been made by John Benton, "Clio and Venus: A Historical View of Medieval Love," in *The Meaning of Courtly Love,* ed. F.X. Newman (Albany: SUNY Press, 1968), pp. 34–37, and has been forcefully exemplified by Georges Duby who traces the appropriation of noblewomen's power and influence by emergent chivalric and clerical institutions in the eleventh and twelfth centuries in *Le Chevalier, la femme, et le prêtre: le mariage dans la France féodale* (Paris: Hachette, 1981).

An excellent literary analysis of the degradation of women's roles in Chrétien's romances from *Erec* to *Perceval* is provided by Marie-Noëlle Lefay-Toury, "Roman breton et mythes courtois: L'évolution du personnage féminin dans les romans de Chrétien de Troyes," *Cahiers de Civilisation Médiévale* 15 (1972), 193–204 and 283–293. For a discussion of female roles in twelfth- and thirteenth-century romance, see Jean-Charles Payen, "Figures féminines dans le roman médiéval français," *Entretiens sur la Renaissance du 12e siècle,* ed. Maurice de Gandillac and Edouard Jeauneau (Paris: Mouton, 1968), pp. 406–428; and "La Destruction des mythes courtois dans le roman arthurien: la femme dans le roman en vers après Chrétien de Troyes," *Revue des langues romanes* 78 (1969), 213–228.

3. Chrétien de Troyes, *Le Chevalier au Lion (Yvain),* ed. Mario Roques, CFMA, 89 (Paris: Champion, 1971).

4. The fact that individual noblewomen occasionally exercised considerable political power, as documented by Andrée Lehmann, *Le Rôle de la femme dans l'histoire de France au moyen-âge* (Paris: Berger-Levrault, 1952) and Régine Pernoud, *La Femme au temps des cathédrales* (Paris: Stock, 1980), is qualified by an analysis of the diminishing legal status and social influence of noblewomen as a class under primogeniture after 1100; see Duby, *Le Chevalier, la femme et le prêtre,* and Suzanne Wemple and Jo Ann McNamara, "The Power of Women through the Family in Medieval Europe: 500–1100," *Feminist Studies* 1 (1973), 126–141. The paradox of woman's position in medieval canon law—spiritually equal to man before God but temporally inferior and dependent—is presented by René Metz, "Le Statut de la femme en droit canonique médiéval," *La Femme: recueils de la Société Jean Bodin pour l'histoire comparative des institutions* (Bruxelles: Librairie Encyclopédique, 1962), vol. 12, 59–113.

5. Chrétien de Troyes, *Le Chevalier de la Charrete,* ed. Mario Roques, CFMA, 86 (Paris: Champion, 1971). On the intertextuality of these two romances see my

"Reading the *Yvain/Charrete*: Chrétien's Inscribed Audiences at Noauz and Pesme Aventure," *Forum for Modern Language Studies* 19, 2 (1983), 172–187.

6. Woman's function as a prize contested by two combative knights represents a modification of woman's function as "gift" in an exchange system which Mauss and Lévi-Strauss posit as a basic structure of social interaction. See Claude Lévi-Strauss, *Les Structures élémentaires de la parenté* (Paris: PUF 1949), pp. 66–86 and 616–617; and, for an application of Lévi-Strauss to gender theory, Gayle Rubin, "The Traffic in Women: Notes on the 'Political Economy of Sex,'" in *Toward an Anthropology of Women*, ed. Raina Reiter (New York: Monthly Review Press, 1975), pp. 171–177. On woman as an object of exchange in feudal marriage arrangements, see Duby, *Le Chevalier, la femme, et le prêtre*, p. 250 and *passim*. Cf. Christiane Marchello-Nizia, "Amour courtois, société masculine, et figures du pouvoir," *Annales E.S.C.* 36 (1981), 969–982.

7. The initial customs in the *Charrete* are Meleagant's "covant" ("pact,"*Ch.* 75) to release the Logrian prisoners if a knight defends Guenevere and the "don contraignant" Arthur accords to Keu to fight Meleagant; the "costume" (*Y.* 2104) in *Yvain* is that which obliges Laudine to marry a knight to defend her fountain against aggressors. Erich Köhler has analyzed these parallel structures, "Le Rôle de la 'coutume' dans les romans de Chrétien de Troyes," *Romania* 81 (1960), 386–397. Köhler's analysis studies the tensions between feudal nobility and kingship embodied in the "custom" rather than the paradoxal structure of gender it reveals.

8. On consent in marriage in the twelfth century see John T. Noonan, "Power to Choose," *Viator* 4 (1973), 420–434, and Jean Leclerq, *Le Mariage vu par les moines au XIIe siècle* (Paris: Le Cerf, 1983), pp. 11–23. David J. Shirt shows how Chrétien incorporates contemporary canonical discussion of consent in *Cligés*, "*Cligés*, a twelfth-century matrimonial case-book?," *Forum for Modern Language Studies* 18 (1982), 75–89.

9. See Duby, *Le Chevalier, la femme, et le prêtre*, pp. 43–51 and 252.

10. See the detailed analysis of this scene by Karl Uitti in his *Story, Myth, and Celebration in Old French Narrative Poetry, 1050–1200* (Princeton: Princeton Univ. Press, 1973), pp. 183–213.

11. On the influence of the *Ars Amatoria* and the *Metamorphoses* in this scene, see Jean Frappier, *Etude sur "Yvain ou Le Chevalier au Lion" de Chrétien de Troyes* (Paris: SEDES, 1969), pp. 72–76.

12. Tony Hunt, "The Dialectic of *Yvain*," *Modern Language Review* 72 (1977), 290.

13. "... (S)ed sunt diversa puellis / Pectora: mille animos excipe mille modis" (Ovid, *Ars Amatoria*, I, 755–756, cited by Frappier, *Yvain*, p. 74.

14. Myrrha Lot-Borodine, *La Femme et l'amour au XIIe siècle d'après les poèmes de Chrétien de Troyes* (Paris: 1909), p. 216.

15. *Etude sur "Yvain,"* p. 153.

16. Marie-Noëlle Lefay-Toury, "Roman breton et mythes courtois," 199.

17. As does G.J. Halligan, "Marriage in Chrétien's *Yvain*," *Journal of the Australian University's Modern Language Association* 34 (1970), 264–285.

18. See Erich Köhler, *L'Aventure chevaleresque: idéal et réalité dans le roman courtois*, trans. E. Kaufholz (Paris: Gallimard, 1974), pp. 198–201. See also Alfred Adler, "Sovereignty in Chrétien's *Yvain*, *PMLA* 42, 2 (1947), 281–305.

19. We can assume that the freed hostages return to the Isle aux Puceles, but, given their King's former irresponsible actions, we cannot assume that their existence will be untroubled.

20. For a concise structural study, see Norris Lacy, "Organic Structure of Yvain's Expiation," *Romanic Review* 61 (1970), 79–84.

21. Although this interpretation has been qualified and nuanced in many ways, it is probably the most prevalent view of Yvain's adventures and is well summed up in Frappier's words on the hero: "Surtout, sa volonté d'expier sa faute et de mériter

le pardon de sa dame par ses exploits, sa parfaite fidelité d'amant, approfondissent et embellissent sa conception du devoir chevaleresque, le rendent de plus en plus sensible à la pitié et à la juste cause des malheureux" (*Yvain*, 160). This conception of Yvain's chivalric duties belongs more to the reader than to the knight. The dissenting view, that Chrétien does not exemplify Yvain's progress in the amatory sphere in the second part of the romance, has been expressed by Tony Hunt, "Chrétien de Troyes' Arthurian Romance *Yvain*, in *Medieval Literature, II: The European Inheritance*, ed. Boris Ford (Penguin: 1983), 126–141.

22. Frappier, *Etude sur "Yvain,"* 160.

23. Lacy, "Organic Structure," 80–81.

24. Peter Haidu, "The Hermit's Pottage: Deconstruction and History in *Yvain* in *The Sower and His Seed*, ed. Rupert Pickens (Lexington, KY: French Forum, 1983), p. 133. Cf. Francis Dubost's semiotic analysis of Yvain's rehabilitation with respect to feminine figures, "Le Chevalier au Lion: Une 'conjointure' signifiante," *Le Moyen Age* 90, 2 (1984), 222.

25. However, for an optimistic view of the ending which also focuses sympathetically upon Laudine, see A.R. Press, "Chrétien de Troyes' Laudine: A 'belle dame sans mercy,'" *Forum for Modern Language Studies* 19, 2 (1983), 165–170.

26. As suggested by Frappier, *Etude sur "Yvain."*

27. In fact, the name "Laudine" never appears in the Guiot manuscript upon which Roque's edition is based. It occurs at verse 2151 in Foerster's edition as edited by T.B.W. Reid, *Yvain* (Manchester: Manchester Univ. Press, 1948). For a discussion of this textual problem, see Alfred Foulet and Karl D. Uitti, "Chrétien's 'Laudine': *Yvain*, vv. 2148–55," *Romance Philology* 37, 3 (1984) 293–302.

28. As argued by Mary Dugan, "Le Rôle de la femme dans *Le Chevalier au Lion*," *Chimères* 15 (1981), 38.

29. A claim for the "feminism" of twelfth-century romance has been made by Payen, "Figures féminines dans le roman médiéval français," 415–417, and "La Destruction des mythes courtois," 214. The charge of Chrétien's "misogyny" has been refuted by Z. P. Zaddy, "Chrétien Misogyne," *Marche Romane* 30 (1980), 305. As my analysis suggests, neither term adequately describes Chrétien's complex rhetorical strategy in *Yvain* or the romance's ideological ambivalence.

I wish to thank Meritt Blakeslee for inviting me to present an earlier version of this article at the International Courtly Literature's session at the MLA Convention in New York, December 30, 1983. I also thank Sarah Kay and Tony Hunt for their invitation to read another version in February, 1984, at the University of Liverpool and the University of Saint Andrews, respectively.

Rewriting Men's Stories

Enide's Disruptive Mouths

E. Jane Burns

Let's begin our discussion of *Erec et Enide* with a different story, not with the well-known tale told by the master author of twelfth-century French romance, Chrétien de Troyes, but with an alternate version of the classic courtly narrative he made famous.[1] Let's begin with a retelling of the traditional Old French adventure story delivered this time from the mouth of a female protagonist in another text altogether, the *Lai du Lecheor* (*The Debaucher's Tale*).[2] This anonymous short narrative from the twelfth century begins by outlining the standard storytelling process for Old French tales of love and adventure as we know it. But the tale soon shifts to a pointed critique of that literary system articulated by one of the courtly ladies figured in the narrative.

The narrator of the *Lai du Lecheor* explains first how Breton storytellers gathered typically to recount their amorous and chivalric adventures in the company of courtly ladies:

> Les plus nobles et les plus beles
> Du pais, dames et puceles.

> ["The country's most noble and most beautiful women,[3] ladies and young ladies," vv. 5–6.]

These well-dressed noble women (v. 10) constitute the audience for courtly narrative along with "clerics, knights, and many people of other professions":

Abridged by the author from "Rewriting Men's Stories: Enide's Disruptive Mouths," Chapter Four of *Bodytalk: When Women Speak in Old French Literature*. New Cultural Studies. (Philadelphia: University of Pennsylvania Press, 1993), 151–202. Reprinted by permission.

> . . . clers et chevaliers,
> Et plusors genz d'autres mestiers;
> Dames i ot nobles et beles,
> Et meschines et damoiseles [vv. 43–46].

They all come to hear the adventures of knights who fashion their past exploits into orally-delivered tales:

> Et la érent conté li fet
> Des amors et des drueries
> Et des nobles chevaleries;
> Ce que l'an estoit avenu
> Tot ert oi et retenu:
> Lor aventure racontoient
> Et li autre les escoutoient

> ["Deeds of love and lovemaking and noble chivalry were recounted there. Everything that had happened was heard and remembered. They [the knights] told of their adventures while others listened," vv. 16–22.]

Women do not figure, it seems, among the storytellers recounting chivalric adventures, nor among the harpers or musicians who carry the prize-winning story to distant lands:

> Chascuns a son fet reconté;
> S'aventure disoit chascuns,

> ["Each one recounted his deed and told of his adventure," vv. 50–51.]

> Car cil qui savoient de note
> En viele, en herpe et en rote
> Fors de la terre le portoient
> Es roiaumes ou il aloient

> ["Those who knew how to play the *vielle*, the harp and the rote carried it [the favorite *lai*] away to other lands where they traveled," vv. 35–38.]

While the Old French pronouns *chascuns* and *cil* used in the preceding examples do not preclude the possible existence of women within a group of

taletellers or musicians, neither do they suggest female participation in these activities.

By contrast, the *Lai du Lecheor* subsequently details one particular storytelling contest in which a female protagonist clearly takes up the role of speaker as eight women break off from the larger group of listeners to talk among themselves. Termed "wise" and "learned," "noble, courtly and esteemed" (*sages, ensaingnies, franches, cortoises et proises*, vv. 57–58), these women become the audience for a single female speaker who critiques the way male storytellers have told their tales. She says:

> Molt oi ces chevaliers parler
> De tornoier et de joster,
> D'aventures, de drueries,
> Et de requerre lor amies:
> D'icelui ne tienent nul plet
> Por qui li grant bien sont tuit fet.
> Par cui sont li bon chevalier?
> Por qoi aimment a tornoier?
> Por qui s'atornent li danzel?
> Por qui se vestent de novel?
> Por qui envolent lor joieaus,
> Lor treceors et lor aneaus?
> Por qui sont franc et debonere?
> Por qoi se gardent de mal fere?
> Por qoi aimment le donoier,
> Et l'acoler et l'embracier?
> Savez i vos nule achoison
> Fors sol por une chose non?

["I have long heard these knights talk about tournaments and jousting, adventures and lovers, questing for ladies. They make no mention of why all these great deeds are undertaken. Why are knights good? Why do they like to fight in tournaments? For whom do young men dress up? For whom do they wear new clothing? For whom do they send their jewels, treasures and rings? On whose account are they genteel and generous? On whose account do they refrain from wrong-doing? Why do they like courting, hugging and kissing? Do you know any reason but one?" vv. 65–82.]

The standard response to this question, in courtly literature and in

the critical commentary on it, is that knights undertake valiant exploits for the lady, the courtly descendent of the troubadour's *domna,* a woman revered and adored by the chivalric lover who puts her on a pedestal and keeps her there.[4] The narrative scenario informs many of Chrétien de Troyes's romances. But the female speaker in the *Lai du Lecheor* provides a different answer to her own rhetorical question, suggesting that there is more to courtly romance than meets the eye, and more than we as readers have previously surmised.

Detailing for her female audience the unseen, unstated element that motivates knightly endeavor, this female storyteller alludes cryptically to a thing (*une chose*) that provides the greatest pleasures, "les granz douçors":

> Ja n'avra nus tant donié
> Ne biau parlé ne biau proié
> Ainz qu'il s'em puisse departir
> A ce ne veille revertir;
> D'ice viénent les granz douçors
> Por coi sont fetes les honors.

> ["Never would anyone [any knight] court so long nor speak so nicely nor plead so sweetly before taking his leave if he did not want to come back to this: from this thing comes the greatest pleasures, the reason why honorable deeds are done," vv. 83–88.]

Then, with a verbal chutzpah wholly uncharacteristic of courtly heroines, the female speaker in the *Lai du Lecheor* states frankly that what is hidden in the Arthurian adventure story, that coveted *chose* concealed behind the accounts of valiant knights and beautiful ladies, is no less than female genitalia. In a most unladylike fashion she speaks of *con* (cunt):

> Maint homme i sont si amendé
> Et mis em pris et em bonté,
> Qui ne vausissent un bouton
> Se par l'entente du con non.

> ["Many men are improved, revived by it, made worthy and good, men who would be worth nothing if not for the thought of/desire for cunt," vv. 89–92.][5]

In this female speaker's view, chivalric prowess is inspired less by medita-

tion on the elegant beauty of the knight's favorite lady than by the eroticized female body that that beauty masks. The female speaker in the *Lai du Lecheor* thus graphically describes the process attested more obliquely in the Old French *Philomena*, whereby the putative lover's interest in the unnamed vagina is concealed behind elaborate descriptions of the heroine's lovely face.[6] This lady storyteller puts it bluntly:

> Nule fame n'a si bel vis
> Por qu'ele eust le con perdu,
> Ja mes eust ami ne dru.

> ["No woman's face is so beautiful that she could keep her lover if she lost her cunt," vv. 94–96.]

We should remember here that this woman's critique is levelled less against the medieval practices of love and prowess than against the narrativizing of courtly behavior into tales which leave something out. The questing knight's stories take no account ("ne tienent nul plet"), she tells us, of female sexual difference, which remains obscured behind descriptions of the lady's beautiful face. If, in other examples of courtly narrative, the *dame's* lavish clothing tends to hide her sexual difference, here the very fabric of the romance narrative itself works to conceal the eroticized anatomy of female protagonists figured within it. Men's stories of love and adventure are cast in this instance as creating an elaborate detour around the formidable female *con,* the unknown territory of female sexuality. Chivalric storytellers talk of love and adventure in order to avoid confronting the female body, says the lovely lady of the *Lai du Lecheor.* Thus do her crass words debunk the fiction of the role she herself is meant to play, revealing it to be an amusing literary convention and a wanting cultural construction of femininity.

The skeptical reader might object here that the words of the outspoken "Lady" in the *Lai du Lecheor* cannot be taken as representing a "real" woman's voice since they originate with the tale's anonymous author, who was most likely male. Indeed, this woman cannot be considered to speak "as a woman," in any totalizing sense, to tell a story utterly her own or wholly distinct from the master narratives already circulating among twelfth-century storytellers. But this is not only because she is a literary character. Our own voices as contemporary women are also constructed in many ways, also conditioned by cultural patterning and inherited literary tradition.[7] Carolyn Heilbrun has cogently explained how women—whether historical women functioning as speakers and writers or their fictional counterparts

who tell their stories in literary texts—have no specifically female plots to guide them, no narrative plots of their own.[8] They must rewrite old stories, engaging and recasting stereotypes in order to resist them.[9]

Resistance to the stereotype of the courtly lady is what I hear in the comments of the female voice in the *Lai du Lecheor*. This is not to say that the female speaker of the *lai* thoroughly repudiates the culturally constructed sexuality represented by the elaborate layers of clothing and adornment that typically comprise the courtly lady's beauty and silence. Such a move is impossible, as Judith Butler has persuasively argued:

> If sexuality is culturally contracted within existing power relations, then the postulation of a normative sexuality that is "before," "outside," or "beyond" power is a cultural impossibility and a politically impracticable dream, one that postpones the concrete and contemporary task of rethinking subversive possibilities for sexuality and identity within the terms of power itself.[10]

If we agree with Butler that "there is no gender identity behind the expressions of gender; that identity is performatively constituted by the very 'expressions' that are said to be its results" (25), we can read the female speaker in the *Lai du Lecheor* as a character who performs within the given cultural construction of femininity to remake or redo it. At least we can choose to read her inscribed voice that way. We can begin to ask how this woman's constructed voice "does" or "redoes" the gender identity that has been imposed upon her, how she operates within a matrix of power relations, repeating its conventions while also displacing them. Our question then becomes: what kind of gender construction is being played out in this purportedly female critique of male storytelling conventions?

When the female speaker in the *Lai du Lecheor* tells her female audience that all men want is *con,* we hear on the one hand the stereotypical reduction of women's anatomy to pleasure-giving genitalia so prevalent in the misogynous registers of Old French farce and fabliau. But we can also see, as in farce and fabliau themselves, how the status of that *con* changes significantly when it speaks, rather than functioning as the object of another's speech. If in asserting that men really want nothing other than *con,* the speaking lady of the *Lai du Lecheor* reiterates the commonplace that men want to possess women as objects, she also reveals that men want what women have, that is to say: the sweet *chose* that women, as subjects, can choose to give or withhold. The *con* typically objectified as an isolated body part has here shifted significantly toward (if not into) the subject position as it be-

comes an integrated part of the speaking female. Delivering her critique of male storytelling within an alternate literary economy of women speaking to women about female anatomy, this talking *con,* by its very existence, calls into question the adventure story's standard objectification of the silenced female body. For even more significant than *having* what men want, this heroine purports also *to know* what men want. She then occupies the subject position to the extent that she knows her object, and says so. With a bawdy flair, this courtly lady refashions her assigned role as statuesque beauty to speak as a knowing, thinking and sexualized body all at the same time.[11] There is no question that this *con* has a head.[12]

If "Erec et Enide" Were "Enide's Romance"

Chrétien de Troyes does not mention *con* in his classic Arthurian tale of love and adventure known by modern readers as *Erec et Enide.* Neither do his female protagonists refer overtly to women's body parts. But I want to take the *Lai du Lecheor* as point of departure for reading Chrétien's romance because it stages a rivalry between men's stories and women's stories that Chrétien's text works hard to obscure. By highlighting the love story between his protagonists along with the hero's reputation and chivalric prowess—the very topic addressed by male taletellers in the *Lai du Lecheor* ("Des amors et des drueries / Et des nobles chevaleries," ["It is about love and lovemaking along with noble deeds," vv. 17–18])—Chrétien diverts our attention away from one of the more difficult questions at the heart of his romance: the status of the woman's voice, her right to speak versus the necessity of keeping her silent.

The issue is not, to my mind, simply one of wifely obedience, nor of love, though the Griselda story lurks barely beneath the surface of this highly complex tale. Whether or not Enide should speak, when and under what conditions she might talk, forms part of a larger narrative problem concerning authorship, or more specifically "who's speaking" the Arthurian adventure story: Who's telling the tale we read/hear, and how might that tale change with a change in the gender of the speaker? The heroine Enide is perhaps best known for parading somnolently through the first 2000 lines of Chrétien's text in utter silence before uttering the first in a series of curt but disruptively uncourtly statements.[13] These moments of female speech, however corrected and appropriated by the end of the tale, allow us to see how the most fundamental rivalry played out in this text exists between the male adventure story and female retellings of it. In this sense *Erec et Enide* provides a particularly apt medieval case study for addressing the questions posed in the longstanding debate between Nancy Miller and Peggy Kamuf over the relative importance of knowing "who's speaking" (male or female) in the literary text and "what difference it makes?"[14]

If we read *Erec et Enide* not as a master narrative of Chrétien de Troyes's rhetorical skill, but as a tale of female voices speaking against that tradition of storytelling, we get a new picture of love and courtliness, romance and adventure. We begin to see how the objectification of the lovely lady, so crucial to the working of the courtly milieu where she provides the inspiration for feats of prowess, the audience for chivalric combat and the supportive listener for tales of adventure, focuses principally on the female body. Yet we also see how the heroine's speech more staunchly resists colonization and appropriation; her constructed voice cannot be fetishized as easily as her fictive flesh.

When Chrétien's lovely heroine Enide "wakes up" from her slumber in the land of silence and begins to talk, she, much like the female speaker in the *Lai du Lecheor*, tells unsettling stories. Altering the standard scenario of courtly romance in many ways, she speaks within but apart from the master narrative, significantly rewriting the very *conte d'aventure* that creates her as a silent object of the heroic knight's desire. From this perspective, Chrétien's romance shows how women, who are essential to the working of the courtly world, can nonetheless make "gender trouble"[15] within it, not only with their bodies but more significantly with the voices that issue from them.

CONJOINTURE: COUPLING FOR/WITH PLEASURE

The pleasure of this text, as is typically the case with Old French romance narratives, resides in the telling of a love story. But whose pleasure is at stake here, and what are its parameters? Chrétien warns in the prologue to *Erec et Enide* that the attentive author must be careful not to silence any material that might bring pleasure to his audience. The storyteller's careful craft involves speaking out, giving voice to thoughts and words in order to please the listener:

> car qui son estuide antrelait,
> tost i puet tel chose teisir
> qui molt vandroit puis a pleisir.

> ["Whoever neglects his learning may easily silence something that would later give much pleasure," vv. 6–8.][16]

The rhyme sounded here between *pleisir* and *teisir* posits a relationship between the author's speech and the pleasure of the text, telling us in essence that to silence literature is to withhold pleasure.

Elsewhere in this romance, however, courtly pleasure is defined, in line with the female speaker's observation in the *Lai du Lecheor,* as deriving from enjoyment of the woman's body. This sexual pleasure takes place in private and in the silence of the medieval bedchamber. When Enide, who is cast throughout the tale as the ideal object of desire, valiantly fends off the amorous advances of the *comte vaniteux,* the Count of Limors, she promises to deliver the carnal union he desires, craftily rhyming *pleisir* with *seisir:*

> Car je ferai vostre pleisir:
> Por vostre me poez seisir.

["I will do your bidding; you can take me as your own," vv. 3357–58.]

Pleisir here connotes the purely physical bliss proffered by the naked woman's body, the kind of pleasure that the count also hopes to attain from his proposed liaison with Enide:

> La dame est moie et je sui suens,
> si ferai de li mon pleisir.

["The lady is mine and I am hers. I will do as I want with her," vv. 4800–01.]

If these two admirers are thwarted in their efforts to woo Enide and seize her body, Erec of course succeeds at this task. And at the end of the forest adventure, when Erec and Enide are reconciled as spouses and reunited as lovers, *pleise* rhymes appropriately with *beise:*

> Ansanble jurent an un lit,
> et li uns l'autre acole et beise:
> riens nule n'est qui tant lor pleise.

["They lay together in bed, hugging and kissing. Nothing could have pleased them so much," vv. 5200–02.]

This scene of erotic reconciliation recalls the incident that sparked the couple's arduous adventure earlier in the romance, the problematic encounter in the bedchamber at Carnant, which is in fact the motor force behind the entire romance. Pleasure, in this case excessive carnal pleasure, is the very reason that Erec and Enide embark on their protracted forest journey. Erec, as we remember, had been so caught up in the actions of *acoler* and *beiser* that he neglected his chivalric duty in favor of love:

> Mes tant l'ama Erec d'amors,
> que d'armes mes ne li chaloit,

> ["Erec loved her so much that he neglected armed combat," vv. 2430–31.]

> si an fist s'amie et sa drue;
> en li a mise s'antendue,
> en acoler et an beisier.

> ["He made her his lover and sweetheart. He put all his attention in hugging and kissing her," vv. 2435–37.]

Within the context of Chrétien's first romance, pleasure then carries two distinct meanings as it derives from two distinct sources: the act of conferring pleasure can come either from the author or his heroine, from the speaking subject who offers the pleasure of his tale to a listening audience, or from the silent object of desire who can potentially provide the pleasure of the female body. The polarity thus implied sets male speech against female sexuality, suggesting a rivalry between *boche d'home* and *corps de femme*, between the romance author and his female protagonist.

Chrétien's avowed project, in full, is to transform the standard *conte d'avanture* into a pleasurable *bele conjointure*. He proposes in the process to weave into his narrative the unspecified *tel chose* generally neglected, he tells us, in the adventure story:

> Li vilains dit an son respit
> que *tel chose* a l'an an despit
> qui molt valt mialz que l'an ne cuide

> ["The peasant says in his proverb that one may hold in contempt *something* that is worth much more than one believes," vv. 1–3.]

But what is at stake in this shift from the grammatically masculine *conte d'avanture* to the feminine *conjointure*? What precisely is this *bele conjoin-*

ture that Chrétien boasts of as his distinctive literary accomplishment? And what is the *tel chose* included or absorbed within it?

The neologism *bele conjointure* has been taken generally to signify a masterful weaving together of diverse narrative elements.[17] Yet if we think of *conjointure* in the sense of coupling, joining, bringing together in amorous liaison or linking in marriage,[18] we see how the romance author has metaphorically transferred the act of coupling with a woman, with her enigmatic *chose*, into the realm of literary creation that is his alone. This is a particularly deft example of colonizing the unknown terrain of the female body by absorbing it into discourse as Luce Irigaray describes it: "the really urgent task is to ensure the colonization of this new 'field,' to force it, not without splintering, into the productions of the same discourse."[19] In a sense, Chrétien's neologism gives his project away, for we can hear within this ostensibly new literary practice of *conjointure* the *con* that it contains and usurps. The pleasure of the heroine's body has become in this instance the pleasure of the romancer's text. Or at least that is what Chrétien's prologue proposes.

MEN'S STORIES: THE *CONTE (COMTE) D'AVANTURE*

The point is driven home even more clearly through a flurry of homophonic resonance that draws on the base sound *con* to outline a process of all-male storytelling. Within the space of four lines, the prologue repeats the word *contes* in various semantic configurations that make it read almost as a verb conjugation, establishing the morphology of the Arthurian adventure story in terms of men who tell tales about valiant men to male listeners.

Chrétien designates the literary world of the *conte d'avanture* as comprising a tale (*contes*) about a count (*contes*), Erec, identified by his patrilineal descent, told regularly before kings and counts (*contes*) by professional male storytellers ("cil qui de *conter* vivre vuelent," ["men who live by storytelling"], vv. 19–22). Women, typically excluded from playing the key roles of creator or heroic subject in the courtly scenario of literary production, are here also absent as storytellers or listeners.[20] One might then wonder where within the Arthurian world, when the *conteur* tells a *conte* to an audience of *contes et rois,*[21] we could locate the female *con*? And how might the sexualized woman's body it represents tell the Arthurian tale differently?

WOMEN'S STORIES: THE *CONTE (CON) DE FEMME*

Readers of courtly romance have long defined the Old French *conte d'avanture* as a tale predicated on the unknown, literally on that which has not yet happened, on "ce qui est à venir," ("what is to come"). It is the unknown dilemma that will befall a knight which gives the hero an occasion to prove his valor and subsequently hear it recorded in stories that bring joy or pleasure to the listener. But what is this unknown terrain that knights are forever conquering? The uncharted territory that they perpetually seek to tame and control echoes hauntingly "these uncharted territories, these dark continents, these worlds through the looking glass / on the other side of the mirror" that Irigaray evokes to describe man's view of female sexuality (*Speculum*, 136). Could it be that in its affirmation of male subjectivity the *conte d'avanture* relocates onto the field of chivalric combat the unknown field of female sexual difference, temporarily substituting coupling between men (*conbatre*) for heterosexual liaison with a woman (*conjointure*)?

The *con* is precisely, we are told euphemistically, what gets Erec into trouble at Carnant, where his dalliance in the marriage bed through actions of *acoler* and *beisier* causes him to neglect chivalric *conjointure* with men in battle:

> N'avoit mes soing de tornoier:
> a sa fame volt dosnoier.

> ["He no longer took an interest in tournaments but preferred to spar with his wife," vv. 2433–34.]

Erec has neglected, that is, the combat itself and the male hugging and kissing that so often accompany it: as in Erec's encounter with Gauvain, "de joie l'acole et anbrace" ("full of joy, he hugs and embraces him," v. 4136) or his combat with Guivret, "Li uns l'autre beise et acole" ("they hug and kiss each other," v. 3900). The trouble with Enide in this scene is that she intervenes literally and problematically between men, splitting the bonds of male *conjointure* through the use of her sexualized body.

But that body and the heroine's sexual identity are inextricably linked throughout this romance with the woman's voice.[22] The testing adventure in particular is undertaken for two express reasons. First, because Enide has seduced her knight with the pleasure of amorous embraces, drawing him away from public tournament and joust. But second, and no less important, because this supposed seductress has exercised her voice, daring to describe her knight's dalliance as "recreantise," or chivalric neglect. The dilemma initiated by the allure of female sexuality in this romance has thus been aggravated by the activity of the companion orifice, the woman's mouth. The avowed purpose of the testing adventure is to bring both offending orifices under control to curtail Enide's erotic activity, enabling Erec to reestablish his prowess as a knight, and to curb the intrusive woman's voice that first enunciated the charge of "recreantise." At the end of the forest adventure Erec makes explicit the link between Enide's erotic misdeed and her speech by pardoning his lover/wife for two related offenses, one sexual and the other linguistic:

> Je vos le pardoing tot et quit
> del forfet et de la parole

["I forgive you everything: the words and the deed," vv. 4892–93.]

Nothing intrinsically harmful characterizes the fateful words that Enide utters at Carnant. Lamenting her role in distracting Erec from fulfilling his chivalric obligations, she proclaims only indirectly and very cautiously his own chivalric neglect (vv. 2492–2500). In describing Erec's failed knighthood, Enide initiates no charge of her own. She simply repeats the laments formerly articulated by Erec's own companions:

> Si conpaignon duel en avoient;
> sovant entr'ax se demantoient
> de ce que trop l'amoit assez

["His companions were grieved on account of this. They often lamented among themselves that he loved her too much," vv. 2439–41.]

Enide reiterates accusations she has overheard: "Par ceste terre dient tuit" ("Everyone around here is saying . . . ," v. 2540). But words formerly pronounced by honorable knights create a radically different effect when they issue from the mouth of a woman. If the laments of Erec's companions-at-arms express concern, while Enide's concern seems also to condemn, it is partially because this woman's speech is linked not to public declaration but to private body functions. We remember that in the scene at Carnant, Enide speaks from the privacy of the bedchamber and more specifically from the very bed where she has "pleased" her failed knight.

And indeed, Erec's instructions to Enide throughout the forest trial effect a *disjointure* from this troublesome female body. He first requires Enide to ride alone ahead of him (vv. 2770–71) where she serves as bait to provoke attackers whom he can vanquish.[23] On many occasions, Erec instructs Enide to stay behind as he joins rival knights in battle elsewhere, in her absence.[24] Indeed the verbal combat that ensues between Erec and his female rival, different from those battles which typically bond men together, actually works to hold the heterosexual couple apart. Because Enide so often rides and sits alone, the largest portion of her speech during the forest trial occurs in the form of monologue, spoken not to Erec but privately to herself (vv. 2829–39, 2962–78, 3100–12).[25] Yet she does speak. If Erec remains deaf to most of this heroine's pointed words during the testing adventure, we hear them all. What we hear is Enide speaking not from the masculinized "head" that would underwrite chivalric norms but from a female body that actively resists them. We hear, in effect, this heroine rewriting the very adventure story she is in, outlining the possibility of other versions that traditionally have gone untold and unrecorded. Her words map out for us the varied ways in which the *conte d'avanture*, when placed in the mouth of a woman, comes out differently.

If the scene at Carnant demonstrates how Enide could damage Erec's reputation as a knight by speaking of his *recreantise*, succeeding scenes reveal how her words could ruin Erec's chivalric identity by voicing stories of his potential failure, his carelessness or ignorance. When Enide first defends her decision to speak out despite Erec's injunction for silence, she posits the knight's possible defeat, citing her fear that the three attackers might harm him:

> Ci vienent poignant aprés vos
> troi chevalier qui molt vos chacent;
> peor ai que mal ne vos facent.

> ["Here come three knights riding after you in hot pursuit. I am afraid they will harm you," vv. 2842–44.]

Her story, not unlike Guenevere's earlier tale of Erec's unchivalrous encounter with Yder's dwarf (vv. 323–30), casts the perfect knight in the role of a loser, one who might be harmed by his opponent, rather than one who effortlessly wins the fray. Enide's second speech paints an equally unchivalric portrait of Erec being struck by one of five rival brigands:

> et li cinquiesmes a vos muet
> tant con chevax porter le puet;
> ne gart l'ore que il vos fiere.

> ["The fifth one is coming toward you as fast as his horse will carry him. He'll soon strike you," vv. 2987–89.]

When Chrétien counters these "women's stories" with reports of Erec's success against both sets of attackers, the difference between his telling of Erec's adventures and Enide's version becomes all the more apparent. Her narrative directly undermines the essence of the adventure story by substituting for the necessary "unknown" a description of what is about to take place, "three knights are coming, five knights are waiting to attack." Her comments not only deflate Erec's skill; they replay the troublesome imbalance of Carnant by placing the heroine in a position of knowing more than her knight does. Even though the entire forest escapade is staged by Erec as a test of Enide, he is made to occupy, at these key moments, a position of apparent inferior knowledge.

Elsewhere Enide justifies her decision to speak by depicting Erec as incompetently forgetful. During the encounter with Guivret she observes:

> Je voi bien que mes sires pansse
> tant que lui meïsmes oblie;
> donc est bien droiz que je li die.

["I see that my lord is deep in thought, so much so that he forgets himself. Thus is it right for me to speak to him," vv. 3748–50.][26]

When fleeing the *comte vaniteux,* Enide breaks her silence to correct Erec's tactical miscalculation, telling him they must speed up if they are to escape:

> Se nos alons an tel meniere
> ne poez de ci eschaper

["If we continue like this you won't escape from here," vv. 3550–51.]

At these moments Enide speaks, however hesitatingly, however awkwardly, as the informed subject playing to Erec's less knowledgeable object. Her "women's stories" are emitted piecemeal and quietly, remaining always under the mystifying cover of wifely obedience and courtly love, though they contest the very terms of woman's subservient place in both marital and courtly contracts.

Enide again moves problematically into the subject position when redressing Guivret for having attacked the wounded Erec. As her pointed words remind this knight of a chivalric code he has apparently forgotten, she alone appears to know how knights should behave:

Que ja n'an valdroit mialz tes pris,
se tu avoies morz ou pris
un chevalier qui n'a pooir
de relever, ce puez veoir.

["Your reputation would never improve for having captured or killed a knight who was unable to get up. You can see that," vv. 5003–6.]

Doesn't he realize, she implies, that his reputation is at stake? And we as readers/listeners overhearing this exchange are made to see how the knight's hard-earned *pris* (worth), established in battle and disseminated through tales of glory, can be threatened by the counter narrative of a woman who would change that story, calling him a *chevaliers maudit* ("a cursed knight," v. 4991.)

With the Count of Limors, Enide condemns outright the feudal trading of women in marriage upon which her own liaison with Erec is based. Flatly rejecting the count's marriage proposal, though it echoes almost exactly the objectifying terms of Erec's earlier offer, Enide now asserts that this commodification of women cannot bring her *joie:*

Cele respont: "Sire fuiez!
por Deu merci, lessiez m'ester;
ne poez ci rien conquester;
rien qu'an poïst dire ne faire
ne me poroit a joie atraire"

["She answers: 'Go away, sir! In God's name, leave me alone. You cannot conquer anything here. Nothing you can say or do will bring me joy,'" vv. 4672–76.]

Having initially ignored the count's threats (vv. 4786–87), she ends by openly defying them along with everything else he says:

Ahi! fet ele, ne me chaut
que tu me dies ne ne faces:
ne criem tes cos ne tes menaces.

["'Ah!' she said, 'whatever you say or do means nothing to me. I'm not afraid of your blows or threats,'" vv. 4806–8.]

Enide could, in theory, have made this statement to Erec as well. She does, after great deliberation, ignore his equally intimidating threats. And if her blanket rejection of the count's speech includes his earlier appraisal of her beauty, we can hear in it an implicit critique of the objectification she suffered from Erec's similarly masterful desire to transform her into something worthwhile. The count offers to fashion Enide, Pygmalion-like, into a countess: "de vos ferai contesse et dame" ("I will make you a countess and a lady," v. 4666). Erec had proposed with equal authority to make her a queen, "la li ferai porter corone," ("I will have her wear a crown," v. 664).

Of course Chrétien leads us to believe that Enide responds differently to the two offers because she is in love with the valiant Erec and thoroughly uninterested in the presumptuous count. But the verbal echo between the two incidents helps us to see how both knights' constructions of woman as obedient *fame* or beautiful *amie* deny a place to female subjectivity. Each time Enide breaks her silence we are reminded pointedly of how men's stories in this romance so often elide the speaking, knowing, female subject.

This is perhaps most apparent in Enide's manipulative encounter with the *comte vaniteux*, when she constructs a tale of future romance and coupling, a love story in which seizing the female body to derive pleasure in sex is paired with taking the prized woman by force from a rival knight (vv. 3356–58; 3379–81). Outlining a chivalric scenario consonant with the courtly exchange of women later codified in the custom of Logres in Chrétien de Troyes's *Chevalier de la charrette*, Enide here describes the standard courtly fight and its resolution: when the attacker attempts to take the lady by force, her defender will fight back fiercely and courageously. The winner gets the woman, to do with as he pleases, for she is now his *amie*:

> si me feites a force prandre;
> mes sires me voldra desfandre,
> qui molt est fiers et corageus.
> Ou soit a certes ou a geus,
> feites le prandre et afoler
> ou de la teste decoler.
> Trop ai menee ceste vie,
> je n'aim mie la conpaignie
> mon seignor, ja n'an quier mantir.
> Je vos voldroie ja santir
> an un lit certes nu a nu.

["So take me by force. My lord, who is very bold and brave will defend me, in earnest or in jest. Have him captured and wounded or have his head cut off. I have led this life too long. I have no interest in my lord's company and do not want to lie about it. I would like to feel you naked beside me in bed," vv. 3381–91.]

The most significant feature of this "woman's story" is not, to my mind, that Enide lies to the count in order to protect Erec's life, although that is the message which the narrator's commentary underscores through phrases such as the following:

> Bien sot par parole enivrer
> bricon, des qu'ele i met l'antante
> mialz est asez qu'ele li mante,
> que ses sires fust depeciez

["She knew how to intoxicate a rogue with words as soon as she put her mind to it. It is better that she lie to him than have her lord cut to bits," vv. 3410–13.]

But we as readers/listeners can witness in this scene a more important sleight-of-hand: Enide "knows how to confuse, confound, dizzy" the listener "through her speech," because when she tells the standard tale of Arthurian romance and adventure, it comes out differently. In fact, it disappears altogether: the narrative she recounts will never take place, at least not the way she tells it here.[27] Though this female storyteller *knows* the requisite narrative elements that make a pleasing courtly tale, when she articulates them from her mouth and body, the story becomes a dream, a trick, a mirage.

When this heroine retells the basic "men's story," it doesn't work; something crucial is lost in the transfer. Or perhaps something is added.[28] But we learn unequivocally from this incident that Enide's story diverges critically from the chivalric model it proposes. It is as if she states here between the lines: "this is not my story; I can tell it, but it will be just a story, a fiction, even a falsehood." Certainly not the kind of story Chrétien boasts of in his prologue as a tale destined to advance the teller's reputation.

Enide's stories, simply put, do not convey the same kind of knowledge (*estuide, escience*) as Chrétien's tale. Neither do they simply reverse the terms of the male/female equation, placing a knowledgeable woman at the top of the chivalric hierarchy. Rather they make "gender trouble" within the system, showing how one could tell the chivalric tale differently, thereby exposing what it hides. One could reveal, for example, as Enide does repeatedly, that knights fall short of the chivalric ideal or that ladies might refuse the commodification and fetishizing that that ideal requires. Enide's words then do not simply posit the woman's story as an antidote or corollary to the chivalric men's story, supplying the "missing half" of a binary equation. Enide's stories in this romance disrupt the most fundamental literary *conjointure* on which male adventure stories are built.[29] They do so by refusing the binary logic governing chivalric practice and substituting for it a logic that rings of Irigaray's paradoxical "both at once," that position forged from holding one view and its irreconcilable opposite view simultaneously. The stance is symptomatic, according to Irigaray, of woman's necessarily indeterminate social positioning. As Diana Fuss explains, "Both at once signifies that a woman is simultaneously singular and double; she is 'already two—but not divisible into one(s),' or, put another way, she is '*neither one nor two*.'"[30] This is precisely what Enide herself later says.

Perhaps the most famous of Enide's lines in this romance occurs when the Count of Limors, who finds her lamenting over Erec's presumably dead body, asks pointedly whether Enide is this knight's wife or his lover:

> Si li comança a enquerre
> del chevalier, qu'ele li die
> s'ele estoit sa fame ou s'amie.

> ["He began to inquire about the knight, asking that she tell him whether she was his wife or his lover," vv. 4648–50.]

Thoroughly undercutting the binary construction of this chivalric world view, Enide responds simply, "L'un et l'autre" (v. 4651), meaning, "both at the same time," and therefore, "neither one alone" or "neither one at all, actually." Enide now answers the count's question without answering it on his terms. By conflating the poles of the dichotomy *fame/amie*, Enide suggests in her cocky response, first of all, that the distinction between *fame* and *amie* is meaningless because the two roles depicted by these terms bear such strong resemblance to one another; and, secondly, that the terms *fame* and *amie* are equally inadequate to describe her current position as a speaking subject.

Indeed, earlier scenes in this romance have established what it means to be a *fame* in the world of Arthur's knights. The *fame* played by Enide was a young woman given away by her father, traded as a commodity that could be made into a lady and a queen. This *fame* was properly subservient to her husband and deferentially silent. The role of *amie* played by ladies vying for the distinction of being tagged "la plus bele" included winners of beauty contests that established a knight's prowess, all of whom remained appropriately silent. To play the part successfully of either *fame* or *amie* in this romance requires that a woman be as beautiful as she is speechless. The perfect courtly heroine, whether wife or lover, must be seen but not heard.[31]

The full import of this heroine's claim to being both *fame* and *amie* consists, to my mind, in her introduction of a third term into the equation, outlining a position lying between the stereotypical extremes of courtly femininity. For if Enide is literally both Erec's beautiful wife and his lover, through marriage and through sex, she rejects the silence that those categories require. Rather than being fully in the knight's possession, as the Old French possessive adjective would indicate—"sa fame ou s'amie"—Enide suggests through her paradoxical linking of traditionally opposed roles, through the *et* of her "l'un et l'autre," that the heroine of Arthurian romance can endow the terms of *wife* and *lover* with new meaning, restructuring their heretofore mutually exclusive relation. Her *conjointure* is not narrative synthesis or stylistic harmony; it is a simultaneously coming-together and holding-apart of the female flesh and its supposedly antithetical speech. In this *conjointure* the *con* is not appropriated into literature or tamed into obedience. It talks.

If Chrétien's *Erec et Enide* shows us, on the one hand, how there is no place for the female subject in tales of adventure, how the romance narrative successfully appropriates the woman's body to its own ends, it also shows how women's speech cannot as effectively be colonized by these tales of love and adventure. Although the beautiful bodies of female protagonists are readily made to conform to and underwrite the tenets of chivalry in courtly romance, their voices more thoroughly resist such appropriation. For when courtly heroines speak, as we have seen, they often rewrite the very story that contains them. Their bodytalk exposes what is hidden within the *conte d'avanture,* what is covered up by the homophony of *contes, comte, conter* that links men together as storytellers and listeners in Chrétien's prologue. Revealing how the female *con* has been appropriated by the *conte d'avanture*, these women's words also show us how the fictionalized bodies bearing that *con* can tell the story differently. When they talk, it matters whose body is speaking.

Notes

1. The following essay constitutes a shortened version of a chapter, by the same title, from my book, *Bodytalk: When Women Speak in Old French Literature* (Philadelphia: University of Pennsylvania Press, 1993).

2. Gaston Paris, "Lais Inédits," *Romania* 8 (1879): 64–6.

3. "Les plus nobles" could also mean the "most noble men" or "the most noble men and women," though the subsequent description of women suggests that they alone are the subjects of this passage.

4. For a critique of this standard interpretation see E. Jane Burns and Roberta L. Krueger, "Introduction" to *Courtly Ideology and Woman's Place in Old French Literature* special issue of *Romance Notes* 25, 3 (1985): 205–211.

5. In his introductory remarks to the *Lai du Lecheor* G. Paris reads this passage as a joke, assuming that properly courtly ladies would neither speak this way nor approve of such uncourtly sentiment. The poet, he contends, places these words in the mouth of a courtly lady to provoke a refined laugh among his listeners who would ostensibly dismiss this woman's speech as improbable and hence insignificant (64). I think her words deserve more serious consideration.

6. For an extended discussion of the process, see E. Jane Burns, *Bodytalk*, chapter 3.

7. See Denise Riley, *Am I That Name?* (Minneapolis: University of Minnesota Press, 1988), 98–114 and Diana Fuss, *Essentially Speaking* (London: Routledge, 1989), 23–37.

8. *Hamlet's Mother and Other Women* (New York: Columbia University Press, 1990), 103–112.

9. Or alternately, as Nancy Miller has argued, women's fiction repeatedly chafes against the "unsatisfactory reality" contained within the maxims of male-defined plots and plausibilities, "Emphasis Added: Plots and Plausibilities in Women's Fiction," in her *Subject to Change* (New York: Columbia University Press, 1988), 25–46.

10. Judith Butler, *Gender Trouble* (London: Routledge, 1990), 30–31.

11. These seemingly independent female voices are absorbed, however, into the larger frame of male storytelling when the narrator explains how everyone joined with the ladies in making a *lai* that brought joy to clerks and knights (vv. 109–118).

12. For a discussion of the head/ass dichotomy used to construct female identity in Old French farce and fabliau, see E. Jane Burns, *Bodytalk*, chap. 1.

13. With the exception of a few brief instances of reported speech (vv. 1385, 1622), Enide remains, throughout the opening scenes of the tale *tote coie* (v. 684). She reverts to this position at tale's end, saying nothing at all during the final coronation.

14. *Diacritics* (Summer 1982), 42–53.

15. I borrow the phrase from Judith Butler's book by the same title.

16. *Erec et Enide,* ed. Mario Roques (Paris: Champion, 1976). All subsequent line references are to this edition. English translations are mine.

17. On *conjointure* see especially Douglas Kelly, "The Source and Meaning of *Conjointure* in Chrétien's *Erec,*" *Viator* 1 (1970), 179–200 and his *Sens et conjointure in the Chevalier de la Charrette* (The Hague: Mouton, 1966). Also, Michelle Freeman, *The Poetics of Translatio Studii and Conjointure in Chrétien de Troyes' Cligés* (Lexington: French Forum Publishers, 1979).

18. Cf. "conjoindre, conjointure" in A.J. Greimas, *Dictionnaire de l'ancien français* (Paris: Larousse, 1969), 132.

19. *Speculum of the Other Woman*, trans. Gillian C. Gill (Ithaca, NY: Cornell University Press, 1985), 137.

20. Though they are present in abundance in the Arthurian court that Chrétien depicts on the following page of our printed text. No less than 500 "demoiseles de hauz paraiges filles de rois gentes et saiges" are said to populate this courtly milieu.

21. Jacques Lacan recognized in the early seventies that courtly love is an affair between men; see *Séminaire XX, Encore* (Paris: Seuil, 1975).

22. For a sensitive and careful reading of *Erec et Enide* that pays special attention to Enide's speech, see Michel André Bossy, "The Elaboration of Female Narrative Functions in *Erec et Enide,*" *Courtly Literature, Culture and Context,* eds. Keith Busby and Erik Cooper (Amsterdam: John Benjamins, l990), 23–38. And equally cogent, Laurie Finke, "Towards a Cultural Poetics of Romance," *Genre* 22 (1989), 25–76.

23. Erec here places Enide in a position of possible rape, as Bossy points out, 28.

24. When Erec fights the first attackers, Enide "waits elsewhere" (v. 2911); after battling the five brigands, Erec brings their horses back to where Enide waits (vv. 3069–72); Erec rides off into the forest to engage the *comte vaniteux* (vv. 3608–11); when battling the two giants, Erec instructs Enide to "wait for me here" (vv. 4296–97) and later returns to her (vv. 4543–44, 4558); Enide also waits apart while Erec fights with Maboagrains at the Joie de la Cort (vv. 5814–15).

25. See Bossy's comment that Enide holds forth most vociferously when Erec is unconscious, 33.

26. John Plummer reads Enide on the model of a feudal counselor whose advice to her lord echoes the tenets of *bien dire* and *bien aprandre* set out in Chrétien's prologue: one who has an obligation to speak the truth and teach the right that will lead eventually to "joy" for the court, "*Bien dire et Bien aprandre* in Chrétien de Troyes' *Erec et Enide*," *Romania* 95 (1974): 380–94. In this reading Enide serves the "higher good" of teaching proper conduct. Indeed it is remarkable how many readings of *Erec et Enide* posit a similar function for the poem's heroine, without adequately recognizing the extent to which this service—whether to chivalry, love, marriage or some other "higher good"—actually absorbs and effaces Enide. For a fuller discussion of the substantial criticism on Enide, see *Bodytalk: When Women Speak in Old French Literature*, 199–200, note 25.

27. Chrétien subsequently narrates instead a fight between Erec and the count in which Erec wins the female prize (vv. 3561–3652).

28. The chivalric narrative Enide provides here differs most obviously from its Arthurian counterparts because of the string of imperative verbs that construct it. Telling the count how to proceed, Enide sets the stage for and orchestrates the plot of his future action in a mode uncharacteristic of the interaction between knights and ladies.

29. Later in the romance, however—during the Joie de la Cort episode—Chrétien absorbs this resistant voice by having Enide recount her past adventures to a long-lost cousin. The narrative remains properly chivalric, focussing on Erec's skills and achievements. For a discussion of this important section of the romance, see *Bodytalk*, 184–96.

30. Irigaray, *This Sex*, 24, 26, cited by Fuss in *Essentially Speaking*, 58.

31. My reading diverges in this regard from that of Barbara N. Sargent Baur who argues that Enide plays the roles of both *fame* and *amie* but not simultaneously because the two cannot be reconciled, "Erec's Enide, 'sa fame ou s'amie?'" *Romance Philology* 33, 3 (1980): 373–87; and from that of Joan Brumlik who claims that Erec wants to kill the outspoken real *fame* and remake Enide as the more pliant and metaphoric *amie*, "Chrétien's Enide: Wife, Mistress and Metaphor," *Romance Quarterly* 35, 4 (1988): 401–14. To my mind, both roles are equally constructed, equally problematic, and more similar than we have previously acknowledged.

"EZ IST IR G'ARTET VON MIR"

QUEEN ISOLDE AND PRINCESS ISOLDE IN
GOTTFRIED VON STRASSBURG'S *TRISTAN UND ISOLDE*[1]

Ann Marie Rasmussen

Arthurian heroines play numerous roles: they can be sorceresses, mothers of great men, ladies who inspire or vex the hero, attendants who counsel and assist another lady.[2] Only rarely, however, are they daughters of mothers or mothers of daughters. Some Arthurian heroines have no parents at all (Lunete and Laudine [*Iwein*]); some have only fathers or male guardians (Condwîrâmûrs [Wolfram's *Parzival*], Queen Guinevere); some have active fathers and passive, ghost-like mother figures whose function is subsumed by the appellative "mother-of-noble-birth" (Enite [*Erec*], Obîe and Obilôt, daughters of King Lyppaut [*Parzival*, Book VII]). In a word, Arthurian heroines appear to be freed from maternal influence, detached from any sort of female lineage. They function in an imaginary world that assigns to men the transmission of knowledge, status, and pedigree across time. The Arthurian heroine ensures the continuity of the male line even as she ennobles and enriches it, while remaining without female ancestors or descendants. Her world most often culminates in a relationship with a male hero, be he lover, spouse, or son. We can imagine this organization of masculine and feminine lineage as a simple graph: the male world in the Arthurian romance occupies the horizontal axis, which stands for genealogy, chronology, movement through time, what Julia Kristeva calls "linear time"; the female world occupies the vertical axis, which stands for space, eternity, biological rhythm, cyclical (seasonal) return—in Kristevan terminology, "monumental time." In this second notion of the temporal, time is the recapitulation of eternal time in the current moment, yet always only a fragment of a larger whole. On our hypothetical graph, such a notion of female time intersects and expands a critical moment of male chronology, of male genealogy. In the Arthurian world, in other words, the past and the future belong to men, the present to women.[3]

Gottfried von Strassburg's epic fragment *Tristan und Isolde* (c. 1210–15) is a significant exception to the rule that heroines in or close to the Arthurian tradition are dispossessed of a female inheritance.[4] In Gottfried's retelling of this tragic story of adulterous love, the hero's destiny is intimately and fatefully intertwined with that of a daughter and her mother who bear the same name.[5] The mother, Queen Isolde, is the sister of the Irish champion Morold (killed by Tristan in battle) and the wise and respected spouse of Ireland's ruler, King Gurmun. The daughter, Princess Isolde (also known as Blonde, or Fair, Isolde), is Gurmun and Isolde's only child, selected to become the bride of King Mark, Ireland's arch enemy and the ruler of Cornwall, but fated to become the lover of Mark's nephew, Tristan. The political and social order of the fictional world within which these characters move is, of course, congruent with the patrilinear organization of the feudal world. Power is controlled by and descends through noblemen; noblewomen are objects whose exchange between patrilinear families on the marriage market secures political alliances while keeping wealth, influence, and power within the noble class. Such a dynastic marriage of convenience between King Mark and Princess Isolde is the premise for the plot of *Tristan*. The plot (that is, the erotic love between Tristan and Isolde), however, comes about because the arranged marriage goes awry, and it goes awry because Tristan, not Mark, shares with Princess Isolde a love potion that is her mother's gift.

What then does it mean that the love potion is the bride's gift from her mother? What happens when we read the crucial intervention of the love potion as a direct outcome of a mother/daughter relation, i.e., of a *diachronic* female relation? To answer these questions, we must reassess the role played by the mother, Queen Isolde, and the relationship between Queen Isolde and Princess Isolde must be placed in the context of the mother/daughter subgenre in medieval German literature.[6]

When Tristan, slowly dying from a poisoned, painful, and fetid wound inflicted by the mortally injured Irish champion Morold, disguises himself as the minstrel Tantris and has himself set adrift before the Irish coast, he uses—indeed must use—deception to obtain a cure from the sole person on earth who can effect it, the poisoner of Morold's sword, Morold's sister, the Irish Queen Isolde. Queen Isolde is indeed a powerful, knowledgeable, and intelligent woman (though even she is fooled by the arch-trickster Tristan, for she does not recognize his wound as the product of her own handiwork!). Her knowledge of government and diplomacy places her alongside other powerful fictional queens (Laudine, Guinevere, Amata, Kriemhild, Hilde, Kudrun, Gerlint), who all wield considerable political influence (whether for good or for evil) in their own right. Moreover, Queen Isolde is an herbalist and physician second to none, a woman whose skills as a healer are augmented by occult powers (clairvoyant dreams, the love potion). These realms of knowledge are conventionally associated in fiction with (magical) female power, and her command of them aligns Queen Isolde with the sorceresses who hold sway without male consorts on the margins of Arthur's world.[7] By being placed at the side of a man, however, Queen Isolde is transferred out of the realm of fairies, myth, and magic (the realm to which all-powerful sorceresses are assigned) and into the realm of historical time, i.e., patriarchy, in a way that diminishes her power. For this sorceress-queen is also a mother who has one child, a cherished and adored daughter to whom, as the unfolding makes clear, she has taught many of her skills, but whom she must nevertheless relinquish—finally, dramatically, and (it would appear) utterly—in marriage, to the patriarchal world.

In preparing Princess Isolde to fulfill her role as a marriageable object of exchange, Queen Isolde is depicted as conforming to a familiar convention about mothers that structures the mother/daughter genre: mothers educate their daughters and guide them into marriage. This "sexual apprenticeship" model is the dominant paradigm for depicting mothers and daughters in medieval German literature, literature which, it must be stressed, was written by men. In the mother's instructions or through her acts, these imagined mothers-of-daughters fashion a notion of female identity that depends on becoming an attractive and compliant object of male desire. This mother does not create autonomous, "self-actualizing" notions of female desire and selfhood; rather, she assumes that female identity is synonymous with sexual identity, and that woman's socio-sexual identity is reactive, shaped in accordance with society's (men's) demands of her. Writing on the comic mother/daughter didactic poem *die Winsbeckin* (c. 1210–50), Trude Ehlert has formulated the concept of the "other-directed" female identity that such a relationship to men and to society implies: "Thus all the mother's teachings are intended to make woman a member of society who causes no problems, an instrument for men to use in perfecting themselves, one that is oriented exclusively toward society and men."[8] This notion of total compliance in society's expectations of women, which Ehlert elsewhere in her article aptly dubs woman's "instrumental function" (Ehlert 44), does indeed function as a kind of dominant ideology throughout the mother/daughter subgenre, including *Tristan und Isolde*. In medieval German literature, however, woman's "instrumental function" can be read not just as an ideal to be lived up to, but also as a convention to be defied, a model to be subverted, and a protocol to be exploited. When inculcating woman's "instrumental function," the mother attempts to reproduce in her daughter the same kind of female identity that the mother herself has acted out or is in the process of acting out. The goal of the mother's teaching is for the daughter to adopt and fulfill her mother's teachings, in other words, for the daughter to replicate her mother, to *become* her mother—for Isolde to become . . . Isolde. The mother/daughter relation is set up to act out a concept of femininity that guarantees continuity at the expense of distinct identities. Or to put it another way, the diachronic female relation represented by the mother/daughter relation has as its overt goal the recapitulation of woman's function as the bearer of Kristeva's "monumental time." The mother/daughter lineage is assigned a paradoxical function indeed, for it implicitly proposes something like female history only in order to undo it.

This paradox surfaces, I think, in virtually all medieval German mother/daughter texts, as they play in distinct ways with contrasts in order to uphold sameness. In texts such as D*ie Winsbeckin* and the fifteenth-century rhymed couplet text "Wie ain muoter ir dochter lernet puolen" ("How a mother teaches her daughter whoring"), the instructress-mothers take virtually diametrically opposed attitudes towards woman's instrumental function (*Die Winsbeckin*: fulfill it; *Wie ain muoter*: exploit it), but both works assume that the daughters become like their mothers.[9] In the comic Neidhartian mother/daughter poems, the pairing of a sexually adventuresome daughter defying her socially conformist mother can be transposed into the pairing of a socially conformist daughter trying to restrain her sex-crazed mother. If these mothers and daughters represent the all-too-familiar construction of femininity as sexuality, in both its alluring and grotesque varieties, they also imagine biological rhythm and seasonal return as feminine, and above all, they postulate that the differences between mothers and daughters (age, station, life experience) are rendered *comically* insignificant by their fundamental sameness as women.

Finally, the paradoxes of this ideology of femininity reverberate profoundly in the epics that pair an evil mother with an exemplary daughter (for example, Heinrich von Veldeke's *Eneasroman* [1170–89]; and the anonymous thirteenth-century epic *Kudrun*, which pairs an exemplary daughter with a good mother and an evil stepmother). These mothers use power according to their own lights, in effect challenging their own instrumental function while seeking to bend their daughters' instrumental function to their own purposes. They fail and die. Their daughters, on the other hand, resist this co-optation, holding out successfully for illustrious marriages that are, by definition, patriarchally sanctioned. Dissimilarity would seem to prevail; the evil mother's usurpation of male power is punished by unmourned death; the exemplary daughter's compliance with male power is celebrated by the story's happy end. And yet the evil mother remains continuous with her exemplary daughter insofar as the evil mother illustrates a threatening rejection of conformist notions of femininity that must be savagely disavowed (the mother's unmourned death) for patriarchal closure (the daughter's happy marriage) to take place. Only the violent expurgation of the evil mother can ensure the survival of the exemplary daughter and perhaps offer some "reassurance" that the exemplary daughter will attempt to fashion daughters who are like her.

The dilemmas of sameness and dissimilarity, of continuity and disruption in the mother/daughter bond, are given unique shape and valence in *Tristan und Isolde*, for the continuity between Queen Isolde and Princess Isolde, I will argue, is both radically disrupted and radically affirmed. Queen Isolde is an exemplary mother; in many respects she is the best "good mother" within the context of the mother/daughter genre.[10] To reread her story, we return to the plot of Gottfried's *Tristan*. As readers will remember, Tristan visits the Irish court twice. The first time he disguises himself as the minstrel/merchant Tantris in order to be cured of the poisonous wound inflicted by Morold; the second time he enters the country as himself, but in secret, in order to kill a marauding dragon and so win the hand of Princess Isolde for his uncle, King Mark of Cornwall. During Tristan's first visit, Queen Isolde not only cures him but recognizes his immense artistic gifts and keeps him on to instruct Princess Isolde. This is an entirely conventional aspect of good mothering, since as a mother Queen Isolde is traditionally responsible for her child's education.

During Tristan's second visit comes the ultimate test of Queen Isolde as a mother, which is also, not coincidentally, the ultimate test of her skill, her mettle, and her resolve. After killing the dragon and cutting out its tongue, Tristan has been overcome by the dragon's poison and falls into a deep stupor. An ambitious Irish seneschal, long enamored of Princess Isolde, comes upon the dead dragon, cuts off its head, and swaggers back to court, where he gleefully announces that he has won the Princess. Both Princess Isolde and her mother forcefully reject a humiliating match with an upstart cheat as an exchange below Princess Isolde's worth, but the King, judicially bound by his vow and the evidence, is powerless to prevent it. Under these somber and threatening circumstances, it falls to Queen Isolde, ably assisted by Brangaene, to save her daughter.

Using her occult powers, the Queen summons a dream that reveals to her the true circumstances of the dragon's killing; she organizes the search for the wounded hero, which is carried out together with Brangaene and Princess Isolde, who finds him; she again heals Tristan, who is near death.

All this happens behind the scenes, as it were, in the women's chambers. It also falls to Queen Isolde, however, to *publicly* orchestrate the repudiation of the seneschal through the still-secret knowledge that the true dragonslayer has been found.

Scholars have not often discussed the scenes in which Queen Isolde successfully carries this out, yet the scenes present, I think, a critical examination of the range and the limits of the power of a wise and well-respected queen.[11] The plan is carried out in two segments, the first private and the second public. Gurmun has set a date for a public hearing to adjudicate the seneschal's claim, and he has summoned his neighbors, vassals, and kin to take part and to advise him. When they are assembled, he seeks their counsel, summons the Queen, takes her aside, and privately confers with her. Revealing that she knows the truth, the Queen comforts and reassures him, and then she tells him to proceed: he should calmly summon the assembly, affirm without fear that he will keep his vow, wait for the two Isoldes to arrive, allow the seneschal to set forth his demand, and then turn things over to her by ordering her to speak: "sô gebietet mir'z, sô spriche ich / vür iuch, vür Îsôt und vür mich" ("When you command me, then I will speak for you, for Isolde, and for myself," ll. 9753–9754).

Evidently this scheme suits the King, and evidently he trusts his wife, for although the Queen tells him no more, he proceeds as she has privately advised. The scene now advances to the public hearing. As the crowd whispers, the Queen and Princess Isolde enter the palace, greet the assembled noblemen, and take their places beside the King. Before the assembly, the seneschal asserts that his love for Princess Isolde has caused him to risk his life to slay the dragon. Brandishing the dragon's head as evidence, he demands the Princess as his rightful reward. At this point the Queen interrupts and throws down the gauntlet, forthrightly accusing the seneschal of deceit. The seneschal attempts to head off this dangerous intervention by demanding that the King speak for himself. This the King does, but only to follow the plan his wife has laid out and formally turn the proceedings over to her.

> "Seneschal," said the queen, "the man who desires as rich a reward as my daughter, Isolde, without having earned it, truly, he covets too much." "Eh gads," said the seneschal, "Lady, you are acting badly, why are you saying this? My Lord, who is to decide this matter, he can surely speak perfectly well for himself. Let him speak and reply to me." The king spoke: "Lady, speak, for yourself, for Isolde and for me!" "With thanks, Lord, I shall do so." (ll. 9820–9831)[12]

In the ensuing battle between truth and deception, conventional notions of femininity and masculinity—in a word, gender issues—become weapons in the struggle. The seneschal deploys conventional notions of gender on his own behalf, first by parading as a dragonslaying he-man, and then by wondering aloud why the Queen is speaking instead of the King, thus impugning the King's masculinity and implicitly (who would dare to do so explicitly?) accusing him of effeminacy. Taking up the battle over who represents "true" masculinity (the candidates being the King, the seneschal, and the Queen herself), the Queen rejects the seneschal's claim while mockingly praising his masculinity (*menlîchen muot*, 'manly heart'). This tempts the seneschal to make a great show of how much he worships the Princess, a show that strikingly recalls the self-abasement in love practiced as a privileged enactment of masculinity by the courtly love poets of both the Old French and the Middle High German schools. As soon as Princess Isolde rejects the seneschal, however, he turns face and launches into a misogynist diatribe on the fickleness of women.[13]

Now conventional notions of femininity have been brought into play. In a marvelously entertaining enactment of mock humility, the Queen *agrees* with the seneschal's assessment of women and then turns his misogyny into an *open* charge of effeminacy against the seneschal. Why doesn't the seneschal just leave womanly ways to weak women such as herself, instead of acting like one by lying and cheating? Goading him unmercifully, the Queen spurns his advances to Princess Isolde in her own name:

> "She [Princess Isolde] is indifferent to many a man who desires her greatly and among those you are in first place. She takes after me in that. I never cared for you, either. I know Princess Isolde feels the same way; in that she takes after me." (ll. 9931–9937)[14]

Queen Isolde then challenges the seneschal to act like a "real man" by owning up to the truth and by stepping down from his deceitful claim; she knows, she proclaims, the identity of the real dragonslayer. Enraged, the seneschal demands the opportunity to fight this unknown challenger, and a combat date is set for three days hence.

In this scene, masculinity is on trial. The Queen is not only defending Princess Isolde from a disgraceful marriage, she is also defending the King from an implied charge of effeminacy, and she is defending her right, as Queen, to speak "as a man" for the King; that is to say, she is defending her right to adopt a position conventionally reserved for men, the exercise of political power. The allegation of effeminacy boomerangs against the seneschal when the Queen entices him into making such a convincing display of his own fickleness that he brands himself, with his own definitions, as "feminine." In tandem with this, the Queen's words and deeds establish that the King is indeed the "real man" on the scene, man enough to trust his smart wife. In return, the male trust in her, so publicly affirmed, undoes the fickleness claimed for herself by the Queen. That, together with her success in revealing the truth, legitimates the Queen's access to public, political speech.

Thus falls to Queen Isolde the paradoxical role of publicly defining herself as a *woman*, by assenting to the misogynist discourse that brands all women fickle, in order to negotiate and set aright the standards of masculinity. It takes a woman to make a man. This consummate performance, which invokes gender conformity (without embodying it) in order to achieve a measure of gender transgression, suggests at least three things: that gender categories are socially constructed and unstable; that definitions of masculinity that undergird male social control rest on misogynist and essentialist definitions of femininity; and that while female complicity is necessary for patriarchy to stand, female collusion with and resistance to male authority are not necessarily antithetical.

In the three-day hiatus between the two public hearings, Princess Isolde discovers Tristan's true identity. Once more Queen Isolde (again aided by Brangaene) is the agent who turns potential catastrophe into success. She restrains Princess Isolde (and herself) from taking revenge on Tristan as Morold's killer, learns of Tristan's mission to win Princess Isolde for King Mark, approves of it, and brings about a reconciliation between King Gurmun and Tristan. Queen Isolde comprehends that King Mark's proposal does not just include a way out of a humiliating alliance, not just a truce between former enemies, but that it also promises the Princess rank and privilege commensurate with her own, namely, the status of a Queen. In other words, Tristan's proposal, on Mark's behalf, opens up for Princess Isolde the possibility of replicating her mother's destiny, of becoming like her mother, of "living up" to her name.[15]

Let me return to the primary issue under discussion: the extent of the Queen's power as it is exemplified in her prominent public role during the seneschal's first hearing. The sequence of private conference preceding public advocacy which the reader has witnessed drives the point home that while Queen Isolde may be rich, wise, beautiful, witty, and sharp, her access to political power is predicated solely on the esteem and love with which her husband the King regards her. She cannot exercise power publicly unless he loves and trusts her enough to command it. This accords well with Susan

Mosher Stuard's description of changes in noblewomen's opportunities for political power during the twelfth and thirteenth centuries (the period of time in which, of course, the many versions of *Tristan und Isolde* were written):

> In the aftermath of this change [the process during the twelfth and thirteenth centuries by which the inheritance of queens was integrated into the crown lands] a queen might still influence a husband or son, and his bureaucracy, or as the surviving parent, she might be trusted with the power of regent during the minority of her son. But neither her office itself nor her inheritance rights and marriage portion sustained her position. Royal women, except those who could claim the right of primogeniture in the event that they had no brothers, lost authority. If they exerted any power at all, they derived it from their intimacy with and access to the reigning king.[16]

What does all this mean with regard to the love potion that Queen Isolde brews for her daughter? It means that Queen Isolde wants her daughter's fate to replicate her own not just sentimentally, but also politically. It means that Queen Isolde intends not just that love find a place in the arranged marriage between Mark and Princess Isolde, not just that, as Hugo Kuhn has pointed out, love "cement" the political alliance between Ireland and Cornwall,[17] but that a Queen's political power find a place in her daughter's marriage. In other words, this epic is not only about romantic love, not only about male power struggles, but also about a noblewoman's *knowledge* of her limited right to political power, and her manipulation of available resources. The mother's gift of the love potion means that while acquiescing in her daughter's (and her own) instrumental function, Queen Isolde still desires to give her daughter a measure of control over it. For as is shown by the paradox of Queen Isolde's first exchange with her husband, she knows, when she orders him in private to command her in public, that for powerful women the rule of love and the exercise of public power are inextricably linked.

What Queen Isolde appears to want for her daughter is that love be the "glue" that holds patriarchal society together. The love potion can be read as a kind of "insurance policy," intended to guarantee that Princess Isolde experience in her arranged marriage not just love but, more important, political power. The mother's promise miscarries calamitously, however: not Mark and Isolde, but Tristan and Isolde drink the potion and become enslaved to each other in an erotic love, characterized by cycles of pain and pleasure that will last until—indeed, bring about—their deaths. The magical agent designed to guarantee that Princess Isolde would become her mother instead violently shatters the desired replication of normative femininity, replacing it, for Princess Isolde, with a fate that could not be more different from her mother's. Princess Isolde is not honored and loved, but rather alternately tyrannized and petted by a suspicious and jealous husband; she is not consulted and given public authority but rather repeatedly tested and even forced to submit to a public ordeal. For her, private deceits and public denial become necessary so that she and Tristan can maintain and endure their passion. Princess Isolde experiences love as a force that is irreconcilable with the normative social and sexual order. Love has become the solvent that threatens to erode the substance of patriarchy.

And it would appear that Princess Isolde's adulterous love for Tristan disrupts the continuity between mother and daughter, too. Just as Tristan is denied an identity as father, since he no fewer than three times refuses the patriarchal role as a feudal lord,[18] so Princess Isolde is separated from a oneness between mother and daughter, insofar as the continuity of such a unity is imagined in normative, patriarchal terms. And yet . . . . It is the love potion, the gift of a loving mother to her cherished daughter, that has dissolved the patriarchal bond of oneness between mother and daughter, that has subverted Princess Isolde's "instrumental function," that has liberated Princess Isolde from the law of wifely obedience, even if it has made her submit to the perhaps even harsher law of passion. With the love potion, Queen Isolde passes her strength, her cunning, and her knowledge to her daughter, including the strength and the wit to defy the conventions that the mother herself embodies. As the epic plays itself out, Princess Isolde acquires more of her mother's traits—her cunning, her wisdom. In the end, when she is summoned as a master physician, the only one with the skill to heal Tristan, it is hard to know whether she is mother or daughter, for in a sense she has surely become both.[19]

The continuity between mother and daughter is not disrupted but transformed. The connection between mother and daughter enacted in *Tristan und Isolde* is based neither on replication nor on rejection, both of which would reenact (though in different ways) the model of the fundamental sameness of all women. Rather, this different kind of mother/daughter continuity allows distinct identities for mother and daughter, for women, while affirming the power of their relation. In connecting sameness and generational change, such a mother/daughter relation brings together the "essentially" synchronic nature of monumental time and the diachronically ordered aspect of linear time without subordinating one to the other, thus confusing the hierarchies these terms imply. The paradox such a female continuum enacts, monumental time with a linear dimension, dislocates the dualities of the patriarchal order it is intended to shore up.[20] In the terms of the Kristevan image graph introduced at the beginning of this essay, the trajectory of this female continuum no longer intersects and amplifies a moment of "masculine" linear time, but rather interrupts and redirects it.

Seen in this way, the female continuum encompasses all the major female figures in the story. It includes Tristan's mother, Blanscheflur, whose passionately loving and dying body bears and grounds the story's fluid dualities. As has long been noted, Blanscheflur's story makes clear from the outset that erotic passion flies in the face of the dominant social order; the intertwining of unconditional love and unconditional sorrow that characterizes Gottfried's conception of erotic love begins with Blanscheflur, who conceives Tristan in a passionate embrace that wrests Rivalin from death.[21] The female continuum includes the "false" Isolde, Isolde-White-Hand, Tristan's wife, whose rage at overhearing of Tristan's passion for another woman leads her to betray him in turn. The death-bringer, obviously bound to the Queen and the Princess by her name, Isolde-White-Hand plays out the lethal aspect of femininity that is bound to manifest itself in a dualistic, patriarchal system. She represents the fracture at the heart of the female continuum.[22]

And finally, the female continuum includes the indispensable Brangaene, niece and cousin, who doubles for both mother and daughter but also eludes their control. As an intimate of both mother and daughter at the Irish court, Brangaene is instrumental in resolving the predicament of Tristan's identity. As a mother surrogate, Brangaene is entrusted with the love potion; she alone shares with the Queen the knowledge of this magic. As a daughter surrogate, Brangaene takes Isolde's place in Mark's bed on their wedding night, substituting her intact virginity (her blood) for Isolde's already broken hymen. As Tristan and Isolde's intimate and confidante, Brangaene is go-between, messenger, victim, betrayer, and co-conspirator. Part sister, part mother, part daughter, Brangaene is many things, but most of all she is never fully defined by any of her roles. She is the agent of chaos and the crosser of borders, the doubling figure who symbolizes the concept of "non-identical identity" characterizing this story's female continuum.

Transformed into erotic love, the discontinuous continuity between Queen Isolde and Princess Isolde disrupts the existing social order and dislodges the hierarchies of justice, law, and gender. The effects of this disruption reverberate even in the narrative organization of the Tristan story. In the world before the love potion, events are ordered as a progression toward a goal (which is the potion itself); afterwards, the meetings and partings of the lovers are the story's events. These episodes share an internal ordering as repetitive cycles that oscillate between separation and unification, suspicion and certainty, denial and affirmation, pain and pleasure. The sequence in which they appear in the narrative, however, has little internal development. In this sense, the narrative organization of these episodes is bewitchingly arbitrary and random: they belong in no particular order and could be rearranged in various ways. And indeed, whereas the various medieval versions of the Tristan legend agree on the sequence of events leading up to the love potion, the events following it are presented in different sequences in the many different versions.[23]

With the love potion, the mother both claims and liberates her daughter. Is the erotic passion that Queen Isolde unleashes "merely" destructive?[24] Does it not also transform women's pursuit of power, which other epics (*Kudrun, Eneasroman, Nibelungenlied*) view in a hostile fashion, into a force that insistently lays bare the elemental contradictions in the social order with which it remains fundamentally (but not essentially) incompatible? In the end, the love between mother and daughter, like the love between Tristan and Isolde, is the source of fierce love—"To me nothing has ever been as dear as you" (*mir wart nie niht sô liep sô duo*, l. 10296), says the Queen to her daughter—and also the source of fierce sorrow. Perhaps the suffering that Princess Isolde shares with Tristan is also a part of Queen Isolde's legacy to Princess Isolde, a transmuted form of her maternal grief at having to surrender her child to the patriarchal order so that mother and daughter may survive.

I close this essay with a historical coda. In the "real" medieval world, historical conditions were such that the ration of power a mother could bequeath to her daughter was modest at best. In fact, we know very little about the lives of ordinary medieval mothers and daughters; the historical record is too paltry, the documents too sparse, much evidence lost, and much, much more never written down. But fragments of this "dark continent" do surface: here, for example, in the testimony of a medieval French noblewoman of low station, Beatrice de Planissoles, interrogated by the bishop of Parmiers, Jacques Fournier, on a charge of heresy in 1320 (some one hundred years after Gottfried's *Tristan* was written) in the village of Montaillou. Her words corroborate the entanglement of the mother/daughter bond with magic and subversion.[25] They also tell us *what* a love potion could be made of.

Beatrice has been shown some "very suspect things" that were found among her possessions. After confirming that these things belong to her, she explains the origin and function of each in turn. About a cloth stained with blood she says:

"These cloths stained with blood are from the menstrual blood of my daughter Philippa and because this baptized Jew [a woman] had told me that if I kept some of her first blood and that if I gave it to her husband or to another man to drink he would never be interested in another woman." (Confession of Beatrice, widow of Othon de Lagleize of Dalou, from the inquisition records of Jacques Fournier, bishop of Parmiers, 1320.)[26]

Two mothers, one fictional, one real—Queen Isolde, married to a king, Beatrice de Planissoles, interrogated by the inquisition and convicted of heresy—both harnessing the forces of a proscribed realm (the supernatural, the marginalized, the knowledge from a pagan universe as represented by "the baptized Jew") in order to guarantee for their daughters a measure of autonomy in a male-dominated world. Love, brought about by ingesting menstrual blood, will render a man's virtually total economic, legal, and social control of his wife accessible to her *on her terms*. Beatrice de Planissoles goes even farther than Queen Isolde, for her potion does not bind her daughter, but merely the daughter's spouse or lover. Thus she seeks to give her daughter the gift of control over the only "commodity" she possesses in patriarchy: her sexuality, her desirability, her instrumental function. In curbing the potential adultery of her husband, Philippa may possibly strengthen marriage, both the institution and her own; yet in gaining power over her husband, she weakens and subverts the medieval convention of male rule in marriage. The control this power gives her can also be read as a form of "marriage resistance" smuggled into the institution of marriage itself.[27] What matter that the voices of these women are brought to us by men? Before us flashes one of those rare moments in medieval history, a moment that illuminates what Adrienne Rich calls the "double-life" of women. For a second, the veil in which recorded history shrouds so much of medieval women's lives is rent and we glimpse truths that can only be discerned as shadows: the shadows of women's embattled and subversive knowledge of their oppression; their collusion and resistance in the struggle for empowerment; their love for one another.

NOTES

1. "In this she takes after me" (l. 9937); thanks to the North Carolina Research Group on Medieval and Early Modern Women for their responses to an earlier draft of this essay. I am grateful to Sally Poor, Helen Solterer, and Robert Sullivan for reading, commenting, and correcting.

2. See Joan M. Ferrante, *Woman as Image in Medieval Literature, From the Twelfth Century to Dante* (New York: Columbia University Press, 1975), p. 120.

3. When considered in this way, the fictional Arthurian world illustrates some

aspects of Julia Kristeva's concepts of time as it is constructed by the symbolic and semiotic orders, as well as the alignment of these orders with enculturated notions and constructions of masculinity and femininity. All Kristeva citations are quoted from *The Kristeva Reader*, ed. Toril Moi (New York: Columbia University Press, 1986).

In her influential essay "Women's Time," Kristeva first elaborates two temporal dimensions: "the time of linear history, or *cursive time* (as Nietzsche called it), and the time of another history, thus another time, *monumental time* (again according to Nietzsche), which englobes these supra-national, socio-cultural ensembles within even larger entities" (189). These two temporal dimensions are then aligned, with the aid of anthropological and psychoanalytic categories, with masculinity and femininity, respectively. Linear temporality "is readily labelled masculine" (193), and is described as "time as project, teleology, linear and prospective unfolding: time as departure, progression and arrival—in other words, the time of history" (192). Monumental temporality is aligned with femininity, and of it Kristeva says:

> As for time, female subjectivity would seem to provide a specific measure that essentially retains *repetition* and *eternity* from among the multiple modalities of time known through the history of civilizations. On the one hand, there are cycles, gestation, the eternal recurrence of a biological rhythm which conforms to that of nature and imposes a temporality whose stereotyping may shock, but whose regularity and unison with what is experienced as extra-subjective time, cosmic time, occasion vertiginous visions and unnameable *jouissance*. On the other hand, and perhaps as a consequence, there is the massive presence of a monumental temporality, without cleavage or escape, which has so little to do with linear time (which passes) that the very word 'temporality' hardly fits: all-encompassing and infinite like imaginary space . . . (191; footnotes omitted).

4. Another significant exception is the *Lai de Fresne* by Marie de France (fl. c. 1160–1190). See Michelle Freeman, "The Power of Sisterhood: Marie de France's "Le Fresne," in *Women and Power in the Middle Ages*, ed. Mary Erler and Maryanne Kowaleski (Athens, Georgia: University of Georgia Press, 1988), pp. 250–64.

5. I quote from Gottfried von Strassburg, *Tristan*, ed. Rüdiger Krohn. 3 vols. (Stuttgart: Reclam, 1984). All translations are my own.

Gottfried's version is a fragment; it breaks off during the second half, as Tristan is contemplating marriage to Isolde-White-Hand. Two medieval German continuations exist, which are of interest primarily as interpretations of Gottfried's work, since both continuers read *Tristan* as the *hero's* tragedy, for whose fall Isolde, as temptress, is to blame. See Rüdiger Krohn's summaries and bibliography in the edition mentioned above.

Gottfried's version reworks, in Middle High German translation, the *Roman de Tristan* by Thomas d'Angleterre (between 1155–1170/80?). Only fragments of Thomas's version survive. As (bad) luck would have it, the fragments that have come down to us from both Old French versions (Béroul, Thomas) are " post-love potion" and do not contain the mother/daughter story. The German version by Eilhart of Oberg, which predates Gottfried's version and may be indebted to Béroul's Old French version, assigns *all* of Queen Isolde's actions, with the exception of brewing and bestowing the love potion, to Princess Isolde. The Queen is not even named. Of these "original" retellings, only Gottfried preserves and elaborates the portions of the story where the mother/daughter plot appears. See Marion Mälzer, *Die Isolde-Gestalten in den mittelalterlichen deutschen Tristan-Dichtungen: Ein Beitrag zum diachronischen Wandel* (Heidelberg: Winter, 1991).

Readers interested in enjoying a panoramic view of the medieval Tristan stories may find the following German anthology of interest: Danielle Buschinger and Wolfgang Spiewok, eds., *Tristan und Isolde im europäischen Mittelalter: Ausgewählte Texte in Übersetzung und Nacherzählung* (Stuttgart: Reclam, 1991).

6. The secondary literature on mothers and daughters in modern literature (primarily approached from the perspective of the woman writer) is so copious that instead of attempting a bibliography I prefer to steer the reader to Marianne Hirsch, *The Mother/Daughter Plot: Narrative, Psychoanalysis, Feminism* (Bloomington: Indiana University Press, 1989). In contrast, very little work has been done on this topic in medieval literature. See Nikki Stiller, *Eve's Orphans: Mothers and Daughters in Medieval English Literature*, Contributions in Women's Studies, 16 (Westport, Conn.: Greenwood Press, 1980), and also Ann Marie Rasmussen, "'Bist du begehrt, so bist du wert': Magische und höfische Mitgift für die Töchter," *Mütter—Töchter—Frauen: Weiblichkeitsbilder in der Literatur*, ed. Helga Kraft and Elke Liebs (Stuttgart: Metzler, 1993), pp. 7–33.

7. See Peter Meister, *The Healing Female in the German Courtly Romance*, Göppinger Arbeiten zur Germanistik, 523 (Göppingen: Kümmerle, 1990).

8. "(Alle Lehren der Mutter) zielen also darauf ab, die Frau zu einem problemlosen Glied der Gesellschaft und einem Instrument der Selbstperfektionierung des Mannes zu machen, das sich nur auf diese Gesellschaft und auf den Mann hin ausrichtet . . ." (Trude Ehlert, "Die Frau als Arznei: Zum Bild der Frau in hochmittelalterlicher deutscher Lehrdichtung," *Zeitschrift für deutsche Philologie*, 105 [1986]: 61).

9. The text "Wie ain muoter ir dochter lernet puolen" is known to scholars as "Stiefmutter und Tochter" ("Stepmother and Daughter"). I use the more descriptive title given to this work in a medieval manuscript, the so-called "Liederbuch der Clara Hätzlerin" ("Clara Hätzlerin's Songbook"), compiled by the professional scribe Clara Hätzlerin in Augsburg, 1470 or 1471. For a list of the manuscripts containing " Stiefmutter und Tochter," see Tilo Brandis, *Mittelhochdeutsche, mittelniederdeutsche und mittelniederländische Minnereden: Verzeichnis der Handschriften und Drucke*, Münchner Texte und Untersuchungen, 25 (Munich: Beck, 1968), Nr. 351.

10. Hugo Bekker compares Queen Isolde (together with Brangaene) to the cowardly and intriguing barons at Mark's court, yet later calls her "prudent" (163) and a "true believer in the bond of married love" (164) for having brewed the love potion. This view of Queen Isolde as a scheming, conventional, yet somehow judicious woman who plays a negligible role in political affairs is not supported by my reading. Hugo Bekker, *Gottfried von Strassburg's "Tristan": A Journey Through the Realm of Eros*, Studies in German Literature, Linguistics, and Culture, vol. 29 (Columbia, S.C.: Camden House, 1987), in particular pp. 154–66.

11. In a recent article, Albrecht Classen argues that Gurmun is a passive and weak king, while Queen Isolde is "in control of government affairs" ("Matriarchy versus Patriarchy: The Role of the Irish Queen Isolde in Gottfried von Strassburg's *Tristan*," *Neophilologus*, 73. 1 [1989], 81). Classen contends that this reflects "a literary model of matriarchy which . . . clearly reflected historical reality of the earlier and high Middle Ages" (86). But the historical evidence for any "remnant" of matriarchy seems dubious at best. In any case, the issue of women's exercise of power is not a question of women's "ancient rights"; it arises anew out of the internal contradictions inherent in any patriarchal social order in any era of history. The pursuit of matriarchy too often begs this more substantial question. All this leads me to the disciplinary question of why the search for matriarchy is viewed in some scholarly circles as an adequate approach to the issue of women's power in the Middle Ages (witness Mälzer, note 5). Setting these doubts aside, in the following I argue that far from supporting Classen's claim that Queen Isolde enjoys supreme power, a close reading of the text reveals the very real limitations and dependencies of that power.

12. "truhsaeze" sprach diu künigîn
    "der alsô rîlîchen solt,
    als mîn tohter ist, Îsôlt,
    ungedienet haben wil,
    entriuwen des ist alze vil."

"ei" sprach der truhsaeze dô
"vrouwe, ir tuot übel, wie redet ir sô?
mîn hêrre, der ez enden sol,
der kan doch selbe sprechen wol.
der spreche und antwürte mir."
der künec sprach: "vrouwe, sprechet ir
vür iuch, vür Îsôt und vür mich!"
"genâde hêrre, daz tuon ich."

13. The seneschal's behavior mimics the misognistic flip-flop between worshiping women and vilifying them that, feminists argue, lies at the heart of courtly love poetry. Queen Isolde herself implies this when she taunts the seneschal by saying that he has set forth his misogynist arguments "just as a courtly knight should" ("rehte alse ein vrouwen ritter sol," l. 9905; the pun on "Frauenritter"—lady's knight/lady's man/ladylike knight—is untranslatable). In terms of status, the seneschal fits the bill for a courtly love poet (a German one, at least): a court official, lower in rank than his love object, probably not of "free" birth, but rather a *ministeriale*. In fact, I think that this whole scene is a deliberate send-up of the notions of courtly love, which are being dismissed as superficial and fickle in an implicit comparison with the soon-to-be-ignited erotic passion shared by Tristan and Isolde.

14. "ir ist der vil unmaere,
    dem sî doch vil liep waere,
    der dû ze hant der êrste bist.
    daz selbe ir von mir g'artet ist.
    ich selbe enwart dir ouch nie holt.
    ich weiz wol, alse entuot Îsolt:
    ez ist ir g'artet von mir."

15. A second hearing of the seneschal's case now follows. At first, it proceeds very much like the first one: the seneschal addresses the King and is answered by the Queen, who summons Tristan. With Tristan's entrance, gender issues have been set aright (the "real man" has appeared) and order has been restored; the King takes over, now fully in charge of the proceedings. The Queen's last public act is to direct mocking barbs at the seneschal, whose kin, humiliated by his obvious lies, force him to back down in disgrace. Before the assembled nobility, King Gurmun and Tristan negotiate and affirm the marriage settlement between Mark and Princess Isolde. During this part of the scene no mention is made of the Queen, although both she and Isolde are clearly still present; affairs of state are again safely in the hands of men.

16. Susan Mosher Stuard, "The Dominion of Gender: Women's Fortunes in the High Middle Ages," in *Becoming Visible: Women in European History*, 2nd ed., ed. Renate Bridenthal, Claudia Koonz, and Susan Mosher Stuard (Boston: Houghton Mifflin, 1987), p. 163. See also Marion F. Facinger, "A Study of Medieval Queenship: Capetian France 987–1237," *Studies in Medieval and Renaissance History*, 5 (1968), 3–47. Thanks to Judith Bennett for this reference.

17. Hugo Kuhn, "Gottfried von Straßburg," *Die deutsche Literatur des Mittelalters: Verfasserlexikon*, vol. 1— (8 vols. to date), 2nd ed., ed. Kurt Ruh. (Berlin: de Gruyter, 1976—), vol. 3, cols. 153–67; here, cols. 163–64.

18. One: Tristan regains his biological father's realm and relinquishes it to his foster father; two: Tristan refuses to let Mark step down for him and goes to win Isolde instead; three: instead of running off with Isolde and marrying her himself, Tristan turns her over to Mark.

19. Joan M. Ferrante hints at this when, in discussing Princess Isolde, she repeatedly summons the image of Queen Isolde: "In a way, she (i.e., Princess Isolde) draws him to her by magic (the poison on Morolt's sword comes from her mother); she gives him new life (her mother cures him of that wound and later of the dragon's poison); and she awakens him to the passion of love (the love-potion, too, comes from her mother)" (*Woman as Image*, p. 93, n. 2).

20. In discussing her concepts of the symbolic order (the order of language, of society, of gender) and the semiotic, which represents (among other things) all meaning that can and must escape the processes of the symbolic, and which therefore is defined as the " truth" of the symbolic order, Kristeva makes a comment that seems particularly relevant here: "The artist (that imaginary committer of incest) suspects that it is from the mother's side that the unverifiable atemporal 'truth' of the symbolic order and its time springs out and explodes" (Julia Kristeva, "About Chinese Women," in *A Kristeva Reader*, p. 154).

21. Blanscheflur herself must have recourse to a mother figure in order to carry out her wishes; she enlists the aid of her old governess [*meisterinne*], who smuggles Blanscheflur into Rivalin's chamber.

22. Thanks to Ulrike Wiethaus, Wake Forest University, for insights that helped me clarify this point. Gottfried's *Tristan* does not include these parts of the story; although Gottfried narrates the courtship of Tristan and Isolde-White-Hand, his story breaks off before their marriage. See also Brigitte Schöning, "Name ohne Person: Auf den Spuren der Isolde Weißhand," in *Der frauwen buoch: Versuch einer feministischen Mediävistik*, ed. Ingrid Bennewitz, *Göppinger Arbeiten zur Germanistik*, 517 (Göppingen: Kümmerle, 1989), pp. 159–78.

23. See, for example, Peter Stein, "Tristan, "*Epische Stoffe des Mittelalters*, ed. Volker Mertens and Ulrich Müller (Stuttgart: Kröner, 1984), pp. 365–94, here p. 365. Progression toward an ending (toward death), reenters the narrative only with the figure of Isolde-White-Hand.

24. Speaking of Thomas's version, Joan M. Ferrante writes: "The woman Tristan loves incarnates the destructive force of love, the all-consuming passion that excludes any other ties. She unleashes the destructive impulse in him, the death-wish, bringing on the surrender of a noble spirit to a passion that must kill him" (*Woman as Image*, p. 93, n. 2).

25. On medieval magic see Richard Kieckhefer, *Magic in the Middle Ages* (Cambridge: Cambridge University Press, 1990), who notes in passing that "while there is no reason to think that women alone practiced magic, both pagan and Christian writers ascribed it primarily to them" (p. 39). The mother/daughter/magic nexus resurfaces in Kieckhefer's book; see pp. 81–82 and 192. We must be careful, however, not to confuse medieval bias with medieval reality. Kieckhefer reminds us that "a particularly important element in the stereotype of the witch was the centrality of women. . . . This bias may owe something to the role of women as popular healers with herbs and charms, but there is no reason to think that women had a monopoly of these or other forms of magic. . . . Ultimately the vulnerability of women in this context must be seen as a corollary to the precarious position women held in late medieval society (and, for that matter, in almost every society through history)" (pp. 197–98).

26. From *Readings in Medieval History*, ed. Patrick J. Geary (Lewiston, N.Y.: Broadview, 1989) p. 542. (Special thanks to Monica Green, Duke University, for pointing out this passage to me.) Beatrice goes on to explain that she never actually administered the potion because she thought it better to wait until Philippa's marriage had been consummated, and this had not yet taken place when she was arrested.

27. The term "marriage resistance" is borrowed from Adrienne Rich, "Compulsory Heterosexuality and Lesbian Existence," in *The "Signs" Reader: Women, Gender, and Scholarship*, ed. Elizabeth Abel, and Emily K. Abel (Chicago: University of Chicago Press, 1983), pp. 139–68, here p. 157.

FEMALE HEROES, HEROINES, AND COUNTER-HEROES

IMAGES OF WOMEN IN ARTHURIAN TRADITION

Maureen Fries

To discuss images of women in Arthurian tradition raises problems of role-definition. In all early European vernacular literature, as Georges Dumézil and his disciples have shown, male heroic roles fall into well-defined types, drawn from actual male functions in Indo-European society.[1] Such characteristically mimetic functions encompass sovereignty, including the lawgiver and seer; battle, embodied in the warrior; and agriculture, with whose third-function figure Dumézil believes the first two warred, and over whom they achieved a victory. While female figures are sometimes found in the third function, their usual position is vague and contrapuntal—often tripartite, as if they had no permanent home, and identified with evil and the color green, as in the Celtic Otherworld and the Druidic as opposed to the Christian religion.[2] I want here to investigate some women in Arthurian literature, to determine whether such negative images are universal or whether there are other female images—both heroic and positive—to be discovered.

Certainly there were very few heroic role models for females in medieval life: they were only infrequently rulers and forbidden to bear arms or enter the priesthood. Additionally, women bore the burden of numerous negative stereotypes. While some of these predated Christianity (witness Hesiod, Demosthenes, and others of the ancients), the Church added to its Judaic heritage in elaborating upon the supposed universal faults of the daughters of Eve. To all women, philosophers, theologians, moral writers, and even romancers ascribed the sins of Adam's partner: they were said to be weak, vain, lustful, and needful of the guidance and headship of men, who were supposed to curb their pride and insubordination in order to make them pure, humble, and submissive.[3] In real life, however, women sometimes

Reprinted with permission from *Popular Arthurian Traditions*, ed. Sally K. Slocum (Bowling Green, OH: Bowling Green State University, Popular Press, 1992), pp. 5–17.

proved themselves the social equals of men. Eleanor of Aquitaine, married serially to the kings of France and England, ruled more land than either of her husbands. Joan of Arc led armies, shocking the Middle Ages not so much by her mysticism as by cutting off her hair and wearing men's clothes. Margaret Paston defended one of her husband's estates, alone with only nineteen servants for support, against a thousand men for over a day.

While most such women are rarely acknowledged in the public records, they do offer historical images of female heroism. "Female hero" may seem at first a paradoxical term, since we are accustomed by long literary tradition to think of the word "hero" as masculine and the word "heroine" as feminine. Yet a structural analysis of any plot reveals that these are, in essence, functional terms: that is, they operate in character slots determined by the significance of actions to the narrative as a whole. A heroine is thus recognizable by her performance of a traditionally identified, female sex-role. But any woman who by choice, by circumstance, or even by accident, escapes definition exclusively in terms of such a traditional role is capable of heroism, as opposed to heroinism. Even in literature, men are not the only world-changers, nor women only their helpers: Antigone is there, and Alice in Wonderland, and Jane Eyre. All three of these—and others—assume the usual male role of exploring the unknown beyond their assigned place in society; and all three reject to various degrees the usual female role of preserving order (principally by forgoing adventure to stay at home). The adventurous paths Antigone, Alice, and Jane choose require the males who surround them to fill subordinate, non-protagonist roles in their stories.

Such female protagonists fit various critics' definitions of the hero. In Northrup Frye's term, they are superior in degree to other men (*Anatomy* 33: the terminology is Frye's). Even more aptly, they fill Joseph Campbell's formulation of the hero as "the man or woman who has been able to battle past his personal and local historical limitations to the . . . primary springs of human life and thought" (*Hero* 20). In their most complete quests, such female heroes, like their male counterparts, are able to undertake journeys to knowledge in which encounters with that which is Other lead ultimately to the decisive encounter with the Self. If completely successful, female (like male) heroes return to their original societies with the prized gift of renewal.

Heroines neither venture forth nor return. They are not knowers but—in Campbell's phrase—"what can be known" (116). The heroine "lures," "guides," and "bids [the hero] burst his fetters"; if he can "take her as she is . . . with the kindness and assurance she requires," he "is potentially the king, the incarnate god of her created worlds" (116). The heroine is Snow White or Sleeping Beauty; she is Andrew Marvell's Coy Mistress;

she is (after the fact) William Faulkner's Emily. If the rose is so often her icon, it is because her greatest virtue is her beauty. And her most desired end is marriage, the target for which that beauty is poised.

Marriage is either absent from, or (at most) incidental to, the literary career of the counter-hero. About a decade ago I defined this type for Arthurian males ("Malory's Tristram"). I want now to redefine it for Arthurian females. Characteristically, the counter-hero possesses the hero's superior power of action without possessing his or her adherence to the dominant culture or capability of renewing its values. While the hero proper transcends and yet respects the norms of the patriarchy, the counter-hero violates them in some way. For the male Arthurian counter-hero, such violation usually entails wrongful force; for the female, usually powers of magic. The counter-hero is the Witch in *Hansel and Gretel*; she is Keats's Belle Dame Sans Merci; she is Becky Sharp, in the novel Thackeray proclaimed was without a hero. Always she is preternaturally alluring, or preternaturally repelling or sometimes both, as in Chaucer's *Wife of Bath's Tale*. But her putative beauty does not as a rule complete the hero's valor, as does the heroine's. Rather, it often threatens to destroy him, because of her refusal of the usual female role.

And more: she does not fight like a man. Male roles corresponding to the Indo-European heroic functions are easy to identify in Arthurian literature: Arthur enacts the king; Merlin, the seer; and Gawain, Lancelot and others, the warrior. But female roles are more fluid and far more ambivalent. Arthurian women are essentially ancillary to the male actors of that literary tradition and must therefore be considered in relation to the male heroic roles they complement or defy: as heroine, female hero or counter-hero. As the heroine represents the most culturally familiar of these female presences, at her (to paraphrase Chaucer in the *General Prologue)* I will begin.

I

The first and most perdurable heroine of Arthurian literature is Guinevere. While she appears by name in fragmentary Welsh writings of uncertain date, such as the triads, her first important role is in the Arthurian section of Geoffrey of Monmouth's twelfth-century *History of the Kings of Britain*. Geoffrey used the fluid medieval genre of *historia*, with its allowance for more invention than would later be decorous, to tell the story of Arthur's marriage. Guinevere, descended from a noble Roman family, is the most beautiful woman "in the entire island" (221). This heroine's beauty and aristocracy are initially seen as an impetus to virtue. At Arthur's recrowning at Caerleon, Guinevere keeps separate but equal status to her husband's, as they banquet in sex-specific groups, the King with his knights and the Queen with her ladies (presumably to emphasize chastity). The Arthurian women attending Guinevere "scorned to give their love to any man who had not proved himself three times in battle. In this way the womenfolk became chaste and more virtuous and for their love the knights were ever more daring" (229). In the mock war of the first Arthurian tournaments, the ladies further arouse their knights to that valor necessary to the achievement and maintenance of their honor.

But honor begins a decline as Arthur decides to wage an offensive war on Rome and appoints his Queen and his nephew, Modred, as co-regents. This precaution, in which the queenship has its Celtic significance of sovereignty and the male co-rule its Pauline significance of protection against womanly weakness, comes to naught. "The news was brought to [Arthur] that his nephew, Modred, in whose care he had left Britain, had placed the crown upon his own head . . . [and] was living adulterously and out of wedlock with Queen Guinevere, who had broken the vows of her earlier marriages" (257).

This social, nuptial and feudal fraud—at the same time incest, bigamy and treason—repeats at a deeper structural level Uther's earlier adultery with Arthur's mother, Ygerna, and is a reminder of Original Sin with its consequences for all fallen human nature. It negates the virtue of Guinevere, Arthur's prime personal and social emblem of control of self and others. Modred, as king's sister's son, a shadow side of Arthur he has overlooked at his peril (Garbaty), is the first of several subsequent antagonists to the King who seize the Queen. Guinevere is here, and is to remain, the instrument around whom the action turns, the other seducers and/or abductors bearing different names but a like function to Modred. That Geoffrey's Guinevere ends her life as a nun vowed to chastity at Caerleon, the scene of her co-coronation with Arthur, indicates her conformation to the heroine's role as reflector of the male hero's values. The performance of penitence for oneself and/or as surrogate for a male was a function of the female in romance as it was in real life.[4]

Such penitence seems to disappear from Guinevere's next appearance as heroine in the twelfth-century *Lancelot* of Chrétien de Troyes. The original role of lover/abductor assigned to Modred is here divided, more or less permanently (an exception being the fourteenth-century *Alliterative Morte Arthure*). To Lancelot falls the function of amorous rescuer, and to a new character, Meleaganz, that of usurper of husbandly prerogatives. In the *Lancelot,* Guinevere would at first appear to be the dominant character, especially in terms of the doctrine of courtly love which informs the romance. His horse killed beneath him, Lancelot mounts near the beginning of the tale a shameful cart because of his eagerness to see the queen; faints upon finding Guinevere's comb, complete with a few strands of her golden hair; pretends to lose his first battle with Meleaganz when the Queen commands him to; and—at a later tournament—begins to win at a similar command. Additionally, he patiently suffers her rejection (because of his hesitation in mounting the cart), attempts suicide at a false report of her death, and breaks through iron bars at her invitation to lovemaking. *Frauendienst*, with its doctrine of womanly superiority, seems to inform the story.

But only on its surface, as further analysis discloses. Romance, as a depiction of the warrior class's idealization of itself, actually centers upon male heroes and not female love-objects. As was consistent with medieval religious, political and moral theories, men are the agents of the action and women—when they are heroines—the instruments. On the level of deep structure, Lancelot glorifies himself in his campaign to save the Queen. Guinevere exists, like other heroines of Arthurian and other romance, to get into trouble the hero must get her out of. The incentive to heroic action, she is at the same time its reward. Functionally, Guinevere is unable to act on her own. She is carried off and imprisoned; fought for and defended; freed and returned home; and fought for again: all at the will of and/or agreement between the males in the tale.

Romance females are patriarchally predicated by passive verbs; to romance males belong the active ones. In the course of Chrétien's romance, Lancelot successfully suffers and survives a death-dealing bed and a lethal sword bridge; defeats various minor knights and succors various minor ladies; lifts a symbolic tombstone to free Arthur's imprisoned subjects, whom he later releases again; attracts admiring younger knights; breaks iron bars to join the Queen; escapes from an inescapable tower. And these are but a sample of his deeds, which climax in his joyous welcome by Arthur and his court after he finally dispatches the abductor Meleaganz. Chrétien's narrative is obviously not *about* Guinevere, no matter how much she is its heroine: it is *about* Lancelot.

To ramify the portrait of Arthurian heroinehood, Guinevere may profitably be compared to two others of Chrétien's characters, Laudine and Enide. Of all Arthurian women, Laudine is the most bound into patriarchal custom. Her fate is tied to the magic fountain which is the heart of her patrimony. Once Yvain kills her husband, Esclados, she is obliged to find another defender for the fountain, to protect her land, since she—as a woman—is forbidden to bear arms. Through the schemes of her damsel,

Lunete (of whom more under the rubric of female hero), she is brought to rationalize her hate for Yvain into a love which allows her acceptance of him as a new husband/fountain-defender.

Like the initial Guinevere, Laudine serves as a pivot for Yvain's growth in knightly prowess. Warned by Gawain of the dangers of uxoriousness, he receives permission from his spouse to renew his skill at arms, for the space of one year. Overstaying his leave, Yvain is publicly rebuked by Laudine's free-roaming damsel (note: not by his wife herself, since she is bound to the patriarchal fountain). The rebuke drives him mad—in Arthurian romance, a cipher for the recognition of sexual transgression (Doob). Cured and aided by a wonderful lion, he performs various deeds of knightly valor, particularly in service to ladies and including Lunete, who again reconciles him to Laudine.

If Laudine represents the ultimate Arthurian heroine, in her extreme passivity and submission to patriarchal custom, then Enide—the only female character in Chrétien whose name is usually linked to her hero's as the title of a romance—is an anomaly: the only heroine who, for part of her story, is also a female hero. The dialectic of this essay requires me to consider the earlier part of Enide's career separately from the later, to which I turn in my next section.

As heroine, Enide seems at first even more archetypal than Laudine. Not a great lady like the latter and Guinevere, she is so genteelly, Cinderella-ish poor that Erec first sees her in a garment full of holes. Nor is her name ever given until she marries Erec—not unusual for medieval romance, in which so many women are known merely as someone's wife or lover,[5] and certainly an indication of her status as instrument of Erec's glorious career. Yet, once married, she displays the same spurious power as Chrétien's other heroines, as Erec—in an opposite and complementary movement to Yvain's— falls into an uxoriousness so prolonged that his father's whole court talks of it. Only when he hears Enide blaming herself for his falling away from knightly activity does Erec take the decisive action which is to turn the character I will designate as Enide I—a heroine—at least temporarily into Enide II—a hero.

But before turning to Enide II's heroic career, let me catalog the characteristics of the Arthurian heroine. Whether the archetypal Guinevere, or Laudine, or Enide I, she is an instrument and not an agent: the still point around which the real action (of the male universe) turns. Her virtues are those universally recommended to medieval women in real life: chastity, obedience, silence (one does well to remember that Enide's troubles as a heroine begin when she speaks too openly). Her chief virtue, however, is always her beauty, the prime impelling force behind her hero's activity. In the case of Chrétien's Guinevere, it is more important than any real virtue and even supersedes the usually important one of chastity. For Chrétien never condemns the adultery of Lancelot and Guinevere. In a romance world where the hero's virtue depended so much upon amorous encouragement from the heroine, a monogamous relationship accompanied by infrequent sexual consummation sufficed as well as marriage (Lanham *passim*). With the female hero, however, absolute chastity seems necessary, and her relationship with the male hero is quite another matter. To this matter I now turn.

II

Female heroes in Arthurian romance fall into two sub-types: the wife-hero, and the virgin. The former role is self-evident, the latter perhaps needs clarification. By "virgin" both I and Arthurian romance understand a woman living with no permanent attachment to a man, and to some extent with a man's freedom of action (as in the original meaning of the word). Arthurian virgin-heroes remain single, at least for the duration of their capacity for heroic action. But, like Arthurian heroines and wife-heroes, they nevertheless share the prime function of devoted service to patriarchal culture.

Arthurian wife-heroes, on the other hand, never play a consistently heroic role in romance. The wife's social definition as *femme couverte*—the legal term for the married woman's identity as a chattel of her husband—allows her only intermittent access to those activities ordinarily (and "properly") associated with males. The most interesting of all such wife-heroes is the character I have designated Enide II.

I left off my discussion of Enide I at the point when she woke her husband with what she thought was a private lament. Her exaggeration of her own responsibility for what is—after all—Erec's choice of uxoriousness focuses attention upon the distinction her beauty brings to her heroinehood. But her self-accusation is also a blaming of that husband who is so attached to that beauty; and Erec's self-pride in his knightly honor is wounded by it. To Erec her remarks indicate that Enide as well as the world has underestimated him, and that therefore she does not love him enough. His subsequent trial of Enide not only matures her and his characters and restores their mutual love but also—and more to my present purpose—turns Enide for a time into a wife-hero.

Enide II's actions during this part of the romance are certainly not the "purgatory of obedience" Jean Frappier has denominated them (72) but rather a loyal and loving *dis*obedience, as well as an assertion of real female prowess. Commanded to wear her best dress (in contrast to her earlier rags) and ride forth with her husband, alone, and—most important—to say no word under any circumstances without his permission, Enide proves her affection and good judgment by defying the medieval wife's expected submission to the male command. In repeated though forbidden speech, she warns Erec of danger and treachery, allowing him to conquer numerous robber knights, two lecherous counts who covet her love, and a dwarf knight who becomes her and Erec's useful friend. Enide further performs incidental, nonheroinic actions such as watching their horses while her husband sleeps and subsisting like a male in the forest, without the lady's usually requisite servants. Impressed by such heroism, Erec assures her he now knows her love is perfect. But his kiss turns her again, as in the archetypal fairy tale, into a heroine. Forsaking heroic action, Enide assumes once more the female roles of nurse and admired beauty—a beauty she had lost while playing the hero. Adventures continue, but henceforth only for Erec.

Like Enide, Guinevere in later versions of her story evinces incidental heroism. Wherever Lancelot and not Modred is her lover, she resists her nephew's attempted incest. In the thirteenth-century *Mort Artu,* the fourteenth-century *Stanzaic Morte Arthur* and Malory's fifteenth-century *Morte Darthur,* Guinevere outwits Modred with the excuse that she must go to London to ready her trousseau; then she seizes the White Tower and holds it successfully against her would-be spouse. Grail-influenced works with their repeated motif of repentance from worldly values also allow for an incidentally heroic Guinevere. In both the *Stanzaic Morte* and Malory, Guinevere's taking of the veil emerges even more specifically than in Geoffrey of Monmouth as a rejection of the worldly heroine's role: Guinevere refuses Lancelot's love in an attempt at salvation for them both. Her spurning of his offer of marriage and even of a final kiss casts her into a heroic mold, but it is a male-inspired one: that of the repentant worldly woman, on the model of Mary Magdalene, Mary of Egypt and other formerly sexual females. As with Enide, this version of Guinevere is at best only partially heroic.

In Arthurian romance, only women who are not married are capable of consistent heroism. These virgins escape male domination and, for a time at least, actualize their title by acting the man. An ancient archetype influencing this model is that of the huntress goddess Artemis/Diana, whose very occupation implies freedom from women's usual social bonds—especially from the house, symbolic of woman's role as keeper of the patriarchal flame. Thus such Arthurian women are frequently connected with both the forest and the moon.

The moon gives her very name to Chrétien's Lunete, the first of the virgin-heroes in Arthurian literature. Like the goddess who stands behind her, she possesses magic powers: her initial gift of a magic ring to Yvain makes him invisible to his pursuers and enables his subsequent success. Additionally, Lunete displays the wit which will come to distinguish Arthurian female heroes—she not only talks her mistress, the heroine Laudine, into marrying Yvain but, at the end of the romance and with similar guile, successfully reconciles husband and wife. Part of Lunete's persuasion of Laudine to marriage is an alleged letter from a certain *Damsel Sauvage*—obviously a counterfeit and covert reference to Lunete's own unbound and comparatively powerful, undomesticated presence. Active where Laudine is passive, she manipulates not only her mistress but Yvain himself. Her freedom emerges also in her physical mobility; at will she is able to leave the fountain to which the patriarchally predicated Laudine is bound. At one point Chrétien even calls her *maistre,* a rare designation—with its connotation of both skill and learning—for a woman during the Middle Ages. In spite of this preternatural cleverness, Lunete is loyal both to Laudine and Yvain. Only when she is condemned to the stake for treason can Yvain aid her as much as she does him, since she is precluded from waging trial by combat (a perquisite of the warrior class).

That combat can nevertheless be mounted in distinctively feminine ways is proved not only by Lunete but by another female character, Malory's Lyonet (the similarity in names is probably no accident). Attached like Lunete to a great lady, in this case her sister, Lyonesse, Lyonet comes to Arthur's court (the mobile virgin as compared to the static lady) to ask him to send her sister relief from a siege by an unwanted suitor. Given Gareth, Arthur's disguised nephew, as a champion, Lyonet derides him for having spent a year (his deliberate choice) as Arthur's kitchen boy. Her sustained scorn spurs Gareth to numerous victories and eventually to marriage with Lyonesse. Like Lunete, Lyonet uses both verbal guile and magic—the latter to ensure the young couple's chastity—as weapons. But, at the end of Gareth's tale, she is wed to his brother Gaheris. Malory's comment here, that she "*was* called *damsel sauvage*" (1:363, italics mine), is both an echo of Lunete's appellation and a reminder that she will be tamed by marriage—as Lunete, at least within Chrétien's tale, was not. Even virgin-heroes have their limits, Lunete in her inability to defend herself against the treason charge, Lyonet in her ultimate fate as a *femme couverte.*

But if they are not as free as males, and also few in number, virgin-heroes have for a time—unlike heroines—the power to change their environments. In their fruitful use of tongue and wit, they resemble the sometime wife-heroes; in their (however limited) magical powers and their mobility, the female counter-heroes. But these latter—the freest, most potent and most feared of Arthurian women—deserve a discussion all their own.

III

Like the heroine, the female hero, whether virgin or wife, exists to encourage male prowess: her agency is "selfless" in that it exists for patriarchal—male rather than female—purposes. Contrariwise, the female counter-hero holds values which are not necessarily those of the male culture in which she must exist. Her actions are as likely to hurt the hero as to help him. Rather than only occasionally exhibiting powers greater than most women, like the female hero the counter-hero consistently fills roles ordinarily attributable only to men.

Such female power, like the female virgin-hero's, has its roots in a mythological archetype. If the virgin-hero is an avatar of Artemis, the female counter-hero derives from a much more powerful figure, the Magna Dea, the Great Mother whose religious worship the early Christian hierarchy found so dangerous that it tolerated, and eventually encouraged, the cult of the Blessed Virgin Mary as a counterbalance. The Arthurian female counter-hero is a fluid figure, always at least double and usually multiple in her manifestations. She appears—as Campbell notes of her mythological forebears—under "a multitude of guises," serving both as "mother of life" and "at the same time mother of death" (302–03).

Her sexually-initiated status is her hallmark: I know of no Arthurian counter-hero who is maiden. Even in marriage, she exhibits an indifference to patriarchal values and a sexual freedom unknown and unknowable to the female hero or the monogamous heroine. Her double nature as nurturer and destroyer illustrates even more aptly than the figures of heroine or female hero the ambiguity and ambivalence of medieval male authors generally, and Arthurian writers particularly, toward women. Thus she can be at the same time the most alluring of presences (her aspect as supernatural beauty) and the most revolting (her aspect as hag).

Both alluring beauty and loathsome haghood appear in the most influential Arthurian female counter-hero, Morgan le Fay. More beneficent splittings-off from her original role emerge in the several Ladies of the Lake who later develop from her archetype: literally watered-down from Morgan (whose name indicates her origins in the greater body of water, the sea), they exhibit that tenet of medieval misogyny which held that no woman should be as strong as a man, or *could* be without some supernatural power. In Morgan's movement as a character in Arthurian tradition emerges such misogyny at work, as she develops from an entirely wholesome into a mainly maleficent presence.

Her literal wholesomeness marks her first literary appearance in Geoffrey of Monmouth's *Vita Merlini* where—not yet Arthur's sister—she performs the office of carrying the dying King to Avalon for healing. As objective correlative to this nurturing function stands the nourishing ambience of her *insula pomorum*. A typical Celtic Otherworld, it is free from death, full of earthly delights, and inhabited by women who—in contrast to the patriarchal actuality of the real world—are its absolute rulers. This second Eden thrives under the reign of Morgan herself—beautiful, a shapeshifter who can change her appearance at will, and learned not only in the healing medicine she hopes to use on Arthur but in such recondite studies as astrology.

This portrait of Morgan as a lovely, learned and potent woman changes early in Arthurian tradition. Incidentally a healer in Chrétien, she acquires (in *Erec*) a lover, Guiomar, upon which liaison the worldly poet makes no comment. In the thirteenth-century Prose *Lancelot*, however, Guiomar becomes Guinevere's cousin and his affair with Morgan a source of shame to them both—and to Arthur, since Morgan is now his sister. Renounced by Guiomar at Guinevere's instigation, an embittered Morgan bears her lover's son after exile from the court. In an obvious quest for power over those who have hurt her, she seeks out Merlin, who also loves her, to teach her many enchantments. In a later work, the *Livre d'Artus,* she uses this newly-learned skill to found her *val sanz retour*, to keep Guiomar in her power and—with the valley's capacity for preventing, through a magic curtain of air, the escape of any knight who enters it—to foil Guinevere and Arthur by entrapping Round Table adventurers. This character elaboration, incidentally coinciding with the growth of women-hatred in the latter Middle Ages (Heer, ch. 13), turns Morgan from a nurturing ruler of a sea-girt paradise into a destructive sorceress who entraps men sexually rather than healing them.

Not only Morgan's healing powers are transformed: even her beauty is put in question. In the Prose *Lancelot,* while her loveliness is praised, she is also seen as ugly, hot (the bodily quality medievals associated with sexuality) and lecherous. To this portrait the Vulgate *Merlin* adds that she was very brown of face. Morgan thus diverges from the pink-and-white complexion and golden hair of the heroine (Harris). Since physical beauty is a coefficient of moral goodness in medieval literature, her darkness emerges as spiritual as well as corporeal. In the *Suite du Merlin,* she is said to have acquired permanent ugliness after yielding to lechery and the devil. In versions influenced by this idea of her ugliness, only through enchantment could she appear beautiful. Such a formulation is clearly an echo of the widespread medieval theological perception of the beautiful woman as the Devil in drag.

Many of these negative themes of hypersexuality, misused power and ugliness masquerading as beauty are summed up in Morgan's appearance in the fourteenth-century English poem, *Sir Gawain and the Green Knight*. Here, the Fay is a repulsive old crone who manipulates the lovely young Lady Bertilak and her husband in an attempted seduction of Gawain, who represents the entire Arthurian ethos. At the end of the poem, Bertilak reveals Morgan's role to Gawain, who (not without blemish) has survived the double beheading and triple hunting/boudoir tests, as an attempted blow against Guinevere. Female counter-heroes are often as much counter to heroines as to male heroes.

Even when married, Morgan refuses male values. While she has variously named husbands in various Arthurian works, her most persistent spouse is Urien, and Yvain becomes their son. But marriage cannot tame her voracious sexual appetite. Taking a lover, Accolon, she gives him Arthur's sword and its even more powerful sheath (it prevents bleeding to death) after having promised her brother to keep it safe. Arthur's regaining of the sword and slaying of Accolon motivate Morgan to even further dirty work against the Round Table. With various other sorceress-queens who serve as narrative doubles to her personality (in Malory three others), she abducts Lancelot in an attempt to seduce him. She also abducts and vamps Alexander le Orphelin, a Cornish hero who, in Malory's version of his adventures, vows to cut off his testicles rather than sleep with her. Adultery is compounded by her plot to kill Urien, prevented only by the intervention of Yvain.

In spite of this murderous and adulterous career, Morgan retains her nurturing function as Arthur's conductress to Avalon after his wounding. But this "good" Morgan is overshadowed by the ubiquitous "bad" woman. She is the most extreme villain of Arthurian romance—even worse than the infamous Sir Breunz sans Pitié. Her gradual change (one can hardly call it growth) from a connector of life with healing, as mistress of Avalon, into a connector of death with illicit sex indicates the inability of male Arthurian authors to cope with the image of a woman of power in positive terms.

Reduction of that power seems to have influenced the later development of the various Ladies of the Lake—also counter-heroes but less strong and much more beneficent than Morgan. The original of these is the great ruler of a sea-kingdom—like Morgan's, a watery version of the Celtic Underworld—who kidnaps the baby Lancelot and rears him among her ten thousand maidens. Taught courtesy, valor, music, and simple, non-knightly combat, Lancelot is sent—at fifteen—to conquer the enemy of the Lady's cowardly son (the purpose of his abduction and fosterage). In terms of the male ethic which governs romance, the Lady's purpose is selfish—not the furtherance of the knight's own career, but a settling of her private grudge, as with Morgan's ultimate manifestations. Unlike Morgan, however, the Lady is eventually refined to the norms of her male culture. In the Prose *Lancelot*, for instance, her purpose alters and her sending Lancelot to Arthur's court to be knighted is its climax. She—or a further avatar (Holbrook)—also gives Arthur Excalibur and, at the end of his career, receives it again from him, besides earlier restoring it to him as he fights Accolon. Obviously the Lady has been retailored to represent the (mostly) nurturing side of the split mother-image, as Morgan has become the (mostly) devouring side.

A combination of these split images appears in the figure of Nimue (also called Niniane and Viviane), who first serves as a devourer and then as a restorer of Arthurian males. Like her sister-avatar, she is called the Lady of the Lake. In a borrowing from Morgan's career, she has the besotted Merlin teach her his magic, but without yielding to him sexually. Shutting Merlin away in a cave, she deprives the male Arthurians of their counselor and reveals her own cunning ambition. But Nimue then becomes the devoted and influential friend of Arthurian society: she saves the King and his knights from Morgan's death-dealing magic mantle; reverses the infatuation of Pelleas and Etard; and, taking Pelleas as her lover, makes him a knight of the Round Table and protects him all his life. Yet even settling down with one man does not hinder her power: she reveals Guinevere's innocence of a murder charge and emerges as one of the three (or nine, depending on the work) queens who bear the King away to Avalon. This last function allies her, of course, with her original—Morgan le Fay.

Whether maleficent like Morgan or (mostly) beneficent like Nimue and the other Ladies of the Lake, all Arthurian female counter-heroes reveal a split tendency. Never completely committed to the knightly ethos which dominates their world, they often act in their own interest instead of the males' (thus differing from the female heroes). Their actions are bold and often sexual. More than the female heroes, they are capable of transforming their environment(s) and doing so for their own benefit. Examined in terms of the prime function of romance as a mirror of the male warrior ideal, these Arthurian women are truly counter-cultural.

IV

And now to sum up. Arthurian heroines are conservative, passive, instrumental non-actors, useful for provoking, renewing and rewarding the actions of their knight-agents. Arthurian female heroes may, indirectly and for a specified time, consciously play female parts to effect transformation of their male-dominant world, but they always act only for knightly benefit. Arthurian female counter-heroes openly refuse to be seen in womanly supportive roles in what is essentially a male drama and attempt to change their woman-hostile world by direct and not indirect action. All of these women, even the comparatively powerful counter-heroes, are limited by their inability to assume such traditional male roles as the warrior one of physical combat. Once, for instance, when Lancelot is wounded with an arrow by a comparatively unimportant *damsel sauvage,* both the Vulgate and Malory make clear that it is only by accident. In place of such usual male roles as warrior and seer, female heroes and counter-heroes must use guile, both verbal and magical. Yet even this does not earn them honor: what is wisdom in the seer is reduced to mere sorcery in his female counterpart. As for heroines, they have only their beauty, a chancy weapon at best.

All three female types hold up a mirror to male social values, not female ones. What goes counter to the predominant and longstanding male-glorifying bias of the tradition, such as the power of the female counter-hero, is seen as subversive. Both society and literature in the Middle Ages so neglected or distorted women's values that female heroes begin as scarce and dwindle practically into non-existence. As Chaucer had his Wife of Bath note, the portrait depends on who paints it, the lion or the man. In medieval Arthurian literature, to make this figure further ironic, the image of the woman is not ever the product of the lioness, but always of the lion.[6]

NOTES

1. Dumézil's ultraproductive corpus spans over half a century, and dozens—probably hundreds—of books and articles. For a convenient summary of his (changing) ideas, see Littleton.

2. See, for example, Dumézil, "Le Trio des Macha." An earlier and differently focused study of female tripartition is Lucy Paton's.

3. For further discussion, see Fries, "Feminae Populi."

4. Perhaps the most vivid enactment of this theme, common in romance as well as in female saint's life, is in the Middle English *Athelston* (ca. 1355–80), where the wife of the Earl of Stane must submit—although pregnant—to ordeal by fire to prove her husband's innocence of treason.

5. An egregious example is the Middle English *Sir Isumbras,* in which an abducted wife survives a forced royal (and bigamous) marriage she insists remain chaste, and makes her original husband a sovereign upon his successor's death—all with no name except "the wife of Sir Isumbras."

6. This paper was presented in a somewhat different form as The Kasling Memorial Lecture for 1985 at the State University of New York College at Fredonia.

WORKS CITED

Athelston. Ed. A. McI. Trounce. EETS 224. London: Oxford, 1951 .

Campbell, Joseph. *The Hero with a Thousand Faces.* 2nd ed. Princeton: Princeton UP, 1968.

Chrétien de Troyes. *Les Romans de Chrétien de Troyes: Erec et Enide, Le Chevalier de la charrete [Lancelot], Le Chevalier au lion [Yvain].* Ed. Mario Roques. Paris: Champion, 1952, 1958, 1960.

Doob, Penelope B. R. *Nebuchadnezzar's Children: Conventions of Madness in Middle English Literature.* New Haven: Yale, 1975.

Dumézil, Georges. "Le trio des Macha." *RHR* 146:5–17.

Frappier, Jean. *Chrétien de Troyes: The Man and His Work.* Trans. Raymond J. Cormier. Athens: U of Ohio P, 1982.

Fries, Maureen. *"Feminae Populi:* Popular Images of Women in Medieval Literature." *Journal of Popular Culture* 14 (1980): 79–86.

———. "Malory's Tristram as Counter-Hero to the *Morte Darthur.*" *NM* 76 (1975): 605–13.

Frye, Northrup. *Anatomy of Criticism: Four Essays.* Princeton: Princeton UP, 1971.

Garbaty, T. A. "The Uncle-Nephew Relationship. Origin and Development." *Folklore* 88 (1977): 221–235.

Geoffrey of Monmouth. *History of the Kings of Britain.* Trans. Lewis Thorpe. London: Penguin, 1966.

———.*Vita Merlini.* Ed. and trans. J. J. Parry. Urbana: U of Illinois P, 1925.

Harris, Adelaide Evans. *The Heroine of the Middle English Romances.* Cleveland: Western Reserve UP, 1969.

Heer, Friedrich. *The Medieval World: Europe 1100–1350.* Trans. Janet Sondheimer. New York: Mentor, 1962.

Holbrook, S. E. "Nymue, the Chief Lady of the Lake, in Malory's *Le Morte Darthur.*" *Speculum* 53 (1978): 761–77.

Lancelot do Lac. Ed. Elspeth Kennedy. 2 vols. Oxford: Clarendon, 1980.

Lanham, Margaret. "Chastity: A Study of Sexual Morality in the English Medieval Romance." Diss. Vanderbilt, 1948.

Littleton, C. Scott. *The New Comparative Mythology: An Anthropological Assessment of the Theories of Georges Dumézil.* Rev. ed. Berkeley: U of Cal. P, 1973.

Livre d'Artus, Le. The Vulgate Version of the Arthurian Romances. Ed. H. Oskar Sommer. 8 vols. Washington: Carnegie Institution, 1908–16. Vol. 7.

Malory, Sir Thomas. *The Works.* Ed. Eugène Vinaver. 3rd ed., rev. P.J.C. Field. Oxford: Clarendon, 1990.

[Estoire de] Merlin. The Vulgate Version of the Arthurian Romances. Ed. H. Oskar Sommer. 8 vols. Washington: Carnegie Institution, 1908–16. Vol. 2.

[Suite du] Merlin. Ed. Gaston Paris and J. Ulrich. 2 vols. Paris: Didot, 1886.

[La] Mort [le roi] Artu. The Vulgate Version of the Arthurian Romances. Ed. H. Oskar Sommer. 8 vols. Washington: Carnegie Institution, 1908–16. Vol. 8.

[Stanzaic] Morte Arthur. Ed. P. F. Hissiger. The Hague: Mouton, 1975.

[Alliterative] Morte Arthure. Ed. Mary Hamel. New York: Garland, 1984.

Paton, Lucy Allen. *Studies in the Fairy Mythology of Arthurian Romance.* 2nd ed. New York: Franklin, 1960.

Sir Gawain and the Green Knight. Ed. J.R.R. Tolkien and E.V. Gordon. 2nd ed., rev. Norman Davis. Oxford: Clarendon, 1967.

Sir Isumbras. The Thornton Romances. Ed. J. O. Halliwell [–Philips]. London: Camden Society, 1844.

STORY, GENDER, AND CULTURE

Leaving Morgan Aside

Women, History, and Revisionism

in *Sir Gawain and the Green Knight*

Sheila Fisher

The anonymous author of *Sir Gawain and the Green Knight* knew how the story would end, both the story of Arthurian history and the story of his own romance. In the end is the beginning, because the end of Arthurian legend in the collapse of the Round Table accounts for the beginning of this poem, for its motivation, its selected and selective emphases, and its design. With a knowledge of the end, the romance focuses on the beginning and on one adventure of one young knight, for this is essentially a poem about beginnings: about the New Year and the first youth of King Arthur; about the young court's solidarity and the first assumption of the pentangle by Gawain.[1] Through its emphasis on beginnings, *Sir Gawain and the Green Knight,* as I will argue in this essay, tries to revise Arthurian history in order to make it come out right. The purpose of this revisionary agenda is nothing less than to demonstrate how the Round Table might have averted its own destruction by adhering to the expectations of masculine behavior inherent in Christian chivalry.

If the end is the beginning, it also serves as the means, the poem's directive for its revisionism. The poem alerts us to the connections between beginnings and ends through the cyclical emphases of its narrative and specifically through the articulations of historical betrayal and of the loss of a civilization that frame the romance: "þe segge and þe asaute watz sesed at Troye" ["Since the siege and the assault was ceased at Troy"] (lines 1 and 2525).[2] Projected onto the Arthurian past, these references to historical gain, loss, and betrayal forecast the Arthurian future. Given these narrative emphases, it is significant that, at the end of the poem, about a hundred lines from the closing reiteration of historical betrayal, we find Morgan le Fay,

Reprinted from *The Passing of Arthur: New Essays in Arthurian Tradition*, ed. Christopher Baswell and William Sharpe (New York: Garland, 1988), pp. 129–51.

who is here not only named for the first (and last) time, but also designated as the generator of the romance, of the complex narrative of Gawain's testing. For Gawain's edification, Bertilak finally reveals Morgan's presence in the plot (and even then, once he has introduced her, it takes him ten lines [2446–55] to get to the point):

> Ho wayned me vpon þis wyse to your wynne halle
> For to assay þe surquidré, ȝif hit soth were
> Þat rennes of þ grete renoun of þe Rounde Table;
> Ho wayned me þis wonder your wyttez to reve,
> For to haf greued Gaynour and gart hir to dyȝe
> With glopnyng of þat ilke gome þat gostlych speked
> With his hede in his honde bifore þe hyȝe table. [2456–62]

> [She guided me in this guise to your glorious hall,
> To assay, if such it were, the surfeit of pride
> That is rumored of the retinue of the Round Table.
> She put this shape upon me to puzzle your wits,
> To afflict the fair queen, and frighten her to death
> With awe of that elvish man that eerily spoke
> With his head in his hand before the high table.]

Morgan's placement is not, as some critics have argued, a flaw in this carefully constructed narrative; it is neither an accident nor an authorial mistake.[3] The poem, as I will argue in this essay, deliberately leaves Morgan aside, positioning her at the end of the narrative when she is, in fact, its means: the agent of Gawain's testing.

Sir Gawain and the Green Knight marginalizes Morgan le Fay because her marginalization is central to its own revision of Arthurian history. If, however, we take our cue from *Sir Gawain and the Green Knight* and re-read the narrative backwards from the perspective of Morgan's agency, we can define the trajectory and the ideology of the poem's revisionism. Morgan and her marginalization are the means to the poem's end, because women are centrally implicated in the collapse of the Round Table and the end of the Arthurian Age. If women could be placed on the periphery, as Morgan is in this poem, then the Round Table might not have fallen. To deny the female would be to save the kingdom, and, in its revisionary agenda, that is precisely what *Sir Gawain and the Green Knight* attempts to do. In the name of a lost but presumably worthy cause, it attempts an uneasy, because necessarily incomplete, erasure of women from the poem. It should not be surprising, after all, that the poet who wrote a Christian dream-vision allegory to offer consolation for the death of a child could write what is, in essence, a political allegory of women's displacement to offer nostalgic consolation for the death of Britain's greatest king.

If Pearl has gone to a New Jerusalem far removed from the transience and decay associated with her death, Arthur and his court, in Fitt I of *Sir Gawain and the Green Knight,* have gone to an old Camelot far removed from the later struggles associated with its own decay and ultimate transience. As one strategy of its revisionism, the poem focuses on a conspicuously youthful court.

> With all þe wele of þe worlde þay woned þer samen,
> Þe most kyd kny3tez vnder Krystes seluen,
> And þe louelokkest ladies þat euer lif haden,
> And he þe comlokest kyng þat þe court haldes;
> For al watz þis fayre folk in hir first age,
> > on sille,
> > Þe hapnest vnder heuen,
> > Kyng hy3est mon of wylle;
> > Hit were now gret nye to neuen
> > So hardy a here on hille. [50–59]

> [In peerless pleasures passed they their days,
> The most noble knights known under Christ,
> And the loveliest ladies that lived on earth ever,
> And the comeliest king, that that court holds,
> For all this fair folk in their first age
> > were still,
> > Happiest of mortal kind,
> > King noblest famed of will;
> > You would now go far to find
> > So hardy a host on hill.]

Although some readers of the romance find Arthur and his retinue more youthful, more "childgered" (86), more "wylde" of "brayn" (89) than they ought to be, still, this is, as other readers have pointed out, a court in its first blush of youth, as green, one might say, as the giant who comes to test its pride.[4] As such, this court is conspicuously removed from later tensions and egoisms, from later intrigue and infighting.[5] It is thus, in the context of its own history, a prelapsarian court. And we see it, significantly enough, in the midst of its celebrations to inaugurate Christmas and the New Year: "Wyle Nw ȝer watz so ȝep þat hit watz nwe cummen" ["While the New Year was new, but yesternight come"] (60). The triple repetition of newness in this one line (that opens the stanza immediately following the long passage quoted above) emphasizes not only the birth of Christ and the rebirth of the year, but the poem's own revisionary regeneration of Arthurian legend.

This revisionary regeneration is a central strategy in the poem's characterization—in what is essentially its rewriting—of Gawain himself. According to one well-known branch of Arthurian legend, the king's nephew is something of a womanizer. Some critics, in fact, have suggested that *Sir Gawain and the Green Knight* actually plays with this aspect of its hero's reputation by making him confront it at Morgan's castle.[6] Another way of putting this would be to say that here the sins that Gawain has not yet committed come back to haunt him. In Fitt III, Gawain stands accused of being someone he knows nothing about, to the point that both he and the Lady will agree, with some justice, that he is not Gawain (1292–93).[7] For the poem does not want its audience to believe that this is the old Gawain either. Were the hero of this romance the womanizer of legend, the problem of the pentangle's appropriateness to him and the challenge in the bedroom would both be, quite obviously, somewhat beside the point, mysteries resolved for the audience by Gawain's reputation before Gawain ever mounts Gringolet or the Lady ever mounts her assault.

If the poem's revisionary agenda is evident in the initial description of Arthur's court, the portrait of Guenevere in Fitt I both emphasizes this agenda and indicates the ways in which the positionings of women are central to it. Indeed, one of the most conspicuous signals of the work's agenda is its rehabilitation of Guenevere. Guenevere and her betrayals of her king are, of course, notorious in the dissolution of the Round Table; she is most famous, in other words, for her association with the end. In *Sir Gawain and the Green Knight,* however, Guenevere is most prominent at the beginning. There are, in fact, few subsequent references to her in the poem: we are told that she sits near (the similarly rehabilitated) Gawain at the New Year's feast (109); Arthur bids her not to be bothered by the Green Knight's talking head (470–73); we later learn that she is not so beautiful as the Lady (945). The last reference to her in the poem is the most telling, for, as Bertilak informs Gawain, the third of Morgan's motives for sending him on his mission as the Green Knight was

> For to haf greued Gaynour and gart hir to dyȝe
> With glopnyng of þat ilke gome þat gostlych speked
> With his hede in his honde bifore þe hyȝe table. [2460–62]

[To afflict the fair queen, and frighten her to death
With awe of that elvish man that eerily spoke
With his head in his hand before the high table.]

If Morgan had had her way, then, the beginning of the poem would be the end of the queen. Yet, by the time this plot against Guenevere has been revealed, it has been delayed so long, both within the narrative and within Bertilak's list of Morgan's motivations, that it seems somewhat beside the point. Had Morgan been successful, however, she might, some would argue, have done her half-brother something of a favor.

With the end of its story and of Arthurian history in view, the poem can figuratively if not literally accomplish Morgan's wishes. As she is portrayed in Fitt I, Guenevere, in one sense, could not be more dead than she already is. In her most detailed appearance in *Sir Gawain and the Green Knight,* she is utterly static. She does not speak (here or elsewhere in the poem). She simply sits and looks, and, perhaps more importantly, she is looked upon.

> Whene Guenore, ful gay, gray þed in þe myddes,
> Dressed on þe dere des, dubbed al aboute,
> Smal sendal bisides, a selure hir ouer
> Of tryed tolouse, of tars tapites innoghe,
> Þat were enbrawded and beten wyth þe best gemmes
> Þat myȝt be preued of prys wyth penyes to bye,
>> in daye.
>>> Þe comlokest to discrye
>>> Þer glent with ȝen gray,
>>> A semloker þat euer he syȝe
>>> Soth moȝt no man say. [74–84]

[Guenevere the goodly queen gay in the midst
On a dais well-decked and duly arrayed
With costly silk curtains, a canopy over,
Of Toulouse and Turkestan tapestries rich,
All broidered and bordered with the best gems
Ever brought into Britain, with bright pennies
to pay.
Fair queen, without a flaw,
She glanced with eyes of gray.
A seemlier that once he saw,
In truth no man could say.]

As the syntactical circlings of this passage show, it is difficult to distinguish Guenevere and her worth from that of her splendid accoutrements. This is Guenevere fresh from the marriage settlement in which she, like most historical medieval women of her class, has been bought.[8] This is Guenevere set at the high table for all to admire, a token of Arthur's wealth, still the chaste queen who is the sign and symbol of the king to whom she refers. Her rehabilitation according to the revisionist directive of *Sir Gawain and the Green Knight* is inscribed in her stasis, in her function as the emblem of Arthur. Because she seems incapable of movement, she seems incapable of the specific movement that would lead her to a treacherous union with Lancelot.

Not moving or speaking, Guenevere here is marginalized to such an extent that she is buried in the plot of the poem.[9] For, if there is never just one margin, there is never just one way to be marginalized. Morgan le Fay is marginalized within the narrative by being placed at the end of the poem. But the poem marginalizes and thereby rehabilitates Guenevere by displaying her at the beginning of its own story, as a token of Arthur, and dissociating her from the end, where, as Morgan le Fay attempts to do in this romance, she will become the agent of his destruction. It is significant, however, that the initial description of Guenevere is placed as close to the opening mention of historical betrayal as Morgan's agency is placed to the closing repetition of "þe segge and þe asaute . . . at Troye." And it is significant, too, that when Guenevere *is* mentioned at the end of *Sir Gawain and the Green Knight,* a desire for her death as well as her own capacity for destruction are projected on to the single figure of Morgan le Fay.

Guenevere and Morgan may be marginalized in very different ways at the beginning and end of the poem, but there is always, of course, the Lady in the middle. In a romance that makes much of beginnings and ends because it is concerned with the end of beginnings, the Lady's placement squarely at the poem's center is significant for many reasons. If Morgan is the means to the end of trying young Gawain (and, by extension, the pride of the Round Table), then the Lady is a stand-in for Morgan, in the middle, literally and figuratively, as Morgan's intermediary, despite Bertilak's rather suspicious attempt in Fitt IV to claim her as *his* agent.[10] Bertilak tells Gawain:

> Now know I wel þy cosses, and þy costes als,
> And þe wowyng of my wyf; I wro3t hit myseluen.
> I sende hir to asay þe. . . . [2360–62]

[I know well the tale,
And the count of your kisses and your conduct too,
And the wooing of my wife—it was all my scheme!]

Although sex with her may temporarily seem an end in itself, it is, or would
be, a means to the end of trying young Gawain. Moreover, it is no accident
that one of the few references to Guenevere comes when Gawain sees the
Lady for the first time:

> Ho watz þe fayrest in felle, of flesche and of lyre,
> And of compas and colour and costes, of alle o þer,
> And wener þen Wenore, as þe wyȝe þoȝt.
> He ches þurȝ þe chaunsel to cheryche þat hende.
> An o þer lady hir lad bi þe lyft honde,
> Þat watz alder þen ho, an auncian hit semed. . . . [943–48]

> [The fair hues of her flesh, her face and her hair
> And her body and her bearing were beyond praise,
> And excelled the queen herself, as Sir Gawain thought.
> He goes forth to greet her with gracious intent;
> Another lady led her by the left hand
> That was older than she—an ancient, it seemed. . . .]

This reference to Guenevere is not simply a conventional aesthetic observation.[11] As the construction of this passage shows, it serves to underline
the Lady's placement between two marginalized females, Morgan and
Guenevere, because she, the woman textually and sexually in the middle, is
the common denominator between them.

If the Lady is the common denominator between these two female
characters, what she denominates is, in essence, femaleness itself. Nor is this
definition of the Lady so obvious, nor so reductive, as it would at first seem.
And while it may seem strange to make much of Morgan's marginalization
when the Lady is at the center of the poem, it is the nature of the femaleness ascribed to and designated by the Lady, and shared by both Guenevere
and Morgan, that needs marginalizing if *Sir Gawain and the Green Knight*
is to succeed in its Christian chivalric revision of Arthurian history. For, rather
than contradicting the poem's agenda of leaving the female aside, the centrality of the Lady works to underline the poem's purpose. Situated as she
is between Guenevere in Fitt I and Morgan in Fitt IV, the Lady is, as Gilbert
and Gubar would define it, "framed" within the poem.[12] That is, she is both

enclosed and "set up," as it were, in the poem's effort to contain and delimit her meaning. The Lady is contained and redefined in the text so that Gawain can be reintegrated, green girdle and all, into the reconstituted court at Camelot.

Indeed, containment, it seems, is the essence of the Lady who is always situated within and associated with enclosed and private spaces. We see the Lady first entering the closet in which she hears Mass on the first day of Gawain's stay in the castle: "Þe lorde loutes þerto, and þe lady als, / Into a cumly closet coyntly ho entrez" ["The lord attends alone: his fair lady sits / In a comely closet, secluded from sight"] (933–34). The poet's choice of the adverb "coyntly" to describe her entrance into the private space of the closet suggests to readers of Chaucer the famous pun on "queynte" as female genitalia, which marks the Wife of Bath's characterization of herself in her prologue.[13] Interestingly, Gawain repeats this adverb again at the beginning of his anti-feminist diatribe: "Þus hor knyȝt wyth hor kest han *koyntly* bigyled" ["They have trapped their true knight in their trammels so quaint"] (2412; emphasis mine). When the Lady emerges from the closet, with her retinue of ladies and with Morgan le Fay some eight lines later, one hardly needs to invoke Freud to catch the associations with female sexuality that the poem is making. And, of course, the Lady's most famous activities within private enclosed spaces occur not merely in Gawain's bedroom, but inside the curtains of Gawain's bed: "and ho stepped stilly and stel to his bedde, / Kest up þe cortyn and creped withinne" ["And she stepped stealthily, and stole to his bed, / Cast aside the curtain and came within"] (1191–92).

The Lady, it might seem, can exercise considerable power even within such containment. But the containment of the Lady within the castle or the closet or the bedroom echoes her containment within the text, a containment that, while it places the Lady at the center, simultaneously underlines her marginalization. She is, as we will see, placed at the center in order to be displaced from it. And it is here that, in order to accomplish its revision of Arthurian legend, the poem takes as its model late medieval social and legal history. For, like her historical counterpart, the medieval noblewoman, the Lady is contained within the castle in order, finally, to be marginalized within aristocratic society.[14] She is so marginalized, in fact, that a poem that names everything, including Gawain's horse Gringolet, never names her. She has no ostensible existence outside the castle walls unless a man chooses to name her (Bertilak generally calls her "myn owen wyf" [2359] or "my wyf" [2361] as if to underline his ownership; Gawain mentions her as little as he can [2497]). She is simply the Lady. That is all there is to know and all we need to know.[15]

Contained as she is within the castle and the poem, the Lady and the femaleness she shares with Guenevere and Morgan become fundamentally associated with privateness. The Lady is associated with privateness because that is the realm she inhabits. But she is so thoroughly associated with privateness that privateness itself becomes feminized in *Sir Gawain and the Green Knight*. Certainly, her privateness is linked to female sexuality, as the possible pun on "coyntly" suggests. The dangers associated with the Lady, the threat she poses to Gawain's life, may ultimately derive from this source and from the poem's inscription of the otherness of female sexuality according to the time-honored tradition of medieval misogyny.[16] But *Sir Gawain and the Green Knight* goes even farther, I believe, in order to suggest the political and social implications of the female's privateness and the fundamental disruptiveness attributed to the female and to the values associated with her in this poem. For it is through the redefinition of this privateness and of the emblematic girdle that the poem accomplishes its revision of Arthurian legend and provides a model of masculine behavior by which the Round Table might have been saved.

As the course of Arthurian history and of chivalric literature makes clear, trouble arises when the knight withdraws from public life to fulfill private desire, when the knight yields to private desire at the expense of public function. And Gawain, with his pentangle and armor locked away somewhere in one of this castle's many private rooms, is in such a precarious situation from the moment that he enters Morgan's castle in Fitt II. The plot of the romance has relegated him to privateness to test how he fares there, for the temptations posed by private desire are essentially the ones that Gawain must overcome both to save his life and to ensure the preservation and continuation of the Arthurian world.[17]

Gawain, in assuming the Green Knight's challenge at Camelot, has ceased to be a private individual. He has assumed the responsibility of acting as a token of Arthur's fame and reputation. In this capacity, he has no room for private desires, or at the very least, his private desires must be trained to the service of the public good. Indeed, when Gawain claims the test, he does so on the basis of relationship to Arthur, who is both his uncle and his king: "Bot for as much as ȝe ar myn em I am only to prayse, / No bounté bot your blod in my bodé knowe" ["That I have you for my uncle is my only praise; / My body, but for your blood, is barren of worth"] (356–57). There can be no more concise statement of the alignment of public and private in the worthy knight than Gawain articulates here. Arthur is in him; he stands for Arthur; and thus he publicizes his king and kingdom in the testings he undertakes. And this, then, is also the meaning of the pentangle, each of whose five interlocked points refers to the way the individual male's private virtues are inextricably interwoven with the public systems of belief, the ideologies, of Christianity and chivalry. The pentangle is a sign of the private male's conscription into the public order. The interconnectedness of these virtues underlines, then, the religious and political stability that would result from adherence to the values encoded in the pentangle.[18]

For Gawain to yield to the Lady would, in fact, involve more than yielding to the otherness of her sexuality. Implied in that yielding to otherness would be the Round Table knight's capitulation to privateness, to private desire, and to the feminization of the private that has been inscribed in this poem. But this romance's rehabilitated Gawain will not yield to mere sexual desire, despite his attraction to the Lady. Certainly, the confrontation at the Green Chapel preoccupies him, perhaps more than his agreement to exchange winnings with his host, and in its own terms, this preoccupation is understandable enough. At this point, however, the poem's revision of Gawain's often spotted past is especially telling. Unlike the Gawain of legend, and even more significantly, unlike Lancelot, this Gawain will not give in to the temptation of mere female flesh, even when, as we have been told, it is lovelier than Guenevere's. At this early stage of the Round Table's career, Gawain is a stronger knight than Lancelot will turn out to be. Gawain is too publicly committed to take his private pleasure and to betray his vows to men, that is, to his king or to his unnamed host, until, indeed, he thinks that his life depends on it.[19]

And then Gawain fails and falls, but not so badly nor so far that the poem cannot reinstate him in its attempt to restore a prelapsarian Camelot. Gawain does not err because of desire for the Lady's body or because of the temptation of her or his sexuality. Rather, he falls because he yields to the desire to save his life, once he has learned of the magical properties inherent in the girdle:

> Þen kest þe knyȝt, and hit come to his hert
> Hit were a juel for þe jopardé þat hym iugged were:
> When he acheued to þe chapel his chek for to fech,
> Myȝt he haf slypped to be vnslayn, þe sleȝt were noble. [1855–58]

> [Then the man began to muse, and mainly he thought
> It was a pearl for his plight, the peril to come
> When he gains the Green Chapel to get his reward:
> Could he escape unscathed, the scheme were noble!]

This is, we might think, a natural enough desire, just as Gawain does at the moment and as Bertilak does later at the Green Chapel, when he judges Gawain:

> Bot here yow lakked a lyttel, sir, and lewté yow wonted;
> Bot þat watz for no wylyde werke, ne wowyng nau þer,
> Bot for ȝe lufed your lyf; þe lasse I yow blame. [2366–68]

> [Yet you lacked, sir, a little in loyalty there,
> But the cause was not cunning, nor courtship either,
> But that you loved your own life; the less, then, to blame.]

But this yielding is particularly dangerous because the desire for life might well be the most natural and instinctive of all. As such, it is the private desire that includes all others within it. To yield to this desire might be only the beginning.

What is more, in political terms, to yield to this desire would spell the end of Arthur's kingdom, of its famous prowess, of its military strength. What would happen, after all, if members of the Round Table, individually and collectively, succumbed repeatedly to the desire to preserve their lives? Gawain may be over-reacting when he speaks later of his "cowarddyse and couetyse" (2374), but he is not entirely wrong. To assume the girdle, as the poem states, "for gode of hymseluen" (2031) is to think primarily of himself. It is to think not of the kingdom's reputation, of its security and solidarity, but of his private desire; it is, in essence, an act of cowardice in which Gawain also shows himself more greedy than he ought to be to save his own private neck.[20] In the feudal and chivalric world of this romance, a man's desire to save his life might be understandable, but wanting "lewté" is no minor political transgression.

The girdle initially signifies life, and specifically Gawain's desire to save his own. Because this private desire is linked in *Sir Gawain and the Green Knight* to the privateness that is the Lady, Gawain's action implicitly betrays the masculine codes of Christian chivalry affirmed as the central values of this poem. When Bertilak has revealed the shape of the testing to Gawain, Gawain's response shows his understanding of the political, ethical, and sexual consequences of his action. Flinging the girdle back at Bertilak, he admits that desire for his life caused him "to acorde me with couetyse, my kynde to forsake, / þat is larges and lewté þat longez to knyȝtez" ["And coveting came after, contrary both / To largesse and loyalty belonging to knights"] (2379–80). His belief that he has betrayed his "kynde" cuts many ways; he has betrayed his nature, which is not only the virtues signified by the pentangle. It is also Arthur, and Arthur's blood, and the values of the Round Table's knighthood. In these terms, to betray his "kynde" is also to betray his masculinity, that is, his fundamental identity, for, in this poem, knighthood and masculinity are in the end the same thing. Without the synonymity of masculinity and knighthood, we are left in a romance world in which masculinity and masculine behavior become synonymous with courtliness, with love dalliance in the bedroom, with the world of ladies and Lancelot, with the world that is contained in Morgan's castle and contained by the narrative. And this is the world from which Gawain has just made a well-timed escape.

After the woman in the middle has compromised Gawain's manhood with her privateness, the poem provides for him, in Fitt IV, a father-confessor to conduct the process of marginalizing the woman and reintegrating Gawain into the court at Camelot. This father-confessor is none other than the Green Knight/Bertilak, whose words to Gawain should carry special weight because he has experienced the dangers of enclosure within the private world of women.[21] Bertilak, after all, can rapidly change color at Morgan's whim.

It is his father-confessor that Gawain has betrayed by failing to return the girdle in the exchange of winnings game. And it is from this father-confessor that Gawain receives an axiom that he should never forget and that will restore his knighthood and his masculinity. In two highly condensed and elliptical lines, Bertilak tells Gawain that "Trwe mon trwe restore, / Þenne þar mon drede no waþe" ["True men pay what they owe; / No danger then in sight"] (2354–55). One need not fear harm if the true man truly restores, that is, if he maintains the essential social contracts between men.[22] Then the true man will truly be a man, because he has not yielded to private and thus feminized desires. These lines might well serve as a motto for a poetic, political, and ethical program that would, in effect, save Arthur's kingdom. By following Bertilak's advice, Gawain in his completed confession and analysis of his motives is a redeemed man, here bought back from the woman with whom he has bargained for his life.[23]

But it is not that easy for Gawain, for the court of Arthur, or for the poem that knows the end of its own story and the end of the story of the Arthurian world. For if Arthur's blood is in Gawain, we learn, when we learn of Morgan's agency, that her blood is in him, too. Bertilak, the great revealer, finally reveals Morgan, at the end of the poem, but not until Gawain has shown himself ready for this revelation. By now, Gawain has sufficiently distanced himself from association with the Lady to guarantee his public reintegration into Arthur's court. By now, in an anti-feminist diatribe that has given many critics pause,[24] he has successfully completed this distancing by claiming that, since all great men fall to women's wiles, he might be excused for following suit:

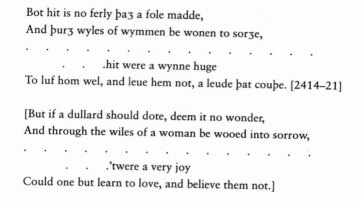

> Bot hit is no ferly þaȝ a fole madde,
> And þurȝ wyles of wymmen be wonen to sorȝe,
>
> .   .   .   .
>
>   .   .   .hit were a wynne huge
> To luf hom wel, and leue hem not, a leude þat couþe. [2414–21]

> [But if a dullard should dote, deem it no wonder,
> And through the wiles of a woman be wooed into sorrow,
>
> .   .   .   .
>
>   .   .   .'twere a very joy
> Could one but learn to love, and believe them not.]

He can learn, then, that not only did Morgan concoct this adventure, but that she is also "Þyn aunt . . . , Arþurez half-suster" ["Your own aunt . . . , Arthur's half-sister"] (2464). Throughout the poem, the woman Morgan has been assigned to a privateness so complete that she cannot be admitted until this point, when Gawain has proven himself protected from the influence of her blood. And yet, by Bertilak's admission, she is always simultaneously lurking at the fringes and inescapably at dead center, related to Arthur and to Gawain, just as her influence is at the narrative center of the romance. The poem forcefully leaves her aside because that is all it can do, but to do that, if it could be done, would be plenty.

And thus the fate of the green girdle, the love token that the Lady wove and wore and gave to Gawain as a sign not only of her, but of his life and his desire to save it. By the time Gawain rides back into Arthur's hall bedecked with the girdle, the Lady has vanished from the realm of its signification. She has been marginalized so that Gawain and the girdle can be publicized. Along the route of the girdle's redefinition and Gawain's return home, Bertilak has claimed that it is his, just as he claims to have pimped for his wife in order to test Gawain's virtue: "For hit is my wede þat þou werez, þat ilke wouen girdel" ["For that is my belt about you, that same braided girdle"] (2358). The girdle has gone from being a sign of Gawain's life and his desire to save it to a sign of his threatened death, his sin and his unkindness, his unnaturalness, all so that it can be, as Bertilak claims, a "pure token / Of þe chaunce of þe grene chapel at cheualrous knyghteȝ" ["token /

How it chanced at the Green Chapel, to chivalrous knights"] (2398–99). The green girdle is a sign now not of the woman, but of the tested man, who has not been found so wanting after all.[25] The woman in the middle has effectively been displaced from the center, to become as marginalized as Guenevere and Morgan. And thus the token is pure, cleansed of female signification, and particularly of male alliance with the female at the expense of bonding with the male. "Trwe mon trwe restore."

But Gawain cannot accept the girdle back so easily. He himself must redefine it in order to associate it directly with his sins, and only marginally with the Lady. And yet the Lady is signified in the specific sin that Gawain links to the girdle: "Þe faut and þe fayntyse of þe flesche crabbed, / How tender hit is to entyse teches of fylþe" ["The faults and the frailty of the flesh perverse, / How its tenderness entices the foul taint of sin"] (2435–36). At this point, the Lady's marginalization and the placement of the female in the poem are complete. The Lady of the girdle is reduced to the corruption of the flesh, in an image that specifically evokes withered, old Morgan, the "auncian," as she has been described in Fitt II (947–69). The Lady, through this rapid deterioration, has been revised. Or perhaps we see here signs of the specific revision that this poem has worked on Morgan herself, because I, for one, find it difficult to understand how Arthur's half-sister could have become so old so soon, unless it were to link her with the corruption of the flesh that, in this poem, becomes linked to the corruption that is women in the center of Arthur's court.[26]

The court, however, is ready to forgive and forget, just as, I would argue, the poem would like to forgive and forget, but primarily to forget as it nears the end of a revisionary agenda that it knows must fail. As a sign of its forgiveness, the court assumes the sign of Gawain's self-defined sin.

> Þe kyng comfortez the knyȝt, and alle þe court als
> Laȝen loude þerat, and lufly acorden
> Þat lordes and ladis þat longed to þe Table,
> Uche burne of þe broþerhede, a bauderyk schulde haue. . . . [2513–16]

> [The king comforts the knight, and the court all together
> Agree with gay laughter and gracious intent
> That the lords and the ladies belonging to the Table,
> Each brother of that band, a baldric should have. . . .]

In the process, the court collectively rehabilitates the girdle by making it a public sign of honor.[27] Interestingly enough, the rehabilitation of the girdle follows the same model as does the rehabilitation of Guenevere in Fitt I. Through this sign, the woman is safely placed within the court, safely placed specifically because she is removed from the dangerous realm of the private and the feminine and published as a token within a masculine world. If Guenevere in Fitt I is rehabilitated because she so surely refers to Arthur, then the publicized girdle is rehabilitated specifically because it now refers to the honor of Arthur's court.

The poem knows, however, that the end is not so easy and that its own means are insufficient to the end. The woman may have been marginalized by leaving Morgan aside, but the process of her marginalization involves her naming. In other words, it involves her publication, her removal from her own sphere of the private so that she can become the public sign of the male. But, as such, the woman as token becomes dangerously current within the court, just as the green girdle, redefined though it might be, is dangerously current in the closing scene at Camelot. For, among the male gazes directed at the static Guenevere in Fitt I is, we can assume, that of Lancelot (who is mentioned only once in the poem [553], included in the brotherhood of knights advising Gawain before his departure in Fitt II). And, unless Guenevere is blind as well as mute, she can, of course, look back.

In its marginalization of women, then, the poem provides a proleptic cure for Arthurian history. If Guenevere had been the static and silent queen, then the Round Table would not have fallen. If men could redefine and thereby control experience for other men, as Bertilak does for Gawain, and, indeed, as the poet does for his audience, then Morgan's power would be diffused. But the poem and its poet know better, because they know the story of Arthur and because women, in the legend and in life, cannot be effectively marginalized. The poem tries to suggest that the life-giving girdle and its giver are ultimately life-threatening. In the historical world of feudal chivalry, however, the bearers of death are not generally women. If our end comes from our beginning, we still know where that beginning starts. If women were legally and politically marginalized within feudal society, they were nonetheless central, biologically, economically, *and* politically, to its continuation. Guenevere's barrenness may thus discount her within this world. But Morgan is, as Bertilak admits, " þe goddes." Although Bertilak makes her magic secondary by attributing it to Merlin, that magic, as Morgan practices it, is powerful stuff. Bertilak may be bent out of shape by it, but he can still grow a new head. It is this regenerative capacity that enables the Green Knight to make his reappearance in Fitt IV.[28] His end, then, is only his beginning and the beginning of the narrative, thanks to Morgan le Fay.

It is no wonder then that the poem's erasure of women, of Guenevere, of the Lady, and of Morgan, is uneasy and incomplete. The odds of Arthurian legend and of human history are against it. Could the female be marginalized, then the Round Table would not have ended. But she cannot be, and it will. Nonetheless, the meaning of this end is not the end of the meaning, not of the "rex quondam rexque futurus" and not of his queen. And not, for that matter, of Morgan le Fay.

NOTES

1. See, for example, Larry D. Benson, *Art and Tradition in Sir Gawain and the Green Knight* (New Brunswick: Rutgers University Press, 1965), pp. 97–98; A. C. Spearing, *The Gawain-Poet: A Critical Study* (Cambridge: Cambridge University Press, 1970), pp. 181 and 222; John Eadie, "Morgain la Fee and the Conclusion of *Sir Gawain and the Green Knight*," *Neophilologus* 52 (1968), 300–01; Robert W. Hanning, "Sir Gawain and the Red Herring: The Perils of Interpretation," in Mary J. Carruthers and Elizabeth D. Kirk, eds., *Acts of Interpretation: The Text in its Contexts 700–1600: Essays on Medieval and Renaissance Literature in Honor of E. Talbot Donaldson* (Norman: Pilgrim Books, 1982), p. 11. In "Myth and Medieval Literature: *Sir Gawain and the Green Knight*," (*Speculum* 18 [1956], 172), Charles Moorman argues that the poem is "a highly compressed allegorical commentary on the entire Arthurian history" and that "the seeds of [its] tragedy were present even in the 'first age' of the youthful and joyous court at Christmas time." Moorman does not argue, as I do, that the poem valorizes the youthful court as part of its revisionist project. In a chapter on *Sir Gawain and the Green Knight* in her thesis, "Mordred's Hidden Presence: The Skeleton in the Arthurian Closet" (Ph.D., Yale, 1985), M. Victoria Guerin offers a thorough analysis of the ways in which the poem follows a revisionist program in its relation to the unnamed Mordred. I am grateful to Professor Guerin for sharing the manuscript of her chapter with me.

2. *Sir Gawain and the Green Knight*, ed. J.R.R. Tolkien and E.V. Gordon, 2nd ed. rev. Norman Davis (Oxford: Oxford University Press, 1967). All quotations of the poem are taken from this edition and are cited by line number. The translation cited is that of Marie Borroff (New York: Norton, 1967). On these lines, cf. Moorman, 164 and 171.

3. See Benson, for example, pp. 32–35. Morgan's traditional enmity toward the Round Table stands as the most frequent justification for her presence in the poem. Most book-length studies of the poem, however, give relatively little emphasis to Morgan's significance to the poem. The exception to the general neglect of Morgan occurs primarily in the articles published on her in the 1950s and 1960s: Denver Ewing Baughan: "The Role of Morgan la Faye in *Sir Gawain and the Green Knight*," *ELH* 17 (1950), 241–51; Albert B. Friedman, "Morgan la Faye in *Sir Gawain and the Green Knight*," *Speculum* 35 (1960), 260–74; Mother Angela Carson, O.S.U., "Morgain la Fee as the Principle of Unity in Gawain and the Green Knight," *MLQ* 23 (1962), 3–16; Douglas Moon, "The Role of Morgan la Faye in *Gawain and the Green Knight*," *NM* 67 (1966), 31–57. The most recent study of Morgan is Edith Whitehurst Williams' "Morgan la Fee as Trickster in *Sir Gawain and the Green Knight*," *Folklore* 96 (1985), 38–56. To date, there has been no comprehensive feminist study of the placement of women in the poem.

4. In addition to the sources cited in footnote 1, see also Moorman, 167–72; Baughan, 244–47; and Friedman, 269.

5. Victoria Guerin's chapter on *Sir Gawain and the Green Knight* offers a comprehensive analysis of this issue in relation to the poem's themes and purposes.

6. For discussion of Gawain's traditional reputation as a "lady's man," see Friedman, 265; Benson, pp. 95 and 103; Spearing, pp. 198–99; W.R.J. Barron, *Trawthe and Treason: The Sin of Sir Gawain Reconsidered* (Manchester: Manchester University Press, 1980), p. 21. Guerin's chapter on *Sir Gawain and the Green Knight* offers a comprehensive discussion of this issue.

7. For a thorough and perceptive discussion of the fluctuation of Gawain's value and identity, see R.A. Shoaf's *The Poem as Green Girdle: "Commercium" in "Sir Gawain and the Green Knight"* (Gainesville: University Presses of Florida, 1984), especially the section, "What *Prys* Gawain?," pp. 34–36. Throughout my discussion of Gawain's activities in the bedroom and of the girdle's meaning, I am particularly indebted to Professor Shoaf's analysis as well as to the bibliography that he generously shared with me before his monograph appeared in print.

8. For a discussion of medieval women's legal, political, and marital rights, see Shulamith Shahar, *The Fourth Estate: A History of Women in the Middle Ages*, trans. Chaya Galai (New York: Methuen, 1983), pp. 11–21, and the chapter on aristocratic women, pp. 126–73.

9. In this essay, my thinking about the placement of women in narrative has been influenced by Sandra M. Gilbert and Susan Gubar's chapter, "The Queen's Looking Glass," in *Madwoman in the Attic: The Woman Writer and the Nineteenth-Century Literary Imagination* (New Haven: Yale University Press, 1984), pp. 3–44, esp. pp. 20–27.

10. Benson, for example, writes that the Lady was "following Bertilak's orders," although he acknowledges Morgan as the source of Bertilak's activities (p. 55). Peter L. Rudnytsky takes the same approach to the Lady in "*Sir Gawain and the Green Knight*: Oedipal Temptation," *AI* 40 (1983), 377. Carson was the first to stress Morgan's responsibility for the plot *and* Bertilak's role as *her* agent (13).

11. Moorman, 167. Moorman's arguments resemble my own here, but he does not associate the Lady, Guenevere, and Morgan, as I believe the poem does, on the basis of the femaleness that they share.

12. I take this idea of "framing women in art" from Gilbert and Gubar, *Madwoman in the Attic*, pp. 13 and 42. My thinking about the significance of Guenevere's placement at Arthur's table was influenced by Susan Gubar's discussion of the dual meaning of Judy Chicago's *Dinner Party*. "But *The Dinner Party* plates also imply that women, who have served, have been served up and consumed." See "'The Blank Page' and the Issues of Female Creativity," reprinted in Elaine Showalter, ed., *The New Feminist Criticism: Essays on Women, Literature, and Theory*, (New York: Pantheon Books, 1985), p. 300 (originally printed in *Critical Inquiry* 8 [Winter 1981]). Hanning also notes that Guenevere in this scene is an "elegant courtly artifact" (11).

13. Speaking of her inexplicable love for Jankyn, the Wife of Bath says: "We wommen han, if that I shal nat lye, / In this matere a queynte fantasye," *The Riverside Chaucer,* ed. Larry D. Benson (Boston: Houghton Mifflin, 1987), III [D], 515–16. The pun on *queynte* as female genitalia occurs frequently enough in Chaucer that it does not seem too much to assume that its possibility would have been familiar to the *Gawain*-poet.

14. For a discussion of medieval women's marital position and rights, see Shahar, pp. 65–125. Throughout my analysis of women's placement within marital, political, and economic systems, I am indebted to Gayle Rubin's important feminist revision of Claude Levi-Strauss' *The Elementary Structures of Kinship* in "The Traffic in Women: Notes on the 'Political Economy' of Sex," in Rayna R. Reiter, ed., *Toward an Anthropology of Women* (New York: Monthly Review Press, 1975), pp. 157–210.

15. For representative interpretations of the Lady as seductress, see Benson, pp. 38–40, and W.A. Davenport, *The Art of the Gawain-Poet* (London: Athlone Press, 1978), pp. 137, 167–68, and 187. Taking a much different approach, Victor Y. Haines, in *The Fortunate Fall of Sir Gawain: The Typology of Sir Gawain and the Green Knight*

(Washington: University Press of America, 1982), argues that while the Lady seems to "corrupt" Gawain in a first reading of the poem, "in the redeemed history of [a] second reading, the lady is benevolent," because she wants to save Gawain's life (p. 145). According to Haines, the Lady operates as an emissary of Mary (not of Morgan) because her love for Gawain is charitable, not concupiscent (pp. 131, 138–42, and 148).

16. Two important feminist contributions to the study of women's relationship to medieval literature include Joan M. Ferrante, *Woman as Image in Medieval Literature: From the Twelfth Century Through Dante* (New York: Columbia University Press, 1975), and E. Jane Burns' and Roberta L. Krueger's "Introduction" to *Courtly Ideology and Women's Place in Medieval French Literature, Romance Notes* 25 (Spring 1985), 205–19.

17. Cf. Shoaf's discussion, pp. 31–46. While Shoaf concludes, "Bertilak's Lady manipulates Gawain until he insists on private value exclusively" (p. 46), he studies Gawain's yielding to privacy in the context of medieval Christian sacramentality and not in the context of the inscription of the female in the narrative.

18. Spearing (pp. 175 and 196–98) and Burrow (pp. 50 and 105) offer representative interpretations of the criticism on the pentangle. In his monograph, Shoaf gives a new reading of the pentangle, which is based in medieval and postmodern sign theory and which gives full weight to the problematics of referentiality in the poem. See, especially, pp. 71–75.

19. Many of my ideas about the configurations of male homosociality in literary texts and the (dis)placement of women within these configurations are indebted to the introduction and first two chapters of Eve Kosofsky Sedgwick, *Between Men: English Literature and Male Homosocial Desire* (New York: Columbia University Press, 1985). While Sedgwick's book primarily discusses later literature, these opening sections are relevant to the study of medieval and early modern texts.

20. Critical disagreement about the poem is sharpest in the divergent interpretations of the seriousness of Gawain's sin. For three recent examples of this divergence of opinion, compare Thomas D. Hill, "Gawain's Jesting Lie: Towards an Interpretation of the Confessional Scene in *Sir Gawain and the Green Knight,*" *Studia Neophilologia* 52 (1980), 279–86; Shoaf, pp. 15–30; and Williams, 51.

21. For representative interpretations of Bertilak's role in Fitt IV, see Moorman, 166; Burrow, pp. 137 and 169; Davenport, pp. 168–73; Spearing, pp. 31 and 221; and Barron, p. 132.

22. Cf. Shoaf, pp. 15–30.

23. See Shoaf's appendix (pp. 77–80) for an indication of the density of commercial images in this poem. For earlier discussions of the implications of the poem's commercial idiom, see Burrow, pp. 76–77 and 88–89, and Paul B. Taylor, "Commerce and Comedy in Sir *Gawain and the Green Knight,*" *PhilQ* 50 (1971), 1–15.

24. The conflicting reactions to Gawain's anti-feminist diatribe is one of the most interesting interludes in the history of the critical tradition on this poem.

25. Shoaf's monograph stands as the most comprehensive discussion of the complex significations of the girdle and of its thematic function within the poem.

26. Tolkien's footnote on Morgan's advanced age (p. 130) has been consistently accepted by most critics who have raised this issue. Others, like Benson (p. 32), associate Morgan's aging with the filth of the flesh whose presence within him Gawain must acknowledge as the wages of his sin. Carson argues, on the basis of the poem's sources, that Morgan and the Lady are one and the same because of the dual nature of Morgan. In Carson's reading, Bertilak is Uriens, and Morgan's traditional characterization becomes attributed to the two central women in the poem (5 and 13). While Carson's reading engages Morgan's centrality in the poem, it does not sufficiently engage the marginalization of Morgan that the poem accomplishes by substituting the Lady for her. Williams offers an analysis similar to Carson's, but bases her discussion on Jungian archetypes (41 and 49).

27. For a representative sampling of the disagreement over the poem's ending, see Moorman, 170; Burrow, pp. 158–59; Spearing, pp. 222 and 230; Benson, pp. 241–42; Edward Wilson, *The* Gawain-*Poet* (Leiden: Brill, 1976), pp. 130–31. Williams' discussion of the concluding presentation of the girdle comes close to my own, but she does not discuss the significance of the erasure of the Lady in the final scene (52).

28. See, for example, Benson, p. 94, and Hanning, pp. 6–7, on the meaning of the natural landscape. The complex meanings that circulate around the natural world in this poem align themselves in interesting ways with what Elaine Showalter has designated as "the wild zone" of female culture, that is, the private world of women's culture that men never see. See "Feminist Criticism in the Wilderness," in *The New Feminist Criticism*, p. 262 (originally published in *Critical Inquiry* 8 [1981]).

ENCHANTED GROUND

THE FEMININE SUBTEXT IN MALORY

Geraldine Heng

Readings on women characters in Malory are by tradition tacitly inclined to concede to the feminine only a supporting place in the Arthurian society of the text. The image of knightly culture on which that civilisation is posited must assume feminine presence and assistance for its completion, yet also constitute the feminine in essentially subsidiary relation to masculinity. Because the female is read as adjunctive (though necessary), a specifically feminine point of view in the work is never fully recovered, but remains only an inchoate potential, subsumed and dispersed within other discourses. A subtextual reading is needed to extricate and identify the outlines of that view, and restore thereby a certain equivalence. The disruptive gestures and energies, intrusions and interruptions that are lodged within surface textuality ultimately point to a submerged second narrative interplaying with and often prompting the first, and marked by a recognisably feminine voice.

To be conscious of the precise borders of a feminine hinterland, it is first necessary to be aware of the feminine origin of many of the enabling conditions for activity. The simplest form of this would be that tissue of gifts and material objects intruded into the narrative by women, which surrounds and underlies the textual drama. These timely insertions advance and mediate action, often by directly instigating it: such, for instance, is the purpose of the white hart and brachet which appear at Arthur's wedding feast to begin the cycles of quest for the Round Table. Indeed, this threefold episode—a prologue of sorts to the later adventures—is exemplary in function, for it lays down the structures of appropriate behaviour toward the feminine, in its explicit criticism of Gawain, even as it instills the right of the

Reprinted by permission from *Courtly Literature: Culture and Context.* Selected papers from the 5th Triennial Congress of the ICLS, Dalfsen, The Netherlands, 9–16 August, 1986. Ed. Keith Busby, Erik Kooper (Amsterdam, Philadelphia: John Benjamins, 1990), pp. 283–300.

queen to arbitrate and judge knightly conduct.[1] Only after the action has been finalised and suitably glossed can the Round Table be formally inaugurated.[2] Women also possess devices that restore, like Isode's brachet which reclaims Tristram to the world after an isolating madness.[3] Objects of protection, like Lyonesse's ring and Lyonet's magical ointment, both so effective in securing Gareth's good reputation, come from women, as do those of harm, such as Morgan le Fay's dangerous cloak, horn and shield. Devices of this nature suggest an extension of female presence in the narrative in the widest sense, since they encompass and symbolically fix the entire realm of human possibility—good and evil, success and failure, protection or destruction.

Perhaps the most enigmatic and dangerous items of this material trove are *swords*, the instruments on which all masculine accomplishment must turn, and therefore pivotal to conceptions of male identity and personal force.[4] These are so strongly associated with feminine sources and ownership as sometimes to be only temporarily accessible to men. The bestowal of Excaleber occasions the first of otherworldly feminine interventions in Arthur's life, when his own sword, an early motif of his royal authority through its free acquisition from stone and anvil, shatters, failing him. The meaning of this replacement is carefully elaborated in a deliberate pointing to the secret powers of the new weapon, contained not in blade but in scabbard or sheath (Lat. *vagina*), a significance to which its royal custodian is at first insensitive. It takes Merlin, an authoritative reader of semiotic categories, to decipher the twin interlocking signs, and repeatedly tutor Arthur on the superior value of the scabbard. We notice that *women* never lose sight of these veiled significances, which they too are able to read: the king in tragic contrast never learns the language of emblems sufficiently, and between the theft of the weapon by Morgan, and its partial retrieval by Nyneve, has his fate irrevocably sealed. But if Arthur is blind to the sword's meaning, he is still able to perceive the borrowed character of its powers, a debt he symbolically acknowledges in the favour he agrees to give for their use, and in his unquestioning assumption that Excaleber is not his to keep or bequeath.[5] The negative image to Arthur's graceful submission is then Balyn, the self-willed knight who rejects such personal obligation. After being permitted by a maiden to establish his worth through the drawing of her mistress's sword, he defiantly asserts his right to its ownership, illegitimately insisting on keeping what is not his. It is instructive that he goes on to destroy the brother who is an alter-ego of himself with the very sword he will not relinquish—a destiny we are told by the prophetic female messenger, arising directly out of its misappropriation.[6] In the two men are thus offered polar models of conduct in response to the feminine: one, acknowledging debt and stewardship with the acceptance of a sword, and the other, repudiating these with the appropriation of a sword. Where Excaleber will protect its masculine custodian, therefore, Balyn's weapon will destroy the very people who are closest in affection to its user, a legacy transmitted even after his death.[7]

It is possible to discover other swords, confirm a pattern of meaning. Galahad's has a girdle woven for it by Percivale's sister out of her own hair; and it is she who is appointed to draw the sword for him out of scriptural history and gird it upon him, a ceremonially significant act.[8] Lancelot's was "lapped . . . in [Guenevere's] trayne" (*Works*, p. 1058) on the day he became a knight, a re-writing of the OF Vulgate Cycle episode where it is the queen, and not the king, who supplies the sword that ritually completes Lancelot's entry into knighthood.[9]

The most suggestive trope for an analysis of feminine authority and presence in Malory, however, is that which is offered to us to describe two kinds of feminine play in the text—the tantalising, doubly-figurative trope of enchantment. In its most familiar conformation, this refers to magic, and magical resources. While only one man, Merlin, is decisively associated with the practice of sorcery, the reference of magic to women is almost casual, reflexive; even nameless figures who make the briefest appearances may possess magical objects and spells, and work enchantment: it is a language depicted by the text as being ubiquitously familiar to women. There is, however, a second level of usefulness to the metaphor of enchantment in a courtly universe: that of the enchantment of love.[10] In a fictive discourse where love is valorised as a formidable motive power, and the female beloved identified with its source and regulation, even a territory of masculine endeavour is a ground of feminine possibility. Each kind of enchantment traces a path by which the feminine may be active in the world, and constructs patterns of intelligibility specific to female interests and presences. Each must therefore be examined in turn.

The function of love, in the society of the narrative, is the displacement of a purely masculine and primarily martial discourse with another of greater civilising value: a sophisticated, feminine-presided discourse of emotion and relation. An ideology of war is only useful for the initial efforts of colonisation and consolidation which enable the establishment of Arthurian society, and for securing its preservation afterward from sporadic external threat. In textual terms this is to be found in the segments of narrative which manifest what we are used to identify as 'chronicle' behaviour,[11] where a fairly warlike Arthur[12] and the 'preromance' heroes of Kay, Lucan and Gryfflet, are the main actors.[13] For the distilling of an actual civilisation in the wake of victory, however, martial energies, always potentially disruptive and dangerous in peace-time, must be sublimated and re-assumed: and an ideology of war is therefore translated into an ideology of arms, or feats of prowess, for love. With this, a masculine orientation, turning upon allegiance to a king, warfare in the company of other men, massive group enterprises, and the goal of personal glory, is displaced and supplanted by a feminine-influenced one: involving instead allegiance to a lady, trial and effort out of the stimulus, inspiration or possibility of love, and in the essentially lonely conditions of the quest.[14] This substitution of orientation has been thought to create a motive logic of "greater moral potentiality" (Singer, p. 82) for the uses of violence,[15] and its dissemination seen to constitute "an extension of the idea of conscience in the broad sense" (Bloomfield, p. 44).[16]

So fundamental to Arthurian society are the ideology of love and the claims of the feminine it inscribes, that those who are ignorant of or antagonistic to their spirit are shown to be necessarily outcast to society. In the fate of Balyn, a knight whose temperament attests a greater affiliation with the "chronicle" than the "romance" mode of assumptions, may be glimpsed the lineaments of such a suggestion. His career is a record of incomprehension and misplacement in a discourse intrinsically foreign to him. When first introduced, Balyn is a man already set apart from his civilisation by an earlier act of transgression against Arthur's family, and seeking reintegration into society through intended appeasement of the king (*Works*, p. 62). Before this can be attempted, however, his separation is further intensified through the addition of a second killing to the first, deepening his offence against Arthur. Whatever the moral stature of the lady of the lake he beheads,[17] Arthur is in her debt for the loan of Excaleber,[18] an obligation the king feels with sufficient force to cause him to expel Balyn from court (*Works*, p. 66). Indeed, it would appear to be out of his negative relations with the feminine, and his limited understanding of the feminine-pervaded discourse of romance society that Balyn's unfortunate fate is determined. We are told that his denial of the sword-bearing maiden's request for the weapon's return will produce his brother's death and his own; and Merlin categorically declares that Balyn will cause the Dolorous Stroke for his responsibility in the suicide of Columbe, whose life he renders unbearable:

> ". . . because of the dethe of that lady thou shalt stryke a stroke moste dolerous that ever man stroke, excepte the stroke of oure Lorde Jesu Cryste. For thou shalt hurte the trewyst knyght and the man of most worship that now lyvith; and thorow that stroke three kyngdomys shall be brought into grete poverté, miseri and wretchednesse twelve

yere. And the knyght shall nat be hole of that wounde many yerys."
(*Works*, p. 72)

That the assumptions of the courtly world to which he would belong
are alien to him is partially indicated by the absence of any genuine relationship of intimacy with the feminine in Balyn's life. He is one of very few
knights in the Arthurian constellation who has no lady, and never wins one,
his closest human bond being, significantly, to another man, a brother who
is in effect a double of himself. Balyn is therefore caught unawares by the
intensity of Columbe's love for Lanceor, and in his wonder at the degree of
commitment to the courtly ethos that would prompt so sacrificial an affirmation as hers, may be sensed his own remoteness and dislocation. Not
being himself familiar to love, his presence is then inimical to the love-
relation,[19] expressing an unintentional antipathy that has even posthumous
consequences, for the world's two most famous lovers of women, Lancelot
and Tristram, are inadvertently made to do battle later at the very site where
Balyn has caused the deaths of Lanceor and Columbe.

Where Balyn's intentions and the outcome of his efforts correspond
most closely is in the domain of warfare, an area in which he appears to be
comfortable and effectual. Here, he is in his appropriate milieu, a "chronicle"
mode of action where his ungovernable and impulsive explosions of violence
are useful.[20] It is only when the application of brute masculine force must
be selectively tempered by obedience to social dictates[21] and the regulation
of emotion—the peculiar specialities of a romance orientation—that his efforts are accordingly futile. His bewilderment then at his consistent failure
to discharge that most basic of chivalric duties, the protection of those in
his care, bespeaks the floundering confusion of a man stranded in a strange
country with a map he cannot read: because the language, though familiar,
has altered its codes of reference. The blank shield he finally accepts as replacement for his own arms is merely the outward mark of his capitulation
to the unbreachable discontinuity between that world and himself, and
acknowledgement of the subsequent loss of coordinates for identity. His
original assertion of independent identity from the feminine, and separation
from the matrix of courtly motivations, tragically concludes with the absence
of all the saving attributes of such a connection. The aridity of Balyn's life,
its squandered resources, and the sad absurdity of his death bear painful
witness to that misplaced adaptation.

The love-relation, which leaves few untouched in one or another of
its forms, is a realm of special possibility for women, since it is indisputably
their ground. Through its projection, not only may women condition an

arena of masculine action by intervening in the process of the "adventure,"[22] but even the most sedentary may manifest a presence in knightly acts. By receiving a knight's dedication and being ascribed his motivations, resources, and accomplishments, a woman is at once immanent in his deeds, her place and influence permanently inscribed in the record of his gestures. Conversely, knightly obedience to and cooperation with the feminine supply effective means for actualisations of feminine will, creating an agency by which women may be active in the world. Knightly actions, where they are an extension of feminine will, are, in this sense, transparent, and have been described as "*Gesta dominarum per milites*, the exploits of ladies through the medium of knights."[23]

Nowhere are the implications of the love-ideology more thoroughly celebrated than in the life and career of that legendary servitor of women, the great Lancelot himself. By his own profession, the meaning of his acts is to be sought only in a strict context of relation with his beloved, and valued only to the degree that they install the advocacy of his lady:

> "And all my grete dedis of armys that I have done for the moste party was for the quenys sake, and for hir sake wolde I do batayle were hit ryght other wronge. And never dud I batayle all only [for] Goddis sake, but for to wynne worship and to cause me the bettir to be beloved, and littil or nought I thanked never God of it." (*Works*, p. 897)

In expressly assigning the queen the purpose and uses of his life, Lancelot subsumes his identity within her own,[24] his volition existing separately only insofar as it is a force for instituting her authority and spatial presence within the world. To this end, it is to Guenevere and not Arthur that he sends defeated knights for their fealty and homage, an act of empowerment underwriting her supremacy in the courtly universe.[25] Indeed, his submission to his lady's will is so perfect[26]—taking precedence even over allegiance to God and concern for his soul—that it is awarded the supreme accolade of being suspected to be founded in supernatural causes. The occasional voicing of female speculation that Guenevere exercises the enchantment of sorcery as much as that of love over Lancelot is perhaps supreme testimony to the power and efficacy of feminine domination through the "spell" of emotion (*Works*, p. 279). Indeed, the characterisation of Lancelot answers the requirements of masculine dedication to feminine will so satisfyingly that it has often been felt to contain the lineaments of an ideal women's fantasy. Lancelot is "an example . . . of what the modern analytical psychologist terms the 'animus archetype,' the dream image of manliness that inhabits the woman's psyche,"[27] largely because he enacts the willing and symbolic capture of the best attributes of masculinity by feminine elements. That he is the premier knight[28] in a theatre of pure masculine ability and the finest specimen of secular civilisation is necessary to establish the pleasure of his voluntary self-subordination. For not only is the obedience and devotion of chivalry's best knight immensely desirable, but it sets in place a paradigm of idealism of special advantage to the feminine,[29] through its assuming the absolute priority of female interests. Lancelot is the most effective agent in the text for the transliteration of female will and desire because the emotional logic of serving a particular lady translates polysemously for him into dedication to a feminine principle, affirmed in the enormous variety of requests successfully made of him by women.[30] Ultimately it is in this that the meaning of his characterisation is to be found, located within a world of feminine purpose without which a Lancelot as we know him would be unimaginable: seen thus, Lancelot's desire, then, is the desire not *for* the feminine, but *of* the feminine.

Yet however fascinating its operations or useful for individual female causes, the enchantment of love defines clear limits in the end for feminine play. By its nature it allows only an indirect presence and vicarious participation for women, since it is dependent on knighthood to work its design. For a direct mode of feminine play, we must look to a different emphasis in the image of enchantment—the actual practice of magic itself. Love is a spell optimistic in attitude, possible only in a collaborative discourse of shared, mutual, emotional interrelation. Magic, on the other hand, is an independent force, and requires little concession from the human counters with which it transacts. Its dispositions therefore lodge formidable sources of power in the text, to far exceed the mechanism of arms. And, because its operations are secret or indecipherable, and may press even the unwilling into service, it is a thing to be feared, particularly by a warrior ethic, for its mysterious compulsion.[31]

An early demonstration of the control available with magical resources occurs at the very beginning of the text where it is Merlin's supervision of war that enables the victories on which Arthurian society rests. His instigation, management and termination of conflicts is almost arbitrary— a measure of the freedom available to a manipulator of magic. Interestingly, the outward sign of such control and freedom is indicated through the metaphor of *writing*: with the completion of the wars, Merlin narrates and glosses them for record by his predecessor magician, so that they erect a permanent testament to the authori(ci)ty of magic (*Works*, p. 37).[32] The suggestion that enchantment gives access to textual control hardly surprises, for the place of its practitioners is a privileged one in the text, analogous to an author's. It is particularly significant, then, that the one masculine practitioner, Merlin, is excised very early from the narrative, and the mantle of authority and authorship quickly passes from him to female users of magic. Where Merlin once shepherded Uther to a night of illicit love with a duped Ygrayne by means of a clever blurring of identities, Dame Brusen later shepherds Elayne to a similar night with an equally-deceived Lancelot by a parallel trick.[33] Where the enchanter once importuned a damosel of the lake for her love, enchantresses of various persuasions—Hallewes, Annowre, Morgan, the queens of North Galys, Estlonde, and the Oute Iles—now importune men for theirs. Indeed, Merlin's own position as advisor and rescuer of Arthur is filled by the very woman who authors his defeat.

The two principal enchantresses who construct different dispositions of power after Merlin's removal—Nyneve, the principal Lady of the Lake, and Morgan le Fay—are incomprehensible merely by the standards of chivalry. Despite their intermittent conflict with each other, the distinction between them is slight, and far less than their mutual distinction from the realm of commonplace mortals that is their occasional tramping-ground. It is only by a clearly partial standard of reference that Nyneve is identified as beneficent and Morgan as malign—estimated, that is, only by the relative usefulness or threat of their presence for knightly society. Both are women possessed of such powers as confer an extraordinary autonomy upon them, an untrammelled freedom to act that is denied others. Released from the normal codes circumscribing mortal relations, they unleash actions which may playfully mimic the gestures of the courtly-chivalric ethos, but without self-conscription. An ironic tension prevails even as they invoke the formalities of contact—positive or negative by Arthurian standards—with knightly culture, suggesting always their distance.

Nyneve's capture and disposal of Merlin is accomplished through a delicately ironic interrogation of the familiar courtly role of the beloved mistress. Only here, the lady is a maiden, who through sexual withholding keeps perfect her control over her professed lover, and intact her personal powers.[34] The discrepancy between the sage maiden, virginal but canny, and the old magician, powerful but besotted, holds considerable potential for humour or pathos, and is perhaps finally elemental in its configuration. It may be inevitable that she supplants him, as spring replaces winter,[35] but the textual attention is to her clever application of the courtly metaphor at hand. Merlin as would-be lover is eager and compliant, revealing secrets and doing her will in his own version of a knight's performance of deeds for his lady's pleasure. She enacts the elusive beloved, whose extraction of his promise not to enforce her, here through sorcery, should conventionally yield to an eventual submission and acceptance of his love. But Nyneve stages instead an alternative outcome, interpolating a scene in which the anticipated sexual surrender is substituted by her ascension to greater power. To approve and confirm her freedom for such extemporising—a freedom once exercised exclusively by Merlin—the text underwrites her intervention by placing responsibility for his demise with Merlin himself, marking him as a victim of his own lust and folly.[36] This is a displacement that perhaps corresponds to textual shifts in orientation. Merlin's presence is largely useful for the setting-up of Arthurian society, and the accurate deployments required for its early success. With the transposition to romance imperatives, however, his presence is superannuated, and a shift of authority to feminine disseminators of enchantment is timely and appropriate.[37] The text dramatises this transition by juxtaposing an ascent with a decline, and insists that it is by the efficacy of the new powers that the old are subjugated: "So by hir subtyle worchyng she made Merlyon to go undir that stone to latte hir wete of the mervayles there, *but she wrought so there for hym* that he come never oute *for all the craufte he coude do* (*Works*, p. 126, emphasis mine). With the supplanting of her predecessor is bequeathed some obligation to the Arthurian world, and Nyneve works with sporadic attention on its behalf. We are given to feel, however, that it is far less central to her interests than it was to Merlin, whose preoccupation with its concerns was obsessive. Our impression, instead, is of her moving in a separate and wholly other reality, her own centres of interest, from which she may he recalled only when more-than-human intervention is exigent.[38] She interrupts when the odds are overwhelmingly weighted by magic against merely human abilities, employing her superior perspective to even the advantage, but does not, unlike Merlin, interfere in the purely human struggle of social destiny.

Having refused to be constructed as a beloved object in the frame of relations proposed by Merlin, Nyneve eventually improvises a construction of her own, with the acquisition of the knight Pelleas for a husband. She does this in a display of her own form of prowess, in playful imitation of the typical chivalric pattern of rescue.[39] Her winning her knight through the defeat of the initial contender for his love is as much a manifestation of feminine desire acting for itself as an independent force in the world, as it is a dispensation of exact justice to two mortals deadlocked by their emotions. To deliver Pelleas from the excesses of Ettarde's cruelty and pride, she enchants him, turning his love away from Ettarde and toward herself, thereby fully transacting Merlin's role by completing the very spell she made Merlin promise never to cast on her, and gaining what she had been unwilling to surrender before.[40] Pelleas is thus a twice-enchanted subject, bound by a spell of magic, and one of emotion. We are told that his lady, true to the familiar pattern of other women practising enchantment, thereafter extends protection to her chosen knight in the form of safeguarding his reputation, by ensuring he is never upstaged by Launcelot in tournament.[41]

If Morgan and Nyneve may be said to differ—and some have argued that they are both merely divided aspects of a single magical being[42]—it is a difference of intensity, rather than of kind. Nyneve, in spite of her occasional compassion for Arthur, is more impersonal in her relations with the Arthurian world, less interested in its quotidian operations. Morgan, on the other hand, is intensely interested in the Arthurian ethos as a stage for her powers, and the disruptions she manufactures for the king and his knights point to a pleasure in their competitive display. Yet underlying the details of their surface gestures is an abiding similarity of nature. Both have a capacity for force that is not containable by knightly society alone, and therefore a level of independence which establishes them as unique. Each selects whom she will love, rather than being herself selected, and is not above a degree of coercion in the exercise of choice. Both are superb readers of the language of signs, whether it is to secretly encode, or to publicly decipher meaning, in the form of such symbolic objects as shield, horn, cloak or sword; and both are represented, finally, in the feminine escort that will deliver Arthur beyond the regions of his geographical authority.

These similarities shared by Nyneve and Morgan are themselves an expression of their dissimilarity from the rest of ordinary humankind. That is to say, they are factors for identifying their otherness within the context of narrative values—constructions to acknowledge the persistence of alternative voices and levels within the text. The presence of enchantresses and enchantment is thus a recognition of alterity in the Arthurian worldview, and of the active pressure of submerged discourses. Distinctions in moral judgment as applied to Morgan and Nyneve therefore tend to be founded less in any genuine opposition of their natures than on a difference in the perception and interpretation of their otherness. Because Nyneve is more detached from Arthurian society, functioning less visibly, the sense of her alienness is, ironically, reduced. By contrast, Morgan's febrile dynamism and repeated appearances on the Arthurian stage are highly visible, and the tension and suspense generated by her acts draw almost continuous attention to her as a foreign presence. Of the two, Morgan is then the enchantress far more recognisable as different, and other, from the human—a condition that is essential, Fredric Jameson shows us, to a definition of someone as evil:

Evil . . . continues to characterize whatever is radically different from me, whatever by virtue of precisely that difference seems to constitute a real and urgent threat to my own existence. So from the earliest times, the stranger from another tribe, the "barbarian" who speaks an incomprehensible language and follows "outlandish" customs, but also the woman, whose biological difference stimulates fantasies of castration and devoration . . . behind whose apparently human features a malignant and preternatural intelligence is thought to lurk: these are some of the archetypal figures of the Other, about whom the essential point to be made is not so much that [s]he is feared because [s]he is evil; [but] rather, [that] [s]he is evil *because* [s]he is Other, alien, different, strange, unclean, and unfamiliar.[43]

To compound the palpable impression of her difference, Morgan is also openly defiant of Arthurian values. Where Nyneve has quietly defeated and replaced Merlin—surely an act as destructive as any of Morgan's[44]—Morgan must hurl gloating challenges at Arthur when she outmanoeuvres him, or boastfully delight in her abilities: "'. . . and tell hym I feare hym nat whyle I can make me and myne in lyknesse of stonys, and lette hym wete I can do much more whan I se my tyme'" (*Works*, p. 152). Furthermore, her energies are unruly, her instincts unabashedly competitive. She desires not one, but several lovers (*Works*, pp. 256–57, 554, 555, 642–43, *passim*), and not only magical power, but the temporal authority of the king. The episode of the False Excaleber is set up so that she and Accolon may enact a replacement of Arthur and Uryens, for expressly ambitious reasons (*Works*, pp. 145–46); and the hostility she bears Guenevere, revealed in the episodes of the magical horn and insinuating shield she directs toward Arthur's court, arises from merely acquisitive hopes. Like Nyneve, she too is linked to Merlin by the text—he is "a devyls son" (*Works*, p 126), she "an erthely fende" (p. 149), a suitable description perhaps for one who is ultimately an overreacher, and whose form of enchanted play testifies to an intense interest in the demonstration and extension of her powers. In the final analysis, however, Morgan's impact is not as destructive as it might superficially seem. The trials she provides Arthur's knights serve to increase their abilities and reputations with successful endurance; and the potentially subversive instruments she sends to Arthur are deflected from their purpose when Nyneve publicly discloses their concealed meanings. Indeed, her last appearance in the text with her sister-enchantress, in the barge to Avalon, offers us a curiously suggestive image for a retrospective revision of her acts. Here she addresses Arthur not agonistically, but as a fellow player in a drama that has now concluded all its scenes, with their former identities irrelevant and discarded. Arthur's last actions have been enigmatic, seeming to indicate his anticipation of the barge and its women,[45] and eager to entrust his final destiny to them. Morgan's greeting to her brother—the only speaking voice among the women—is accordingly affectionate, concerned: "'A, my dere brothir! Why [ha]ve ye taryed so longe frome me? Alas, thys wounde on youre hede hath caught overmuch coulde!'" (*Works*, p. 1240). The tones are the gentle, chiding ones of a protectrice and healer, not those of a mortal enemy, and in them may be discerned a suggestion of the final instability and impermanence of all constructed identity. An affinity between them is at once suggested: the bond perhaps of two actors finally away from the pageant, who need no longer play their temporarily assigned roles.

In Malory's text, I have attempted to show, is a subtext of feminine presences—direct and indirect manifestations which together inscribe a range of play that perhaps yields, in the fullest sense, what has been called "the recovery of a possible operation of the feminine in language."[46]

NOTES

1. Three models in the treatment of women are posed by the examples of Gawayn, Tor, and Pellynor, constituting intertextual commentaries. See Sir Thomas Malory, *The Works of Sir Thomas Malory*, ed. Eugène Vinaver (Oxford: Clarendon Press, 1967), Book III (henceforth referred to as *Works*).

2. Though the "Rounde Table" is mentioned in Book II (*Works*, p. 62), it does not in fact formally exist till Book III (p. 120). Significantly, the object designating the knightly order—the round table itself—has by this time come to be associated with Guenevere. When it first appears in Wace's Arthuriad, it is only associated with Arthur. In the chronicles, it is the king, of course, who exclusively "arranges the entire symbolic system, presides over its rites and orders its meaning" (Charles Méla, "Perceval," in *Literature and Psychoanalysis: The Question of Reading: Otherwise*, ed. Shoshana Felman [Baltimore: Johns Hopkins Univ. Press, 1982], p. 258). That a shift has occurred to connect the *queen* with this symbolic object is appropriate to romance.

3. Originally given Tristram by a princess of France, King Faramon's daughter (*Works*, p. 378). We notice that Tristram's hound, Husdant, in earlier traditions (Béroul, Thomas) is not specifically a feminine gift, but merely appears as Tristram's hunter.

4. There is a ritual acknowledgement of the importance of the sword, of course, in knighting ceremonies. Where these must be truncated of necessity, as for instance in the battlefield, they are abbreviated to the investment with the sword and the neckblow, which may stand in for other features. See Robert W. Ackerman, "The Knighting Ceremonies in the Middle English Romances," *Spec.*, 19 (1944), p. 294.

5. Arthur seems to know precisely what has to be done with Excaleber, and, in his chastisement of Bedyvere upon the latter's failure twice to carry out instructions, what nature of response to expect from the casting of the sword upon the waters. From Bedyvere's initial reluctance to comply, we might guess that it would be a very real temptation indeed to keep the weapon for its "precious stonys" and splendour, or to pass it on as a gift for loyal service. Arthur must be admired for doing neither. On the question of the sword's return to water, and its having come from a lady of the lake, we might note the interesting though arguable point that swords from the Anglo-Saxon

and Medieval periods that have been recovered from rivers, lakes or boggy ground seem to have survived best. See H.R. Ellis Davidson, *The Sword in Anglo-Saxon England: Its Archaeology and Literature* (Oxford: Clarendon Press, 1962), and R. Ewart Oakeshott, *The Sword in the Age of Chivalry* (London: Arms and Armour, 1981).

6. I disagree with Jill Mann's contention that in keeping the sword, Balyn is merely "taking the adventure" assigned to him (see "'Taking the Adventure': Malory and the *Suite du Merlin*," in *Aspects of Malory*, eds. Toshiyuki Takamiya and Derek Brewer [D.S. Brewer, 1981], pp. 71–91). An adventure *might* have been assigned to him, one intended for him, had he returned the sword. His refusal signifies, rather, a flouting of the adventure-that-might-have-been, in favour of one of his own definition—a declaration of autonomy with unfortunate consequences for himself and all who encounter him. It is willful self-assertion being recorded here, and not submission to chance, despite Balyn's—untrustworthy—claim to the contrary. The text goes on to depict him as notoriously inadequate in comprehension.

7. Merlin predicts that Lancelot will slay Gawain with it, "the man in the worlde that he lovith beste" (*Works*, p. 91).

8. It is a brief knighting ceremony in itself, making Galahad her knight.

9. Guenevere's claims to Lancelot's loyalty are thus established over the king's, making *her*, and not Arthur, his symbolic overlord. See H. Oskar Sommer, ed., *The Vulgate Version of the Arthurian Romances* (Washington: Carnegie Institution, 1910–1912), Vol. III, pp. 131, 137.

10. I avoid applying the term "courtly love" here because of the instability of its status as a critical concept and its fluctuating meaning, which automatically render any application controversial and troublesome. See, e.g., the discussions in Richard Barber, *The Knight and Chivalry* (Ipswich: Boydell and Brewer, 1974); Roger Boase, *The Origins and Meaning of Courtly Love* (Manchester: Manchester Univ. Press, 1977); Julia Kristeva, *Desire in Language: A Semiotic Approach to Literature and Art*, ed. Leon S. Roudiez, trans. Thomas Gora, et al. (New York: Columbia Univ. Press, 1980); Jacques Lacan, "God and the *Jouissance* of Woman," in *Feminine Sexuality: Jacques Lacan and the* Ecole Freudienne, eds. Juliet Mitchell and Jacqueline Rose, trans. Jacqueline Rose (New York: Norton, 1982); F.X. Newman, ed. *The Meaning of Courtly Love* (Albany: State Univ. of New York Press, 1968); Denis de Rougemont, *Love in the Western World*, trans. Montgomery Belgion (Princeton: Princeton Univ. Press, 1983); Irving Singer, *The Nature of Love, Vol. II: Courtly and Romantic* (Chicago: Univ. of Chicago Press, 1984).

11. It is a mode apparently designed for the subsidiary role of framing actions to the main narrative interest—romance. The movements between what I call "chronicle" and "romance" modes are generally unobtrusive—mediated perhaps by the very nature of the model Professor Benson sees Malory's tales as comprising: the "brief prose cycle" (Larry D. Benson, *Malory's Morte Darthur* [Cambridge, MA: Harvard Univ. Press, 1976], p. 4). In a cycle, we would expect the beginning and end of a society to be very different from the treatment of its routine existence, and any sense of possible disjunction we might feel is accordingly minimised. To further ease the transitions, characters like Gawayn appear in both modes.

12. But even here the narrative makes him an Arthur who takes orders from Merlin, acting almost as a (royal) lieutenant. Malory's Arthur, even in the so-called "chronicle" sections, never has the control and stature of Geoffrey's, La3amon's or Wace's, or even that of the figure in the ME Alliterative *Morte Arthure* (Valerie Krishna, ed., *The Alliterative Morte Arthure: A Critical Edition* [New York: B. Franklin, 1976]).

13. Once a society *has* emerged, the characterisation quickly turns against these "chronicle" heroes, favouring instead the younger, women-serving knights of the Round Table, even as the figure of Arthur himself recedes and diminishes in stature. They are superseded in prowess, with Kay transmuting into a male shrew and a butt of jokes, and Arthur into a slightly buffoonish and ineffectual romance king. Not only is he typically powerless to affect the comings and goings of his knights, but

he mutates into someone who takes falls in tournaments, and has to be re-horsed by Lancelot.

14. The knight may of course be accompanied by a maiden or a dwarf, or be temporarily in company. But the model is now *individual*, and not group activity—a paradigmatic "individualism" that arises largely out of a relation to the feminine. I owe the distinctions in this section to Peter Haidu's discussion of romance (Peter Haidu, "Romance: Idealistic Genre or Historical Text?," in *The Craft of Fiction: Essays in Medieval Poetics*, ed. Leigh A. Arrathoon [Rochester, MI: Solaris Press, 1984], p. 31).

15. Presumably because love of another, as opposed to love of self, is outward-directed, and implies a degree of altruism previously unthinkable. "Pagan love of fame was being brought under control" (Morton W. Bloomfield, "The Problem of the Hero in the Later Medieval Period," in *Concepts of the Hero in the Middle Ages and the Renaissance*, eds. Norman T. Burns and Christopher J. Reagan [Albany: State Univ. of New York Press, 1975], p 44).

16. "The great invention of the medieval romancers was to link love to glorious deeds so as to make love the direct cause and heroic personal identity and social position [only] the indirect consequences" (Cesare Segre, "What Bakhtin Left Unsaid: The Case of the Medieval Romance," in *Romance: Generic Transformation from Chrétien de Troyes to Cervantes*, eds. Kevin Brownlee and Marina Scordilis Brownlee [Hanover: Univ. Press of New England, 1985], p. 35).

17. Whatever the ethical status of this lady of the lake, the enmity between Balyn and herself is oddly expressed in terms of a gender jurisdiction, with each of them being responsible for deaths in the other's family along sexually-divided lines, in a strangely elemental blood-struggle for dominion. Merlin is also singularly unconvincing here in his retrospective vindication of Balyn. Why did he not call the lady of the lake "the falsist damesell that lyveth" (*Works*, p. 67) on the occasion of her presenting Excaleber to Arthur? We might notice instead that Merlin's later downfall, which he is able to foresee, but unable to prevent, is accomplished by *another* "lady of the lake." Perhaps a suggestion of competing spheres of influence and power exists here.

18. Balyn thus not only denies recognition of his debt to the sword-bearing maiden for her part in the drama at Arthur's court (which enables his moral worth to be proven), but with the slaughter of Excaleber's owner, he prevents Arthur from fulfilling *his* debt as well. Courtly society depends on the acknowledgement of just such relationships of duty and obligation, a basis of order.

19. His interventions are as disastrous for false lovers as for true ones—witness the case of Garnysh of the Mount and Duke Harmel's daughter.

20. Though in fact his best (and least morally ambiguous) accomplishments even in this realm are performed when he takes direction from Merlin. Interestingly, Balyn's story is literally sandwiched between "chronicles" and "romance" sections of the Arthuriad, between the close of wars and the start of the cycles of quest and adventure. Needless to say, his making off with Lyle of Avilion's sword does not itself constitute a genuine "quest" as such.

21. His acts of destruction nearly always coincide with defiance of social law as well. For instance, he retains his sword in Pellam's hall in a rude breach of custom, and kills Garlon, his host's brother, under Pellam's roof, and without issuing prior warning or challenge.

22. In a courtly society not at war or under foreign threat, the identity-forging requirements of "adventure" (see Mann) are most often to be met in service to the feminine, whose causes prompt and invite a wide field of knightly activity. Since female interests are thus quintessential to the formation of masculine personality, the agents of chance—like Fortune herself—typically tend to be feminine.

23. Hermann J. Weigand, *Three Chapters on Courtly Love in Arthurian France and Germany* (Chapel Hill: Univ. of North Carolina Press, 1956), p. 33.

24. See Whitehead's sensitive reading of the final, moving events in the Lancelot-Guenevere relationship, where even Lancelot's "resolution to retire from the

world . . . is an act of self-identification with his lady" (F. Whitehead, "Lancelot's Penance," in *Essays on Malory*, ed. J.A.W. Bennett [Oxford: Clarendon Press, 1963], pp. 110–13).

25. While also simultaneously "bring[ing] his relation to Guenevere to the center of action" (Benson, p. 90). Where the OF Vulgate Cycle has a number of knights send their captives to surrender to the queen, Malory re-works the features of the story to emphasise Lancelot's unique subservience to Guenevere. See Benson, pp. 82–88, for an account.

26. Even the act of fathering Galahad, so necessary to the Grail Quest element, is depicted as involuntary, the result of wily manipulations by Elayne and Dame Brusen. Maureen Fries is of course correct in positing a suspect Tristram as the foil to Lancelot's unswervingly loyal character ("The Tragic Pattern in Malory's *Morte Darthur*: Medieval Narrative as Literary Myth," in *The Early Renaissance* (Acta 5), ed. Aldo S. Bernado [Binghamton: State Univ. of New York Press, 1979], pp. 81–99). The sordid affair with Segwarydes' wife, and his marrying of the second Isode testify to a corrupt fidelity. Ironically, it is Tristram's love that should be perfect, since unlike Lancelot he is constrained to love by a magic potion. It speaks much for the power of freely-given love that it is Lancelot who is the superior lover.

27. Heinrich Zimmer, *The King and the Corpse: Tales of the Soul's Conquest of Evil* (New York: Pantheon Press, 1956), p. 133.

28. See Benson (pp. 224, 231) on the re-suscitation of Lancelot's supremacy after the Grail Quest section with the healing of Sir Urré, and Malory's careful placing of the Quest within the "context of worldly chivalry." To Jessie Weston, Galahad is merely "his father's representative" in a spiritual context, "vicarious achiever of the quest" for Lancelot (*The Legend of Sir Lancelot du Lac* [London: David Nutt, 1901], p. 142). We might note that Lancelot's first name is "Galahad" (*Works*, p. 126), and see Galahad as a Lancelot stripped of the adulterous relationship with Guenevere that is anathema to the clerical mind.

29. The more attractive younger knights in particular are linked to Lancelot in surreptitious ways by the text and their lives similarly manifest a brand of idealism that is inextricable from a pervasive feminine presence. See especially the characterisations of Gareth, La Cote Male Tayle, and Alysaundir le Orphelyne.

30. That is, all but requests of a sexual nature are effective. Obviously, obedience to Guenevere would preclude compliance to others in this area, though Lancelot is lamentably attractive to women (see, e.g., the importuning of him by the two Elaynes, Hellawes, Morgan and the three queens, the maiden who frees him from Mellygaunce's captivity, etc.). From the earliest traditions, and even in the so-called parallel tradition of the MHG *Lanzelet* (Ulrich von Zatzikhoven, trans. Kenneth G.T. Webster [New York: Columbia Univ. Press, 1951], Lancelot's characterisation has been of a man to whom women are irresistibly drawn, and whose adventures invariably involve the feminine. In Malory's text, women recognise him even when he is disguised.

31. That enchantment is feared by warriors is axiomatic in all literatures, including the oral. Underlying that response are the competitive structures of two divergent forms of power with a similar goal—domination. Warrior culture, so visible in its trapping, is naturally fearful of a force whose operations are mysterious and invisible, and which it suspects of being more efficacious than (merely) human physical strength.

32. There is, moreover, a manifestly literary quality to many of Merlin's displays of power, several of his forecasts turning upon a trick of writing: since he is able to bring about what he "foresees" through manipulation of those around him, who co-operate with his arrangements, his assertions, like any author's notes-in-progress, are intrinsically self-fulfilling. The implication of this handling is detectable in Merlin's love of dramatic disguise, hoax and deception, each instance of which playfully puts his audience in doubt of the relationship between the appearance of a thing, and its

referent—to fracture the signifying process so that he remains the most accurate reader of signs in the sections he inhabits.

33. The basis of Merlin's trick is merely the creating of a slide between signifier (here, a person's appearance) and signified (that person's identity), switching "meanings" between Uther and the Duke of Cornwall for a night. Dame Brusen does precisely the same thing, confusing the codes of identity (Elayne's with Guenevere's) through the substituted sign of the queen's ring. From Merlin's manipulation, Arthur, king in the secular realm, is born, while from Brusen's comes Galahad, a spiritual king of a spiritual country.

34. An inner fragmentation would seem to attend the loss of virginity, dramatised in folklore and myth by the motif of sudden loss of magical powers with the onset of sexual experience. Brünhilde, in the *Nibelungenlied*, is a notable literary example. Power passes on with the surrender of one's sexual being to another. Something of this may possibly glimmer in the idea of sexual withholding that is one strain in the original configuration of courtly love in lyric poetry. By retaining intact her physical and psychic self, Nyneve continues to hold a palpable form of power over him who loves her.

35. In Merlin's complete resignation to his projected end may be sensed a faint shadow of mythic inexorability, and the structure of cyclical replacement. "'A,' sayed the kyng, 'syn ye knowe of youre evil adventure, purvey for hit, and putt hit away by youre crauftes, that mysseadventure.' / 'Nay,' seyde Merlion, 'hit woll not be.'" (*Works*, p. 125).

36. "And allwayes he lay aboute to have hir maydynhode, and she was ever passynge wery of hym and wolde have bene delyverede of hym, for she was aferde of hym for cause he was a devyls son, and she cowde not be skyft of him by no means" (*Works*, p. 126). The text justifies Nyneve's response by making Merlin too pressing and importunate, and her "wery" resistance only natural. The bringing back of the old slur on Merlin's origins weighs against him conclusively.

37. In the chronicle versions of Geoffrey, Wace and La3amon, Merlin is of course not even associated with the Arthuriad at all, but only the "Utheriad," so to speak.

38. What this "other reality" might be like is far plainer in the OF Vulgate Cycle or the MHG *Lanzelet*, where she is clearly an otherworldly fay, ruling a feminine domain.

39. Through magic, a woman's equivalent of a knight's skill at arms, and a means of accomplishing a purpose by her own efforts. Pelleas' assigned role in the episode is that of the besieged "lady" who requires succour from a distress he is unable to alleviate on his own.

40. Nyneve is now also a representative of divine authority, as Merlin once was. Where Merlin used to discourse on the will of God, chastising Arthur for squandering his military resources and for sexual incest (*Works*, pp. 36, 44), Nyneve now delivers God's judgment to Ettarde for excesses of cruelty and pride (*Works*, pp. 171–72).

41. We note that Lyonesse similarly guarantees Gareth's reputation with a magical ring of invulnerability (*Works*, p. 345). Like a number of other knights, Pelleas virtually disappears from the narrative after the formalisation of his relations with his lady. There are occasions when he accompanies Nyneve to court as her consort described in much the same way as when wives or mistresses accompany male personages on celebratory occasions ("So agayne the feste of Pentecoste cam the Damesell of the Laake and brought with hir sir Pelleas . . . . " [*Works*, p. 179]).

42. For L.A. Paton this is the "fairy mistress" who is healer and protectress, seductive *amie* and vengeful antagonist, schemer and shape-shifter—an elemental goddess who exists outside the realm of human morality and for whom its categories are inapplicable, perhaps impertinent (Lucy Allen Paton, *Studies in the Fairy Mythology of Arthurian Romance* [Boston: Athenaeum, 1903]).

43. Fredric Jameson, *The Political Unconscious: Narrative as a Socially Symbolic Act* (Ithaca: Cornell Univ. Press, 1981), p. 115. Jameson observes that romance is a medium for women ("the most characteristic protagonists of romance") because of the room it makes for *guile* as an operating force, over the "sheer physical power" that distinguishes a masculine medium (p. 113). In this light, Morton Bloomfield's lament for the absence of "a hero of any sort worthy of note in the English tradition between Beowulf and Spenser"—by which he means an *epic* hero of supremely and unambiguously masculine proportions—is significant. He finds instead a proliferation of protagonists in the later Middle Ages (Bloomfield, pp. 33–37). This "de-heroicisation" of literature and proliferation of characters testifies of course to a widening and varying of an original concept of heroism narrowly male, and which makes possible, and is itself the effect of, and entrance of the feminine and feminine kinds of heroism into textual life, that were previously (by definition) excluded.

44. Nyneve has in fact removed from Arthurian society a significant source of benevolent patronage, but escapes censure for having accomplished this discreetly, away from general observation. Her habitual understatement, and Morgan's customary overstatement, leads to their respective vindication and vilification by society.

45. "Though Arthur returns Excalibur to the Lady of the Lake to signal his mortal distress, it seems a signal arranged with Morgan, for she immediately appears with the greeting 'A, my dere brothir!' (III, 1240) and bears Arthur away" (Myra Olstead, "Morgan le Fay in Malory's *Morte Darthur*," *BBIAS*, 19 [1967], p. 138).

46. Luce Irigaray, *Ce Sexe qui n'en est pas Un* (Paris: Minuit, 1977), p. 74.

"LE DONNE ANTICHE E' CAVALIERI"

WOMEN IN THE ITALIAN ARTHURIAN TRADITION[1]

Regina Psaki

The Italian adaptations and translations of the Arthurian material have generally fared poorly at the hands of modern critics; the tendency to measure all medieval Arthurian literature against Chrétien de Troyes's "ideal" model has been an unfortunate constant in Arthurian criticism. In their travels across medieval Europe the Arthurian tales, both oral and written, were shapeshifters. Many who study this material claim that its incarnation in each language was somehow anomalous (read "inferior") with respect to its sources in French courtly culture. Wolfram's *Parzival*, both secular and at the same time much more spiritual in its ethical concerns than the *Conte del Graal*; the Old Norse shorthand translations of Old French courtly romances, adapted for a sterner setting; the Tuscan refashionings adapted to the noncourtly politics and ideology of the *comune*: all foreground those elements that suit the new environment, discarding some we may consider essential to the original. Personae and episodes are familiar, but all modify what medievalists have taken to be the heart of the French sources. The symbolic landscape of *aventure*, the itinerary of self-discovery and maturation, and the intricate psychological play of love and duty, of self and beloved, of loyalty to lord and lover, are categories codified in Chrétien's "biographical" romances. In fact, however, even in France these categories have already declined by the early thirteenth century. It is unproductive, therefore, to measure later works in other national literatures by the standard of those romances that nineteenth- and twentieth-century esthetics and ideology have dubbed "canonical."

Nonetheless, critics frequently *have* made precisely these comparisons, to the invariable disadvantage of the later authors. Presenting a global judgment on the Italian Arthurian material, for example, Antonio Viscardi described an entropy in its trajectory:

In the course of the fourteenth century a degeneration set in, which reduced the tone of Arthurian composition in Italy to monotony and triviality. This tendency had already manifested itself in the previous century in the French Prose *Tristan* and in the compilations in which the amours of various lovers are interspersed with the quest of the Grail. The heroes lose their distinguishing characters. Tristan is identical with Lancelot, and Lancelot with Perceval . . . . The Prose *Tristan* was the source of many versions in Italian and bequeathed to them its banality.[2]

Viscardi's emphasis on the declining individuality of the heroes betrays his adherence to the biographical model, a paradigm within which all later cycles with their multiple protagonists must perforce be devalued. If the Italian prose romances, composed for an educated and relatively upper-class audience, can generate such hostility, it will come as no surprise that the *cantari*, performed orally before a much less sophisticated public, are similarly found wanting.[3] Michelangelo Picone compares the production of Chrétien de Troyes and Marie de France, "created to entertain, but above all to form and educate, the refined courts of Northern Europe," to that of the *canterini*, "whose only purpose was to provide their assiduous and voracious listeners with a kind of collective escapism . . . [and] automatic patents of nobility."[4] Picone, a balanced and refined critic, is unusually harsh here, caricaturally elitist and francophile, scornful of the audience and producers of the *cantari*. His distaste for the quotidian, literal, and capitalistic lives of the new consumers of the Arthurian material is embarrassingly intense.[5] For him the *cantari* retain of their rich originals

> only the external scaffolding: a certain technical nomenclature, an heuristic patrimony of themes and motifs, a repertory of personae and of topical events; definitively gone however is the spirit which informed those personae and events, the semantic tension underlying the superficial manifestation of those themes and motifs. *Aventure* in the *cantari* is no longer an *iter*, a passage toward the Truth. . . . it has become instead . . . a label, serving only to catalogue; it is resolved in pure story, in brute narration . . . completely absent is every allusion to possible *other* senses, to latent levels of meaning.[6]

I present these judgments at such length both because they reflect a consensus on the post–twelfth-century Arthurian material and because they foreground those privileged aspects of early romance that later versions discard.

The parameters of the Chrétien-centered model of romance include exquisite and self-conscious artistry; a biographical focus on the maturation of the (male) individual; an intellectual and ideological agenda that makes the motifs of "adventure" and "quest" point beyond themselves to a transcendent spiritual humanity; and an itinerary of love and self-recognition that seems to elevate the female beloved to the status of virtual equal. But does the twelfth-century model actually privilege the female pole of the gender spectrum in an equal measure with the male? Are the "donne antiche e' cavalieri" of the romances Dante invokes in *Inferno* V really complementary and symbiotic?

In her book *Woman as Image in Medieval Literature*, Joan Ferrante sketches a positive picture for women in twelfth-century literature, which becomes more grim in the thirteenth century; she also notes, however, that the courtship plot of twelfth-century courtly romance "would seem to demand a real woman, but more often yields a symbol."[7] Roberta Krueger develops this insight in scrutinizing Chrétien's *oeuvre*:

> In most romances, the lady is neither the principal protagonist—the subject of the narrative's action—nor the narrator, the subject who speaks. Within the adventure, she is typically an object of exchange or an object of desire. . . . The [*Charrete*'s] female characters . . . are blank figures who appear suddenly and anonymously . . . their status and motivations are unexplained. . . .[8]

Krueger's description of the women of Chrétien's *Chevalier de la Charrete* also fits the female figures in the later compilation romances. Whatever other transformations occur from the twelfth to the thirteenth centuries, then, for women in Arthurian romance very little actually changes. They are still essentially corollary to the male hero, still extrinsic, and still more the bearers than the makers of meaning.[9] With the multiplication of stories in the compilation-model romances, the position of female figures has become only slightly more extrinsic than in the biographical model. The itinerary of the romance is still a *male* maturation and bonding, and Erec's is the lesson the community of knights learns best: no recreantise! Any attempt, therefore, to examine Italian Arthurian women always slides into a study of Arthurian men. Narrators, focalization, plot, characterization, all make it impossible to focus on the female characters independent of their male counterparts.[10] Why is this the case? What are the mechanisms by which our gaze is constantly directed back to the male protagonists?

I will now examine how the male-centered focus discounts two categories of women: the "heroines" Isotta and Ginevra in the late-thirteenth-century *Tristano Riccardiano*,[11] the early fourteenth-century *Tavola Ritonda*,[12] and the fourteenth-century *cantari*;[13] and other female figures both in the prose romances, and in those *cantari*—the *Ponzela Gaia, Brito da Brettagna, Liombruno, Bel Gherardino, La Donna del Vergiù*, and *Fiorio e Biancifiore*—that use Arthurian material only as settings or as markers of courtliness.[14] In this essay I offer a pragmatic narratological analysis with a feminist agenda, and I examine the following categories: the female characters' presence in or absence from the plot; their reward or punishment by the plot; the use of narrative focalization to program the reader's allegiance; the representation or suppression of women's thoughts, ideas, and motivations; overt narratorial praise or blame; the representation of women as physical and ethical individuals; and their status as pretext for or generatrix of adventure, and ultimately of narration itself.

Women in the plot of both romances and *cantari* are, to varying degrees, peripheral; we as readers follow the path of the hero. The story does not remain at home with the heroine, waiting at Camellotto, Tintoile, or the Gioiosa Guardia for the knight to return; it follows him in his adventures.[15] During these adventures various female figures swim into the ken of both knights and readers with the unpredictability of shooting stars:[16]

> E in quel punto, ecco davanti da lui, per uno picciolo sentiero, venir una donzella a cavallo; ed era scapigliata, e venia gridando, facciendo lo maggior lamento del mondo. Tristano, veggiendo la donzella in tale maniera, ebbe gran maraviglia; e sì la priega ch'ella gli dica, per cortesia, suo grave duolo . . .

> ["At that moment, a maiden on horseback suddenly appeared on a narrow path in front of him. She was all disheveled and rode crying, making the greatest lament in the world. Tristano was astonished by this sight, and asked the maiden to tell him, for courtesy's sake, why she was so very sorrowful" *Tav. Rit.* LIX.]

These secondary characters stand for adventures, or initiate them, or implore help, or pose challenges. They represent the unknown; they are never the familiar figures with whom the reader identifies; they are themselves interpretative objects, symbols (as Ferrante noted), mysterious agents. They remain firmly outside the spectrum of possible protagonists; they are instead the burdens or rewards assigned to the protagonists.

The "heroine" of the romances essentially inspires gallant deeds and song,[17] and waits until the hero returns to love her again.[18] But by far her most frequent impact on the plot is to provoke quarrels and violence among men. Most notably, the adulterous love of Tristano and Lancillotto for Isotta and Ginevra continually breaches the tenuous peace between Tristano and Marco, and between Lancillotto and Artù. It is only a small step from seeing the romances as chronicling the separations and reunions of the lovers, to reading them as chronicling the separations and reconciliations of Tristano and Marco, and Lancillotto and Artù.[19] When Tristano recovers from the madness brought on by his belief that Isotta had betrayed him, his first thoughts are not of her but of Marco: "Sono io al presente amico o nimico dello re Marco, mio signore e mio zio?" ("Am I at present a friend or an enemy of my lord and uncle, King Marco?" *Tav. Rit.* LXXII). In the *cantare* "Ultime imprese e morte di Tristano," Marco's reaction to the news that Tristano and Isotta is telling: "Lasso! la mia vita grava: / io veggio ben che Tristan non m'amava" ("Alas! my miserable life—I see clearly that Tristano did not love me," 6). In the T*avola Ritonda* the two adulterous couples are virtual mirror-images, dancing with Artù and Marco a stately minuet that occasionally intensifies to a frantic pace.[20] The women, objects of desire to all the male protagonists, provoke the various battles, betrayals, and vendettas between them; this is made explicit when Ginevra learns of Artù's defeat and disappearance:

> E la reina, intendendo le parole, immaginando sì come ella era istata cagione di tanto male, si affisse di dolore; e fu quello dolore sì corale, che passò per mezzoo del cuore, e di sùbito cadde morta. . . . E qui pone fine il nostro libro e a tutte storie e cavallerie ed avventure e battaglie e torniamenti che fatte furono per li cavalieri erranti.

> ["When the queen heard these words, she realized that she had been the cause of so much evil and was overcome with remorse. So sharp was her sorrow that it cut her heart in two, and suddenly she fell down dead. . . . So ends our book and with it all the stories, the chivalry, the adventures, the battles, and the tournaments made by the knights errant," *Tav. Rit.* CXLV.]

If a modern reader might instead indict Morderette's adulterous love and pursuit of Ginevra, or Artù's own hidden sin in fathering him, the medieval author (and, perhaps, audience) have no difficulty in identifying the flaw at the heart of the Arthurian dream of chivalry with Ginevra's transgressions—much more serious somehow than Isotta's.

It is worth noting that while Lancelot and Guinevere receive the lion's share of the attention in the French and English material, the Italian material very clearly favors Tristan.[21] This is abundantly clear in the *Tavola Ritonda*—which, much more than the *Tristano Riccardiano*, attempts to unite the various cycles into an interlaced whole—despite the narrator's occasional efforts to establish parity.[22] Tristano's superiority elevates Isotta, again despite the narrator's occasional perfunctory attempts to equate the two heroines.[23] When the two queens hear that Lancillotto and Tristano are dead, Ginevra's lament is four lines long, and Isotta's twenty-four (*Tav. Rit.*, CVI). The status of the principal female characters derives from the status of their male counterparts, and in any case the scope and importance of Isotta and Ginevra are strictly limited.

The minor female characters too have clearly limited roles. They are objects of exchange from the very opening of the *Tavola Ritonda*, in which knights seize ladies from the knights they defeat (I). Both the *Tristano Riccardiano* and the *Tavola Ritonda* confer a notable ambiguity on Tristano's winning of Isotta for his uncle, an ambiguity that reduces her agency at the same time as it legitimizes their later adulterous love:

> E lo ree Languis disse: "Io la voglio dare pur a ttee e nonn ad altrui."
> E .T. disse: "Io la voglio pur per lo ree Marco, inpercioe ch'io igli l'òe
> promessa." E lo ree Languis disse a .T.: "E promettimi tue queste cose
> sì come cavaliere?" E .T. disse che ssì. Allora si prese lo ree madonna
> Isotta per mano e .T. la sposa per lo ree Marco.

> ["And King Languis said, 'I want to give her to you and to no one
> else.' Tristano said, 'But I want her for King Marco, because I prom-
> ised her to him.' King Languis said to Tristano, 'Do you promise me
> this as a knight?' And Tristano said yes. Then he took madonna Isotta
> by the hand and Tristan married her for King Marco," *Tris. Ricc.*
> LVI.]

The Gaia Pulcella, daughter of Fata Morgana, is an object of exchange in the *Tavola Ritonda* in the narrative of Sir Burletta of the Desert, who had tried unsuccessfully to rape her. To Sir Burletta's indignation, Lancillotto intervened, fought him, and restored the girl to her father. When Burletta recounts this to Tristano, the latter says of Lancillotto, "Imperò che grande ingiuria fue quella ch'egli fece a voi: ma di ciò mi foe grande maraviglia, ch'egli non eè usato di fare tali cose" ("It seems a great injury that he did you, but I marvel at it greatly, for it is not like him to do such things,"

LXXXI). This episode, on the surface extraordinary, is in fact emblematic of the way women function as symbolic currency in these romances.

If women are not the protagonists and are in fact dangers and distractions to the honor and solidarity of the real male protagonists, then it is not surprising that they remain ciphers to us. They rarely serve as narrative focalizers; that is, we rarely see the action through their eyes or from their perspective. In the *Cantare di Fiorio e Biancifiore*, for example, even when we might expect to be following the abducted Biancifiore, the narration keeps us firmly tracking the young Saracen lover, who traces his Christian beloved with the help of those who notice the resemblance between them:

E la sera giunse in un albergheria,
ed immantenente che s'è dismontato
dice la donna de l'albergatore:
—Messer, voi m'asomigliate a Biancifiore.
E Fiorio disse: —Gentil donna mia,
quello ch'io vi dico non vi sia in pesanza:
quando ci albergò la druda mia,
Biancifiore, la prima speranza?

["That evening he arrived at an inn, and as soon as he had dismounted the innkeeper's wife said to him, 'My lord, you look to me just like Biancifiore.' And Fiorio said, 'My dear lady, do not be displeased by what I say: when did my love lodge here, Biancifiore, my best hope?'" 78–79.]

Similarly, when Marco steals Isotta from the tower where Tristano had left her, we see the event reported twice from the position of the two men, but never from that of the queen:

. . . trovando la bella Isotta, sìe la presoro, e appresso la puosoro sovr'uno ricco e portante palafreno; e tale fecioro di Brandina. . . . Essendo al palagio, lo re fae imprigionare la reina in una grande e ricca camera, e quivi la serra a tre chiavi. . . . E allora cavalcano verso la torre. Ed essendo davanti, trovarono tutto il campo scalpitato d'orme di cavagli; e nella torre non truovano Isotta nè Brandina. . . . E sappiendo sì come la reina era tolta per lo re Marco, sì come gli pastori gli diceano; a lui gli mancarono i cinque sentimenti, e non sentia niente; e 'n tale maniera giacque per mezza ora.

["Finding the beautiful Isotta, they took her and set her on a rich palfrey; they took Brandina as well. . . . When they reached the palace, the king had the queen imprisoned in a big, luxurious chamber, locking her in with three keys. . . . Then (Tristano and Governale) rode to the tower, and when they arrived they saw that the field outside was all marked by horses' hooves, and neither Isotta nor Brandina was in the tower. . . . When (Tristano) found out from the shepherds that King Marco had taken the queen, all five senses deserted him and he felt nothing, lying there like that for half an hour," *Tav. Rit,* XLVI–XLVII.]

The narration subtly but forcefully positions us to track events from the stance of the male protagonists, to follow what they, not the female figures, see and feel.[24]

Narrative focalization is ultimately a more vital index of the author's presentation of women than the representation or suppression of the heroine's thoughts. As is common in medieval literature, we must interpret the motivations of most of the characters from their behavior and from terse narratorial commentary, rather than from any depiction of their reflections. We see these characters for the most part from the outside. When in the *Tavola Ritonda* Marco has foolishly promised and given Isotta to Palamides, the narrator tells us,

E Tristano udendo tali novelle, fece vista d'uomo impazzato; e andava gridando per la sala, "L'arme, arme!" e dicendo: —Ahi, Palamides, ahi Palamides! bene ti puoi e ti dei tener contento, che pur ne se' venuto alla tua di quello tesoro che tanto tempo ài desiderato!

["Tristano, hearing such news, looked like a madman and went shouting through the court, 'Arms! My arms!' and saying, 'Oh, Palamidesso, Palamidesso, how happy you must be now that you have gained the treasure you have wanted for so long!'" XLII.]

We are more likely to see the actions than the thoughts of any given character; at most, we will see a brief description of state of mind, as in this representation of the same episode from the *Tristano Riccardiano*:

E quando .T. intese queste parole, sì *ne fue molto dolente, più che neuno altro cavaliere* e disse: "E Iddio, e cchi uddio mai parlare di cosie malvagi cavalieri, sì come sono quegli di Cornovaglia, che per diliveragione di loro donna non vollero prendere arme?" . . . Molto fae grande pianto .T. tutta la notte per madonna Isotta e in quella notte non dormì egli nè poco ned assai.

["And when Tristano heard these words, *he was more sorrowful than any other knight,* and said, 'Oh, God, who ever heard of such base knights as these of Cornwall, who would not even take up arms to free their lady?' . . . Tristano made a great lament for madonna Isotta all night long, and that night he did not sleep, either much or little," LXXIII–LXXIV, emphasis mine.]

When the Italian texts do reveal what a character is thinking, the expression used is "dire in sè" ("to say to oneself"), or "dire nel suo cuore" ("to say in one's heart"), as though vocabulary were lacking for reporting a protagonist's inmost thoughts.[25]

Interestingly, narrators are most likely to expand on the thoughts of female *antagonists.* When a woman forces her attentions on an unwilling protagonist, the narrator typically condemns her perfidious and irrational desire at some length.[26] This departure from usual narrative practice signals an unease about women who attempt to compel men sexually, an unease that was wholly absent from, for example, the treatment of Sir Burletta's attempted rape of the Gaia Pulcella (*Tav. Rit.,* LXXXI). As Roberta Krueger notes, women are allowed to seem powerful insofar as they are indifferent and immobile:

> Woman's "power" is a fiction of the male subject who needs her to resist so that he can desire her. If we reformulate this from a feminist perspective, woman's "impenetrable divinity" marks her displacement from the position of the desiring subject, a displacement that male desire and the enigma of woman continually enact.[27]

When women in the Italian romances articulate an active desire that is not mutual, they disturb the universe far more than the knight who rapes or abducts. Moreover, the horrified and innocent object of their attentions announces, scandalized, "ch'i' non farei cotale fallo al signor mio" ("I would not do such a wrong to my lord"), even when, as in *Bel Gherardino,* the young man owes no loyalty at all to the lady's husband.[28] Unleashed female desire, transformed into savage female revenge, exceeds any cruelty knights can inflict on each other; the Duchess of "La Donna del Vergiù" wants to have her victim "squartare . . . dall'inforcatura insino alle reni" ("quartered . . .

from his groin up to his kidneys," 28). Small wonder, then, that men appear in Dante's *Inferno* V as the helpless accomplices of lust, secondary accessories to what is in its desperate violence depicted as a woman's crime.

Other means of characterizing the heroines in the Italian Arthurian material include physical and moral description of them, their actions and speeches, and overt narratorial commentary. Without exception the initial introduction of the female characters follows that of the male protagonists. We know Lancillotto before we meet Ginevra, Tristano before Isotta, the *cavaliere* before the Donna del Vergiù, Liombruno before madonna Aquilina, and so on. The stories center unequivocally on a male protagonist, who is soon provided with a female counterpart. Introductions of women are briefer and more general than the extensive portraits we find in twelfth-century French romance.[29] Never do we see a catalogue of her moral qualities analogous to that devoted to Tristan's "four virtues" of prowess, loyalty, love, and courtesy, nor do the narrators of romances and *cantari* ever describe the appearance of the heroes. The heroine's role is to be beautiful and beloved, more than to find someone beautiful and love him, and the narrator keeps the reader's eye firmly on this man's-eye view of the women.

The actions of the heroines, which also characterize them powerfully, do not usually originate with the Italian authors; the *cantari* as well as the romances follow their French sources fairly closely. The Italian authors retain the curious blamelessness of the protagonists, male and female, no matter what their errors or falls from grace. After Braguina's heroic subterfuge in "lending" her virginity to the deflowered Isotta, the queen orders her killed to prevent her ever revealing the secret. The narrator of the *Tristano Riccardiano* resolutely refrains from commenting on this treachery, speculating on its cause, or excusing Isotta on the grounds of emotional distress. While the inscribed audience—the servants ordered to kill Braguina, and Braguina herself—offer all the horrified commentary necessary, theirs is no real condemnation. Not only does Braguina return gladly to Isotta because she prefers her own lady's unkindness to the kindness of any other,[30] but the scene of the would-be murder is more comic than pathetic:

> E ll'uno deli servi sì disse a Braguina: "Egli ee pur bisongno che ttue muoi in questo diserto, e noi percioe sì tt'avemo menata quae per ucciderti." Allora disse Braguina: "Ditemi, servi, fate voi queste cose per volontade dela reina?" E' servi sì rispuosero e dissero che ssie. Allora incomincioe Braguina forte mente a ppiangere. E ll'uno deli servi sì disse all'altro: "Uccidila," e quegli rispuose e disse: "E cche no l'uccidi tue?"

["One of the servants told Braguina, 'I'm afraid you have to die in this wilderness, and so we've brought you here to kill you.' Then Braguina said, 'Tell me, servants, are you doing these things at the queen's behest?' And the servants answered and said that they were. Then Braguina began to cry bitterly. And one servant said to the other, 'Kill her,' and the other answered, 'Well, why don't you kill her?'" *Tris. Ricc.*, LXVII.]

Neither the narrator nor the characters really hold Isotta accountable for her betrayal. Like her elaborately staged ambiguous oath,[31] it is not figured as blameworthy: these are simply the shifts to which her irresistible, indeed supernatural, passion reduces her. At one point in the *Tavola Ritonda*, a knight brings to Tintoile an enchanted horn that will identify unchaste ladies (XLIII). Naturally the horn incriminates Isotta; Dinasso the seneschal defends her with dazzling illogic, dissuading Marco from burning all the ladies who fail the test. Isotta's guilt with regard to the king is not a serious offense, and we are not invited to condemn her.

Ginevra is also curiously invulnerable to blame in the romances and the *cantari*, even though she and Lancilotto have no magic love philter to attenuate their guilt. The evil that Ginevra, Isotta, and our heroic knights commit is always to be overlooked on the grounds of ignorance or *forza maggiore*. Tristano, for example, indulges in occasional infidelities (including an absent-minded marriage) for which no one condemns him.[32] Bel Gherardino, abandoned by his fairy mistress for revealing the secret of their love, yields to the Sultan's wife when she threatens to cry rape:

Ed ella il prese co molta baldanza,
  dicendo: —Se tu non fai quel ch'io desio,
io griderò, che non è mia usanza,
  e farotti morire, in fé di Dio.
E in quel punto gli gittò il braccio al collo,
  e così il prese per forza e baciollo.
    Ed e', veggendo che non può stornare
  che egli non faccia il suo comandamento,
fra suo cuore disse: "E' mi conviene pure fare,
  ed io ne vo' fornire il suo talento."
E sì la prese sanza più indugiare,
  e del grande desio, ch'è pieno d'alimento,
al suo volere di quelle rose colse,
  e poscia per più volte se ne tolse.

["She took hold of him boldly, saying, 'If you don't do what I want, I will scream, which is not my habit, and have you killed, by God's faith.' At that she threw her arms around his neck, seized him by force and kissed him. And he, seeing that he cannot get out of doing what she commanded, said to himself, 'I have to do it anyway, and I want to satisfy her desire.' So he took her without further delay; of that great desire, abundantly fueled, he gathered the roses as he pleased, and then gathered them several times more," 22–23.]

The protagonists, in other words, because they are the focus of our attention, are *a priori* not blameworthy; the narrator can condemn the antagonists as cruel or uncourtly.[33]

The unconcern with psychological realism and interior moral development is consistent with the generally external and social concerns not only of Italian Arthurian romance, but of the particular stage of the Arthurian romance on which it draws, the thirteenth-century compilation model. As Picone points out (though I disagree that this proves the inferiority of the *cantari* vis-à-vis twelfth-century French source material), the emphasis placed on naming, recognition, and personal integration in Chrétien and Marie exists only formally, not essentially, in the Italian romances and *cantari*.[34] Knights learn, forget, relearn, change, and abandon their names without any implied loss or recovery of identity in a real sense. They travel incognito and fight their best friends (or assist their mortal enemies) without the ensuing recognitions carrying any particular symbolic freight. The obligations of chivalry imply less an individual ethical integrity and integration than a pedestrian concern with keeping the roads safe.[35] The positive influence women could exercise on the knights who loved them devolves into a rather mechanical inspiration, prescribed like iron for anemia. Sir Viano advises King Artù to summon the queen and her ladies to inspire the king's knights, to turn the tide of the battle; the mysterious and elevated "good" thus becomes "a kind of a tonic which, when taken, produces instant valor and chivalric worth."[36] These transformations, however, characterize thirteenth-century Arthurian romance and are not to be read as signs of a uniquely Italian "simplification" and "consumerist adaptation" for an inferior class, as Picone claims.[37] Indeed, the compilation model's perfunctory treatment of this motif works to unveil the male-female dynamic mystified in the twelfth-century romances. The larger cultural shifts mirrored in the later texts require further study before we can assess the works on their own terms.

The role of women in the Italian Arthurian material is thus ultimately consistent with their roles in the French sources. Despite the many innovations in Arthurian romance after the twelfth century, the male-centered focus of the earliest romances continues in later French romance and in foreign adaptations. The presence, even exaltation, of female principals in Arthurian and other fantasy texts works to occlude the actual relegation of women and femininity to the margins of the male universe.[38] Women fill many object-functions in the structural schema of the romances: they are objects of desire and objects of exchange,[39] motivating forces, rewards, temptations, distractions, and origins or pretexts of adventure.

To conclude this essay, I would like to consider this last role. Women are connected not merely causally to adventure, magic, and mystery; they are related metaphorically as well. In the Arthurian world, women and adventure are figural equivalents, with their compelling appeal, their incomprehensible logic, their incontrovertible rules. Adventure is the nearest analogue to the pursuit of the woman, the pursuit of the story, that the narrative labyrinth enacts. The unbending parameters of the other, to which the protagonist can only submit, are articulated explicitly in the *Tavola Ritonda*'s episode of the "Isola della Malvagia Usanza" (Isle of the Evil Custom), in which knights must compete in prowess and ladies in beauty. The losers, of course, die: the knights in battle, and the ladies, tellingly, by decapitation. No one seems to want to uphold this hideous adventure, but no one can change it:

> Avvegna che quella usanza trovata nè ordinata fosse per lui, sìe gli conveniva mantenerla e accrescerla, per la ubedienza, a tutto il suo podere; e per tale convenente si provvede. . . . Allora messer Tristano, vedendo tale stremo e cattivo partito, e che quivi non valeva prodezza nè combattere, mal volentieri si recòe a tagliare la testa alla dama; ma pure a Brunoro e a lei egli la tagliò, chè altro non gli valeva. . . .

> ["Even though (Brunoro) had not ordained this custom, he had to maintain and augment it, in compliance, with all his power, and for this necessity he readied himself. (XXXV). . . . Then Sir Tristano, seeing himself in such an extreme and bitter situation, and that here his prowess as a fighter was worth nothing, reluctantly made up his mind to cut off the lady's head, but only hers and Brunoro's, since he could do nothing else," XXXVII.]

The terms of the various adventures assume the inflexibility of laws of nature. These arbitrary and unreasonable demands are clearly analogous only to the various requirements of the *domna*: the Queen capriciously orders

Lancelot to fight his best or his worst, in the *Charrete*; Isotta reproves Tristano for imaginary infractions of the "rules" of love; the various fairy mistresses impose silence on their lovers, and punish them for breaking it (*Liombruno, Bel Gherardino, Ponzela Gaia*). There is no apparent logic to the commands of the women, who belong to that arbitrary and irresistible world of the Other figured in the knights' periodic contact with an Otherworld.

To say that adventure and women in the Arthurian world are virtual equivalents, rendered strange and distant in order to be desired and pursued, is not to reduce the itinerary of Arthurian narrative to a banal quest for sexual pleasure, union, or restoration. On the contrary: the itinerary of Arthurian narrative is rather the pursuit of narrative itself, not its achievement; and the pursuit of the female beloved is its own object.[40] Thus, as soon as Tristano and Isotta (or Lancillotto and Ginevra) do achieve perfect union, the narrative must separate them in order to start over again. The female figure in Arthurian romance can essentially be defined as all that is not the male subject, all that he lacks, all that drives him. The enigma of femininity in Arthurian romance is the desired object that affords no greater pleasure than its endless pursuit.

Despite the changes the Arthurian material underwent in Italy, the women of the Italian Arthurian tradition retain the female role in French romance. The Italian tradition, rather than reflect a new "mercantile" ideology as has been suggested,[41] emulates the second wave of French Arthurian literature, the decline-and-fall compilations, as distinct from the "biographical," symbolic, consciously hypersubtle first wave of twelfth-century romance. In this context, the role of women in driving behavior, inspiring excellence, embodying obscure power vis-à-vis a male protagonist, remains consistent across frontiers of language, political structure, and class. While single episodes or works may push at the parameters of that role, making room for the autonomous female characters we find in both literatures, female characters eventually subside into a conventionally "feminine" role. This is all but inevitable, since they, like the adventures knights pursue and the endless narration that writers and readers seek, must remain "outside" the male subject, an endlessly receding object of desire.

NOTES

1. I know of no essay on women in the Italian Arthurian tradition, but on Italian Arthurian literature generally, see: Daniela Delcorno Branca, *I romanzi italiani di Tristano e la Tavola Ritonda* (Firenze: Olschki, 1968), *Il romanzo cavalleresco medievale* (Firenze: Sansoni, 1974), and others; Joan Ferrante, *The Conflict of Love and Honor: The Medieval Tristan Legend in France, Germany and Italy* (The Hague:

Mouton, 1973); Edmund G. Gardner's *The Arthurian Legend in Italian Literature* (New York: Dutton, 1930), still not superseded; Donald L. Hoffman, "The Arthurian Tradition in Italy," in *King Arthur Through the Ages*, vol. 1, ed. Valerie M. Lagorio and Mildred Leake Day (New York: Garland, 1990), pp. 170–188; H. Krauss, "Der Artus-Roman in Italien," in *Le roman jusqu'à la fin du XIIIe siècle*, eds. Jean Frappier and Reinhold Grimm, GRLMA (Heidelberg: Winter, 1978); Pio Rajna, *Le fonti dell' "Orlando furioso"* (Florence, 1900); and Viscardi's article cited in note 2.

2. "Arthurian Influences on Italian Literature from 1200 to 1500," in *Arthurian Literature in the Middle Ages: A Collaborative History*, ed. Roger Loomis (Oxford: Clarendon Press, 1959), p. 424.

3. The *cantare* was a short narrative form whose basic unit was the eight-line stanza (the *ottava*); it flourished between roughly 1250 and 1500. Most *cantari* are anonymous; they were performed publicly to musical accompaniment, though no such accompaniment survives, and they treated epic, Breton, mythological, Carolingian, and hagiographical material. For the history of this narrative form, and speculation thereon, see the various contributions to *I cantari: Struttura e tradizione*, Atti del Convegno Internazionale di Montreal, 19–20 March 1981, eds. Michelangelo Picone and Maria Bendinelli Predelli (Firenze: Olschki, 1984).

4. ". . . creati per intrattenere, ma soprattutto per formare ed educare, le raffinate corti del Nord dell'Europa . . . canterini aventi come unico scopo quello di consentire a degli ascoltatori attenti e onnivori una specie di evasione collettiva . . . delle patenti improvvisate di nobiltà." "La 'matière de Bretagne' nei cantari," in *I cantari: Struttura e tradizione*, 90–91 (my translation).

5. See Picone, 90.

6. " . . . soltanto l'impalcatura esterna: una certa nomenclatura tecnica, un patrimonio euristico di temi e motivi, un repertorio di personaggi e di avvenimenti topici; definitivamente scomparso è però lo spirito che informava quei personaggi e quegli avvenimenti, la tensione semantica sottesa alla manifestazione di quei temi e di quei motivi. *L'aventure* nel cantare non configura più un *iter*, un'approssimazione verso la Verità. . . . è diventata invece . . . un'etichetta avente semplice funzione di inventario; essa viene completamente risolta in racconto puro, in narrazione bruta . . . del tutto assente è ogni allusione a possibili sensi *autres*, a livelli di significato latenti." (93–94)

7. *Woman as Image in Medieval Literature* (New York: Columbia University Press, 1975), pp. 11, 65.

8. "Desire, Meaning, and the Female Reader: The Problem of Chrétien's *Charrete*," in *The Passing of Arthur*, ed. Christopher Baswell and William Sharpe (New York: Garland, 1988), pp. 34, 36.

9. The terms are Laura Mulvey's, from her "Visual Pleasure and Narrative Cinema," in *Screen*, 16.1 (1975), 6–18. Susan Gubar similarly notes a "long tradition identifying the author as a male who is primary and the female as his passive creation—a secondary object lacking autonomy, endowed with often contradictory meaning but denied intentionality." "'The Blank Page' and the Issues of Female Creativity," *Critical Inquiry*, 8.2 (1981), 247.

10. On narrative's capacity for a predominantly male perspective, or the ability of female readers to enjoy such narrative, see (for example) Judith Fetterley's discussion of the "immasculated" reader, "taught to . . . identify with a male point of view. . . . Intellectually male, sexually female, one is in effect no one, no where, immasculated." *The Resisting Reader: A Feminist Approach to American Fiction* (Bloomington: Indiana University Press, 1978), pp. xx–xxii.

11. E.G. Parodi, ed., *Il Tristano riccardiano* (Bologna, 1896); republished in M.-J. Heijkant, *Tristano riccardiano* (Parma: Pratiche, 1991). References are to the chapters of this edition.

12. *La Tavola ritonda o l'istoria di Tristano*, 2 vols. (Bologna: Romagnoli, 1964–65). References are to the chapters of this edition. I quote with slight modification

Anne Shaver's English translation, *Tristan and the Round Table* (Binghamton, N.Y.: Medieval and Renaissance Texts and Studies), 1983. All other translations are mine.

13. *I cantari di Tristano*, ed. Giulio Bertoni (Modena, 1937); *The Chantari di Lancellotto*, ed. E.T. Griffiths (Oxford: Clarendon Press, 1924).

14. References are to octave numbers in the following editions: *Ponzela Gaia*, ed. G. Varanini (Bologna, 1957); *Brito da Brettagna, Liombruno, La donna del Vergiù*, ed. Ezio Levi, in *Fiore di leggende: cantari antichi, serie I: cantari leggendari* (Bari: Laterza, 1914); *Bel Gherardino* and *Fiorio e Biancifiore*, ed. Domenico De Robertis, in "Cantari antichi," *Studi di filologia italiana*, 28 (1970), 67–175.

15. E.g., *Tavola Ritonda*, CIV; L; XCIII; C, and *passim*.

16. Krueger notes this phenomenon in the *Charrete* (34).

17. 17. E.g., *Tavola Ritonda*, CXXIV.

18. In the *Tavola Ritonda*'s definition of chivalry, she must not marry him, because the "cura e la pigrizia" ("responsibilities and laziness") of marriage might distract him from valor (XLII).

19. Eve Kosofsky Sedgwick explains that women serve both to occlude and to enact a "homosocial contract" by which males locate themselves in an essentially male order. See *Between Men: English Literature and Male Homosocial Desire* (New York: Columbia, 1986).

20. The two couples share various symmetrical amorous idylls at the Gioiosa Guardia, and are stolen away by the Dama del Lago for a similar experience at the Castello del Lago (CV–CVII).

21. D. Delcorno Branca, *I romanzi italiani*, 89, 95–104.

22. The narrator establishes six "generazioni" ("categories") of knights, and places Tristano and Lancillotto in the highest (XLII). When they unwittingly fight each other, however, either the combat is interrupted or Tristano wins; when they fight as allies, Lancillotto kills seventy-five knights while Tristano kills one hundred seven (L).

23. The narrator tells us that at twelve Isotta and Ginevra were two of the three most beautiful women in the world (XX).

24. On the mechanisms of the male gaze and spectator identification, see Laura Mulvey, "Visual Pleasure and Narrative Cinema"; Teresa De Lauretis, ed., *Alice Doesn't: Feminism, Semiotics, Cinema* (Bloomington: Indiana University Press, 1984); Jacqueline Rose, *Sexuality in the Field of Vision* (London: Verso, 1986).

25. E.g., The *chantari di Lancellotto*, I.23.

26. E.g., the Duchess in "La Donna del Vergiù;" the Bellices episode in the two Tristano romances; the Sultaness in *Bel Gherardino*; and Arthur's queen in *Ponzela Gaia*.

27. "Desire, Meaning, and the Female Reader," 42.

28. *Bel Gher.*, II.22; *Donna del vergiù*, 20.

29. See Alice M. Colby, *The Portrait in Twelfth-Century Literature* (Geneva: Droz, 1965); *Tav. Rit.*, XX.

30. "io voglio imprima lo male che mia donna mi vorrà fare, che lo bene d'un'altra donna," *Tris. Ricc.*, LXX.

31. *Tav. Rit.*, LXIV, and *Tris. Ricc.*, LXXXVII.

32. Tristan deflowers a Jewish maiden, Aigua della Spina, in the month between her marriage and its consummation (*Tav. Rit.*, XXV); he also ogles the daughter of the Fata Morgana, the Gaia Pulcella (*Tav. Rit.*, LXXX), just before meeting Sir Burletta and hearing of his attempted rape of this same maiden.

33. One *cantare*, *Il cavaliere de lo falso scudo*, does indicate God's displeasure with the two queens' unholy prayers for their lovers (7–8), but it is anomalous in Italian Arthurian works.

34. "La 'matière de Bretagne' nei cantari," 95–97.

35. Delcorno Branca, "Il cavaliere delle armi incantate," 113. In *I cantari*, pp. 103–126.

36. Anne Shaver, *Tavola Ritonda*, p. xv.

37. "La 'matière de Bretagne' nei cantari," 91.

38. As Roberta Krueger notes, "Her privilege as a literary figure is less an indication of 'real' power than a male mystification of femininity, one that obscures the reality of her historical decline" ("Desire, Meaning, and the Female Reader," 34).

39. Krueger, 34.

40. On romance as about the writing of romance, see Michelle A. Freeman's influential article, "Chrétien's *Cligés*: A Close Reading of the Prologue," *Romanic Review*, 67 (1976), 89–101.

41. We should guard against generalizing from the experience of the *comune* in Florence to the literary productions of the Venetian republic, the Angevin court of Naples, and the *signorie* of the Po Valley, all of which contributed to the body of Arthurian material in Italy.

Fairies' Tales

FAIRY GODMOTHERS
AND FAIRY LOVERS

Laurence Harf-Lancner

At the beginning of the twelfth century, only one type of imaginary woman, the heiress of the ancient Fates, deserved the name of fairy. But the characteristics of the supernatural lover soon came into focus; in her turn, she became a fairy.

FAIRY GODMOTHERS

The folklore theme of the fairy godmother develops into a true topos in vernacular literature, even as it remains solidly anchored in the collective imagination. A text from the fourteenth century, a distant echo of the *Canon episcopi* and of Burchard of Worms's penitential, bears witness to this. Entitled *Demandes et reponces tres curieuses* ("Very careful questions and answers"), it expounds Christian doctrine in the form of a dialogue between master and student:

> "Mestre, que dites vous de ces fames qui dient qui vont en loerre et des estries et des ames et de ces guibelins qui souloient, et de ces mors que len voit, et de tiex choses. Mon enfant les fees ce estoient deablez qui disoient que les gens estoient destinez et faes les uns a bien les autres a mal, selon le cours du ciel ou de la nature. Comme se un enfant naissoit a tel heure ou en tel cours il li estoit destine quil seroit pendu ou quil seroit noie ou que il seroit riche, ou quil espouseroit tele dame, ou telez destinees. Pour ce les appeloit len fees, quar fee, selon le latin, vaut autant comme destinee, fatatrices vocabantur."

Translated and abridged from pp. 27–42[1] of Chapter 2 of *Les Fées au Moyen Age: Morgan et Mélusine: La Naissance des fées* (Paris: Honoré Champion, 1984). By permission. Translated by Michael E. Ford. Edited by Thelma S. Fenster.

["'Teacher, what do you say about these women who, they say, go out on the prowl, and about sorceresses and beings, and about these goblins that once were, and about these dead that one sees, and about such things?'—'My child, those fairies were bewitched who said that people were destined and fated, some for good and others for evil, according to the course of the heavens or of nature. For example, for a child born at such and such an hour or at such an alignment, it was destined that he would be hanged or drowned or become wealthy, or that he would marry a certain lady, or other such fates. For this reason one called them fairies because fairy, according to the Latin, means much the same as fated; they used to be called *fatatrices*.'"][2]

From the contamination in the collective mind between the Latin Parcae and benevolent ladies, a contamination to which Burchard's testimony bears witness, a typical scene of medieval narrative literature was born that would become the most characteristic theme of fairy tales after the Middle Ages: when a child comes into the world, a meal is prepared for the fairies who come to decide the destiny of the newborn. The good outcome of this meal depends upon the benevolence of the visiting fairies.[3]

The romance of *Amadas et Ydoine* ("Amadas and Ydoine") offers the most remarkable illustration of the fairies' meal. To escape from a husband who horrifies her, Ydoine solicits the assistance of three *sorcières* ("sorceresses"). The talents of these ladies, experts in *encantement* ("enchantment") and the *mauvais ars* ("black arts"), are then evoked; these talents will be met with later: they will be attributed to fairies when the desire for rational explanation unites fairies and witches. Here, on the contrary, the separation is complete. The witches use their power: *des vis l'une a l'autre figure / Müer par art et par figure* ("to change, by art and by fashioning, one visage into the other's face"); then they go on to pass themselves off as what they are not: fairies.

The eve of the wedding [between the heroine, Ydoine, and the Count of Nevers, whom Ydoine does not love], the witches use enchantment to have themselves conveyed in the darkest hours of the night to the side of the Count of Nevers. They paralyze him so effectively that *il ne set s'il dort u s'il velle* ("he does not know if he's asleep or awake"):

Et puis se müent a mervelle
Em beles figures de fees:
Si se tignent a Destinees.
Pour Cloto se tient la premiere,

Pour Lachesis l'autre sorcière,
Et la tierce pour Atropos
Qui tout bien met arriere dos;
As trois Destinees se tienent
Par qui toutes coses avienent.

["And then, marvelously, they change into comely forms of fairies:
thus they look like the Fates. The first looks like Clotho, the second
sorceress like Lachesis, and the third like Atropos, who forgets all
good; they look like the three Fates by whom all things happen."][4]

The assimilation of fairies to the Fates, and the mention of the names
of Clotho, Lachesis, and Atropos, explicitly identify the fairies as the Parcae.
Thus, only these names come from clerical culture in a scene otherwise entirely inspired by the traditional theme of fairy godmothers:

Devant son lit sans atargier
Une touaille rice et grant,
Bele et blance, traient avant,
Et d'argent trois coupes mult beles,
Trois cuilliers et trois esquïeles,
Et a blans mances trois coutiaus,
Et puis aprés trois simeniaus;
Mengieres ont et viandes chieres,
Et boires de maintes manieres.

["Without delaying, in front of his bed they brought forth a great and
rich cloth, lovely and white, with three very beautiful silver cups, three
spoons, three bowls, and three knives with white handles, and then
afterwards three little cakes. They have foods and costly meats, and
many types of beverages."]

The setting of this scene, designed to persuade the reader of its visi-
tors' fairy-like nature, rests principally on these preparations for the meal,
which suggest that the image of the fairies is inseparable from the meal itself. The witches complete the picture by citing adventures that have befallen
the count's entourage in order to fix in the unfortunate count's mind the
certainty of the witches' divinatory power. Getting to the quick of the matter, they claim to conjure up the Count's birth and that of Ydoine to recall
the destiny that they purportedly imposed upon the two protagonists. The

folklore motif of a fairy's vengeance then surfaces: one of the fairies, deprived of a knife and thus not able to participate in the feast, sounds a dissonant note with a maleficent gift, whereas her companions compete in generosity. The motif is in fact doubled here because Ydoine and her future spouse, each as unlucky as the other, have both supposedly incurred the anger of fairies: at their births, one witch had claimed to have been deprived of a knife, while the other was deprived of a spoon. Thence comes the cruel stroke of fate by which the witch chooses to afflict the Count of Nevers: if he has the misfortune to go near his wife he will die within the year. Thus Ydoine, though married, can still remain faithful to Amadas.

This surprising scene draws all its richness from the juxtaposition of two levels of the marvelous: the fairy marvelous, and enchantments; of these, the first is completely foreign and inaccessible to humans, while the second is reserved for mortals who enter into contact with the supernatural world and derive from it powers that place them above their own kind. Nowhere else is this identification of the fairies, Fates, and Parcae as explicit as is their link with the good fairies who visit hospitable places. But if the theme of the fairies' meal is less frequent in medieval literature than in the domain of folklore,[5] the theme of fairy godmothers enjoys a consistent favor throughout the Middle Ages.

In the *Roman d'Escanor* ("Romance of Escanor"), composed around 1280 by Gérard d'Amiens, Gawain's marvelous gift—a last trait of his mythical origin—through which his strength rises and falls with the course of the sun, is accorded to him, along with prowess and courtesy, by good fairies.[6]

[. . .]

A fairy's maleficent gift can justify the origin of the evil custom that the hero must destroy. Thus the entire structure of *Les Merveilles de Rigomer* ("The Marvels of Rigomer") rests upon the dual quest that must successively lead two heroes, Lancelot and Gawain, from the kingdom of Logres to wild Ireland to challenge the spells of Rigomer. These spells, which strike the entire Irish kingdom with a kind of lethargy whose successive waves reach out little by little even to Arthur's kingdom, are the work of a wrathful fairy:

> C'est un castiaus fait de mervelle,
> "Qu'une fee fist fremer
> En une roche desor mer . . .
> Mais bien soiés fis et certain
> Que nus n'i vait armes porter,
> Mius ne l'en venist deporter.
> —Sire, dïent li compaignon,

Comment et par quele raison?
—Signor, dist il, bien le sai dire:
Par une fee qui ot ire,
Quant ma damoisiele fu nee,
Si li douna tel destinee
Que ja n'i venra chevaliers
Qui s'en repairt sains ne entiers
Que il ne soit mors u navrés
Ou pris u par armes oltrés;
Si est mis en la destinee
Que ma dame n'ert mariee
Dechi que chil venus sera
Qui les navrés respasera
Et chiaus qui sont emprisonés
Gietera fors a volenté."

["There is a marvelously fashioned castle, which a fairy caused to be built upon a great rock above the sea. . . . But you can be sure and certain that no one goes there bearing arms, And even less does one come away with them.—'Sire,' the companions ask, 'How and for what reason?'—'Lords,' he says, 'I can indeed tell you: a fairy who was angry when my damsel was born gave to her such a fate that never would a knight come here who might leave hale or whole, and not be dead or injured or made prisoner or vanquished at arms. Thus is it fixed in her fate that my lady will not be wed until one will have come who will cure the wounded and free willingly those who are imprisoned.'"][7]

Gawain undertakes the adventure of Rigomer after Lancelot. He leaves the court accompanied by the principal knights of the Round Table. Each of the quest companions finds ample opportunity to prove his valor, often in a confrontation with the other world. In one of these adventures some fairy godmothers again appear. In a cemetery, Cligès extracts the shaft of a lance that is buried in a dead knight's wound; he summons him back to life and finds himself immediately forced into combat by this living dead man. But not the slightest injury penetrates the flesh of the knight, who explains:

"Quatre fees out a mon naistre
Si me destina li plus maistre

Qu'en mon vivant plaie n'aroie
se jou a Rigomer n'aloie."

["'There were four fairies at my birth. The principal one destined that
in my life I would not have a wound as long as I stayed away from
Rigomer.'"]

Disobeying the order of the fairy, the knight of the perilous cemetery goes
to Rigomer, where he confronts the great knight whom only Lancelot succeeds in vanquishing. He is then injured:

"Adonc revint a moi li fee
Si me redona destinee:
Tant comme el corps ai le tronçon
Si sui en joie sans tençon.
Qant li tronçons est for saciés,
Si sui dervés, bien le sachiés."

["'Then the fairy came back to me and she again gave me a destiny: so
long as I have the lance shaft in my body I have joy without conflict;
when the lance shaft is drawn out, I fly into a rage, know that well.'"][8]

Cligès finally rids himself of this dangerous adversary by driving the weapon
once more into the wound and by piercing the heart of the knight, behind
whom the image of the vampire rises up.

Thus, in *Les Merveilles de Rigomer* the fairy godmothers assume their
usual function of justifying the source of an evil custom or of a formidable
adventure. But in this romance, too, where one by one all the marvels of
the adventurous forest surge up and then disappear, two images of fairyland
clearly and equally coexist: one is inseparable from the image of Destiny,
the other is linked to the type of amorous encounter of a mortal hero (here,
Gawain) with a supernatural woman (the fairy Lorie).

[Late epic heroes, too, have fairy godmothers. In *Huon de Bordeaux*
("Huon of Bordeaux") the hero is welcomed into the fairy kingdom of
Auberon, a hero born of the union of Julius Caesar and Morgan.* Auberon's
inexplicable supernatural qualities come from the gifts of fairies bestowed
when he was a newborn. In the first continuation of *Huon*, too, fairies are

---

* This paragraph and the next, placed within brackets, represent an abridgement of the
original. *Ed.*

present at Esclarmonde's birthing of Clarisse, attending first to the mother (like the womb fairies of folklore), then to the child.

In the *Roman d'Aubéron* ("Romance of Aubéron"), a false preamble to *Huon*, Brunehaut, Aubéron's maternal grandmother, receives gifts from the fairies at her birth that elevate her above ordinary mortals. Julius Caesar is born of the union of Brunehaut and Caesar, Emperor of Rome. Julius Caesar marries Morgan la Fee; three fairy godmothers assist at Morgan's delivery and at the birth of the twins, George and Aubéron.]

But these fairy godmothers represent an essentially decorative form of the marvelous and have no dramatic role or symbolic function or any particular resonance in the medieval imagination. Fairy lovers, on the other hand, with their comings and goings between the other world and the human one, form the framework of the Breton romance. Nameless at first, they too come to be called fairies.

FAIRY LOVERS

As early as the twelfth century, the supernatural women who divide their time between the other world and the human one are also cast as fairies: more beautiful than the most beautiful among mortal women, they immediately inspire love. About 1150, Geffrei Gaimar in his *Estoire des Englés* ("History of the English"), evokes the fatal beauty of Alftrued. Here, King Edgar sends his counselor Edelworth to a young woman; he wishes to be sure that, by her grace, the daughter of his vassal justifies her reputation and merits the rank of queen. Edleworth is dazzled:

> Tant lesguarda vis e colur,
> E cors e mains, le bele flur,
> Kil quidat bien ke co fust fee
> Kele ne fust pas de femme nee.

["He looked so intently at her face and complexion, her body and her hands, the beautiful flower, that he believed this was a fairy, that she was not of woman born."][9]

The fairy here has no link whatever with the Parcae and can in fact be taken for any sort of otherworldly woman. How, then, can the heroines of the *lais* of *Lanval, Graelent, Guingamor, Désiré,* or those mysterious feminine figures who haunt the adventurous forests of the *Chevalier de la Charrete* ("Knight of the Cart"), of Aymon de Varennes's *Florimont,* of the *Elucida-*

tion,[10] of the *Deuxième Continuation* ("Second Continuation" [of Chrétien de Troyes's "Perceval"]) be designated, other than as fairies—even if the authors are less explicit than in the case of fairy godmothers? They all belong to the beyond, sylphs whose common traits (their superhuman beauty and magical powers) fall under the rubric of their fantasy nature.

Yet, the romance texts from the years 1160–1220 that most clearly affirm the supernatural nature of these characters at the same time deny them the denomination "fairy." The hero meets a *pucelle* ("maiden"), a *demoiselle* ("damsel"), a *dame* ("lady"), or a *meschine* ("girl") of noble extraction who, when she has granted him her love, is henceforth designated as *s'amie* ("his sweetheart") or *sa drue* ("his lover").[11]

[...]

The word "fairy" therefore almost never appears in a number of works that would seem to call for it. The use of a thoroughly imprecise vocabulary to designate the fairy could certainly be a stylistic bow in the direction of the fairy marvelous, itself based upon a mystery knowingly maintained. But it is also true that the name "fairy," a word not previously attached to the new mythical form that invades romance beginning in the twelfth century, was only just coming to be used. In spite of the imprecision of the qualifiers, we nevertheless need hardly hesitate about the fairy nature of certain female characters. Supernatural appearances are in fact nearly always preceded by a whole series of indications that replace, in a flattering way, an explicit naming and that make of the fairy encounter a veritable topos inherited from tales of the marvelous, where it constitutes the first narrative sequence.

It is also the case, however, that as of the first romances of the twelfth century, there are fairy lovers who are designated as such. The mysterious "Orva la fee" of the *Roman de Troie* ("Romance of Troy"), in whom some scribes saw Morgan le Fay, gives Hector the gift of a mount as a sign of love; rejected, she pursues him with her hate:

> Hector monta sor Galatee,
> Que lui tramist Orva la fee,
> Qui mout l'ama e mout l'ot chier
> Mais ne la voust o soi couchier:
> Empor la honte qu'ele en ot,
> l'en haï tant come el plus pot.

> ["Hector mounted Galatee, which Orva the fairy gave him, who loved him very much and held him very dear. But he did not wish her to

sleep with him; for the shame that she felt because of that, she hated him as much as she could."][12]

The supernatural protectrice of the Knight of the Cart [hero of Chrétien de Troyes's *Lancelot, or the Knight of the Cart*] receives the explicit appellation of "fairy," just as Morgan herself does in [Chrétien's] *Erec et Enide* ("Erec and Enide").[13] Like the Dame du Lac, the *fada de Gibel* ("fairy of Gibel") in the romance of *Jaufre* lives in an underwater kingdom.[14] The descendants of the *sylvaticae* ("wood nymphs"), the beautiful unknown women who suddenly appear in the forest from which they seem to be a veritable emanation, little by little take the name of fairy. Therefore, when Nicolette, hiding in the forest, is found near a fountain in a framework that suits a supernatural apparition, the shepherds take her immediately to be a fairy.[15] Likewise, when [in the poem *Le Vair Palefroi* ("The Grey Palfrey")] the grey palfrey brings to William [the hero] his ladyfriend, the watchman thinks he sees a fairy in this beautiful young girl who emerges from the night and whom God gave to William to console him for his lost love.[16] Thus the word "fairy," missing from stories that would seem to call for it, appears here in two texts that seek to create the illusion of the marvelous.

In the *Lancelot-Grail* cycle, many adventures are plotted along the lines of marvelous tales, and many of the female characters could be called fairies. The term, however, is applied to two characters alone: Morgan and the Dame du Lac; and it is always accompanied by a comment. It is never said of Morgan that she is a fairy; rather, she is titled *Morgue la fee* ("Morgan la Fay, Morgan the Fairy").[17] The *Huth Merlin*, which evokes the lake of the fairies when Excalibur is mentioned, withholds the denomination of fairy from Morgan as well as from Viviane.[18] The *Vulgate Merlin*, on the other hand, employs the designation *Morgue la fée*, but always followed by a comment: Morgan is a good pupil who profited so well from her scholarly lessons that she gained the surname of *Morgue la fée* ("Morgan the Fairy") or *Morgue la faée* ("Morgan endowed with magic powers"):

> et li rois Neutres de Garlot rot l'autre fille qui estoit bastarde qui avoit non Morgains; et par le consoil de tous les amis ensemble la fist li rois aprendre letres en une maison de religion et celle aprist tant et si bien qu'elle aprist des arz et si sot merveille d'un art que l'en apele astrenomie et molt en ouvra toz jorz et sot molt de fisique, *et par celle mastrie de clergie qu'ele avoit fu apelee Morgain la faee.*

["and King Neutre of Garlot also had the other illegitimate daughter who had the name Morgan; and heeding the advice of all his friends together, the king had her learn letters in a house of religion and she learned so much and so well that she learned about the arts and thus she knew an art that is called astronomy and she used it every day and she knew a lot about potions *and by this mastery of learning was she called Morgan, endowed with magical powers.* "][19]

The constant use of *Morgain la faée* in the thirteenth-century manuscript [of *Merlin*] edited by A. Micha, of *Morgain la fée* in the manuscript dated 1316, edited by O. Sommer, seems to indicate a confusion between the noun [*fée*] and the adjective [*faée*] and also between two character types that were originally quite distinct: the fairy [*fée*], a supernatural woman; and, the woman who is *faee* ("enchanted," or "endowed with magical powers"), a mortal woman in contact with the other world in an active way (that is, she herself possesses magical powers), or associated with the other world in a passive way (that is, she is the object of an intervention by the fairies). The frequency of these notations reveals a desire both to clarify and to give a rational explanation, but it also shows a certain imprecision in the semantic register of the word "fairy."

The Lady of the Lake is never described as a fairy in the *Lancelot Grail*, with one exception. That exception is significant, however: in the famous scene of the abduction of the young Lancelot (*Or dist chi li contes que la damoisele qui lanselot emporta el lac estoit une fee* ["Now the story says that the damsel who carried Lancelot off into the lake was a fairy"]), followed by a definition that likens fairies to crafty enchantresses.[20] The characteristic desire of the prose romance to explain, apparent in this definition (as in the entire cycle), by describing the fairy characters in a rational way also reveals how moveable fairy traits were at the beginning of the thirteenth century.

Thus one sees emerge, in a way parallel to that of the fairy godmothers, a second type of fairy figure who enters French literature with the Matter of Britain: woodland and water deities who constantly mingle with humans, just as they do in their supernatural kingdom, which is never very far from the world of humans. But unlike the fairy godmothers who inherited their name along with their function from the Fata, these ladies of the fountains and woodlands become fairies only little by little, as their character develops in the romance.

During the thirteenth century the character of the supernatural lover develops. Thus in *Les Merveilles de Rigomer*, the good fairies from Ireland's forests multiply their benevolent interventions, helping Arthur's knights to destroy Rigomer's spells and erasing the image of the disquieting fairy godmothers. Lancelot tastes of their hospitality after having conquered it. Entering a deserted dwelling at night, he must confront a demonic apparition: cats guarding a coffin attack him. But this formidable test is meant only to eliminate the unworthy. Two damsels in white then lead Lancelot to their lady, whose fairylike character is merely suggested (*Onques ne fu plus biele fee* ["Never was there a more beautiful fairy"]), and who claims sovereignty from *ma dame Lorie / qui provoste est de nostre loi* ("my lady Lorie, who is the magistrate of our law"). Gawain, the hero destined to triumph over the spell, deserves the love of Lorie the fairy, whose protection accompanies him throughout his quest. Imprisoned by a knight, he is freed by

> Lorie
> La dame de Roche Florie,
> Une fee qui bien l'amoit
> Et mout grant poesté avoit.

["Lorie, the lady of Roche Florie, a fairy who loved him well and who had very great power."]

Later, his companion, asleep in the forest, is carried off by fairies:

> Fees en la forest manoient,
> Qui tot lor couvenent savoient.
> A lui vinrent, si l'en porterent
> El bos ou eles converserent.
> En .I. bel liu dedens lors tre,
> La ont le chevalier entré.
> Moult l'ounererent et siervirent,
> Por que biel chevalier le virent.

["Fairies dwelt in the forest, who knew their entire covenant. They came to him, and they carried him away into the wood where they lived together. They brought the knight into a beautiful place inside their tent. Much did they honor and serve him, for they saw he was a fair knight."][21]

He finds his companion again shortly afterward, having himself been carried off by Lorie, who saved his life by arriving on her magic ship, unexpected and unannounced, to prevent her friend from falling into the water.

She accompanies Gawain to Rigomer and grants her favors to him as the knight destined to overcome the marvels. When, after his victory, Gawain is offered the hand of Dionise, the lady of Rigomer, Lorie opposes the marriage because of her love for the hero. The knight then returns to Brittany, the fairy to her kingdom of Roche Fleurie. She intervenes one last time, shortly before the break in the romance: during the adventure that sets Lancelot against a monster, the panther, she tends the knight's wounds with a magic ointment and makes him the gift of a horse.

The fairies of *Les Merveilles de Rigomer*, always called fairies, do not at all resemble the heroines of the fairy *lais*: living communally in the forest, they obey the orders of their *provoste* ("magistrate"), the fairy Lorie, in whom one may glimpse a character who later will appear in literature as the Queen of the Fairies. Similarly, in *Claris et Laris* ("Claris and Laris," begun 1268), the fairies reside in a *valee delitable* ("delightful valley") in the heart of Broceliande, where they live united and in perfect agreement. Laris questions one of them:

> Icele con bien enseignie
> Li dist, que Morgans iert nommee,
> La suer Artus, et estoit fee,
> Et ses compaignes voirement
> Estoient fees ensement,
> Qui la gent par le mont feoient;
> Laienz herbergiees estoient
> Pour tant, que li leus iert estables
> Et deduisanz et convenables.

> ["Like a courteous person, she said to him that she was named Morgan, the sister of Arthur, and she was a fairy, and her companions were truly fairies as well, who enchanted people throughout the world; they were lodged there because the area was untroubled and lovely and agreeable."]

The fairies here, as in *Rigomer*, are supernatural women ("fairy" is synonymous with "goddess")[22] whose realm is of this world and accessible to all travelers: they do not hide from humans who, for their part, have no fear of them. In addition, the power to enchant people (*faer*) attaches to their "fairy" nature, a power that may be understood as the ability to fix the destiny of people at birth, but also, in a wider sense (and as corroborated by the role of the fairies later on in the tale), as something like the power to intervene in all human affairs and to redirect their flow at will. The other world is situated with geographic precision, and its female inhabitants, far from hiding their supernatural character, lay claim to their fairy nature.[23] In the fourteenth century, in *Meliador*, when Froissart recounts the abduction of Sagremor during the Hunt for the White Stag in a forest where *i ot fées* ("there were fairies"), he first introduces the ladies of the river as nymphs and Diane's damsels, and later as fairies.[24] The narrative schema is borrowed from fairy lais like *Graelent* or *Guingamor*, but here the fairies are clearly specified: the mythical figure has in the meantime become a literary type.

Two parallel texts bear the proof of this emergence of a second type of fairy character in the thirteenth-century romance. Jean de Haute Seille's *Dolopathos*, written in Latin about 1200, was translated into French about 1220 by Herbert de Paris. One of its stories is that of the swan children: the hero surprises a mysterious young girl while she is bathing and he requires her to follow him while he steals her golden necklace. The young woman is the victim of her jealous mother-in-law, who replaces the children that the young woman brings into the world with animals; she is saved by her children, who have inherited a half-human, half-animal nature from their mother. Jean de Haute Seille always calls the swan woman a *nympha* ("nymph"), finding in scholarly culture the mythological figure that most closely resembles the heroine of his story.[25] A score of years later, Herbert de Paris translates *nympha* as "fairy."[26] It all suggests that Jean de Haute Seille, writing in Latin between 1184 and 1212, did not have available the word *fata* ("fate") to describe the swan woman—the same character that Herbert de Paris, writing in French around 1220, calls a fairy. Two systems of opposition are thus brought to light: first, a chronological opposition; second, a linguistic one.

Around the year 1400, the two romances of *Mélusine* [one written by Jean d'Arras, the other by Coudrette] designate the heroine as a fairy, the manuscripts oscillating between two nouns, *fée* and *faée*.[27] Beginning with the prologue, Jean d'Arras evokes, by the term *faee*, the supernatural women who come to offer themselves to mortals; among these women is the one who built Lusignan. King Elinas meets a beautiful lady in the forest who sings more sweetly than *seraine, faee ne nuimphe* ("siren, woman of magic powers or nymph"). But in the account itself of the loves of Melusine and Raimondin, the word *fée* ("fairy") reappears only one other time, at the end of the romance, uttered by Melusine herself, who in fact denies that her children are a fairy's sons.[28] Throughout the narration, the three fairies of the romance (Presine, the supernatural friend of Raimondin's father, and Melusine herself) are never called anything but *dame* ("lady") or, for Presine and Melusine, by their names.

For Coudrette, who brings back the word of the lord of Parthenay, Melusine is both fairy and woman of magic powers (*femme faee*):

> Le chasteau fut fait d'une fee
> Si comme il est par tout restrait,
> De laquelle je sui estrait,
> Et moy et toute la lignie
> De Partenay, n'en doubtez mie.
> Melusine fut appellee
> La fee que vous ay nommee.

["The castle, completely remote, was made by a fairy, from whom I come, both I and the entire line of Partenay, do not doubt it. She was called Melusine, the fairy whom I have named to you."]

Melusine is treated as a *femme faee* by a Raimondin blinded with grief after his son Geoffroi's crime.[29] The reader senses, therefore, a hesitation between *fée* and *faée* in the work of Jean d'Arras and of Coudrette, as well as a certain parsimonious use of the term. In the *lais* [mentioned above], the absence of the word fairy is most reasonably explained, first, by a lack of equivalence between the semantic register of the word fairy and the character herself, and, second, by the genre itself of the *lai*, which often flirts with a willingly maintained mystery. But in the romances of Jean d'Arras and Coudrette, Melusine is designated as a fairy only in the prologue and in the epilogue—that is to say, at the moment when she is above all the ancestor of the Lusignans: in the prologue, builder of the fortress and founder of a line of descent; in the epilogue, banshee announcing mourning. In the course of the same story, however, her human nature dominates in order to make her a more reassuring character.

The Middle Ages therefore knew two types of fairies: the Parcae, whose classical image had been profoundly transformed by popular tradition; and, the ladies of the forest whose path often crosses that of mortals. In the twelfth century the latter became fairies when they entered into learned culture and as the word fairy became progressively disjoined from the character of the Parcae. At the beginning of the thirteenth century the two folklore types, previously distinct, melted into one new figure, fully literary, both loving goddess and mistress of destiny. After the Middle Ages, fairies would have no other countenance, and the fairies of our popular tales have often felt the influence of this romance creation.[30]

1. Pages 31–34 of chapter 2 treat epics and appear here in synopsis, enclosed in square brackets. Discussion of some non-Arthurian works has been eliminated. Excisions are indicated by ellipsis marks, also within square brackets. *Ed.*

2. *Demandes et reponces tres curieuses*, Bibliothèque Nationale MS ffr. 2458, f° 38.

3. See Stith Thompson, *Motif Index of Folk Literature*, F 311.1, Fairy godmother; F 312, Fairy presides at child's birth; F 316, Fairy lays curse on child; F 361.1, Fairy takes revenge for not being invited to feast; A 463.1, The Fates; M 301.12, Three fates, "norns," prophesy at child's birth.

4. *Amadas et Ydoine*, ed. J. Reinhard, ll. 2089 ff. [An extended narrative of thwarted love, *Amadas et Ydoine* is not an Arthurian work. *Ed.*]

5. It can be found again in the *Jeu de la Feuillée* by Adam de la Halle (ll. 564 ff.) and in *Perceforest*, where the fairies are goddesses named Lucina, Venus, and Sarra. See J. Lods, *Le Roman de Perceforest* (Paris, 1959), Appendix.

6. Gérard d'Amiens, *Escanor*, ed. H. Michelant (Tübingen, 1886), ll. 2787–2821. [A romance, grounded in Arthurian fictions, in which Gawain figures importantly. *Ed.*]

7. *Les Merveilles de Rigomer*, ed. W. Foerster (Dresden, 1908), ll. 6880–6918. [An Arthurian work dated in the last decade of the twelfth century or first half of the thirteenth, *Les Merveilles de Rigomer* borrows heavily from Chrétien de Troyes's *Chevalier de la Charrete*, among others. English translation by Thomas Vesce (New York: Garland, 1988). *Ed.*]

8. *Les Merveilles de Rigomer*, ll. 9403–06, 9417–22.

9. Geoffrei Gaimar, *L'Estorie des Englés*, ed. T.D. Hardy and C.T. Martin (London, 1888), ll. 3661–64.

10. The *Elucidation* is a prologue, probably of the thirteenth century, to the *Conte del Graal* of Chrétien de Troyes and his continuators. *Ed.*

11.

	pucelle	demoiselle	meschine	s'amie	dame	drue	la bele
Lanval	10	3	1	7	3		
Graelent	4	12	1	11	2		
Guingamor	5	2	2	3	1	1	
Désiré	7	7	2	12	3		
Florimont	6	10		6			
Elucidation	15	3					
Second Continuation							
1. Fairy of the Chessboard*	5	10			2		1
2. Fairy of the Tomb†	5	1					
3. Carimedic's "amie"‡	1				7		

* See synopsis in *The Continuations of the Old French "Perceval" of Chrétien de Troyes*, vol. IV, *The Second Continuation*, ed. William Roach (Philadelphia: American Philosophical Society, 1971), pp. xx, xxxi. *Ed.*

† For synopsis see Roach, ed., pp. xxvii–xxviii—*Ed.*

‡ In the story of the unfinished bridge; see synopsis in Roach, ed., pp. xxix–xxx—*Ed.*

Concerning the Fairy of the Chessboard, it is also said that she resembled a fairy by her beauty, "de biauté resambloit fee," l. 28131. (The figures refer to the number of occurrences of each term.) Likewise, the flower girls of the *Roman d'Alexandre* ("Romance of Alexander") are never anything but "maidens," but one of them is "more beautiful than a fairy."

12. Benoit de Sainte Maure, *Le Roman de Troie*, ed. L. Constans (Paris, 1904–12), ll. 8023–28. [One of the romances based on the Matter of Rome that antedate Chrétien de Troyes's romances. *Ed.*]

13. Chrétien de Troyes, *Le Chevalier de la Charrette* ("The Knight of the Cart"), ed. Mario Roques (Paris, 1970), l. 2345; *Erec et Enide*, ed. Mario Roques (Paris, 1952), ll. 1907, 2358.

14. *Jaufré*, ed. C. Brunel (Paris, 1943), l. 10654. [An Arthurian poem in Provençal, from ca. 1225. *Ed.*]

15. *Aucassin et Nicolette*, ed. Mario Roques, 2nd ed. (Paris, 1969), XVIII, p. 20: *vos estes fee* ("you are a fairy"), and XXII, p. 23: *Sire, nos estiiens orains ci entre prime et tierce, si mengiens no pain a ceste fontaine*, . . . *et une pucele vint ci, li plus bele riens du monde, si que nos quidames que ce fust une fee, et que tos cis bos en esclarci.* ("Sir, we were here between prime and tierce, and thus ate our bread at this fountain, . . . and a maiden came here who was the most beautiful creature in the world, and who illumined all the forest, and we thought she was a fairy.")

16. Huon le Roi, *Le Vair Palefroi*, ed. A. Langfors (Paris, 1957), ll. 1181–82. Cf. *Aye d'Avignon* ("Aye of Avignon"), ed. S.J. Borg (Paris, 1967), ll. 1031–38, where the heroine is mistaken for the fairy of a spring.

17. *Lancelot*, ed. A. Micha, LXXVIII, 1: *.II. dames dont l'une avoit nom Morgue la fee et l'autre sebile la roine* ("two ladies one of whom was named Morgan la Fay and the other Queen Sibyl"); LXXXVIII, 4: *l'an apele Morgue la fee* ("they call her Morgan la Fay").

18. *Merlin*, ed. G. Paris and J. Ulrich (Paris, 1886), I, p. 195: *en un lach ou fees habitent* ("in a lake where fairies live"); and p. 197: *Nus n'i enterroit sans le congiet as fees* ("No one would enter there without leave from the fairies").

19. Robert de Boron, *Merlin*, ed. A. Micha (Paris, 1980), § 72, p. 245. The corresponding passage in Sommer's edition is in V. II (*Estoire Merlin* ["Story of Merlin"]), p. 73. See also the *Livre d'Artus* ("Book of Arthur"), ed. Sommer, p. 136: *Morgan la Fe que ensi li mistrent non les genz du roiaume de Logres por ce quele ouroit de maintes merveilles* ("Morgan le Fay, as she was named by the people of the kingdom of Logres, because she worked much magic; and *ibid.*, p. 164).

20. *Lancelot*, ed. Micha, VIa, p. 19.

21. *Les Merveilles de Rigomer*, ll. 2578, 2594–95, 10627–30, 11763 ff.

22. *Claris et Laris*, ed. J. Alton (Tübingen, 1884), v. 3661–69, 29325. [Claris and Laris are two friends in this long, two-part Arthurian romance. In the first part, Laris is carried off by a fay named Madoine and rescued later by Claris. *Ed.*]

23. Ibid., l. 8232: *La fee que Laris ama* ("The fairy whom Laris loved"), ll. 8240, 10757, 10768, 10771, 16104, 17326, 28968, 29310 (*Ceanz est li manoirs aus fees / Qui vont par estranges contrees* ["Therein is the residence of the fairies, who inhabit strange lands"]).

24. Froissart, *Meliador*, ed. A. Longnon (Paris, 1895), ll. 28366, 28824–25, 30343.

25. Jean de Haute Seille, *Historia septem sapientum (Dolopathos)* ("Legend of the Seven Sages, or Dolopathos"), ed. A. Hilka (Heidelberg, 1911), pp. 81, 85, 86, 87. [A largely non-Arthurian prose work: a frame story and tales set in Sicily during the reign of Augustus Caesar. *Ed.*]

26. Herbert de Paris, *Li Romans de Dolopathos* ("Romance of Dolopathos"), ed. C. Brunet et A. de Montaiglon (Paris, 1856), l. 9233: *Lai trovait baignant une fee* ("There he found a fairy bathing"); ll. 9469, 9476, 9859, 9873, 10091, 10118.

27. Jean d'Arras, *Melusine*, ed. L. Stouff (Dijon, 1932), p. 3: *les faes* ("women with magic powers," or "enchantresses") in the manuscript edited by L. Stouff become *fayes* and *fees* ("fairies") in two other manuscripts; the *faée* (pp. 3, 4, 5, 311) becomes *fee* ("fairy") in manuscript E (see p. 5, n. 1).

28. Ibid., pp. 259–60: *Et toutesfoiz je vueil bien que vous sachiez que je sui ne qui fu mon pere, afin que vous ne reprouvez pas a mes enfans qu'ilz soient filz de mauvaise mere, ne de serpente, ne de faee, car je suis fille au roi Elinas d'Albanie et a la royne Presine, sa femme, et sommes .III. seurs qui avons esté durement predestinees*

et en griefz penitances ("Yet I want you to know who I am and who my father was, so that you will not reproach my children for being sons of a bad mother, or of a serpent, or of a sorceress; for I am the daughter of king Elinas of Albany and of queen Presine, his wife, and we are three sisters who have been harshly destined and done hard penances").

29. Coudrette, *Mélusine*, ed. E. Roach (Paris, 1982), ll. 70–76, 3798.

30. These two types of fairies gave rise to two clichés: *plus habile qu'une fée* ("more nimble than a fairy," that is, the fairy spinner, the Parca); *plus belle qu'une fée* ("more beautiful than a fairy," that is, the fairy lover).

FROM THE LAKE TO THE FOUNTAIN

LANCELOT AND THE FAIRY LOVER

Anne Berthelot

This article is based on certain episodes in the Prose Lancelot, *in the edition of Alexandre Micha (Geneva: Droz, 1979), in particular volume IV: the poisoned fountain, pp. 133–59; the second encounter of the healer damsel with Lancelot, pp. 215–22; the damsel of the well, pp. 300–07, 330–32; the damsel at court, pp. 354, 367–71. A summary follows here of the relevant events of those pages.*

[*The poisoned fountain*: Having sent a damsel to tell Queen Guenevere that he is well, Lancelot, in the company of an old woman, leaves the abbey where he has spent the night. He comes upon a sparkling fountain and, before it, two knights and two damsels picnicking. One of the damsels, whose brother is one of the knights, is struck dumb by Lancelot's beauty. But soon, Lancelot falls mortally ill, for the water of the fountain from which he had drunk so thirstily has been poisoned by the venom of two snakes. Lancelot swells up hideously. The damsel, brought sharply out of her frightened trance by her brother, attends to Lancelot with herb-lore. After about two weeks, he is healthy once more, but she is not, for she has fallen in love with him.

Bors and Lionel, and a damsel from Arthur's court, arrive at the residence of the damsel and her brother, where Lancelot is recuperating. They tell Lancelot that the queen has taken to her bed, sick with worry for him. She has sent him a ring. Because he isn't yet well enough to travel, Lancelot sends some locks of his hair back to the queen with Lionel. . . . Lionel advises Guenevere to urge the king to declare a tournament about a month hence, and says that he and Lancelot will attend; she does so. When Lionel returns to Lancelot with this news, however, Lancelot laments that he will

Translated from "Du lac à la fontaine: Lancelot et la fée-amante." *Médiévales: Langue, Textes, Histoire*, special issue, "Au pays d'Arthur," 6 (1984): 5–17. Trans. Thelma S. Fenster, with Anne Berthelot. With permission.

not recover soon enough to be at the tournament. Lionel then talks to the healer damsel, who is languishing with love for Lancelot. Should she die of unrequited love, Lancelot will not be cured; thus she advises that he adopt a different manner. And indeed, Lancelot himself tells Lionel that he was improving until the healer damsel herself took sick. Lionel advises Lancelot to tend to the damsel, but Lancelot thinks of his love for and loyalty to the queen. Lionel points out that if Lancelot should die (because the healer damsel has died), then the queen will die of chagrin, and Lancelot will be the cause of her death, thus of a "disloyalty." Lancelot bids Lionel go to court and explain all this to the queen, to ask her whether he should die. But even before leaving, Lionel tells the damsel that Lancelot agrees to do her will, and she then goes and administers her healing arts. By the time Lionel has returned from the queen with the order that Lancelot satisfy the damsel, the hero is already much better.

The day comes when the healer damsel asks Lancelot to keep his side of the bargain. He reveals the love that exists between himself and a lady, and the damsel finds a solution: they need not have carnal relations as long as Lancelot is always willing to accept her as his love, to love her as a maiden and the queen as a *dame* ("married noblewoman"). She declares that she'd be happier remaining a virgin for love of Lancelot than if she were the richest lady in the world. She asks Lancelot for a gift to seal their love and he gives her a silken belt that Guenevere had once given him; she in turn gives him a golden clasp that he wears at his neck out of love for her. . . . (pp. 133–59).

Second encounter of the healer damsel with Lancelot: Much later Lancelot arrives at a fountain and sits down. When the moon comes up, he sees three armed knights, then four squires; the squires have with them none other than the healer damsel to whom Lancelot had pledged himself. After a bitter exchange between the damsel and one of the squires, who then tries to force her, Lancelot saves her. He and the damsel go off to the castle of her cousin, where they dine and spend the night. In the morning Lancelot departs for another adventure, but not before the damsel ascertains that Lancelot will go to the tournament at Camelot, where she promises to see him again. . . . (pp. 215–22).

The damsel of the well. Lancelot is left by enemies to die in a deep and stinking well where there are worms and snakes that attack him up and down. As he is lamenting his fate, a damsel comes along who, when she learns of his noble extraction, determines to rescue him. She procures a rope from her chamber and ties one end of it around an oak tree while Lancelot hoists himself up holding the other end. It turns out she is the daughter of the very man who put Lancelot in the well, and one of his servants has seen her (pp. 300–07). Later, the damsel and the hero ride away, eventually stopping at the home of a widow lady. She sees that Lancelot's leg is swollen (from snake bites) and since she herself has no healing powers, she sends for her sister, who does (pp. 330–32).

The healer damsel at court: The queen is at her window, gazing down upon the ladies and damsels who have come to see the tournament. She notices the damsel who had cured Lancelot of poisoning and to whom he had given the belt. Guenevere recognizes the belt as one she had once presented to Lancelot and realizes that she had given Lancelot permission to do this damsel's will; she becomes angry (p. 354). . . . The queen sends for the healer damsel and tells her a story: she explains to her that she has a friend whose lover the damsel has stolen away. She tells her about the belt (that it had been given to the lover by the lady) and warns her that she (the damsel) might die because of it. The frightened damsel explains everything that passed between her and Lancelot, at the end of which the queen is satisfied that the damsel deserves the belt. She invites her to remain her companion, which the damsel happily agrees to do (pp. 367-71).] *Ed.*

By its size *Lancelot* constitutes the most considerable portion of the *Lancelot-Grail* cycle. But where its meaning is concerned, it may appear in certain respects to be but a parenthesis in the cycle, since its hero is the model of earthly chivalry who, by his adulterous love for Queen Guenevere, has renounced the celestial glory granted later to his son Galahad. That son must be born, however, and his birth occurs in the *Lancelot*, which all too often is discussed exclusively for the role of that birth episode because it foreshadows the Holy Grail. But numerous other threads "interlace" in the *Lancelot,* and other motifs and other characters play their proper role, sometimes using the episode in which Galahad is conceived as a means of showing off or as a moment in the attainment of their own goals.

That is the case for the episode of the *damoisele a la fontainne* ("damsel at the fountain"): with her as intermediary, the romance, as if in training, seems to be rehearsing in advance the amorous episode with the Fisher King's daughter, future mother of Galahad. In fact, the character of the damsel, named late,[1] encountered often in but a small number of pages, pitted victoriously against Guenevere then suddenly gone, is much more than a redundancy of the romance in a feminine constellation where positions have already all been assigned.

At first the function of the episode in the romance's economy appears weak: once more Lancelot is lost—that is, the court and the queen are "questing" for him desperately. In fact, he is obliged to accomplish a valorous deed that he pledged to the not-very-worthy character of an "old woman," who guides him to the required location. On the way, he comes upon a very beautiful fountain, and on its edge a damsel drawn on the model of the fairy lovers of the Breton *lais*. She fills a hole in Lancelot's biography: having been raised by a fairy (the Lady of the Lake) and desired by another (Morgan), he has a right to this magic encounter at a fountain. Unfortunately, the Grail, its existence already palpable, watches over the morality of "erring" as well as of wandering knights and the fountain is poisoned, if not by that one, too symbolic poisonous snake, at least by *II culuevres granz et hideuses et longues . . .* ("Two great, long, hideous snakes"). What was supposed to be but a halt in the knight's journey thus becomes the object of an unexpected development, like Lancelot himself when he: *commence a enfler plus et plus et tant qu'il devint ausi gros com I tonnel* ("begins to swell more and more and such that he became as big as a barrel," p. 136), to the great dismay of the participants—or of the readers.

Once the adventure is ended (not without difficulty) by Lancelot's healing, the damsel, in great danger of disappearing from the text as from Lancelot's memory, leaves her fountain and succeeds, by who knows what topographic shortcut, in placing herself further down along the hero's designated path. There she loses her power and becomes a simple *pucelle deconseillee* ("damsel in distress"), such as one finds in abundance in strange forests. Now saved from rape by her *ami* ("sweetheart") Lancelot, who thus *guerredone* ("rewards") the healing she dispensed to him, she seems to erase from Lancelot's mind all memory of the episode of the Grail Castle,* to which Lancelot will never again allude. Sent [afterward] to the court, she attracts Guenevere's suspicion by *affichant* ("showing off") the belt that Lancelot gave her. The queen will react in the same way (that is, with suspicion and with a close interrogation) when Galahad's mother, accompanied by her son, comes to court. But the symbolic value of the belt (the image of chastity, whereas Galahad is the image of an undeniable error), and the oratory talents of the damsel, disarm the queen, who offers her hospitality (almost) without second thoughts. The hospitality is fatal, however, in that it withdraws the damsel from the romance arena in order to reduce her to a simple object of discourse, an object of *gab* ("taunt," "joke") between Lancelot and the queen, whose sense of humor is not brilliant:

> Et de vostre novele amie, fait ele *par gabois*, cele qui vos gari de l'envenimement, c'aves vos fait? (. . .) Certes vos l'avez bien laissie,

---

*This episode at Corbenic occurs in between the two instances with this damsel. *Tr.*

si est moult bele et moult cortoise et vos ama bien par amors et vos lui, jel sai vraiement. ("And what of your new sweetheart, she said tauntingly, the one who cured you from the poisoning, what have you done with her? (. . .) You have surely left her; yet she is very beautiful and very courtly and she loved you truly and you her, I know that well.")

Thus love for the damsel is not dangerous, for it is purely a matter of words and signs: contenting herself with an object as an *enseigne* ("sign") of love, the damsel has no more existence than it does; she is but an "illustration," like those in the contemporary "Arts of Love."[2] And, after having been welcomed into the bosom of Guenevere's followers, she loses her individuality. All the wandering damsels furnished by the text so that Arthur's knights may have adventures submit to an analogous fate: absorbed into the indeterminate entourage of the unique "lady" that is Guenevere, they may detach themselves from it, but only sometimes, in order to play the monodic and anonymous role of queen's messenger. Unlike the Fisher King's daughter, who remains outside the court and partly succeeds in creating another pole of attraction, the damsel of the fountain seems to melt away under Guenevere's radiance, and Lancelot will be able to serve his two "sweethearts" in one form and in one kind:* the queen; the romance [with the birth of Galahad] has now entered into the Grail era. The compensation for this rapid disappearance is the ubiquitousness that seems to be the damsel's gift.

Although there are twenty pages for the poisoned fountain episode as compared with fifteen pages (in Micha's edition) for the episode at Corbenic and the conceiving of Galahad, the fountain episode is treated in an offhand manner in most summaries of *Lancelot*.[3] This adventure, unremarkable among so many others by virtue of its conformity to a certain number of models, is nonetheless charged with *senefiance* ("meaning"): it plays the role of romance matrix with regard to events that follow, whose correct interpretation needs to return to that adventure as if to their source. The damsel at the fountain strongly resembles the bearer of the Grail, the Fisher King's daughter [future mother of Galahad]; but it is important to determine whether the link that unites them is typological in nature (the healer damsel preceding Galahad's mother as Isaac prefigures Christ), or whether the (chronologically) second damsel may be the inverted reflection of the first.

---

*The French here is "la seule espèce" and has theological overtones, as in the Catholic mass the bread and wine are the two "espèces." Tr.

The damsel who carries the Grail is only the second in a series of three (of course!) maidens with whom Lancelot deals in this "branch" of his adventures. She is the only one whose story, "forgotten" by Lancelot for excellent reasons, cannot be retransmitted by the usual means—that is, by the reciting knight to clerics poised to record, and from there into the book being read. Like the persistent heterogeneity of the Grail matter, the "publication" of this lacuna in Lancelot's account, a story that can come only from other "sources," in a way signals that the episode of the Fisher King's daughter is an interpolation: it inverts the sign of an already-encountered section, passing from the profane to the sacred, or from magic to the purely romance story.

The damsel at the fountain will remain anonymous throughout her interventions in the romance, which is thus forced to resort to complicated circumlocutions to designate her. When Lancelot accepts her officially as sweetheart, he does not ask her name: one does not ask a fairy her identity. This anonymity allows the healer damsel to blend without difficulty with the damsel who, after the visit to Corbenic, pulls Lancelot out of a well, where he has been imprisoned. In fact, these figures lend themselves so easily to resembling one another that Micha, in his Table of Contents (vol. IV), indicates that "Lancelot sends the damsel who had healed him at the fountain as messenger to the queen," whereas this messenger is apparently the damsel of the well, whom Lancelot in turn subsequently liberated and escorted for some time. Both *garissent* ("protect") Lancelot from a serious danger, bearing at least in part in both cases on the *envenimement* ("poisoning"). In both cases too, health is restored in two stages: the damsel of the well first frees Lancelot from the well without troubling about the poison; then, after a long ride on horseback, Lancelot sees that his legs are swollen and demands care. At that point there is another doubling: just as the damsel at the fountain, although smitten with Lancelot, does not think of caring for him until her brother invites her sharply to do so, the damsel of the well has no part in Lancelot's healing, deferring it instead to a widow lady, who is also a relation; the widow lady is not able to provide the care but appeals to her healer sister, who will be reabsorbed instantaneously into the text margins after having fulfilled her function. The symmetry between the two scenes, and between the two feminine figures who evolve in them, is perceptible in these formulas:

1. [Widow lady:] je ai une moie seror qui plus en set au mien esciant. que fame del monde ("I have a sister who knows more about that, in my view, than any woman in the world," p. 331).

2. [Address to the Damsel of the Fountain by her brother:] Ha, bele douce seror (. . .) Ja soliez vos plus savoir de la force des herbes que pucele qui soit au monde, et d'anvenimement oster d'antre home ne cuit je pas qu'il sait si sachant el monde ("Ah, sweet and lovely sister (. . .) You used to know more about the strength of plants than any maiden in the world, and as for curing a man of poisoning, I don't think there is a more knowledgeable person in the world," p. 136).

In addition to the insistence on sisterly relations in both passages, the key word *savoir* ("knowledge") and the healer's excellence are elements that can be found in both: if each is the best, it is only normal that they be confused with one another!

The evolution in two stages can be found in the fountain episode, in the form of Lancelot's "relapse": remarkably healthy after two drastic treatments, he falls ill once more and "will die within the week" when the healer damsel ceases her cure because of her own sickness. There is a doubling of the episode, in which for the first time Lancelot's "double" is drawn with particular clarity: his cousin Lionel takes his place just as well in regard to the queen (whom he informs) as to the damsel (to whom he promises the hero's faith without having his endorsement). The rectification operated by Lionel[4] for the profit of this cousin whom he so resembles signals in passing that the poisoning has to do with love, and that the failure, or the attempt to lie "by omission," are punished by the reappearance of the illness so that the sequence may be replayed correctly.

Between these two analogous and symmetrical *envenimements* is placed the *enivrement* ("intoxication")* thanks to which Galahad's conception may take place. A single stage this time, unless the conjoined appearance of the Grail and its female bearer constitutes a new variant on poisoning, the venom penetrating first the eyes, as the physiology of love would have it. In any case, the *boivre* ("drink") furnished by Brisane† is carefully paralleled with the water drunk by Lancelot at the fountain. As at the fountain, the knight *si ot talant de boivre a ce qu'il ot eu chaut a venir* ("desired to drink because of the heat to come," p. 208). The liquid contained in the cup that is so like the Grail itself evokes, at the price of a slight contradiction in terms, the "sycamore" fountain: . . . *le boivre qui plus estoit clers que fontaine et de coulor a vin* ("the drink that was clearer than a fountain and

---

*At Corbenic, Lancelot is drugged into believing that he is making love to Guenevere, whereas in reality his partner is the Fisher King's daughter. This will lead to the birth of Galahad. *Tr.*

† Brisane is governess to the Fisher King's daughter. *Tr.*

[was] the color of wine," p. 208). In the absence of the term *envenimement*, that of *poison** is used straightforwardly, and Lancelot's unbounded thirst can finally only be compared with what took hold of him at the fountain. Further, the vocabulary of the two scenes can be interpreted entirely in a metaphorical manner and as if in service to the same theory of love: at the origin of this sentiment necessarily lies a mystical element, or at least a supernatural one—as, for example, Lancelot's exceptional and "angelic" beauty in the eyes of the damsel of the fountain. It is also important that several signs be present whose order of appearance and whose apportioning among the characters are almost a matter of indifference: whereas the damsel, in love with Lancelot, interprets her love as a true malady *dont ele garra bien se Dieu plest* ("from which she'll soon recover, God willing"), it is Lancelot who suffers physically and in that way makes concretely visible the metaphorical pain of the "fairy."

In the episode of the fountain as in that of the Grail, the key characters are framed or reinforced by other figures who signal, inside the scene, elements that the simple narration cannot render sufficiently redundant, and who relaunch the action whenever contemplation (of the Grail, of Guenevere's face—which, for Lancelot, is superimposed upon the Grail— or simply of Lancelot's own beauty) threatens to bring the text to its death. These figures comment upon or, if necessary, moralize the action, and in both cases finally blur the damsel's responsibility. The most interesting of these intermediaries is the *maîtresse* ("governess") of the Fisher King's daughter Brisane, whose name underlines her likeness to Brangain, Yseut's lady-in-waiting, of whom she can reasonably be called a reflection. At this stage of *Lancelot*, Brisane is gifted with remarkable knowledge; there is nothing she does not know about the love between the knight and Guenevere, which puts her on a par with Morgan or with the Lady of the Lake. The strategic effectiveness with which Brisane uses her knowledge, the better to fool Lancelot, the better to *enfantômer* ("trick") him with a mirage of Guenevere, raises doubts about the damsel of the fountain some dozens of pages earlier.

The damsel of the fountain now in fact does not seem to be the custodian of Lancelot's "secret": she justly bases her reasoning on the fact that courtliness requires him to accept her love, at a time when he loves another; but, faced with the hero's reluctance, she seems to have no doubts about the identity of the *haute dame* ("noble lady") whom she cannot equal. Further,

---

* Whereas *envenimement* is here a strong term, *poison* is a weaker term, including all kinds of magic and fatal drinks. *Tr.*

although she assumes an absolute passivity at the beginning of the episode, and takes care at every opportunity to make clear that she counts for nothing in the course of events, the text shows by certain indices that she is a priori a more important character than might appear: presented as having all the attributes of a fairy, which persist in spite of the textual jumble that tends to integrate her into a socially ordinary universe, she is in a sense the "internal" object of the narration even before Lancelot is poisoned: her feelings are described straightforwardly, and the ripening of her love precedes the unfortunate happenstance that pushes Lancelot to drink the poisoned water. After the damsel has fallen in love and therefore ill, and has confessed that fact to her brother, a finally-thirsty Lancelot approaches the fountain where he had arrived some time earlier, as if he had been obeying some injunction left silent by the romance, and drinks. The *conte* ("tale") knows that the situation intersects with a magic scenario, to which it conforms, without any of the characters being truly aware of this intrusion of another logic, a "supernatural" one, in the rational and chivalric logic of the romance.[5]

If, however, in this first movement, magic causality acts discreetly without being taken on by any of the spokespersons of the text, Lancelot's relapse is clearly attributed to amorous blackmail. Not on Lancelot's part, however, for he is asleep at the moment when the damsel of the fountain declares her love to him in the language of detailed courtly rhetoric; once awakened, he prefers not to ask for any details about his healer's enigmatic words, which avail themselves of an amorous register where Lancelot never *s'aventure* ("ventures"), except with Guenevere. It is Lionel, infinitely less courtly than his cousin, and outside the "magic circle" of adulterous love, who receives the message of the healer damsel and perceives its threat:

> Sire, fet ele, je nel diroie a vos ne a autre, mais toutes voies dites a vostre signor *qu'il s'ocist et autre por sa biauté*, que mar fust il onques si biaux. (. . .) Lyon antandi bien ceste parole, et bien sot qu'ele volt dire, mais onques ne fist semblant qu'il l'eust oïe; (. . .) si s'an voloit aler, quant ele le rapele et li dist: Biaux sire, dites a vostre seignor qu'il morra dedans VIII jorz, *s'il ne prant autre conroi* de soi et ce sera moult granz pechiez, *se il par defaute se laisse morir.* ("Sire, says she, I won't tell you or anyone else; but nevertheless, tell your lord *that he is killing himself and another by his beauty*: woe that he was ever so handsome. Lionel well understood her words and knew well what she meant but he gave no sign that he had heard her; (. . .) thus he made to leave, when she calls him back and says: Fair lord, tell your

lord that he will die before the week is out if *he does not do some-thing about the situation he is in*, and it will be a great sin *if he al-lows himself to die simply by default*.")

The text is not more explicit. But Lancelot, informed by Lionel—that is, by someone whom he can *entendre* ("understand")—*en devint touz esbahiz, car bien connoist la senefiance des paroles* ("became upset, for he well knew the meaning of the words," p. 150). This *senefiance* ("mean-ing") is one that Lionel, not inclined toward euphemisms, summarizes straightforwardly:

> Sire, que vos vaut le celer? Vos poez morir ou vivre, se vos volez. (. . .) si sai bien qu'ele morra, se vos ne l'aseurez de vostre amour ("Sire, of what use to you is concealment? You may die or live, if you wish. [. . .] I know surely that she will die if you do not assure her of your love," p. 150).

The damsel of the fountain is from that point in a position of strength: hold-ing Lancelot's life in her hands and, as a consequence, the life of the romance that is based on him, she has a vast power, comparable to the power of the writer himself.

Although the damsel of the well doubles the damsel of the fountain, no mastery as radical as that of her original, or of the constellation com-posed of the Fisher King's daughter and Brisane, can be read into her inter-ventions. Nor does the situation demand it, since she appears in a phase of the denouement, when all elements are hastening toward the recording room that is Arthur's court. However, seeing, in a premonitory dream,[6] that Lancelot saves her from the pyre to which she is condemned, she imposes her mark on the story, constraining him silently to conform to the model that has been proposed to him—or imposed on him. Proliferating in the text to the point where long-foreseen episodes are in some way reduced to hav-ing a very small place, or conjured away, the multiple figure of the damsel becomes an obsession that constructs on Lancelot's path a series of obstacles paralleling the obvious meaning of the story.

In different degrees, what's at stake in each of these encounters is turn-ing Lancelot away from a univocal courtly love, making him know, instead of variants of the chivalric quest based on brave acts undertaken for the honor of the lady, the gamut of relations with women that monodic *fin'amor* ("true love") prohibits. The three appearances of the damsel correspond to three transgressions in the amorous order: at the ideal level, the first is the most important, since it introduces a rival to Guenevere and demands of the knight a long-term commitment made in full awareness. Lancelot's second "fault," although apparently more serious by virtue of its consequences (material: Galahad; and spiritual: madness of Lancelot), bears only on love's *surplus* ("sexual congress") and rests upon a bit of trickery performed at the knight's expense; from Lancelot's point of view, he remains faithful to Guenevere. If he betrays anyone when he visits the Grail castle, it is the damsel of the fountain, his "new sweetheart," whom he denies even as he respects the terms of the contract that binds him to the queen: *Il me samble, fet il, que de damoisele ne vi je onques si bele; de dame ne di je mie* ("'It seems to me,' he says, 'that I have never seen such a beautiful damsel; I am not speaking of a lady,'" p. 206). As the damsel's knight and friend, it would be *courtois* ("courtly") of Lancelot to make an equal exception in her favor; this omission points to Guenevere's lasting preponderance, beyond Lancelot's rhetorical commitments.

Further, at the fountain itself, Lancelot submits only regretfully to the test imposed upon him [to love the damsel]. Instead, it is Lionel who acts, who precipitates matters, while his cousin temporizes and defers to the discretionary power of the queen,* who assures the damsel, by *procuration* ("sending back an official representative" [that is, Lionel]), of Lancelot's faith:

> Par foi, fait Lions, je i [à la reine] alasse mout volontiers, mes je vous voi si atorné que je ne croi pas que vous fussiez vis tant que je revenisse et por ce couvient il que *vos* preigniez *hatif conroi*. Atant s'em part Lyonnel del pavillon et vient a la damoisele qui molt estoit deshetie et la salue *de par Lancelot* et li dist: Damoisele, *mes sires vos mande* (. . .) *il vos promet* que vos des ore mais poez faire de lui comme de vostre chevalier et de vostre ami, se il vos plaist ("'By my faith,' says Lionel, 'I would go there [to the queen] very gladly but I see you in such a bad state that I don't believe you'd live until I returned; and for that reason, you must make a swift decision.' At that Lionel leaves the pavilion and comes to the damsel, who was quite distressed, and greets her on Lancelot's behalf and says to her: 'Damsel, my lord sends to you [. . .] [that] he promises you that from now on you may do with him as with your knight and sweetheart, if you please,'" p. 153).

---

*By sending Lionel to ask the queen if he (Lancelot) should die; see introductory synopsis. Tr.

The least one can say is that Lionel is clearly extrapolating on the information furnished to him by Lancelot. But it is the double or the phantom of the knight that participates in this engagement. By contrast, at the moment of the visit to Corbenic, there is error, transfer, and metamorphosis as fecund as that which, in the romance's past, allowed Arthur's birth.[7] If Lancelot, drugged and not in control of himself, accomplishes the act expected of him, his relations with the daughter of the Fisher King are no less indirect, resting upon the mediating work of an image, of an amorous representation alone able to create the brief illusion of an agreement.

Lancelot passes completely unaware through these stages of a "sentimental education," done in the manner of a cyclical romance: the tests are not seen as such, and they may not even be perceived; locked in a seamless sphere of courtly values, the "queen's knight" tirelessly superposes them onto the new situations that are presented to him. It is the others (Lionel or Brisane, the damsel of the fountain, or the Fisher King's daughter) who take advantage of available resources to achieve the desired result. The surroundings give an impression of a certain suppleness, whereas Lancelot himself remains intact, unshaken, from beginning to end conforming to the "typical" nature of his character. At the end of each episode he barely consents to ratify what others have done "for him," in his name: upon awakening next to the daughter of the Fisher King, his murderous impulses are replaced *in extremis* by the ecstatic contemplation of the young lady's beauty—and that is perhaps the true treason in regard to Guenevere, the recognition of a certain willingness to fall into the trap that has been set for him. Insofar as the damsel of the fountain is concerned, Lancelot's move to conform to the speech that another undertook in his name is even clearer:

> Celui jor avint aprés disner que Lanceloz fu remés tout seul el pavillon fors de la pucele qui gari l'ot et il fu assis en son lit et la commença a resgarder, si la vit de si grant biauté et tant li plot que, s'il n'amast la roine de si grant amor, il ne se tenist pas qu'il ne feist la volenté a la damoiselle ("That day it happened after lunch that Lancelot remained alone in the pavilion except for the maiden who had cured him, and he was seated on his bed and began to look at her, and saw that she was of such great beauty and she pleased him so much that if he didn't love the queen with such a great love, he could not have prevented himself from doing the damsel's will," p. 155).

At this moment Lancelot is absolved of all fault in advance by Guenevere's "blank check," which Lionel has just brought to him; unluckily, he puts off the moment of "doing the damsel's will" until the queen's permission is no longer in force. But even then the error he commits toward his lady is less serious, according to the code of courtesy, than the one he commits in *faussant* ("falsifying") his promise to the healer damsel, forcing her to find, in his stead, the *cote mal taillee* ("the ill-fitting cloak"*) that prevents a recalcitrant knight from *faillir du tout* ("completely failing") at his word. The healer damsel is not satisfied with this compromise, not any more than the romance is, and that explains the second attempt at seduction, successful this time, that Lancelot endures at Corbenic: the bearer of the Grail is effectively the avatar of the damsel of the fountain, substituting the magic of poisons for the casuistic blackmail that led her nowhere. The number of apparitions into which she is fragmented hardly matters: Lancelot indeed has a "new sweetheart."

To complete the gamut of treasonous acts by the "perfect lover" toward his lady, the second appearance of the healer damsel [as the damsel in distress] and the episode of the damsel of the well place the "sweetheart" under the "safe conduct" of her knight errant (something quite new for Lancelot) and obtain from him a written recommendation. These are apparently mere details after the crucial "faults" that have already been committed, but they are nonetheless details that introduce a central motif in medieval literature, that of the all-powerful *écrit* ("written text"), and they make a "cleric" of Lancelot in the most extraordinary way: *Lanceloz fait les lestres teles com il veut, com cil qui estoit fondez en clergie tant qu'a celui tans ne trovast on nul chevalier plus sage que lui* ("Lancelot writes the letter as he wishes, like one who was a trained cleric such that at that time no one could find a knight as wise as he," p. 346).[8] This letter makes official the situation of Lancelot's "new sweetheart," and confers on her the status of not being punished, a status that is nearly equal to Guenevere's. Guenevere, *enchantée* ("enchanted" / "delighted") by the message, goes so far as to facilitate a last meeting with her lover, something that does not accord with her habitual jealousy. The only problem that then arises comes from the ambiguity of Lancelot's formulas: prey to a knight's usual difficulties of remembering, aggravated in his case by three recent imprisonments, Lancelot seems to confuse in the same formula the damsel of the fountain and the damsel of the well—rightly enough, since, structurally speaking, they form just one. But the queen generously reserves her power to pardon for the maiden who brings the letter [the damsel of the well], for she believes that this maiden has cured Lancelot from his *envenimement* (the only poisoning

---

*The *cote mal taillee* also has connotations of a rather bad compromise. *Tr.*

she has heard about), and because of that confusion she at first treats the maiden with the belt* with an inquisitional rigor.

Three characters, therefore, join to constitute a single image of woman and of love, antagonist of the queen. The episode of the Fisher King's daughter ought not take a preponderant place in the interpretation of the text: whatever the Grail's function elsewhere in the Arthurian romance in general, here it has a different value, and what happens backstage at Corbenic belongs to the area of amorous experimentation more than to mystical experience. One might wonder, however, whether the apparent succession of three damsels who are but one in Lancelot's adventures, each incarnating an aspect of love, constitute a profane allusion to the Holy Trinity: the founding love of the damsel of the fountain would correspond to the age of the Father; the redemptive love of the Fisher King's daughter would correspond to the age of the Son through the intermediary of Galahad; "scriptuary" love, symbolic of the damsel of the well, would correspond to the age of the Spirit.[9]

There are, in any case, three types of human love: spiritual (because the platonic relations that the damsel of the fountain consents to undertake with Lancelot, putting a good face on bad luck, form a singular prelude to the mystical marriage that will unite Galahad and Perceval's sister in the Quest for the Holy Grail); carnal (which will give birth to the promise of a romance future, but also to the promise of the unavoidable end of any romance, in the person of the eschatologically oriented Galahad), literary (through the extra *mise-en-abîme* of the story constituted by Lancelot's ambiguous letter in favor of his multiform sweetheart). In this rivalry between two *arts d'aimer* ("arts of love"), and in spite of Lancelot's return to the court—final but temporary—it isn't clear that Guenevere carries the day. All these temptations placed on the knight's path seem to derive from deliberate intention, from a conceptualized general scheme that aims at reconquering, step-by-step, terrain lost to the queen. And even more than the damsel of the fountain, resuscitated like a mirage composed of persistent images of the fairy lover in the structure of a text that she embarrasses; much more than the damsel of the well, simple reflection of an other who is already a shadow; more than the daughter of the Fisher King, who, in accomplishing her virtuous sin, serves interests other than her own, there is in the *Lancelot* an explicit rival of Guenevere: she is the Lady of the Lake or, by antiphrasis, Morgan and her sorceress companions, who never cease to attack Lancelot and his lineage. Relations between the queen and "Niniane" are not always excellent: even if Guenevere sometimes appeals to the fairy to find their com-

---

*That is, the damsel of the fountain. *Tr.*

mon lost *protégé* (and she does, just before the beginning of the fountain episode), the Lady of the Lake's answers, or her personal messages to the queen, are not always models of kindness. If, for example, it is completely normal for the Lady, former "pupil" of the all-knowing Merlin, to know about the love between Lancelot and Guenevere, her intentions in sending the *bouclier fendu*[10] ("split shield") hardly seem more pure than those of Morgan, who takes every occasion to denounce the lovers. In this double-edged gift can be found the echo of a threat and the fairy's insistence upon underlining her part in the development of the romance.

With regard to Lancelot, Guenevere occupies the archetypal position of the bad queen, a Potiphar's wife,[11] whose attempt at seduction this time has not only succeeded but even changed its sign to become the perfect in-carnation of courtly love. There is a true usurping of power that operates to the detriment of the Lady of the Lake and to Guenevere's benefit; a usurp-ing or, more courteously, a passing of powers: at the edge of the forest of adventure, where the romance magic of the fairy ends, the queen takes in charge the "Fair Unknown" that Lancelot is and opens the door of the civi-lized world—that is, of the chivalric world—to him. A certain hostility none-theless subsists between the two ladies, representatives of incompatible prin-ciples. When Guenevere sends for help from her rival,[12] she procures for Niniane the desired opportunity to intervene once more in the development of the romance fiction.

Paradoxically, Lancelot finds himself all alone again. Yet a supernatu-ral intervention remains in suspense and cannot be politely rejected with-out having its chance to operate with lasting effect. If the Lady of the Lake is called upon to help, the text is obliged to keep account of this invitation and to report its consequences: a rediscovered Lancelot will therefore be lost a second time in order to be saved by a character straight out of the Lake. The name of the Damsel of the Fountain itself plagiarizes the name of the Lady of the Lake, in an immediately meaningful way; and, where Lancelot is concerned, she will choose a compromise concerning her virginity that recalls the ambiguity of the title "lady" conferred on the very virtuous *Blanche Serpente* ("She Snake"),[13] tricking Merlin in order to preserve her chastity! Yet, intervening like a *dea ex machina* through a tear in the romance fabric (the contradiction inherent in the episode of the poisoned fountain is underlined by Guenevere's surprised remark to Lionel: . . . *par foi, fait ele, vos dites merveilles, car ancore n'a il gueres que I damoisele vint çaiens qui nos dist qu'il ert sains et haitiez* ["by my faith, she says, you speak most strangely, for a damsel came here quite recently who told us that he was sound and healthy," p. 145]) the Damsel of the Fountain does not have to bear the freight of an inhibiting romance past and, most especially, resides outside the incredibly branching lineages that multiply interdictions in amorous relations. In that form, as later in the shape of the Fisher King's daughter, she can bring to fulfillment the impossible love, impossible because of the incestuous (but falsely so) relation between Lancelot and the Lady of the Lake.* At the same time, contributing to delaying indefinitely Lancelot's return to court (that is, to the absence of adventures), she assures the lengthening of the romance, and even acts as link—she who belongs to the generation of the fathers by virtue of her connection with the supernatural—with the second generation, that of the sons, that of Mordred and Galahad, beyond the Arthurian parenthesis in *Lancelot*. In addition, she returns Lancelot to the moment when he received his education at the lake, which was never completed, and she causes a new discourse, that of the theory of love, to penetrate into the heart of the romance, rather than herself being an illustration of it. Thus the episode of the poisoned fountain, though not of course the central point of the *Lancelot*, is seen to be a sequence as important for other reasons as that of Galahad's conception: the damsel of the fountain allows the romance to experiment with new stylistic techniques and to reestablish an equilibrium between court and forest, between the social universe of the queen and the adventurous universe of the fairy.

NOTES

1. The name Amable, attributed to her by an "appendix" of the "Agravain." (Cf. G.D. West, *An Index of Proper Names for French Arthurian Prose Romances*, University of Toronto Romance Series 35 (Toronto: University of Toronto Press, 1978) appears nowhere in the episodes under study here; it comes instead from a naming frenzy that often seizes a second generation of continuators.

2. The model for these texts is the *Tractatus de Amore* ("Treatise on Love") by Andreas Capellanus, where the author passes in review all the possible cases of declarations of love according to the social origin of the protagonists, and rules on cases of *rupture pour trahison* ("break-up due to betrayal").

3. The episode is mentioned, but details of it are not given; it suffices to consult the Table of Contents in Micha's edition, however, to appreciate its richness.

4. Lionel, brother and opposite of Bohort, represents the anti-courtly side of Lancelot, of whom he is the living image (as Galahad, Guenevere, and others notice).

5. From a certain point of view, a fountain-with-fairy is just as displaced from Arthur's realm and from the romances of the Round Table as Morgan, who, perpetually banished, maintains herself only in the margins of the royal territory, against the will of her brother.

6. See, in regard to the dream in Lancelot, the article by Mireille Demaules, "Ecriture et imaginaire du rêve dans le *Lancelot en prose, Médiévales* 3 (1983): 18–27.

7. In Robert de Boron's *Merlin*, Merlin uses magic and "herbs" to give Uther Pendragon the "semblance" of the duke of Tintagel and to permit him to approach

---

*We recall that Lancelot was raised by the Lady of the Lake. Tr.

Ygerna (*Merlin: Roman du XIIIe siècle*, ed. Alexandre Micha, Textes littéraires français 281 [Geneva: Droz, 1979], pp. 225–28).

8. Such a vocabulary is generally used to depict Merlin; in this way a "spiritual" family, in which his mother is Niniane, the Lady of the Lake, and his father is Merlin, is sketched out in the background for Lancelot.

9. Might it be possible to discern in this section of the *Lancelot* the influence of Joachim de Flore's theories? (See *Joachim de Flore in Christian Thought: Essays on the Influence of the Calabrian Prophet*, ed. Delno C. West [New York: Franklin, 1974].)

10. The two halves of the shield that represent a lady and a knight join by *merveil* ("magic") when the love between Lancelot and the queen is consummated. In the prose *Tristan*, Morgan sends an emblematic shield to Arthur to explain his shame to him: it represents a knight dominating a king and a queen. (See *Le roman en prose de Tristan, le roman de Palamede, et la compilation de Rusticien de Pise: analyse critique d'après les manuscrits de Paris*, ed. Eilert Löseth [Paris: Bouillon, 1891; repr. Geneva: Slatkine, 1974], paragraph 190.)

11. See the *lai* of *Lanval* in the *Lais* of Marie de France. The queen attempts to seduce the hero; then, humiliated by her failure, she accuses him of having tried to rape her.

12. The romance seems to forget this messenger for a long time; it apologizes for that, moreover, on account of the illness of the maiden and her imprisonment by Claudas (ed. Micha, vol. V, 151 ff.). But at the level of magic as well as textual causality, it suffices to call for Niniane's aid for her to be able to intervene immediately.

13. For this surname and for a more complete biography of the Lady of the Lake, see the *Prophecies Merlin* by Richard of Ireland, ed. Lucy A. Paton, New York: Heath; London: Oxford University Press, 1926–27.

Nymue, The Chief Lady of the Lake, in Malory's Le Morte Darthur

Sue Ellen Holbrook

The account of Merlin's disappearance from the world most often repeated is that he was imprisoned by the woman he loved after having taught her all the magic art that she desired to know. All the major versions in medieval literature, except the Vulgate *Merlin* Sequel, identify the woman in question as the Lady of the Lake,[1] and all but the *Prophecies de Merlin* provide another name as well, written with several spellings that seem to be scribal variations of each other.[2] It has become convenient to call the Lady of the Lake "Niniane" as she appears in the Vulgate *Lancelot* and the *Suite du Merlin,* "Viviane" in the Vulgate Sequel, and "Nymue" in Sir Thomas Malory's *Le Morte Darthur.*[3] As the object of Merlin's fatal love the Lady of the Lake has achieved notoriety, but it is necessary to remind readers that she is by no means generally represented in medieval fiction as evil and that her place in Arthurian legend is not confined to being the cause of Merlin's disappearance. Malory's Nymue especially does not fit the label "wiley temptress" inevitably applied to Merlin's lover, and even more than her counterparts is worth being recognized in the fullness of the roles given her.

Although scholars have not been blind to Nymue's presence in *Le Morte Darthur,* the attention has been incidental. After the last generation of sorting out issues, Malory criticism can now afford, among other things, to peer at Malory's echelon of minor characters as something besides clues to sources, chronology, biography, or unity. Those who appraise *Le Morte Darthur* for its storytelling should benefit from an ampler acquaintance with Nymue, for she is a sturdy, memorable adjunct in the supporting cast that enriches this work's narrative world. The focus of the present essay, then, is Nymue, its object to define what she is like, viewed not merely in the isolated, and in this case even paltry, Merlin affair, but as she appears in the

First published in *Speculum,* 53.4 (1978): 761–77. Reprinted by permission.

whole of Malory's Arthuriad whether approached as a collection of assorted tales or as a unified narrative sequence. The first portion takes up the sticky problem of Nymue's names and which incidents are properly ascribed to her; the second portion touches upon Malory's sources for the passages involving Nymue; and the third looks in detail at Nymue's appearances in *Le Morte Darthur*.

Several things may be learned. For one, contrary to what has been thought, Malory has two Ladies of the Lake—not three or more, and not one, who is now good, now bad, now dead, now alive—and one of them is indeed Nymue. Further, we see the ways Malory, responding to a precedent in his sources, ameliorates Nymue's part in Merlin's disappearance and expands her role of benign helper, his changes promoting consistency and continuity in line with his narrative habit overall. Finally, and especially useful to those of us occupied with the larger legend surrounding Merlin and the Lady of the Lake, we find that far from being the bawd of fabliau or the femme fatale of romance, in *Le Morte Darthur* Nymue, the Chief Lady of the Lake, has a secure identity as the bold and helpful female who ever "dyd grete goodenes vnto kynge Arthur and to alle his knyhtes."[4]

In approaching a discussion of Nymue as she appears in Malory's *Le Morte Darthur*, we must solve the problem of names before singling out which incidents belong to her. Unlike other medieval narratives, where most of the personnel tend to remain anonymous, Malory's long work abounds with names for nearly everybody. Sometimes names which are slightly different evidently refer to the same character, as in the case of "Breuse saunce pyte" and "the broune knyght wyhtoute pyte," and sometimes names which are very alike evidently refer to different characters, as in the case of "Bryan of the Ilys" and "Bryan de les yles." And, since medieval spellings of proper names normally tend to be inconsistent, Malory's reader may be all the more inclined to hesitate before recognizing who is who, relying on epithets or allusions to kindred and previous incidents as supportive identification. Tracking down Nymue is additionally complicated because she has a second name, "the Lady of the Lake." In short, then, one cannot assume at the outset that every time the name "Nymue" or some variant thereof appears it designates the same character, nor that every time the epithet "Lady of the Lake" occurs it designates the same character, let alone that "Nymue" and "Lady of the Lake" both refer to the same character.

Fortunately, the spellings of Nymue's name are not wildly diverse. In the Caxton text of *Le Morte Darthur* the name "Nymue" occurs four times, "Nyneue" twice, and "Nynyue" once, while in the Winchester MS the name "Nynyve" occurs five times and "Nenyve" twice. The Caxton and Winchester, then, share only one variant, "Nyny*ue*" or "Nyn*ve*." Interestingly, "Nymue" is unique to the Caxton text, and although in using the letter *m* it is related to the spellings "Nymyane," "Nymiane," and "Nimiame" found in Lovelich's *Merlin* and the Middle English prose translation of *Merlin*[5]— both close in date to *Le Morte Darthur*—it is distinguished by the position of the vowel *u*, which evidently prevents it from being interchangeable with *v* as in the other variants. Not having ascertained the manuscript Caxton used for his edition, we cannot say whether or not this version of the name is Caxton's own editorial contribution. In any event, it is the name repeated most often in the Caxton text, and since only Caxton's text of *Le Morte Darthur* had been published until 1947, Malory's readers have become accustomed to knowing his character as "Nymue."[6]

Further, it is only reasonable to conclude that in *Le Morte Darthur* the name "Nymue," or its orthographic variants, does designate the same character in each instance, for the accompanying epithets and allusions all link up. Of particular importance is Nymue's alias, "the Lady of the Lake." In the seven separate incidents using the name "Nymue," six also use the epithet, "damosel(s) of the lake," "Lady(ies) of the lake," or "chief lady of the lake." The phrases "one of" the damosels or ladies of the lake and also "chief lady" imply that there is someone in *Le Morte Darthur* besides Nymue known as "the Lady of the Lake," as indeed there is. This Lady of the Lake is the woman whom Arthur sees "goyng vpon the lake" (Bk. 1, ch. 25) where her sword Excalibur is held aloft by an emerging arm clothed in white samite. She gives Arthur Excalibur in exchange for his promise to fulfill a future request. A little later, in the tale of Balin, she comes to court to demand that Arthur keep his promise by decapitating either Balin or a certain damosel whose sword Balin has taken. Arthur rejects her request as unseemly, "I maye not graunte neyther of her hedes with my worship" (Bk. 2, ch. 3), while Balin accuses her of falsehood and treachery, declaring that she "was the vntruest lady lyuynge / and by enchauntement and sorssery she hath ben the destroyer of many good knyghtes / and she was causer that my moder was brente thorow her falshede and trechery." In revenge he cuts off her head. Arthur reproaches Balin for killing a woman who was under his safe conduct and buries the Lady of the Lake nobly. Malory's own earlier line of exposition, "whan Balyn was redy to departe he sawe the lady of the lake that by her menes had slayne Balyns moder," gives objectivity to Balin's accusation; hence the surprising termination of her presence is justifiable even though ignoble.

In Malory's source for these two episodes, the woman is anonymous, merely "une damoiselle," without any titular connection to a lake.[7] Malory

alone gives her the name "Lady of the Lake" and then takes pains to disso-
ciate her from Nymue, perhaps as much because of Balin's accusation of
falsity as because she has become a moribund character. It is easy to see why
Malory, with his penchant for naming all characters, would have named the
giver of Excalibur as he did. Although it is not her arm that thrusts Excalibur
aloft here in a lake near Caerleon or that arises from a "water" to retrieve
Excalibur later after the battle on Salisbury Plain, her dwelling place is apparently under or near the lake, for "within that lake is a roche / and theryn
is as fayr a place as ony on erthe and rychely besene" (Bk. 1, ch. 25), and
when Arthur sees her she is, of course, "goyng vpon the lake." Further, if
Malory were already aware of the Dame du Lac as a personage in the French
romances, it must have seemed appropriate to him to give her title to the
source of Excalibur, Arthur's sign and implement of greatness, an identification which subsequently ran afoul of the woman's role in the Balin episode.[8]

There are four other references to a damosel or lady of the lake di-
vorced from the name "Nymue," but three of these plainly do refer to Nymue
and the fourth probably does so as well. The damosel named "Nymue" in
the adventure of Pellinor receives the additional appellation "damoysel of
the lake" in the next tale, which tells of her relationship with Merlin. The
two references to "the damoysel of the lake" that follow the story of Merlin's
entombment occur in incidents directly connected in plot and personnel.
Since the "damoysel of the lake" is additionally identified in the first of these
incidents as she who "had put Merlyn vnder the stone," who, in turn, had
previously been identified as "the damoisel that kyng Pellinore broughte to
the courte / and she was one of the damoysels of the lake that hyȝte Nyneue,"
she obviously must be Nymue, too. Again, the "chyef lady of the lake" who
is mentioned in the "Healing of Sir Urre" must be Nymue, for on another
occasion the name "Nynyue" is conjoined with the epithet "chyef lady of
the lake," presumably to distinguish Nymue from the Lady of the Lake who
had given Arthur Excalibur and had been killed by Balin. The only reference to "the lady of the lake" open to confusion is the passing allusion, "And
after that the lady of the lake confermed hym sir Launcelot du lake," but
since within both the internal chronology and the formal structure of *Le
Morte Darthur* the other Lady of the Lake had died before Lancelot was
born, it is plausible to assume that Malory did have Nymue in mind here.
Further, although R.H. Wilson prefers to count this Lady of the Lake as a
third character with the same title, nothing latent in this brief reference requires such a separation.[9]

Altogether, then, Nymue appears in ten distinct actions or references
spread throughout *Le Morte Darthur*. In order, she takes part in the tale in-

volving Pellinor's adventure (Bk. 3, ch. 5, 12–15); the episode of Merlin's infatuation and death (Bk. 4, ch. 1, 5); the stories of Arthur's battle with Accolon and Morgan's magic mantle (Bk. 4, ch. 9–10, 16); the adventure of Gawain, Pelleas, and Ettard (Bk. 4, ch. 23–24, 29); the Tristram section where Arthur's life is endangered by Lady Annowre (Bk. 9, ch. 16) and again where Galahad's *enfance* is narrated (Bk. 11, ch. 3); the tale of the poisoned apple (Bk. 18, ch. 8); the tale of the healing of Sir Urre where she is included once as part of a previously untold story concerning Servause le Breuse and again in connection with the Pelleas affair (Bk. 19, ch. 11); and finally in the scene of Arthur's "dolorous deth & departyng" (Bk. 21, ch. 6). Basically, Nymue's several appearances sort out into five kinds of parts: the damosel who is brought to court by Pellinor, who shuts the doting Merlin into his living grave, who saves and weds Pelleas, who protects Lancelot, and who aids Arthur and his queen. Are not such parts incompatible, do they not cause a conflict in characterization? Surprisingly, the answer is no. Indeed, within the obvious internal chronology and narrative sequence of *Le Morte Darthur*, Nymue develops with acceptable logic: initially a damosel in distress, transitionally a sorcerer's apprentice, finally a benevolent sorceress on the side of good knights and particularly Arthur's court. To be sure, we have a character who is not cut from whole cloth, and the seams are visible; nevertheless, Nymue emerges as a consistently sympathetic figure, memorable more as Pelleas's beloved wife than as Merlin's fatal lover.

It is informative to begin with a general notice of Malory's sources, even though analogous material has not been recovered for all portions of *Le Morte Darthur*, nor with the possible exception of the alliterative *Morte Arthure*, have the medieval texts of Malory's known sources been preserved.[10] For the early part of *Le Morte Darthur*, Malory used the *Suite du Merlin* and retained all four of Niviene's parts. The adventure with Pellinor and the incidents of Arthur's battle with Accolon and Morgan's mantle are basically similar in both Malory's version and the *Suite*'s. Malory's treatment of Nymue's relationship with Merlin, however, is considerably different from the *Suite*'s although related to that branch rather than the Vulgate Sequel's; it reflects an influence by the *Lancelot* and perhaps by the *Prophecies* as well.[11] The story of Gawain, Pelleas, and Ettard is also found in the *Suite*, but Malory apparently gives it a wholly new denouement in which Nymue has a unique role. Nymue's aid to Arthur when he is beset by Annowre grows from a mere seed in the corresponding adventure in the prose *Tristan* where one of the Lady of the Lake's damosels is minimally involved.[12] The reference to the Lady of the Lake's giving Lancelot his name does not, however, seem to be in Malory's source for that segment of the Tristram section.[13]

In the tale of the poisoned apple, for which Malory drew upon the *Mort Artu,* Nymue's entire role is Malory's addition. No definite source exists for the healing of Sir Urre, and it remains plausible that Malory created the whole story, certainly at least the roll call of names in which the two allusions to Nymue occur. The link there with Pelleas comes, of course, from Malory's own story, while in connecting her with Servause le Breuse, Malory refers to the French book. In the little story he appends, Servause flickeringly resembles Segurant le Brun of the *Prophecies,* in both name and deed, for both do not joust with Lancelot thanks to promises made to the Lady of the Lake and both are involved in exploits with dragons and giants.[14] The rhetorical device of citing spurious authority notwithstanding, Malory's vignette of Servause and Nymue may have been sparked by a memory of the *Prophecies'* Segurant le Brun. For the scene of the ship taking Arthur away from his last battle, Malory drew upon the *Mort Artu* and also the English stanzaic *Le Morte Arthur,* but the presence of Nymue among the women in the ship is unique to his version.

In summary, then, as far as one can tell, Malory kept all four of Nymue's parts in the *Suite,* one of which, the relationship with Merlin, is quite changed; chose only one reference from the prose *Tristan,* which he enlarged; excluded all from the prose *Lancelot;*[15] and added several (four to six depending upon Servause and the christening of Launcelot) of his own invention. Looking at Malory in light of all the relevant narratives, whether or not he consulted them, one will be rewarded by several discoveries. In combining Merlin's lover with a character involved in other activities, Malory did not go against the grain of the written tradition. In making those other activities exhibit a protective, kind woman capable of foreknowledge and enchantment, again Malory did not violate the trend of his predecessors. In developing her particularly as a friend to Arthur's court, he took advantage of the specific example embedded in the *Suite.* In creating sympathy for Nymue in her role as the woman who caused Merlin to disappear from the world, Malory controverted the immediate story in the *Suite* but stayed in tune with the other major versions. Finally, by craft or by accident, Malory surpassed all his predecessors in achieving a minor figure whose presence may be felt recurrently at crucial points and whose intermittent appearances form a definite pattern and flow consistently from a single, unambiguously benign character.

Nymue first enters Malory's Arthuriad as part of "a straunge and a merueillous aduenture" at the celebration of Arthur's marriage to Guenevere and the establishment of the Round Table fellowship. Nymue arrives on a white horse pursuing her white brachet, which, having run into the hall after a white hart, had been taken away by one of the knights. She appeals to Arthur "not to haue this despyte" (Bk. 3, ch. 5), when suddenly another knight rides in and abducts her "with force," Nymue's yells making Arthur glad she is gone. Merlin orders Pellinor to retrieve Nymue and either to bring back the knight as well or to slay him. When Pellinor catches up with Nymue, she has become the bone of contention between her cousin Meliot of Logris, who "wold lede her to her kin," and her abductor Hontzlake of Wentland, who claims with a lie to have obtained her "by my prowesse of armes" (ch. 12). Pellinor asserts his own right to the lady, "for I haue promysed hit kynge Arthur," and offers to fight with each to obtain her. In the ensuing battle, Hontzlake unethically kills Pellinor's horse, but Pellinor victoriously cleaves Hontzlake's head to the chin, whereupon Meliot respectfully yields his cousin to him, requesting that "as ye be a true knyghte / put her to no shame nor vylony" (ch. 13). That night Meliot honors Pellinor with hospitality and a new horse, pleased that "suche a noble man shalle have the rule of my cosyn," and Pellinor, with equal good will, invites Meliot and his brother to come to Arthur's court.

In this part of the adventure, Nymue merely provides a situation, the pattern of which will recur throughout Arthur's reign, for demonstrating the qualities Arthur desires in his knights. In following the adventure Nymue has initiated, Pellinor fulfills a promise to his king and displays courage, martial excellence, courtesy, and good will. With efficiency and justice he kills a man guilty of kidnapping, lying, and unfair fighting. By example and invitation he converts others to the Arthurian court ethic, which is formalized through the oath sworn upon the completion of this wedding-time adventure. Further, in aiding and swearing not to dishonor a woman, Pellinor acts upon another ideal incorporated into the code: "alweyes to doo ladyes / damoysels / and gentylwymmen sucour" (ch. 15). Pellinor's personal lesson in the succour of women is learned ironically, however, for in his zeal to recover Nymue, he had by-passed a damosel with a wounded knight, who both die because he does not heed the damosel's cry for help. He mourns his mistake to Nymue, later repents to Guenevere, and ultimately learns from Merlin that the damosel was his own daughter and the knight would have married her and come to Arthur's court. Further, Pellinor's failure to respond to the damosel will one day cause his friend to leave him to die. Nymue's first appearance, then, is inauspicious, though the incident of Pellinor's failure to aid a woman in which she is involved is itself significant and far-reaching.

Mainly passive in the first segment of Pellinor's adventure, on the trip back to Camelot Nymue reveals an unshrinking and practical nature with the capacity to direct action. For instance, when she is thrown from her horse so that "her arme was sore brysed and nere she swouned for payne," she simply informs Pellinor that "myne arme is oute of lythe where thorow I must nedes rest me" (ch. 13). In the *Suite*'s version of the accident, the lady is far more distressed, declaring that she is going to die and requiring lengthy ministrations before her fear and pain are assuaged.[16] Malory's abridgement provides Nymue, perhaps unintentionally, with heroic endurance. Then, when Pellinor awakens from a nap (Nymue merely resting) and impetuously starts to resume the trip even though it is night, Nymue points out that "it is so derke that ye may as well ryde backward as forward." Her amusing common sense proves fortuitous, for they overhear some passing knights divulge espionage at Camelot and a plot to poison Arthur by the northern chieftains. Though obtained incidentally, this information is important at this hinge of the Arthuriad, for it shows that Arthur's strong fellowship now forms a serious threat to the opposing chieftains, although further trouble rears in Arthur's struggle to establish his rule. Nymue's sensible quality shows again when she and Pellinor come across the corpses of the damosel and knight by-passed earlier, for it is through her fitting advice that the distraught Pellinor buries the knight as is honorable and takes the damosel's head with him, both penance and evidence for his regrettable deed.

Through the episode of Pellinor's adventure, then, Nymue is introduced into Malory's narrative world as a woman who clamors when she needs help but is stoic when injured, acts with common sense, and gives worthy advice. The details of the white hart, brachet, and horse which heralded her entrance might originally have signalled that she is either one of the goddess Diana's followers, i.e., a virgin huntress, or a messenger from the fairy world. Malory, however, presents her as a mortal woman, who is defenseless physically, subject to abduction and rape, and dependent upon men to help and rescue her and also to maintain her sexual honor. Curiously, we first see her in *Le Morte Darthur* in an appeal to Arthur for aid while in subsequent appearances it is she who aids Arthur's court. Further, we first see her distressed by men, while later in the Arthuriad she is able to defend herself, other women, and also men against either sex, not through prowess of arms, of course, but through enchantments and superior knowledge of events. We have here one of the visible seams made in the *Suite du Merlin* or before, and preserved by Malory, as various stories were attached to the Lady of the Lake figure that may once have belonged to someone else. For the present purpose, however, it is appropriate to take note of the seam, not to tease it open in search for origins. If within the logic of *Le Morte Darthur* a defenseless maiden can turn into a stalwart defender practiced in supernatural craft, that is sufficient. Further, the difference in Nymue's initial appearance and her subsequent roles may be seen as a reciprocal effect, good perpetuating good, especially as Malory does provide a transition through his treatment of Nymue's relationship with Merlin, from whom she learns the art of enchantment. Since in the *Suite du Merlin* the damosel in Pellinor's adventure is anonymous, becoming linked by name to Merlin's beloved only at the end of the narrative, Malory's naming this character "Nymue" as soon as Pellinor catches up with her at least suggests that he was far enough ahead in his knowledge of the "French book" to be aware that Pellinor's damosel and Merlin's beloved were the same.

Nymue's second appearance in *Le Morte Darthur*, the famous relationship with Merlin that ends in his entombment, follows quickly upon her adventure with Pellinor. The introduction to this episode relates not that Merlin fell in love, as the other versions have it, but that Merlin fell "in a dottage" on her and "wold lete haue her no rest but alweyes he wold be with her," being, in short, as Malory says, "assotted" (Bk. 4, ch. 1). There is no mention of love either pretended or genuine on Nymue's side or even of indifference or hostility. One does sense, however, an ulterior motive in her receptive behavior, for "euer she maade Merlyn good chere tyl she had lerned of him al maner thynge that she desyred." After unspecified time passes, Merlin warns Arthur that he will not live much longer and is destined to "be put in the erthe quyck," helpless even in his foreknowledge and with all his crafts, for otherwise "it wylle not be." Malory, like the writers before and after him, allows Nymue, who will make Merlin go and stay under the rock that is to be his living grave, no choice in being the instrument of this destiny.

It is a laconic story that Malory goes on to tell, but in effect his Nymue has more to excuse than to blame her. Merlin goes everywhere with Nymue, trying often by his "subtyle craftes" to detain her some place privately, until she makes him swear to practice no enchantment upon her or he will never have his will with her. She is deceptive here, in implying that she will give in to him if he does not enchant her, evidently in order to protect herself rather than out of opportunism. This motive is reiterated when Malory says bluntly that "alweyes Merlyn lay aboute the lady to haue her maydenhede." Tired of this pressure and afraid of this "deuyls sone," Nymue wants him to go away but cannot find a way to be rid of him. Finally, by her "subtle wyrchynge" (which probably does mean enchantment, though it may also be no more than sly persuasion), she makes Merlin go under a great stone to describe to her the marvels he says are there. When he does so, she "wroughte so ther for hym that he came neuer oute for alle the crafte he coude doo," thus fulfilling his prediction of his end. At the close of chapter five, the entombed Merlin tells Bagdemagus that he can only be helped by her that put him there; Nymue's implicit refusal to do so is regrettable but part of the destiny.

Malory's version is notable on several counts. He intimates that Nymue learns sorcery, "all maner thynge," from Merlin but unlike other versions never states that she inveigles from Merlin the secret that keeps him entombed. Further, her motives for incarcerating him are that she is tired of his sexual interest and also that she is afraid of him. The implications of the story are that she wanted to learn Merlin's crafts and was willing to tolerate his attention until she had done so while yet preserving her virginity. To be sure, Malory has given us virgins more beleaguered than Nymue is, but her resistance to the urgent Merlin is not unworthy. For Malory's Merlin is distinctly lecherous. The line between passionate love and concupiscence may depend on one's moral perspective, but when Malory, who takes pains elsewhere to display the difference between "virtuous love" and "licours lust," refers not once to love but only to "dottage" and gives Merlin no more than an incessant desire to have the damosel's "maydenhede," we must admit that the traditional fatal love has diminished into patent lechery. Our sympathy is thus thrown towards Nymue in this affair.

It is disturbing to see Merlin end ignominiously, yet Malory has, after all, presented a mortal Merlin throughout his narrative, not an omnipotent being immune to human folly. Seeing Merlin become a lecher surprises us partly because this is the only sexual relationship Malory has depicted him in and partly because the more widely known image of Merlin portrays him as a romantic lover rather than as a lustful man. The narrator of the Vulgate Sequel particularly emphasizes the superfluity of Viviane's guards against sexual intercourse with Merlin, declaring twice that he had no reputation as a man determined upon carnal knowledge of women.[17] In the Vulgate Sequel Merlin is chastely attracted to Agravadain's daughter,[18] while in the *Suite* he has been in love with Morgan le Fay,[19] and in the *Prophecies* he has actually seduced Morgan.[20] In all the major versions except Malory's, Merlin is in love with as well as sexually desirous of the woman, and the irresistible longing that taps his powers and life until they run dry and he is lost to the world can be viewed, following E.S. Ownbey, as the upsurge of his human side,[21] his mantic knowledge deriving from his diabolic ancestor, his capacity for emotion from his human mother.

Nymue's protection of her virginity is significantly essential in all medieval variations of the story, perhaps being based originally on a traditional link between sexual continence and mantic prowess.[22] In Malory's sympathetic treatment, at least, it also reflects the medieval ideal that chastity in women is a virtue. It is not to be thought that Malory seized a feminist opportunity to lower the estimable Merlin in order to raise Nymue, yet the effect of the incident in his retelling is to lighten this Lady of the Lake's deception. Certainly, Malory's Nymue is more acceptable than the *Suite*'s Niviene, who secretly hates and plots against Merlin all along. Although the inclination to condemn Nymue for her role in Merlin's sad end is hard to overcome, the reader who overlooks Nymue's need to defend her chastity as it is presented in the *Morte Darthur* version and her relative innocence throughout will also miss the slender but sure thread of congruity perceived by Malory when, following the pre-Tennyson tradition, he identified Merlin's fatal beloved with the benevolent ally of Arthur's court. For, in Malory's subsequent use of Nymue, she carries on, in a circumscribed way, Merlin's role as enchanter and prescient advisor, whose skills, knowledge, and loyalty are dedicated to Arthur and his court.

For the story of Gawain, Ettard, and Pelleas, Malory creates a role for Nymue that she has nowhere else in literature—the savior and beloved wife of Sir Pelleas. The good knight Pelleas, "moost man of prowesse," loves the proud Ettard, vowing "neuer to leue her tyl she loued hym" (Bk. 4, ch. 22), no matter how much he must suffer. Ettard hates him of course because she "coude neuer be quyte of hym." Gawain, moved by Pelleas's plight, promises to help but instead takes the willing Ettard for himself. Discovering the two in bed making love, Pelleas is anguished by Gawain's falseness but decides not to slay them because he "wylle neuer destroye the hygh ordre of knyghthode" (ch. 23). He lays his naked sword across their throats as a sign that he has discovered the betrayal but has chosen not to kill them. Relinquishing his sword signifies his defeat as well, and returning to his own pavilion, he intends to go to bed and die. Ever courteous, he bequeaths his goods to his loyal retinue; ever romantic, he asks his men to take his heart when he is dead and bear it to Ettard between two silver dishes, telling her he saw her lie with the false Gawain.[23] In the meantime, when Ettard, who believed that Gawain had already slain Pelleas, wakes up to discover Gawain's double deceit, she recognizes Pelleas's nobility in letting Gawain live and, blaming Gawain, realizes that "al ladyes and damoysels may beware by yow and me." Gawain simply leaves, and the conclusion of the story, in which Nymue gains her importance, centers on Nymue, Ettard, and Pelleas.

Upon learning that Pelleas has been betrayed in love and refuses to arise again, Nymue guarantees that he will not die for love and that the lady who caused his plight will be put in a similar one. Pelleas is as extreme in his dedicated misery as Ettard is in her haughty hatred, yet Nymue sides with the knight and intervenes because "it is no Ioy of suche a prowde lady that wylle haue no mercy of suche a valyaunt knyght" (ch. 23). She acts, then, upon the axiom that the beloved should pity the suffering lover when that lover has all the qualities idealized in the concept of chivalry. Confirming with her own eyes that Pelleas is "so lykely a knyght," Nymue punishes Ettard and revives Pelleas by reversing their states. Through enchantment, which Nymue tells Ettard is the righteous judgment of God, Ettard is made to love Pelleas until nearly out of her mind, while Pelleas awakens in utter hatred of her. Leaving Ettard to die for sorrow as she would have left Pelleas to do, Nymue commands Pelleas to "take your hors / and come forthe with me oute of this countrey / and ye shal loue a Lady that shal loue yow" (ch. 24). Not only does she save his life and justly punish his tormentor, but she also awards him a lady with whom love can be requited. The lady is, of course, herself.

When Pelleas finishes telling Nymue how Ettard had treated him, saying, "And now suche grace god hath sente me / that I hate her as moche as euer I loued her thanked be our lord Jhesus," Nymue pointedly replies, "thanke me." Malory's deft touch with dialogue here puts an edge to Nymue's character. To tell Ettard that God has made her mad with love is a clever strategy, truthful since God would have had to sanction the enchantment, yet trenchant since being convicted in a righteous judgment seems more devastating than being victimized by a sorceress, who might be whimsical or scheming. With Pelleas, on the other hand, Nymue has more to gain, namely, the man himself, by taking her due credit. The imprecise syntax of the narrative does not tell the reader whether Nymue enchanted Pelleas into loving her as well as into hating Ettard, but Nymue's motives do not seem selfish, and since she had started to act on Pelleas's behalf even before she met him, she cannot be accused of having manipulated the situation in her favor.

Nymue does not concern herself at all with Gawain. She punishes Ettard for being merciless to a true lover, not for being unfaithful to him with Gawain, their brief encounter being simply the springboard for Pelleas's plunge into an undeserved dying for love, and she ignores Gawain even though he broke his word to a fellow knight. At the end of Book 4, Malory states that in the future Pelleas and Gawain never become friendly yet neither do they take up their quarrel in battle, for Pelleas "spared hym for the loue of kyng arthur / But oftymes at Iustes and turnementes sire Pelleas quyte sire Gawayne" (ch. 29). Interestingly, Nymue prevents Pelleas from ever fighting with Lancelot, yet she takes no hand in separating Pelleas from Gawain. In the Pelleas story, then, Gawain, as the betrayer, seems to be important only in setting up a situation in which a proud woman is justly humbled and fittingly chastized for extreme scorn and a lovesick man is justly saved and fittingly rewarded for extreme devotion. It is a good story, in the medieval fashion, with a satisfying ending: no longer the wearied virgin, "the damoysel of the lake reioysed syr Pellas and loued to gyders durynge their lyf dayes" (ch. 24).

Why did Malory put his denouement into the hands of Nymue, Chief Lady of the Lake? Perhaps the echo of the name "Pellinor" in "Pelleas" combined with the notion of having an enchantment resolve a story that has both the economy and the fantasy of fairy tale underneath its courtly themes. Having learned the art of enchantment, the damosel Pellinor brought to court has aided the king himself this way a few chapters earlier, as we shall soon discuss; why not summon forth the same character? In any case, the choice is successful and Nymue's part deftly developed. Again, as with Pellinor, the tale does not revolve around Nymue but around Pelleas, to whom Malory later refers as "the lover." Still, we see that through his typical way with dialogue, act, and epithet, Malory has sketched Nymue as clever, firmly opinioned, quick to intervene where warranted, capable of receiving and returning love equally, and, like Malory's other passionate heroines, constant to the one man she loves.

Malory links Pelleas and Nymue in warm allusion to their love three more times in the later part of his Arthuriad. One of these references occurs when Malory lists Pelleas's name in the incident of the healing of Sir Urre, another episode apparently unique to Malory. Malory names all 150 knights who were there, a glorious roll call, superb in itself for the sheer sounds and, as an anticipatory eulogy, charged with the awareness that the fellowship will not be "whole together" much longer. While naming, Malory sometimes digresses to extend an identification, to append a story, or to remind us of what a certain knight had done, and coming to Pelleas, he says: "Sir Pelleas that loued the lady Ettard / and he had dyed for her loue had not ben one of the ladyes of the lake / her name was dame Nymue / and she wedded sire Pelleas / and she saued hym that he was neuer slayne / and he was a ful noble knyghte" (Bk. 19, ch. 11). This glowing remembrance, along with the other two conjunctions, which will be discussed later, allows Nymue's identity as Pelleas's savior and beloved to outshine her image as the maiden through whom the assotted Merlin was shut in a rock.

Malory brings Nymue into *Le Morte Darthur* twice in specific association with Lancelot, a link which is related to Nymue's role as Arthur's ally. First, in the *Tristram* section, she is fleetingly referred to in the passage telling of the birth of Galahad: "and they crystened hym Galahalt / & wete ye wel that child was wel kepte and wel nourisshed / & he was named Galahalt by cause syr Launcelot was so named at the fontayne stone / And after that the lady of the lake confermed hym sir Launcelot du lake" (Bk. 11, ch. 3). This is the only vestige of Nymue's prototype as the fay who raised Lancelot that Malory provides, although in the Merlin episode he does include Nymue's visit, in Merlin's company, with Ban and Elaine where they see Lancelot as an infant. Though not developing the story of the Lady of the Lake's guardian relationship to Lancelot, Malory apparently inserted the reference since it clarified a point about Lancelot's name. Obviously, he saw no conflict in this role for Nymue and the other parts he gives her to play.

Secondly, in the "Healing of Sir Urre," where Nymue is named in conjunction with Pelleas, she is also mentioned as having prevented Lancelot from ever fighting with Servause le Breuse. She accomplished this by exacting from each independently a promise to fulfill a request when asked; the request, of course, turns out to be never to fight with each other. Servause, described here as a slayer of giants, dragons, and wild beasts, does not appear elsewhere in *Le Morte Darthur* nor is he a known figure in other Arthurian narratives, although he does resemble Segurant le Brun of the *Prophesies*. Whether Malory invented or somewhere found this vignette with the Lady of the Lake's intervention between the two good knights, her role does fit that prototypal one of Lancelot's protector. We should be reminded too that Malory gave Nymue credit for keeping Lancelot and Pelleas from ever fighting with each other, although there her primary interest was in Pelleas. All three of these links with Lancelot are congruent with Nymue's role as Arthur's ally, and since Lancelot is Malory's particular hero, it is fitting that he found Arthur's ally some way of being happily associated with him, too.

Nymue enters *Le Morte Darthur* on five occasions in sympathetic aid of Arthur. In her next two appearances after the Pelleas story, she thwarts plots to kill Arthur by power-hungry Morgan le Fay. In Arthur's battle with Morgan's lover Accolon, who is treasonously using Excalibur against the king, Nymue comes into the field "for loue of kynge Arthur / for she knewe how Morgan le fay had soo ordeyned / that kynge Arthur shold haue ben slayne that daye / and therfor she cam to saue his lyf" (Bk. 4, ch. 9). As the fight worsens, Nymue "beheld arthur / how ful of prowesse his body was" (ch. 10) and by an enchantment causes Excalibur to fall out of Accolon's hand, whereby Arthur retrieves it and wins the battle. Her arrival on the scene is sudden but no more so than the dramatic rescues regularly effected by minor and major characters throughout tales of adventure.[24] It is especially significant that Nymue aids Arthur in this particular plot of Morgan's to steal his sword and scabbard, for Merlin had warned him about such treachery when foretelling his own demise and how Arthur would miss him. Nymue's first act as Merlin's replacement, then, is continuous with Merlin's concern for Arthur in this matter of treachery over the sword and scabbard. In the next episode, which is directly connected with this one, Nymue privately advises Arthur not to wear the mantle sent by Morgan ostensibly as a peace offering, but instead to command the messenger to put it on first. Arthur's trust in her counsel is confirmed, for as soon as Morgan's damosel puts on the mantle, she "felle doune dede / and . . . brente to coles" (ch. 16).

Nymue aids Arthur again in an adventure primarily told to show Tristram's prowess and readiness to "amend foul deeds" and to "help noble men." The sorceress Annowre, having failed to seduce Arthur, attempts to have him slain, but "thenne the lady of the lake that was alwey frendely to kynge arthur / she vnderstoode by her subtyl craftes that kynge arthur was lyke to be destroyed" (Bk. 9, ch. 16). Knowing too that only Lancelot or Tristram can help, Nymue sets out looking for either one. Finding Tristram, she hastily brings him to Annowre's castle, where the sorceress herself is about to decapitate Arthur, and while Tristram dispatches Annowre's knights, Nymue blocks her retreat by crying to Arthur, "lete not that fals lady escape." When Arthur cuts off Annowre's head, Nymue hangs it by the hair from her saddle-bow. The detail of the head, reminiscent of her advice to Pellinor to carry his daughter's head, is a fitting sign of the benevolent sorceress's victory over the malevolent one who wanted the king's head. Sorceresses and severed heads are, again, remnants of the myth material woven into Arthurian narrative, but in this incident, Nymue is primarily a brave, resourceful, alert aide, whose means of help are not only human but characteristically female. Her extraordinary power is only her foreknowledge, "vnderstoode by her subtyl craftes," for enchantment plays no part, and she relies on men for the necessary battle work. One might have expected Nymue to use an enchantment, as she did in the Accolon battle, but the situation has called for one of the best fighters in the ranks; after all, it is a vehicle for Tristram's chivalry, which her use of an enchantment would have usurped. Too, Nymue's methods of rescue here are in line with Malory's tendency to reduce the supernatural.

In the episode in which Guenevere is wrongly blamed for poisoning Patrice, Nymue, again referred to as she who wedded Pelleas, is praised "for euer she dyd grete goodenes vnto kynge Arthur / and to alle his knyghtes thurgh her sorcery and enchauntementes" (Bk. 18, ch. 8). Here the great goodness Nymue does for Arthur is in fact done directly for Guenevere. In a portion of the incident unique to Malory, Nymue, hearing that Guenevere had been accused, comes to court to confirm that Guenevere was in no way guilty and to reveal that it was Pinel who had plotted the poisoning in order to murder Gawain, whose brothers had killed Pinel's cousin, Lamerak. Although Lancelot has already saved Guenevere from burning at the stake for the alleged poisoning, Nymue's disclosure is not superfluous, for it has effects both within the story and on the narrative structure. It emphasizes Guenevere's unquestionable innocence here and shows Lancelot winning the Queen's quarrel without equivocation, where might and right do coincide. In Lancelot's two subsequent rescues of Guenevere from alleged treason, her innocence is a degree more ambiguous in each; this structural gradation fits into the pattern of increasing conflict enmeshing the characters in this part of the Arthuriad.[25] Nymue's revelation, in its reminder of the feud between the families of Lamerak and Gawain, also drops a sharp sign that strife is active among the Round Table knights. Further, without Nymue's confirmation, the knights, though not we readers, might have continued to mistrust the Queen despite their necessary acquiescence to the verdict achieved through trial by combat, and so it is indeed for the good of Arthur's court that Nymue makes the truth known.

Aiding the Queen may be a reflection or vestige of Nymue's traditional role as Lancelot's protector, but it is also clearly her function as Arthur's ally, the function Malory specifically developed for her. Furthermore, it is very appropriate for Nymue to aid Guenevere, whom Malory defends as a true lover, for Nymue's relationship with Pelleas exemplifies true love, and, in a telling detail, "sire Pelleas the louer" is one of Guenevere's special retinue of knights who fight for her in the subsequent episode of Melygant's abduction. Finally, we may appreciate the balance Nymue's aid to Guenevere gives to her role as Arthur's friend. In all her other instances of help, she defends men, either from the pernicious influence of women or from fighting against each other. Given the infrequent opportunity medieval heroines have to help each other, for their roles are nearly always in relation to men, either to save them or to be saved by them, it is a nice touch indeed for Nymue to aid a woman, the Queen herself.

Nymue's final appearance in *Le Morte Darthur* is again unique to Malory. Identifying Nymue as "the chyef lady of the lake / that had wedded Pelleas the good knyght and this lady had doon moche for kyng Arthur" (Bk. 21, ch. 6), Malory places her with the other weeping women in the ship which leads Arthur away from his last battle. Where does the barge go, to Avalon where Arthur will be healed or to the chapel beside Glastonbury where he will be buried? The scene's description, the dialogue, the narrator's comments, the epitaph on the tomb, "Hic iacet Arthurus Rex quondam Rex que futurus," yield no commitment to the belief either that the king is dead or that he lives somehow still. Nymue's place in the ship of ambiguous destination is part of the balanced hope and grief in the mystery of Arthur's death. Nymue, who has always aided Arthur and prevented his death before, is there along with Morgan le Fay, who has consistently tried to destroy Arthur. By using Nymue as a counterbalance, Malory retains Morgan's legendary association as the healing goddess of Avalon without letting her presence seem incongruent with her preceding role; that is, she continues to be a negative presence, her solicitous healing power notwithstanding, because she is off-set by Nymue. By placing Nymue in the ship as well as Morgan, Malory extends both the influence of good and the influence of evil, of creation and of destruction, into Arthur's departure. As R.M. Lumiansky pointed out, the deliberate balance of Morgan and Nymue is enhanced by the other two named queens, for one, the Queen of Norgales, is a malicious confederate of Morgan, while the other, the Queen of the Wastelands, is the benign aunt of good Perceval.[26] Although Lumiansky is incorrect in thinking that Nymue is also the lady who gave Arthur Excalibur, he nevertheless makes a valid observation in his argument that Arthur "is accompanied by the same two supernatural forces, for evil and for good, which he has regularly faced in the events of his life recorded throughout Malory's book."[27] Morgan and Nymue need not be interpreted as "supernatural" forces, but what is basic to the structure and tone of the scene is that the enemy is balanced by the friend, thus thickening the ambiguity wrapped around Arthur's death. It is effective, too, that Nymue be remembered in this passage specifically as the lady who wedded Pelleas and kept him away from mortal danger, and with whom "he lyued to the vttermest of his dayes . . . in grete reste"—a poignant reminder of the stable love idealized in the "hoole book of king Arthur and of his noble knyghtes of the Rounde Table."

Although, like nearly all medieval literary heroines, Nymue, the Chief Lady of the Lake, receives her light from the male heroes whose orbit she moves in—serving as Pellinor's quest, Merlin's paramour, Lancelot's guardian, Arthur's ally, Pelleas's wife—and although she is but one dot of light in the richly populated expanses of *Le Morte Darthur*, she is nonetheless a luminary. Like the gleam Alfred, Lord Tennyson took her name to mean,[28] she appears intermittently at strategic turns, enhancing the narrative and appealing to our attention in the quick, bright way characteristic of the details which give to *Le Morte Darthur* its glow.

NOTES

1. Lucy Allen Paton has argued that the Lady of the Lake is a Celtic fee distinct in origin from the lover of Merlin (*Studies in the Fairy Mythology of Arthurian*

Romance, 2nd ed. [1908; repr., New York, 1970]); nevertheless, by the time of the earliest extant work in which either figure appears, the Lady of the Lake is also Merlin's beloved.

2. There are over a dozen variations, ranging from "nymenche" to "uiuane"; most scholars seem satisfied that all could be scribal corruptions of each other. Although there is no manuscript authority for the definitive or earliest spelling of the name, Paton and others have accepted "Niniane" as the basic form; A.O.H. Jarmon, however, has raised the possibility that "Viviane" is the earliest form ("A Note on the Possible Welsh Derivation of *Viviane*," *Gallica* [Cardiff 1969], p. 8). Paton tends to use "Niniane" as the standard name, although Gaston Paris and Jacob Ulrich consistently adopt the spelling "Niviene" in their edition of the Huth *Suite du Merlin (Merlin* [Paris, 1886]); H. Oskar Sommer consistently prints "uiuane" in both of his editions of the Vulgate *Merlin* Sequel *(Le Roman de Merlin* [London, 1894] and *Lestoire de Merlin* in *The Vulgate Version of the Arthurian Romances* [Washington, 1908]).

3. Although the spelling "Nymue" does not occur at all in the Winchester MS of *Le Morte Darthur,* it does occur four out of seven times in William Caxton's edition, the only text familiar to readers until the 1947 edition of the Winchester MS by Eugène Vinaver.

4. The edition being used for quotations from Malory is the Caxton text as reprinted by H. Oskar Sommer, *Le Morte Darthur* (1889; repr., New York, 1973); passages are cited by book and chapter only, not page. For several reasons, Malory scholars have, over the last twenty-five years, become used to consulting the Winchester MS version as edited by Vinaver rather than the Caxton version. Not everyone who has compared the two texts, however, is convinced that the Caxton should be rejected. The present author resorts to the Caxton both by way of convenience for Victorian scholars interested in later Arthuriana, students, and other readers, who are likely to read *Le Morte Darthur* in editions based on Caxton, and by way of signalling that the Caxton version should perhaps be brought out of eclipse. Quotations from Sommer's edition have been checked against the Pierpont Morgan Library copy of Caxton.

5. "Nymyane" and "Nymiane" occur in Lovelich's *Merlin*, "Nimiane," "Nimiame," and "Nimyane" in the prose *Merlin*.

6. In fact, before Sommer's 1889 edition of Caxton's text of *Le Morte Darthur,* many editions (all but Southey's and Strachey's) printed the name "Nimue" at least five times, because they were reprints based not on Caxton's 1485 edition but on Wynkyn de Worde's 1529 edition in which, among other modifications towards consistency, the spelling of the name also tends to be regularized.

7. "Ensi qu'il tenoient parole de l'espee, atant voient une damoisele qui venoit par de viers la mer . . . Li rois prent l'espee et moult en merchie la damoisiele" ["As they talked of the sword, they see a damsel coming from the sea . . . The king takes the sword and thanks the damsel profusely" *(Merlin,* ed. Paris and Ulrich, 1: 197–198)]. In the story of Balin, "endementiers qu'il parloient par laiens de ces choses, atant es vous une damoisiele tout a chevel qui laiens entra . . . et li rois regarde la damoisiele et connoist que est cele qui l'espee li douna" ["while they spoke there of these things, here comes a damsel on horseback who entered there . . . and the king looks at the damsel and knows it is she who gave him the sword"] (1: 218). (All translations from Old French in these notes are mine. *Ed.*)

8. Paton remarks that in the "strange sequel to the story of Arthur's finding of Excalibur," it is the "feature of the sword" that led the original author of this episode to merge the giver of the sword and the fay whose death caused Balin to leave the court (pp. 199–200, nl).

9. "Addenda on Malory's Minor Characters," *JEGP* 55 (October, 1956), 580.

10. For the suggestion that Malory used the Thornton MS copy of the alliterative *Morte Arthure,* the sole version now extant, see William Matthews, *The Ill-Framed Knight* (Berkeley, 1966), pp. 99 and 213.

11. The compressed nature of the episode in both the *Lancelot* and Malory may cast a false resemblance between the two versions, but it is notable that only the *Lancelot* and Malory explicitly conjoin a cave and Cornwall in the locus of Merlin's imprisonment. Paton suggests that "the influence of some such story as that of the *Prophecies* may be at work" (p. 221).

12. "Enfin une des demoiselles de la dame du Lac lui avait ôté la bague et la'avait jetée dans une rivière" ["Finally one of the damsels of the lady of the Lake took the ring from him and had thrown it in a river"] (in the analysis of *Le Roman en prose de Tristan*, E[ilert] Löseth [1891; repr., New York, 1970], p. 59, section 74a).

13. The unedited state of the numerous prose *Tristan* MSS makes a definite conclusion difficult to reach. However, Sommer reports that Galahad's name is not mentioned in the parallel passage of the French romance *(Le Morte Darthur, 3: 192)*; an analogous reference does not occur in the version edited by Paulin Paris, *Les Romans de la table ronde*, 5 (Paris, 1877); such a reference, or even the basis for it in the relevant portion of the prose *Tristan* is not noted by either Löseth (p. 276, n5, section 388a) or Vinaver *(The Works of Sir Thomas Malory*, 2nd ed. [Oxford, 1967]), pp. 1524–1525.

14. See *Les Prophecies de Merlin*, ed. Lucy Allen Paton (New York, 1926), 2: 438–439 (Dame du Lac prevents joust between Lancelot and Segurant), 206 (pursuit of dragon), 447 (combat with giant); for commentary on the Segurant episodes in the *Prophecies, see* 1: 279–292.

15. Although we do not know exactly all the contents in the manuscript Malory was using, it is likely that some of the Dame du Lac's appearances in the *Lancelot* were in Malory's immediate source.

16. "Et celle chiet a terre si felenessement seur le brach seniestre que elle cuida bien avoir l'espaulle desliuee, si a si grant angoisee que elle se pasme. Et quant elle revint de pasmisons, elle s' escrie: 'Ha! sire chevaliers, morte sui!' . . ." ["And she fell down so violently on her left arm that she thought her shoulder was dislocated, and thus she has such great anguish that she swoons. And when she revived, she cries: 'Ha! Sir knight, I am dead!'"] *(Merlin.* ed. Paris and Ulrich, 2: 120–121).

17. "Mais nous ne trouons mie lisant que onques merlins requesist uilounie" ["But we don't find in reading that Merlin ever demanded anything vile"] *(Lestoire de Merlin*, p. 280); ". . . non mie por ce que li contes fache mention que merlins touchast onques a feme carnelment" ["not at all because the tale mentions that Merlin ever touched a woman carnally,"] (p. 421).

18. "'Si la regarda merlins moult angoiseusement & pensa en son cuer qui moult seroit bur nes qui auoec tel pucele porroit dormir. & se ne fust fait il la grant amor que iai a uiuiane mamie iou la tenisse encore a nuit entre mes bras" ["Merlin looked at her with great anguish and felt in his heart that a man would be lucky who could sleep with such a maiden. 'And were it not for the great love I have for Viviane, my love, I would hold her in my arms tonight,'"] *(Lestoire de Merlin*, p. 404).

19. *Merlin,* ed. Paris and Ulrich, 1: 266.

20. *Prophecies*, ed. Paton, 1: 169. Another allusion to Merlin's amorous activity occurs in the *Parlement of the Thre Ages*, where Merlin holds Galyan captive in a bower of his own making so that no other man can take her from him (ed. M.Y. Offord, EETS 246 [1959; repr., London, 1967], lines 606–609).

21. "Merlin and Arthur," Vanderbilt University thesis, 1932, pp. 141–142.

22. On the requisite of chastity in magicians, see, e.g., Alfred Nutt, *Studies on the Legend of the Holy Grail* (repr., New York, 1965), p. 247.

23. Cf. Frederick Whitehead, "On Certain Episodes in the Fourth Book of Malory's *Morte Darthur*," *Medium Ævum* 2 (October, 1933), 205.

24. Cf., Vinaver, p. 1347, n. 144, 19–23.

25. See also R.M. Lumiansky, " The Tale of Lancelot and Guenevere: Suspense," in *Malory's Originality*, ed. Lumiansky (Baltimore, 1964), p. 226.

26. "Arthur's Final Companions in Malory's *Le Morte Darthur*," *Tulane Studies in English* 11 (1961), 17–18.

27. Ibid., p. 18.

28. "In the story of *Merlin and Nimuë* I have read that Nimuë means the 'Gleam'," quoted by Hallam Tennyson in note to *Merlin and the Gleam* in *Demeter and Other Poems* (1907–08; repr. New York, 1970), p. 370.

ARTHUR, ARGANTE, AND THE IDEAL VISION

AN EXERCISE IN SPECULATION AND PARODY

Judith H. Anderson

One of the more luridly colorful figures in *The Faerie Queene* is Argante, the aggressively lustful giantess of Book III. She first appears bearing the Squire of Dames "athwart her horse," bound fast "with cords of wire, / Whom she did meane to make the thrall of her desire."[1] Within stanzas, she has discarded the Squire, replacing him with the mightier Sir Satyrane, whom she plucks by the collar right out of his saddle and evidently hopes to subject to her service, for "ouer all the countrey she did raunge, / To seeke young men, to quench her flaming thrust." Whomever she finds most fit "to serue her lust,"

> She with her brings into a secret Ile,
> Where in eternall bondage dye he must,
> Or be the vassall of her pleasures vile. [III.vii.50]

The reprehensible Argante is also the twin sister of Ollyphant, or elephant, with whom she is said to have been locked in sexual intercourse at birth. These incestuous twins are therefore a nightmarish parody of the immaculate birth of the twins Amoret and Belphoebe two cantos earlier. Incest, from Latin *incestus*, is the supreme expression of unchastity, as A.C. Hamilton notes, and this fact emphasizes the parodic relation between Belphoebe, exemplar of chastity in Spenser's poem, and the lascivious Argante.[2]

Spenser takes Ollyphant, the name of Argante's twin brother, from the giant in Chaucer's *Sir Thopas*, a tale on which Spenser drew frequently and specifically in Book I for Prince Arthur's dream of his beloved elf queen,

---

Reprinted from *The Passing of Arthur: New Essays in Arthurian Tradition*, eds. Christopher Baswell and William Sharpe (New York: Garland, 1988), pp. 193–206.

the Queene of Faerie.[3] In the Letter to Ralegh, Spenser wrote that his own sovereign Queen, Elizabeth, bears two persons, "the one of a most royall Queene . . . the other of a most vertuous and beautifull Lady." "This latter part," he added, "in some places I doe express in Belphoebe," who bodies forth chastity. The former part—"the person of . . . the Queene, and her kingdome in Faery land"—he expresses in the Faerie Queene herself, the idealized figure whom Arthur loves and for whom he searches the length of Spenser's poem.[4] Through both connections, on the one hand, as a parody of Belphoebe's birth, and, on the other, in the shared Chaucerian origin of Ollyphant's name and Arthur's vision of the Faerie Queene, the genealogy of Argante thus touches distantly the person of Queen Elizabeth.

Argante's own name has never been accounted for satisfactorily. Whereas most editors pass over it in conspicuous silence, Hamilton follows Joel Belson in glossing it as a coinage from Greek *argos* (ἀργός), meaning "bright," "shining," "white, or "swift-footed," and related to the Greek words *arges* (ἀργής) meaning "bright," "shining," "white," or "vivid," and *argas* (ἀργᾶς), meaning "shining" or "white."[5] This gloss, as Belson explains it, seems to me somewhat forced, however, since Argante is said to be afire, not alight, with fury and lust; since her "sun-broad shield" suggests enormousness—indeed enormity—not brilliance; and since her dappled horse, not she, accounts for the speed with which she enters the poem.[6] In fact, if we try to base Argante's name on Greek coinages, the word *argos* (ἀργός) or "idle," "yielding no return," seems to me an equally suitable candidate, because we can connect it with Spenser's use of *idle* elsewhere in the poem, meaning "useless" or "degenerate in moral terms" and occasionally punning on *idyll,* or "place of pleasure," a meaning relevant to Argante's island bower, her "secret Ile" of lust.[7]

But I doubt that the primary source of Argante's name is to be found in coinages from the Greek. Instead, it is to be found in Arthurian legend. In Laȝamon's *Brut,* King Arthur, mortally wounded at the battle of Camelford, addresses these words to his successor: "And I will fare to Avalun, to the fairest of all maidens, to Argante the queen, an elf most fair, and she shall make my wounds all sound; make me whole with healing draughts." Reinforcing Arthur's words, Laȝamon subsequently adds, "the Britons believe yet that he is alive, and dwelleth in Avalun with the fairest of all elves."[8] While in Laȝamon, two women merely bear Arthur over the sea to Avalon, in Geoffrey of Monmouth, an undoubted Spenserian source, Avalon is specified to be an isle or island and thus the kind of land mass that Spenser's Argante (not to mention Spenser's sovereign) inhabits.[9]

Belson, Hamilton's source in glossing Argante's name, was aware of the occurrence of Argante in Laȝamon's *Brut,* but he refers to it only as an example of his belief that Argante is a variant of the name Morgan in medieval literature, for it is usually Morgan le Fay who reigns in Avalon. Rather than consider the relation of Laȝamon's Argante to Spenser's, Belson is intent on the relation of Spenser's Argante to the "'morgans' or sea women of Breton folklore who were said to dwell in under-sea palaces" and in French folklore were said to have a "craze for human men" that could never be sated because men died at their touch.[10] Unfortunately, Belson's bridge from Spenser's Argante to these frustrated morgans is his belief that the names Argante and Morgan were interchangeable and that Spenser and his readers were aware of this possibility. The only evidence for their interchangeability, however, is the presence of Argante, instead of Morgan, in Laȝamon's *Brut* and the older scholarly speculations of our own century based upon it, which are, to put the matter mildly, highly conjectural.[11] Moreover, the morgans of folklore do not even match Argante very closely, for she is an island or land creature, not a sea woman, and at her touch men like Satyrane or the Squire of Dames may get bruised but they do not perish. In view of these difficulties, it is not surprising that Hamilton adopted Belson's Greek etymology of Argante's name and passed over his hypothesis that Argante is really Morgan and therefore based on the morgans of myth. Yet the facts remain that Spenser uses the name Argante and that the apparent source of this name either is Laȝamon's *Brut* or is represented by it, since a number of scholars argue that Laȝamon drew on Welsh, Irish, or French sources for his poem, which now are lost.[12]

Before I pursue further the relation of Laȝamon's Argante to Spenser's, I should raise more directly the question of whether Spenser might have encountered the *Brut.* Laȝamon's long poem, which contains the first version of Arthur's life in English, is generally considered of thirteenth-century origin. Its subject is the history of the Britons, who are depicted as the descendants of Trojan Brutus; about a third of it treats the story of Arthur. Although Laȝamon's Middle English is difficult, it is not inaccessible, and the main argument against the likelihood that Spenser knew it is the absence of a printed edition of it during the Renaissance and its survival to this day in only two Cottonian manuscripts, if modern editions are excepted.[13] Indeed, the main reason that few readers have noticed the coincidence of Argante's presence in Laȝamon and in Spenser is very probably the scarcity of modern editions of the *Brut* until fairly recently.

Yet the provenance of the two known manuscripts of Laȝamon's *Brut* is English, and Laȝamon, an English priest in Worcestershire with ties to

Ireland, was presumably drawing on oral and written legend in greatly elaborating his major source, the French *Brut* of Wace. Neither Laȝamon's poem nor his putative sources, therefore, were entirely beyond Spenser's reach, which, Rosemond Tuve has repeatedly assured us, must have extended to manuscript sources.[14] Spenser's demonstrable interests in British history, Arthurian legend, and older poetry in English would surely have recommended Laȝamon's poem to him, had he met it. Noteworthy here, perhaps, is the fact that Spenser's particular interest in the story of Brute was strong enough for him somehow to have produced five Welsh words in two lines of verse, which actually scan, in the account of Brutus Greenshield that Arthur finds in Alma's chamber of memory, amid "rolles,"

> And old records from auncient times deriu'd,
> Some made in books, some in long parchment scrolles,
> That were all worme-eaten, and full of canker holes. [II.ix.57][15]

Aside from Spenser's historical interests and the availability or unavailability to him of a manuscript of Laȝamon's *Brut,* there is nothing outside his *Faerie Queene* itself to influence our judgment of the one piece of hard evidence of a relationship between Spenser and Laȝamon that we have—the name *Argante.* Simply assuming this relationship for the present, I would like to explore its potential for significance in *The Faerie Queene,* to see what kinds of meanings it might release and in what kinds of patterns participate, thereby to measure its plausibility on internal grounds.

From what we have seen already, Spenser's perverse Argante is a simple antitype of the chaste Belphoebe and shares, through the origin of her brother Ollyphant's name, a distant tie to Prince Arthur's vision of the elf queen, and in these radically deflected ways parodically approaches the idea of Elizabeth I. This is parody that the origin of Argante's name as Laȝamon's elfish queen of fairies enforces so considerably as to alter its status from tentative suggestion to far-reaching and metamorphic fact. With Laȝamon to hand, the very structure of the episodes surrounding a center of Book III, the Gardens of Adonis, begins to participate in parody. On both sides of the idealized Gardens, there is thwarted love. In the cantos on their far side, such compromised and dishonorable figures as Argante, the Witch and her son, False Florimell, and the Squire of Dames dominate the scene. On their near side and in sharp contrast are the honorable figures of Belphoebe and Timias, who alludes to Sir Walter Ralegh as conspicuously as Belphoebe does to Elizabeth.[16] From the perspective of the thwarted love of Timias for Belphoebe, plus the recognition of Argante as a monstrous parody of the Faerie Queene, Argante's figure can be read as a terrible reflection of and on Elizabeth's notorious exploitation of courtly flirtation with her younger male courtiers. Here I would emphasize that this reading is unlikely to occur merely on the basis of contrast between Belphoebe and Argante, chastity and unchastity. It is simply not a meaning truly available without reference to Laȝamon's *Brut*.

If we once recognize in Argante a distorted reflection of the Faerie Queene, we can make sense of other resonances latent and perhaps suppressed in Argante's figure. For example, should we also choose to derive her name secondarily from the Greek coinages I earlier discussed, we can recover a sardonic commentary on the rewards of the courtier's life that is substantially more detailed and realistic than is an animated fantasy of lust. Greek *argos,* meaning "useless" or "yielding nothing," refers to a lack of return on untilled land or to a lack of return of money—to the absence of yield, then, on land or money. We need only connect this word (as I did earlier) with its Greek homonym *argos,* or "shining" and "bright," and thence with the related *arges* and *argas,* "shining," whose root, *arg-,* shared with the latter *argos,* comes in Latin and French to mean "silver" and "money"— *argentum* and *argent/argenté,* respectively—more nearly to suggest Argante's name and to find in the giantess a sour but typically Spenserian reflection on the niggardly rewards of courtiership under Elizabeth's thumb.[17]

As antitype to an idealized elf queen, Argante correlates more generally with the ambivalent treatment of Arthur, at times throughout Spenser's poem but most conspicuously in Book I, when, paradoxically, the poem also most idealizes him. Here, Arthur's figure, embodying in the poem the perfection of all the virtues, is imprinted with complicating, compromising, and completing elements of meaning and history. In the course of the poem, Argante proves to be just one of the skeletons in Prince Arthur's closet.

When Arthur is first introduced, the poet concludes a lengthy description of him by focusing on the wondrous shield he carries, which can dispel illusion and turn men to stone. The shield, we learn, was made anciently for Arthur by Merlin:

> Both shield, and sword, and armour all he wrought
> For this young Prince, when first to armes he fell;
> But when he dyde, the Faerie Queene it brought
> To Faerie lond, where yet it may be seene, if sought. [I.vii.36]

The "he" who died refers logically and syntactically in the last two of these lines to Arthur, the "he" who fell to arms in the line immediately preceding, rather than to Merlin, and yet the temporal clause, "when he dyde," is the more unsettling precisely because of its initial unobtrusiveness, its insidious subordination, its failed ambiguity.[18] The poet's use of the word *but* ("But when he dyde"), rather than *and,* points up the discontinuity present in Arthur's death, even as the pronoun *he* momentarily masks it, and the combined influence of the two words further contributes to the oddly emphatic, oddly evasive effect. It is as though the poet were simultaneously inviting us to overlook Arthur's death and refusing to let us do so.

Acknowledged to be dead in time even when first introduced in the poem, the young Prince Arthur is conspicuously an image, a poetic figure tied and not tied to British history. His youth itself, not yet possessed of rule, and his romantic quest for an ideal, distance him both from the mighty king dominant in legendary history and from the very human and fallible warrior of the Arthurian cycles. At the same time, of course, the figure of Spenser's Arthur is conceived in allusion to British history, not only through his name and descriptive details like the dragon on his helmet, but also through the canto-long catalogue of the British rulers who preceded him, a mnemonic event in which Arthur himself participates in the House of Alma. This Arthur exists in the space between history and imagination, between what has been and what might be, between the forces that engendered the Arthur of legendary history and the glimpse, elusive but inspiring, of the Faerie Queene. He is at once a figure of pure and open potential and, insofar as he is in some sense truly Arthur, a figure embedded in the failures of history.

From this point of view, the complicating and potentially subversive elements of parody in Arthur's dream of the Faerie Queene, which have attracted attention of late, make sense. The dream itself alludes to that of Chaucer's comic Sir Thopas; numerous verbal details within it echo the Redcrosse Knight's dream of a false Una earlier in Spenser's poem; and several of its lines recall Chaucer's Wife of Bath's Prologue and his *Troilus and Criseyde,* both tales of humanly vital but immoral or ephemeral love.[19] Even as Arthur expresses the Faerie ideal that motivates him, these echoes and allusions parodically qualify his vision, though they do so without destroying or overwhelming its positive force. They both threaten *and* enrich it by adding dimensions to it undeniably present in human history. Without such dimensions, Arthur's dream would not be moored to what has preceded him, whether in Redcrosse's Christian story, in Chaucer's poetic world, in the Arthurian cycles, or in the consciousness of the race. With them, the dream has a basis in history and human reality, morally mixed for ill and good as these must always be.

The ambivalences that cluster around Arthur's figure when the poet first describes him similarly indicate parody of various sorts.[20] The dragon on his helmet bespeaks his kinship to Uther Pendragon (or "dragon's head") and reflects the fiery dragon in the sky that foretold Arthur's birth, but in a Book in which the cumulative symbols of evil are serpentine forms, it signals as well the demonic force that the figure of Arthur harnesses.[21] In this last sense, Arthur's dragon is like the brazen serpent of Moses in the wilderness, like that in Fidelia's cup, and like those associated with wisdom and healing in classical myth—on the caduceus, for example, or in the figure of Asclepius.

Atop Arthur's crest, "A bunch of haires discolourd diuersly" exactly replicates a line describing Archimago impersonating the Redcrosse Knight and thereby parodically recalls evil illusion more precisely than is ever the case in Arthur's dream. The replicated line charges Arthur's figure with the ambivalent potency earlier possessed by evil alone. Arthur's figure, taken whole, redirects this potency, rather than being drawn by its presence into alliance with Archimago's disguise. Arthur's crest itself, for example, is said to be comparable "to an Almond tree ymounted hye . . . Whose tender locks do tremble euery one / At euery little breath, that vnder heauen is blowne" (I.vii.32). Throughout Book I—from the Wandering Wood, to Fradubio's grove, to Orgoglio's fountain of lust and beyond—trees, often trembling, are associated with the theme of fleshly nature and, to this point, with temptation and failure. Now, however, the trembling of a tree suggests a world in concert with heaven, and the specification of the tree as an almond alludes to Aaron's rod in Numbers (17.5–8) that budded and yielded almonds as a sign of his election by God.[22] Like the tree of life into whose balm Redcrosse falls in his final fight with the Dragon, the tree and the theme it embodies are here repossessed by a positive power. And yet, even as they are repossessed, allusive parody is present as both threat and human relevance. Nature redeemed, or repossessed, is not *natura impeccabilis,* nature incapable of sinning.

But two parodic touches in the description of Arthur take us closer to Argante. Both suggest pride, which from the beginning of Book I participates in the ambivalent potency of the natural world. This ambivalence underlies and accounts for most Spenserian parody and is, indeed, the axis around which Spenserian types and antitypes revolve.

The first of the prideful parodies occurs when Spenser uses the word "haughtie" to describe Arthur's helmet (31). This word recalls Orgoglio's "haughtie eye" some fifteen stanzas earlier and anticipates the Dragon's crest in canto xi (15). Sixteenth-century meanings of *haughty* range from negative, through neutral, to positive ones. It can simply mean "high, lofty," in a literal sense or "imposing in aspect"; more positively, it means "high-minded" and "aspiring," exalted in "character, style, or rank"; and yet its earliest meaning, which persists throughout the period, is the one still current: "high in one's own estimation," "proud," and "arrogant."[23] While Arthur's helmet is defensive armor and thereby implies his haughtiness to foes, it also carries his identifying crest and with it once again the trace of a double potential for evil or good. In this the "haughtie helmet" resembles the word *pride* itself when it first appears in Book I to characterize the trees in the Wandering Wood—those "loftie trees yclad with sommers pride" (i.7). Here, if only for a moment before *pride* is redefined as an obstruction of heaven's light, it carries the natural and innocent meaning, "prime," "flowering," "splendor," and glances at the ambivalence of the natural world for evil or good, pain or pleasure, anarchy or energy.[24]

The second parodic touch of pride in the description of Arthur is more insistent than his haughtiness. It alludes to the House of Pride and specifically to the characterization of Lucifera, that "mayden Queene," whose figure is an early antitype in the poem to that of the virgin Queen, Elizabeth, and therefore potentially a parody of her. Twice in this characterization the phrase "exceeding shone" occurs: thus Lucifera's

> . . . bright blazing beautie did assay
> To dim the brightnesse of her glorious throne,
> As enuying her selfe, that too exceeding shone.
>
> Exceeding shone, like *Phoebus* fairest chylde. . . . [I.iv.8–9]

Like the "glistring gold" of Lucifera and her throne, which is at once an extension of and rival to her discontented self, the "glistring ray" of Arthur's wondrous shield "so exceeding shone . . . That *Phoebus* face it did attaint" (vii.34). That Arthur's pride is in the shield whose power is God's is a meaning that carries the promise of redemption and the threat of presumption. It is a meaning inscribed in biblical history and in the history of Britain.

My point has been that, from an early stage of *The Faerie Queene*, parody is evident in connection with Arthur's own idealized figure and with the ideal he pursues, the elf queen of his vision. Argante, as a parody of this queen, is an immensely stronger and more destructive instance of the broader parody whose roots spread over Book I, but she is hardly alien to Spenser's methods or to the ambivalence and oppositions of his points of view. The potential parody of the virgin Queen present in Lucifera becomes in Book

III more directly a criticism of her "ensample dead"—her lifeless or un-worldly example—in the person of Belphoebe, and in Book IV it emerges in the loathsome figure of Slander, "that queane [or queen] so base and vilde" (III.v.54, IV.viii.28).[25] As a monstrous fantasy and a fleeting nightmare not quite suppressed, Argante is a shocking parody of the Faerie Queene in Book III but, sadly, once recognized, one that is hard to ignore or forget. As such a parody, moreover, she is an assault on the object of Arthur's quest, and, if we trust the sequence of cantos and books in *The Faerie Queene,* she is an assault from which this quest never fully recovers. Never, after the final half of Book III, is the possibility of Arthur's finding the Faerie Queene in any sense viable.

NOTES

1. All Spenserian references are to *The Works of Edmund Spenser: A Variorum Edition,* ed. Edwin Greenlaw et al., 11 vols. (Baltimore: Johns Hopkins Press, 1932–57), cited as *Var.*; *The Faerie Queene* is cited as *FQ.* The present reference is to *FQ* III.vii.37.

2. Edmund Spenser, *The Faerie Queene,* ed. A.C. Hamilton (London: Longman, 1977), p. 373. *Faute de mieux,* I use the term *parody* throughout this essay to approximate the phenomenon of reflection in a fun-house mirror—in this case a reflection often more sobering than comic. To my mind, one can parody a person's status or behavior and, indeed, a person's identity or style of life. Indeed, one can parody any manner or form that the mind has fashioned. Parody of Elizabeth I, of the virgin Queen, is the parody of an image, idea, or conception of Elizabeth. Spenserian parody typically and ironically reflects actual texts—Chaucer's or Spenser's own, for example—and textualized ideas, such as the virgin Queen or Belphoebe.

3. In the *1590 Faerie Queene,* "Chylde *Thopas*" is the confounder of Ollyphant (III.vii.48, *Var.,* III, 412).

4. *Var.,* I,168.

5. Hamilton, ed., p. 373; Joel Jay Belson, "The Names in *The Faerie Queene*" (Ph.D. Columbia University), 1964, p. 35. Liddell and Scott, s.v., ΑΡΓΌΣ, ἀργής, αργᾶς. On the relationship of these Greek words, see Julius Pokorny, *Indogermanisches etymologisches Wörterbuch* (Bern: Francke, 1959), pp. 64–65, who discusses their proto–Indo-European root, *arg-*. Hamilton, I should note, cites only *argos* to gloss Argante's name. Belson cites both *argos* and *arges* but not *argas*.

6. *FQ* III.vii.39, vs. 8; 49, vs. 8; 40, vs. 4; 37, vs. 3.

7. *FQ* III.vii.50. Liddell and Scott, s.v. ἀργός.

8. "Layamon's *Brut,*" in *Arthurian Chronicles Represented by Wace and Layamon,* intro. Lucy Allen Paton (1912; rpt. London: J. M. Dent, 1928), p. 264. Laȝamon, *Brut,* ed. G. L. Brook and R. F. Leslie, EETS 227 (London: Oxford University Press, 1978), II, 750:

And ich wulle uaren to Aualun.' to uairest alre maidene.
to Argante þere quene.' aluen swiðe sceone.
& heo s[c]al mine wunden.' makien alle isunde.
al hal me makien.' mid haleweiȝe drenchen.

. . . .
Bruttes ileueð ȝete.' Þat he bon on liue.
and wunnien in Aualun.' mid fairest alre aluen. [14277–80, 14290–91]

9. Galfrido Monemutensi, *Brittannie vtriusq[ue] regu[m] et principium origo & gesta insignia* ([Paris]: Jo. Badius Ascensius, 1517), Fo. xciv, VII.vii: "in insulam Auallonis"; Geoffrey of Monmouth, *The Historia Regum Britanniae*, ed. Acton Griscom (London: Longmans, Green, 1929), p. 501.

10. Belson, pp. 35–37; Lewis Spence, *The Minor Traditions of British Mythology* (London: Rider, 1948), pp. 27–28. There is no foundation in Spence for Belson's suggestion that the morgans of Ushant live "on" the island.

11. For example, Lucy Allen Paton, *Studies in the Fairy Mythology of Arthurian Romance*, 2nd ed. (1903; rpt. New York: Burt Franklin, 1960), pp. 26–28; J.D. Bruce, "Some Proper Names in Layamon's *Brut* Not Represented in Wace or Geoffrey of Monmouth," *MLN*, 26 (1911), 65–68.

12. J.S.P. Tatlock, *The Legendary History of Britain: Geoffrey of Monmouth's Historia Regum Britanniae and Its Early Vernacular Versions* (Berkeley: University of California Press, 1950), pp. 483–531, esp. pp. 515–29; Spence, p. 27; Paton, pp. 26–34; Bruce, pp. 65–69. For a recent assessment, see *Dictionary of the Middle Ages*, ed. Joseph R. Strayer (New York: Scribner's Sons, 1983), II, s.v. *Brut*.

13. *Dictionary of the Middle Ages*, II, s.v. *Brut*. Cf. Carrie Anna Harper, *The Sources of the British Chronicle History in Spenser's Faerie Queene* (1910; rpt. New York: Haskell House, 1964), pp. 24–27.

14. Rosemond Tuve, "Spenser and Some Pictorial Conventions" and "Spenserus," in *Essays by Rosemond Tuve*, ed. Thomas P. Roche, Jr. (Princeton: Princeton University Press, 1970), pp. 112–62, esp. 112–18.

15. The Welsh words occur in *FQ* II.x.24: "That not *Scuith guiridh* it mote seeme to bee, / But rather *y Scuith gogh*, signe of sad crueltee." See also Charles Bowie Millican, *Spenser and the Table Round: A Study in the Contemporaneous Background for Spenser's Use of the Arthurian Legend* (Cambridge: Harvard University Press, 1932), p. 202, n. 5; cf. p. 78.

16. On the allusion to Ralegh, see James P. Bednarz, "Ralegh in Spenser's Historical Allegory," *SSt*, 4 (1983), 49–70.

17. Edmond Huguet, *Dictionnaire de la langue française du seizième siècle* (Paris: Didier, 1925), s.v. *Argente, Argenté*. Lewis and Short, s.v. *Argentum*, relate *arges* and *argas* etymologically to *argentum*. Henry Gibbons Lotspeich, *Classical Mythology in the Poetry of Edmund Spenser* (1932; rpt. New York: Cordian, 1965), s.v. *Giants*, suggests that Argente, "an alternative name for Luna, daughter of Hyperion," in Boccaccio's *De genealogia deorum gentilium* (IV.16) may account for the name and size of Spenser's Argante. But the name remains Argente, not Argante, in Boccaccio, and, as Belson observes, the incidental size of Argente does not persuasively account for "the psychotic lustfulness which Argante typifies [for this] is, by nature, of monstrous and gigantic proportions" (35–37).

18. Cf. the reference to Merlin's death in *FQ* III.iii.10.

19. I have treated this dream in greater detail in "'A Gentle Knight was pricking on the plaine': The Chaucerian Connection," *ELR*, 15 (1985), 166–74, esp. 172–73. See also Patricia A. Parker, *Inescapable Romance: Studies in the Poetics of a Mode* (Princeton: Princeton University Press, 1979), pp. 83–86.

20. On these ambivalences, see Kenneth Gross, *Spenserian Poetics: Idolatry, Iconoclasm, and Magic* (Ithaca: Cornell University Press, 1985), pp. 128–43, esp. p. 133. In Gross's reading, parodic elements reflect the poet's concern with idolatry, with the threat and power of the image as image. Wonderfully perceptive and persuasive as I often find Gross's ideas and analyses, I consider this meaning too specialized fully to account for the widespread use of parody in *The Faerie Queene*.

21. On the dragon, see Hamilton, p. 103. On serpentine forms, cf. Jane Aptekar, *Icons of Justice: Iconography and Thematic Imagery in Book V of "The Faerie Queene"* (New York: Columbia University Press, 1969), pp. 87–107, esp. p. 103; pp. 125–39.

22. For a similar view, see Kathleen Williams, *Spenser's Faerie Queene: The*

World of Glass (London: Routledge & Kegan Paul, 1966), p. 22. Gross, pp. 133–34, gives short shrift to the positive force of the description of Arthur. The suggestion that a positive reading is moralistic obfuscates the fact that the moralism, if that's what it is, is Spenser's. *The Faerie Queene* is much more than simply moralistic, but moral it sometimes—indeed, more than sometimes—is.

23. *OED,* s.v. *Haughty,* 1–3.

24. *OED,* s.v. *Pride sb1, II.7, 9.*

25. On Belphoebe's "ensample dead" and the "queane" Slander, see my essay "'In liuing colours and right hew': The Queen of Spenser's Central Books," in Maynard Mack and George deForest Lord, eds., *Poetic Traditions of the English Renaissance* (New Haven: Yale University Press, 1982), pp. 47–66.

Iseult and Guenevere in the Nineteenth Century

Iseult of Brittany

A New Interpretation of Matthew Arnold's *Tristram and Iseult*

Barbara Fass Leavy

Matthew Arnold was pleased with his version of the Tristram and Iseult legend. He was especially proud of having gotten to the story before Richard Wagner popularized it, and Arnold thought that he himself had done the better job. An audience unfamiliar with Wagner, however, did not find *Tristram and Iseult* easy to read. Such narrative details as the drinking of the love potion are only alluded to, and the story, told in flashbacks from the deathbed of the hero, was not easy to follow. Modern readers are less likely to face such difficulties. Nevertheless, critics of Arnold's poetry find themselves in much the same situation today that his general readers did in the past: "*Tristram and Iseult,* though it will stand as the most brilliant of Arnold's poems on love, is not an easy work to approach or to comprehend."[1] The major problem concerns Part III, the conclusion of the poem. In it, a widowed Iseult of Brittany tells her children an ancient tale from her country. She relates how Merlin and Vivian were traveling together in a forest, how they stopped to rest (and, implicitly, to make love), and how Vivian imprisoned Merlin in a magic plot of ground from which she left him to follow her own way. The end of Iseult's story is also the end of Arnold's poem.

Explanations for the presence of this tale in *Tristram and Iseult* vary, as do opinions about whether Arnold added Part III as an afterthought or whether it was part of his plan from the outset. Some critics find the story added merely to provide comic relief in a tragic poem, but this is a rather lame interpretation—especially since the story of Merlin and Vivian is far from comic in any sense of that word. Others find a parallel between Tristram and the Irish Iseult on one hand, and Merlin and Vivian on the other, but at least one Arnold scholar admits that the analogy is inept.[2] Nothing but a consuming love unites Tristram and Merlin. In their *Commentary,*

Reprinted by permission from *Victorian Poetry* 18 (1980), 1–22.

Tinker and Lowry even suggest a parallel between Iseult of Brittany and Merlin: both have been the victims of a "disastrous love."[3] Tinker and Lowry argue that the final episode of the poem may "be interpreted as her conscious, though indirect, presentation of her own case to Tristram's children" (p. 124).

In their reading, Tinker and Lowry emphasize the central role Iseult of Brittany plays in Arnold's poem. In the legend, as in Wagner, the usual heroine is Tristram's mistress, Ireland's Iseult, and the triangle involves her husband, King Mark of Cornwall. Iseult of Brittany plays but a minor role in the drama, a role that portrays her as a deceitful woman. Quite different is Arnold's triangle; according to G. Robert Stange, the "whole tendency of Arnold's treatment of the legend is toward a balanced opposition, a contrast between two kinds of women and two kinds of love, an issue which is not even suggested in earlier versions." Stange expresses surprise that through a startling "shift of emphasis Iseult of Brittany becomes the central figure of the poem" (p. 257). In fact, critics generally find themselves wondering whom the poem *is* about. It is divided according to the subtitles "Tristram," "Iseult of Ireland," and "Iseult of Brittany." I will argue with Paull F. Baum that from "beginning to end the poem is her poem, the Breton Iseult's."[4] But I will also offer an entirely new reading of the poem to explain the significance of Arnold's unique focus of interest.

Arnold's *Tristram and Iseult* portrays a young wife and mother who has spent her youth at stereotyped female tasks while the men she knew were occupied with more exciting pursuits. As she tends her dying husband in the dutiful fashion that would be expected of her, he, in turn, longs only for his mistress, who is herself bored with a tedious marriage. Moreover, in a Shelleyan fashion, Tristram expects his wife to accept calmly his passion for another. After he dies, she does continue to care for their children in a faultlessly maternal fashion, living an existence whose monotony and emptiness are described so emphatically that the description cannot possibly be read as a minor element in the poem. But here the narrative takes a surprising direction: the stoical, long-suffering wife has an extraordinarily rich fantasy life, one in which she reveals what the poet in another work calls the "buried life," a fantasy existence in which she can draw on a legend of her own country, the story of Merlin and Vivian, to project herself imaginatively into the role of her rival and conceive of a relationship in which she is the adventurous and dominating rather than passive and submissive partner. In short, Arnold's poem offers one of the most extraordinarily astute examples of female fantasy in nineteenth-century literature.

The basis for identifying Iseult of Brittany with Vivian exists in a source for Arnold's version of Merlin's tale, the essay by Villemarqué in the

Revue de Paris.[5] Baum has analyzed this source in detail, but has failed to take up Villemarqué's depiction of the Druidesses who inhabit the Brittany forest in which legend has it that Merlin is buried. Vivian is one of these shape-changing fairies about whom Villemarqué has a great deal to say. A major theme in his discussion is of crucial importance to a reading of Arnold's *Tristram*: the Druidesses of Brittany are very unhappy about their *inability to bear children*. Villemarqué refers to them as "ces vierges du druidisme, á qui une loi fatale refussait les noms de mére et d'épouse" (p. 55). For this reason, they frequently serve as nurses to other women's babies, for they are also the "bonnes fées auxquelles on voue les petits enfans, et qui veulent parfois leur servir de mére pour se consoler de ne pouvoir l'être" (p. 48). One of the longer stories about them that Villemarqué relates comes from a thirteenth-century manuscript, "Le Roman de Brun de la Montagne," and it is important because—as will be seen later in this essay—it describes one of these frustrated would-be mothers in details that Arnold would later employ to portray Iseult of Brittany, a real mother who could in her buried life imagine herself a Vivian. In the medieval tale, Butor de la Montagne decides to take his newborn infant to be blessed by the fairies. One of these is so taken with the child that she is not content merely to hold and bless it, relinquishing it as she must when the cock crows. The next day she arrives at the castle where the baby lives, and, claiming that she has lost her own child, begs to be allowed to serve as a nurse to the newborn. Villemarqué describes at some length her tender ministrations towards the child, whom she "baisa toujours en chantant" (p. 52), returning to her forest after he slept, but then only until she could once again return to offer him her attentions. Arnold plays a variation on this theme when the children of Iseult are asleep at night and their mother's imagination is free to roam in ways that are not revealed until she expresses her own visions of the forests of Brittany and the legendary lovers, Merlin and Vivian, who are associated with them.

In short, it is the thwarting of a Vivian's maternal instincts that Arnold read about in Villemarqué. Would it take much of an imaginative sleight of hand in an age that recognized only too ruefully the existence of "two voices" and "divided aims" to toss the coin and conversely imagine that a mother might be a frustrated Vivian? The shape-changing motif itself would sustain this double vision.

A proper Victorian wife could never openly confess to a secret longing to be Vivian. A clue to the response she might receive were she to reveal her buried life can be found in a note added to a later edition of another source for Arnold's poem, John C. Dunlop's *History of Fiction*. A footnote to Tristram's story records Robert Southey's dismay at learning that the Arthurian hero whom some legends praise is reported in others as an adulterer. Southey's moral disgust is reflected in his question, "Who could bear Desdemona represented as an adulteress?"[6] Who indeed! The question itself hints at buried longings that dare not be exposed to conscious awareness. Arnold would not have read this note, added to Dunlop more than forty years after his poem was written. Nevertheless, Southey's reaction remains interesting within the context of Arnold's poems. First, it recalls the passage in "The Terrace at Berne" in which the beautiful Marguerite is unaccountably depicted as a prostitute. Second, it reflects both the antithesis and the synthesis that exist in the Iseult of Brittany-Iseult of Ireland duality. (Was there ever a more Desdemona-like heroine than the Breton Iseult?) Was Arnold himself indulging in a common Victorian fantasy? For Southey's disgust also points to the popular (although now disputed) assumptions about Victorian female sexuality. Wives were expected to be uninterested in sex, and the innocence of young girls was assiduously guarded. Is it not possible, then, that part of the Victorian "buried life" could be described by a popular, if distasteful, saying that every man wants his wife to be a whore in bed, and that Iseult's projection of herself as Vivian represents a corresponding female fantasy?

Again, the desire to have a wife who behaved as a courtesan was hardly a wish that the well-bred Victorian man could admit to, and it is ironic that his projection of the wish on to her might be unwittingly accurate. The wife and the courtesan formed polar opposites, and as Peter Cominos expresses it, there was an "unbridgeable gulf formed between the chaste and the unchaste."[7] And yet the very denial of shared sexual impulses between the proper lady and her fallen sister is evidence that the idea had occurred to someone. In *The Other Victorians,* Steven Marcus quotes from William Acton that

> it is a delusion under which many a previously incontinent man suffers . . . to suppose that in newly married life he will be required to treat his wife as he used to treat his mistresses. It is not so in the case of any modest English woman. He need not fear that his wife will require the excitement, or in any respect imitate the ways of a courtezan.[8]

From this statement, one is hardly surprised to read further in Marcus that in Victorian pornography, wives as well as prostitutes are sexually excitable and active. The suppression of such an idea so that pornography becomes its only medium of expression is significant for a reading of *Tristram and Iseult* and an understanding of how Iseult of Brittany sees herself in Vivian. To quote from Cominos once more, in Victorian times "the respectable ideal of purity represented unadulterated femininity; her opposite represented the *projection* of those rejected and unacceptable desires and actions that must be destroyed to keep women pure beings."[9]

Sex is not the entire story. Many aspects of the proper Victorian wife's personality had to be repressed and her lack of freedom is reflected in the constrained life of Brittany's Iseult. It is ironic that the only essay given over to Mrs. Matthew Arnold (a corrective to the usual scholarly attention to the mysterious Marguerite), an article that purports to establish Arnold's contentment within his marriage, also reveals how many of her husband's needs Frances Lucy Arnold could not satisfy. In addition, the reader is left with the distinct impression that she was damned with faint praise: "Several contemporaries have left general one-sentence estimates of her."[10] It does not matter then whether Arnold's Marguerite was fact or fiction. Indeed, if she were but a figment of his imagination, as he claimed, all the more significant. No wonder Arnold was drawn in the Villemarqué essay to the motif of the shape-changing fairies, Vivians who also longed to be gentle mothers. And when he created in *Tristram and Iseult* a wife most critics think represents Mrs. Arnold, she was not one who stayed in the background, but was rather the center of his poem. In light of the conclusion of the poem, this seems less an homage to his marriage partner than a recognition of the implications of choosing a wife about whom no one cared to write more than one line. But in projecting his fantasy onto her, Arnold succeeded in providing an uncannily accurate depiction of female fantasy.

To read Part III of *Tristram and Iseult* as a projection of the Breton Iseult's fantasies has the virtue of clearing up the difficulties critics almost unanimously admit to in interpreting the poem. The remainder of this essay will undertake an exposition of *Tristram* that focuses both upon the organic relationship of Part III to the rest, specifically Part I, and the way in which Part III parallels Part I as it provides the contrast between Iseult's real life and her imagined existence as Vivian.

One of the links between the parts is the relationship of both the Tristram legend and the story of Merlin to Keats's "La Belle Dame sans Merci." In both Arnold and Keats an ailing knight is introduced with a similar question: "What Knight is this so weak and pale" (Arnold, 1. 9)[11] "Ah, what can ail thee knight at arms, / Alone and palely loitering" (Keats). The image of Keats's "wretched wight"[12] can be found in Tristram, who is called a "fever-wasted wight" (I. 107), and in the portraits of both Iseults, each of whom at some point in the poem is described as pale and wasted. More significant is the comparison between Iseult of Brittany, whose "looks are mild, her fingers slight" (I. 30), and Keats's fairy, whose "foot was light, / And . . . eyes were wild." Arnold has preserved Keats's rhyme while modifying his diction in a manner that will prove significant.

Despite the change of meaning, the contrast between Iseult's mildness and the fairy's wildness, the allusion to Keats's poem is but one of many. But the allusion does *not* make the seemingly logical connections, that is between La Belle Dame sans Merci and Iseult of Ireland, each a temptress who has lured the hero away from the world to which he belongs. Instead, Arnold has drawn his reader's attention—even if by way of contrast—to La Belle Dame and Iseult of Brittany, preparing the way for the conclusion of the poem, in which Tristram's wife imagines herself a temptress, a Vivian whose resemblance to the light foot of Keats's fairy lies in her freedom: "But she herself whither she will can rove—/ For she was passing weary of his love" (III. 223–224).

This developing identification between Iseult of Brittany and Keats's fairy is reinforced by a reading of Villemarqué's description of the Breton Druidesses (e.g. Vivian). Again, one would expect Arnold to pick up details from their portraits for his own of Tristram's mistress. But once again the reverse is true; it is his hero's wife who resembles them. According to Villemarqué, "leur peau était plus pure que neige; elles portaient de blanches robes de soie et des couronnes d'or" (p. 51). Arnold's depiction of Iseult of Brittany seems almost an expanded translation of this passage:

> What Lady is this, whose silk attire
> Gleams so rich in the light of the fire?
> The ringlets on her shoulders lying
> In their flitting lustre vying
> With the clasp of burnish'd gold
>
> . . . .
>
> I know her by her mildness rare,
> Her snow-white hands, her golden hair;
> I know her by her rich silk dress. (I. 24–28, 50–52)

The Druidesses possess skin "plus pure que neige"; Iseult of Brittany is known in legend, Malory, and in Arnold's poem by her "snow-white hands." In both passages the ladies wear robes of silk; and in both instances, gold (crowns or clasps) adorn their persons. Now admittedly, white skin, silk robes, and gold ornament are hardly original to either Villemarqué or

Arnold. Yet the poet has spent much time on the description of Iseult of Brittany's appearance, and very little on that of her rival. More crucial, if Vivian in Part III is to be linked with Iseult of Ireland, as she is by those critics who read the final story as an analogue to Tristram's fated love affair with his uncle's wife, then it is very strange that Arnold has gone out of his way to endow Tristram's wife rather than his mistress with Vivian's physical appearance. But in so doing, he prepares the way in Part I for her final fantasy, her vision of herself as the woman whose appearance she has possessed all along.

Other structural resemblances between Arnold's and Keats's poems illuminate Iseult's fantasy, for, as will be seen later, they help explain the meaning of her imagined transformation. One of the changes that Arnold made in Villemarqué's story of Merlin and Vivian brings his own poem still closer to Keats's. In Villemarqué, Merlin and Vivian are walking in a forest when she imprisons him. In *Tristram and Iseult* she is riding on horseback, a detail which again invokes Keats's analogue to the legendary Arthurian material. In both poems the man falls asleep with his enchantress, either to dream of thralldom or to wake up literally imprisoned. Finally, a recurrent image in *Tristram* evokes the concluding image of Keats's knight, who, awakened from his dream, wanders disconsolate about the scene of his tryst: "And this is why I sojourn here, / Alone and palely loitering." Arnold's Tristram, similarly "Thinn'd and paled before his time" (I. 108), is more than once portrayed as a sojourner—"Whither does he wander now?" (I. 189)—also searching for a lost love:

> Ah! he wanders forth again;
> We cannot keep him; now, as then,
> There's a secret in his breast
> Which will never let him rest. (I. 243–246)

In summary, Keats's "La Belle Dame sans Merci" is reflected both in Parts I and III of *Tristram,* providing a link between the beginning and the end of the poem. But the significance of Arnold's borrowing from Keats does not stop here. Keats's ballad, and its many sources and analogues so popular in England, form a pattern into which *Tristram and Iseult* easily fits. The story of the man who leaves the world (and often a wife in it) to seek a more blissful existence with a supernatural mistress in her magic realm was commonly told in nineteenth-century Europe.[13] Such stories depicted man's dilemma in being torn between mundane reality and a more carefree or more passionate existence. It was not unusual to conceive of his split psyche as embodied in two women (in this sense Arnold had ample precedent for his conception of the Tristram triangle), his wife representing the seemingly inferior part of himself:

> There were two Iseults who did sway
> Each her hour of Tristram's day;
> But one possess'd his waning time,
> The other his resplendent prime.
>
> . . . .
>
> She is here who had his gloom,
> Where art thou who hadst his bloom? (I. 68–71, 76–77)

Arnold's contribution to this basic story in his time, however, is less obvious in *Tristram and Iseult* than it is in one of his most popular poems, "The Forsaken Merman." And it will be significant to note that in this well-known work, the protagonist is a woman. For Margaret there is no merging of reality with yearning imagination, but only an oscillation between the productive demands, not always unhappy, of her everyday existence on the one side, and the symbolic world of her musings on the other. During the day she spins and sings joyfully,

> Till the spindle drops from her hand,
> And the whizzing wheel stands still.
> She steals to the window, and looks at the sand,
> And over the sand at the sea;
> And her eyes are set in a stare;
> And anon there breaks a sigh,
> And anon there drops a tear,
> From a sorrow-clouded eye,
> And a heart sorrow-laden,
> A long, long sigh;
> For the cold strange eyes of a little Mermaiden
> And the gleam of her golden hair. (ll. 96–107)

When, a few years later, Arnold depicted a similar scene in Part III of *Tristram,* its unique applicability to the life of women, rather than the plight of mankind in general, was emphasized. Iseult of Brittany, left alone to care for her children, peacefully if not joyfully fulfills the duties of each day. The embroidery she takes up each night has much in common with Margaret's spinning, and she too pauses or stops at times, although the exact cause of her distraction, other than concern for her children, is left deliberately vague:

> and there she'll sit
> Hour after hour, her gold curls sweeping it;
> Lifting her soft-bent head only to mind
> Her children, or to listen to the wind.
> And when the clock peals midnight, she will move
> Her work away, and let her fingers rove
> Across the shaggy brows of Tristram's hound
> Who lies, guarding her feet along the ground;
> Or else she will fall musing, her blue eyes
> Fixt, her slight hands clasp'd on her lap. (III. 82–91)

It is ironic that Margaret, who has deserted her children in the otherworld, and Iseult, who is so irrevocably bound to hers in this, should enact so similar a routine. But the important question is raised only in *Tristram:*

> And is she happy? Does she see unmoved
> The days in which she might have lived and loved
> Slip without bringing bliss slowly away,
> One after one, to-morrow like to-day? (III. 6467)

This question, and its relation to Arnold's choice of a female heroine in poems whose traditional conflicts are usually centered on a male figure, pick up added meaning from a very important influence on the poet, Homer. For behind the image of Margaret's weaving and Iseult's embroidery (there is also an image of a woman darning in "The Scholar Gipsy" and weaving is crucial to the Philomela story) stands the classical and archetypal figure of Penelope, the virtuous and faithful wife. She, in turn, easily becomes the ideal Victorian housewife as the latter has been recently described: "Sentiment's favorite domain in Victorian times was near the warm cozy hearth of the home where the wife, sweet, passive and long-suffering, waited patiently for the return of her husband."[14] Homer's epic bears a noteworthy relationship to Arnold's work as a whole, and to *Tristram and Iseult* in particular,[15] mainly because of the prominence in his poetry of the wanderer image. But as clear as it is in his poems that Odysseus was a more important symbol to Arnold than critics acknowledge,[16] so is it equally clear that "Penelope" was ordinarily to remain at home. His wanderers are invariably men, whether they are on long journeys, eternal quests, or short hunting trips.

"The Church of Brou" provides the typical example of the male-female relationship that forms the central conflict in *Tristram and Iseult:*

> In the bright October morning
> > Savoy's Duke had left his bride.
> From the castle, past the drawbridge,
> > Flow'd the hunters' merry tide.
>
> Steeds are neighing, gallants glittering;
> > Gay, her smiling lord to greet,
> From her mullion'd chamber-casement
> > Smiles the Duchess Marguerite. (I. 5–12)

Even Iseult of Ireland leaves on her sea journey only when she is so commanded by her father or summoned by Tristram. In only three poems is a woman conceived of as a wanderer, and significantly in all three are joined the themes of her wandering and of illicit sexual passion. One instance has drawn much critical attention; it is, again, the puzzling treatment of Marguerite that is at issue:

> Or hast thou long since *wander'd* back,
> Daughter of France! to France, thy home;
> And flitted down the flowery track
> Where feet like thine too lightly come?
> > ("The Terrace at Berne," ll. 17–20; italics added)

In another instance, Philomela, victim rather than perpetrator of her eternal travels, is, like Odysseus, a "wanderer from a Grecian shore." It would not be going too far to say that Arnold's "Philomela," with its theme of rape, incest, and infanticide, could be read as a nightmarish inversion of respectable Victorian domesticity. The horrendous outcome of the story was, moreover, the personal nightmare of a poet for whom stoic acceptance and quietude were a precious goal: eternal passion, eternal pain.

For a man to be an Odysseus was to be for Arnold immature, unsettled, alienated; and the famous letter he wrote to his sister shortly before he married makes clear that for him family life was a haven for a wandering spirit that threatened his stability, however reluctantly he might relinquish his freedom. But for a woman to be an Odysseus was far worse, especially since the respectable Victorian woman was raised not only to curb her own instincts, but ultimately to help her husband curb his. Hence it is significant that in Part III of *Tristram and Iseult* the substance of Iseult's fantasy lies not so much in her love affair, but in her freedom to end love affairs when she pleases—in short, in her freedom to wander, to abandon her role as Penelope, and to assume that of a female Odysseus.

In Part I of *Tristram and Iseult* the Odysseus-Penelope motif is worked out through the reiterated themes of Tristram's wandering and the steadfastness of Iseult of Brittany. His journeys are both actual and symbolic, as various time levels interact within this portion of the poem. The narrator describes not only the present scene in which a dying Tristram awaits his mistress, but presents as well the flashbacks in which the legend of Tristram and the two Iseults is recounted. At times the flashbacks and his memories merge to become one, and it is Tristram's wandering mind that we follow back through the years. His early and tranquil love for his "timid youthful bride" (I. 214) is described so that at first she seems less a Penelope than a Naussica:

> —Whither does he wander now?
> Haply in his dreams the wind
> Wafts him here, and lets him find
> The lovely orphan child again
> In her castle by the coast;
> The youngest, fairest chatelaine
> Whom this realm of France can boast
> Our snowdrop by the Atlantic sea,
> Iseult of Brittany. (I. 189–197)

Such memories of these early years soothe him in his feverish state, and the narrator encouragingly begs,

> Hither let him wander now;
> Hither, to the quiet hours
> Pass'd among these heaths of ours
> By the grey Atlantic sea;
> Hours, if not of ecstasy,
> From violent anguish surely free! (I. 228–233)

But this second best will not long content Tristram, and the lure of ecstasy causes him to "[wander] forth again," to follow the "secret in his breast / Which will never let him rest" (I. 243–246).

In contrast to Tristram's wandering,

> Thy lovely youthful wife grows pale
> Watching by the salt sea-tide
> With her children at her side
> For the gleam of thy white sail.
> Home, Tristram, to thy halls again! (I. 269–273)

Her role as Penelope is one for which Brittany's Iseult has been trained since childhood. Once again the time sequence in the poem is deliberately blurred as youthful and adult reality merge while she sorrowfully hovers over her ill husband:

> Is it that a deep fatigue
> Hath come on her, a chilly fear,
> Passing all her youthful hour
> Spinning with her maidens here,
> Listlessly through the window-bars
> Gazing seawards many a league,
> From her lonely shore-built tower,
> While the knights are at the wars?
> Or, perhaps, has her young heart
> Felt already some deeper smart,
> Of those that in secret the heart-strings rive
> Leaving her sunk and pale, though fair? (I. 37–48)

Of all the emotions in this poem of tragic passion, those of Brittany's Iseult remain the most complex, because they are the least specifically articulated. The passage is fraught with merely suggestive possibilities. First of all, it depicts a young woman trapped in her role, gazing "listlessly" through barred windows, her separation from the active life emphasized. In contrast, the men in her life are free to roam, to follow the adventures that war represented in the Arthurian tales. Second, the source of her fear is left deliberately vague. The imminent death of her husband revives emotions long familiar to her, associated with her maiden years and buried deep in her unconscious.

To repeat, it is the blurring of past and present that creates the mood of the passage, for the final impression is of a young woman experiencing deep emotional conflict that saps all vitality as she buries her secret desires. The nature of this conflict may have to do with the battle Cominos has described as perpetually ongoing in the personality of the Victorian lady as she "waged her battle between sensual desire and duty at an unconscious level."

For respectable Victorians "'Innocence' or 'pure-mindedness' or 'inherent purity' was an exalted state of feminine consciousness, a state of unique deficiency or mindlessness in their daughters of that most elementary, but forbidden knowledge of their own sexuality" (pp. 156–157).

Innocence is probably the most emphasized characteristic of Iseult of Brittany in Part I. There is, again, the reference to Tristram's "timid youthful bride," with its unmistakable sexual implications. Her looks further emphasize her purity, the whiteness of her skin and hands an almost clichéd symbol. Also stressed is her youth; and she is named the "sweetest Christian soul alive." Moreover, her beauty is not such as would imply passion, but is rather the "fragile loveliness" of a "patient flower" or "snowdrop," an image of frigidity as well as delicacy (I. 49–55, 72). The asexual childishness that these descriptions imply is at one point in the poem made explicit: "Sweet flower! thy children's eyes / Are not more innocent than thine" (I. 325–326).

This juxtaposition of sexual innocence and motherhood would not have seemed at all unusual to the Victorian mind. William Acton wrote that the "best mothers, wives, and managers of households, know little or nothing of sexual indulgences. Love of home, children, and domestic duties are the only passions they feel" (Marcus, p. 31). In addition, Victorian man, trained to view his own fleshly desires as part of his lower nature, would depend upon his wife's innocence to help him conquer his animal instincts. Or so the scholarship on the subject tells us. But D.H. Lawrence, much of whose writing is directed against the remnants of Victorian sexual attitudes, has warned us to heed the tale and not the teller. What is noticeable in *Tristram and Iseult* is that Arnold depicts the effect of Iseult's purity in such a way that her innocence seems almost the wound from which Tristram is dying.

To pursue this subject it is necessary to quote more fully a passage partially quoted in another context:

> There were two Iseults who did sway
> Each her hour of Tristram's day;
> But one possess'd his waning time,
> The other his resplendent prime.
> Behold her here, the patient flower,
> Who possess'd his darker hour!
> Iseult of the Snow-White Hand
> Watches pale by Tristram's bed.
> She is here who had his gloom

> Where art thou who hadst his bloom?
> One such kiss as those of yore
> Might thy dying knight restore! (I. 68–79)

The diction—"prime," "waning," "bloom," "restore"—suggests that what is at stake is actual sexual potency; Iseult of Ireland possessed Tristram's prime, his wife merely his waning time. And sexual potency is no less than a matter of life and death. Iseult of Brittany watches ineffectually by (not in) Tristram's bed as the life ebbs out of him. One might argue that this is the appropriate place for the wife of a sick man: at his bedside. But the poem suggests that the scene has another significance. The passion of a kiss from Ireland's Iseult might arouse enough energy in Tristram to save his life. Finally, then, innocence is death and only sexuality bestows life:

> Does the love-draught work no more?
> Art thou cold, or false, or dead,
> Iseult of Ireland? (I. 80–82)

The theme of impotence was explicitly presented by Dunlop in an appendix to the 1816 edition of his *History of Fiction* (too explicitly for the Philadelphia editors of the book, who omitted the passage in their 1842 edition). In the brief passage, a beautiful and even seductive Iseult lies asleep in the arms of her husband. He kisses her, but then memories of his mistress keep him from going any further:

> Tristan se couche avec Yseult sa femme. Le luminaire ardoit si cler, que Tristan pouvoit bien voir la beauté d'Yseult: elle avoit la bouche vermeille et tendre, yeux pers rians, les sourcils bruncs et bien assis, la face claire et vermeille comme une rose a l'aube du jour. Sy Tristan la baise et l'acolle; mais quante il lui souvient de Yseult de Cornouailles, sy à toute perdue la voulonté du surplus. Cette Yseult est devant lui, et l'autre est en Cornouailles qui lui defent que à l'autre Yseult ne fasse nul riens que a villeinie lui tourne. Ainsi demeure Tristan avec sa femme; et elle qui d'acoller et de baiser ne savoit riens, s'endort entre les bras de Tristan.

> ["Tristan lies down with Yseut, his wife. The light burned so clearly that Tristan could see Yseut's beauty: she had a red and tender mouth, merry blue eyes, brown and well-arched eyebrows, a face that was bright and pink like a rose at dawn. Tristan kisses and hugs her; but

when he remembers Yseut of Cornwall, he lost all desire for lovemaking. This Yseut is before him, and the other is in Cornwall, who prevents him from doing anything to the other Yseut that might turn into vileness. Thus Tristan remains with his wife; and she, who knew nothing of hugging and kissing, falls asleep in Tristan's arms," I, 491.]

The passage weakens arguments, such as Stange's, that earlier versions of the Tristram and Iseult legend did not present a balanced contrast between two kinds of women and two kinds of love. In addition, the passage suggests that Arnold quite consciously altered his sources and that what is noticeably original in his version is the innocence of Brittany's Iseult, who—again—is pictured by but never in her husband's bed. What Arnold has depicted in this poem is the double tragedy, for man and for woman, of Victorian attitudes towards sexuality. For Iseult of Brittany, repressed desire is associated with the symbolic barred windows through which she can only gaze listlessly at a life closed to her forever. Her education and upbringing have fitted her for no tasks beyond motherhood, so that in Part III of the poem it is said of her unhappy existence that a "noisier life than this / She would find ill to bear, weak as she is" (III. 100–101). Critics have found in Tristram's wife an example of that stoic acceptance Arnold is supposed to have extolled, but it is impossible to applaud an acquiescence on her part to a life in which playing games with her children—that is, a perpetuation of her own childhood—is her only recreation.

On the other side, her husband has also been victimized by the assumptions that governed her life, his own sexuality being thwarted by the role he is forced to play with respect to his wife. The Tristram legend embodied within it not only the dualism between duty and love, but a social system which in Victorian England created polar opposites in woman, the one side denied the desires that were in reaction projected so emphatically on to her opposite that she could be conceived of as a diabolical temptress.

The dichotomization of women into the Eve and Mary prototypes is hardly unique to Victorian times. But something new had been added: the century was particularly aware of the existence of two voices. They were, for Arnold, the cause of "this strange disease of modern life, / With its sick hurry, its divided aims" ("The Scholar Gipsy," ll. 203–204). His desire for unity in such a world is reflected in much of his prose writing as well as his poetry. It is a desire particularly noteworthy in *Tristram and Iseult* because of lines that do not appear in the final version of the poem in a passage he obviously had some difficulty with. In Part II, after Iseult of Ireland has come to Tristram's side too late to save his life, he asks her to approach his wife and request that she, Iseult of Ireland, be allowed to stay at his side. Counting on the obedience as well as the goodness of his wife, he orders, "Say, I will'd so, that thou stay beside me" (II. 95). Two other versions of this line, however, suggest a quite different meaning: "Say I charg'd her, that ye live together. / Say, I charg'd thee, that thou stay beside her" (p. 145n). What has finally been discarded depicts the strong desire that somehow a union be established between the two Iseults. Why did Arnold reject this conception? Of course, one can only speculate. The rejected lines do have a Shelleyan ring which might have led Arnold's audience to unfortunate conclusions. Even a relatively modern, enlightened reader probably finds it difficult to read the Romantic poet's letter to his first wife, in which he asks Harriet to come and live with him and Mary as their sister, without thinking that Shelley was insensitive, mad, or both. To expect your wife and mistress to live in harmony and become friends is asking, for most people in any event, too much. Yet the request is highly significant, for it reflects the yearning on the part of the man that somehow his life might be fulfilled if only he could find one who combined the qualities of both wife and mistress, who thus might allow him a deeper satisfaction than life had bestowed by forcing him to choose between them.

What is striking in *Tristram and Iseult* is that Tristram's dying wish, that somehow wife and mistress would unite as one, is fulfilled after his death through his wife's own fantasy. Pragmatically, she is the only one left alive in the poem to satisfy his wishes and is specifically referred to as the "young surviving Iseult" (III. 5). But this pragmatism has happy dramatic results for the poem: the dream of a temptress to be a mother, as was the case in the stories recounted by Villemarqué, is nowhere near as enthralling to the reader as the dream of a mother to be a temptress. In addition, a "fallen" woman can quite openly and consciously long to be a respectable member of society, since her very dream would thus suggest a conscience at least potentially pure. The contrary is not true. The desire of a "good" woman to lead the life of her counterpart involves feelings that must be so deeply repressed that they surface only through unconscious fantasy.

Cominos writes of the repressed Victorian woman that she "became subject to motives and desires of which she was not aware. . . . Repressed Victorian sexuality reasserted itself in indirect ways in the symbolic disguises of dreams and fantasies and in the symptoms of commissions wherein acts alien to the actors themselves were carried out" (p. 164). One of the resultant patterns of behavior that Cominos emphasizes is what he calls the "urge towards domination," which is a reaction against the usual submissiveness and passivity experienced by the Victorian woman. Interestingly, there are two themes in Part III of *Tristram and Iseult,* particularly in the Merlin and Vivian story: one of these has to do with freedom; the other, quite explicitly, with Vivian's domination and control over Merlin, he becoming literally her prisoner.

The beginning of Part III of *Tristram* establishes a crucial context for the tale of Merlin and Vivian, a tale not actually told until the climax and end of the poem. A seemingly unimportant change that Arnold made in an earlier conception of the poem is significant. Originally the wording of the fifth and sixth lines was a description of how "one bright day, / Drew Iseult forth" to play with her children out of doors. The revision of what can be found in the Yale manuscript of the first sixty-three lines of Part III establishes Iseult as one of Arnold's rare female wanderers: "The young surviving Iseult, one bright day, / Had wandered forth. Her children were at play" (III. 5–6). Now it has been noted that when Arnold's women explicitly "wander," as in the case of Marguerite or Philomela, they do so within the negative context of illicit sexual passion, unsettled lives, and alienation. If Tristram's wife were merely on an aimless walk now, Arnold would probably have chosen another word to describe her sojourn. That Iseult "wandered" forth now suggests her uneasy state of mind and Arnold's commentary on a potentially dangerous mood. It is at this point that she calls her children to her to narrate "an old-world Breton history" (III. 37).

There are two noteworthy aspects to the telling itself. First, the story elicits from the children a reaction that is vague enough to create some ambiguity as to what Arnold intended:

> From Iseult's lips the unbroken story flow'd,
> And still the children listen'd, their blue eyes
> Fix'd on their mother's face in wide surprise
>
> .   .   .   .
>
> And they would still have listen'd, till dark night
> Came keen and chill down on the heather bright. (III. 45–47, 50–57)

What is it that has so surprised the children? Merely the story of Merlin and Vivian? Unlikely, for children are with ease able to suspend their disbelief in a world of fairy tales. Their "wide surprise" may more likely be attributed to their having caught something of their mother's uncharacteristic mood; they may be reacting, that is, more to the teller than to the tale.

Significantly, the story itself is told in motion, Iseult wandering with her children, although on safely warm, dry roads. But reality eventually beckons:

> when the red glow on the sea grew cold,
> And the grey turrets of the castle old
> Look'd sternly through the frosty evening-air
> Then Iseult took by the hand those children fair,
> And brought her tale to an end, and found the path,
> And led them home over the darkening heath. (III. 58–63)

The end of the yet untold (for the reader) tale coincides with the journey homewards, with Iseult's abandonment of her wanderer role and her assumption once more of her role as mother providing the safety of a home that "look'd sternly" at her to remind her of her responsibilities.

Once home, mother and child-woman again merge to become one; no longer free to wander, Iseult

> moves slow; her voice alone
> Hath yet an *infantine* and silver tone,
> But even that comes languidly; in truth,
> She seems one *dying in a mask of youth*
> And now she will go home, and softly lay
> Her laughing children in their beds, and play
> Awhile with them before they sleep. (III. 72–78, italics added)

But there is a crucial difference between the once-child and the still child-woman. She is no longer really innocent; it is clear that she has crossed the line into the realm of experience, her voice alone retaining its "infantine and silver tone." Marriage to Tristram, suffering his passion for another, her *experience* with sexuality and motherhood have to have awakened in her some of those buried impulses that made her maidenhood trapped and languid. And thus it is not really true, as the poem says, that the stories she tells her children mean for her now what they may have meant when, a child, she learned them. Her innocence is indeed but a "mask of youth," a lie perpetrated to keep her imprisoned in her status as child-woman:

> the tales
> With which this day the children she beguiled
> She gleaned from Breton grandames, when a child,
> In every hut along this sea–coast wild.
> She herself loves them still, and, when they are told,
> Can forget all to hear them as of old. (III. 106–111)

As of old? Only so if one can attribute special meaning to the "Breton grandames." Such figures play a significantly ambiguous role in the literature Arnold would have known. For example, the influence on *Tristram* of Keats's "The Eve of St. Agnes" has been noted by some critics, although restricted to the pictorial imagery in the poem, especially the description of the tapestry in Part II. In Keats's poem, Angela, intended to protect Madeline's purity, actually cooperates in the young virgin's seduction by Porphyro. Angela is modeled on the nurse in *Romeo and Juliet,* who similarly cooperates with Romeo and his designs on Juliet. Shakespeare's nurse, in turn, is thought by some to be modeled on Chaucer's Wife of Bath, a woman of unrestrained sexual impulses, whose main target for abuse is a treatise extolling virginity. Angela, Juliet's nurse, and the Wife of Bath all have stood on end the role each would have been expected to play as the experienced guardians of young women's chastity, just as the fallen woman would be seen as the resultant counterpart of unguarded innocence, seduced unawares.

Therefore it is possible that Iseult of Brittany, hearing the story of Merlin and Vivian from Breton grandames, might have been made aware all along of the sexual implications of the tale. If so, then her education has not been entirely pure, and her fantasy life may have been fed from the outset by the legends of her country, legends whose meaning she has recognized from the start.

The tale of Merlin and Vivian itself forms a striking contrast with the description of Iseult of Brittany in Part I of *Tristram.* Whereas Iseult stares listlessly out of barred windows while the men of her court are at war, Vivian travels with Merlin, the two of them wanderers together. He is on foot and she is on horseback, but lest it be thought that the difference suggests her helplessness, to which he is chivalrously deferring, a special point is made of how, after he suggests a resting place, she "Nodded, and tied her palfrey to a tree" (III. 212). Her control of her own horse, her independence in action, prepare the way for her final imprisonment of him. Vivian, of course, has won her dominance over Merlin through typically feminine beauty and wiles, and that "he grew fond, and eager to obey / His mistress, use her empire as she may" (III. 183–184), does not imply more than that the battle of the sexes involves inequality from the outset. Cominos points out that "in the Victorian battle of the sexes, women were disarmed of the weapon of their sexuality" (p. 163). Not so Vivian, and her passive assent to Merlin at this point in the poem seems but a pose intended to disarm him.

The next section of the passage is properly demure, less suggestive, for example, than the corresponding section of "La Belle Dame sans Merci," where, to the extent that Keats could make it clear, the sleep of his knight follows upon sexual satisfaction. Merlin's deep sleep is not so explicitly described, although a reference is made to Vivian's "sleeping lover" (III. 218). What thereupon ensues is an incantatory description of Vivian's spell, in lines evocative of the magic conclusion to "Kubla Khan":

> Nine times she waves the fluttering wimple round,
> And made a little plot of magic ground.
> And in that daisied circle, as men say,
> Is Merlin prisoner till the judgment-day. (III. 219–222)

The final lines in this episode are also the climactic lines of the entire poem: "But she herself whither she will can rove—/ For she was passing weary of his love" (III. 223–224).

And this is the story Iseult of Brittany told her children, as she wandered with them from their home, which finally beckoned her with stern reminders of duty and responsibility. It is a story in which the contrasts to her own life are clear. She is bound in her role as Penelope. She was so bound in her youth, yearning after the adventuring heroes she knew; she was so bound in her marriage, waiting on her homebound shore for Tristram's sails to appear; and she is so bound now in an existence where every day will be "To-day's exact repeated effigy" (III. 95). Is it any wonder that she is drawn by a tale of one who "whither she will can rove"? Moreover, she has been the passive partner in her love relationship, suffering a martyr's role, expected even to tolerate her husband's love for another. Vivian, in contrast, chooses her lovers as she will, discarding them as she pleases, for it is she who dominates in her affairs with men. She is also sexually free, her travels with her lover an expression of desires she has no need to repress, her role as a temptress one in which she has no need or inclination to deny her sexuality. As Cominos writes, women in Victorian England "were either sexless ministering angels or sensuously oversexed temptresses of the devil" (p. 167). In Iseult's fantasy, the imprisonment of Merlin by such a temptress is no less than the revenge exacted by the ministering angel whose enforced asexuality was, again, symbolically represented by her own prison, the barred windows by which she was constrained.

It has already been suggested that Arnold may have projected upon Iseult of Brittany Victorian man's forbidden desire for synthesis, his wish that his wife share the attributes of his mistress (real or imagined), an idea vehemently denied in such popular works as Acton's. This psychological mechanism has been made part of the theory involved in a recent anthropological study of "Gypsy Women: Models in Conflict"—a study that bears comparison to *Tristram and Iseult* because the Carmen-Micaela dichotomy that arises from myths of the gypsy woman as temptress corresponds to the motif of the two Iseults. Bizet's librettist and Arnold were working out the same pattern. But the reality, notes Judith Okely, is that gypsy women are in fact bound by sexual codes more stringent than women outside their group, and she argues that each woman projects upon the other characteristics her own culture insists be repressed. Okely's depiction of this interrelationship between gypsy and female outsider corresponds to the interrelationship between the fairies of Brittany who long for the motherhood denied them, while mothers constrained by domestic duties long for the life of the footloose Vivian. In addition, Okely extends this mutual projection to relations between the sexes, and what she has to say may illuminate the division that took place in Arnold's poem and in his age as women were divided into the mutually incompatible temptress and angel: "Just as men may be dissatisfied by the ideal woman and ideal role they have created for themselves, so may women be troubled by alternative images and tendencies within themselves. Both men and women protect themselves by giving these tendencies, oversimplified, to an alien people."[17]

The battle of the sexes, as Cominos has described its manifestation in Victorian culture, does divide men and women, husband and wife, into alien camps. Yet, Arnold's depiction of the fantasy life of Brittany's Iseult is too astute and too sympathetic to be only a projection on to her of his own forbidden impulses. It is, however, difficult to speculate about what might account for this unusual insight into the female psyche. Arnold was extremely circumspect about his personal life, and if *Tristram and Iseult* does reveal some of his conflicts about married life, he would have endeavored to bury the clues as well as the feelings. In addition, Arnold did not write on the question of woman's role in society. Thus one can only be tentative about the source of the poet's insight into woman's repressed fantasies.

A. Dwight Culler has provided a source of help in his study of "Monodrama and the Dramatic Monologue," for although Arnold's poem does not fit perfectly the genres Culler is studying, *Tristram* can nevertheless be viewed in the same context. As Culler writes,

> One may say that there arose in the decades immediately before and after the turn of the century several related art forms that focused on a solitary figure, most frequently a woman, who expressed through speech, music, costume, and gesture the shifting movements of her soul. That the figure was solitary and that virtually the entire text

consisted of her utterance was evidence of an attempt to focus on her subjectivity; that she was feminine was a further indication that the drama was one of passion.[18]

Two points about the classical tradition behind many of these monodramas are significant here. First, figures from ancient literature who served as models for such treatments of feminine passion were often deserted or betrayed women—Œnone and Dido, for example. Second, Culler has noted the part that the prosopopoeia played in the education of students during this period. As part of their training in rhetoric, they wrote speeches in which they took the part of persons not themselves (and, presumably, frequently quite alien to themselves) whose feelings they were nevertheless encouraged to depict and whose cause they were to plead. From these points alone one could partially account for Arnold's portrait of Iseult of Brittany and for his attempts to reconstruct sympathetically her emotions as a betrayed wife. In addition, "passion" was Arnold's theme in *Tristram* much as it was the theme of the monodrama:

> And yet, I swear, it angers me to see
> How this fool passion gulls men potently;
> Being, in truth, but a diseased unrest,
> And an unnatural overheat at best. (III. 133–136)

This passage is, however, puzzling. What, specifically, is the source of the passion from which Arnold's narrator is recoiling? Has it to do with the illicit love of Tristram, which is about to be recounted through Merlin and his enthrallment by Vivian? Or, perhaps, is the passion Iseult's, a temporary welling up of strong feelings which, were they to find no utterance, would result in her failure to achieve the quietism Arnold seems to have advocated?

For there is one other possibility that can be explored to show that Arnold might have recognized (as the result of personal experience or imaginative projection) and even sympathized with the repressed desires of women to live existences quite different from the ones allowed them, but that this recognition and sympathy do not necessarily imply approval. One of the functions of storytelling is to supply the medium through which emotions otherwise forbidden can find outlet. This compensatory feature of the narrative has in recent years drawn the attention of folklorists who try to determine what role folktales play in the societies that retain them as part of their culture. One theory, propounded by anthropologist J.L. Fischer, is that it is in the best interests of a society to allow its people some outlet for the tensions built up in the conflict between personal desires and the "demands of other members of the society that the individual pursue his personal goals only in ways which will also contribute to, or at least not greatly harm, the welfare of the society."[19] There is evidence in *Tristram and Iseult* that Iseult's final story serves the function that many folklorists attribute to the folktale.

The articulation of her repressed fantasies by Iseult of Brittany through the story of Merlin and Vivian does not, in fact, come in the poem until the reader has some assurance that all is well with the teller and with her family. Nothing specific about Iseult's inner-life is at first known except that it is allowed to surface only after her children have been put to sleep each night. The reader nevertheless learns from the outset that Iseult has told them a story and that she "brought her tale to an end, and found the path, / And led them home over the darkening heath" (III. 63–64). Having been assured that some disequilibrium expressed earlier through Arnold's use of the wanderer image has been restored, the reader then learns the source of Iseult's tension through Arnold's poignant description of her bleak day-to-day existence. And then—only then—the story itself is told, with its final climactic protest. But Iseult's fantasy life has already been rendered harmless, for Arnold has established for the reader, as well as for himself, that the status quo has remained undisturbed. It is perhaps within the haven of this security that Arnold can retain enough sympathy for his heroine to allow himself to explore her buried life, creating as a result one of the most sympathetic, insightful portraits of female dependency and resultant fantasy to come to us from his age.

NOTES

1. G. Robert Stange, *Matthew Arnold: The Poet as Humanist* (Princeton Univ. Press, 1967), p. 254.

2. Howard W. Fulweiler, *Letters from the Darkling Plain: Language and the Grounds of Knowledge in the Poetry of Arnold and Hopkins* (Univ. of Missouri Press, 1972), p. 77.

3. C.B. Tinker and H.F. Lowry, *The Poetry of Matthew Arnold: A Commentary* (Oxford Univ. Press, 1940), p. 124.

4. *Ten Studies in the Poetry of Matthew Arnold* (Duke Univ. Press, 1985), p. 39.

5. Theodore de la Villemarqué, "Visite au Tombeau de Merlin," *Revue de Paris,* 41 (1837), 45–62.

6. (London, 1888), I, 207.

7. "Innocent Femina Sensualis in Unconscious Conflict," in *Suffer and Be Still: Women in the Victorian Age,* ed. Martha Vicinus (Indiana Univ. Press, 1972), p. 166.

8. (New York, 1966), p. 29.

9. "Innocent Femina," p. 168. Cominos' views have been disputed by Carl Degler in "What Ought to Be and What Was: Women's Sexuality in the Nineteenth Century," *The American Historical Review,* 79 (1974), 1477. For the purposes of this

essay, however, the controversy is not important; as I will try to show, Arnold's poem seems almost an illustration of Cominos' essay.

10. Patrick J. McCarthy, "Mrs. Matthew Arnold," *TSLL*, 12 (1971), 647.

11. Citations are to *The Poems of Matthew Arnold*, ed. C.B. Tinker and H.F. Lowry (Oxford Univ. Press, 1963).

12. Arnold could have known Keats's other version of line 1.

13. Lionel Trilling is only one of the critics who have pointed out, for instance, that Arnold was probably familiar with the popular tale of *Undine. Major British Writers*, ed. G. B. Harrison (New York, 1959), II, 597.

14. Helene E. Roberts, "Marriage, Redundancy or Sin: The Painter's View of Women in the First Twenty-Five Years of Victoria's Reign," *Suffer and Be Still*, p. 48.

15. To argue for the importance of the *Odyssey* in Arnold's poems is counter to prevailing scholarly opinion. Warren D. Anderson contrasts Arnold with Joyce, citing Arnold's Oxford lectures to prove that Arnold "ignored" this particular Homeric work. See *Matthew Arnold and the Classical Tradition* (Univ. of Michigan Press, 1965), pp. 89–90. Also see Ellen S. Gahtan, "'Nor help for pain': Matthew Arnold and Sophocles' *Philoctetes*," *VN*, No. 48 (Fall. 1975), pp. 21–26. The resemblance between the Philoctetes and Tristram stories is striking; in the former, Odysseus plays a major role and may have contributed to some of the motifs in *Tristram and Iseult*. Arnold was sensitive to any comparisons between himself and Tennyson, and for this reason he might have muted the obvious evidence for the influence on his own poetry of Odysseus' wanderings. For evidence of this sensitivity see the *Letters of Matthew Arnold 1848-1888*, ed. George W.E. Russell (New York, 1896) I. 375: "I am rather troubled to find that Tennyson is at work on a subject, the story of the Latin poet Lucretius, which I have been occupied with for some twenty years."

16. Subtle identifications between himself and Odysseus can be found in the letters. One of these can be seen in the famous letter to his sister in which he describes the "aimless and unsettled" nature of youth, which for him threatens a gulf across which he fears he may never again be able to have close personal contact with his family. He intends to fight these tendencies within himself that isolate him from those he loves, although to leave the freedom of youth "is a melancholy passage from which we emerge shorn of so many beams that we are almost tempted to quarrel with the law of nature which imposes it on us" (*Letters*, I, 17). The sea journey here is but a metaphor for his state of mind; in another letter he writes to his wife that he is on his way home from one of the journeys his work as school inspector has necessitated: "My face is now set steadily homewards," he writes his Penelope, "Chamouni, Geneva, Dijon, Paris, London, Fox How. Kiss my darling little boys for me" (*Letters*, I, 86). Years later, in another letter to his sister, he reveals that these business trips hardly satisfied his wanderer impulses: "Much as I could have desired to see Greece, too, and the East, I know that my time is not yet come" (*Letters*, 1, 230).

17. In *Perceiving Women* (London, 1975), p. 79.

18. *PMLA*, 90 (1975), 375.

19. "The Sociopsychological Analysis of Folktales," *Current Anthropology*, 4 (1963), 259.

In Defense of Guenevere

Carole Silver

In chapter two of The Romance of William Morris *the author discusses Morris's* The Defence of Guenevere and Other Poems, *which she describes as "brief, intense, concentrated distillations of experience. . . . They are— or can be made to appear—complex, ambiguous, paradoxical, and ironic" [13]. Morris's volume is traditionally divided into three parts: the Malory poems (which are derived from* Le Morte D'Arthur*), the Froissart poems (drawn from Froissart's* Chronicles*), and the "fantasies" or "dreamlight" poems, which stem from folklore and legend [17]. [Ed.]*

The vast creative and destructive power of earthly love is the subject of the Malory poems. Morris's preoccupation with rejected lovers and fatal women mingled with his excited discovery of Southey's edition of *Le Morte D'Arthur* to create two of the most powerful poems of the division, "The Defence of Guenevere" and "King Arthur's Tomb." Counterpoised against these, he wrote two additional poems, again based on Malory, which examine the tensions between earthly and heavenly love, "Sir Galahad: A Christmas Mystery," and "The Chapel in Lyoness." Additionally, he began but did not complete a number of Arthurian works, "The Maying of Queen Guenevere," "Saint Agnes [sic] Convent," and "Sir Palomydes' Quest."[1]

The influence of *Le Morte D'Arthur* pervades them all. Morris is fond of developing hints and implications from his source into major incidents or motifs in his own poems. He attempts to create original works that elaborate upon yet are true to what he envisions as the essence of the source with which he is dealing. Thus, the Malory poems are poems of brilliant, flashing

---

Originally published as part 2, chapter 2, of *The Romance of William Morris* (Athens, Ohio: Ohio University Press, 1982), pp. 17–32. Reprinted with permission of The Ohio University Press/Swallow Press.

color, the colors of chivalry and heraldry; their settings—bowers, tourney fields, and chapels—are drawn from Malory's realm of magic and romance. Even the structure of the poems, complex, elaborate, contrapuntal, attempts to capture the richness of Malory's interwoven tales; their utterance imitates what Morris thought was the quality of Le Morte D'Arthur's stylized prose. Investigating the effects of love on character, Morris examines the motivations of Malory's figures, analyzing emotions at which Malory only hints. Concerning himself, before Tennyson, with the mixture of love and sin that marked the final days of Arthur's court, Morris dramatizes the tragedy and examines the reasons for it.[2] "The Maying of Queen Guenevere," a fragment seemingly intended as the first poem in a cycle, presents a brief picture of the frustration of Meliagraunce in loving Guenevere who "laughs aloud" (1:xix) at his passion for her. Thus, it introduces the Meliagraunce incident in "The Defence." "Sir Palomyde's Quest" seems intended as a treatment of the plight of Iseult and Palomydes, both paralleling and contrasting with the relationship between Guenevere and Launcelot. In Palomydes, Morris had found an image of the worthy but unloved lover of a fatal woman;[3] in Guenevere he now found both the pre-Raphaelite image of beauty and the romantic concept of the fatal woman, loved and desired by all—but doomed to destroy herself and those who adore her. Meredith Raymond suggests that the four Arthurian poems form two pairs of diptychs[4] and that Guenevere is the central figure in the first group. Her portraits in "The Defence" and "King Arthur's Tomb" illuminate each other. By understanding the queen's complex nature as revealed in the first poem, the reader can more fully comprehend her actions in the second.

"The Defence" and "King Arthur's Tomb" are integrally related to each other, though each can stand on its own. They are also closely related to Malory, for Morris both alludes to his source and weaves an elaborate counterpoint around it.[5] As Laurence Perrine indicates: "Morris has . . . taken one of Malory's characters in a moment of stress and brought her intensely alive."[6] He has based his poem on Malory's account of Guenevere's second trial for treason and adultery, a crisis arising from her harboring of Launcelot in her chamber. In the course of her defense, Guenevere mentions her first trial, the result of Meliagraunce's accusation that she has lain with one of the ten wounded knights captured during her kidnapping. In both cases, with Malory's story in mind, the reader realizes that although the queen is unquestionably guilty of adultery, the specific charges against her are false. Gauwaine's accusation—that Launcelot and Guenevere had been making love in her chamber when they were trapped there by Agravaine and his companions—is probably incorrect.[7] Malory first has Launcelot announce his intention of going to speak with the queen and then refuses to discuss the next occurrence:

> And then, as the French book saith, the queen and
> Launcelot were together. And whether they were abed or
> at other manner of disports, me list not hereof make no
> mention, for love that time was not as is nowadays.[8]

Malory is not being coy, for on an earlier occasion he tells us plainly that "Sir Launcelot went unto bed with the queen . . . [and] took his pleasance and his liking until it was in the dawning of the day."[9] He simply does not *know* what happened on this specific occasion, and he suggests, moreover, that sexual intimacy need not have occurred:

> But the old love was not so; men and women could love
> together seven years, and no lycours lusts were between
> them, and then was love, truth, and faithfulness: and lo,
> in likewise was used love in King Arthur's days.[10]

Morris probably read Malory as suggesting the queen's innocence in this instance and built from it one of the fine ironies of the poem. Morris follows Malory in indicating that the second accusation against Guenevere is equally untrue. She is "innocent," for it is Launcelot, rather than one of the wounded knights kidnapped with her, who has entered through the barred window of her chamber and enjoyed her favors. Thus, Launcelot can truthfully, if ironically, swear with certainty "that this night there lay none of these ten wounded knights with my lady,"[11] and she can do the same. Meliagraunce is "shent" (1:8) for selecting the wrong man.

Moreover, Guenevere hews down Gauwaine's proof of her guilt in this incident—the presence of blood stains on her bed—more conclusively than just by suggesting that a queen does need to offer proof of innocence.[12] The blood is Launcelot's, but Guenevere provides a suggestion of its origin calculated to arouse sympathy for her. She will not say she has been forced, she tells us: not in this way will she defend "The honour of the lady Guenevere" (1:7) even on judgment day. But this is just what she implies; she suggests what she wishes her audience to believe—that Meliagraunce, "Stripper of ladies" (1:7), has attempted an assault on her virtue—but that she is too much a queen to discuss it.

Yet, far more important than her specific objections to Gauwaine's charges are Guenevere's revelations of her true inward nature.[13] The moral ambiguities within the poem are quite deliberate; they stem from Guenevere's character, not Morris's uncertainty about it. The queen does not know whether she is morally guilty; she is uncertain of the rightness of her position, certain only of the strength of the love that has placed her in it. She can defend her love, indeed, she will not deny its worth or power, but she cannot always defend the adultery that it has caused; thus she attempts at times to deny the latter and always to minimize its importance. She hints at her actions, half confessing through double-meaning statements, slipping, through the imagery she uses, into temporarily admitting adultery, then withdrawing into a stance of innocence and ostensibly retracting the statements she has made. Denying, finding excuses, equivocating, she always stops short of full confession. The keynote of the poem—and of Guenevere's character— is the poem's first word, "But" (1:1). With it, we are thrown into the whole moral structure of Guenevere's nature.

The quality of Guenevere's argument is revealed at the very beginning of the poem. The meaning of her first statement to the judges who have decided to burn her at the stake is certainly double:

> God wot I ought to say, I have done ill,
> And pray you all forgiveness heartily!
> Because you must be right, such great lords— (1:1)

On one level she is sarcastically flattering her audience, saying that the lords in their wisdom and rank are not to be contradicted; but she may also mean that she *has* sinned and *should* ask forgiveness. That she does mean the latter, as well as the former, is shown by her next argument. When she asks the lords to identify with her in the matter of the "choosing cloths" (1:2) she is asking them to understand her moral dilemma and the reason for her wrong choice. The lords are to suppose they were about to die, "quite alone and very weak" (1:1), and were then to choose between heaven and hell without knowing which was which—just as she has had to do. In describing the instruments of choice, she subtly slants the argument. One of the two cloths is described as "blue,/ Wavy and long, and one cut short and red" (1:2). "No man could tell the better of the two" (1:2), says Guenevere, but this is untrue. All—especially those acquainted with Morris's color symbolism—would do as she had done and choose "heaven's colour, the blue" (1:2); all would be shocked to discover that blue, with its connotations of spirituality, means hell.[14] Guenevere is ostensibly pleading that the wrong choice in her life was made unwittingly, but she is also suggesting that the choice was logical and the one all would have made. Her argumentative skill a most makes the reader forget that she *is* confessing; in saying that she had chosen hell, she means not only unhappy love, but adultery, a path of action that will lead to hell. She seeks to excuse her sin by suggesting its universality, and she blames it upon the moral confusion in the universe: things are not what they seem. But she still must admit that, whatever the cause, she has done wrong.

The refrain which follows the incident appears at first to be Guenevere's repudiation of what she had just admitted:

> Nevertheless you, O Sir Gauwaine, lie,
> Whatever may have happened through these years,
> God knows I speak truth, saying that you lie. (1:2)

But it may be interpreted in another way as well. The queen, answering the letter rather than the spirit of Gauwaine's charge, may well mean that she has been innocent in the particular incident of which she is accused, though guilty on other occasions.[15] When the refrain next occurs, after her confession of her love for Launcelot, its second line is slightly altered. "Whatever may have happened" (1:2) becomes "Whatever happened on through all those years" (1:5). The statement is no longer conditional; Guenevere is openly confessing her love, perhaps even her adultery, though again protesting her innocence on the particular occasion cited. Uttering the refrain one last time, she moves back to the conditional tense ("Whatever may have happen'd") but stresses the length of time she and Launcelot have loved and suffered—"these long years" (1:10). Her stressing of the long years brings to mind Malory's defense of her affair—its delayed and inevitable consummation. But it brings to mind, as well, the many years of the lovers' dalliance. Ambiguity is reintroduced every time Guenevere utters the refrain.

The queen reveals herself even more directly when her speech works against its intentions, when she slips into saying too much. She says more than she intends when she pleads for kindness from Gauwaine, asking him to "Remember in what grave your mother sleeps" (1:6)—ostensibly not to condemn her to his mother's ignominious death. Her conscious point is that punishing adultery brings nothing but shame and fear to the avengers of it; she implies that Gauwaine is already haunted for his deed. But, in so doing, she slips into identifying herself with Gauwaine's unfortunate but guilty mother, Margawse. Again, in discussing her interview with Launcelot in her chamber, in describing them as "children once again, free from all wrongs/ Just for one night" (1:9), she suggests other nights less free from wrong.

But Guenevere's most important revelations are made through the images in which she describes herself and her love. Suggesting that her beauty is a "gracious proof" (1:9) of her innocence, she equates her external loveliness with her inner spiritual perfection in the time-honored medieval tradition. But the images in which she describes herself are the sensual ones of "Body's Beauty" rather than "Soul's Beauty." We are shown the "passionate twisting of her body" (1:2), and she demands that her male judges notice the rising of her breast, "Like waves of purple sea" (1:8), the movement and brightness of her hair, the grace of her long throat and rounded arms, and the shadows lying in her hand "like wine within a cup" (1:8). The long red-gold hair and pillar-like neck suggest Elizabeth Siddal, Rossetti's model and mistress, but, more significantly, they suggest the opulent sensuousness of Guenevere's own nature.[16]

The terms in which she describes the growth of her love for Launcelot are both descriptions of madness and images of a fall. On her first meeting with him, she has been "half mad with beauty" (1:4). Overwhelmed with joy at the fertility of the spring, she has exchanged kisses with him. The birth of nature has been paralleled by the birth of passion. Love has overpowered her, making her lips, "curl up at false and true," her soul seem "cold and shallow without any cloud." She informs her judges that, in internal chaos, she has moved beyond the accepted rules for human conduct. Her marriage vow has become only "a little word, / Scarce ever meant at all" (1:3), for she has forgotten the significance of marriage. She admits that with moral sense, public opinion, and religious and legal sanctions unimportant to her, her only stay has been love; there is nothing to keep her from adultery.

Loving Launcelot is described as the process of "slipping"

> . . . slowly down some path worn smooth and even,
> Down to a cool sea on a summer day;
> Yet still in slipping there was some small leaven
>
> Of stretched hands catching small stones by the way,
> Until one surely reached the sea at last,
> And felt strange new joy as the worn head lay
>
> Back, with the hair like sea-weed; yea all past
> Sweat of the forehead, dryness of the lips,
> Washed utterly out by the dear waves o'ercast. (1:4)

Sliding down a path "worn smooth and even" perhaps because so many have taken it, she has been initially ambivalent about her fall. She has stretched out her hands to catch "small stones" with which to temper it, but she has yearned to immerse herself in the sea. The sea, when reached, has substituted "strange new joy" for fear, frustration, and anticipation. It is a joy in love—a distinctly sexual passion suggesting the release of spent desire.

Ironically, her self-vindication backfires; in pleading "temporary insanity," in dwelling upon the mitigating circumstances, she convinces the reader that she has done what she will not quite openly admit. One of the strengths of the poem is that her central argument—moral confusion—is what convinces the reader that she is an adulteress. The reader is to appreciate her consummate rhetoric, her methods of handling her judges—she seduces, cajoles, and threatens them—and the variety of pleas by which she seeks to win sympathy and time, but he is not to ignore her duplicity. For example, what she says she will say and what she does say are quite different. She states that she will not review the past, but her purpose is to do just that, slanting events to win her audience's sympathy and their belief in the omnipotence of love. She says that she has told her judges everything:

> all, all, verily,
> But just that which would save me; these things flit. (1:10)

She has not done so, for she breaks off her argument just at the point at which she would have to incriminate herself, telling of Launcelot's plans for their flight and life together. She cannot do so without revealing that she knows that Launcelot will come to rescue her. She can say with some accuracy, "All I have said is truth, by Christ's dear tears" (1:10), for she has omitted important evidence and made statements whose double meanings have allowed her confession to go unheard. Skillfully, she gives her auditors, and many readers, the impression that she could prove her total innocence if she chose, that she has left the strongest part of her case unstated.

Guenevere's defense is not, of course, to be fully believed. In this sense, the poem's title is ironic. Guenevere intends a speech of self-vindication, but her words and actions persuade the reader of her adultery. The final turn of the poem, however, reinforces its ultimate ambiguity. The reader is forced to recognize that the adultery is less meaningful than the love itself. One believes in her love for Launcelot, in the overwhelming power of the passion that has undone her. The most persuasive part of her argument is her defense of the necessity of erotic passion:

Must I give up for ever then, I thought,

That which I deemed would ever round me move
Glorifying all things; for a little word,
Scarce ever meant at all, must now I prove

Stone-cold for ever? (1:3)

Love, the force that moves the world and the impetus behind all being, is the difference between life and death in life. "Bought/ By Arthur's great name and his little love" (1:3), Guenevere has been forced to seek love outside her marriage of convenience and with a man other than her kingly, chilly husband. Thus, she must be partially pardoned and fully sympathized with. She has indeed suffered, and she realizes that passion has undone her, driving her—except for a few sea-moments—to pain and near madness. She does not yet recognize, in her cruelty to her opponents, her glee at the death of Meliagraunce, and her threats to destroy her enemies and the kingdom, the signs of her moral and emotional deterioration. All that she knows as yet is that passion is her *raison d'être* and that, to preserve it, she will stop at nothing. The rest of the lesson will come in "King Arthur's Tomb."

On the other hand, what the reader is to recognize in "The Defence of Guenevere" is the power of an ambiguous figure who is beyond morality, who represents the poet's mixed anima, creative and destructive, deadly and life-giving both. Morris's genius is in his refusal to render a smug verdict upon her. His testimony, as well as hers, is to the formidable power of erotic passion which can dissolve all other values in it.

Morris's profound psychological grasp of illicit romantic passion is displayed once again in "King Arthur's Tomb." The poem is both a sequel to the "Defence" and a further analysis of the love that leads to death, this time as it affects both Launcelot and Guenevere. The poem's source is Malory's account of the last meeting of the lovers, though, as David Staines indicates, Morris has telescoped several incidents in the final pages of Malory.[17] But his inspiration is visual as well as literary, for the poem's imagery comments on Rossetti's watercolor, *Arthur's Tomb*, which Morris had purchased. The painting shows a tormented Launcelot leaning over a tomb with the figure of Arthur carved on it; Launcelot's lips are seeking those of the queen who kneels, resisting, in the foreground. The lovers are confined and trapped by the apple trees surrounding them and separated by the cold marble of the tomb. In the grass of the foreground is a coiled snake—a mirror image in Morris's poem—which untwists itself near Guenevere's form.[18]

Both Rossetti's painting and Morris's poem, thus, seem to illustrate Malory's terse lines: "Wherefore, madam, I pray you kiss me and never no more." "'Nay,' said the queen, 'that shall I never do.'"[19] But Rossetti's single scene becomes a triptych in Morris's poem. Two separate panels frame the central tableau. The first is devoted to Launcelot's trip to Glastonbury and to his shining memories of the "old garden life" (1:11) which he shared with Guenevere; the second to the queen's mingled memories of her past love and the pain it has brought, thoughts which have haunted her on the night before she and Launcelot meet at Glastonbury. Thus, the poem contrasts the past of each of the characters, utilizing brilliant, heraldic color to suggest its vitality and beauty, with their present states, seen as the cold grays and blacks of bleak reality. For example, Launcelot's visual memory of the queen, shining in the morning light, clothed in green and holding scarlet lilies like Saint Margaret, forms an ironic contrast to her image when he meets her at Glastonbury in the poem's present:

> all her robes were black,
> With a long white veil only; she went slow,
> As one walks to be slain, her eyes did lack
> Half her old glory, yea, alas! the glow
>
> Had left her face and hands; (1:15)

The contrast between past and present is further sharpened by the poem's lack of logical transitions.[20] The utterance is an attempt to capture the time-sense and impact of dream, specifically of nightmare. Scenes and memories shift in dream logic; time is either blurred or frozen into everlasting moments. For the severing of the lovers is seen as a nightmare to both, and it will be over only when they die.

In "King Arthur's Tomb," Morris fully develops the *Liebestod* theme that he had sketched in the early prose tales. The love that leads to death and partakes of it is emphasized by the many images of entwinement that run through the poem.[21] The lovers' beings are entwined and their entanglement is destroying them, but their separation means their deaths. When separated from Guenevere, Launcelot is dead-alive. Yet, when they meet and she rejects him, he asks her to slay him instead. As he arises from his swoon, bloodied on the hands and head, he has been symbolically crucified. When Guenevere renounces her lover, all she desires is death: her wish is granted, for the poem ends with the tolling of her bell of passage. For the lovers enmeshed in their tragic passion, the only resting place is the tomb.

Guenevere comes to self-knowledge before her end. When, in the central scene, she comes forth to meet Launcelot at the tomb he does not know is Arthur's, she knows that "a blight/ Had settled on her" (1:14–15). The blight is spiritual as well as physical, for she comes persuaded of her sin and sickness, determined to renounce Launcelot forever—destroyed by the love that had once made her bloom.

Unlike Malory's character who confesses her sin with calm dignity, Morris's Guenevere must go through an intricate process of self-vindication leading finally to self-recognition. She begins by offering a defense of her actions, this time with God and Launcelot as her audience. Though she insists, "I am not mad, but I am sick; they cling, / God's curses, unto such as I am" (1:17), she realizes only gradually that she has become what she had predicted she would become in the "Defence," if she were guilty of adultery:

> A great queen such as I
> Having sinn'd this way, straight her conscience sears;
> And afterwards she liveth hatefully,
> Slaying and poisoning, certes never weeps,— (1:5)

At Glastonbury, she has been unable to weep, and her beauty, the "gracious proof" of her innocence, has faded. The agony of guilt has consumed her and made her cruel. She has become what her attendants call her, a "tigress fair" with "claws" (1:20).

Moreover, while Launcelot's thoughts have been of love and freedom, hers have been meditations on damnation. Fearing a hell which would be a continuation of the worst moments of her earthly life, an eternity of being called a harlot by a churl, she has come to ask God's pardon. The God she prays to is no disembodied spirit to her; she loves His beauty, yearns to kiss His feet, and coaxes Him as if He were her lover. She reminds Him, as she has reminded her judges in "The Defence," of how beautiful she is. And she sees Him as an object of erotic passion: "I cannot choose/ But love you, Christ, yea, though I cannot keep/ From loving Launcelot" (1:16). Indeed she sees the two as rival lovers and she wishes to be allowed to keep both. Unable to resolve her conflict, she strikes out at Launcelot, and, through him at herself. Entwined as they are, in scourging him she beats herself, and in humiliating him she shames herself.

Her justification is that God has given her the grace, in renouncing Launcelot, to save his soul. Guenevere may, indeed, have to purge Launcelot spirit and her own by fire, but the smell is not of redemption but of burn ing flesh, as Morris dwells on the agony of the renunciation. Guenevere's opening words to Launcelot, when they meet at Arthur's tomb, establish the tone of her attack. "Well done!" she says sarcastically to her lover, who kneels in exhaustion near the monument; it is right to pray "For Arthur, my dear lord, the greatest king/ That ever lived" (1:16). Attempting to wound Launcelot by her sudden preference for her husband, she refuses her lover a single, final kiss of parting. Instead, with God's name on her lips, she ironically offers him a more sexual greeting:

> Across my husband's head, fair Launcelot!
>> Fair serpent mark'd with V upon the head!
> This thing we did while yet he was alive,
>> Why not, O twisting knight, now he is dead? (1:17)

Her confession of past adultery and sneering suggestion that they make love on the tomb are not unexpected, but her description of Launcelot as a twisting serpent is initially surprising. Her taunt is connected both with Rossetti's painting and with Launcelot's coat of arms, which in a cancelled portion of "The Defence" is described as "the great snake of green/ That twisted on the quartered white and red" (1:xx). Guenevere finds her lover's heraldic emblem symbolic of his behavior. She sees him as the serpent in the garden, the tempter of herself as Eve, and the cause of her fall.[22]

She initially refuses to accept the responsibility for loving Launcelot, though she cannot disavow the passion itself. She argues that the affair has been Arthur's fault and Launcelot's, not hers. Arthur has been cold to her, merely kissing her "in his kingly way" (1:18) and thrusting her at his friend as he tells her to cherish the knight who is his "banner, sword and shield" (1:18). Launcelot, she indicates, has been all too eager to accept her. Attacking him, she insists that she has been the one to suffer and that he has forced her into a life of lies, ruined her in her role as queen, and dishonored her person and reputation. Projecting her own guilty view of herself onto him, she accuses him of emotional disloyalty, of thinking her changeable in love and mood, "uncertain as the spring" (1:19).

As the poem continues, and Guenevere's self-awareness increases, she admits the validity of her last charge, ascribing it, correctly, to her own sense of self and to the perceptions of her attendants. Her plea for their forgiveness: "Forgive me! for my sin being such . . . / Made me quite wicked" (1:20) marks the beginning of her understanding of her condition. While Launcelot has envisioned her as the pure Saint Margaret, she sees herself as the woman of Samaria and as Mary Magdalen. When she imagines

> . . . Mary Magdalen repenting there,
> Her dimmed eyes scorch'd and red at sight of hell
> So hardly 'scaped, no gold light on her hair (1:20)

the image is of herself. She cannot see the glory of repentance, only its pain, for the agony is all that she has experienced. The last step in self-realization occurs when, remembering a joust in the "old garden days," she hears the names called out by the opposing knights—"Iseult" and "Guenevere" (1:22). "The ladies' names bite verily like steel" (1:22), she screams, for they remind her of Iseult's and her own adultery.

But as she moves from identifying herself with God to recognizing herself as a fallen Eve, a Magdalen, and a common harlot, she is driven almost insane by the realization. Thus, she bursts into a brutal, obsessively repetitive attack on her lover. Compulsively repeating Arthur's description of Launcelot as his "banner, sword and shield," she calls her lover a banner and shield besmirched by the *bend sinister* of bastardy and a "crooked sword" (1:22) that has scarred its bearer's arm. Reiterating her charges, she damns him as a Malay blade secretly "poison'd with sweet fruit" (1:22), as a reaper's sickle stained with the deadly hemlock it has cut, and, in both cases, Arthur's murderer. Branding Launcelot as a false protector of Arthur and herself—*traitor* to both—she will not even permit him to imagine peace through death. He "dare not pray to die," she screams, "Lest . . . [he] meet Arthur in the other world" (1:22).

When she sees Launcelot swoon and believes him dead, her own ordeal is over. Wishing for her own demise, she echoes Malory's queen in lamenting the absence of the kiss of parting she has refused to give her lover: "Never, never again! not even when I die" (1:23).[23]

Obsessed by guilt, revenging herself upon her lover and herself for her discovery that earthly love can destroy, repudiating that love, but still chained to it, Guenevere gains the only possible release from her pain. The bell that Launcelot hears as he returns to consciousness is the knell announcing her death.

Although erotic love is seen as blasting the bodies and souls of those enslaved by it in "King Arthur's Tomb," Morris does not find a comfortable solution in espousing celestial love as its alternative. Meredith Raymond is correct in stating that the second pair of Malory poems, "Sir Galahad: A Christmas Mystery" and "The Chapel in Lyoness," examine "spiritual love and heavenly grace," thus balancing the first pair.[24] But "Sir Galahad" and "The Chapel" emphasize the trials and frustrations of eros, and the rewards of heavenly love seem strangely weak.

Galahad, the virgin knight, replaces Guenevere as the central figure in the poems and both his character and his adventures are less closely linked to Malory than were Guenevere's. Morris's real interest is firmly rooted in this world, and his Galahad is a man of it, suffering the pains and doubts of earthly existence. Morris either creates his own Malory-like incidents or greatly amplifies brief statements from his source. For example, while Malory mentions that Galahad is benighted in a deserted hermitage, the episode in the hermitage which constitutes the "Christmas Mystery" is Morris's invention. Morris's concerns are psychological rather than supernatural; he traces the thoughts of the virgin knight during "the longest night in all the year" (1:24)—which is also the dark night of his soul. While the rebirth associated with Christmas does come to Galahad, the emphasis falls on his pain as much as on his promised redemption. Galahad thinks much upon his chastity, wondering "what thing comes of it" (1:24). He compares his plight to those of Palomydes and Launcelot and initially decides that it would be better to be Palomydes, who has the hope, even if vain, of ultimately winning Iseult's love, or Launcelot who, despite his sin, has "Guenevere's arms, round, / Warm and lithe, about his neck" (1:25). His most vivid memory is of an unknown knight taking leave of his lady before departing on the quest of the Sangreal. Their "last kisses" sink into Galahad's mind, provoking his intense loneliness and frustration. His most powerful grief arises at the thought that "no maid will talk/ Of sitting on my tomb" (1:25). Though comforted by Christ, who reassures him that God's love is best and that sexual love, vain and illicit in the lives of Palomydes and Launcelot, cannot offer the rewards of heaven, Galahad cannot fully and freely renounce earthly love. He will indeed refrain from the vain lusts of the flesh, but his quest for the Grail becomes, as Ralph Berry indicates, more a sexual sublimation of his desires than an alternative to them.[25] Most significantly, "Sir Galahad" ends on a note of defeat. Morris makes clear, long before Tennyson's bitter treatment of "The Holy Grail," that the pursuit of a purely spiritual goal can bring destruction. The reader learns that Sir Lionel and Sir Gauwaine have been shamed, Sir Lauvaine wounded, and that "poor merry Dinadan" lies "hack'd and dead" (1:30); "In vain they struggle for the vision fair" (1:30). Galahad's successful quest and triumph are never witnessed.

"The Chapel in Lyoness," while indicating Galahad's movement toward perfection, does not show that he has lost his frustrations or relinquished his sympathy for erotic love. Its central theme is the motif Morris had reiterated in the early tales: the hope for a fleshly reunion of lovers in a paradise devoted to them. Sir Galahad finds Ozana Le Cure Hardy lying wounded within a deserted chapel. Like the maimed king in the Percival romances, Ozana is suffering a wound of the soul, a result of a failure or inability to aid his mysterious lady,[26] and Galahad diagnoses the malady. Lamenting that "there comes no sleep nor any love" (1:33), Ozana yearns for death and a heavenly reunion with his lady. It is Galahad who frees him, bringing him a rose sprinkled with dew and the precious water of rebirth, symbols of purification and salvation. Only after Galahad has blessed him and given him the kiss of passage, can Ozana, pressing a lock of hair from the head of his beloved, find the peace of death. It is the virgin Galahad who sees the vision of Ozana's reunion with his lady. He sees Ozana's "wasted fingers twine"

> Within the tresses of her hair
>   That shineth gloriously,
> Thinly outspread in the clear air
>   Against the jasper sea. (1:34)

Galahad's question, uttered when the knight has died—"Ozana, shall I pray for thee?" (1:34)—requires a negative answer. Ozana, in a heavenly rapture that has little to do with God, needs no prayer, for he has been united with the woman who is his soul. It is Galahad, the lonely visionary, who needs the reader's prayers and evokes the reader's sympathies.

Thus, in the Malory poems, does Morris establish his concern with the deadly effects of desire and the desirable elements of death. Finding few rewards in either heaven or earth, he creates a group of tormented, frustrated, and memorable characters. Through the figure of Galahad, he adds to the portraits of rejected lovers the image of the hero doomed to isolation, but sympathizing with the pains of others. In the portrait of Guenevere, he not only creates a superb fatal woman, but depicts the ambiguous nature of the anima herself. In all the poems of the group, he reveals his considerable, if precocious, understanding of the conflicts within the human psyche.

NOTES

1. Two other poems may be included in the Malory group, though they are less central to it. "Near Avalon" utilizes Malory in its title and employs Guenevere as a symbol of love's fatality, and "A Good Knight in Prison" employs Launcelot as the figure who rescues the captive knight. See 1:xix for "The Maying of Queen Guenevere": see 24: 68–69 for "St. Agnes [sic] Convent," a fragment of the dramatic monologue of Iseult of Brittany, consisting of her reflections on her wretched present and the happier past she experienced in loving Tristram; and see 24: 70–71 for "Palomydes' Quest," a fragment, dealing with Palomydes' dreams of capturing the Questing Beast and winning fame and the love of Iseult of Cornwall. (All references—volume and page numbers in parentheses—are to *The Collected Works of William Morris*, ed. May Morris, 24 vols. [New York: Russell & Russell, 1966]. —Ed.)

2. Morris's volume appeared a year before the first series of Tennyson's *Idylls of the King* (1859). He knew the early Tennyson poems: "Morte D'Arthur," "Sir Galahad" (which he disliked), and the fragment "Sir Launcelot and Queen Guinevere." Only the last—with its images of spring and description of the passionate kiss of the lovers—seems to have influenced him, and the appearance of the *Idylls* may well have made him abandon his own plan for an Arthurian cycle.

3. See Chapter 1 [of *The Romance of William Morris* (Athens, Ohio: Ohio University Press, 1982)] and note 1 above. Morris's identification with Palomydes clearly intensified. The rejected knight was the subject of Morris's contribution to the Oxford Union frescoes: *How Sir Palomydes loved La Belle Iseult with exceeding great love out of measure, and how she loved not him but rather Sir Tristram*, and was mentioned in the canceled opening of "The Defence" (1:xx). Morris's painting of Jane Burden was seemingly first named *La Belle Iseult* (before its title was changed to *Guenevere*) and perhaps he again visualized himself as Palomydes. Indeed, his one physical description of the knight is of a man with "red heavy swinging hair" (1:21) like his own.

4. Meredith Raymond, "The Arthurian Group in *The Defence of Guenevere and Other Poems*," *Victorian Poetry* 4 (1966): 213.

5. The following discussion of "The Defence" appeared, in slightly different form, in my article "'The Defence of Guenevere': A Further Interpretation," *Studies in English Literature: 1500–1900* 9 (1969): 695–702.

6. Laurence Perrine, "Morris's Guenevere: An Interpretation," *Philological Quarterly* 39 (1960): 241. See also Mother Angela Carson, "Morris' Guenevere: A Further Note," *Philological Quarterly* 42 (1963): 131–34. For recent articles which concentrate on the poem see Raymond, "The Arthurian Group"; Robert L. Stallman, "The Lovers' Progress: An Investigation of William Morris' 'The Defence of Guenevere' and 'King Arthur's Tomb,'" *Studies in English Literature: 1500–1900* 15 (1975): 657–70; and Dennis R. Balch, "Guenevere's Fidelity to Arthur in 'The Defence of Guenevere' and 'King Arthur's Tomb,'" *Victorian Poetry* 13, nos. 3–4 (1975): 61–70.

7. Perrine, "Morris's Guenevere," p. 237. See also Carson, "A Further Note," pp. 132–34 for an explanation of Guenevere's probable innocence on the occasion of Launcelot's visit.

8. Sir Thomas Malory, *Le Morte D'Arthur*, intro. Sir John Rhys, 2 vols. (London: J.M. Dent, 1906), 2:324.

9. Ibid.

10. Ibid., 2:314–15.

11. Ibid., 2:326.

12. Perrine, "Morris's Guenevere," p. 239. In indicating that the queen's body cannot be defiled, Guenevere suggests her awareness of the doctrine of the king's two bodies. As queen royal, she is above judgment and incapable of evil; as queen natural, she is graceful and beautiful in proof of innocence.

13. Guenevere, like the other fatal women of the volume, is not intentionally evil. She is to be compared to Yoland in "The Tune of Seven Towers," and the nameless lady in "Concerning Geffray Teste Noire." Her role as an embodiment of love's fatality is made evident in the lyric "Near Avalon" (1: 40).

14. It is clear that the color blue is also associated with King Arthur. See Balch, "Guenevere's Fidelity," pp. 61–70, for a reading of the symbolism of the cloths which differs from mine.

15. The role of Gauwaine as the accuser in the poem is not, as Perrine thinks in "Morris's Guenevere," p. 235, a mistake. Morris casts Gauwaine in this role to create an important antagonist to Guenevere and to make the accuser someone who understands the ramifications of adultery and its punishment. Moreover, Morris compresses the events that follow the incident, for it is as a result of Launcelot's killing of Gauwaine's relatives during the rescue of Guenevere that Gauwaine becomes the enemy of the lovers.

16. Morris's description of Guenevere resembles Rossetti's studies and paint-

ings of Lizzie Siddal, which were executed during the early 1850s—especially the study for *Regina Cordium*, which shows Lizzie before her illnesses, and before Rossetti had fully spiritualized and desexualized his portraits of her. The implications of Morris's selection of her as a prototype for Guenevere are interesting: they suggest the strength of Morris's worship of Rossetti and the adoption of Rossetti's ideal standard of beauty and/or they suggest Morris's sexual attraction to Lizzie. Since she seems to have disliked Morris, his choice of her as an ideal may have reinforced his identification with Palomydes.

17. David Staines, "Morris' Treatment of His Medieval Sources in *The Defence of Guenevere and Other Poems*," *Studies in Philology* 70 (1973): 444. Morris changes the scene of the parting from Almsbury to Glastonbury, since the latter place is the site of Arthur's tomb—a monument which provides much of the poem's drama. He again compresses events described by Malory in order to make the death of Guenevere simultaneous with the severing of the lovers.

18. *Arthur's Tomb*, dated 1854 but actually completed in 1855, was initially purchased by John Ruskin. The faces of the lovers are those of Rossetti and Lizzie, and the painting depicts Launcelot leaning over the Queen, who appears to be resisting him. The symbolic use of the images of apple trees and of a snake suggests that Rossetti is treating the incident as an analogy to the Fall.

19. Malory, *Morte D'Arthur*, 2:395.

20. Despite his appreciation of the poem, Swinburne failed to recognize the relationship between the poem's intense passion and broken utterance, and found it in need of "combing and trimming." He felt that the work, though powerful, "had not been constructed at all; the parts hardly hold together; it has need of joists and screws, props and rafters" (Algernon Charles Swinburne, *Essays and Studies*. 4th ed. [London: Chatto and Windus, 1897] pp. 112–13).

21. See, for example, "This he knew also; that some fingers twine, / Not only in a man's hair, even his heart, / (Making him good or bad I mean,) but in his life" (1:11), and Guenevere's cry of anguish, "not / Ever again shall we twine arms and lips" (1:17).

22. Guenevere describes Launcelot's serpentine "long lips" (1:18) cleaving to her hand and imagines his body "curl'd, . . . in agony" (1:22). All her images of him are phallic, and he is equated with a viper and a sword.

23. Cf. Malory's account of Guenevere's final speech to Launcelot: "Through this man and me hath all this war been wrought, and the death of the most noblest knights of the world; for through our love that we have loved together is my most noble lord slain. . . . Therefore, Sir Launcelot, I require thee and beseech thee heartily, for all the love that ever was betwixt us, that thou never see me more in the visage" (*Morte D'Arthur*, 2:394).

24. Raymond, "Arthurian Group," pp. 214–15.

25. Berry [Ralph]. "Defense of Guenevere" [*Victorian Poetry* 9 (1971): p. 277–86], p. 279.

26. One possible explanation for Ozana's plight is that he is being punished for his failure to aid Guenevere. Malory mentions him as one of the ten knights who failed to save her from Meliagraunce's attack and could not, because of his wounds, defend her at her trial.

ANOTHER LOOK

Julia Margaret Cameron's Photographic Illustrations to Alfred Tennyson's *The Idylls of the King*

Joanne Lukitsh

In the fall of 1874 Alfred Tennyson asked the photographer Julia Margaret Cameron (1815–1879), his friend and neighbor on the Isle of Wight, to do photographic illustrations of his *Idylls of the King*. These photographs were to be reproduced as wood-engraved frontispieces to a new cabinet edition of Tennyson's *Works*. The eventual result of Tennyson's seemingly casual request of a friend was Cameron's only publication of her original photographs in book form: *Illustrations to Tennyson's* Idylls of the King *and Other Poems* (London: Henry S. King and Company, 1875, two volumes). Cameron's photographic illustrations of literature were related to the Victorian interest in *tableaux vivants* and fancy dress. The interplay of fantasy, role-playing, and social self-importance active in Victorian family theatricals figured in the production of the *Illustrations;* in her photographs of the *Idylls of the King* Cameron featured the experiences of the women characters of Camelot: the women exert power over the men, without challenging the order of Arthur's kingdom. This examination of the *Illustrations* gives an account of the production and content of the volumes and considers how a prominent woman artist applied Tennyson's interpretation of the Arthurian story—and its tremendous contemporary popularity—to her artistic program.

Alfred Tennyson's Freshwater neighbor was a photographer of wide renown, whose work had been exhibited in London, Paris, Berlin, and Vienna. Cameron began to work in photography at the age of 49, in 1864. Up to that time, Cameron's energies had been devoted to her family, her husband, Charles Hay Cameron, a distinguished jurist, and their six children. Julia Cameron was related by birth, marriage, and social connections to some of the most distinguished figures of the period. Tennyson and Henry

Reprinted by permission from *Arthurian Literature VII*, ed. Richard Barber (Woodbridge, Suffolk/Wolfeboro, NH: Boydell & Brewer, 1987), pp. 145–57. Figures are a partial selection from original article.

Taylor were her close friends and John Herschel was the godfather of one of her sons. Cameron socialized with William Holman Hunt, John Ruskin, Dante Gabriel Rossetti, and other prominent people at Little Holland House, her sister's salon outside of London. In 1864, Cameron decided to "ennoble" photography: her "out of focus" technique, expressive lighting, and elevated subject matter distinguished her images from commercial photography. She also wanted her photography to earn money for her sons' education. Cameron actively promoted her work, seeking recognition and sales; her photographs won the praise of her famous friends, many of whom posed for portraits and wrote favorable reviews in the press. (Cameron's portraits of Victorian men of mark are now regarded as some of the finest accomplishments of nineteenth-century photography.) In addition to portraiture, Cameron assembled family members, servants, and friends to pose for her camera in *tableaux vivants,* scenes from literature and history. Subjects of women were a major theme of Cameron's photographic illustrations, a theme she shared with contemporary women artists in other media. Cameron illustrated inspirational and heroic women characters, but her subjects, such as her numerous studies of the Madonna, generally glorify the conventional Victorian roles of woman as wife and mother.[1]

When Tennyson asked Cameron to do photographic illustrations of his *Idylls of the King,* he was making a request of an accomplished photographer with an established point of view. He was also, as Cameron herself explained, asking a favor. Cameron described the cabinet edition project and her decision to publish the *Illustrations* in a series of letters written to Sir Edward Ryan, a family friend, in November–December, 1874. Cameron wanted Ryan to use his influence to get the *Illustrations* reviewed in the London *Times.* She wrote Ryan on November 29, 1874:

> About three months ago Alfred Tennyson walked into my room saying, "Will you think it a trouble to illustrate my Idylls for me?" I answered laughingly, "Now *you* know, Alfred, that *I* know that it is immortality to me to be bound up with you that altho' I bully you I have a corner of worship for you in my heart & so I *consented.* — I have worked for three months putting all my zeal and energy to my high task. But my beautiful large photographs are reduced to cabinet size for his people's edition and the first Illustration is transferred to Wood-cut and appears now today when *1200* copies are issued.

[Three Cameron photographs were reproduced as wood-engravings: "King Arthur," "Elaine," and "Maud" (from the Tennyson poem *Maud*).]

I do it for friendship not that I would not gladly have consented to profit if profit had been offered. Doré got a fortune for his *drawn* fancy Illustrations for these Idylls—Now one of my large photographs, take one for instance illustrating Elaine who is May Prinsep (now Hitchens) at her very best would excite more sensation and interest than all the drawings of Doré—and therefore I am producing a volume of these large photographs to illustrate the Idylls, 12 in number all differing (with portrait of Alfred Tennyson) in a handsome half morocco volume priced six guineas—I could not make it under for it to pay at all.

The photographs will also be sold singly at 16/- each to those who prefer single copies—then the set would come to £10/8/- for the 13 pictures without binding whereas the *book* is only six guineas. It will make a beautiful Xmas gift book or Wedding gift book—the Elaine of May Prinsep and the Enid of another lovely girl are as all agree *not* to be surpassed as Poems and Pictures, and the King Arthur all say is a magnificent Mystic mythical a real embodiment of conscience—with piercing eyes and spiritual look and air.

. . . I have taken *180* pictures to obtain 12 successes—this is the work of the last three months and then the experience and labours of 10 previous years have all been brought into play.

The hiring of armour and models has all cost me a great deal and I *hope* to get one single grain of the momentous mountain heap of profits the poetical part of the work brings to Alfred. *Then I can help my youngest boy who has not yet had one farthing from us.*[3]

There were eventually two volumes of the *Illustrations*, identical in title and format; the first, described above by Cameron, was published in late December–early January, 1875; the second, with subjects from both the *Idylls* and other Tennyson works, was published in May, 1875.[4]

Cameron's belief in her artistic achievement and her dissatisfaction with the meager wood-engraved reproduction influenced her decision to publish the *Illustrations,* but the commercial prospects offered by the *Idylls of the King* clearly motivated her action. Cameron's favorable comparison of her photographs to the engravings of the *Idylls* (published in 1867–68) by the popular French graphic artist Gustave Doré gives an indication of Cameron's high opinion of her work and her expectations for its sale.[5] Cameron's work on the cabinet edition had included non-*Idylls* subjects ("Maud" was one of the photographs reproduced in wood-engraving), but the first volume of the *Illustrations* was devoted exclusively to the *Idylls*.

(By using the same title for both volumes, however, Cameron did allow herself the option to include non-*Idylls* subjects—as she did in the May, 1875 publication).

Tennyson's involvement with the project had commercial value, as is evident in the expansion of Tennyson's role in the publication described in another Cameron letter to Ryan, dated December 4, 1874.

> Alfred Tennyson *asked* me to illustrate his Idylls *for this people's edition* . . . it seemed such a pity that they should only appear in the very tiny reduced form in Alfred's volume (where I gave them only as a matter of friendship) that he himself said to me, "Why don't you bring them out at their actual size in a big volume at your own risk" and I resolved at once to do so. And I am sure if it is favourably noticed in the *Times* I shall make a *success* of it after all my labour.[6]

Tennyson's involvement with the project was noted in the review which was eventually published in the London *Times* and in a review published in *The Morning Post.*[7]

In her November letter to Ryan, Cameron described the format used for both volumes of the *Illustrations*: a frontispiece photographic portrait of Alfred Tennyson and twelve photographic illustrations. Each photograph is preceded by a separate page with an excerpt from the Tennyson text. These excerpts are reproduced in a facsimile of Cameron's handwriting and Cameron also inscribed titles and text excerpts on the mounts of the individual photographs. The average size of the albumen photographs in the *Illustrations* is 32 x 20 cm. Cameron's photographs are generally this large, but as components of a book the images dominate the space of the viewer; the intensity of the experience of examining the volume is augmented by the impress of Cameron's personality in the inscriptions and text excerpts. The *Illustrations* was dedicated to the Crown Princess and featured a sonnet in honor of Cameron written by Charles Turner, Alfred Tennyson's brother. The twelve photographs in the first volume of the *Illustrations* were arranged to follow the course of the *Idylls of the King*, but the subjects featured were not representative of the course of the *Idylls* in 1875 (three chapters, "The Coming of Arthur," "Pelleas and Ettaree," and "The Last Tournament" were omitted entirely).[8] The second volume of the *Illustrations* features photographic illustrations to three subjects from the *Idylls* and to Tennyson's poems, "The May Queen," "The Princess," "Mariana," "The Beggar Maid," and "Maud."[9]

Cameron ordered the sequence of the *Idylls of the King* subjects in the first volume of the *Illustrations* to follow the course of Camelot, from the springtime and optimism of "Gareth and Lynette" to the winter mysteries of "The Passing of Arthur." In the first photograph Lynette gazes on the sleeping Gareth in the cave surrounded by honeysuckle. In the second photograph, Enid stands at the cedarn cabinet and reflects upon the "faded silk/ A faded mantle and a faded veil" which she had worn at her first meeting with Geraint; in the third photograph Enid sings, from Geraint's recollection of their first meeting, the song of fortune and its wheel. Vivien's

Collection of the J. Paul Getty Museum, Malibu, California, Julia Margaret Cameron, "Gareth and Lynette," 1874, Albumen, 13^1/$_8$ × 10^7/$_{16}$ in.

Collection of the J. Paul Getty Museum, Malibu, California, Julia Margaret Cameron,
"And Enid Sang," 1874, Albumen, 13⁷/₈ × 11¹/₄ in.

seduction of Merlin and his subsequent imprisonment in the oak tree are
the subjects of the fourth and fifth photographs. These images are followed
by two photographs of Elaine: the first as she guards the shield of Lancelot
which became the focus of her dreams of love; the second as she sings her
song of love and death after Lancelot has rejected her love and claimed his
shield. In the eighth image the Pale Nun binds Sir Galahad with the sword
belt she has woven. Guinevere and Lancelot's final embrace before Mordred's
intrusion is the subject of the ninth photograph. In the tenth Guinevere lis-

tens to the song of the Little Novice. In the final photographs of the volume of the *Illustrations* King Arthur prepares for battle and, in the last image, asserts his identity as the king. In the second volume of the *Illustrations* there are three more subjects from the *Idylls*: the transport of Elaine's body to Camelot, its presentation at court, and the final departure of King Arthur on the mysterious barge, from "The Passing of Arthur."

Of the fifteen photographic illustrations of the *Idylls*, eleven are from the idylls of Enid, Vivien, Elaine, and Guinevere, the group which Tennyson published in 1859, and the group which Gustave Doré illustrated in four volumes published in 1867–68.[10] Cameron believed her work was superior

Collection of the J. Paul Getty Museum, Malibu, California, Julia Margaret Cameron, "Vivien and Merlin," 1874, Albumen, 12¹/₂ × 10⁷/₈ in.

to Doré's engravings of the *Idylls* and their popularity encouraged Cameron to publish her photographs. It is likely that Doré's engravings also influenced Cameron's selection of subjects. Doré and Cameron both illustrated Vivien's seduction of Merlin and his imprisonment in the oak tree, the parting of Lancelot and Guinevere (Doré illustrated the characters at their embrace at the road of the divided way), Guinevere and the Little Novice at Almesbury, the transport of Elaine's body to Camelot, and its presentation at court. The similarities of subject do not extend to their visual representation: Doré's virtuoso rendition of scenic detail, atmospheric lighting, and individual expression are far removed from the generalized illumination, shallow space, minimal indications of setting, and limited range of facial and gestural expression of Cameron's photographs.

There are two Cameron photographs whose compositions were inspired by Doré's engravings, but whose final forms differ for reasons indicative of the specific context and intentions of Cameron's photographs of the *Idylls of the King*. In Doré's engraving of the imprisonment of Merlin in the oak tree, Merlin sits upon the oak tree. In the Cameron photograph of the same subject, Merlin stands before the oak tree. Cameron apparently wanted her model to sit upon the oak tree, but there were problems with the exposure of the photographic negative. The model for "Vivien" discussed the experience of posing for this photograph in an article published in 1886, after Cameron's death:

> I very much objected to this [posing as Vivien] because Vivien did not seem to be a very nice character to assume, but when Mrs. Cameron said a thing was to be done it had to be done and so my objections were overruled. My troubles however were not over, for in addition to my having to portray the objectionable Vivien, I discovered, to my dismay, that she had designated her husband for Merlin. As for Mr. Cameron, with his silvery hair and long white beard, being an admirable representative of the patriarch there could not be a shadow of a doubt, but would he laugh?—the point was soon settled, laugh he did and most heartily.

Cameron posed "Merlin" sitting upon the tree trunk, but there were problems with the exposure. "Vivien" continued:

> It was more than mortal could stand to see the oak beginning gently to vibrate and know that the extraordinary phenomenon was produced by the suppressed chuckling of Merlin . . . with all the latitude

Mrs. Cameron allowed herself in the way of "out of focus" and "sketchiness" Merlin had moved far too much, there were at least fifty Merlins to be seen [on the negative].[11]

In a letter of December 15, 1874, Cameron described her project: "Tennyson himself is very much pleased with this ideal representation of his *Idylls*."[12] The mundane exposure problems of a chuckling husband altered Cameron's original compositional intentions, but did not impair the final achievement of an ideal representation.

The role-playing of Victorian family theatricals was considered by the individuals and their intimate audiences as an opportunity to express aspects of one's own character; Cameron evaluated her husband's portrayal of Merlin from this perspective in a letter to Ryan.

> My husband is exceedingly well thank god. He appears in character!! in this book. Can you guess his character—you ought to know his tendency!! He sends you his love and so do I.[13]

Cameron wrote of the model for Vivien:

> . . . she is not wicked eno' for she is a sweet girl, but she is lissome and graceful and piquant I think.[14]

The model for King Arthur was William Warder, a Freshwater, Isle of Wight porter. In contrast to Charles Cameron, Warder's personal character was apparently of little interest to Cameron and Ryan:

> Alfred Tennyson himself is very much interested in my work and has been up here perpetually to see how I am going on. He approved of my King Arthur greatly. He always says that his Arthur is an embodiment or I might say incarnation of *Conscience*. That he was "the principle of conscience moving among his knights" and certainly my King Arthur has eyes that search into one and is *mythical* and spiritual in the highest degree. I must not detain you with details altho' I know you take a lively interest in matters great and small concerning your friends.[15]

Cameron didn't speculate on the personal qualities which enabled Warder to embody an "Incarnation of *Conscience*." A sense of social-self-importance, with a shared interest in idealism and fantasy, underlay the shared

Collection of the J. Paul Getty Museum, Malibu, California, Julia Margaret Cameron, "Elaine 'The Lily Maid of Astolat,'" 1874, Albumen, 13⁹/₁₆ × 11¹/₈ in.

assumptions within which Cameron worked. From this position of social influence, Cameron was able to present photographs derived from family activities for the edification of the public, and expect sales and recognition.

A second change in composition between a Doré engraving and a Cameron photograph is the evolution of Cameron's representations of Guinevere. In another article about Cameron, published in 1897, the model for Guinevere complained about posing all day lying at the foot of the model portraying King Arthur. This scene, from the final parting of Guinevere and King Arthur, was depicted by Doré but is not found in the extant copies of Cameron's *Illustrations*. In a prototype copy of the *Illustrations* there is a photograph of Guinevere standing alone, preceded by a text excerpt describing Guinevere's jealousy of Elaine (. . . and rose again, / And moved about her palace, proud and pale).[16] In later editions, Cameron replaced this subject with the image of Guinevere and the Little Novice. Through this substitution Cameron represented Guinevere in remorse and minimized her role as Elaine's rival. This presentation of Guinevere's relationship to Elaine is especially significant because of Elaine's prominence in Cameron's photographs of the *Idylls of the King*. Elaine's idyll is represented in four photographic illustrations, the most of any character, and told from the point of view of her fantasy of ideal love. In the first of the four photographs Elaine gazes at the shield which Lancelot had entrusted to her; by the second photograph Lancelot has rejected Elaine's love, claimed his shield, and left her desolate and insane. Elaine's dying request was that her body be taken to Camelot and presented at court; two photographs illustrate the fulfillment of Elaine's wishes.

Through the use of visual parallels between the photographs of Elaine and King Arthur, Cameron elevated Elaine's fantasy of love into one of the major events of Camelot. Elaine and King Arthur are the only characters represented in visually continuous, paired sequences, and both are represented on boats, symbolic of their passage into immortality. Parallels between Elaine and King Arthur exist in Tennyson's text, establishing an equivalence between Elaine's dream of an ideal love and King Arthur's dream of an ideal society; through her sequencing of photographs in the first volume of the *Illustrations* Cameron went beyond a thematic equivalence between Elaine and King Arthur. The photographs in the first volume conclude with two images of King Arthur. These final—and only—images of King Arthur visit his presence retrospectively upon all of the events in his kingdom (this sequence is maintained even with the three *Idylls of the King* photographs in the second volume of the *Illustrations*). The weight of the final images of King Arthur prevents the visual parallels with images of Elaine from mitigating his magisterial importance. Instead of being King Arthur's peer, Elaine stands as an important figure in her own right. The photographs of Elaine in the second volume of the *Illustrations* substantiate her importance by representing Elaine as the creator of her own immortality: the fulfillment of her last wish that her body be presented at the court of Camelot.

Elaine's prominence in Cameron's photographic illustrations of the *Idylls of the King* illuminates the importance of the other women characters in the *Illustrations*. As with images of Elaine, their importance is not overt but becomes apparent in connections and continuities among the photographs in the *Illustrations*. The women characters are active, the men passive and reactive: Lynette watches over a sleeping Gareth, Vivien seduces and imprisons Merlin, and the Pale Nun inspires Galahad. Enid's wifely loyalty is honored, but Guinevere's adulterous relationship with Lancelot is represented sympathetically, both at her parting from Lancelot and her remorse at the song of the Little Novice. Guinevere is not represented grovelling at the feet of King Arthur; instead, the viewer assumes her point-of-view as she looks up at the King's face disappearing into the mists. Cameron's emphasis upon the woman characters also suggests additional reasons for her choice of subjects. Vivien's seduction and imprisonment of Merlin and the Pale Nun's inspiration of Galahad are major events within their respective idylls, while Lynette's reflection upon the sleeping Gareth is a comparatively minor event. Within Cameron's arrangement, however, Vivien and the Pale Nun are powerful women who influence men's actions, and Lynette's maternal solicitude takes on the power of the "utter peace and love and gentleness" of the world.[17]

Cameron succeeded in her endeavor to secure a review of the *Illustrations* in the London *Times*; the publication was also reviewed in *The Morning Post*. Discussion of the photographs in these reviews is confined to appraisals of Cameron's effectiveness in her selections of models and their poses; neither review discusses the predominance of the women characters or any general theme in the selection of subjects. Both reviews also read as if they had been written by Cameron, including mention of the fact that the oak tree from "Vivien and Merlin" was taken from Tennyson's own grounds—knowledge unavailable from an examination of the photographs.[18] The *Times* review concluded, "We sincerely hope that this artistic volume may be as profitable to Mrs. Cameron as its preparation has been laborious."[19] It is not known if the *Illustrations* was profitable, but Cameron did produce a second volume in May, 1875. Five months later Cameron moved with her husband and sons to their family estate in Ceylon; this move marked the end of Cameron's active involvement with photography. She died in Ceylon in January, 1879.

The Idylls of the King provided Cameron with an opportunity for commercial profit and with the means for fantasy. As is apparent in her discussion of her husband's portrayal of Merlin, the production of the *Illustrations* touched upon expressions of fantasy which were appreciated to different degrees by different audiences. Cameron's women characters of Camelot extend female influence to an extent not present in her other photographs (even in the non-*Idylls* subjects of the *Illustrations*). The combination of female power and deference to male authority suggests Cameron's own situation: a prominent, ambitious artist who sought to change the standards of photographic representation, make money at the same time, and who deferred to her husband's wishes to move to Ceylon. Cameron's homage to Elaine honors woman's purity and innocence, and also brings to mind the character of the Lady of Shalott, with implications of the creativity of woman in a sphere outside the maternal.

Collection of the J. Paul Getty Museum, Malibu, California, Julia Margaret Cameron, "The Parting of Sir Lancelot and Guinevere," 1874, Albumen, 13^{15}/₁₆ × 11^{1}/₁₆ in.

JULIA MARGARET CAMERON'S *ILLUSTRATIONS TO TENNYSON'S* IDYLLS OF THE KING
AND OTHER POEMS

Titles within quotes are from inscriptions to the photographs from the copies of the *Illustrations* in the collection of the J. Paul Getty Museum, Santa Monica, California, USA.

Volume 1 (December 1874–January 1875)

Gareth and Lynette

Enid

And Enid Sang

Vivien and Merlin

Vivien and Merlin

Elaine, "the Lily Maid of Astolat"

Elaine

Sir Galahad and the Pale Nun

The Parting of Sir Lancelot and Queen Guinevere

[The Little Novice and Queen Guinevere in the Holy House of Almesbury]

King Arthur

"The Passing of Arthur"

Volume 2 (May 1875)

["For I'm to be Queen of the May, Mother, I'm to be Queen of the May"]

["He thought of the sharp look Mother gave him yesterday" / "They call me cruel hearted, I care not what they say"]

["So now I think is near [sic]—I trust it is—I know" / "The Blessed Muse went that way my soul will have to go"]

[The Princess]

["O hark"]

["Tears from the depths of some divine despair Rise in the heart, and gather to the eyes"]

["Mariana—She said I am aweary aweary I would that I were dead"]

[King Cophetua and the Beggar Maid]

[Elaine]

[Elaine "And reverently they bore her unto the Hall"]

["The Passing of Arthur"]

[Maud "There has fallen a splendid tear" / "From the passion flower at the gate"]

1. Helmut Gernsheim, *Julia Margaret Cameron: Her Life and Photographic Work*, rev. ed. (Millerton, NY, 1975), is the standard source on Cameron. An excellent article on the *Illustrations* is Charles W. Millard's "Julia Margaret Cameron and Tennyson's *Idylls of the King*," *Harvard Library Bulletin* 21 (April, 1973), 187–201. My research for this article was done in conjunction with the exhibition and catalogue, *Cameron: Her Work and Career,* for the International Museum of Photography at George Eastman House (Rochester, NY, 1986). A version of this article was presented at the Symposium on Arthurian Studies, the 21st International Congress on Medieval Studies, Kalamazoo, Michigan, in 1986. I would like to thank Debra Mancoff, Beloit College, for her support of my work with Arthurian imagery.

2. Alfred Tennyson, *The Works of Alfred Tennyson,* cabinet edition in ten volumes (London, 1874–75). The Cameron photographs were reproduced as the frontispieces to volumes 6, 7, and 9.

3. Cameron to Ryan, November 29, 1874, Gilman Paper Company Collection; the Cameron letters are reprinted with the permission of the Gilman Paper Company, New York, NY. Other correspondence pertaining to the first volume of the *Illustrations* is reprinted in Gernsheim, *Cameron,* pp. 44–48.

4. As Cameron mentioned in her letter to Ryan, individual photographs of *Idylls of the King* subjects were also sold. "The Parting of Sir Lancelot and Queen Guinevere" was reproduced in wood-engraving on the cover of the American journal *Harper's Weekly* on September 1, 1877; the accompanying article discusses Cameron's photographs of the *Idylls* but not the gift book.

Millard ("Cameron and Tennyson's *Idylls of the King*," p. 190) found no evidence of the size of the edition of the *Illustrations,* a question complicated by the number of extant prints which have been disbound from volumes. Millard describes variations in inscriptions on the mounts of the photographs, in the colors of photograph mounts, and photographic compositions among the extant copies; the existence of these variations suggests that Cameron was closely involved with the production of the individual copies of the *Illustrations,* and that the edition would not have been very large.

In the Gernsheim Collection, Harry Ransom Humanities Research Center, University of Texas at Austin, there is a "Miniature edition" of the *Illustrations* (photographs measuring $3^{1}/_{2}$ x $4^{1}/_{4}$"), which Gernsheim believes may have been a prototype for a cheaper edition of the *Illustrations,* which was never published (Gernsheim, *Cameron,* pp. 178–79). Cameron also included *Idylls of the King* subjects in a miniature album which she gave to her son, Henry Hirschel Hay; this album was reprinted in 1975 by Lunn Gallery/Graphics International (Washington, DC) as *An Album: Julia Margaret Cameron.* Gernsheim gives May, 1875 as the publication date for the second volume of the *Illustrations (Cameron,* p. 178). This date is confirmed by the May 1, 1875 date of the copyright registrations for the three subjects of "The May Queen." The photographs for the first volume of the *Illustrations* were registered for copyright on December 8, 1874.

5. Cameron actively promoted her photographs in exhibitions and through her printseller, Colnaghi and Company, London; it is interesting to speculate that it was the commercial prospect offered by the *Idylls of the King* which encouraged her to publish her photographs in book form for the first time.

The Doré engravings were published by Moxon and Company, London; *Vivien* was published in 1867 and *Guinevere, Enid,* and *Elaine* in 1868. Cameron knew Doré and took his portrait in 1872 (reproduced in *Cameron: Her Work and Career,* p. 72).

6. Cameron to Ryan, December 4, 1874, Gilman Paper Company Collection.

7. "Poetry and Photography," London *Times,* February 1, 1875; "Mrs. Cameron's New Photographs," *The Morning Post,* January 11, 1875, reprinted in Gernsheim, *Cameron,* pp. 48–49.

8. For a summary of the chronology of the *Idylls of the King*, see John D. Rosenberg, *The Fall of Camelot* (Cambridge, MA, 1973), pp. 156–57.

9. It is possible that another Moxon publication, the famous "Pre-Raphaelite" 1857 edition of Tennyson's *Poems* influenced Cameron's selection of non-*Idylls* subjects in the second volume of the *Illustrations*; "The May Queen," "Mariana," and "The Beggar Maid" were published in *Poems*. Michael Bartram in *The Pre-Raphaelite Camera: Aspects of Victorian Photography* (London, 1985), p. 142 relates John E. Millais's illustration of "Mariana" in this edition to Cameron's version of the subject, and Millard ("Cameron and Tennyson's *Idylls of the King*,") pp. 187–201 relates Daniel Maclise's illustration of "The Passing of Arthur" to Cameron's version of the subject. All of the non-*Idylls* poems of the second volume of the *Illustrations* pertain to the subject of woman.

10. Gustave Doré, *Vivien, Enid, Elaine, Guinevere* (London, 1867–68).

11. "A Reminiscence of Mrs. Cameron by a Lady Amateur," *The Photographic News* 30 (January 1, 1886), 2–4.

12. From a letter enclosed with a prototype copy of the first volume of the *Illustrations* in the collection of the Metropolitan Museum of Art, New York, NY; the letter is reproduced in full in Gernsheim, *Cameron*, p. 48.

13. Cameron to Ryan, November 29, 1874, Gilman Paper Company Collection.

14. Cameron to Ryan, December 6, 1874, Gilman Paper Company Collection.

15. Cameron to Ryan, December 4, 1874, Gilman Paper Company Collection.

16. The prototype copy is in the collection of the Metropolitan Museum of Art, New York, NY; this version of the illustration of Guinevere is also used in a copy of the *Illustrations* in the collection of the Tennyson Research Centre, England (Millard, "Cameron and Tennyson's *Idylls of the King*," p. 192). The photograph of the "proud and pale" Guinevere is described in the London *Times* review and listed in the copyright registrations for December 8, 1874.

17. This quote is from the text excerpt to "Gareth and Lynette" in the first volume of the *Illustrations*.

18. In addition to asking Ryan for his assistance, Cameron also wrote A. D. O. Wedderburn requesting a review of the *Illustrations* in the *Times*. This information is from a sale catalogue, Sotheby Park Burnet, London (December 9, 1983, lot 102, five letters, December 4–December 12, 1874, with a copy of the *Illustrations*).

19. "Poetry and Photography," London *Times*, February 1, 1875.

THE WOMAN'S EYE

FOUR MODERN ARTHURIAN ILLUSTRATORS

Muriel Whitaker

In 1891 William Morris established the Kelmscott Press to counteract the ugliness that marred most nineteenth century books and that, in his view, signified a decadent society. Taking as his models illuminated manuscripts and early printed books, he defined a beautiful book as one in which every element of the architecture was treated as part of an integrated whole. The type must be black and legible, the words well spaced, the paper and ink of excellent quality, and the decoration—initials, title page, borders, frames, and illustrations—must harmonize with the appearance of the text.[1] Although the Kelmscott Press did not long survive its founder's death in 1896, it had an enormous influence not only on other private presses that soon appeared but also on commercial publishers who saw a market for fine books illustrated by established artists. Some of the artists who received commissions were women who shared Morris's ideal of the book as a work of art.

The strong prejudice against women that had long existed in the fine arts was less noticeable in the decorative arts, since many of these had traditionally come within a woman's domestic sphere. Embroidery, lacemaking, ceramics, watercolor painting, and book illustration were regarded as genteel arts that women could practice in the home. Beginning with such domestic creations as Christmas cards, valentines, and the decoration of personal letters and books for children, Kate Greenaway (1846–1901) and Beatrix Potter (1866–1943) proved that women could make the profession of illustrating pay. Under the umbrella of the Arts and Crafts movement, many women shed their amateur status to become partners or competitors of professional men.[2] Four who did so were illustrators of Arthurian works: Eleanor Fortescue Brickdale, Jessie M. King, Dorothea Braby, and Annegret Hunter-Elsenbach.

Eleanor Fortescue Brickdale[3] (1872–1945) belonged to an upper middle-class family, some members of which were interested in art, at least as a leisure activity. At the age of seventeen, Brickdale began to attend the Crystal Palace School of Art where her instructor was Herbert Bone, the artist who had designed eight or possibly ten tapestries illustrating Alfred, Lord Tennyson's *Idylls of the King*.[4] Woven in 1879–80 at the Royal Windsor Tapestry Manufactory, they treated narrative situations and symbolic flora in a way that Brickdale later adopted. By 1897 she was not only studying at the Royal Academy Schools but was showing her work at Academy exhibitions. A black and white drawing, "Sir Lancelot du Lake," was based on the ballad account of the hero's battle against Sir Tarquin in Thomas Percy's *Reliques of Ancient English Poetry*. The subject may have been suggested by Sir John Gilbert's oil painting completed in 1886. Although the situations are identical—two knights jousting beneath a shield-laden oak as a maiden watches—the "woman's eye" is apparent in Brickdale's interpretation of the literary text. Unlike Gilbert's weak, distressed maiden shrinking into the background, Brickdale's damsel, looking composed and curious, occupies the foreground while the knights are relegated to the middle distance behind the strong diagonals of trunks and branches. A reviewer complained that "the black horse of the knight to the right is only deduced by Socratic methods after some study as to what the patches in question *cannot* be intended to represent."[5] The artist never mastered this traditional chivalric image, solving the problem by omission. Though the *Studio* reviewer prophesied that Brickdale would take a notable position among "the few of her sex" who have excelled in black-and-white decorative art,[6] she found that her métier was color.

In 1911 the Leicester Galleries in London exhibited twenty-eight watercolors based on Tennyson's first set of *Idylls of the King* (1859). Individually named "Enid," "Vivien," "Elaine," and "Guinevere," they originally appeared under the title *The True and the False*. The four types of women that the title subsumes are the model wife, obedient, meek, and true; the *femme fatale*, an archetype that Mario Praz characterizes as one that "united in itself all forms of seduction, all vices, and all delights"; the sacrificial virgin; and the faithless wife. Tennyson's central theme, the conflict between Sense and Soul, was intended to have direct relevance to Victorian society. Thanks to technological advances in color printing, twenty-one of Brickdale's watercolors were reproduced in Hodder and Stoughton's 1911 limited edition of 350 copies, signed by the artist.

That Tennyson had fixed views about the artist's relationship to a literary source is revealed in John Ruskin's letter[7] to Margaret Bell (April 3–4, 1859) describing a visit to Holland House where he found the poet engaged in argument with the painter G.F. Watts:

[Tennyson] was maintaining that painters ought to attend to at least what the writer *said*—if they couldn't to what he meant—while Watts and I both maintained that no good painter could be subservient at all: but conceive everything in his own way,—that no poems ought to be illustrated at all—but if they were—the poet *must* be content to have his painter in partnership—not a slave.

Tennyson's evocation of the Middle Ages relied not on accurate historical detail—in fact, he regarded the period as one "that hover'd between war and wantonness"—but on images that would summon up a secondary world of the imagination inhabited by a mythic society of knights and ladies who performed their roles in castles, perilous forests, enclosed gardens, and wasteland chapels. Using recounted vision and dream, he added a psychological "inner world" that was both mundane and transcendent. He established a chivalric milieu through such concrete words as painted shield, casque, charger, "old and rusty" armor, lances and "golden-hilted brand." There are references to oaken settles, boards on which feasts are spread, stained glass windows and sculpted doorways, with occasional purple passages such as the description of Arthur's chair:

> And from the carven-work behind him crept
> Two dragons gilded, sloping down to make
> Arms for his chair, while all the rest of them
> Thro' knots and loops and folds innumerable
> Fled ever thro' the woodwork . . . .
> And, in the costly canopy o'er him set,
> Blazed the last diamond of the nameless king. ("Elaine," ll. 434–43)[8]

Costume, too, is an element in his medievalism, as when he describes the dress that Earl Doorm offers Enid:

> a splendid silk of foreign loom,
> Where like a shoaling sea the lovely blue
> Play'd into green, and thicker down the front
> With jewels than the sward with drops of dew. ("Enid," ll. 685–89)

Not surprisingly, the contemporary artist J.C. Horsley described him as "the painter's poet."

His depiction of characters in moments of emotional significance provided artists with scenes that could be detached from the narrative. He created settings in a Pre-Raphaelite way, focusing on individual details. Botanical forms were observed from nature but, when appropriate, could bear the weight of symbolism.

Eleanor Brickdale was an ideal illustrator of Tennyson's works because she shared the poet's love of the English countryside, his delight in sensuous imagery, and his moral awareness. In her illustrations for the *Idylls*, she avoids scenes of chivalric encounters, preferring to place her characters in garden or court settings. Her castle furnishings seem patterned on the medieval reproductions that firms like William Morris & Co. manufactured for the "artistic houses" of wealthy industrialists.[9] Elaine's tower room contains a high table with Gothic arches, a curtained bed covered by a scarlet spread, a footstool, and a carved chest. A shield is propped before the heroine, who embroiders on a case of crimson silk Sir Lancelot's "azure lions, crown'd with gold."

Costuming the characters in court dress provided scope for painting jewel-like colors and opulent fabrics. Like many Pre-Raphaelite artists from Dante Gabriel Rossetti on, Brickdale may have found models for her fur-trimmed houpelands, tight fitting hose, extravagant headdresses and *robes royales* in the British Museum's fine illuminated manuscripts such as the fifteenth–century Harley MS 4425 (*Roman de la Rose*) or in such artists' aids as Henry Shaw's *Dresses and Decorations of the Middle Ages* (1843) or F.W. Fairholt's *Costume in England* (1846). Since costume could signify not only period, class, and occupation but also emotional states, and since color was an important aspect of costume symbolism, Brickdale's attention to these aspects of her illustration had didactic as well as aesthetic importance. Tennyson's lines often provided specific details that she could incorporate. For example, to illustrate "so loved Geraint / To make her beauty vary day by day, / In crimson and in purples and in gems" ("Enid," ll. 8–10), she paints a fair-haired woman and man both gorgeously dressed in fifteenth-century style. Crimson and purple are aristocratic colors. Later, humiliated and placed under an order of silence, Enid rides in a dress of "faded silk, a faded mantle and a faded veil" denoting her sadness and her husband's contempt. Vivien's dress, as she lies at Merlin's feet in the forest of Broceliande, Tennyson describes thus:

> A twist of gold was round her hair; a robe
> Of samite without price, that more exprest
> Than hid her, clung about her lissome limbs,
> In color like the satin-shining palm. ("Vivien," ll. 219–22)

Gold signifies power, green deceit. These are also the colors associated particularly with Celtic fays. Again Brickdale effects a literal translation, adding serpentine patterning to the palm-green gown.

Another element in conveying the poet's theme of "Sense at war with Soul" is found in physical appearance. Arthur, "ideal manhood closed in real man," has "a golden head," hair like "a sun that ray'd from off a brow / Like hillsnow high in heaven," a curly golden beard, steel-blue eyes, and a clear face. Lancelot has "night-black hair," "large black eyes," and a face scarred and lined by "the great and guilty love he bore the Queen." Brickdale reproduces the dark hair and eyes in her frontispiece illustration and an easel painting. But by choosing to illustrate the narrative moment when "Sir Lancelot went ambassador, at first, / To fetch her, and she took him for the King," she avoids the necessity of painting a face ravaged by divided loyalties. The young Guinevere glitters "like May sunshine on May leaves / In green and gold." Brickdale also dresses the golden-haired queen in scarlet (passionate love) and gold (sovereignty) or in blue (fidelity in love). Elaine has a stream of golden hair (virginity), blue eyes, and a perfect body—the features of an ideal medieval beauty. In Brickdale's painting illustrating the lines "at which the King / Had gazed upon her blankly and gone by" ("Vivien," ll. 158–59), Vivien has plucked eyebrows and auburn hair (a common feature of Pre-Raphaelite fatal women) that is coiled snake-like over her head. The leopard skin flung over her flame-colored gown relates her visually to Frederick Sandy's oil painting, *Morgan-le-Fay* (1862–63).

While medieval costumes and castle settings are intended to create a sense of remoteness, both poet and artist used the English landscape of their own time as a setting for the romance characters. Tennyson's idea of wilderness came from Cornwall, a source perhaps reflected in the Gothic extravagance of the perilous forest through which Enid and Geraint ride. Brickdale's landscape sources were the Surrey countryside where she grew up and the woodlands, meadows, and gardens surrounding the country houses of relatives and friends in Gloucestershire, Shropshire, and the Forest of Dean. Landscape is the most important feature of "Farewell, fair lily." Presenting to the viewer the back of his scarlet cloak and high-crowned hat, Lancelot gazes downstream where the lily-maid's barge can distantly be seen. With the kind of botanical accuracy that Ruskin approved—"paint from nature"—the artist recreates the luxuriant growth of high summer—magenta splashes of sorrel and foxglove, coarse-leaved burdock, sedges, bullrushes, waterlilies clogging the lethargic stream, oaks and elms with sun glinting off their leaves. A riot of flora characterizes the paradisal days "Before the coming of the sinful Queen"—foxgloves, snapdragons, blackberry bushes, and grasses from which "spirits mad with joy" hang suspended.

Just as Tennyson used the cycle of the seasons as a source of aesthetic and didactic patterning, Brickdale relates passing time to moral conditions. Tulips bloom in Enid's walled garden to suggest pristine innocence. The walled garden in which Vivien attempts to trap "the blameless king" contains autumnal leaves and ripe apples. The latter image with its associations of a lost paradise conveys the woman's success in tempting Merlin, as well as the decay of the Camelot world.

Brickdale chose to illustrate lines of text that presented women characters in emotionally charged situations. That she consciously loaded her paintings with allegorical images is evident from her own explication of "The Lovers' World":[10]

> Here you may see disclosed mysteries of Spring, the Springtime of Youth, of the World, of Love. As a flower-sheath drops and shows the bud, so has Love unfolded and shown to this girl Life, Song, Colour, and Music. . . . The Rainbow promises all Hope, the White Dove all Peace, and the Brown Turtle-Dove all Constancy. Over her head is the Dream-king, the Veil and the Wreath of Myrtle—Myrtle the Crown of Life, as Laurel is the Crown of Fame, and Cypress the Crown of Death. . . .

Both the familiar Pre-Raphaelite practice of charging botanically accurate plants and flowers with symbolism and the popularity of symbol dictionaries like Kate Greenaway's *Language of Flowers* (1884) would have prepared viewers to understand polysemous images.

The rose, symbol of passionate love and transient beauty, is Guinevere's flower. Seated beside a cupid-topped fountain in a May garden dominated by a flowering chestnut, the Queen prophetically sniffs a rose bud. The floor of the bedroom where the lovers spend "their last hour" is strewn with red roses. When Elaine tells Lancelot of her desire "to be with you still, to see your face, / To serve you and to follow you thro' the world," the garden contains lilies (purity) and yews (death). At the foot of the hollow oak (decayed Wisdom) where Vivien seduces Merlin are bracken, brambles, and sharp grasses through which writhes a snake. One of the most complexly allusive scenes illustrates "As in the golden days" ("Guinevere," ll. 377 ff), a reminiscence of a paradisal May. The Queen, her golden hair loose, wears an ermine-trimmed *cote* embroidered with roses.[11] She is surrounded by standard roses, lilies, doves, and blue columbines. The fact that

Figure 1. "The Queen who sat betwixt her best / Enid and lissome Vivien, of her court / the wiliest and the worst." Eleanor Brickdale Fortescue's watercolor illustration for Alfred, Lord Tennyson. The Idylls of the King. *London, New York, Toronto: Hodder and Stoughton, 1911. From the Tennyson Research Centre, Lincoln, by permission of Lincolnshire County Council.*

the garden of love is juxtaposed to a Gothic church and that the recollection takes place in the convent at Aymesbury encourages a dual reading, since each image has both secular and religious significance. The rose represents passionate love and the Virgin Mary; the blue columbine folly and the Holy

Spirit; lilies, purity, innocence, and immortality; and doves, the birds of Venus, also stand for the Holy Spirit. The double set of significances may allude to the fact that Guinevere is about to gain salvation by exchanging erotic love for the life of a nun devoted to the pursuit of spiritual love. Brickdale's final illustration shows the completion of the process, as the Queen, wearing a nun's habit, prepares to dispense loaves of bread to the poor, following the lines:

> Walk your dim cloister, and distribute dole
> To poor sick people. . . .
> And so wear out in almsdeed and in prayer
> The sombre close of that voluptuous day.
>
> ("Guinevere," ll. 677–682)[12]

Once again a garden provides the background. The cloister's delphiniums and golden lilies would realistically have grown in any Edwardian woman's perennial border. In this context, appearing behind the penitent, they signal religious faith and salvation.

In response to the first extensive exhibition of her watercolors at the Dowdeswell Galleries, London, in 1901, Walter Shaw Sparrow wrote an article that, in effect, examines the genus "lady artist."[13] Should a woman of genius, he asks, "make herself the imitative slave of men-artists and their ways of work, or should she, controlled by 'her sweet and wayward earthliness,' keep us all in mind of the old saying that Intuition is to her sex both Impulse and Law?" Presenting himself as a "pen-knight" defending the woman artist, Sparrow asserts that a woman's genius depends on her "heart" and her intuition. Imagination in its highest form "lady artists" have never yet possessed. They are more like bees than skylarks. Allowing for the limitations inherent in her gender, Sparrow finds much to praise in Brickdale's watercolors: her intuition that allows her to respond to a subject with feelings rather than words; a "scenic manner" of treating character; an aptitude for imitating favorite styles; an ability to observe nature accurately; a good eye for color; and a delight in human nature.

It is true that this artist was not particularly original. She relies on a familiar Pre-Raphaelite repertoire—truth to nature in painting landscape, the expansion of meaning through allegorical images and symbolic colors, the representation of beautiful women who are either innocents or destroyers. Her skill in fitting suitable images to the text required more than "heart" and intuition. One feels that Tennyson would have approved her attention to "what the writer *said*."

Brickdale's Scottish contemporary Jessie M. King[14] (1875–1949) was criticized for being too original. The daughter of a strict Presbyterian minister, she had to hide her schoolgirl drawings and watercolors under hedges to prevent their being destroyed by disapproving parents. Later, when she entered the National Art Competitions in South Kensington open to art students from all over Britain, she was denied prizes for illustration because her work did not reflect an established tradition. In the judges' view, "a student's business was to be neither individual nor artistic."[15] King's individualistic style was formed at the Glasgow School of Art, which she attended from 1892 to 1897. Realizing that her gift was for linear expression, her enlightened teacher, Francis Newbery, allowed her to concentrate on plant drawing and decorative illustration. As one of the Glasgow Girls, she was instrumental along with Charles Rennie Mackintosh, Margaret and Frances Macdonald, and others in promoting an Art Nouveau variation known as the Glasgow Style. Influences included William Morris, who introduced beauty into nineteenth-century industrial design; Aubrey Beardsley, who developed the whiplash line and stylized floral decoration in the course of illustrating Malory's *Morte Darthur*; continental Symbolist painters like Jean Delville and Jan Toorop, who created a world of dreams, visions, and spells as an escape from reality; Celtic illuminated manuscripts with their interlaced zoomorphic and human forms; and Japanese prints with their two dimensional treatment of space, their linearity, and their use of patterned costume.

What differentiated the Glasgow Style from other forms of Art Nouveau were its attenuated plants and people, its emphasis on geometric forms such as rectangles, circles, parabolas, and grids, and its fondness for specific motifs that acted as identifying signs. In particular, the "Glasgow rose" appeared on furniture, jewelry, stained glass, metal work, textiles, and book illustrations designed by Newbery's students. It is thought to have evolved from the circles of pink linen from which Jessie Newbery created geometric appliqué roses. The multifoliate rose became King's predominant image.

By 1902 King's literary illustrations were well enough known to warrant a full length *Studio* article by Walter R. Watson. He praised her as "an artist who has acted in a dual capacity. She has not only illustrated the meaning of prose and poetry by her conception of the thoughts of the poet or author, but has produced designs for the decoration of the covers of books which have given them added value which true art ever gives where beauty is coupled with utility." He added that the artistic personality that her work revealed depended on the power of her imagination (the quality that Sparrow had denied to women). Imagination enabled her "to pass through and beyond the outward and merely physical limitations, and to search the essential life and reason which animate it."

In 1903 she illustrated *The High History of the Holy Graal*, translated from the Old French *Perlesvaus* by Sebastian (Septimus) Evans and published by J.M. Dent in both deluxe and standard editions.[16] This venture into medievalism along with her designs for William Morris's *Defence of Guenevere and Other Poems*, which John Lane brought out the following year, established her as a decorator of fine books.

Because Sebastian Evans, the translator of *Perlesvaus*, shared with his friend Edward Burne-Jones a devotion to the Grail legends, he had asked that artist to decorate the first edition, published in 1898. That Burne-Jones was dissatisfied with the result is revealed in a letter to Evans, March 22, 1898:[17]

> But I did all I could for the Graal. The reproductions didn't look a tithe as nice as the drawings—but there was nothing to do but let them pass—the publishers hurried—I had them twice done—and perhaps they are better than I think, but wood engraving is the only art for such work no doubt—the other is a wretched compromise.

With her fine pen-and-ink drawings photographically reproduced, Jessie M. King proved that opinion inaccurate.

The High History of the Holy Graal begins at the narrative point where Britain has fallen on evil times because of Perceval's failure, on his first visit to the Grail Castle, to ask, "Whom does the Grail serve?" King Arthur, Gawain, Lancelot, and Perceval undertake the quest to find the castle, ask the question, and restore the land. Their adventures are described to the point when Perceval frees the Grail Castle from the King of Castle Mortal, and achieves the golden cup awarded to the most worthy knight. He then sails off in a mystic ship, its white sail marked with the knight's red cross—"nor never thereafter did no earthly man know what became of him." One quotation must suffice to convey the strange magic of the Grail terrain that Perceval encounters in the great Lonely Forest:

> He looketh amidst the launde and seeth a red cross. He looketh to the head of the launde and seeth a right comely knight sitting in the shadow of the forest, and he was clad in white garments and held a vessel of gold in his hand. At the other end of the launde he seeth a damsel likewise sitting, young and gentle and of passing great beauty, and she was clad in white samite dropped of gold . . . out of the forest

PERCEVAL·SEETH·THE·QUESTING·BEAST

Figure 2. "Perceval Seeth the Questing Beast." Jessie M. King's illustration for Sebastian Evans, trans. The High History of the Holy Graal. *London: Dent; New York: Dutton, 1903. Courtesy of the University of Alberta Library, Edmonton.*

issued a beast, white as driven snow, and it was bigger than a fox and less than a hare. The beast came into the launde all scared, for she had twelve hounds in her belly, that quested within like as it were hounds in a wood. (p. 198)

King provided thirty-six headpieces and twenty-two full-page illustrations, some with the black-and-red borders that Morris had used in his Kelmscott books. She generally chooses scenes in which a beautiful damsel either assists, implores, or confronts one of the heroes. Her women conform to a type characterized by luxuriant hair, often held back from the face with a rose, a long jaw, and pointed chin emphasized by her habit of presenting faces in profile. Their loose, billowing gowns and mantles, embroidered or patterned with roses, are defined by whiplash lines suggesting freedom and energy. The capaciousness, contrasting with the constricting clothing that women actually wore both in late medieval and Edwardian times, exemplifies woman's desire to free herself from socially imposed restriction.

The artist's knights wear the flamboyant plate armor suggested by fifteenth-century models; it features elongated sabatons, many-jointed greaves, beaded gardes-de-bras, and chainmail lamboys. Their cloaks, the banners fluttering from their lances, and the caparisons of their horses are embroidered with roses. Perceval's shield combines roses with the traditional red cross. Shields often form a motif in the decorative headpieces or, drawn in red ink, become corner-stops in a double picture frame that distances the viewer, adding to the sense of remoteness from reality that the scenes evoke.

To emphasize vertical line, King draws tall, fluted columns with elaborate floral capitals; dripping candles in spiraling candlesticks looped with rose garlands, fruit, and jewels; dark crosses; and elongated angels with shredded wings like those that flank the crucifix above Guinevere's coffin. Streaking clouds, surging cloaks, and blown branches convey the demonic energy of the devil knights who "come through the forest with such a rushing." Streams of stars convey the mystical spirit associated with the Grail (a symbol of divine grace), as when Perceval sees the questing beast or Gawain sees the Grail procession.

So skilled was Jessie M. King in the art of bookbinding and decoration that in 1899 she was appointed tutor in Book Decoration and Design at the Glasgow School of Art. For a deluxe copy of the *High History* she provided a Vellucent binding, reproducing in tints of pale green, rose, and gold the black and white illustration titled "Perceval winneth the golden cup." The images of the knight and golden-haired lady, along with a border design of rose bushes, Perceval's shield and fans were imposed on a pale yellow wash. Since the whole design was applied to the underside of translucent vellum, the effect was magical, particularly as the luminosity was increased by mother-of-pearl inlays.

In 1903 Jessie M. King also decorated for Routledge's Broadway Booklets series Tennyson's *Morte D'Arthur*, *Guinevere*, and *Elaine*, providing a frontispiece and three black-and-white illustrations for each. Her next major commission was to provide twenty-four full-page illustrations and forty-one headpieces and tailpieces for William Morris's *The Defence of Guenevere and Other Poems* (1904), published by John Lane.[18] This collection of poems, inspired largely by Sir Thomas Malory's *Morte Darthur* and Froissart's *Chronicles*, appeared first in 1858. It was, as Morris admitted in a letter to Andreas Schew almost thirty years later, "exceedingly young also and very mediaeval."[19] The title poem was remarkable in being the first literary presentation of Lancelot and Guinevere's tragic love affair from the woman's point of view. In the Arthurian poems— "The Defence of Guenevere," "King Arthur's Tomb," "Sir Galahad, A Christmas Mystery," and "The Chapel in Lyoness"—the combination of castle, chapel, and graveyard settings with the psychological tensions revealed by soliloquy, vision, and dream provided the artist with opportunities for expressing her peculiar double vision. Juxtaposed to solid stone walls, square castle towers, diamond-paned windows, and the convent's paved floor, all clearly defined by heavy black lines, are ethereal rose bushes created by whorls of minute circles and black dots, crosses hung with roses and starry ellipses, and Lancelot's face imposed on disintegrating rays of sunshine. The latter image appears to illustrate the lines:

> And every morn I scarce could pray at all
> For Lancelot's red golden hair would play
> Instead of sunlight, on the painted wall,
> Mingled with dreams of what the priest did say.
>
> ("King Arthur's Tomb," ll. 305–308)

The composition shows King's effective use of verticals as the characteristic attenuation of her designs is enhanced by the crucifix on the wall, a Romanesque column, a two-light window, the lines of Guinevere's cloak, an elongated priest with a crucifix and an elaborate candelabrum with three tapers. The diagonal beam of light connects the lovers, adding vibrancy to the otherwise static scene.

Another example of King's ability to merge waking and dreaming worlds through imagination, memory, and vision occurs in "Sir Galahad, a

Christmas Mystery" where the hero wakens from sensuous dreams to censorious angels, the foremost holding a scarf embroidered with the exhortation, "Galahad, rise and be arm'd." In "The Chapel in Lyoness," another Grail knight, Bors, dreams that a beautiful woman, defined by roses and stars, bends over him, obscuring the cross. The line's nervous intensity conveys the heroes' physical and psychological confusion.

As in Aubrey Beardsley's illustrations for Malory's *Morte Darthur*, the knights are subordinate to the powerful woman who formally and psychologically dominates many compositions. Confronted by Gawain and four other accusers in "She threw her wet hair backward from her brow," the Queen, as tall as a tree, taller than the wall, fills most of the picture space as, with hands pressed to her head, she conveys her anguish. The lightly drawn men on the periphery gaze vacantly at the wall behind her. In "But stood turn'd sideways listening," Guinevere's heavy, rose-decorated hair, voluminous gown, and provocatively curved body draw the eyes away from the almost hidden accusers and the rescuer Lancelot, palely appearing beyond the wall. But King's women are not the contemptuous, medusa-locked aggressors of Beardsley. Lacking blatant sensuality and demonic energy, they represent Arthur Symon's ideal decadence that aims "to fix the last fine shade, the quintessence of things; to fix it fleetingly; to be a disembodied voice and yet the voice of a human soul."[20]

When we compare Eleanor Brickdale and Jessie M. King, we note that the former, by depicting real English flowers, real English landscapes, and the kind of furniture to be found in late Victorian and Edwardian houses, created a tangible world of mundane experience that legitimized the characters' reality. In contrast, King's larger-than-life characters inhabit a mystical world of stylized plants, life-enhancing halos, streaming petals, and stars. The artificiality of pure decoration denudes of naturalism the trees, shrubs, flowers, and clouds, making them images in a dream. Disintegrating lines convey a medium that is beautiful, transient, and on the point of dissolution.

King was the complete decorative artist, producing batik panels (e.g., "How the Queen went a-Maying"), mosaic panels in colored and mirror glass, tempera on wood, watercolor on paper and vellum, ceramics, designs for Liberty scarves, menu covers, and pageant costumes, including "The Holy Grail," Lady of the Lake, Queen Morgan le Fay, and Sir Perceval. With her husband E.A. Taylor, she taught art classes in Paris, and from 1915 until her death she was part of the artist's community in Kirkcudbright, Scotland, where she created for herself a *persona* by going about in a wide-brimmed hat, black cloak, and silver-buckled shoes. Her idea of a beautiful book was much like Morris's:

A page of type, beautifully set, a little ornament beautifully surrounded by type, a chapter heading, symbolic or treating of the matter in the chapter and summing up in it something of the whole trend of thought in that chapter, is to me what book Decoration means.

Her imaginative recreations were a response to these questions: "How can I simplify? How can I convey the essence with the minimum amount of information? In short, how can I tell everything without showing everything?"[21] Today, Jessie M. King is regarded as the best book illustrator that Scotland has produced.

One of the most successful of this century's private presses is the Golden Cockerel Press. Founded in 1920 by Harold Taylor with the intention of publishing works by young, unknown writers, it established a reputation for book design under Robert Gibbings's ownership. Himself a well-known wood-engraver, Gibbings aimed at producing illustrated books in which the engravings were part of a page's total design. Christopher Sandford, who bought the press in 1933, had a different view. He believed that the artist should be allowed to do full-page illustrations as well as head-and-tail pieces. In that way the artist's role became as important as those of the author and printer. His maxim was that "the illustrations should at the same time illustrate the subject of the book, complement its design, be pictures each in its own right, sometimes if not always provide the added charm of pleasing patterns and decorations, and finally reveal the magic of the artist's own inspiration."[22]

Dorothea Braby (1909–) is a wood engraver, portrait painter, and book illustrator who received her training in London, Florence, and Paris. Like Eric Gill and Robert Gibbings, she valued the art of wood engraving because it allowed the artist to take responsibility for the final product, unobstructed by the inadequacy of photographer, block maker, or printer. "No motion has obscured the translation from the idea to actuality," she wrote in her essay, *The Way of Wood Engraving*.[23] When the Golden Cockerel Press offered her a commission to provide six color engravings for Gwyn Jones's prose translation of the Middle English romance *Sir Gawain and the Green Knight* (1952), she accepted, despite her view that "the colour print in which a different block must be cut or engraved for each colour is the most laborious and roundabout way in existence in which to create a small colored picture. Unless the print has something special to say, the amount of work entailed is hardly justified."[24] The color range, consisting of dark green, leaf green, pink, and deep rose, suggests the antitheses basic to the texts' aesthetic

pattern—warmth and cold, natural and supernatural, courtliness and barbarity, sensuous castle life, and rigorous forest hunts.

What Gwyn Jones describes as "the gracious and aristocratic air, the polished manners and good breeding" of the characters, Braby conveys through fifteenth-century costumes similar to those that the Limbourg brothers painted in the Duke of Berry's *Très Riches Heures*. Challenging Arthur's court at their Christmas feast, the Green Knight is not a macabre giant, but as the poet describes him, a well-proportioned man with a broad back and small waist. His form fitting *cote hardie* is patterned with birds, his dark green mantle trimmed with fur, and his axe elegantly looped with ribbon. In his Bercilak form, wearing a capacious houpeland with inset patterned sleeves and a fur hat, the bearded host exudes an air of confidence, geniality, wealth, and power. Gawain is equally elegant in a dagged floor-length forest green mantle, patterned and bordered with leafgreen designs; his belted fur-trimmed houpeland is cut to reveal yellow-green hose. A minstrel playing a lute, a serving boy in tight hose and doublet carrying a heaping platter of fruit, a canopied bed where the bare-breasted lady, in a green gown with rosy patches indicating the shape of her thighs, caresses Gawain's arm suggest the pleasures of castle life. But the wild hunt passing outside, the snake-like girdle at the foot of the bed, the dog preparing to attack a bone as Gawain and Bercilak exchange kiss and fox pelt—both symbols of deceit—convey an underlying menace that is realized in the final print. Wintery branches reach out skeletal fingers, the horse neighs in terror, and the enormous axe that the Green Knight is about to raise commands the foreground.

For this deluxe edition of 360 copies the inks and paper were especially made. Christopher Sandford's leather binding was chosen to match particular inks. The artist consulted the translator about every pictorial detail. The result admirably fulfills Sandford's ideal of author, artist, and printer cooperating to produce a beautiful book.

Annegret Hunter-Elsenbach (1948–) is a Canadian painter who has taught herself the art of making fine bindings. Between 1978 and 1981 she created a unique art object, an illustrated edition of Tennyson's early poem, *Morte d'Arthur* (1842). This work demonstrates the degree to which a fine book allows the artist to express personal tastes, skills, and conceptions in

---

Figure 3 (facing page). Bercilak's lady tempts Sir Gawain a third time. Dorothea Braby's color engraving for Sir Gawain and the Green Knight, *trans. 2nd ed. Gwyn Jones. London: The Golden Cockerel Press, 1936. Courtesy of the Golden Cockerel Press, London.*

an opulent manner. Hunter-Elsenbach is responsible for the calligraphy (Gothic lettering in ebony ink on handmade paper), the seven watercolor illustrations, the endpapers' patterning of dead and broken reeds, the leather binding, and the design of the silken case with brown velveteen lining. The illustrations are minimalist, as the artist selects only the essential elements from the text. A stark chapel, "a broken chancel with a broken cross," huddles against a cliff. Excalibur, like a child's sword made of lathes, lies among "the many-knotted waterflags / That whistled stiff and dry about the marge" of the grey lake. The three queens, characterized by spikey crowns, stand in the "dusky barge," their long mauve gowns and undulating white veils seen only from the back. To illustrate "so like a shattered column lay the king," Arthur's hooded head is pictured, as finely chiseled as an effigy. The unifying image, shown in each illustration, is the full moon "brightening the skirts of a long cloud," or rather the layers of streaked clouds that horizontally divide the sky. The funereal color range of grey, mauve, indigo, and black substantiates the poetry's sombre mood.

Each full-page illustration is interleaved with Japanese-style paper in which are embedded strands of straw-colored fibre. Forming their own broken-reed patterning, they suggest the winter-death metaphor that dominates the poet's and the artist's conception. The burgundy and black leather triangles of the cover direct us to Excalibur, its blade formed of parti-colored

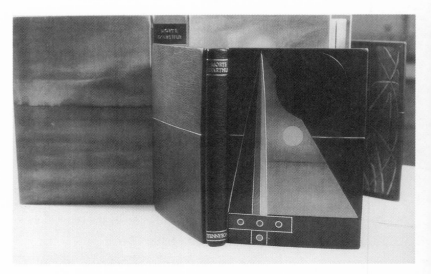

Figure 4. Cover bindings, interleaf and slipcase by Annegret Hunter-Elsenbach for Alfred Lord Tennyson's Morte Darthur, 1981. *Photograph courtesy of The Bruce Peel Special Collections Library, University of Alberta, Edmonton (photo by Carolynne Poon).*

white and black leather, its pommel inset with gold, green, red, blue, and topaz "oasis" onlays imitating the text's jewels:

> For all the haft twinkled with diamond sparks,
> Myriads of topaz-lights, and jacinth work
> Of subtlest jewellery. (*Morte d'Arthur* ll. 56–58)

Triangles and sword combine to form "the barge with oar and sail" that carries the king to Avalon, under the full moon, a black leather circle. The main sail is a silken representation of a lake and sky, ghostly under its white moon. As well as representing a sail, the triangle provides the setting for Excalibur's final appearance. The desolate landscape in understated blues and misty greys and greens is repeated on the case where the white moon is darkly mirrored in the water. Shoreline evergreens and leafless willows strongly suggest a lake in the Canadian wilderness.

Does the work of these women substantiate the idea that gender differences affect an artist's interpretation of a particular text? Brief comparisons of specific works might be illuminating. In the mid-1860s Edward Moxon, Tennyson's publisher, commissioned the Alsatian Gustave Doré to provide thirty-six drawings that could be reproduced as steel engravings in folio editions of *Elaine* (1866), *Enid* (1866), *Guinevere* (1866), and *Vivien* (1867). This artist's strength was his ability to create a landscape imbued by the wildness and strangeness appropriate to romance. The castle-topped crags of the Vosges and Savoy and the serpentine roots and dead trees of dense continental forests are the usual backgrounds in which he places Tennyson's characters. Chivalric activities and male participants are the principal subjects. In *Vivien*, for example, only four of nine illustrations show the distanced woman (a lazy-looking gypsy), the rest being devoted to pirates, to Merlin and a squire, and to Arthur and his knights riding in the forest, so dwarfed by the surrounding scenery that they seem inconsequential. Tennyson's central interest, the personalities of the women who represent "The True and the False," is of little concern to Doré. Elaine and Enid are indistinguishable from each other, both being depicted with Saxon braids, languid attitudes, and vapid expressions quite at variance with their strong-minded prototypes. In Guinevere's scenes of significant emotion, "The Parting," "The Dawn of Love," and "The King's Farewell," we are shown only her back. The fact that Doré did not understand English sufficiently well to make a close study of the text, along with his inability to depict credible women or to appreciate moral implications, made him an unsatisfactory illustrator of *The Idylls*.

In contrast, as we have seen, Eleanor Brickdale made women the central figures in her interpretation, depicting them in eighteen of her twenty paintings. Her fondness for enclosed gardens and small rooms effects the kind of closure that focuses the viewer's attention on the human figures, unlike Doré's engravings where romantic scenery diverts the eye. As well, Brickdale was alert to moral issues, filling her paintings with allegorical images that control the viewer's response. Doré was undoubtedly the better artist, but Brickdale was a more sensitive transmitter of the poet's intention.

William Morris's poem "King Arthur's Tomb" in *The Defence of Guenevere* volume was inspired by Dante Gabriel Rossetti's watercolor *Arthur's Tomb* (1855). Both were based on Malory's description of the lovers' last meeting at Almesbury, when Lancelot begs for a final kiss:

> "Madame, I praye you kysse me, and never no more."
> "Nay," sayd the quene, "that shal I never
> do, but absteyne you from suche werkes." (XXI, 10)

If we compare Rossetti's watercolor with Jessie M. King's black-and-white illustration for Morris's poem, we again find that "the woman's eye" perceives the subject with a difference. To increase the drama and point up the triangular relationship between Lancelot, Guinevere, and Arthur, Rossetti shifts the scene from Almesbury, the convent where the Queen has become a nun, to Glastonbury, the scene of Arthur's burial. Lancelot's scarlet surcoat (the color denoting passionate love), the stiff muscularity of his body, the brightness of his red hair and beard, the intensity of his gaze as he projects himself toward Guinevere over the effigy of her dead husband make him the dominant figure.

Guinevere in a nun's black habit, white wimple, and veil (though still wearing a golden crown) shrinks back, holding a restraining hand between her face and her lover's. The fact that she is squarely set beneath an apple tree and that a snake slithers through the grass conveys an allusion that Rossetti used again in his Oxford Union mural. Woman, the temptress, caused the fall of man. The tomb's pictorial panels, which show Arthur knighting Lancelot and the Grail's appearance at the Pentecostal feast, recapitulate the hero's dual disloyalty to king and God, failures for which Guinevere is responsible.

Jessie M. King's illustration for the line "He did not hear her coming as he lay" effects a role reversal. Because of the massive blackness of the nun's habit and her black headband with its enormous rose, the woman encroaches formally and symbolically on the white space that contains Lancelot in a

HE·DID·NOT·HEAR·HER·COMING·AS·HE·LAY·

Figure 5. "King Arthur's Tomb." Jessie M. King's illustration for William Morris, The Defence of Guenevere and Other Poems. *London: John Lane, 1904. Courtesy of* The Bruce Peel Special Collections Library, *University of Alberta, Edmonton.*

posture of abasement at the Queen's feet. Her freely flowing hair, unrestrained by the white veil that lightly dotted lines barely outline, refutes the idea that in taking the veil Guinevere has surrendered her power as a woman. The thorny cross behind her is circled by stars, forming a halo that seems to sanctify the Queen. Her hand is extended in a gesture of blessing and forgiveness above the dispirited head of her lover and the stony head of her husband. Serious but serene, she is manifestly free of the bitterness, scorn, and fear that beset the Queen in Morris's text.

Dorothea Braby's illustrations may instructively be considered alongside Virgil Burnett's lithographs for *Sir Gawain and the Green Knight*, trans. Keith Harrison (London: Folio Society, 1983). While Braby does not dismiss the evil that threatens Arthurian chivalry, she emphasizes the pleasures of castle life—the fashionable costumes bespeaking wealth and taste, the feasting, music, love-making, and hunting that beguile the participants. The elegant elongation of the ladies' trains, the young woman's sinuous golden girdle and necklace with pendant emerald, the courteous dialogue conveyed by gesture and stance create an air of refinement. This is a world of wish-fulfilling dream where women are valued as mediators of civility.

Burnett chooses to focus on the nightmare elements symbolized by the wasteland outside the castle walls. His Green Knight, a grim destroyer with flat head, narrowly set eyes, sharp nose, and downturned mouth, grips his serviceable axe with a menacing air. The equally grim Gawain, silhouetted against a dark castle, stares fixedly ahead. Lady Bercilak exudes deceit as she sits by a guttering candle with a sharp-edged knife on the table before her. The most complex illustration shows a naked Gawain trapped by sharp thorns and tenacious roots as he tries to escape from the demonic castle. A pigsnout helmet, the Green Knight's battle-axe, gravestones, and barred windows proclaim the enveloping danger. In the central doorway, the white figure of the lady, who has ensured his failure by persuading him to accept the girdle in secret, stands like a phallic symbol directly above the hero's head.

There is a basis in the text for both interpretations. The woman artist chooses to recreate the atmosphere of castle life in Old French romances that Erich Auerbach describes thus:[25] "The setting is fixed and isolating . . . refined and elegant. Women play an important part in it; the mannerly ease and comfort of the social life of a cultured class has been attained." The male artist reiterates medieval mysogyny, presenting woman as a malign destroyer of man's happiness and peace.

An examination of four women who have illustrated Arthurian texts in this century reveals a progressive development of decorative ingenuity, an increasing sense of their authority as artists, and a significant change in reception. While critics discussing Brickdale and King found it necessary to qualify the term "artist" by means of an accompanying "lady" or "woman," no such discrimination would be considered appropriate to Braby or Hunter-Elsenbach. Brickdale remained fixed in late Pre-Raphaelite romanticism, accepting the images of women that male writers and artists had created in the nineteenth century. King moved away from Pre-Raphaelite stereotypes to develop a style immediately recognizable. Within the fairy-tale framework, she presented women who, free from the demonic impulses of the Beardsleyan *femme fatale*, were capable of acting decisively and feelingly. Dorothea Braby called wood engraving "the philosopher of the arts," because it required such self-control and discipline. This artist was extraordinary in her ability to produce from the action of a sharp tool on hard wood illustrations that seem to have grown directly from the literary text. Patient skill was required to produce a finished print from a number of blocks, each incomplete in itself, and to harmonize the colors so that the lighter ones would not be overwhelmed in the printing process. Whereas Braby was an equal partner with the translator and printer of *Sir Gawain and the Green Knight*, Hunter-Elsenbach made herself master of the entire art work, writing the text herself in elegant script, painting the illustrations directly onto the page, and producing end papers, bindings, and slipcase. Her *Morte d'Arthur* is as complete an example of artistic independence as it would be possible to find in the art of the book. Unaffected by considerations of the maker's gender or personality, it is simply a work of art.

NOTES

1. Morris's views on this subject have been collected in *The Ideal Book, Essays and Lectures on the Arts of the Book by William Morris*, ed. William S. Peterson (Berkeley: University of California Press, 1982).

2. Anthea Callen, *Angel in the Studio: Women in the Arts and Crafts Movement 1870–1914* (London: Astragal, 1979).

3. Her name also appears as Fortesque-Brickdale and Fortescue-Brickdale.

4. See Muriel Whitaker, *The Legends of King Arthur in Art* (Cambridge: Brewer, 1990; and Rochester, N.Y.: Boydell, 1991), pp. 235–36 and illustration plate 28.

5. E.B.S., "Eleanor F. Brickdale, Designer and Illustrator," *Studio* 13 (1898), 104.

6. Her black-and-white work included an illustrated edition of Tennyson's *Poems* (1905) with eighteen large and fifty-five small line drawings. For additional information about Brickdale see Jan Marsh and Pamela Gerrish Nunn, *Women Artists and the Pre-Raphaelite Movement* (London: Virago, 1989).

7. Van Akin Burd, ed., *The Winnington Letters* (Cambridge, Mass.: Harvard University Press, 1969), p. 150.

8. The first set of *Idylls of the King* was published in 1859 with the titles "Enid," "Vivien," "Elaine," and "Guinevere." The title "Enid" was changed to

"Geraint and Enid" in 1870; the poem was divided into two parts—"The Marriage of Geraint" and "Geraint and Enid"—in 1873. Similarly, the second idyll became "Merlin and Vivien" in 1870; the third became "Lancelot and Elaine" in 1870. For ease of reference, line references are taken from Alfred, Lord Tennyson, *Idylls of the King*, ed. J.M. Gray (New Haven: Yale University Press, 1983).

9. See T.S. Gibson, "Artistic Houses," *The Birth of The Studio 1893–1895* (Woodbridge, Suffolk: Baron, n.d.), pp. 38–49.

10. This painting along with the artist's description is reprinted in Callen, pp. 206–07.

11. This costume seems to have been inspired by the one that Queen Victoria wore when she appeared as Queen Philippa at a costume ball in 1842, with Prince Albert as Edward III. The pair are recorded in Sir Edwin Landseer's painting.

12. The same lines inspired Sir William Reynolds-Stephens's bronze and ivory statuette, "Guinevere's Redeeming" (1905, Castle Museum, Nottingham). See Whitaker, 233–35.

13. Walter Shaw Sparrow, "On some watercolour pictures by Miss Eleanor Fortescue-Brickdale," *Studio* 23 (1901), 31–44.

14. On her life and work see Jude Burkhauser, ed., *"Glasgow Girls": Women in Art and Design 1880–1920* (Edinburgh: Canongate, 1990) and Colin White, *The Enchanted World of Jessie M. King* (Edinburgh: Canongate, 1989).

15. Walter R. Watson, "Miss Jessie M. King and her Work," *Studio* 26 (1902), 177–88.

16. *The High History of the Holy Graal* translated from the Old French by Sebastian Evans LLD with decorative drawings by Jessie M. King (London: Dent; New York: Dutton, 1903). Evans's source was Bibliothèque Royale MS ll,145, edited by M. Ch. Potuin for "La Société des Bibliophiles Belges" in 1866.

17. Burne-Jones Papers, XXV, 211, Fitzwilliam Museum, Cambridge.

18. William Morris, *The Defence of Guenevere and Other Poems* (London: John Lane, Bodley Head, 1904). King also provided gilt designs for the cover and spine.

19. Critics inevitably compared the medievalism of Morris and Tennyson. Richard Garnett in the *Literary Gazette*, March 1858, x/ii, 226–27 wrote, "The difference between the two poets obviously is that Tennyson writes of mediaeval things like a modern, and Mr. Morris like a contemporary. . . . Tennyson is the modern *par excellence*, the man of his age; Rossetti and Morris are the men of the middle age; and while this at once places them in a position of inferiority as regards Tennyson, it increases their interest towards ourselves."

20. Arthur Symons, "The Decadent Movement in Literature," *Harper's New Monthly Magazine* (November, 1893).

21. White, p. 124.

22. Julia Bigham, *An Introduction to the Golden Cockerel Press* (London: Victoria and Albert Museum, 1987), p. 17.

23. Dorothea Braby, *The Way of Wood Engraving* (London: *Studio*, 1953) p. 9.

24. Braby, p. 70.

25. Erich Auerbach, *Mimesis: the Representation of Reality in Western Literature*, trans. Willard R. Trask (Princeton: Princeton University Press, 1953), p. 131.

LOOKING AT ELAINE

KEATS, TENNYSON, AND THE DIRECTIONS OF THE POETIC GAZE

Constance W. Hassett and James Richardson

CRITICAL APPROACHES

A curiosity of the history of Tennyson's Arthurian poems is that he learned only long after he had written the "Lady of Shalott" that the heroine he had chanced upon in an 1804 edition of the medieval "Cento Novelle Antiche" was "evidently the Elaine of the Morte d'Arthur": he had never "heard of the latter" when he "wrote the former." Tennyson's confusion suggests the newness of Arthurian material in 1832, when he first published "The Lady of Shalott," and this freshness may in turn account for the remarkable afterlife of his poem in Victorian painting. The revised "Lady of Shalott" in the successful 1842 *Poems,* the illustrations by Hunt and Rossetti in Moxon's 1857 edition, and the 1859 publication of "Elaine" (later "Lancelot and Elaine") in *Idylls of the King* fueled something like a craze: art historian Muriel Whitaker has located "at least eighty" subsequent versions of the Lady of Shalott/Elaine motif. Though artists sometimes turned directly to Malory, as Tennyson himself did for his *Idylls*, there is no doubt that "Tennyson's influence in popularising this material was paramount."[1]

The very intensity of this rediscovery of medieval sources suggests, of course, that Victorians were largely discovering themselves. The poets most drawn to Arthurian legends were less likely to translate or faithfully renarrate the tales than to elaborate the lyric or dramatic intensity of their most hopeless and passionate situations. Tennyson's "Lady of Shalott" and its inheritors, Arnold's "Tristram and Iseult," Morris's *Defence of Guenevere* volume, Swinburne's book-length *Tristram of Lyonesse* are fever dreams of doomed yearning or erotic luxuriousness. They make of the legends containers for passions too large, too violent, and too strange for the Victorian parlor, for the novel, and for realism in general—and too real. Not surprisingly, recent criticism has found these poems of erotic extremity newly interesting and revealing. In particular, it has found in the Victorian fascination with Tennyson's "Lady of Shalott" and "Lancelot and Elaine" and their pictorial and poetic sequels an opportunity to raise interesting questions about the representation of women. Put simply, the image of Elaine floating past Camelot beautiful and dead on her barge can be seen as an instance of the recurrent Victorian image of a woman "killed into art." As Elisabeth Bronfen has shown in her encyclopedic *Over Her Dead Body*, the "watching" of dead and unconscious women in nineteenth-century poetry and painting is so ubiquitous as to define a subgenre. Her illustrations from art and literature range from austere speculation to kitschy soft porn, and a list of analogues by poets in the neighborhood of Tennyson would be similarly various, stretching from the melodramatic self-absorption of D.G. Rossetti's "My Sister's Sleep" to the literal necrophilia of Swinburne's "The Leper." The motif invites both sensation and sentimentality. But as in the poems of Christina Rossetti spoken *by* the dead lady, or in Browning's "My Last Duchess," or his "Porphyria's Lover," where a strangler overwrites both his victim's and his own interiority with the fantastic rationalization "I am quite sure she felt no pain," the image can be used with sharp critical self-consciousness.[2]

We hope to contribute to the discussion of "aesthetic death" by suggesting that Tennyson's two very different Elaines represent very different sides of the medievalizing impulse, and more specifically that in managing Elaine's death he makes unexpected—and uneven—contributions to the Victorian analysis of gender. Even more basically, we hope to complicate and enrich the notions of reading, identification, and spectatorship that have underlain recent critical assessments of nineteenth-century poetry.

Discussions of the dead lady motif—so naively celebrated in Poe's oft-cited "the death of a beautiful woman is, unquestionably, the most poetical topic in the world"—almost inevitably focus on the denial of female interiority and the privileging of the male gaze. For many critics the difficulty with narratives like Elaine's lies in their celebration of "the beauty of female muteness and reification." For Sandra Gilbert and Susan Gubar in *The Madwoman in the Attic,* images of women in male-authored texts encode an endemic "scorn of female creativity" that has "powerfully coercive and monitory effects" on "the self-images of women writers." They find Tennyson's poem especially offensive in this regard: because the Lady's "last work of art is her own dead body," she too helps "enforce" a masculinist "injunction to silence."[3]

Equally relevant, given the popularity of the Lady of Shalott/Elaine motif with Victorian painters, is Griselda Pollock's castigation of oppressive masculinism in the visual arts. Like Gilbert and Gubar, Pollock worries about the consequences for creative women's sense of their own "possibilities and ambitions" and "how women can speak/represent within a culture which defines the feminine as silenced other." Pollock is especially attentive to the female as a visual sign of the masculine genius, the "passive, beautiful or erotic object of creativity."[4] A similar concern with the female as aesthetic object has led Laura Mulvey to a broad critique of "the manipulation of visual pleasure." Borrowing Freud's identification of scopophilia as "one of the component instincts of sexuality," one that mediates the masculine fear of castration through representations of the female, Mulvey concludes that "in a world ordered by sexual imbalance, pleasure in looking has been split between active/male and passive/female" roles.[5] The gendering of spectatorship *per se* has provided another basis for objecting to the "The Lady of Shalott": the poem ends with the Lady's transformation into a fetishized icon serving only to soothe unconscious masculine anxiety. Thus Deborah Cherry disapproves of Rossetti's drawing of Lancelot scrutinizing the dead Lady of Shalott because "the sensuous curves of the constructed feminine body, the fairness of the feminine face are presented for the pleasure of the masculine gaze." And Carl Plasa, writing about the very stanza that Rossetti illustrates, regrets its "reactionary orientation": "Though Lancelot reflects 'a little space,'" he goes on "to re-articulate, with 'she has a lovely face,' the orthodox perception of women as the object of the 'masculine' gaze."[6]

These critiques, the best of them powerful, have two features in common: resistance to representations of gender imbalance and a hypothesis of their consequences, viz., the repression of potentially creative women who identify with the silenced and viewed females of traditional art. Moreover, in working to discredit the hierarchical structure of sexual difference, these critics tend to subscribe to the binary opposition that sets the observing male against the exhibited female, his articulate speculativeness against her silent physicality, and his dominance against her subordination.

But resentment of the "reactionary orientation" or of "the sadistic-aggressive impulses underlying" certain representations of women may not tell the whole story and may underestimate the complexity of gendered responses to particular works of art. In a comprehensive study of the most flagrantly misogynistic of spectatorial genres, the hard core film, Linda Williams discovers repeatedly that viewers—whether male or female—engage in bisexual identification with the principals of any given scenario. And when she retraces the theoretical steps whereby Mulvey accounts for the gendered split in the structure of visual pleasure, she returns to Freud's analysis of scopophilia. Unlike Mulvey, she finds his analysis faulty: Freud is guilty of accepting at face value his culture's negative evaluation of the female body. This leads to the error of reinscribing as a psychoanalytic "reality" a fear of female lack that is culturally constructed. Having thus undermined the easy dichotomy between active/male and passive/female roles, Williams concludes that visual pleasure is a matter of identifying "alternately or simultaneously" with and across one's own gender.[7]

The value of Williams's commentary on a liminal genre lies, for our argument, in its joining of literary critical insight with what might be called plain common sense; viz., the realization that imaginative sympathy is not dependent on the biological sameness of the reader/viewer and the represented figure. To be sure, most aesthetic genres would prove hopelessly unpleasurable if this were the case. Where gender is concerned, it is manifestly true, as Myra Jehlen has noted with particular explicitness, that many a male author "has represented at least part of himself as female." In particular, as Gerhard Joseph long ago demonstrated, Tennyson's early poetic identifications are with female figures. Tennyson takes the story of the Lady of Shalott, and in a certain sense her gender, as his own. It is only with his 1842 volume that he no longer primarily "projects himself" into "female protagonists."[8] Jehlen attributes women's cross-gendered "metaphorical potential" to the social circumstances that leave both women and writers alienated from public life (211). In a very different but compatible analysis, Barbara Johnson locates the symbolic affinity of female and author in the alienation that is constitutive of language *per se*. The "denial of female interiority and subjectivity and the transformation of the woman's body into an art object" is powerfully symbolic of every artist's loss of "autonomy and intentionality" in the work itself. Johnson sums up her argument with the striking assertion that the representation of a female as "objectified and denied interiority is not in itself a function of her gender" (275).

Criticism is often well served by the kind of literalism that looks freshly at generic distortions that have become "conventional," but certain of the analyses we have cited are weakened by bluntly "realist" assumptions that arguments like those of Williams, Jehlen, and Johnson will help us to complicate. First of all, some of these discussions seem to assume that "looking at a woman" across a room is an exact analogue for reading about a woman. They posit a rigidly coherent and gendered self whose response to art is determined entirely by its biological sex. We will operate on the rather different assumption that named characters in poems are often hardly characters, much less people, and that the viewing of a "real" visual object and the reception of a poem's word-image are substantially different. At the same time, following feminist theorists who have seen the collapse of the male/female opposition as a valuable theoretical move, we will suggest possibilities for reading that allow cross-gendered identifications, and propose a notion of "gaze" that includes, as if by reflection, the anxiety of being looked at.

THE POETRY OF SENSATION: CHARACTERS AND ABSENCES

In a review of the 1830 *Poems, Chiefly Lyrical,* Tennyson's closest friend Arthur Hallam linked him with Keats who, ten years dead and out of print, was at last finding readers in Oxford and Cambridge circles:

> They are both poets of sensation rather than reflection. Susceptible of the slightest impulse from external nature, their fine organs trembled into emotion at colours, and sounds, and movements, unperceived or unregarded by duller temperaments . . . they lived in a world of images.[9]

Hallam's essay downgrades the reflective, philosophically explicit, and recurrently didactic poetry of "What oft was thought but ne'er so well expressed," recommending instead, "sensation," emotion, and the inexplicitness of the image. These, surely, had been deployed, though perhaps not quite with a Keatsian or Tennysonian density, in earlier ages. But they will now be the hallmarks of a poetry that, haunted by emotions and images, will yearn, whether powerfully or mawkishly, against language's borders with the sensuous and the unparaphrasable.

That is, the heightened receptivity Hallam praises is subject to excesses and strains that his own somewhat tremulous adulation mirrors, and it was bound to draw scorn from readers who withheld the empathy it so longingly solicits. Their recoil could be startling in its crudity. J.W. Croker, one of the notorious "snuffers-out" of Keats, was still around in 1833 to condescend to Tennyson as the latest star, or suckling, in the *"milky way* of poetry of which the lamented Keats was the harbinger" (Jump 66) and his sneer is neither isolated nor entirely irrelevant. Readers more intelligent and much more admiring than Croker have sensed in the swooning sensitivity of Keats and Tennyson—and Hallam—something they wanted to call feminine or effeminate, child-like or childish, hyperesthetic or morbid. Hazlitt's diagnosis—"effeminacy of style, in some degree corresponding to effeminacy of character"—is a typical version of the "worries about the feminization of men" that Susan Wolfson tracks so insightfully through the nineteenth-century response to Keats. A parallel case could be constructed for Tennyson. "School-miss Alfred," Edward Bulwer-Lytton gibed, and another critic dismissed him as "pretty-pretty, full of womanly talk and feminine stuff" (Jump 12). "Feminine stuff," indeed, for the two poets share not only an aesthetic of heightened receptivity and a "world of images" but a predilection for imaging their own receptivity and inexplicitness in terms of women. "To a degree unmatched by other male Romantic poets," Wolfson says, "Keats tends to represent ecstatic or visionary experience as an erotic encounter with a female or feminized figure," and the early Tennyson was alternately adored and deplored for his fairies and mermaids, Marions and Marianas, Lilians and Elaines. Like Swinburne, author of the reviled "Hermaphroditus," like that "intellectual hermaphrodite" Rossetti ("He is the Blessed Damozel . . . he is Lilith . . . in petticoats or pantaloons"), Keats and Tennyson are experienced by some anxious readers as veritable pools of Salmacis. Moreover, this is how they come to experience themselves, for they sense, perhaps mostly unconsciously, that the enabling sensibility of their art is something their culture knows as "feminine."[10]

But let us begin with a poem that, at least in summary, seems a ready-made example of "manly" art, a poem that seems to endow its hero with the masculine privilege of the gaze. Keats's "The Eve of St. Agnes" was beloved of Victorian painters and poets who were reading and illustrating Tennyson and Malory, and it is hard to think of a more erotic canonical poem. Madeline is preparing for bed on St. Agnes Eve when, according to legend, "Young virgins may have visions of delight / And soft adorings from their loves receive" (47–48).[11] Porphyro sneaks into the castle of his enemies "That he might gaze and worship all unseen" (80), secretes himself in Madeline's chamber, and watches her undress and dream. As is apparent even from this outline, any interpretive case carried into this maiden chamber will have to make room for the voyeuristic thrill of invisibility. Madeline will be the blank slate that fantasy overwrites. Porphyro's gaze will be invasive and riskless. Resolving not to assume automatically that what happens in a poem is like "reality," let us "gaze" with Porphyro:

> And still she slept an azure-lidded sleep,
> In blanched linen, smooth, and lavender'd,
> While he from forth the closet brought a heap
> Of candied apple, quince, and plum, and gourd;
> With jellies soother than the creamy curd,
> And lucent syrops, tinct with cinnamon . . . (262–67)

"Half-anguished," unable to embody his desire, Porphyro engages in the kind of imagistic indirection fundamental to the poetry of sensation: he sets a table. The slide from erotic Madeline to exotic food is not merely local. Throughout this poem, the erotic and the more generally sensuous, mutually displaced, are difficult to distinguish at all. When, in the next stanza, Porphyro fills "baskets bright" with "glowing hand," his hand takes on their silver and the baskets are flushed with desire. Yearning is everywhere and nowhere for everything and nothing, and the viewing of Madeline is only a temporary organization of oceanic desire and pervasive ghostliness, intensity and absence, into the single "perspective" of Porphyro's "gaze." "Perspective" is, of course, a construct both depending on and supporting exactly the notion of self that is unstable in Keats and Tennyson: a "gaze" presupposes a self located at a single point that watches, at some distance, something located securely outside the mind. But these distinctions dissolve in "Ode to a Nightingale," which begins its climactic phase with "I cannot *see*" and then begins mixing senses with the effect of "spreading" and confusing perspectives and objects.

The same thing happens at Madeline's bedside. "Lavender'd" means scented with lavender, but it flickers through the mind as a *color* that bleeds, partially through consonance, to the "blanched linen," and that associates itself with the faint "azure" of Madeline's lids, especially since "azure-lidded" and "lavender'd" are re-blendings of conspicuously similar sounds. "Smooth" will wander in the mind from the sheets to Madeline, to the oral viscosity of the lines themselves, and "soother" confuses "soothing" with the already-heard "smooth." Blendings and blurrings proliferate. Keats foregrounds—indeed he narrates—the play of the signifier. Words are, as the passage puts it, "tinct" by each other. Are there any distinct "objects" here, is there any woman separate from the background? There are words, Keats's synesthesia says, and once inside us (which is the only place they are), they blur and change and reflect each other, creating meanings so rich and disorganized that it makes no sense to imagine ourselves somehow separate from them and watching "what they describe" through some kind of window. Both ends of the gaze, not to mention what comes between them, are destabilized.

Anticipating "objection" to the poem, Keats himself admitted that "in my dramatic capacity I enter fully into the feeling: but in Propria Persona I should be apt to quiz it myself."[12] Most readers of this romance episode, if not exactly compelled to dial 911, will remain realists enough to feel some uneasiness about Porphyro's scheme, which the poem seems to excuse on the intersubjective grounds that Madeline is also "looking at"—dreaming of—him. Porphyro and Madeline see not each other but a fantastic dream of love. Like the Lady of Shalott's, their desire is in this way objectless, and both poems in their early stages defend their yearning imaginations against the limitation that any particularization of their objects would bring.

It is this parallelism and complicity of the dissolved or unspecified object with a dissolved or unspecified viewer that we wish to examine. Wolfson, for example, notes that Keatsian texts showing "women subject to the male gaze frequently involve figures of male *vulnerability*" (326; italics added). Here we need to return briefly to the difference between real sights and verbal images. If you see a body in "real life" (or even in a painting), you see one. If a poet *instructs you* (or himself) to see one, memory or something like it *supplies* what cannot be before the eyes. This second-hand image is fainter than the present and as blurry and unstable as memory: it cannot be held, stared at; it feels half-there, already lost. Yeats saw this half-absence historically as endemic to the poetry of sensation. "When the tide of life sinks low there are pictures, as in the *Ode on a Grecian Urn*," he says, developing what sounds like the post-structuralist notion that representation is absence with "the pictures make us sorrowful. We share the poet's separation from what he describes." The imagery of the poetry of sensation, that is, simultaneously strains for intensity and accuses itself of lost immediacy, secondariness, and irremediable ghostliness. "It is life in the mirror . . . ," [13] Yeats concludes, completing the transit from Keats's urn to Tennyson's Lady of Shalott. Keats loves Madeline's vagueness because he loves his own half-absence and inexplicitness, but she also becomes a figure for the unavoidable secondariness of any verbal/mental image and of the self itself. Tennyson's version of this Romantic insight, *his* "image of the Image" is the Lady of Shalott's mirror. In it, she sees "Shadows of the world" (58) that she must weave into her poem/ tapestry. "Life in the mirror" is neither presence nor absence, neither life nor death: she finds reflected both "two young lovers lately wed" and a "funeral" and reaches the halfway mark of the poem half-concluding "I am half sick of shadows" (71).

When the world stares *back*, however, everything changes. The fantasist, infinite and vague, is reduced to one particular person seen by another. Both "The Eve of St. Agnes" and "The Lady of Shalott" are stories of a gazer exposed to this narrowing and metaphorically fatal return of the gaze. They are part of a tradition of poems of embowered yearning that runs from Keats through Tennyson to the Rossettis, Morris, Swinburne, the Aesthetes, and the early Yeats in which the Romantic autonomy of the imagination is problematized, its reality questioned.[14] "Do I wake or sleep?" cries Keats in "Ode to a Nightingale"—and fantasy can be asserted only within the charmed circle that a poem holds open and whose collapse is nervously anticipated. "If ye sing not, if ye make false measure, / We shall lose eternal pleasure" (I, 463) Tennyson's Hesperides chant.

At the *beginning* of "The Lady of Shalott," the Lady occupies the ostensibly "male" position—she is more like Porphyro than Madeline, much more gazer than gazed-upon. Concealed in her tower, she watches the reflections of the passing world in her mirror. Tennyson specifically withholds her from the gaze of the world "But who hath seen her wave her hand? / Or at the casement seen her stand?" (23–24), and he cuts from the original published version of the poem the two lines—"She leaneth on a velvet bed / Full royally apparelled"—that give the *reader* the clearest view. The 1842 version hides the Lady until her exposure, like Porphyro's, can signal the collapse of her world apart. Like him, she begins as an unseen watcher. Like his, her isolation is both her power and her failure: it protects a unified, all-possible, and in a sense immortal self that is unnarrowed by a definite life, unlimited by exchange with others. Like Porphyro, the Lady of Shalott is a yearning imagination whose transition "from the region of shadows into that of realities" (as Tennyson himself put it[15]), is both desired and dreaded.

Perhaps, in psychologizing at such length, we have seemed to assume the distinctness and "reality" of the "characters" of these poems. Approaching the poetry of sensation from his own direction, Browning once griped about Tennyson's "Pelleas and Ettarre," "I should judge the conflict in the knight's soul the proper subject to describe: Tennyson thinks he should describe the castle, and the effect of the moon on its towers, and anything *but* the soul."[16] The complaint suggests a critical caution. "The Eve of St. Agnes" and "The Lady of Shalott," like many poems in their tradition, are more landscape or background than they are "soul." We must recall that the method of the poetry of sensation blurs figures with their background and even with each other. "The Lady of Shalott," in fact, opens with thirty-five lines of a landscape:

> Willows whiten, aspens quiver,
> Little breezes dusk and shiver
> Through the wave that runs forever
> By the island in the river . . . (10–14)

Tennyson is remembering how windstruck willows turn up the paler undersides of their narrow leaves, how aspens quake even on windless days, how little gusts darken their paths along the water, but his precision is in the service of dissolution. All glimmer and flow, this is the soft focus landscape in which the Tennysonian self typically unfocuses. It is his version of Keatsian half-absence.

There is no character here, but there are emotions, inexplicit, fleeting, mixed. The falling dipodic rhythm, formulaic and relentlessly rhymed, translates as compelling, compelled, even nervous? The landscape certainly seems to be: in the whitening of the willows there are suggestions of snow or shock or instant aging, and "whiten," "quiver," and "shiver" all have undertones of fear. A poem's emotions come from all directions, and their assembly in the mind washes over the tenuous boundaries between characters and between characters and background: there is no way to know who sees this landscape. Only later do we understand that we have already begun to feel the Lady's blended dread and desire, and to live her diaphanous "life in the mirror."

SWAN SONGS: POETIC SWOON AND THE EXPOSURE OF THE GAZE

Fluidity of self and spreading of identification are simultaneously presuppositions and aspirations of nineteenth-century poetry, and Keats is their theorist: "When I am in a room with People . . . the identity of everyone in the room begins to to [sic] press upon me that, I am in a very little time an[ni]hilated," he says in a famous letter illustrating his hyper-receptivity, and it is difficult—and not just in this letter—to distinguish that receptivity from imaginative projection: "The camelion Poet" he insists and re-insists, "has no Identity—he is continually in for—and filling some other Body." The poet is "everything and nothing" and "has as much delight in conceiving an Iago as an Imogen."[17]

The dissolution of poetic (and readerly) identity is experienced continuously in the swarming emotions and blurring perspectives of Keats and Tennyson, but its nature and consequences are perhaps clearest when it rises into the *narration* as a "poetic death," as it does in "Ode to a Nightingale" or "The Lady of Shalott." In his great ode, the heartbroken Keats's desire to *be* the heartbreaking song of the nightingale depends on his ability to "fade far away, dissolve, and quite forget" the self-consciousness which the nightingale has "never known." He aspires to pure reception, which he imagines as a kind of erotic death, a ravishment by sensation: "Now more than ever seems it *rich* to die."

This surely is a perfect example of the surrender of the will in a straining after luxurious intensity that Hazlitt gendered as feminine, and that readers have found distasteful or threatening—and not just our poor repressed ancestors. Anyone who has brought "Ode to a Nightingale" or "The Lotos-Eaters" into a classroom will have discovered that their blandishments are still considerably more troubling than Ulysses's exhortation, "To strive, to seek, to find, and not to yield," whether from their readers' over- or underestimation of the virtue of willpower we do not presume to guess. Keats, to return to the *Ode, is* yearning to be subject not just to his senses but to a *song*, and to his *own* song. He wants the poem to come so strongly and effortlessly, with such a "full-throated ease" and fade and flow that he seems to read it or hear it. He pulls back from this metaphorical death, from this pure subjection, when he remembers that the vanishing point he has imagined is an insentience— "to thy high requiem become a sod"—disabled even from hearing the song, much less "writing" it. To "write" is inevitably to divide into a person who writes and a person who reads (and so is to "read"). In asking to be delivered from this self-division, Keats imagines a "poetic death" that dissolves the distinction between actor and acted-upon, power and powerlessness.

Here, again, the poetry of sensation revises the rigid binary of "active" and "passive." What Keats and Tennyson see in female surrogates is their own dissolution, the swooning receptivity that is the very process of their poetry of sensation. They participate not only in looking but, simultaneously, in the exposure of being looked at. A curiously literal example is Tennyson's "The Merman." This early poem involves kissing a lot of mermaids under water and its dismissal by reviewer "Christopher North" (John Wilson) as "distinguished silliness" is as accurate as we could hope to be. But Wilson continues in a gruffly embarrassed aside "we humbly presume . . . he ["Alfred"] is all the while stark-naked under the sea" (Jump 54–55). This hint about self-exposure illuminates not just this poem but the free-floating and ambiguous sexuality of Tennyson's early work as a whole. The gaze imagines the gaze back. The ravished voyeur is the ravishing exhibitionist, a scenario and a feeling delayed only until the pendant on the following page. There, the young Tennyson is, as usual, more interesting, truer to himself, as a woman. He becomes "The Mer*maid*" and auto-, hetero-, and homo-erotic positions blur into one another:

> . . . that great sea-snake under the sea . . .
> Would slowly trail himself sevenfold
> Round the hall where I sate, and look in at the gate
> With his large calm eyes for the love of me.
> And all the mermen under the sea
> Would feel their immortality
> Die in their hearts for loving me. (I, 215)

One thinks of the four-way gaze of Rossetti's "How They Met Themselves," where a couple (who in the way of Rossetti couples look very much like each other to begin with) meet their doubles. But more to the point is the curious power of the mermaid over her audience, a power that radiates also from the poetic dying of the Lady of Shalott. The Lady lets go of her life and swoons downstream, "leaves upon her falling light." With this, the poet-swooner risks becoming pure reception, an object (Keats's "clod"), but her poetic dying is poetry itself. Doomed, slipping downriver, "The Dying Swan" of an even earlier Tennyson poem utters the swan song that ravishes "the soul / Of that waste place with joy / Hidden in sorrow." "Prevailing in weakness," the swan's dirge is "a carol free and bold . . . As when a mighty people rejoice" (I, 254). The Lady of Shalott, who is actually compared to a dying swan in the 1832 version (I, 394), is also "bold" in dying. She becomes a terrible prophet, looking "down the river's dim expanse / Like some bold seer in a trance," and as she flows towards Camelot, the amazed onlookers "crossed themselves for fear." The poetic dying that looks like passivity and "effeminacy" is revealed as the source of poetic authority.

But this final episode of "The Lady of Shalott" is more complex. When the murderous lover of Browning's "Porphyria's Lover" (is *his* name Porphyro?) opens Porphyria's dead eyes, he does so "warily" as if they were "a shut bud that holds a bee," lest the gazed-at gaze dangerously back. Both of our gazers, Porphyro and the Lady of Shalott, are quite literally exposed by the "return of gaze" that Browning's speaker fears and that Tennyson indulges in the merman/mermaid pair. In both "The Lady of Shalott" and "The Eve of St. Agnes" there is a "break" when the embowerment of consciousness collapses. Madeline wakes. Her gaze back literally astonishes: "he sank, pale as smooth-sculptured stone" (297). And it stings "How chang'd thou art! How pallid, chill, and drear!" (311) she says. For each of these lovers, the infinity of fantasy and desire collapses into one self, one life, one moment. Madeline, horrified, sees the mortal who is really there. For his part, Porphyro dies into the single, small (and naked) soul hearing "Wait, *you're* not my dream." It is not his dream either: it is a dreaded passage in the history of love's long morning-after somehow condensed to a glancing second in its night-before.

In the "Lady of Shalott," Tennyson lays out the emotional ambiguities of this moment of exposure as phases of a narrative. First the Lady sees in her mirror a sight so much sharper and more momentous—"The sun came dazzling through the leaves, / And flamed upon the brazen greaves / Of bold Sir Lancelot"—than any she has seen before in her dimly flickering and shimmering world that it almost seems to glare in, exposing her. She leaves her mirror and her web and looks out the forbidden window. The curse has fallen curse has fallen and, as in "The Eve of St. Agnes," it is both love and the limitation of identity. Like Porphyro she is seen, or she is split so that she sees herself. She experiences herself, at any rate, as an object, a mere name: "And round about the prow she wrote / *The Lady of Shalott.*" She embarks on that long, poetically powerful downriver swoon in which she herself, her death, and her song are indistinguishable: "Singing in her song she died."

When the Lady's corpse floats into Camelot, the revelers are awed into silence by her "rich" Keatsian death. Then in the strangely clipped and controversial ending (added in 1842), the Lady comes under Lancelot's gaze:

> But Lancelot mused a little space;
> He said, 'She has a lovely face;
> God in his mercy lend her grace,
> The Lady of Shalott.'

Here is the most conventional aspect of "the gaze:" the Lady is reduced to just another pretty face. More to the point is the more-than-poignant frustration of this ending: our amazement and consternation are the clearest sign that the Lady has served as the "entry" to the poem. Readers crash into four lines whose casual obliviousness leaves no place to put the turbulence carried from the previous one hundred seventy, and forcefully experience what the Lady of Shalott does: the irrelevance of their most loudly tempestuous emotions to the world just inches beyond the skull.

Like the end of "The Kraken," where a sea beast seems to die of being seen ("Then once by men and angels to be seen / In roaring he shall rise and on the surface die" [I, 270]), the Lady's arrival resounds with Tennyson's fears of aesthetic exposure and betrayal. This is often translated weakly as "dread of reviewers" or "fear of life in the real world," but the Lady's dangers are mortal individuality and misrecognition, offenses not against delicacy but against justice. A vastly possible life has become a silent and "lovely face"; it is now only what others make of it. As with the Lady, so with "The Lady of Shalott." No poet can die utterly into her poem. Even at the moment of greatest intensity, there is someone—an interior Lancelot—who watches, knowing that the poem is just a few still words trying to recall the cyclone of feeling. In the end, the Lady is uncomprehended, but that dreaded result, paradoxically, turns out to be what Tennyson's anxiety requires. Lancelot's look is fastened on a mere icon in a way that virtually celebrates Tennyson's own subjective absence from art. This sets a limit to exposure; her mute arrival says to the *external* Lancelots, "Gaze on this corpse, it is *not* the Lady of Shalott."

"Lancelot and Elaine" ends with a corpse, too, but also with a difference. In the much more worldly world of the *Idylls,* even innocence seems staged. Elaine, unlike the Lady of Shalott, elaborately imagines her entrance: Lancelot, she thinks in an echo of the Lady's poem, will "muse at me" (1048), and she carries a letter designed to control the response to her arrival and supplement the exhibition of her corpse. Embracing the illusion that "I shall speak for mine own self" (1264–74), she plays out what Bronfen, following Derrida, calls a naive hope for "good writing," the "desire for full and true presence" (144) in her icon and text. The futility of Elaine's effort is attributable not to writing's erasure of the expressive self (as in "The Lady of Shalott") but rather to the fact that public versions of her story are already under construction. The first of these has to do with guilt: though in "The Lady of Shalott" "nobody is to be blamed" for the Lady's death, in "Elaine" the ascription of blame is crucial to the *Idylls'* moral allegory of the fall of Arthur's kingdom. Second, Elaine has already become an object of jealousy and scandal because Gawaine has "buzzed abroad / About the maid of Astolat" (718–21). This thematic concern with gossip is authentically Malorian, but very different from Tennyson's early anxiety about aesthetic self-exposure: in "Lancelot and Elaine" we are encouraged not to inhabit characters as self-projections, but to see them from the outside, as we would in society, or even in the marketplace. If Tennyson has a single entry to *this* story it is Lancelot, not Elaine, and we see her importance this time mainly in the energy the poet invests in fending her off.[18]

Midway through "Lancelot and Elaine," Lancelot deflects Lavaine's hero-worship by pointing out Arthur:

> . . . in me there dwells
> No greatness, save it be some far-off touch
> Of greatness to know well that I am not great:
> There is the man. (447–50)

It is a conspicuously stirring moment in an idyll that has far too many flats. Said Tennyson, "When I wrote that, I was thinking of Wordsworth and myself" (Ricks I, 435n). The moment resounds not with the young poet's sense of all he might do, but with the fiftyish literary figure's realization that he has gone very far indeed, but not as far as he once dreamed. In his much-praised recent book on Tennyson, Herbert Tucker explains "My account of the career ends in 1855 because the career halts then" (190). William Morris agreed, both in the general assessment of decline and specifically as to the date. Carlyle would have substituted 1842, others 1850. Whether or not one finds a steep decline in Tennyson's later work, it is certain that by 1858, when he began the first version of "Lancelot and Elaine," he was leading a very different life from the poet who found himself in the Lady of Shalott in the early 1830s. The Tennyson of the *Idylls* was Poet Laureate, married with children, a commercial success, a tourist attraction, a friend of monarchs and defender of the realm, a worldlier and perhaps even a more "masculine" person. Stability does not preclude poetry, and Hippolyte Taine's 1860's condescension to Tennyson's poetry as "made expressly for . . . wealthy, cultivated, free business men . . . part of their luxury as of their morality" (Jump 273) is an exaggeration possible only to a reader who learned the career backwards from its public climax rather than followed it through its tortured uncertainties; but it is possible. Even before his marriage and institutionalization Tennyson had begun to cease throwing himself, dreading and desiring, into the gaps between words and passions, between soul and soul. He had ceased, for better or for worse, being a Tennysonian Romantic.

Reading "Lancelot and Elaine" as an allegory of Tennyson's poetic career is reductive but useful. Tennyson cannot be Arthur/Wordsworth (or Arthur Hallam, who was more often on his mind as a pattern for the King[19]), and though there were a good number of Victorians who would have allowed him to be considerably more than either, their overestimation is both thrilling and embarrassing, like a claim he has made for himself and wants to be excused from. "What profits me my name / Of greatest knight?" says Lancelot, "Pleasure to have it, none; to lose it, pain" (1402–04). And he *will* not be the Lady of Shalott, his earlier Romantic self. The Elaine of the Idyll is infantilized: Tennyson defends himself against sympathy with the claims of the Romanticism she represents (and one of those claims is "sympathy" itself) by making her into a stage he has hopelessly outgrown. Far from an erotic object, she is hovering, oppressive, scanning Lancelot's face for signs of the love he cannot feel for her. She "lived in fantasy" (396) and, in a parody of her predecessor's world-weaving, she makes a case for Lancelot's adored shield that duplicates its design. She is enraptured by an image in both the traditional and modern senses of the word. She is, in an odd way, a fan.

Far from a tantalizing half-absence, Elaine is the overknown, and she symbolizes to Lancelot the dangers of *being* overknown—commodified, taken for an image, i. e., "the Tennysonian," a term that had entered the language not very far into the century. In this idyll, misrecognition is constitutive and paradoxical. There would be no story without misreadings of behavior: Guinevere's, Arthur's, Gawaine's, Elaine's. And yet Lancelot enters a tournament with Sir Torre's unknown shield so that (or so Guinevere tells him to say) he can get a response to what he really is and does rather than to his "image." He can only be known by being misrecognized.

In this particular world of mirrors, that is, Lancelot has no anxiety of exposure. He has learned aesthetic detachment only too well, and there is no danger he will mistake his work, the diamonds hard won over nine years of tournaments, for himself. He does not care if they are misprized, feeling only "half disdain / At love, at life, all things . . ." when a jealous Guinevere tosses them out a window and they have "past away" in the stream flowing by the castle. In case we have missed their likeness to the Lady of Shalott, the next sentence glides the barge bearing the dead Elaine directly over the spot where the diamonds have "flashed" into the waters. Lancelot is leaning against the window, and though Elaine is passing "close underneath his eyes," there is no immediate response, not even the "musing" that she had predicted. Perhaps that is because it all happened so long ago, back in 1832. What is in the tableau is the impossibility of both his old innocence and of his new experience. Tennyson now looks out from a tower far more worldly but no less a trap than the one he looked out from decades before. And what we see is perhaps what the strange "break" at the end of the "Lady of Shalott" foresees but cannot bear to admit: that the Lady's greatest misreader was already, and necessarily, Tennyson himself.

NOTES

1. The Italian and Malorian sources are detailed in Christopher Ricks, ed., *The Poems of Tennyson*, 3 vols. (Berkeley: University of California Press, 1987), I, 387; III, 261–62. Tennyson cited from this edition, hereinafter Ricks. Muriel Whitaker, *The Legends of King Arthur in Art* (Cambridge: Brewer, 1990), pp. 217–18.

2. Elisabeth Bronfen, *Over Her Dead Body: Death, Femininity and the Aesthetic* (New York: Routledge, 1992). For Rossetti, see Constance W. Hassett, "Christina Rossetti and the Poetry of Reticence," *Philological Quarterly*, 65 (1987), esp. 499–500. For Browning, see U.C. Knoepflmacher, "Projection and the Female Other: Romanticism, Browning and the Victorian Dramatic Monologue," *Victorian Poetry*, 22 (1984), 139–59.

3. "The Philosophy of Composition," *Essays and Reviews* (New York: Literary Classics of the United States, 1984), p. 19. Barbara Johnson, "*Les Fleurs du mal armé*: Some Reflections on Intertextuality," in *Lyric Poetry: Beyond New Criticism*, ed. Chaviva Hosek and Patricia Parker (Ithaca: Cornell University Press, 1985), pp. 273–74. Sandra Gilbert and Susan Gubar, *The Madwoman in the Attic: The Woman Writer and the Nineteenth-Century Literary Imagination* (New Haven: Yale University Press, 1979), pp. 34, 29–30, 43, 34.

4. Griselda Pollock, *Vision and Difference: Femininity, Feminism and the Histories of Art* (London: Routledge, 1988), pp. 10, 15, 91.

5. Laura Mulvey, "Visual Pleasure and Narrative Cinema," in *Visual and Other Pleasures* (Bloomington: Indiana University Press, 1989), pp. 59, 62.

6. Cherry, item 198, *The Pre-Raphaelites*, exhibition catalogue (London: Tate Gallery, 1984), p. 266. Plasa, "'Cracked from Side to Side': Sexual Politics in 'The Lady of Shalott,'" *Victorian Poetry*, 30 (1992), pp. 260, 259.

7. Bram Dijkstra, *Idols of Perversity: Fantasies of Feminine Evil in Fin-de-Siècle Culture* (New York: Oxford, 1986), p. 42. Linda Williams, *Hard Core: Power, Pleasure, and the "Frenzy of the Visible"* (Berkeley: University of California Press, 1989), p. 215. For an astutely Lacanian analysis of the way "fashion photography scopophilically poses its [female] models" for female spectatorial pleasure, see Diana Fuss, "Fashion and the Homospectatorial Look," *Critical Inquiry* 18 (1992), pp. 713–37.

8. Myra Jehlen, "Archimedes and the Paradox of Feminist Criticism," in *Feminist Theory: A Critique of Ideology,* ed. Nannerl O. Keohane, et al. (Chicago: University of Chicago Press, 1982), p. 211. Gerhard Joseph, *Tennysonian Love: The Strange Diagonal* (Minneapolis: University of Minnesota Press, 1969), p. 72.

9. Unsigned review reprinted in John D. Jump, ed., *Tennyson: The Critical Heritage* (New York: Barnes and Noble, 1967), p. 36. Hereinafter Jump.

10. Susan J. Wolfson, "Feminizing Keats," in *Critical Essays on John Keats,* ed. Hermione D'Almeida (Boston: Hall, 1990) 317, 318, 325. Robert Buchanan, "The Fleshly School of Poetry: Mr. D.G. Rossetti," in *Victorian Poetry and Poetics,* ed. Walter E. Houghton and G. Robert Stange, 2nd ed. (Boston: Houghton Mifflin, 1968), p. 891.

11. John Keats, *Complete Poems,* ed. Jack Stillinger (Cambridge, Mass.: Harvard University Press, 1982). All references to this edition.

12. To Richard Woodhouse, 21, 22 September 1819. *The Letters of John Keats,* ed. Hyder Edward Rollins, 2 vols. (Cambridge: Harvard University Press, 1958).

13. W.B. Yeats, *Explorations* (New York: Macmillan, 1973), p. 163.

14. See, for example, James Richardson, *Vanishing Lives: Style and Self in Tennyson, D.G. Rossetti, Swinburne, and Yeats* (Charlottesville: University of Virginia Press, 1988).

15. Hallam Lord Tennyson, *Alfred Lord Tennyson: A Memoir by His Son,* 2 vols. (New York: Macmillan, 1897) I, 117.

16. *Dearest Isa: Robert Browning's Letters to Isabella Blagden,* ed. Edward C. McAleer (Austin: University of Texas Press, 1951), p. 328.

17. To Richard Woodhouse, 27 October 1818.

18. Herbert F. Tucker, *Tennyson and the Doom of Romanticism* (Cambridge: Harvard University Press, 1992), p. 116.

19. For a more intimate account of Tennyson's identifications with the figures of the *Idylls,* see Cecil Y. Lang, "Tennyson's Arthurian Psycho-Drama," Tennyson Society Occasional Paper Number 5 (Lincoln: The Tennyson Society/Tennyson Research Centre, 1983).

REVISIONARY TALES

GUENEVERE AND MORGAN
IN THE TWENTIETH CENTURY

THE FIGURE OF GUENEVERE
IN MODERN DRAMA AND FICTION

Elisabeth Brewer

Both in medieval and in modern fiction, the figure of Guenevere personifies the feminine ideal, and in so doing indicates our changing attitudes to women and to sexual morality. In the last hundred years in particular, her character has undergone many changes, some of them startling. In 1895, a dramatic version of the Arthurian story[1] was put on in London by the famous Victorian actor and producer Henry Irving, specially written for him by his friend J. Comyns Carr. With sets and costumes designed by the Pre-Raphaelite artist Burne-Jones, music by the composer Arthur Sullivan, and Ellen Terry starring as Guenevere, the show—it must have been almost a musical, and quite spectacular at that—was an instant success. The play seems to have started a fashion for Arthurian drama: in the next ten to fifteen years, many plays based on the Arthurian legend were put on in little London theatres, and at least three centred specifically on Guenevere.

William Morris once remarked that the best way to deal with old stories was to close the book and retell them as new stories for yourself, and the late nineteenth-century dramatists who took the story of Guenevere as the basis of their plots certainly did that. The "most noble Christian queen" of Malory's *Morte Darthur* now becomes the weak little woman of nineteenth-century convention. Guinevere herself talks of the weakness of women in Comyns Carr's play, and we later see her swoon in Morgan's arms from fear that Lancelot's love for her has been revealed. (She swoons in Malory, too, of course, but from excessive weeping or depth of feeling, as when Lancelot comes to see her for the last time.) Our late Victorian Guinevere, however, begins a love-scene with the confession: "Not brave am I, but blest

---

Reprinted from *Arturus Rex: Acta Conventus Lovaniensis*. 1987. Mediaevalia Lovaniensia series I/Studia XVII. Vol. 2. Eds. Willy Van Hoecke, Gilbert Tournoy, Werner Verbeke (Leuven: University Press, 1991), pp. 479–90.

in my great need, / On thee to lean, and unto thee to yield / My love, myself, and my fond helplessness." She is represented as so clinging that Lancelot has actually to shake her off, saying "Let me go!" when Mordred attacks. "O, for my sake take care!," she quavers; later sending a message to Arthur, "tell him that I cling / To one more noble."[2]

Guenevere as the little woman draws attention to the wish-fulfillment fantasy in these plays. The macho image of the male in his gleaming armour (Henry Irving as Arthur had a striking suit of black plate-armour) contrasts with the yielding helplessness of the Queen, overcome by the emotions that she cannot control. Her relationship with Lancelot is all tenderness and faith: there are no attempts to present her as jealous, spiteful and demanding as she often is in Malory. But where Malory disclaims knowledge of what Lancelot and Guenevere are doing when they are alone together, these playwrights often show delicately explicit love-scenes: "One kiss, the last! O God, the very last," Guenevere murmurs.[3] "Yes, even when I sit here by his side . . . I cannot stop the heaving of my breast." "When you are by my side the darkest place / Is radiant."[4]

The glamorisation of adulterous passion as represented in these Guenevere plays suggests the much more liberal attitude to illicit sexual relationships at the end of the nineteenth century. There are hints, too, that Arthur is perhaps to be regarded as sexually inadequate, and that a wife is entitled to more than he is able to give: "Lips in his creed were only made for prayers / And bodies for anointing," the queen complains. She must "live estranged from love / And yearn in vain for those small tenderings / That, costing nothing, are beyond all worth / In 'complishing a woman's happiness."[5] Arthur—perhaps rather surprisingly—agrees, on being charged by Guenevere with neglect, that their love lacks "full expression."[6] He has been too busy; they must both put England first, he insists. In another play,[7] when Arthur is brought home dying, Guenevere amongst the nuns claims: "I've thought and prayed / For him who did not know / One half the streams that flow / Thro' every woman's dream." And later these nuns, instead of being shocked at the disgraceful moral lapse of their queen, chorus "Oh Knights! This was your Queen / Whose beauty is forgiven," thus displaying a much more lenient attitude than Tennyson had done in his Idyll, *Guinevere*, in 1859. Nothing is said about guilt. The more tolerant light in which Guenevere's infidelity to Arthur is viewed can surely be related to the pioneering work in methods of birth-control and the psychology of sexual relationships being carried on by progressives such as Marie Stopes and Havelock Ellis, work which was contributing in practical ways to a radical change of attitude.

Nevertheless, romance predominates, and the love-death motif so strongly emphasised by Wagner in *Tristram and Isolde* also creeps into the Lancelot and Guenevere story to heighten its emotional impact. "Oh that we two, we two together now . . . Might put to see on life's receding tide," says Lancelot as he catches Guenevere to his breast.[8] "Together we go forth into the night . . . In life, / In death, we are together still," Guenevere says to the dying Lancelot at the end of this play when, with Arthur already dead, she clasps her lover in her arms, before falling lifeless upon his body in the last scene.

These plays further draw our attention to the decay of faith, as well as to changes in moral attitudes between the mid-century when Tennyson wrote, and its final decades. Secular attitudes prevail, even though Guenevere often still retreats to a nunnery. In Morley Steynor's *Lancelot and Guenevere*, Lancelot intercepts her on her way to take refuge in the convent, bursting from some bushes and declaring that their vows are "all the more sacred and binding since / No law save Love's own law had sanctioned them."[9] To such an extent is passion, even in an illicit relationship, regarded as uncontrollable and indeed self-justified, that although Morgan le Fay in Ernest Rhys's *Gwenevere* states that the queen's unfaithfulness had "broken the king," she is, again, never even reproached.

In all these plays, the story of the last days of the Round Table is scaled down and domesticated: the larger perspective of Malory and indeed Tennyson is missing, despite the characters' frequent assertion of the need to put England first. Guenevere's emotions dominate these dramas, and from the dignified but guilty Victorian matron of the *Idylls*, she now, as the feminine ideal changes, gradually becomes a more girlish, even elfin figure, "lonely as a child," roaming "loveless through Arthur's halls."[10] We are called upon to sympathise with her plight, rather than to disapprove. But though the subject of these plays is Guenevere's situation and predicament, there is very little psychological realism, as Bernard Shaw was quick to point out in reviewing Comyns Carr's *King Arthur*.[11] Guenevere has become the white ghost of the character set before us by Malory. Her internal struggle with temptation is presented in the sketchiest terms, and similarly we see nothing of the working of Lancelot's mind.

In Tennyson's Guinevere we see a mature woman, whose faithlessness and deception of Arthur over many years is therefore the more reprehensible. But in Morley Steynor's play Guenevere first appears as a beautiful young girl of seventeen, and she and Lancelot (who is only a year older) still behave like young lovers even when many years are supposed to have passed. Their love has a virginal quality, embodying the romantic dreams of the era. Similarly, Ernest Rhys presents his Guenevere as a wild, simple maiden when she arrives at Camelot riding on a palfrey, accompanied by Merlin. Indeed, Morgan le Fay is prompted to exclaim on seeing her "This is no queen!" Later Guenevere herself declares "I'm tired of being queen," like a peevish child. The image is still more romanticised in Graham Hill's tragedy, where she is first seen as "A fair white maid with streaming hair of gold . . . / A gleaming amber torrent to her feet. / She seemed like sunlight glinting from a rock / And where she walked the sombre earth was sewn / With a lithemoving skein of gold."[12] The gleaming amber torrent of her hair conjures up a Pre-Raphaelite image, but she is no mere re-incarnation of the temptress whom Dante Gabriel Rossetti was painting some decades before. Rather, she gives expression to that yearning for a return to a pre-industrial pastoral society which had been described in William Morris's *A Dream of John Ball*[13] and *News from Nowhere*,[14] as well as in his last romances. The lovers can thus be seen to be acting in accordance with the precepts of Edward Carpenter, lecturer, writer, and Socialist, who was a pioneer of the "free love" movement. In his book *Love's Coming of Age*,[15] he complained that "sexual embraces seldom receive the benison of Dame Nature, in whose presence alone, under the burning sun or the high canopy of the stars and surrounded by the fragrant atmosphere, their meaning can be fully understood: but take place in stuffy dens of dirty upholstery and are associated with all unbeautiful things." In the same year as his book was published, Helen and Edward Thomas (the poet) became lovers in a secret glade on Wimbledon Common, as Helen records in her book *As It Was*.[16] So, not for Lancelot the problem of iron window-bars firmly embedded in castle walls. The sighing wind enhances the wistful melancholy and adds a touch of nature-mysticism to these romantic outdoor encounters.

The shared dream of regaining the unspoilt natural world of course pervades the work of very many other contemporary writers in the early twentieth century. Robert Louis Stevenson expresses this new pastoralism in his once-popular poem, "I will make you brooches and toys for your delight / Of birdsong at morning and starshine at night."[17] In Graham Hill's play, Guinevere claims that she "draws her being from the lowly earth." She is "caught by every breath of life and swayed / As leaves are lift and rustled by the breeze."[18] Elsewhere, in her own words, she is "Not a queen, but a kind of dreamer / Pleased with green leaves" whose association with the natural world is further emphasised as she thinks of the home that she has left to become Arthur's bride. "The green leaves every afternoon / At home will be left wondering / Where I am, who used to sing / Against the blackbird there, and play / The leafy afternoons away."[19] The main function of the natural imagery associated with Guenevere, of course, is to increase the sense of pure, natural, elemental passion.

The mood is continued in the early 1920s, in Chester Keith's *Queen's Knight*. Guenevere is portrayed as a rogueish, wilful girl, given to wandering in the fields and hunting in the forest, looking like "some embodiment of Spring."[20] Keith updates the forest bower of Gottfried's Tristram, as did the earlier twentieth-century writers, in which passion runs riot more energetically than ever. Lancelot first meets Guenevere in a glade of the forest where he crushes her to him, "kissing her again and again till her lips were almost bruised with the adorable roughness that is Passion's crowning glory." Here, she enjoys the free forest life with almost childlike ecstasy, we are told, roaming on foot and crowning herself with flowers.[21]

So the Arthurian legend offered a perfect basis for wish-fulfillment fantasies about romantic love, against a vaguely medieval background enhanced by natural scenery. The image of Camelot with its noble knights of the Round Table still enabled writers to glamorise the battles and the hand-to-hand encounters which were felt to be the very stuff of chivalry. A strong vein of patriotism runs through the plays: Guenevere is England's Queen, and the potential glory and significance of this balances the wildwood nymph image also projected. But the dream of Camelot was, for many writers, to be shattered by the horrors of the First World War. The vision of chivalry faded, and the image of the Waste Land later came to dominate the imagination.

The twentieth-century writer most deeply interested in the figure of Guenevere is of course T.H. White, in *The Once and Future King*. His famous re-telling of the story is, like Tennyson's, firmly based on Malory's *Le Morte Darthur*. White endeavoured to depict Guenevere with the psychological realism of the modern novel, and indeed, was very successful for the most part in doing so—the portrait is on the whole a well-rounded and convincing one. White explores the complex relationship between the three main characters: Lancelot is at first jealous of Guenever, because he has to share Arthur with her, then attracted to her when he realises that, in a moment of exasperation, he has "hurt a real person."[22] Arthur perceives at once that Lancelot and Guenever are in love: from the beginning White sets out the complexity of the situation, and accounts for everything. Guenever is credited with the virtues of courage, generosity and honesty—and we soon see that she is a much more positive character than most early twentieth-century versions allowed her to be. She is also shown as being unable to comprehend Lancelot's more spiritual nature: "A bold and extroverted queen" is how White elsewhere sums her up, though he does also describe her later as looking like a woman who has grown a soul.[23]

Though in *The Once and Future King*, White allows Guenevere to remain "the romantic mistress of a nation," he frequently makes a point of showing her in an unflattering light. For Arthur and Lancelot she is just Jenny, and we see her stripped of dignity, creating ugly scenes when jealousy of Elaine gets the better of her—for example, "Guenever was stiff, as if she were in a rigor, and her face was drained white—except that there was a red spot on either side of her nostrils. She looked as if she had been seasick. She was alone. 'So,' shouted the Queen, moving her hand so that they could see a ball of handkerchief in it, which she had torn to pieces. 'Traitor! Traitor! Get out of my castle with your strumpet.'" Soon, as her anger increases in this scene, we are told that in her trembling, her hair has begun to come down. "She looked hideous."[24] We are allowed no illusions about the decorous homelife of royalty—Guenever, like the rest of us, is made of common clay.

Two years later—White emphasises that she is now forty-two—we see Guenever trying to regain Lancelot as her lover. She is overdressed; she has put on too much makeup, and put it on badly. But "Under the clumsy coquetry, the undignified clothes, there was the human cry for help. The young eyes were puzzled, saying: It is I, inside here—what have they done to me? I will not submit. Some part of her spirit knew that the powder was making a guy of her, and hated it, and tried to hold her lover with the eyes alone. Another part said: I am not old, it is illusion. I am beautifully made-up. See, I will perform the movements of youth. I will defy the enormous army of age."[25] Lancelot's continued rejection of her makes her petulant, cruel, contradictory, miserable. But as White explains, her tragedy is that she was childless; there was nothing for her to do. Unless she felt like a little spinning or embroidery, there was no occupation for her—except Lancelot. Her situation is thus very like that of some middle-aged, well-to-do women in the present century, living empty and frustrated lives. She becomes increasingly more neurotic, "growing madder every day,"[26] increasingly bitter because she has not been able to bear Arthur a son, and White remorselessly shows us how she is ageing. But since White takes realism so far, it is strange that in one respect he makes no attempt to explore the psychology of the Queen. We are never told of her emotions on the three occasions when she is threatened with death at the stake. From Malory, whose interests lie elsewhere than with the personality of the queen, it would be unreasonable to ask more, perhaps, than such terse statements as that "then the queen was led forth without Carlisle, and there she was despoiled into her smock."[27] The anatomy of love is the very stuff of romance, of course; the anatomy of fear would be inappropriate in such a mode, and so we are left to imagine for ourselves what her state of mind would have been.

Of recent decades, since historians turned their attention to the Dark Ages in their search for the Arthur of history, many writers have preferred a Romano-British setting for their retellings of Arthur's story. However, placing Guenevere in the world of the Dark Ages has not prevented writers from making her a thoroughly modern young woman at the same time, and it is interesting to see the image and the emphases that emerge from these more recent versions. As early as 1944, Edward Frankland's *The Bear of Britain* goes to rather extreme lengths in order to convey a sense of the crudity and barbarism of the period. The romantic reader will be amazed to find that Guenevere, in keeping with more modern attitudes towards sexual morality, is in some of these novels presented not merely as unfaithful, but as promiscuous or even as a former prostitute. It is a measure of the distance that we have come—is it progress or regress?—since Tennyson wrote his *Guinevere*. Many writers, however, do still manage to make her attractive, and it is clear that they mean her to embody a late twentieth-century ideal.

Godfrey Turton, in *The Emperor Arthur*,[28] presents the young Guinevere as beautiful and haughty, in a very down-to-earth manner, in a sixth-century setting. Guinevere deputises for Arthur at official functions like a member of the royal family at the present day; takes to her bed with headaches, and ages noticeably in the course of the novel—we are told that she "hasn't worn well." But Turton, unlike other retellers of the story, does confront Guinevere's predicament when she is brought to judgment, and attempts to give some indication in realistic terms of what her reaction might have been. He shows us the Queen, haggard but stately, dressed with impeccable elegance, and with her hair done in the Roman manner, facing her accusers with dignity. But when she hears her sentence, her screams ring dramatically through the church, and she shrieks, "No, no, you can't do that to me. I appeal to Caesar." Guinevere's accusers are fanatical monks, who are determined to punish her for her adultery, and one of them hoists her onto his back and carries her off to the fire which has already been made ready for her nearby. She is, of course, rescued in the nick of time.[29]

The description of the incident lacks subtlety, as can easily be seen, but it is unusual insofar as it does make an attempt to present the Queen with some psychological realism, even though the dialogue is trite, at a point in the narrative which other writers pass over.

Most recent retellings update the figure of Guenevere in terms of the images created by the modern media. In Catherine Christian's *The*

Pendragon,[30] Guenevere is first seen as a spirited horsewoman, a lithe and lively outdoor girl, riding a magnificent chestnut horse. The knights who are escorting her find it hard to keep up, because she rides like an Amazon. She has wonderful hair, of course—the description rather reminds one of the shampoo advertisements—"moon-gold, glinting hair—rippling down to her waist, little, soft curling tendrils blowing all about" her grave, intent face. She naturally also has a perfect figure.

The image of the athletic, healthy young woman, so familiar in the cinema and on the television screen, recurs again and again. In Victor Canning's *The Crimson Chalice*,[31] for example, Gwennifer, whose deep, dark blue eyes, fair hair and poppy-bright lips suggest feminity, is nevertheless dressed like a boy in short leather trews. She is known for her wildness, swears like a trooper, and is able to school a horse and ride as well as a man. More feminine, though also a keen horsewoman, is Mary Stewart's Guinevere in *The Last Enchantment*:[32] she is inclined to outride her escort and plunge about in marshes and forests, to the great anxiety of those who are responsible for her safety. In the same author's most recent Arthurian romance, *The Wicked Day*,[33] Guinevere has matured. Still lovely, she has gained in depth of character and understanding. Here we have the *Vogue* Guenevere, one might almost say the Laura Ashley Guenevere: we see her walking in the garden in a gown of soft dove-grey, with her two silver-white greyhounds, cutting fragrant branches of lilac, or sitting in her pretty rose-bower, doing a little embroidery. It creates a new, improved view of the Dark Ages. She is shown as at the same time the elusive vision of men's desires, the lovely consort of the king, a creature of gaiety and wealth and power and happiness, and as a lonely woman who has to live with fear.

These modern Gueneveres thus show how our images of the heroine and our expectations as to how she will behave have changed in the course of time. The authors are now much more explicit about, and make much more of sexual matters, and in this respect we can see that a new race of liberated young Gueneveres has sprung up in the last few decades. In Victor Canning's novel, Guenevere is so anxious to become pregnant that she takes a succession of lovers, ruthlessly having them killed if she thinks that they are likely to talk. It is all for Arthur's sake, however, and she remains in every respect a true wife to him. Fortunately, Arthur is understanding.

Recent authors also tend to be less reticent on the subject of Meliagaunt's carrying off of Guenevere when she went a-Maying, and to turn the episode into a case of rape with rather more graphic detail than is to be found in earlier re-tellings. Our modern anxieties about rape, perhaps, find indirect expression through these recent fictions.[34]

Finally, in the nineteen-eighties, Queen Guenevere seems to have become a superwoman, a successful executive and administrator whose role is not merely to attend state functions as a graceful consort, but to rule. In Gillian Bradshaw's *In Winter's Shadow*,[35] for example, Guenevere has to work hard, in partnership with Arthur, to keep the kingdom together. She would rather be a plain man's wife, she claims, than the empress that she is. Through labyrinths of plots and politics she has to grope her way in her struggle to outwit Mordred. She has clearly been an efficient organiser; and in addition to tending the sick, has also gone in for fund-raising for Arthur's campaigns.

For the Guenevere of the nineteen-eighties, however, it is not enough to be efficient as an administrator and stateswoman. The Arthurian superwoman must also have experienced pregnancy and childbirth. She cannot, of course, bear a son and heir to the throne without perverting the story, but authors such as Parke Godwin in *Firelord*[36] find ways of liberating her from the charge of sterility. In *Firelord*, she has a stillborn baby daughter early in the course of the novel, so that she has been a mother, at least technically. Her love for Lancelot was, it seems, the result of losing her baby. "I failed," she says pathetically to Arthur. "Failed how? You never failed in your life!" he replies reassuringly.[37] Even the experience of motherhood is seen in terms of a career. Parke Godwin returns repeatedly to the idea that Guenevere is a ruler: competence is everything to her. Arthur rules the north through her; and after his death she is left to rule the kingdom, always impeccable in public, "the flawless product of her women's maximum efforts."

In the *Idylls of the King* Tennyson humiliated his Guinevere, as only a Victorian male writer could. Of course he had the good of the nation at heart: as Laureate, he felt it his duty to do what he could to uphold moral standards. Mr Gladstone, it seems, valued the poem to the extent that he used to read it to the fallen women and prostitutes whom he endeavoured to reclaim. One can only speculate as to what he might have said by way of introduction to the reading, and as to what were the reactions of his hearers. Through the *Idylls*, Tennyson expressed his anxieties about the future of Britain: "all my realm / reels back into the beast, and is no more," says Arthur despairingly, looking back upon the divisive loves of Lancelot and Guinevere, Tristram and Iseult.[38] His comment represents the very real fear of the late Victorians, that if, as Darwin had shown, there was such a thing as evolution, upward movement towards higher forms might have a counterpart in downward movement towards degeneration. It would be ungrateful to complain when a poet has striven to communicate a serious message to his society, and Tennyson's Guinevere, humiliated though she is, remains a majestic figure, impressive in her contrition and her sorrow.

When we come to T.H. White's *The Once and Future King*, we meet a vibrant Guenevere who is at times strident, but with whom once again we can sympathise. White, for all the brilliance of his psychological analysis, belittles Guenevere, however, as only a modern realist writer could. No subsequent re-teller of the tale can excel Malory: White reinterprets *Le Morte Darthur* for us, enabling us to see Guenevere as a real woman, to see into her mind and her motives, to understand and to forgive. But do we need so detailed an analysis? Towards the end of the story Malory in fact gives us quite enough clues for us to form for ourselves a very good idea both of Guenevere's charm and of her insensitivity and corroding jealousy.

White knew that he could not reach the high notes as Malory could. "If you want to read about the beginning of the quest for the Grail, about the wonders of Galahad's arrival . . . and of the last supper at court, when the thunder came and the sunbeam and the covered vessel and the sweet smell through the Great Hall—if you want to read about these, you must seek them in Malory. That way of telling the story can only be done once."[39] And when Lancelot and Guenever are together, and Mordred and his gang make their attack, we can see how the demands of realism diminish the regal splendour of Malory's Guenevere. Lancelot turns to the Queen and takes her in his arms. "Jenny, I am going to call you my most noble Christian Queen. Will you be strong?"—"My dear"—"My sweet old Jenny. Let us have a kiss."[40] And so on. In fact, the attempt at updating diminishes the realism rather than the reverse. Malory alone is able to perform the astonishing feat of making Guenevere noble, high-minded and majestic amid the disasters at the end of the story, and at the same time her old self still—mean, heartless and totally uncomprehending of Lancelot's genuinely more spiritual nature. The very contradictions in her character, appearing again and again to the very end, make her a "real person," as White would say.

Guenevere, then, has in the course of the last hundred and thirty years been liberated—for better or worse—from the stern demands of Victorian morality. She remains a symbol of changing attitudes to sex, but her liberation has in many cases vulgarised her and often made her a less interesting figure, although of course it gives us White's delightful comedy and the varied portrayals of some more recent fictions. The new views of Guenevere provide some very intriguing reflections, as in a far-distant mirror, of the changing images of woman in the twentieth century, but not entirely without loss. We no longer censure Guenevere—all is understood, all is forgiven. She is set free to become a private person, the image of young loveliness, or professional competence, and we do not demand that she should maintain the dignity of "England's Queen." Charles Williams in his *Taliessin* poems[41] presented Guenevere—the queen in the rose-garden—as a symbolic figure rather than as a fully realised individual, and as such she was able to communicate significant meanings about the potential role and influence of women in society. But such moral earnestness no longer seems possible: the latest fictions are straightforward romances more reminiscent of Mills and Boone than of the great retellings of the past.

NOTES

1. *King Arthur: A Drama in a Prologue and Four Acts*, produced by Sir Henry Irving at the Lyceum Theatre, London, on January 12, 1895.

2. Graham Hill, *Guinevere: A Tragedy in Three Acts*, acted at the Court Theatre, London, October 1906.

3. Hill, *Guinevere*, Act II.

4. Morley Steynor, *Lancelot and Guenevere: A Play in a Prologue and Four Acts* (London, 1909), but performed at the Bijou Theater, London, in 1904.

5. Hill, *Guinevere*, Act II.

6. Hill, *Guinevere*, Act III.

7. Ernest Rhys, *Gwenevere, A Lyric Play* (London, 1905).

8. Hill, *Guinevere*, Act III.

9. Steynor, *Lancelot*, Act IV.

10. Francis Coutts, *King Arthur* (London, 1907), p. 154.

11. *The Saturday Review*, Jan. 9, 1895, p. 93.

12. Hill, *Guinevere*, Act I, Sc. 1.

13. (London, 1888).

14. (Boston, 1890; London, 1891).

15. (London, 1896), p. 16.

16. (London, 1926), p. 54

17. *Collected Poems* (London, 1950), p. 251.

18. Hill, *Guinevere*, Act II, Sc. ii.

19. Rhys, *Gwenevere*, Act I.

20. (London, 1920), p. 113.

21. Ibid., p. 162.

22. *The Once and Future King* (London and New York, 1958). All references are to the Fontana Library edition, 2nd impression (1965), p. 331.

23. White, *The Once and Future King*, p. 560.

24. Ibid., p. 391.

25. Ibid., p. 455.

26. Ibid., p. 483.

27. *Works of Sir Thomas Malory*, ed. Vinaver (London, 1954), Book XX.

28. (London, 1968).

29. Turton, *The Emperor Arthur* (London, 1985), p. 283–86.

30. (London, 1979).

31. (London, 1976).

32. (London, 1978).

33. (London, 1983).

34. See, for example, Marion Bradley, *The Mists of Avalon* (London, 1983).

35. (London, 1982).

36. (New York, 1980; London, 1985). Reference is to the English paperback edition, Futura (London, 1985).

37. Ibid., p. 311.

38. Tennyson, *The Passing of Arthur* (1869).

39. White, *The Once and Future King*, p. 432.

40. Ibid., p. 566.

41. *Taliessin through Logres* (London, 1938) and *The Region of the Summer Stars* (London, 1944).

Heterosexual Plots
and Lesbian Subtexts

Toward a Theory of Lesbian Narrative Space in
Marion Zimmer Bradley's *The Mists of Avalon*

Marilyn R. Farwell

Nearly two-thirds of the way into Marion Zimmer Bradley's *The Mists of Avalon,* the central character, Morgaine of the Fairies, now an old woman, returns to her home in Avalon after years of exile. She brings with her a younger self, Lancelot and Elaine's child, Nimue, to become a priestess of the goddess, and she encounters a former self in Raven, the woman sworn to serve the goddess with her silence. In the dark of the night, Raven enters Morgaine's sleeping quarters and awakens her. With ritualistic fervor, Raven removes her own cloak, takes Morgaine in her arms and touches "her slowly, with ritual silence and significance" (639). Raven quietly gives Morgaine the silver crescent, the ritual ornament of the priestess, and Viviane's ritual knife, items that Morgaine left behind when she fled in anger from Avalon and her Aunt Viviane's control. Then, in an act of bonding, each pierces herself: "from the breastbone she [Raven] pricked a single drop of blood, and Morgaine, bowing her head, took the knife and made a slight cut over her heart" (639). In an already sexually charged scene, the tension becomes stronger in their next exchange: "Raven bent to her and licked the blood away from the small cut; Morgaine bent and touched her lips to the small, welling stain at Raven's breast, knowing that this was a sealing long past the vows she had taken when she came to womanhood. Then Raven drew her again into her arms" (639–40). In the italicized words in this passage, which indicate her thoughts as they often do throughout the book, Morgaine recounts her heterosexual passions, Lancelot and Accolon, "*Yet Never,*" she says of this reunion with Raven, "*have I known what it was to be received simply in love*" (639–40).

Adapted by permission of New York University Press from *Lesbian Texts and Contexts: Radical Revisions*, edited by Karla Jay and Joanne Glasgow. Copyright © 1990 by Karla Jay and Joanne Glasgow.

While this short scene, two pages in a book of 876 pages, does not contain the romantic tension that Bradley lavishes on the great heterosexual affairs of the text—Igraine and Uther Pendragon, Morgaine and Lancelot, Morgaine and Accolon—it is an unmistakably charged lesbian scene. Only three other hints of lesbianism are apparent in this text, each one centering on Morgaine and each a short interlude in Morgaine's heterosexual life. Yet because this scene represents Morgaine's return to her home, to her mother, the goddess, and, of course, a return to herself and the old powers of priestess which she forswore earlier in the novel, it is a pivotal scene. From this powerful experience she also gains the strength and courage to attempt the difficult mission which occupies the rest of her journey. But how in a basically heterosexual text are we to read this short but erotic and undeniably lesbian section? We could read it as an innocent but intense religious ritual devoid of real sexuality or as a curiosity in a long book that might need curiosities to sustain itself. We could also excuse the lesbian proclivities, as often happens in life and in literary criticism, with the insistence that one encounter does not make either character a "real" lesbian, in effect denying or ignoring what happened. The problems with both attempts to minimize the importance of this scene are the facts: it is an intensely erotic scene, and it is a crucial if not *the* crucial scene of the book. What we must ask instead is how the strong lesbian overtones function in the text as a whole, especially in a novel which cannot, without violence, be called lesbian.

I believe that current feminist discussions of narrative theory are relevant in reading the lesbian content of this text. Twentieth-century narrative theory has taught us that heroic stories, of which *Mists* is a feminist version, are replete with codes and patterns repeated endlessly; feminist critical theory has taught us that these codes are decidedly patriarchal. Feminist literary theory has been eager to recognize the possibility of disruptive plots and spaces that position women as subjects of their own stories. In this search, theorists have, at times, acknowledged the importance of women's relationships, erotic and otherwise, and at other times have minimized their importance. In current continental theory, on which many contemporary feminist theorists depend, male thinkers like Derrida and Foucault have sought a new space for the worn-out (male) subjectivity which has structured the Western narrative. They have described that space of "alterity" or otherness as female, but not as lesbian. In her analysis of continental male thinking, Alice Jardine states that:

> Not only are the abstract spaces of female alterity in contemporary
> thought gendered female (Freud-Lacan's "unconscious," Derrida's

"écriture," Deleuze's "machines," Foucault's "madness"), but so too are the main characters of its theoretical fiction. Evidence for this ranges from the privileging by psychoanalysis of the focus on female hysterics to the emphasis by contemporary philosophy on those bodies which have escaped Western society's definition of "the normal male": the insane, the criminal, the male homosexual. (115)

In some ways it is a relief not to have lesbian included on that list, but many feminist theorists, whatever their theoretical allegiances, have explored the importance of women's bonding, often termed lesbian whatever the sexuality of the women, as a powerful tool for breaking narrative codes.

In her lucid account of new themes that are emerging for biographers of women, Carolyn G. Heilbrun points to the importance of the almost hidden realm of women's friendships, "from passionate bodily love to friendships between women married or living with men" (108). But Heilbrun stops far short of connecting heterosexuality with the old narrative script as other theorists have done. Rachel Blau DuPlessis, for example, has argued that "the erotic and emotional intensity of women's friendship cuts the Gordian knots of both heterosexuality and narrative convention" (149). In a comparable book on women writers' transgression of male heroic stories, Lee R. Edwards attacks the stranglehold that heterosexuality has exercised on heroines because tradition has "derived female identity from an equation linking limited aspiration and circumscribed activity to institutionalized heterosexuality." The female hero must then attempt to nullify "these conjunctions and the conclusions they require" (237). Although she minimizes the potential for women's love to be a disruptive force in the narrative, her original insight coincides with that of DuPlessis: to inscribe female desire in a plot demands a questioning of heterosexuality. Other critics have extended this logic and defined certain metaphoric and structural transgressions of the narrative as lesbian. Barbara Smith opened a new critical category when she suggested that Toni Morrison's *Sula* is a lesbian novel not because Nel and Sula are lesbians—they decidedly are not—but because the novel provides a critique of heterosexual institutions (189). Monique Wittig and Luce Irigaray write of the need to disrupt language and genre by opening new spaces which privilege lesbian as the place of the new alterity. In defining lesbian, they go beyond the sexuality of characters and position lesbian in the revision of the binary structures of male/female, subject/other, presence/absence of Western narratives. Thus, they provide a basis for my development of the idea of lesbian narrative space as a disruptive space of sameness as opposed to difference which has structured most Western narratives.[1]

In *Alice Doesn't*, Teresa de Lauretis offers one of the strongest feminist analyses of a narrative structured by gender difference, but, at the same time, she does not imagine the transgression of this narrative structure in a homoerotic space outside the construction of difference. De Lauretis argues that most of the giants of twentieth-century narrative theory have ignored the gender dimension of narrative structure. The Soviet theorist, Jurij Lotman, is a primary example of someone who identifies different narrative spaces without any consciousness of the gender implications of his divisions. Lotman orders narrative by a simple division, as de Lauretis states:

> Lotman finds a simple chain of two functions, open at both ends and thus endlessly repeatable: "entry into a closed space, and emergence from it." He then adds, "Inasmuch as closed space *can be interpreted* as 'a cave,' 'the grave,' 'a house,' 'woman,' (and, correspondingly, be allotted the features of darkness, warmth, dampness), entry into it *is interpreted* on various levels as 'death,' 'conception,' 'return home' and so on; moreover, all these acts *are thought of as mutually identical.*" (118, de Lauretis's emphasis)

In other words, one space is active and mobile, the other passive and inert. De Lauretis adds that these spaces are also coded by gender, for symbolically and psychologically the male is defined by the active principle, the female by the passive. Using Freud's Oedipal paradigm, she interprets the movement of the narrative in terms of sexual desire, and since male desire is the only desire Freud recognized, the active space must be male; the female space must be that which is overcome (the monster) or that which is desired (the princess). The female is either the obstacle or the reward. Moreover, characters do not determine spaces, but spaces the characters, for women can occupy male space and men—although less likely—can occupy female space: "In this mythical-textual mechanics, then, the hero must be male, regardless of the gender of the text-image, because the obstacle, whatever its personification, is morphologically female, and indeed, simply, the womb" (118–19). Difference is not only in the gender identities of the characters but in the narrative spaces which they occupy. Rosalind in *As You Like It* is not a feminist in drag when she dons the weeds of a man, but simply an occupant of male space, a situation which reinforces rather than transgresses the master narrative.

Crucial, then, to this heroic narrative is what is crucial to all of the master narratives: the construction of difference according to the dichotomies which structure Western thought, those dualities such as active/passive, mind/body, presence/absence, which ultimately rely on the gender dualism, male/female. What de Lauretis does not acknowledge nor analyze is the fact that this dualism, this division of narrative space by gender, is also necessarily heterosexual. When Monique Wittig argues that sex differences are based not on nature, but on economic, political, and ideological structures, she concludes that these differences construct not only a system of domination but also an "unnatural" system of heterosexuality: "The category of sex is the political category that founds society as heterosexual" ("Category" 66). Thus, the same narrative structure that identifies narrative space in gendered terms, that reinforces gender difference symbolically, also reinforces heterosexuality, for in defining the movement of male desire, the active space, into and through the passive space, morphologically female, we have a narrative reenactment of the heterosexual act. The master plot is not just androcentric or phallocentric, it is also basically heterosexual. The question is how female desire can be encoded in a structure which claims her desire as his desire or more accurately as the end of his desire.

This transgressive act cannot be found, I believe, among some of the popularly accepted "feminist" narratives which rely on the gender identity of certain characters. From de Lauretis's distinction between characters and narrative space we can conclude that lesbian can occupy heterosexual space and a heterosexual can occupy what I propose to call lesbian narrative space, just as male and female characters can occupy the oppositely gendered narrative space. This distinction allows us to avoid calling a text feminist which in fact reinforces the structurally gendered spaces, or naming a text about lesbians transgressive that merely replicates gendered ideas. For example, Sigourney Weaver as Ripley in the movie *Aliens* has been hailed as a new feminist hero in the same way that Rosalind in *As You Like It* has often been offered as an example of Shakespeare's feminism. Within the structural view of narrative, neither text can be called disruptive of patriarchal codes. Ripley, the courageous leader and hero of this science fiction movie, is not a female Rambo; she is carefully saved from that fate by the discreet presence of a foil—Vasquez, a woman far too threateningly masculine to be allowed heroic status in a popular film—and by her motherly devotion to the little girl. We cannot, however, ignore some of the tension created by a woman occupying male space. Barbara Creed indicates how conservatism and radicality can exist in the same text, for while the process of birth is depicted in horrid detail, at the same time the combination of male and female characteristics in Ripley does depict a different kind of hero in "a period of profound social and cultural change" (65). Yet, I believe, conservatism wins out because Ripley does occupy the same narrative space as Rambo. She moves through the female space as obstacle in the form of the planet controlled by the horrible mother who grotesquely gives birth to her eggs. She conquers that space and emerges triumphantly from it; in the process she distances herself from the female by destroying the female insect and by calling her a "bitch." Despite the minor part the romantic interest plays in the movie— if it played a larger part Ripley would automatically be forced into female space—the plot remains heterosexual and patriarchal because the movement of the male space into the female space maintains the old structural codes.

Shakespeare's Rosalind is allowed that brief moment in the Forest of Arden when, by wearing male clothing, she is given male space in the narrative, space to malign women and to control the action. Arden is a magical place which is constructed as female: it is a realm of nature, of the momentary suspension of rigid dichotomies, and of love and intuition. It is also a brief sojourn into homosexual territory, for Rosalind's assumed name, Ganymede, is synonymous in the Renaissance with a male homosexual, and Phœbe's passion for Ganymede/Rosalind is the most direct threat to conventional heterosexuality. But homosexuality is never possible structurally. When difference is threatened by sameness, Shakespeare quickly returns to the comfortable dualism. The momentary gender reversal of Rosalind and Orlando and the seeming suspension of rigid dichotomies are disallowed when the implications include the valorization of sameness, including lesbian passion. Rosalind thus emerges from her sojourn as male moving through female space before any serious reconsideration of the codes can occur, and takes her place in the old dichotomies; she returns to marriage, women's "weeds," and the "real world."

In this analytical context many lesbian novels cannot be considered radical transgressors of heterosexual codes, for often and with considerable vigor the dualities of the male active and the female passive spaces are reconfirmed. Gillian Whitlock's recent essay on Radclyffe Hall's *The Well of Loneliness* has given us a more complex view of this novel; she argues "that the book is a political intervention in which Hall starts the process of producing a 'reverse discourse,' a space for other lesbians to speak for themselves and so move forward toward self-definition" (560). This space, which includes the deconstruction of many categories of gender and genre, is cut short in the end, for "Stephen finally lacks the courage and the vision to make the break with old orders" (575). But while Stephen does seem to challenge gender dichotomies on one level, the novel depends structurally on the maintenance of gender difference. Stephen is identified with male desire, she moves through female space and almost wins the female as her reward; but her desire, like Rosalind's, cannot ultimately possess male space. The oxymoron, female hero/male desire, must be subverted, for otherwise it would de-stroy the romance genre of which it is a part. Mary is the passive figure with whom we are structurally comfortable and who in the end can become a "real woman" and go with a "real man." As with *Aliens*, the fact that the narrative space contains an oxymoron is potentially deconstructive, but the novel, like the movie, cannot draw out the implications without destroying itself. It cannot validate sameness above difference. Even current popular lesbian novels are structured in a way that reaffirms codes of sexual differ-ence. Anne Cameron's *The Journey* is such an example. Anne and Sarah play out the gender roles in their journey through the early West to win a place of their own. Anne hunts, Sarah cooks. Their adventures are replete with the tensions of violence that structure novels built on sexual difference, al-though unlike the lesbian despair that informs Hall's novel, this one ends triumphantly, making it what Catherine R. Stimpson has called a lesbian novel of "enabling escape" (244). *The Journey* replicates the male adven-ture story with only slightly different characters occupying the traditional narrative spaces.

The question remains, then, how can the old narrative structure be changed to allow for the existence of female desire? Because female desire within the dichotomous structures of Western thinking is inconceivable—Freud, we will remember, allowed women no desire of their own—I believe that only in the space of sameness can this desire emerge. This space is cre-ated when women forge what Adrienne Rich calls a "primary presence" of themselves to one another (*Lies* 250) or exhibit what Rich elsewhere calls a "primary intensity" for one another ("Compulsory" 648), thus defying a world that has defined them only by their relationships to men. Such a con-centration of one woman on another disturbs if not destroys Western dual-isms. The result is a space defined by fluid instead of rigid boundaries. My use of the word *lesbian* in this context is metaphoric, for while sexuality can be a part of the construction of sameness, it is not a necessary part. This metaphoric use is not without its problems, some of which I have addressed in another essay (100–104).[2] But the fact remains that contemporary theo-rists have often designated that space outside of categories of difference as lesbian, what Elaine Showalter in another context has called the "wild zone" in women's writing and theory (263). Monique Wittig's definition of *lesbian* can serve as the key for this metaphoric definition. *Lesbian,* she has argued, is that space which is "not-woman," which is not dependent on the catego-rization of difference that resides in the dualisms of man and woman ("One Is Not Born" 150). *Lesbian* is a word that denotes, then, a new positioning of female desire, of the lover and beloved, of the subject and object.

Wittig's *The Lesbian Body* is one of the strongest enactments of this new space and new subjectivity. In this experimental text, the traditional Western dichotomies of lover and beloved become a fluid exchange of subject and object, placing the subjects "outside of the presence/absence and center/margin dichotomies" (Shaktini 39). In the deconstruction of the Western idea of lover and beloved, based on domination and heterosexuality, Wittig refuses characters' identities, linear plots, and simple representation. One of her central devices, a "j/e," enacts the destruction of old language patterns. Wittig describes her own effort: "The j/e with a bar in *The Lesbian Body* is not an *I* destroyed. It is an *I* become so powerful that it can attack the order of heterosexuality in texts and assault so-called love, the heroes of love, and lesbianize them, lesbianize the symbols, lesbianize the gods and goddesses, lesbianize men and women" ("Mark" 11). In her lyrical conclusion to *This Sex Which Is Not One,* Luce Irigaray plays with the same fluctuating boundaries between lover and beloved, I and you: "We are luminous. Neither one or two. I've never known how to count. Up to you. In their calculations, we make two. Really, two? Doesn't that make you laugh? An odd sort of two. And yet not one. Especially not one. Let's leave *one* to them" (207). Her attempts to describe their relationship in a new language mean the destruction of the old lovers' dichotomies and the reinscription of a divisionless economy/text: "You? I? That's still saying too much. Dividing too sharply between us: all" (218). Confusing the boundaries between subject/object and lover/beloved undercuts the heterosexuality which is based on this dualism. The point in the narrative where this deconstruction begins is what I would call lesbian narrative space. It happens most often when two women seek another kind of relationship than that which is prescribed in the patriarchal structures, and when it occurs in the narrative, it can cast a different light on the rest of the novel, even on those portions that seem to affirm heterosexual patterns.

With this definition of a lesbian narrative space we can return to *The Mists of Avalon* and propose a reading which takes into account the homoeroticism and the primary presence of women to one another that is portrayed in the central scene between Raven and Morgaine. On the surface, Marion Zimmer Bradley's narrative neatly bifurcates the world between two geographical areas that symbolically and stereotypically represent male and female principles. The male Christian world of Britain is in the process of assuring the sexual dichotomization of a world that had once been ruled by women. As if in punishment for woman's previous ascendancy, the priests and especially a viciously portrayed St. Patrick, insist that women are sinful, weak, unreasonable and, at best, passive helpmates to their husbands.

As women have done throughout history, Arthur's wife, Gwenhwyfar, becomes the patriarchal enforcer of Christianity's negative view of women. The women of Camelot dutifully fulfill the roles of giddy onlookers, gossiping while they spin, and ignoring the greater political and moral issues of their day. On the other hand, while Avalon is slowly fading into the mists because people no longer believe in its values, it still remains the sanctuary for strong feminist values. It worships the goddess along with the gods, its religious island is peopled by priestesses who guard and develop the powers of the Sight, and ultimate authority is vested in the Lady of the Lake. In one way, Avalon is like the Forest of Arden, full of possibility, intuition, the Sight, and a kind of magic beyond empiricism and beyond what Lancelot calls the place where "the real struggles of life are taking place" (146).

But Avalon also reinforces a sexual division which underscores its basic heterosexuality. Its great religious festival is the marriage of King Stag to the Goddess to ensure the fertility of the land. "What of the flow of life between their two bodies, male and female, the tides of the Goddess rising and compelling them?" Morgaine seems to ask when the much-desired Lancelot retreats from making love to her (324). Morgaine does enact this ceremony twice in her life, once with Arthur, her brother, and once with Accolon, her lover in old age. But because of her upbringing in Avalon, Morgaine firmly believes that a woman's body is her own to give to whomever she wishes; she accepts none of the Christian-imposed values of the sinfulness of sex, especially for women outside marriage. The ritual marriages are ceremonial and unbinding as are the number of affairs that Morgaine has, one with Kevin the Harper and another, under the nose of her husband, Uriens, with Accolon. In one way it could be argued that this female sexual autonomy is a new positioning of female desire, for while in the Christian world dualisms imply hierarchy, in Avalon they do not. But at the same time this heterosexuality points to the importance of difference in structuring Avalon as well as Camelot. The place to look for narrative transgression, I believe, is not in the tension between Avalon and Camelot, or in the idealized feminine world of Avalon, but in the momentary revelation of sameness as the core of Avalon.

Several short passages of homoeroticism ask us to restructure that neat dependence on dualism that orders the rest of the novelistic landscape. Instead of positioning female desire within the dualistic system which fosters our way of thinking, the lesbian scenes position desire outside that structure and therefore outside the controlling realm of male desire. While, then, female desire is accorded autonomy in the heterosexual world of Avalon, its true source of autonomy is in the lesbian narrative space constructed by sameness. As a subtext, the lesbian becomes the core of female tension and autonomy. A new story cannot be created by a redefinition of difference, as the world of Avalon attempts to do, but instead must be constituted by the more transgressive sameness.

The relationship of Raven and Morgaine becomes, then, the essence of Avalon, a place of fluctuating boundaries, of no division between self and other, a place where sameness thrives. Avalon as a whole depends upon the exchange of roles among the women, who are mother, daughter, sister, and goddess to one another and to themselves. These relationships are intensified in Raven and Morgaine's love scene. Early in the text, both Morgaine's and Raven's names are given as other names of the goddess, affirming their interchangeability: "'She is also the Morrigán, the messenger of strife, the great Raven'" (136). A fluid exchange of mother-daughter roles seems to attend the central love scene. Bradley describes Morgaine's final feelings in this scene as a meditation on her mother: "It seemed to Morgaine, half in a dream, that she lay in the lap of her mother . . . no, not Igraine, but welcomed back into the arms of the Great Mother . . ." (640). That connection is made in an earlier homoerotic scene when Morgaine, having wandered in the fairy world, describes her sexual encounter with a maiden as a memory: "She remembered that she had lain in the lady's lap and suckled at her breast, and it did not seem strange to her at all, that she, a grown woman, should lie in her mother's lap, and be kissed and dandled like an infant" (405). As with Shug and Celie in Alice Walker's *The Color Purple,* the two women become mother and daughter to one another at the same time, with no warped, psychological insights attending the exchange. Of their lovemaking, Celie reports, "Then I feels something real soft and wet on my breast, feel like one of my little lost babies mouth. Way after while, I act like a little lost baby too" (97). In another, much shorter, lesbian scene between Morgaine and Raven, immediately before the great event that will destroy Raven and send Morgaine with the holy relics into hiding, Morgaine becomes the mother, cradling Raven "like a child" and once again they enact the unity they experienced earlier: "She held Raven against her, touching her, caressing her, their bodies clinging together in something like a frenzy. Neither spoke, but Morgaine felt the world trembling in a strange and sacramental rhythm around them . . . woman to woman, affirming life in the shadow of death" (765).

All of the depictions of women loving women in Avalon are made without negative comment. Only in the Christian world is there any tension or shame about homoerotic desires. In the fairy world, Morgaine, "to her surprise, . . . found the maiden—yes, she looked somewhat like Raven—twining her arms around her neck and kissing her, and she returned the kisses without surprise or shame" (405). It is Lancelot who is tormented by his relationship and attraction to Arthur and whose potential homosexuality is scorned. Mordred recounts a story about Lancelot to the court "'something of a ballad made when they thrust a harp into his hand and bade him play, and he sang some lay of Rome or the days of Alexander, I know not what, of the love of knightly companions, and they jeered at him for it. Since then, his songs are all of the beauty of our queen, or knightly tales of adventure and dragons'" (713). The only hint of homosexuality in the Christian world that is free from this pain occurs between Raven and Morgaine the night before they enter Camelot for the great Pentecostal feast.

Sameness, then, is in one way not a threat in Avalon; in another way it destroys Avalon's reliance on heterosexuality and on gender difference for meaning. This sameness does not depend on whether or not these characters are lesbian but on the space they create which outlaws difference from its midst. This lesbian space also seems to be the strength and core of Avalon. When Morgaine returns home, she is given the courage to complete her task in the act of love with Raven. And again with the love scene immediately before the great event in Camelot, Raven and Morgaine come together "woman to woman" as in prayer: "priestesses of Avalon together called on the life Goddess and in silence she answered them" (766). Sameness, ironically, undercuts the stark symbolic gender differences which are created in the rest of the text and undercuts the heterosexuality which informs the rest of the narrative. At the center of Avalon is the contradiction which deconstructs its faith in heterosexuality and the novel's symbolic structure. Thus, Morgaine's journey reverses the normal, gender-identified movement of the narrative. Symbolically she moves from the female space of Avalon to and through the male space of Camelot, but the core of that female space—that which gives her power and strength—is sameness, is her connection with another woman. The space of movement in this novel is at its center defined by female desire, the desire of one woman for another, for Morgaine is at home only when she is in the arms of another woman.

I am not arguing that *Mists* is ultimately a more transgressive novel than others mentioned earlier and seemingly dismissed, but rather that, in opening a new narrative space, the reader can forge a subtext that explores female desire while the main text does not. The subtext gives us the possibility for a transgressive narrative that can be more fully realized in other narratives or that can be part of our readings of other texts that seem to reinforce the bonding between heterosexuality and the narrative. With the recognition of a truly transgressive space, we will no longer have to settle for a few narratives that pass as radical.

1. In choosing to use the words *sameness* and *difference* I have been influenced, in part, by Toni A.H. McNaron's paper delivered at the 1988 MLA session, "When Chloe Likes Olivia: Lesbian Literary Theory."

2. Ahistoricism and essentialism are the central problems which have plagued the attempt to define lesbian metaphorically. I believe that some of those problems are eliminated when one speaks of lesbian as a space rather than as an essence.

WORKS CITED

Bradley, Marion Zimmer. *The Mists of Avalon.* New York: Ballantine, 1982.

Cameron, Anne. *The Journey.* San Francisco: Spinsters/Aunt Lute, 1986.

Creed, Barbara. "From Here to Modernity: Feminism and Post Modernism." *Screen* 28, no. 2 (1987): 47–67.

de Lauretis, Teresa. *Alice Doesn't: Feminism, Semiotics, Cinema.* Bloomington: Indiana Univ. Press, 1984.

DuPlessis, Rachal Blau. *Writing beyond the Ending: Narrative Strategies of Twentieth-Century Women Writers.* Bloomington: Indiana Univ. Press, 1985.

Edwards, Lee R. *Psyche as Hero: Female Heroism and Fictional Form.* Middletown, CT: Wesleyan Univ. Press, 1984.

Farwell, Marilyn R. "Toward a Definition of Lesbian Literary Imagination." *Signs* 14 (1988): 100–18.

Heilbrun, Carolyn G. *Writing a Woman's Life.* New York: Norton, 1988.

Irigaray, Luce. *This Sex Which Is Not One.* Trans. Catherine Porter. Ithaca: Cornell Univ. Press, 1985.

Jardine, Alice A. *Gynesis: Configurations of Woman and Modernity.* Ithaca: Cornell Univ. Press, 1986.

McNaron, Toni A.H. "Mirrors and Sameness: Lesbian Theory through Imagery." MLA Convention. New Orleans, 29 Dec. 1988.

Rich, Adrienne. "Compulsory Heterosexuality and Lesbian Existence." *Signs* 5 (1980): 631–60.

———. *On Lies, Secrets, and Silence: Selected Prose 1966–1978.* New York: Norton, 1979.

Shaktini, Namascar. "Displacing the Phallic Subject: Wittig's Lesbian Writing." *Signs* 8 (1982): 29–44.

Showalter, Elaine. "Feminist Criticism in the Wilderness." In *The New Feminist Criticism: Essays on Women, Literature, and Theory.* Ed. Elaine Showalter. New York: Pantheon, 1985. 243–70.

Smith, Barbara. "Toward a Black Feminist Criticism." *Women's Studies International Quarterly* 2, no. 2 (1979): 183–94.

Stimpson, Catharine R. "Zero Degree Deviancy: The Lesbian Novel in English." In *Writing and Sexual Difference.* Ed. Elizabeth Abel. Chicago: Univ. of Chicago Press, 1982. 243–59.

Walker, Alice. *The Color Purple.* New York: Harcourt, 1982.

Whitlock, Gillian. "'Everything Is Out of Place': Radclyffe Hall and the Lesbian Literary Tradition." *Feminist Studies* 13 (1987): 555–82.

Wittig, Monique. "The Category of Sex." *Feminist Issues* 2 (1982): 63–68.

———. *The Lesbian Body.* Trans. David Le Vay. New York: Morrow, 1975.

———. "The Mark of Gender." *Feminist Issues* 5, no. 2 (1985): 3–12.

———. "One Is Not Born a Woman." In *Feminist Frameworks: Alternative Theoretical Accounts of Relations Between Women and Men.* Ed. Alison M. Jagger and Paula S. Rothenberg. New York: McGraw, 1984. 148–52.

THE FIRST AND LAST LOVE

MORGAN LE FAY AND ARTHUR

Raymond H. Thompson

When we think of love in Arthurian literature, it is the affairs of Tristan and Iseult, Lancelot and Guenevere, that spring first to mind, followed by those of Uther and Ygraine, Merlin and Nimuë. These, after all, contributed to the rise and fall of kingdoms. Yet an equally important love affair is starting to find a place in Arthurian tradition: the love between Arthur and Morgan le Fay. It dates, however, not from the Middle Ages, but from the decade of the 1980s, even though its roots reach back as far as the twelfth century, and perhaps earlier if the arguments of some Celticists can be accepted.[1]

In medieval tradition the relationship between Morgan and Arthur has proved fascinatingly ambiguous. She first appears in Geoffrey of Monmouth's *Vita Merlini* (ca. 1150) as the eldest and most beautiful among nine sisters on the Isle of Avalon (3:334–35; see also 2:302). She is noted not only for her ability to fly through the air and change her shape, but also for her kindness and great skill in the art of medicine, and thus Arthur is brought to her to be healed of his mortal wound after the Battle of Camlann. Morgan is later identified by Chrétien de Troyes, not only as a skilled healer, but also as Arthur's sister.[2] In the French verse romances she remains a powerful and generally benevolent fay, but in the prose romances her reputation steadily declines (Bogdanow).

In the Vulgate Cycle (ca. 1215–35) Morgan continues on good terms with her brother, whom she carries off in a boat after the Battle of Camlann. After her affair with Guiomar is broken up by his cousin, Guenevere, however, she grows to hate the Queen and constantly seeks either to seduce Lancelot from her side or to expose their affair. In the Prose *Tristan* she sends

Reprinted from *The Arthurian Revival: Essays on Form, Tradition and Transformation*, ed. Debra Mancoff (New York: Garland, 1992), 230–47. Amended by the author.

to Arthur's court a magic drinking horn from which no unfaithful lady can drink without spilling, though it is intercepted by one of Arthur's knights and redirected to Mark's court in Cornwall. In the Post-Vulgate Cycle, Morgan, here the wife of King Urien and mother of Yvain, becomes Arthur's enemy after he executes one of her lovers, and she uses another lover, Accolon, in her plot to take her brother's life. To this end she steals Excalibur and its sheath, which gives magical protection against wounds. Although Arthur recovers the sword, Morgan escapes with the sheath.

From a fay untouched by time Morgan degenerates into a mortal who must conceal her age through magic arts. Her once-prized favors are condemned as promiscuity in romances that extol the devotion of courtly lovers; the famed healer now schemes to destroy others, almost invariably with humiliating results. This was the figure inherited by Malory, but she attracted little attention elsewhere in English literature (with the exception of *Sir Gawain and the Green Knight*) until rediscovered by modern authors, especially writers of fantasy.

To many of these she is little more than a convenient villain: Jane Curry's *The Sleepers* (1968) and Penelope Lively's *The Whispering Knights* (1971) portray her as an evil enchantress from the past who threatens a new generation of heroes. Yet some authors view her enmity to Arthur with sympathy and understanding: in both Sanders Anne Laubenthal's *Excalibur* (1973) and *Excalibur!* (1980), by Gil Kane and John Jakes, Morgan seeks revenge for what she considers the murder of her father and the callous treatment she and the rest of her family experience at Uther's hands. In Phyllis Ann Karr's *The Idylls of the Queen* (1982) she offers a spirited and convincing defence of her conduct toward Arthur and Guenevere (184–200).

Nor does she always assume the role of antagonist. In Georgene Davis' play *The Round Table* (1930), Morgan (or Morgana as she is called here) not only takes over the role of Morgause as mother of Mordred, Gawain, and their brothers, but was, we are told, truly loved by Arthur before they learned that they were brother and sister. Since this relationship precedes the events covered in the play, it is merely mentioned in passing.

Interestingly, Morgan and Morgause again exchange their traditional roles in Sharan Newman's Guinevere Trilogy (*Guinevere*, 1981; *The Chessboard Queen,* 1983; and *Guinevere Evermore*, 1985). Arthur is but one of the many lovers Morgan welcomes to her bed, and both are unaware of their relationship at the time. Once she discovers it, however, she uses Mordred as a tool against Arthur to avenge what she believes was his father's degradation of her mother.

In Catherine Christian's *The Sword and the Flame* (1978; published a year later in the United States as *The Pendragon*), Margause (Morgause) hates Arthur because his father murdered hers, though Mawgan (Morgan) serves her half-brother loyally. The tradition of true love between Arthur and his half-sister is introduced, however, by the device of providing another half-sister, named Ygern. Raised together as children, they love each other truly and plan to marry, until told of their relationship. Thereafter, Arthur can find no happiness in his dynastic marriage with Guinevere. After Ygern is raped by a Saxon raider, she gives birth to Medraut who is reared by Margause. Ygern trains as a Priestess of the Old Faith on Avalon, she rises to become Lady of the Lake, as the Chief Priestess is known, and she comes at last to bear the mortally wounded Arthur to Avalon in her barge. Three days later he dies with his head resting in her lap.

Five works, all published in the 1980s, take the final step of focusing upon the love between Morgan le Fay and Arthur: Parke Godwin's *Firelord* (1980), Marion Zimmer Bradley's *The Mists of Avalon* (1982), Joy Chant's *The High Kings* (1984), Joan Wolf's *The Road to Avalon* (1988), and Welwyn Wilton Katz's *The Third Magic* (1988).

In Godwin's *Firelord*, a historical novel with some elements of fantasy, Arthur genuinely loves Guenevere, who rules by his side with great skill. He recognizes, nonetheless, that Morgana (as Morgan is called here) is his first and deepest love. From her he learns not only passion and joy, but also an appreciation of life and its beauty. He learns, moreover, that "we're human because we care" (89). Ironically, after an all too brief period of happiness, it is this caring that separates them.

Morgana is one of the Prydn, a nomadic people who range north of Hadrian's Wall and are known to outsiders as Faerie. More far-sighted than her companions, she wants to save them from the extinction that threatens them because of their inability to adapt to a changing world. Arthur has his own obligations, however, to Britain as a whole rather than to one small tribe. Consequently, at the moment of decision he chooses to ride south to warn the Britons of impending invasion, rather than stay to help Morgana. Once there, he takes up his responsibilities again, compelled by the country's need for a strong leader.

Yet despite the sacrifice of personal happiness, his love for Morgana endures, and it leads him into conflict with Guenevere when she arranges the murder of Morgana and her family. Deeply hurt by the death of the woman who, in his own words, "touched my soul once and never let go" (275), he imprisons the Queen, regardless of the disastrous political consequences—consequences that lead his country to the brink of civil war. That

Guenevere's imprisonment should result from Arthur's love for another woman, rather than from her own affair with Lancelot, is ironic, but this change from the traditional pattern is a measure of Arthur's feelings for Morgana. He can forgive Guenevere's affair since it injures only himself; yet he cannot overlook her actions when they claim the life of the one he loves.

Morgana's love for Arthur remains equally strong, despite his abandonment of her. Nor does it prove any less disastrous, for it causes her to neglect their son Modred. The effect of this upon his character is explored in greater depth in the short story "Uallannach" (1988), where Modred explains why he blames Arthur and sets the ambush in which both he and his father are slain.

The incest motif is muted in Godwin's novel. Arthur and Morgana are no more than cousins: his mother, Ygerna, was a changeling, left by her Prydn mother in place of a dead infant, so that she might survive in a hard year. Not only are Arthur and Morgana unaware of the relationship at the time, but it is not a barrier since marriage between cousins is customary among the Prydn. Since Morgana dies before Arthur, she cannot bear him to Avalon in a boat after Camlann, but she does come to him in a vision as he lies dying, taking by the hand what he describes as "the last and best of me" (395), so that they may "run home forever under the hill" (396).

In Bradley's fantasy novel *The Mists of Avalon* Mordred is conceived during a ritual in which Morgaine, as a priestess of the Old Religion centered on the Holy Isle of Avalon, takes on the role of the Mother Goddess, welcoming her consort, the new King Stag. He, it turns out, is none other than her half-brother, Arthur, but they recognize each other too late. Such unions are accepted in the Old Religion, but since both the young people were raised partly as Christians, they react with shock and despair at what they believe to be a sin. Morgaine conceals her pregnancy from Arthur, fostering her son with her sister Morgause.

What complicates the situation is that the two do genuinely love each other. Since their mother neglected them both, Morgaine was left to take care of her little brother. Although later separated, they form a bond that is reinforced by their physical union. The ritual is, moreover, spiritual as well as physical, and since both are virgins it has all the more impact. Little wonder then that Arthur, who confesses to his sister, "I have always loved you" (181), remains deeply in love with her for the rest of his life, even though forced to repress his feelings. Morgaine loves him in return, and though she does fall in love with other men—or imagines that she does—her feelings for them never run as deep, nor prove as enduring. Indeed the author herself, in an interview by Parke Godwin, observes that Morgaine is "the educated and intelligent woman who could have, and should have been Arthur's co-queen, and far more intelligent than he ever was" (8).

What drives them apart is, of course, the feeling of guilt at a relationship deemed sinful by the church, whatever the pagan attitude. The gulf widens when Arthur yields to Gwenhwyfar's insistence that he support the Church against all other faiths. This is seen as a betrayal by Avalon, and it accounts for Morgaine's later enmity against her brother, leading eventually to her plot to steal Excalibur and its protective sheath, and then to kill him, with the aid of her lover, Accolon.

Despite this their love endures. When she comes in the barge to the dying Arthur, he murmurs, "Morgaine . . . you have come back to me . . . and you are so young and fair . . . I will always see the Goddess with your face . . . Morgaine, you will not leave me again, will you?" (868). To which she responds, "'I will never leave you again my brother, my baby, my love,' . . . and I kissed his eyes. And he died, just as the mists rose and the sun shone full over the shores of Avalon" (868).

Joy Chant's *The High Kings* creates a dramatic narrative frame for a number of stories told in traditional Celtic style. Among them is an account of Arthur's meeting with a beautiful maiden who promises to help him in his quest for suitable weapons if he will sleep with her. Arthur accepts the bargain willingly and, after a night of lovemaking that was his "first knowledge of women" (172), he is instructed how to enter a hall beneath a lake where he may win the sword Caledvolc (as Excalibur is called here). The powers of this weapon are impressive: "So long as Caledvolc, the hard falcon of battle, is in your hand, there shall be no warrior who can stand against you, and while its sheath is at your side there will be no hurt upon you. Go now: but return to me tonight (172)." "Every word I shall remember, but none so clear as that!" (172) he responds enthusiastically. Thus guided, Arthur wins both sword and sheath, but he is dismayed to learn from Merthin (Merlin) that the maiden is no other than his half-sister Morgen. Grieved at the thought of the sin between them, he rejects her when they meet again. She, on the other hand, sees "no sin, but great discourtesy," and she tells him further:

> There is Sovereignty in the friendship of my thighs, that you have rejected. The blessings of the first night shall be yours, but not the second. In might and glory no man shall equal you, and Britain shall never forget your fame; but this fate also is on you—that you shall never have the love of a woman, and never one to keep faith with you, and never peace in the arms of one, until you lie in my lap again! (174).

Her prophecy proves accurate, for all the women whom he takes to his bed prove faithless, even his wife Gueneva. She steals Caledvolc and gives it to her lover Modrat; he in turn grievously wounds Arthur with it at the Battle of Camlann, for the protective sheath had been lost earlier during the hunt for the boar Troit. Morgen comes for her brother in a boat, promises to heal him of his wound in Avalon, and bears him to the island, his head laid in her lap as she had foretold. Their son in Chant's account is not Modrat, who is Arthur's foster son (a tradition found in *The Dream of Rhonabwy* 140), but rather Amros. The King kills the young man in a fit of guilt-inspired rage, though he afterwards regrets the deed bitterly.[3]

The most unequivocal love affair between Arthur and Morgan is developed in Joan Wolf's historical novel *The Road to Avalon*. Merlin is a Romanized British prince, friend and chief advisor to Ambrosius and his brother Uther. He is also the father of Igraine, Morgause, and, by a second wife (named Nimuë), of Morgan. Arthur is the son conceived out of wedlock by Uther and Igraine, and later raised with Morgan (who is one year younger) and Cal, the son of Merlin's Steward, Ector. They fall in love and plan to marry, unaware of their kinship. When told, Arthur wants to proceed regardless, but Morgan, who has a strong sense of duty, refuses lest such a marriage foment opposition to Arthur's succession. They had, however, already become lovers, and Morgan discovers that she is pregnant. She conceals her condition from Arthur, aware that he would insist upon their marriage, and fosters Mordred with her half-sister Morgause.

Once Arthur is secure on the throne, he proposes to Morgan again, but again she refuses him. He needs, she believes, a legitimate heir, but she can bear no more children because she was damaged by the hard birth of Mordred. Reluctantly Arthur marries Gwenhwyfar. She, ironically, cannot provide an heir either, and when she turns for comfort to Bedwyr (who takes over Lancelot's role as the Queen's lover), Arthur and Morgan become lovers again, having done what they can to fulfil their duty to the kingdom.

Arthur is mortally wounded at the Battle of Camlann, though his enemy there is Agravaine rather than Mordred, for the latter grows up to be a likeable but naive young man. Carried to Avalon, here the estate first of Merlin, then of Morgan, Arthur dies in her arms. "'We will be together,' he told her. 'Believe that. This is only for a little while. We were always meant to be together, you and I'" (358).

Welwyn Wilton Katz's fantasy *The Third Magic* differs from the other books in that it departs radically from tradition in developing the characters of Arthur and Morgan. Most of the action takes place on the world of Nwm, where a ruthless struggle is being waged between the First

Magic of the Circle, wielded by women, and the Second Magic of the Line, wielded by men. As part of their efforts to bring other worlds under their control, both sides "mission" representatives to Earth. The Morrigan is reborn as Morrigan, daughter of Ygerne and half-sister of Arthur; the M'rlendd becomes Merlin the magician; both seek to influence Arthur with their teachings.

The Morrigan, however, has a twin brother named Arddu, who is taken prisoner by the Line. Using his mental pattern, the Line tries to draw back the Morrigan, but instead catches Morgan Lefevre. Morgan is a modern Canadian teenager, over on a visit to Tintagel. She is also a descendant of the Morrigan and almost identical to her remote ancestor.

Morgan and Arddu succeed in escaping from the Line. They find the sword Excalibur, and take it to its resting place in a Castle of Glass, where they also find the Grail Cup, the Bleeding Head that talks to them, and a stone ring. By inserting Excalibur into the ring they are taken to Earth in time for Arthur's attempt to claim the kingship by drawing the same Excalibur from the same stone ring.

Although Morgan and Arddu initially resent each other, as companions in adversity, however reluctant, they learn to appreciate and take care of each other, and eventually they fall in love almost without realizing it. By contrast the Morrigan loses her struggle with Merlin, who succeeds not only in gaining dominance over Arthur, but also in raping her. The child of this union is Mordred. In a last desperate act of revenge she kills Arthur when he draws the sword from the stone ring. Moreover, driven to madness by Merlin's magic, she also kills her twin brother when he tries to prevent her, then herself starts to dissolve in flames. Amid this ruin, Morgan works powerful magic in her turn, for she is the descendant of both the Morrigan and Merlin, wielder of the Third Magic that reconciles the opposition of the first two. "Make things right," she wishes (199), and looks up to find that she has become Morgan LeFay; that Arddu has become King Arthur, triumphantly brandishing Excalibur; "and the legends were there, waiting to be made" (200).

Among these legends is Mordred, whom Morgan must preserve. He is, after all, her ancestor and thus crucial to her existence. "And so Mordred must live to kill Arddu, and she, who loved Arddu, had no choice but to allow it" (200). Yet she also has a vision of "herself on a raven-strewn battlefield taking Arddu's dead body in her arms and then thrusting his sword into this same flat, holed stone, taking them both back to Nwm" (201). "So that," she realizes, "was the source of the legend of Morgan LeFay taking the dead King Arthur to be reborn in a magical land!" (201).

Turning from the individual texts to consider all five works as a group, we can discern, amid the many variations, a basic pattern in accounts of the love between Morgan le Fay and Arthur. In the novels of Bradley, Wolf, and Katz, the basis of their love is established during their childhood together. This marks a departure from the romance tradition in which Merlin takes Arthur from his parents almost immediately after his birth, to be reared in the household of Sir Ector until he claims the throne. The change allows Morgan and Arthur to achieve a closeness that endures despite later differences between them. This feature we may call the "Childhood Bond."

Both are unaware that they are related when they sleep together and conceive a child who cannot be freely acknowledged. In Chant's version, however, only Arthur is ignorant of his partner's identity, while the feature is excluded from Katz's novel, and muted in the novels of Godwin and Wolf by making the kinship more distant. Not only does the love they share make it natural for Morgan to take over Morgause's traditional role as the mother of Mordred in these novels, but furthermore an affair between Morgan's sister and Arthur would unnecessarily complicate a relationship already beset by obstacles. Additionally the attempts to make the kinship more distant reflect the authors' concern to win sympathy for the lovers from an audience for whom incest remains a taboo. An affair with both sisters would alienate that sympathy. This feature we may call the "Incest Motif."

In the accounts by Bradley, Chant, and Katz Morgan helps Arthur win Excalibur and its protective sheath, and to dispose properly of the sword after the Battle of Camlann. Only Bradley has her plot to steal them back earlier, although Katz makes her keeper of the stone ring in which the sword is set. By taking over the role traditionally assigned to the Lady of the Lake, Morgan gains stature as Arthur's benefactor, without whom many of his achievements might have proved impossible. This feature we may call the "Excalibur Motif." It does not appear in the historical novels, where such supernatural elements are either suppressed or rationalized.

After an all too brief period of happiness together the lovers are separated, either because of concern over incest, or because of the conflicting demands of duty. In Katz's novel the separation is perpetuated after the return to Nwm, since Morgan must go back to twentieth-century Earth to be born as herself. Only Bradley has her marry Uriens and plot against Arthur. This feature we may call the "Separation," and it is essential so that Arthur may marry Guenevere.

Morgan is a noted healer, and in all versions except Chant's she displays particular skill in herblore. Bradley and Chant link her with Excalibur's magical sheath that protects Arthur against wounds, while Katz gives her possession of the stone ring that enables her to transport him back to Nwm for revival. Although the medieval romances stress her magical power rather than the less exotic herb lore, this skill, which we may call the "Healing Motif," is firmly attached to Morgan from the earliest accounts.

Mordred is responsible for Arthur's fatal wound, although in Wolf's novel the wound is inflicted by accident rather than design. He is Arthur's son by Morgan in the novels by Godwin, Bradley, and Wolf, although he is raised by their sister Morgause in the latter two. This reflects the older tradition that Morgause, not Morgan, is the mother of Mordred. Katz makes him the son of the Morrigan and thus Arddu's nephew; Chant divides his role between Amros and Modrat, Arthur's beloved foster-son. He is attracted to Guenevere in the versions by Chant and Wolf. This traditional feature we may call "Mordred's Revenge."

Arthur sets forth on his final journey in Morgan's arms. In the fantasies she bears him to an Otherworld Avalon, for healing or burial; in the historical novels by Wolf and Godwin, she awaits him in Avalon, a place in this world to which the dying Arthur is carried by his faithful followers. This we may call the "Journey to Avalon," and it has persisted from earliest accounts.

This survey reveals that the love between Morgan and Arthur is developed primarily by modifying traditional accounts of their youth. Events after the marriage of Arthur and Guenevere preserve the established pattern, except that only Bradley has Morgan marry Uriens. Even then she is no more than the stepmother of Uwaine. The decision to initiate this love at the outset of their careers was probably influenced by two narrative considerations. First of all, since medieval literature has less to say about the earlier years of both Morgan and Arthur than about their later years, modern authors can more readily introduce new material without violating firmly established tradition. Second, a first, forbidden, love between the two offers what to a modern audience is a credible psychological explanation for the failure of Arthur's marriage to Guenevere, and for the curious combination of love and hate that marks the relationship between sister and brother.

The pervasive theme developed in all accounts of love between Morgan and Arthur is the conflict between love and duty, a favorite in modern treatments of the Arthurian legend. In Godwin's *Firelord* Arthur abandons Morgana to save Britain from the Saxons; in Bradley's *The Mists of Avalon* Morgaine opposes Arthur when he supports Christianity against other religions; in Chant's *The High Kings* guilt drives Arthur from Morgen's side; in Wolf's *The Road to Avalon* Morgan refuses to marry Arthur because of her concern for the good of Britain; in Katz's *The Third Magic* Morgan leaves

Arddu in order to fulfil her destiny, to be born on Earth and perhaps reconcile her parents.

A combination of four factors has, I believe, been responsible for this innovative development in the role of Morgan le Fay within Arthurian tradition (for there is no conclusive evidence of a love affair between her and Arthur prior to the twentieth century, whatever may have been the relationship between their Celtic antecedents). In the first place, the widespread sympathy for the figure of Arthur, who is often perceived as an undeserving victim of betrayal by his wife and best friend, encourages attempts to provide him with a true love, e.g., *Lionors: King Arthur's Uncrowned Queen* (1975), in which Barbara Ferry Johnson expands upon Malory's brief mention of Arthur's youthful affair with the daughter of Earl Sanam (1:38).

Second, the recent popularity of fantasy as a literary genre, combined with the growth of interest in the occult and in pagan religions such as Wicca, has increased the amount of attention paid to magic workers like Morgan (Bradley viii; Thompson, *Return* 187). It is inevitable, therefore, that some novels should treat her sympathetically. Yet why should Morgan be chosen for the role of Arthur's true love, however well disposed towards both figures might be the author?

One explanation lies in the ambiguous relationship between the two in medieval tradition. A bond exists between them that is strong enough to withstand the differences that drive them apart in the later texts, and this bond constitutes the third factor. That it has survived is due, in no small part, to the account of Arthur's last journey to Avalon to be healed of his mortal wound, his head resting on the lap of Morgan le Fay. The potency of this image has remained undiminished through the ages, and it has encouraged speculation on the nature of the relationship between the two.

There is, however, a fourth factor. That four out of the five authors— indeed five out of six, if we can include Christian—are women suggests that the love story of Morgan and Arthur is of particular interest to them.[4] The rejection of such romantic, but essentially passive, heroines as Guenevere, Iseult, and Ygraine, in favor of the more independent-minded Morgan le Fay—a figure prepared to take the initiative and accept the consequences as boldly as any man—would seem to reflect changing attitudes on the part of a growing number of women in contemporary society.

This is not to claim that Morgan attains freedom of choice without difficulty or cost. She must constantly struggle against pressures to conform to convention. In the novels of Wolf and Katz her decision not to marry Arthur leads to the sorrow of separation, as she herself recognizes. She does, furthermore, make mistakes, for she can give way to pride, impetuousness, and anger, particularly in the novels of Godwin and Bradley. Yet in this she is no different from male counterparts such as Kay, Gawain, and Arthur himself, and they may all have inherited these qualities from their Celtic predecessors.[5] Moreover the mistakes are part of a necessary learning process that enables the growth of wisdom and maturity. Thus at the conclusion of *The Mists of Avalon* Morgaine reflects, "I did the Mother's work in Avalon until at last those who came after us might bring her into this world. I did not fail. I did what she had given me to do. It was not she but I in my pride who thought I should have done more" (876).

Nor, it must be added, does freedom of choice mean freedom from responsibility. Like the other characters Morgan feels obligations to people whom she cares about. Indeed in Wolf's *The Road to Avalon* her rejection of Arthur's proposal of marriage results from concern for his prospects rather than her own—an action that might appear to be a regression to a patriarchal view of the male-female relationship. It stems, however, not from a wish to see Arthur win power for its own sake, but from awareness of the people's need for a strong ruler in their time of peril, as he reluctantly recognizes: "She was going to sacrifice them both for the good of Britain" (86). It thus reflects a female concern for protection of the community instead of the male drive for power and dominion (Spivack 8, 163–68), and Morgan's self-sacrifice contrasts starkly with the ambition and pride of Agravaine: the former wins for Britain a period of peace and prosperity that the latter malevolently destroys.

Moreover the choice to follow the path of duty is Morgan's own, as is the later choice to resume her affair with Arthur; here, as in the novels of Bradley and Katz, she emerges as the more self-reliant of the two. In Wolf's novel, as so often in Arthurian fiction, the protagonists who follow the stern path of duty must sacrifice personal happiness for the wider good, but it is a sacrifice that they courageously make.[6]

Morgan's role in Arthurian tradition is clearly undergoing another radical reinterpretation. The supernatural fay of the earliest accounts, which are more closely based upon Celtic sources, becomes the evil witch in later medieval romances, reflecting the different role of women in the societies of the pre-Christian Celts and Christianized peoples of medieval Europe (Chant 26–27). Now the witch is giving way in her turn: first to the admirable opponent, more sinned against than sinning;[7] next to the true love and worthy companion, without whose help Arthur's vision is doomed. This reflects another change in the role of women in society. In the first stage women must fight for their independence against male dominance, stirring up resentment and hostility in the process; in the second stage they offer reconciliation, in recognition that the best hope for a better world lies in co-operation, rather than competition, between men and women.

Yet now the cooperation offered is one between equals. The old sub-jugation of women to men has served only to cripple both, to pit Arthur and his knights of the Round Table against Morgan and her sisters. The betrayal of Ygerne by Uther and Merlin leads to the betrayal of Arthur by Morgan, Morgause, and eventually Guenevere. To break this cycle the unscrupulous pursuit of power must be replaced by equal justice and respect for all, women and men alike. Only when the visionary realm of Arthur becomes the vi-sionary realm of both Morgan and Arthur can it hope to endure.

At present the reconciliation between the two seems unattainable in this world and must await their departure for Avalon. With the exception of Parke Godwin all the writers responsible for the sympathetic treatment of Morgan are women, and this situation mirrors the reluctance of men in contemporary society to surrender power.[8]

Yet it has always been a mistake to underestimate Morgan's deter-mination to fight for her rights, as many an opponent has learned to his cost. As a consequence she places herself alongside those other heroes of Arthu-rian tradition who demonstrate heroic defiance and self-assertion, even in the face of daunting odds. Like them Morgan accepts that there is a price to pay for making one's own choices in life. But she is no more afraid to pay it than are they. A new hero is emerging in Arthur's realm, a queen truly worthy, at last, not only of the Once and Future King, but also of a new generation of women who are seizing responsibility for their own lives. She is Morgan le Fay, Arthur's first love. And his last.

NOTES

1. See Paton 11–12, 148–66; Loomis, "Morgain la Fée and the Celtic God-desses"; Loomis, "Morgain la Fée in Oral Tradition"; Matthews 91–93.

2. *Yvain* 2947–51; *Erec* 4193–202. Morgain is also identified as Arthur's sis-ter in Etienne de Rouen's *Draco Normannicus* (ca. 1169).

3. In an appendix to his *Historia Brittonum* (9th century) Nennius describes the tomb of Arthur's son Amr, slain by his own father (61).

4. In Christian's *The Pendragon*, Mawgan/Ygern may be viewed as the fission-ing of a single character (as is the case with the Morrigan/Morgan Lefevre in Katz's novel). All the elements of the basic pattern in the love relationship between Morgan and Arthur appear, except the Incest and Excalibur motifs.

5. The character of the Celts is discussed by Chant 10–12; see also her bibli-ography 198–200. The influence of Celtic legends upon Arthurian tradition is explored by Loomis among others: see Loomis, *Celtic Myth,* Lacy, "Loomis," and Parins 408.

6. See also Rosemary Sutcliff's *Sword at Sunset* (1963), for example. In her "Author's Note" she comments that she has "kept the theme, which seems to me to be implicit in the story, of the Sacred King, the Leader whose divine right, ultimately, is to die for the life of the people" (vii).

7. Morgan is the protagonist of Fay Sampson's Daughter of Tintagel sequence,

which consists of *Wise Woman's Telling* (1989), *White Nun's Telling* (1989), *Black Smith's Telling* (1990), and *Taliesin's Telling* (1991). Her relationship with Arthur in this sequence is ambivalent: despite the hostility that divides brother and sister, at a deeper level they are drawn to each other by feelings of love; see *White Nun's Telling* 143 and *Taliesin's Telling* 67. They are driven apart by pride and by fate, with dire results for both.

8. For the treatment of women in modern Arthurian fantasy and in medieval Arthurian romance, see Spivack 7–15; Thompson, "Arthurian Legend" 232–34, and "For quenys."

WORKS CITED

Bogdanow, Fanni. "Morgain's Role in the Thirteenth-Century French Prose Romances of the Arthurian Cycle." *Medium Aevum* 38 (1969): 123–33.

Bradley, Marion Zimmer. *The Mists of Avalon*. New York: Knopf, 1982.

Chant, Joy. *The High Kings*. Rev. ed. London: Unwin, 1987.

Chrétien de Troyes. *Le Chevalier au Lion (Yvain)*. Ed. Mario Roques. Classiques Français du Moyen Age 89. Paris: Champion, 1960.

———. *Erec et Enide*. Ed. Mario Roques. Classiques Français du Moyen Age 80. Paris: Champion, 1952.

Christian, Catherine. *The Sword and the Flame: Variations on a Theme of Sir Thomas Malory*. London: Macmillan, 1978. (Published in the U.S. as *The Pendragon*. New York: Knopf, 1979.)

Curry, Jane. *The Sleepers*. New York: Harcourt, 1968.

Davis, Georgene. *The Round Table: A History Drawn from Unreliable Sources*. Rutland: Tory, 1930.

The Dream of Rhonabwy. *The Mabinogion*. Trans. Thomas Jones and Gwyn Jones. Everyman's Library 97. London: Dent; New York: Dutton, 1949. 137–52.

Etienne de Rouen. *Draco Normannicus*. *Chronicles of the Reigns of Stephen, Henry II, and Richard I*. Ed. Richard Howlett. Vol. 2. London: Longman, 1855, 589–707.

Faral, Edmond, ed. *La légende arthurienne. Etudes et documents*. 3 vols. Bibliothèque de l'Ecole des Hautes Etudes 255–57. Paris: Champion, 1929.

Sir Gawain and the Green Knight. Ed. J.R.R. Tolkien and E.V. Gordon. 2nd ed. rev. by Norman Davis. Oxford: Clarendon, 1967.

Geoffrey of Monmouth. *Vita Merlini*. In Faral 3: 306–52.

Godwin, Parke. *Firelord*. New York: Doubleday, 1980.

———. "The Road to Camelot: A Conversation with Marion Zimmer Bradley." *SF & Fantasy Review* 7.3 (April 1984): 8.

———. "Uallannach." In *Invitation to Camelot*. Ed. Parke Godwin. New York: Ace, 1988, 83–107.

Johnson, Barbara Ferry. *Lionors*. New York: Avon, 1975.

Kane, Gil, and John Jakes. *Excalibur!* New York: Dell, 1960.

Karr, Phyllis Ann. *The Idylls of the Queen*. New York: Ace, 1982.

Katz, Welwyn Wilton. *The Third Magic*. Vancouver: Groundwood Douglas, 1988.

Lacy, Norris J. "Loomis, Roger Sherman." In Lacy et al., *Encylopedia* 282.

———, et al. eds. *The New Arthurian Encyclopedia*. New York: Garland, 1991.

Laubenthal, Sanders Anne. *Excalibur*. New York: Ballantine, 1973.

Lively, Penelope. *The Whispering Knights*. London: Heinemann, 1971.

Loomis, Roger Sherman. *Celtic Myth and Arthurian Romance*. New York: Columbia University Press, 1927.

———. "Morgain la Fée and the Celtic Goddesses." *Speculum* 20 (1945): 183–203 .

———. "Morgain la Fée in Oral Tradition." *Romania* 80 (1959): 337–67.

Malory, Thomas. *The Works of Sir Thomas Malory*. Ed. Eugene Vinaver. 3rd ed. rev. by P.J.C. Field. 3 vols. Oxford English Texts. Oxford: Clarendon, 1990.

Matthews, Caitlin. *Arthur and the Sovereignty of Britain: King and Goddess in the Mabinogion.* London: Arkana-Penguin, 1989 .

Merlin. Ed. Gaston Paris and J. Ulrich. 2 vols. Paris: Didot, 1888.

Nennius. *Historia Brittonum.* In Faral 3: 2–62.

Newman, Sharan. *The Chessboard Queen.* New York: St. Martin, 1984.

———. *Guinevere.* New York: St. Martin, 1981.

———. *Guinevere Evermore.* New York: St. Martin, 1985.

Parins, Marylyn J. "Scholarship, Modern Arthurian." In Lacy et al., *Encyclopedia* 402–11.

Paton, Lucy Allen. *Studies in the Fairy Mythology of Arthurian Romance.* 2nd ed. Roger Sherman Loomis. New York: Franklin, 1960.

Le roman de Tristan en prose. Ed. Renée L. Curtis. Vol. 1, Munich: Hueber, 1963; Vol 2, Leiden: Brill, 1976; Vol. 3, Cambridge: Brewer, 1985.

Sampson, Fay. *Black Smith's Telling: Book Three in the sequence Daughter of Tintagel.* London: Headline, 1990.

———. *Taliesin's Telling: Book Four in the sequence Daughter of Tintagel.* London: Headline, 1991.

———. *White Nun's Telling: Book Two in the sequence Daughter of Tintagel.* London: Headline, 1989.

———. *Wise Woman's Telling: Book One in the sequence Daughter of Tintagel.* London: Headline, 1988.

Spivack, Charlotte. *Merlin's Daughters: Contemporary Women Writers of Fantasy.* Contributions to the Study of Science Fiction and Fantasy 23. Westport: Greenwood, 1987.

Sutcliff, Rosemary. *Sword at Sunset.* London: Hodder, 1963.

Thompson, Raymond H. "Arthurian Legend in Science Fiction and Fantasy." In *King Arthur Through the Ages.* Ed. Valerie M. Lagorio and Mildred Leake Day. 2 vols. New York: Garland, 1990, 2: 223–39.

———. " 'For quenys I myght have inow . . .': The Knight Errant's Treatment of Women in the English Arthurian Verse Romances." *Atlantis* 4 (1979): 34–37.

———. *The Return from Avalon: A Study of the Arthurian Legend in Modern Fiction.* Contributions to the Study of Science Fiction and Fantasy 14. Westport: Greenwood, 1985.

L'Estoire de Merlin. Ed. H. Oskar Sommer. 8 vols. In *The Vulgate Version of the Arthurian Romances.* Volume 2. Washington, DC: Carnegie Institution, 1908-16.

Joan Wolf. *The Road to Avalon.* New York: NAL-Penguin, 1988.